CATO'S LETTERS

CATO'S LETTERS

OR

Essays on Liberty, Civil and Religious, and Other Important Subjects

FOUR VOLUMES IN TWO

BY JOHN TRENCHARD AND
THOMAS GORDON

Edited and Annotated
by Ronald Hamowy

VOLUME ONE

Liberty Fund   Indianapolis

This book is published by Liberty Fund, Inc., a foundation established to encourage study of the ideal of a society of free and responsible individuals.

The cuneiform inscription that serves as our logo and as the design motif for our endpapers is the earliest-known written appearance of the word "freedom" (*amagi*), or "liberty." It is taken from a clay document written about 2300 B.C. in the Sumerian city-state of Lagash.

Editorial matter © 1995 by Ronald Hamowy. All rights reserved.
Printed in the United States of America.
PAPERBACK COVER ILLUSTRATION: "The Election: Humours of an Election Entertainment." From *The Works of William Hogarth . . . by the Rev. John Trusler. To Which Are Added, Anecdotes of the Author and His Works, by J. Hogarth and J. Nichols* (London: Jones and Co., 1833).

Library of Congress Cataloging-in-Publication Data
Trenchard, John, 1662–1723.
    Cato's letters, or, Essays on liberty, civil and religious, and other important subjects / by John Trenchard and Thomas Gordon : edited and annotated by Ronald Hamowy.
        p.   cm.
    Originally appeared from Nov. 1720 to Dec. 1723 in the London journal.
    Includes bibliographical references and index.
        ISBN 0-86597-128-5 (set : hardcover : alk. paper). — ISBN 0-86597-129-3 (set : pbk. : alk. paper). — ISBN 0-86597-130-7 (vol. 1 : hardcover : acid-free paper). — ISBN 0-86597-131-5 (vol. 1 : paperback : acid-free paper). — ISBN 0-86597-132-3 (vol. 2 : hardcover : acid-free paper). — ISBN 0-86597-133-1 (vol. 2 : paperback : acid-free paper)
        1. Great Britain—Politics and government—1714–1727—Sources. 2. Church and state—Early works to 1800. 3. Liberty—Early works to 1800.   I. Gordon, Thomas, d. 1750. II. Hamowy, Ronald, 1937–   . III. Title.
DA499.T7   1995
320.941′09033—dc20   95-17578

Liberty Fund, Inc.
8335 Allison Pointe Trail, Suite 300
Indianapolis, Indiana 46250-1684

C 10 9 8 7 6 5 4
P 10 9 8 7 6 5 4

Contents

VOLUME TWO

VOLUMES THREE AND FOUR OF THE SIXTH EDITION
No. 69 through No. 138

AN APPENDIX CONTAINING ADDITIONAL LETTERS BY CATO
No. 1 through No. 6

INDEX

Publishing History of Cato's Letters

1. *A Collection of Cato's Letters in the London Journal*. London: Printed for J. Peele, 1721. 36 pp. [Comprising Letters 1–7 (November 5–December 17, 1720). The first letter is mistakenly dated October 8, 1720.]

2. *A Collection of Cato's Political Letters in the London Journal, to December 17, inclusive, 1720*. 2d ed. With a new preface. London: Printed for J. Roberts, 1721. 36 pp. [See entry 1.]

3. *The Second Collection of Cato's Political Letters in the London Journal, continued to the End of January, 1720*. London: Printed for J. Roberts, 1720. 60 pp. [Comprising Letters 8–14 (December 24–January 28, 1720).]

4. *A Continuation of the Political Letters in the London Journal, to January 28, 1720*. London: Printed for J. Roberts, 1720. 60 pp. [See entry 3.]

5. *A Collection of Cato's Political Letters in the London Journal, to December 17, inclusive, 1720*. 3d ed. With a preface to the whole work. London: Printed for J. Peele, 1722. (Bound with *The Second Collection of Cato's Political Letters in the London Journal, continued to the End of January, 1720*.) 84 pp. [Entries 2 and 3, to which is added a new preface.]

6. *The Third Collection of Cato's Political Letters in the London Journal, continued to the End of March, 1721*. London: Printed for J. Roberts,

1721. 64 pp. [Comprising Letters 15–22 (February 4, 1720–March 25, 1721). In addition, this collection contains a four-page letter, signed "Coriolanus," which does not appear in subsequent editions and which apparently was written by neither Trenchard nor Gordon.]

7. *The Fourth Collection of Cato's Political Letters in the London Journal.* London: Printed for J. Peele, 1721. 52 pp. [Comprising Letters 23–29 (April 1–May 13, 1721).]

8. *The Fifth Collection of Cato's Political Letters in the London Journal.* London: Printed for J. Peele, 1721. 64 pp. [Comprising Letters 30–38 (May 20–July 22, 1721).]

9. *The Sixth Collection of Cato's Political Letters in the London Journal.* London: Printed for J. Peele, 1722. 64 pp. [Comprising Letters 48, 55, 56, and 59–63 (October 14, December 2, December 9, and December 30–January 27, 1721).]

10. *The Seventh Collection of Cato's Political Letters in the London Journal.* London: Printed for J. Peele, 1722. 94 pp. [Comprising Letters 64–73 (February 3–April 21, 1722).]

11. *The Eighth Collection of Cato's Political Letters in the London Journal.* London: Printed for J. Peele, 1722. 58 pp. [Comprising Letters 75, 76, and 80–85 (May 5, May 12, and June 9–July 14, 1722).]

12. *The Ninth and Last Collection of Cato's Political Letters in the London Journal.* London: Printed for J. Peele, 1723. 64 pp. [Comprising Letters 86–93 (July 21–September 8, 1722).]

13. *A Collection of Cato's Political Letters in the London Journal.* London: Printed for J. Peele, 1721–23. 7 vols. in 1. [Entries 5–10, bound in one volume.]

14. *A Collection of Cato's Political Letters in the London Journal.* London: Printed for J. Peele, 1722–23. 9 vols. in 2. [Entries 5–12, bound in two volumes.]

15. *A Collection of Cato's Letters in the British Journal.* London: Printed for T. Woodward and J. Walthoe, 1723. 3 vols.

16. *Cato's Letters*. London: Printed for W. Wilkins, T. Woodward, J. Walthoe, and J. Peele, 1724. 4 vols. [Comprising the 138 letters, all undated, that form the body of the work.]

17. *Cato's Letters; or, Essays on Liberty, Civil and Religious, and Other Important Subjects*. 3d ed., carefully corrected. London: Printed for W. Wilkins, T. Woodward, J. Walthoe, and J. Peele, 1733. 4 vols. [Comprising all 138 letters, dated and marked as to author, plus an appendix of six letters by Gordon.]

18. *Cato's Letters; or, Essays on Liberty, Civil and Religious, and Other Important Subjects*. 4th ed., corrected. London: Printed for W. Wilkins, T. Woodward, J. Walthoe, and J. Peele, 1737. 4 vois.

19. *Cato's Letters; or, Essays on Liberty, Civil and Religious, and Other Important Subjects*. 5th ed., corrected. London: Printed for T. Woodward, J. Walthoe, 1748. 4 vols.

20. *Cato's Letters; or, Essays on Liberty, Civil and Religious, and Other Important Subjects*. Berwick: Printed and Sold by R. Taylor, 1754. 4 vols. [Pirated?]

21. *Cato's Letters; or, Essays on Liberty, Civil and Religious, and Other Important Subjects*. 6th ed., corrected. London: Printed for J. Walthoe, T. and T. Longman [etc.], 1755. 4 vols.

22. *The English Libertarian Heritage: From the Writings of John Trenchard and Thomas Gordon in "The Independent Whig" and "Cato's Letters."* Edited by David L. Jacobson. American Heritage Series. Indianapolis: Bobbs-Merrill, 1965. Reprinted with a foreword by Ronald Hamowy, San Francisco: Fox & Wilkes, 1994. [Contains excerpts from thirty-two of the letters and a lengthy introduction on Trenchard and Gordon by the editor.]

FACSIMILE EDITIONS

1. *Cato's Letters; or, Essays on Liberty, Civil and Religious, and Other Important Subjects*. Photofacsimile edition of the 3d ed., corrected [1733]. New York: Russell & Russell, 1969. 4 vols. in 2.

2. *Cato's Letters; or, Essays on Liberty, Civil and Religious, and Other Important Subjects*. Photofacsimile edition of the 6th ed., corrected [1755]. New York: Da Capo Press, 1971. 4 vols. in 2.

Editor's Note

The text of the letters has been taken from the 1755 edition, printed in London in four volumes. This was the sixth edition, and despite its being replete with typographical errors, it was marked as a "corrected" edition.

This new edition offers minimally modernized versions of the letters, which were quite readable as they originally appeared. Certain guidelines affecting spelling, capitalization, punctuation, and other aspects of style have been applied throughout, with consistency as one goal and fidelity to the meaning and spirit of the text as another.

Thus, spelling has been modernized, but only to the point where the flavor of the eighteenth-century text was not jeopardized. Such words as *haveing*, *belye*, and *jackells*, for example, have been rendered in their modern forms as *having*, *belie*, and *jackals*, while other words, such as *politick* and *oeconomy*, have been left to stand as examples of eighteenth-century orthography. British spellings have not been Americanized. Outright spelling errors, however, have been silently changed.

In modernizing the punctuation, extraneous marks such as dashes following commas or semicolons were deleted. To the modern reader these marks are duplicative and distracting. Punctuation has rarely been added except in two cases: missing apostrophes were silently affixed to possessives and missing quotation marks were added where the context called for them and when it appeared that the quotation was, in reality, a quotation and not a paraphrase. Often the original text indicated quoted material by italicizing it; in these instances quotation marks were substituted. Where the original text *did* employ quotation marks, closing marks were sometimes missing; these have been silently added.

Longer quotations, in accordance with modern practice, have been set off in indented blocks except where the quotation was extremely long. Although the reader should have no problem in determining where Trenchard and Gordon are repeating the words of another author, quotation marks have been added to the beginning of each paragraph of all extended non-indented quotations.

Capitalization has been extensively modernized, especially because the original text capitalized almost all nouns. The original capitalization has been preserved for the italicized summaries preceding each letter. In all other cases capitals have been retained only for proper nouns and certain titles. Thus, where the word "King" did not appear to refer to a specific monarch or was not employed in a formulaic expression, it became "king."

Italics, as has been noted, have been eliminated when their purpose was to indicate quoted material. In addition, the italicization of proper nouns, standard in the original text, has also been dropped. Other elements that were italicized, such as short maxims, book titles, and foreign words, have been left as they appeared in the sixth edition.

A Note on the Dates of Cato's Letters

The legal calendar in England until December 31, 1751, was the Julian, or Old Style, calendar, which was eleven days behind the Gregorian, or New Style, calendar in use throughout the rest of Europe, except Russia. Additionally, until the end of 1751 the beginning of the new year did not begin until Lady Day, March 25. Thus, Letter 9, dated December 31, 1720, is followed by Letter 10, dated January 3, 1720, since there was no change of year on January 1. If these two dates were translated into the Gregorian calendar—currently in use—Letter 9 would carry the date January 11, 1721, and Letter 10 would be dated January 14, 1721 (eleven days after January 3, to which would be added a change of year). To avoid confusion, the original dating of these letters has been retained, although the reader should keep in mind that the dates attached to Cato's letters are Old Style. On the other hand, all dates that appear in the editor's notes, unless otherwise indicated, are in New Style.

A Note on the Notes

All notes to the text preceded by a number are the editor's. Because *Cato's Letters* is likely to be of interest to readers in a variety of disciplines, identification is supplied for all but the most prominent people and historical events to which the authors allude. In addition, translations (and sources) are given for all Latin quotations in the text, despite the fact that the authors—here one refers particularly to Thomas Gordon—occasionally employed rather florid translations. Definitions are offered for those English words that are either archaic or border on being archaic. Because of the exigencies of space, identifications and definitions have been provided only at the first mention of the person or event or at first use of the word. When classical figures are first identified, the name under which they are generally indexed has been italicized, in part because of the confusion that often attaches to Roman names when attempting to distinguish the nomen from the cognomen and when determining under which of these the person is most often cited.

Acknowledgments

The research for this project was undertaken at several libraries, and I should like to take this opportunity to express my
appreciation to their staffs for the help shown me. They are the
British Library, London; the Library of Congress; the University
of North Carolina Library, Chapel Hill; the University of Alberta
Library; the Stanford University Library; and the Huntington
Library in San Marino, California.

Because of the nature of this project, spanning a vast array
of historical specifics from widely differing areas, I have, at one
point or another, called upon the help of a large number of people. To all of them I owe a debt of gratitude for their time and
patience. Most particularly, I should like to thank Professor Daniel
Gargola of the Department of History of the University of Ken-
tucky, who provided the Latin translations that appear in the foot-
notes. Among the many others who were kind enough to help me
with points of historical or technical detail are Professor William
M. Bartley of the University of Saskatchewan, Professor Doris Ber-
gen of the University of Vermont, Dr. David Hayton of the Insti-
tute of Historical Research, University of London, Professor
Dwyryd Jones of the University of York, Professor Robert Knecht
of the University of Birmingham, Dr. Ron McCail of the University of Edinburgh, Professor John Miller of the University of
London, Professor Roy Pinkerton of the University of Edinburgh,
Dr. Christopher Storrs, and Professors Ehud Ben-Zvi, George

xviii

Rothrock, Alistair Small, and Nicholas Wickenden, all of the University of Alberta.

I am especially indebted to Professor Harry Dickinson of the University of Edinburgh, who was unfailingly generous with his time and energy in helping me to track down some of the more arcane references appearing in the letters. His help was a reminder of one of the more rewarding aspects of scholarship: a sincere sense of collegiality.

I should also like to express my gratitude to those students who assisted me in the preparation of this edition: Michael Francis, Dusten Stewart, Oleg Roslak, and, especially, Leonard Szabo, whose master's thesis centered on *Cato's Letters*. Allen James and Robert Cole, who acted as my research assistants, worked with diligence and energy on my behalf.

Finally, my greatest debt is to Clement Ho, for his patience and unfailing help throughout the whole of this project.

Introduction

On November 5, 1720, the *London Journal*, one of the numerous opposition newspapers then in circulation, launched a series of letters under the pseudonym "Cato."[1] They attacked the government on a wide range of issues, which, over the course of the three years the letters were to appear, dealt with almost every aspect of political theory and practice then regarded as pertinent to contemporary British life. The letters were written with such vigor and eloquence that they soon made the *London Journal* the nation's most influential paper and a particularly vexatious irritant to the administration. The immediate occasion of the letters was the bursting of the South Sea Bubble, which had precipitated a financial crisis of huge proportions earlier that year. The authors of the letters, John Trenchard and Thomas Gordon, had taken the position, shared by the more radical Whigs and soon borne out by the evidence, that the crisis was due in large part to the machinations of the officers of the South Sea Company, who had connived with members of the government and of the royal court to bilk the public, even at the cost of triggering a financial debacle.

1. The name was chosen to honor Cato the Younger (95–46 B.C.), the implacable opponent of Julius Caesar whose unswerving dedication to republican principles and liberty won him immense admiration in the eighteenth century. When it became clear that Caesar's forces would triumph over those of the Senate, Cato fortified himself in the city of Utica and, rather than flee or be captured alive, stabbed himself after reading Plato's treatise on the immortality of the soul.

The arguments with which Trenchard and Gordon attacked the alliance between the South Sea directors and members of the government who sought to manipulate the price of South Sea stock to their own advantage reflected the authors' broader views on the nature of politics and the proper limits of government. But the South Sea crisis was by no means the sole concern of *Cato's Letters*. Of the 138 letters comprising the original collection,[2] only about a dozen are devoted to the subject and to the dangers inherent in such financial enterprises, while the remainder range over a wide variety of topics of public concern, including questions of public morality and, most importantly, theoretical discussions of the idea of liberty and the nature of tyranny. The political convictions expressed in the letters are at almost every turn consistent with the natural law and natural rights theories earlier embraced by the radical Whig writers and particularly by John Locke in his *Second Treatise of Government*. The authors of *Cato's Letters* closely echo Locke in defining political authority in terms of inalienable rights and in claiming that we derive our liberty directly from our nature as human beings. "All men are born free," they state. "Liberty is a gift which they receive from God himself; nor can they alienate the same by consent, though possibly they may forfeit it by crimes."[3] The theoretical principle upon which Cato based the authority and compass of government is our inherent right to defend ourselves against those who would trespass against our lives, liberty, or property. The notion that the laws of nature and the contract by which civil society is established constrain the sovereign to safeguarding the lives and estates of his subjects, possibly the most important legacy of Lockean theory, informs the whole of *Cato's Letters*. This proposition defines the limits of legitimate state action for both Locke and Cato. When government seeks to impose constraints upon our natural and absolute liberty beyond those necessary to enforce "the laws of

2. Beginning with the third edition of the *Letters*, published in 1733, Gordon appended six letters to the collection, bringing the total number of letters in the series to 144. These six supplementary letters were originally published in the *British Journal* between August 24 and December 7, 1723, and were written by Gordon under the pseudonym "Criton."

3. Letter 59 (p. 406).

agreement and society," it becomes despotic and must eventually fall to revolution.

Trenchard and Gordon's radicalism is evidenced by their particular fondness for the Whig revolutionary martyr, Algernon Sidney, whose *Discourses Concerning Government* was one of the leading treatises on the rights of resistance to tyrannical government. Two notions—that the rights of Englishmen rested on the ancient constitution, and that these self-same rights had their origin in the laws of nature, from which our rights are derived directly prior to the establishment of civil society—appear throughout Sidney's work and were embraced by all radical Whigs. And Sidney's views pervade the whole of *Cato's Letters*, two of which are nothing more than extended quotations from the *Discourses*.[4]

Trenchard and Gordon's apprehensions regarding tyranny in part account for their particular concern with the danger posed to England by Jacobites and papists. Religious questions, especially those having political implications, were of crucial interest to the authors, who were writing in a period beset by Jacobite plots and conspiracies. This in great measure accounts for their rabid anti-Catholicism. Popery was widely associated with the worst excesses of Stuart rule and with the most barbarous and depraved forms of superstition and oppression, and opposition to it was an intrinsic part of the radical orthodoxy to which Trenchard and Gordon subscribed; they saw in the Church of Rome an instrument dedicated to undermining the Revolutionary Settlement of 1688 and to restoring Stuart despotism. Their abhorrence extended to all those who embraced High Church views, which they judged equally pernicious. Indeed, Trenchard and Gordon's Low Church credentials were beyond dispute. They had earlier that year cooperated in writing and publishing an anonymous weekly entitled *The Independent Whig*,[5] which, in passionate lan-

---

4. Letter 26 (pp. 188–94), on the effects of general corruption, and Letter 37 (pp. 262–66), on good and evil magistrates.

5. *The Independent Whig* began publication on January 20, 1720 and went through fifty-three numbers; its last issue appeared on January 4, 1721. Of these, twenty-two were written by Gordon, eighteen by Trenchard, and ten by a third writer, later identified by Gordon only by the letter C. Evidence sug-

guage, advanced the primacy of the individual conscience over ecclesiastical authority. The periodical proved enormously popular and was quickly reprinted in book form, going through at least seven editions in Great Britain and two in the American colonies by 1747.[6] The same distrust of church hierarchy and an equal sympathy with latitudinarian principles pervade *Cato's Letters*. Trenchard and Gordon regarded the clergy's pretensions to civil power as no less inimical to a free commonwealth than an unconstrained monarchy.

Together with a series of attacks on the authority of the clergy, *Cato's Letters* offers a vigorous defense of freedom of conscience and speech. The authors hold that our consciences are the most integral part of our being and as such are exempt from all regulation by the civil magistrate. Our innermost religious convictions are contingent upon our will alone and subject only to the authority of God himself. Freedom of conscience is the first of our natural rights, Trenchard and Gordon maintain, and the immunity of our convictions from the jurisdiction of government is the clearest implication of the law of nature. "Every man's religion is his own," Cato observes, "nor can the religion of any man, of what nature or figure soever, be the religion of another man, unless he also chuses it; which action utterly excludes all force, power, or government."[7]

Natural law, which dictates the limits of state action, precludes any attempt to constrain men in questions of religious belief. We may plead and entreat, we may reason and debate, but

---

gests that this might have been Arthur Collins, a personal friend of Gordon's who was later to win acclaim as the author of "The Peerage of England." There is nothing to support the claim, made by David L. Jacobson, that "C" refers to Anthony Collins, the deist philosopher. See David L. Jacobson, ed., "Introduction," in *The English Libertarian Heritage: From the Writings of John Trenchard and Thomas Gordon in "The Independent Whig" and "Cato's Letters"* (San Francisco: Fox & Wilkes, 1994): xxiv.

6. In addition, the collection appeared in French in 1767, in a translation by Baron d'Holbach, under the title *L'Esprit du Clergé, ou le Christianisme primitif vengé des enterprises et des excés de nos prêtres modernes*. The title is, in fact, a translation of the supplementary title to the English fifth edition (2 vols.; London: J. Osborn, 1735).

7. Letter 60 (p. 414).

we may go no further. "The utmost length that the power of the magistrate can in this matter extend beyond that of exhortation, which is in every man's power, can be only to make hypocrites, slaves, fools, or atheists."[8] Trenchard and Gordon would, of course, have limited the extension of the principles of religious freedom to Protestant dissenters, but this does not weaken the theoretical argument put forward in the letters, which set forth a defense of freedom of conscience unmatched for its breadth and vigor in the literature of the period.

It was Thomas Gordon's Low Church sympathies that first brought him to the attention of John Trenchard, who had already established himself as a political writer of some note. Gordon had authored a series of pamphlets defending Benjamin Hoadly, Bishop of Bangor, whose sermon "The Nature of the Kingdom of Christ," preached before the King in March of 1717, had quickly become a *cause célèbre*. Hoadly had contended that the Gospels provided no textual support for the existence of any visible church authority. The claim incited a huge number of pamphlets both attacking and defending Hoadly, and for a time the Bangorian Controversy, as it came to be known, was regarded as a litmus test for radical Whigs.

Gordon recounts in the Preface to *Cato's Letters* that he first made the older man's acquaintance at a London coffee house. Trenchard was, at the time of their meeting in 1719, fifty-seven years old and had already attained a reputation as a forthright defender of radical Whig views. Indeed, one contemporary described him as "a man of severe principles with regard to liberty and very much esteem'd by persons of judgment and sense," and noted that he was "the only man in his time who on political subjects wrote what he thought and wrote it for no other reason but because he thought it and that it would be of service for his country to know it."[9]

---

8. Letter 66 (p. 467).

9. *An Historical View of the Principles, Characters, Persons, &c. of the Political Writers in Great Britain* (London: Printed for W. Webb, 1740); facsimile edition (Los Angeles: William Andrew Clark Memorial Library, University of California, 1958): 15.

Trenchard was apparently impressed with the style and wit of Gordon's recently published essays supporting Bishop Hoadly and attacking the pretensions of the clergy. Their meeting led to Gordon being appointed Trenchard's secretary, a relationship that quickly grew into a collaboration on the authorship of *The Independent Whig*.[10] Nothing better confirms the approval with which this periodical was received by the British public than the sustained reprinting of the book version for a full thirty years. The success of the series cemented the relationship between the two authors and quickly led to the weekly publication of the series of letters signed "Cato."

Little is known of Gordon's life before his meeting with Trenchard.[11] He was born in Kirkcudbright, Scotland, toward the end of the seventeenth century and was apparently educated at a Scottish university, possibly the University of Edinburgh, where a Thomas Gordon was awarded a degree in law in 1716. Whether or not Gordon became a member of the Scottish bar, the sources agree that he came to London as a young man and seems to have

10. The series proper was preceded by two pamphlets, *The Character of an Independent Whig* (London: J. Roberts, 1719) and *Considerations offered upon the approaching Peace and upon the importance of Gibraltar to the British Empire, being the second Part of the "Independent Whig"* (London: J. Roberts, 1719). Both essays were very well received, each going through five editions within the twelve months following their first appearance. As was customary with the political tracts of the period, they were published anonymously. While the British Library and National Union catalogues credit them both to Gordon, it seems most unlikely that Trenchard did not have a hand in their composition.

11. Biographical information on Gordon and Trenchard appears in William Anderson, *The Scottish Nation: Or, the Surnames, Families, Literature, Honours, and Biographical History of the People of Scotland* (3 vols.; Edinburgh: A. Fullarton & Co., 1867), *s.v.* "Gordon, Thomas" (2:334–35); *Biographia Britannica: or, the Lives of the Most Eminent Persons Who Have Flourished in Great Britain and Ireland* (6 vols.; London: Printed for J. Walthoe, 1766), *s.v.* "Trenchard, John" (6 [Part 2: Supplement]: 175–77); J. M. Bullough, "Thomas Gordon: The 'Independent Whig': A Biographical Bibliography," *University of Aberdeen Library Bulletin* 3 (1918): 598–612, 733–49; Alexander Chalmers, *The General Biographical Dictionary: Containing an Historical and Critical Account of the Lives and Writings of the Most Eminent Persons* ("A new edition"; 32 vols.; London: Printed for J. Nichols and Son, 1812–1817), *s.v.* "Gordon, Thomas" (16:106–7), and "Trenchard, John" (30:18–20); Robert Chambers, *A Biographical Dictionary of Eminent Scotsmen* (4 vols.; Glasgow: Blackie & Son, 1825), *s.v.* "Gordon, Thomas" (2:474–76), and the *Dictionary of National Biography* (22 vols.; London: Smith, Elder, & Co., 1908–9), *s.v.* "Gordon, Thomas" (8:230) and "Trenchard, John" (19:1125–26).

made his living as a tutor in languages prior to his meeting with Trenchard.

Unlike Gordon, Trenchard came from a family of substance. He was born in 1662, the son of a Somerset landowner, and educated at Trinity College, Dublin, where he studied law. In 1690 he left the legal profession to become one of the commissioners of forfeited estates in Ireland. A substantial legacy from an uncle and a felicitous marriage, combined over the course of the next few years with inheritances from his father and from his mother's family, provided Trenchard a considerable fortune that enabled him to devote himself exclusively to the task of writing on contemporary politics.[12]

He was particularly active in the controversy regarding standing armies, authoring two important pamphlets on the subject toward the end of the 1690s,[13] in which he assailed the idea of a standing army as a device of despots. As with most Whigs of the period, who saw an intimate connection between civil liberty on the one hand and religious liberty on the other, both Trenchard and Gordon were deeply concerned with questions of church authority and doctrine. Indeed, some ten years before the publication of *The Independent Whig*, Trenchard had turned his hand to questions of religious belief in *The Natural History of Superstition*,[14] a pamphlet of some fifty pages, in which he adumbrated some of the remarks on superstition and fear of the mysterious that appear in *Cato's Letters*. But, despite these publications, which achieved a fair degree of popularity, by far the most important of Trenchard's contributions was *Cato's Letters*.

As I have indicated, despite the broad range of issues with which the letters were eventually to deal over their three-year pub-

---

12. Trenchard in fact entered the Commons as an MP from Taunton in 1722 and served in that capacity until his death the following year. His tenure there was apparently unexceptional, although it did allow him the opportunity to speak against Walpole's proposal to remit £2,000,000 owed the government by the South Sea Company.

13. John Trenchard, assisted by Walter Moyle, *An argument shewing that a standing army is inconsistent with a free government, and absolutely destructive to the constitution of the English Monarchy* (London, 1697), and John Trenchard, *A short history of standing armies in England* (London 1698).

14. (London: Sold by A. Baldwin, 1709).

lishing history, they were originally prompted by the bursting of the South Sea Bubble in 1720. Indeed, no less than a dozen of the letters concern themselves with the details of the financial and political crisis that followed the collapse in the value of South Sea stock, and a number of others make passing reference to the South Sea directors and to the actions of Parliament in dealing with those responsible for the crash. Inasmuch as the particulars surrounding the crisis figure so prominently in the letters[15] and since questions of public and private finance played such a pronounced role in shaping and giving direction to British politics in the period between the Glorious Revolution and the South Sea disaster, it would be appropriate to provide some history of the South Sea Company prior to its collapse.

The origins of the crash lay in the spectacular growth of long-term national debt in Britain, brought about in large measure by the expenses incurred in the wars of King William III and Queen Anne. The South Sea Company, established in 1711, was itself a creature of this debt.[16] Indeed, the Company's first Governor was Robert Harley, Earl of Oxford, at the time Chancellor of the Exchequer and chief minister to Queen Anne.[17] Harley, while in office, conceived a scheme whereby a newly established company, in return for certain monopoly privileges, would relieve the government of the heavy burden of public credit under which it operated. Under the terms of the original act by which it was set

---

15. See especially Letters 2 through 12, 21, 22, and 92, which deal at great length with the attempts of Parliament and the administration both to investigate and punish those responsible for the swindle and to salvage the remnants of the South Sea Company.

16. The South Sea Company and the financial crisis of 1720 brought about by the South Sea Bubble are dealt with in John Carswell, *The South Sea Bubble* (London: The Cresset Press, 1960); Virginia Cowles, *The Great Swindle: The Story of the South Sea Bubble* (New York: Harper & Brothers, 1960); John G. Sperling, *The South Sea Company: An Historical Essay and Bibliographical Finding List* (Boston: Baker Library, Harvard Graduate School of Business Administration, 1962); and P. G. M. Dickson, *The Financial Revolution in England: A Study in the Development of Public Credit, 1688–1756* (London: Macmillan, 1967): 90–198. Peter Dickson has supplied a useful summary of the events in "The South Sea Bubble, 1720," *History Today* 4 (May, 1954): 326–33.

17. Unlike the Bank of England and the East India Company, the South Sea Company was granted a charter by a Tory Parliament and was governed from its inception by a Tory directorate.

up, the South Sea Company agreed to consolidate approximately £9,500,000 of unfunded government debt[18] by an exchange of government securities for shares at par in the Company. In return, the government agreed to pay the Company an annuity of £550,000. In addition, the Company was granted a monopoly of trade "to the South Seas" (that is, to Spanish America) and, in 1713, was awarded the *Asiento*, a contract with the King of Spain to act as supplier of 4,800 slaves per year to the Spanish possessions in America, a concession granted to the Company for a period of thirty years.

The economic exploitation of the Spanish possessions in the New World does not appear to have ever been regarded as a priority by the Company's directors. The Peace of Utrecht of 1713, which ended the War of the Spanish Succession, provided no commercial advantages to England in Spanish America beyond the *Asiento*, and, in fact, the Spanish colonial system continued to effectively close off English trade to this area. Nor was the *Asiento* of any real value. While the Company did engage in shipping slaves to the Spanish possessions in the New World between the last months of 1713 and the renewal of hostilities with Spain in 1718, the trade was plagued by difficulties and seems to have actually lost money for the Company.[19] In any case, the outbreak of war between England and Spain in August of 1718 put an end to the Company's trade with Spanish America and doubtless encouraged the Company's directors to seek profits once again in the area of public finance.

At the same time, the British government, now straining under a public debt of approximately £31,000,000 (exclusive of the amount owed the three great companies: the South Sea Company, the East India Company, and the Bank of England), viewed the conversion of this debt into the stock of one of the quasi-public companies as the only effective means by which it could free itself of this encumbrance while preserving the principle of the inviolability of its obligations. John Law's Mississippi Company, which had recently

18. That is, government debt not secured by liens on customs and excise revenues.
19. Sperling, *South Sea Company*, 20–21.

been established in France as a device to consolidate the French national debt while promising enormous financial returns, struck many in Britain as a model for the British government to emulate if it were to stay abreast of France as a European power. The British administration was therefore quite receptive to the proposal put forward in November of 1719 by John Blunt, then a director and the dominating influence in the South Sea Company, that the Company incorporate the national debt into the Company's capital.[20] The proposal was put before the Commons in January of 1720 and passed in almost unaltered form, receiving royal assent in April of that year. The centerpiece of the scheme was the conversion of the whole of the national debt of £31,000,000 into South Sea stock. In return for the right to undertake this conversion, the Company agreed to pay the government from between £4,100,000 and £7,500,000—depending upon the percentage of paper offered for conversion—and to reduce the interest rate the government was required to pay on its securities. Holders of government securities would be offered the opportunity to surrender their government paper in return for shares of the Company. By the terms of the agreement with Parliament, the Company was empowered to issue one South Sea share at a par value of £100 for every £100 of debt converted. It thus followed that if the market value of a share of stock sold by the Company were higher than par, say £600, the Company would be in the position to issue, in this instance, five additional shares, or £3,000 of stock, for conversion or sale. Indeed, if it were not for the surplus occasioned solely by the fact that the market price of its stock was well above par, the Company would have been unable to pay the fees owed the government, nor would it have been possible to distribute the substantial bribes promised those in positions of authority.

Government creditors were induced to surrender their government annuities for South Sea stock in the expectation of large capital gains. Indeed, the Company itself had very little else to recommend it, inasmuch as it produced nothing and possessed

20. I have dealt with the outlines of the South Sea Bubble in "Cato's Letters, John Locke, and the Republican Paradigm," *The History of Political Thought* 11 (1990): 273–94, from which this account is borrowed.

no tangible assets. Its capital consisted of debts owed the Company, the greatest part of which were government obligations. In fact, its sole secure asset was the government annuity it was to receive in return for converting the £31,000,000 of public debt to which it had agreed. Nor was the company capable of remitting the £7,500,000 it had promised the government for the right to assume its debt. This amount could be raised only if newly issued stock could be exchanged for publicly-held government obligations at prices far above the par value of South Sea stock. So long as the market for its stock continued to rise, the Company was able to pay off its obligations, meet the substantial costs of its bribes, and handsomely reward those who had the foresight to sell before the market finally collapsed. The Company, severely overextended, could maintain itself only by selling its surplus stock at higher and higher prices. But the moment the expectation of further advances ceased, a precipitous fall in the price of South Sea stock was inevitable.

The pervasive air of speculation that had sustained not only the price of South Sea stock but also a host of other questionable ventures that had sought to raise capital during the spring and summer of 1720 was finally dissipated in late August. An outflow of foreign money, which had earlier helped sustain the market, and the government's issuance of writs against four smaller companies suspected of contravening the recently passed Bubble Act,[21] contributed to the pressures that soon led to a frenzy of selling throughout the market.

There can be little doubt that the intrigues of the officers and directors of the South Sea Company and of the large number of ministers and public officials who were later implicated in the scandal were at least partially responsible for the speculative mania that seized the London Exchange in 1720, leading to the collapse of the market. The London Exchange had at least a thirty-year history of extensive dealings in the shares and bonds of private

21. The "Bubble Act," which received royal assent on June 11, 1720, was passed at the instigation of the South Sea directors, who thought its enactment would reduce the amount of speculation in the stock of companies competing with the South Sea Company for funds. The act sought to check the widespread, unregulated creation of joint stock companies and to prevent their diverting their charters to unauthorized ends.

companies, and it had served as a center of public credit for far longer. Yet it had never experienced anything like the events of 1720. A group of unscrupulous financiers had conspired with a government riddled with corrupt ministers to defraud large numbers of investors in a company whose solidity appeared guaranteed by the fact that the Company's chief asset was the credit of the government itself.

Trenchard and Gordon's seeming fears concerning the effects that flourishing commercial activity might have on political life are in reality not fears at all but, when read against the background of radical Whig ideology, an elaborate critique of government intrusion into the world of trade. For Cato, political corruption arises when men's rights are either ignored or unprotected by law, conditions which occur as consequences of the dishonesty or lack of diligence of magistrates.[22] When the purposes that motivate men originally to enter into civil society are thwarted and their natural rights are violated, then justice demands that the violator be punished. In calling for the punishment of the malefactors responsible for the South Sea swindle, the authors of *Cato's Letters*, echoing Locke, invoke the "universal and everlasting maxim in government," unalterable by statute, custom, or positive institution, that "the benefit and safety of the people constitutes the supreme law."[23] It was the alliance between the manipulators of credit and a corrupt Court that Trenchard and Gordon so vigorously censured. In assailing the South Sea scheme with such intensity, they were not opposing the newly developed instruments of finance that were dictated by an advanced commercial society, as some historians have suggested.[24] Rather, they were taking issue with those financial arrangements that were nothing more than

22. Indeed, Cato argues that the corruption of a people can originate only in the deceit and chicanery of a duplicitous Court and not in the actions of men in their capacity as private individuals. See Letter 94 (pp. 672–73).

23. Letter 11 (p. 87).

24. See especially Pocock's *The Machiavellian Moment: Florentine Political Thought and the Atlantic Tradition* (Princeton: Princeton University Press, 1975): 467–77, and Isaac Kramnick, *Bolingbroke and His Circle: The Politics of Nostalgia in the Age of Walpole* (Cambridge, Mass.: Harvard University Press, 1968): 243–52. For an extended discussion of the role of civic humanist thought in *Cato's Letters*, see Hamowy, "*Cato's Letters*, John Locke, and the Republican Paradigm," 273–74.

extensions of the Court; that is, they opposed the intervention of the government into the marketplace on the grounds that such intrusions by the Court provided an almost unlimited opportunity for political corruption. In this, the authors of *Cato's Letters* were joined by the other radical Whigs, who sought harsh and rapid punishment for all those responsible for mulcting the public, officers of the South Sea Company and members of the government alike.

On October 14, 1720, the price of South Sea stock, which that July had reached £950, dropped to £170 per share, and the first of Cato's letters was printed in the *London Journal*[25] on November 5. The letters continued to be published there until September 8, 1722, although the outspoken nature of the *Journal* aroused such resentment among ministerial officials that several attempts were made to suppress the paper. Cato's letters especially were unceasing in assailing government policy and in calling for severe and swift punishment of those who perpetrated the South Sea swindle. In May of 1721 a Parliamentary committee was struck to deal with the numerous "libels" levelled by the press against the government. The following month, the committee sent for, among others, both Thomas Gordon and the *London Journal's* publisher, John Peele, but they managed to avoid arrest and the government apparently dropped the matter. Some two months later, however, the *Journal's* office was raided, its printing press smashed, and its staff arrested. In addition, one of the *Journal's* chief writers, Benjamin Norton Defoe (the natural son of the writer Daniel Defoe) was charged with seditious libel,[26] but this seems not to have discouraged Trenchard and Gordon, and the letters continued as before.

25. The *London Journal*, published every Saturday, began its existence as *Thursday's Journal*, which was founded as one of the more radical Whig journals in the fall of 1719. In December of that year it switched its publication date from Thursday to the more customary Saturday. The *London Journal* is discussed at some length in Charles Bechdolt Realey, *The London Journal and Its Authors, 1720–1723* [Bulletin of the University of Kansas, Humanistic Studies, Volume 5, Number 3] (Lawrence, Kansas: University of Kansas Department of Journalism Press, 1935), and K. L. Joshi, "The London Journal, 1719–1738," *Journal of the University of Bombay* (Arts and Law Section) 11 (September, 1940): 33–66.

26. In its issue of August 12, 1721, the *London Journal* had printed an account of the examination of several of those suspected of complicity in the South Sea swindle by the Commons' secret committee of inquiry. The account, complete

Subsequently, the Walpole government[27] entered on a policy of bribing political writers rather than taking legal action against them, and this proved to be a far more effective means of silencing the opposition than the threat of legal action. Defoe himself seems to have reached an "accommodation" with the government whereby the charges against him were dropped in return for his switching allegiances to support of the Walpole ministry. More crucially, in the fall of 1722, Elizée Dobrée, then owner of the *London Journal*, approached the Under Secretary of State, proposing that the *Journal* undergo a political conversion and become a supporter of the government in return for a substantial subsidy. To this the government quickly acquiesced. As a consequence, beginning with Letter No. 94—dated September 15, 1722—Cato's letters were no longer published in the *London Journal* but appeared in the newly founded *British Journal*. The letters continued to appear until July 27, 1723, when Trenchard and Gordon published their final letter in the series. Trenchard's health, Gordon informs us, had always been delicate, and by the late summer of 1723 he had begun to suffer from the effects of what was to prove his final illness. Trenchard died on December 16, 1723, some nine days following the date of the last of the six letters written by Gordon that Gordon later appended to the third edition (1733) of *Cato's Letters*.

With Trenchard's death, Gordon apparently re-examined a number of his political beliefs. It seems clear that Walpole's policy of bribing the opposition press was as successful with Gordon as it had earlier proved with Defoe and with the proprietor of the *London Journal*. Fortunately, the political adjustment required was not substantial, since Walpole's Whiggish views, especially those on the High Church clergy's Jacobite sympathies, were becoming

---

with names, was prefaced by a biting attack on "the aiders, confederates, and abettors, to whom we owe the natonal calamities we labour under." Defoe wrote the introduction to the account, apparently at Gordon's instigation, and, as a consequence, was charged with libel.

27. One of the leading Whigs in the House of Commons, Sir Robert Walpole was appointed Paymaster General in 1720. In the following year he was made First Lord of the Treasury (a post he had held several years earlier) and Chancellor of the Exchequer, thus achieving such a dominant position in the government that he is credited with being Britain's first prime minister.

more radical. Doubtless as a reward for his new political insights, Gordon was soon made First Commissioner of Wine Licenses by the Walpole administration, a sinecure he held for the remainder of his life. In 1728, five years after the last of Cato's letters had appeared, Gordon published the first volume of his translation of Tacitus, dedicated to his one-time political enemy, Walpole.[28] To these he prefaced his "Political Discourses on Tacitus," in which he provided a summary of his political views at the time. The political discourses were very well received and the translation apparently proved to be quite lucrative.[29]

Indeed, Gordon lived in quite prosperous circumstances following the death of his friend and mentor. In 1728, as a consequence of his participation in *The Independent Whig*, he received a considerable bequest from a Dr. Walsh, a physician of some means who appears to have been greatly impressed with the sentiments expressed in that paper. And, some time after the death of Trenchard, his widow—who is reported to have relied heavily on Gordon's advice in managing the fortune left her by her husband—became Gordon's wife. Although Gordon continued occasionally to address political and ecclesiastical questions,[30] his later years were devoted primarily to his translations of Tacitus and Sallust. Now a wealthy man, Gordon grew increasingly comfortable and corpulent. The remainder of his life appears to have been unexceptional; he died on July 28, 1750.

Of the numerous publications credited to either Trenchard or Gordon or both, certainly *Cato's Letters* stands as the most signifi-

---

28. Thomas Gordon, trans., *The Works of Tacitus* (2 vols.; London: Printed for Thomas Woodward and John Peele, 1728 and 1731).

29. Gordon undertook a similar exercise some years later with a translation of Sallust, but with less success. See Thomas Gordon, trans., *The Works of Sallust, translated into English, with political discourses upon that author* (London: Printed for Thomas Woodward and John Peele, 1744).

30. His more important political pamphlets were all published between 1721 and 1723—during the period when *Cato's Letters* were being written—and dealt with subjects touched on in that work, the South Sea crisis, the Atterbury plot, and the nature of liberty. See especially *The Conspirators; or, The case of Catiline* (London: J. Roberts, 1721); *Francis, Lord Bacon, or, The case of private and national corruption and bribery* (London: Printed for J. Roberts, 1721); *Three political letters to a noble lord concerning liberty and the constitution* (London: J. Roberts, 1721); and, *An Essay towards preventing the ruin of Great Britain* (London: J. Roberts, 1721).

cant. Of the forty some political weeklies then published, the *London Journal*, in which Cato's letters first appeared, soon surpassed all its competitors in influence and importance as a consequence of Trenchard and Gordon's contributions. Its paid circulation reached somewhere between 10,000 and 15,000, substantially higher than any other paper, including the official *London Gazette*.[31] Nor was the *Journal's* distribution limited to London. It was apparently readily available in most of England's large cities and in the countryside surrounding them and was considered an invariably reliable source for news regarding the actions of the government.[32]

The authority that the letters commanded was immense. They were regarded by many as the definitive voice of those who opposed the efforts to whitewash the South Sea directors; indeed, the leader of the Parliamentary opposition to Walpole's attempts to deal leniently with those implicated in the swindle, Lord Robert Molesworth, was commonly thought to be one of the authors of *Cato's Letters*. Molesworth, whom one historian has described as "the most influential among the liberal Whigs,"[33] was a vocal enthusiast of the letters, and Gordon reports that he actually submitted several for inclusion in the series, although none was published. The letters were so well-received that even while the later ones were appearing in the *London Journal*, groups of earlier letters were published in collected form by several London presses. The whole collection was first published—in four volumes—in 1724 and went through at least six editions by 1755.[34]

31. See Laurence Hanson, *Government and the Press, 1695–1793* (Oxford: Clarendon Press, 1936): 84–85.

32. *Ibid.*, 106. See also K. L. Joshi, "The London Journal, 1719–1738," 41–43.

33. Caroline Robbins, *The Eighteenth Century Commonwealthman* (New York: Atheneum, 1968): 91. Molesworth's *An Account of Denmark*, which relates Denmark's transition to absolute tyranny, was published anonymously in 1694 and was often cited by Whig writers as a particularly appropriate example of the dangers facing limited monarchies.

34. In addition, a French translation by J. L. Chalmel of the seventeenth letter on the danger of bad governors was published in 1790 under the title *Dix-septième lettre de Caton, traduite de l'Anglais de Thomas Gordon* (Paris: A. Baudoin). The catalogue of the Bibliothèque Nationale lists a Dutch translation of the letters: *Brieven over de vryheid en het geluk onder een goede regeering; in 't Engelsch uitgegeeven op den naam van Cato* [Letters concerning the liberty and happiness of people under good government] (3 vols.; Amsterdam: K. van Tongerlo and F. Houttuyn, 1754), but strangely notes that this work is not a translation of *Cato's Letters*.

The natural rights doctrines reflected in *Cato's Letters*, with its emphasis on the proper limits of government and the right of resistance to a tyrannical magistrate, contributed greatly to the work's popularity in the American colonies. Although the letters were never published in book form in America, copies of the English editions appeared in many booksellers' catalogues and were readily available in the various colonial libraries.[35] Equally important, the letters received wide publicity in the American press. American newspapers frequently quoted extensively from them, and they were constantly invoked in the colonists' controversies with the Crown. In 1722, even while the letters were still appearing in London, the Philadelphia *American Weekly Mercury* began reprinting them in defense of the rights of free men and against the claims of arbitrary government. This journal was soon joined by newspapers in New York, Boston, and South Carolina.[36]

So highly regarded did the letters become in the colonies that the arguments Trenchard and Gordon advanced in *Cato's Letters* frequently served as the basis of the American response to the whole range of depredations under which the colonies suffered. Freedom of speech and conscience, the rights possessed by all Englishmen both by virtue of their constitutional heritage and by their nature as human beings, the benefits of freedom, the natural restraints on government, the nature of tyranny, the right of men to resist oppressive government—all these notions found an eager reception in the colonies. The American press regularly quoted or paraphrased from the letters, and its authors were frequently alluded to as the "divine" or the "immortal" Cato. Writing of Cato's reception in colonial America, one historian has concluded: "No one can spend any time in the newspapers, library inventories, and pamphlets of colonial America without realizing that *Cato's Letters*

35. Lundberg and May report that *Cato's Letters* appear in no less than thirty-seven percent of the library and booksellers' catalogues surveyed in the fifty years prior to the Revolution (David Lundberg and Henry F. May, "The Enlightened Reader in America," *American Quarterly* 28 [1976]: 262–93). Donald Lutz estimates that Trenchard and Gordon were among the ten most cited thinkers during the period 1760–1805 (Donald S. Lutz, "The Relative Influence of European Writers on Late Eighteenth-Century American Political Thought," *American Political Science Review* 78 [1984]: 194).

36. Milton M. Klein, *The Politics of Diversity: Essays in the History of Colonial New York* (Port Washington, N.Y.: Kennikat Press, 1974): 67.

rather than Locke's *Civil Government* was the most popular, quotable, esteemed source of political ideas in the colonial period."[37]

Of all the writings accountable for transmitting and developing the radical Whig thought of John Locke and his contemporaries in the Augustan Age,[38] *Cato's Letters* stands out as the most important, both in the contours and direction the work gave to English libertarianism and in its immense popularity in Britain and the American colonies. From its first publication in the 1720s through the revolutionary era that ended the century, its impact on both sides of the Atlantic was enormous. Its arguments against oppressive government and in support of the splendors of freedom were quoted constantly and its authors were regarded as the country's most eloquent opponents of despotism. Indeed, in the minds of many, the sentiments that had been expressed by Joseph Addison in his tragedy of Cato, which first appeared in 1713, applied as much to the authors of *Cato's Letters* as to the great Roman defender of liberty:

> While Cato lives, Caesar will blush to see
> Mankind enslaved, and be ashamed of empire.[39]

RONALD HAMOWY
University of Alberta

---

37. Clinton Rossiter, *Seedtime of the Republic* (New York: Harcourt, Brace and Company, 1953): 141. Similarly, Bernard Bailyn notes that "the writings of Trenchard and Gordon ranked with the treatises of Locke as the most authoritative statement of the nature of political liberty." *The Ideological Origins of the American Revolution* (Cambridge: Belknap Press, 1967): 36.

38. That is, those writers whom Caroline Robbins has described as Commonwealthmen.

39. *Cato: A Tragedy*, Act IV, scene iv.

CATO'S LETTERS

TO JOHN MILNER, ESQ.; OF GREAT RUSSEL-STREET BLOOMSBURY.[1]

Sir,

As shy as I know you to be of publick notice and eclat, let me for once draw, if not you, your name at least, from that recess which you value in proportion to the measure of felicity that you derive from it, and to your contempt for the blaze and tumult of publick life: A taste to which I have the pleasure of finding my own so entirely conformable.

Quiet passions and an easy mind constitute happiness; which is never found where these are not, and must cease to be, when these cease to support it. Mighty pomp and retinue, glaring equipages, and the attendance of crowds, are signs, indeed burdens, of greatness, rather than proofs of happiness, which I

1. Attorney and philanthropist, and a good friend of both Trenchard and Gordon, Milner at one point sat on the Middlesex bench and for a number of years was an officer of London's Foundling Hospital. He died in 1753 at the age of eighty-one.

1

doubt is least felt where these its appearances are most seen. The principal happiness which they seem to bring, is, that other people think them marks of it; and very imperfect must be that happiness which a man derives not from what he himself feels, but from what another imagines. We may indeed be happy in our own dreams, but can never be happy by the dreams of others.

Happiest of all men, to me, seems the private man; nor can the opinion of ill-judging crowds make him less happy, because they may think others more so. He who can live alone without uneasiness, who can survey his past life with pleasure, who can look back without compunction or shame, forward without fear or rebuke; he, whose every day hath produced some good, at least is passed with innocence; the silent benefactor, the ready and faithful friend; he who is filled with secret delight, because he feels his heart full of benevolence, who finds pleasure in relieving and assisting; the domestic man, perhaps little talked of, perhaps less seen, beloved by his friends, trusted and esteemed by all that know him, often useful to such as know him not, enjoys such high felicity as the wealth of kingdoms and the bounty of kings cannot confer.

Imaginary happiness is a poor amends for the want of real. Nor can a better reason than this be urged against envying any man's grandeur and state, however mighty it be, however easy it appear. A great lot is ever accompanied with many cares; and whoever stands constantly in the eyes of the world, will be apt to feel a constant concern (perhaps even to anxiety) how to become his station and degree, or how to raise it, or how to keep it from sinking. The more he is set to view, the more glaring will be any blot in his character, and the more magnified: Nay, malignant eyes will be seeing blots where there are none; and 'tis certain, that, with all his grandeur, nay by the means and help of his grandeur, it will be always in the power of very little people to mortify him, when he can no ways in return hurt them: And thus the least man may become an overmatch for the greatest.

Men are more upon a level than is generally believed; or rather the advantage is commonly where 'tis least imagined, if we take our estimate where it ought to be taken, from the state and measure of their passions; since from this source their happiness or misery arises. Greatness accompanied with vexations, is worse than an humble state void of anxiety; and he who aims not at an elevated lot, is happier than he, who, having it, fears to lose it.

Happiness is therefore from within just as much as is virtue; and the virtuous man enjoys the most.

If with this goodness of mind he be also a wise man, and a master of his passions; if to good sense he have joined other laudable accomplishments, a competent acquaintance with books, with a thorough knowledge of the world, and of mankind; if he be a benevolent neighbour, a useful member of society, perfectly disinterested, and justly esteemed; if he have served and saved great numbers; if he be daily protecting the innocent, daily watching and restraining the guilty; his happiness must be complete, and all his reflections pleasing.

Who this happy man is, where this amiable character to be found, is what I pretend not to inform you; though I am persuaded that few that know you, will ask that question. My purpose here is, to desire your permission to prefix your name to the following edition of Cato's Letters, *as well as to what I have said of Mr. Trenchard. He esteemed you as much as one man could another: You lived in a long course of intimacy with him: I have long lived, to my great advantage and pleasure, in an equal course of intimacy with you. You saw most of these papers before they came out, and many of them were first left to your perusal and judgment. You know in a great measure which were his, which were mine; and no man else whosoever was concerned or consulted. You know what motives produced them; how remote such*

*motives were from views of interest; and that whilst
they continued in full credit with the publick, they
were laid down, purely because it was judged that the
publick, after all its terrible convulsions, was again
become calm and safe.*

*You can vouch, that, as these letters were the
work of no faction or cabal, nor calculated for any
lucrative or ambitious ends, or to serve the purposes of
any party whatsoever, but that they attacked falsehood
and dishonesty in all shapes and parties, without tem-
porizing with any, but doing justice to all, even to the
weakest and most unfashionable, and maintaining
the principles of liberty against the practices of most
parties; so they were dropped without any sordid composition, and without any consideration, save that
already mentioned. They had treated of most of the
subjects important to the world, and meddled with
publick measures and publick men only in great
instances.*

*You know that in the character which I have
here given of Mr. Trenchard, I have set him no
higher than his own great abilities and many virtues
set him; that his failings were small, his talents
extraordinary, his probity equal; and that he was one
of the worthiest, one of the ablest, one of the most useful men, that ever any country was blessed withal.*

You know all the writings which he ever pro-

*duced, and saw most of them before they were pub-
lished. You know that whatever he wrote was occasional, the effect of present thought, and for
immediate use, and that he never laid up writings in
store; an undertaking quite opposite to his turn; and
all his acquaintance knew that he could never submit
to such a task.*

*I mention this last particular in justice to him,
that he may not be answerable for any work in which
he had no share. Because I have been told that some,
who knew nothing, or very little of him, perhaps never
saw him, have fathered upon him writings which he
never wrote; from no kindness to him, but purely
because they were not disposed to let me be the author
of a work which found such favourable reception from
the world,[2] though it was written several years after
that worthy man, my friend, was dead. You, who are
one of his executors, and saw all his papers, know, as
the other executors perfectly do, that he left no writings at all behind him, but two or three loose papers,
once intended for* Cato's Letters, *and afterwards
laid aside; which papers of his, with some of mine of
the same sort, you have in your hands.*

2. In 1728, the first volume of Gordon's two-volume translation of the works
of Tacitus appeared; it contained the *Annals*, to which was prefixed Gordon's
Political Discourses on Tacitus. The second volume, containing the *Histories*, the
Germania, and the *Agricola*, was published in 1731 and continued Gordon's discourses on the author.

As you have for many years seen whatever I intended for the publick, you know by what intervals I translated Tacitus, and when it was that I wrote the discourses upon that author, since you perused both as I produced them, and the discourses prefixed to the first volume were not begun till three years after his death; nor those to the second till two years after the former. You can therefore vouch what an absurd falsehood they are guilty of, who would ascribe these discourses to him, to whose valuable name I ever have done, I ever shall do, all honour and exact justice. Had he really written and owned that work, 'tis more than probable, that the same slanderers would have attributed it to somebody else.

I should not have once mentioned this ridiculous falsehood, which you and many others know to be a complete one in all its parts, had it not in some measure concerned the publick. Let this detection be the punishment of the little malicious minds who invented it; nor can there be a greater, if they have one honest passion remaining, that of shame or any other, to represent them to themselves in their own miserable colours, lying, envious, and contemptible. It is a lot sufficiently wretched, to be obliged to hate one's self; and to be hardened against just shame and remorse, is almost as bad. Doubtless it were better to have no soul, than to have a lying and mali-

cious one; better not to be, than to be a false and spiteful being.

Unhappily for these undiscerning slanderers, who, whilst they mean me a reproach, make me a compliment, many of the reflections in the discourses upon Tacitus, are illustrated from books that have been written, and from facts that have happened since Mr. Trenchard's death, some of them long since his death.

It may be proper here to mention another mistake which has generally prevailed; that a noble peer of a neighbouring nation, now dead, had a chief, at least a considerable hand in Cato's Letters.[3] *Though what I have already said in this address to you abundantly contradicts this mistake; yet, for the satisfaction of the world, and for the sake of truth and justice, I here solemnly aver (and you well know what I aver to be strictly true) that this noble person never wrote a line of those letters, nor contributed a thought towards them, nor knew who wrote them, till all the world knew; nor was ever consulted about them before or after, nor ever saw any of them till they were published, except one by accident.*

3. The reference is to Robert, first Viscount Molesworth (1656–1725), a zealous opponent of the South Sea directors in Parliament, who was thought by many to have been one of the authors of *Cato's Letters*. Molesworth was an Irish peer, and Gordon's allusion to "a neighbouring nation" refers to Ireland, on whose Privy Council Molesworth sat.

I am far from mentioning thus much as any reflection upon that able and learned nobleman, who professed a friendship for Mr. Trenchard and myself, and was so fond of these letters, that, from his great partiality in speaking of them, many people inferred them to be his own. I must add, that he sent once or twice, or oftener, some papers to be published under Cato's name; but as they were judged too particular, and not to coincide with Cato's design, they were not used. He afterwards published some of them in another form. What heightened the report of his being the author of Cato's Letters, *was, that there then came forth a public print of his lordship, with a compliment at the bottom to him, as Cato. I have been told, that this was officiously done by Mr. Toland.[4]*

My regard for the memory of Mr. Trenchard obliges me to take notice also of some men, who, since his death, have thought fit to have been very intimate with him; though, to my knowledge and yours, he hardly ever conversed with them, and always strove to shun them, such of them especially as he found to be void of veracity.

Let me add, that these letters are still so well received by the publick, that the last edition has been

4. John Toland (1670–1722), a Whig writer of great versatility, whose interests in deism brought him into conflict with the Church of England. Toward the end of his life he was partly supported by the generosity of Lord Molesworth.

long since sold off,[5] and for above three years past it was scarcely possible to find a set of them, unless in publick auctions. I mention this, that the present edition may not seem owing to the frequent quotations made from them in our late party-hostilities. I flatter myself, that, as these papers contain truths and reasons eternally interesting to human society, they will at all times be found seasonable and useful. They have already survived all the clamour and obloquy of party, and indeed are no longer considered as party-writings, but as impartial lessons of liberty and virtue. Nor would it be a small recommendation of them to the world (if the world knew you as well as I know you) that they have ever had your approbation. I am therefore very proud, upon this publick occasion, to declare, that I have long experienced your faithful friendship; and that I am, with very great and very sincere esteem,

SIR,
*Your most faithful and
most humble servant,*
T. GORDON

---

5. The "last edition" to which Gordon refers was published anonymously in 1724. This occurred nine years prior to the release of the third edition of *Cato's Letters*, which was the first in which this "Dedication" appears.

❧ THE PREFACE.

The following letters, first printed weekly, and then most of them gathered into collections from time to time, are now brought all together into four volumes. They were begun in November, 1720, with an honest and humane intention, to call for publick justice upon the wicked managers of the late fatal South-Sea scheme; and probably helped to procure it, as far as it was procured; by raising in a nation, almost sunk in despair, a spirit not to be withstood by the arts and wealth of the powerful criminals. They were afterwards carried on, upon various publick and important subjects, for nigh three years (except a few intermissions, which will appear by the dates) with a very high reputation; which all the methods taken to decry and misrepresent them could not abate.

The pleasing or displeasing of any party were none of the ends of these letters, which, as a proof of their impartiality, have pleased and displeased all parties; nor are any writers proper to do justice to every party, but such as are attached to none. No candid man can defend any party in all particulars; because every party does, in some particulars, things which cannot be defended; and therefore that man who goes blindly in all the steps of his party, and vindicates all their proceedings, cannot vindicate himself. It is the base office of a slave, and he who sustains it breathes improperly English air; that of the Tuilleries or the Divan would suit him better.[1]

1. The Tuileries palace was, until its destruction in 1871, the Parisian residence of the French sovereign. The Divan refers to Turkey under the Sultanate.

11

The strongest treatise upon the liberty of the press could not so well shew its great importance to civil liberty, as the universal good reception of these papers has done. The freedom with which they are written has been encouraged and applauded even by those who, in other instances, are enemies to all freedom. But all men love liberty for themselves; and whoever contends for slavery, would still preserve himself from the effects of it. Pride and interest sway him, and he is only hard-hearted to all the rest of the world.

The patrons of passive obedience would do well to consider this, or allow others to consider it for them. These gentlemen have never failed upon every occasion to shew effectually, that their patience was nothing increased by their principles; and that they always, very candidly and humanely, excluded themselves from the consequences of their own doctrines. Whatever their speculations have been, their practices have strongly preached, that no man will suffer injustice and violence, when he can help himself.

Let us therefore, without regarding the ridiculous, narrow, and dishonest notions of selfish and inconsistent men, who say and do contradictory things, make general liberty the interest and choice, as it is certainly the right of all mankind; and brand those as enemies to human society, who are enemies to equal and impartial liberty. Whenever such men are friends to truth, they are so from anger or chance, and not for her own sake, or for the sake of society.

I am glad, however, that by reading and approving many of *Cato's Letters*, they have been brought to read and approve a general condemnation of their own scheme. It is more than ever they did before; and I am not without hopes, that what they have begun in passion, may end in conviction. Cato is happy, if he has been the means of bringing those men to think for themselves, whose character it has been to let other men think for them: A character, which is the highest shame, and the greatest unhappiness, of a rational being. These papers, having fully opened the principles of liberty and power, and rendered them plain to every understanding, may perhaps have their share in preventing, for the time to come, such storms of zeal for nonsense and falsehood, as have thrown the three kingdoms[2] more than once into convulsions. I hope they have largely helped to cure and remove those monstrous notions of government, which have been long instilled by the crafty few into the ignorant many.

It was no matter of wonder that these letters should be ill understood, and maliciously applied, by some, who, having no principles of their own, or vile ones, were apt to wrest Cato's papers and principles to favour their own prejudices and base wishes. But for such as have always professed to entertain the same sentiments of government with Cato, and yet have been offended with his sentiments; as this their offence was neither his fault nor intention, I can only be sorry for their sakes, that the principles which they avowed at all times should displease them at any time. I am willing to believe, that it was not the doctrine, but the application, that disobliged them. Nor was Cato answerable for this; themselves made it, and often made it wrong. All candid and well-bred men (if Cato may be reckoned in the number) abhor all attacks upon the persons and private characters of men, and all little stories invented or revived to blacken them. These are cowardly and barbarous practices; the work and ambition of little and malicious minds: Nor wanted he any such low and contemptible artifices to gain readers. He attended only to general reasonings about publick virtue and corruption, unbiassed by pique or favour to any man. In this upright and impartial pursuit he abused no man's person; he courted no man's fortune; he dreaded no man's resentment.

It was a heavy charge upon Cato, which however wanted not vouchers (if they were in earnest) that he has spoken disrespectfully, nay, insolently, of the King. But this charge has been only asserted. If it were in the least true, I should be the first to own that all the clamour raised against him was just upon him. But the papers vindicate themselves; nor was any prince ever treated with more sincere duty and regard, in any publick or private writ-

2. The kingdoms of Scotland, Ireland, and England.

ings, than his present Majesty[3] has been in these. In point of principle and affection, his Majesty never had a better subject than Cato; and if he have any bad ones, they are not of Cato's making. I know that this nation cannot be preserved, if this establishment be destroyed; and I am still persuaded, that nothing tended more to his Majesty's advantage and popularity, or more to the credit of his administration, or more to the security of the subject, than the pursuing with quick and impartial vengeance those men, who were enemies to all men, and to his Majesty the most dangerous of all his enemies; a blot and a curse to the nation, and the authors of such discontents in some, and of such designs in others, as the worst men wanted, and the best men feared.

In answer to those deep politicians, who have been puzzled to know who were meant by Cicero and Brutus: Intending to deal candidly with them, and to put them out of pain and doubt, I assure them, that Cicero and Brutus were meant; that I know no present characters or story that will fit theirs; that these letters were translated for the service of liberty in general; and that neither reproof nor praise was intended by them to any man living. And if these guessing sages are in perplexity about any other passage in Cato's letters, it is ten to one but the same answer will relieve them. There was nothing in those letters analogous to our affairs; but as they are extremely fine, full of virtue and good sense, and the love of mankind, it was thought worth while to put them into English, as a proper entertainment for English readers. This was the utmost and only view; and it was at least an unkind mistake to suppose any other.

In one of Brutus's letters it is said, "We do not dispute about the qualifications of a master; we will have no master."[4] This is far from being stronger than the original: *Nisi forte non de servitute, sed de conditione serviendi, recusandum est a nobis.*[5] From whence some have inferred, that because Brutus was against having a

3. George I, the Elector of Hanover, who succeeded to the British throne in 1714 and reigned until his death in 1727.

4. See Letter No. 23 (Apr. 1, 1721).

5. "Lest we protested not against slavery, but rather against the terms of our bondage." Cicero, *Epistulae ad Brutum*, 25.4.

master, therefore Cato was against having a king: A strange con-
struction, and a wild consequence! As if the translator of Brutus's
letters were not to follow the sense of Brutus: Or, as if there were
no difference in England between a king and a master, which are
just as opposite as king and tyrant. In a neighbouring country,
indeed, they say that their monarch is born master of the kingdom;
and I believe they feel it; as they do with a witness in Turkey.[6] But
it is not so here: I hope it never will be. We have a king made and
limited by the law. Brutus having killed one usurper, was opposing
another, overturning by violence all law: Where is the parity, or
room for it?

The same defence is to be made for the papers that assert
the lawfulness of killing Caesar. It has been a question long
debated in the world; though I think it admits of little room for
debate; the only arguments to be answered being prejudice and
clamour, which are fully answered and exposed in these papers.
What is said in them can be only applicable to those who do as
Caesar and Brutus did; and can no otherwise affect our free and
legal government, than by furnishing real arguments to defend it.
The same principle of nature and reason that supported liberty at
Rome, must support it here and every where, however the circumstances of adjusting them may vary in different places; as the foundations of tyranny are in all countries, and at all times, essentially
the same; namely, too much force in the hands of one man, or of a
few unaccountable magistrates, and power without a balance: A
sorrowful circumstance for any people to fall into. I hope it is no
crime to write against so great an evil. The sum of the question is,
whether mankind have a right to be happy, and to oppose their
own destruction? And whether any man has a right to make them
miserable?

Machiavel puts Caesar upon the same foot with the worst
and most detestable tyrants, such as Nabis, Phalaris, and
Dionysius.[7] "Nor let any man," says he,

6. The "neighbouring country" is France. "With a witness" carries the sense of
"with a vengeance."

7. All three were infamous Greek tyrants. *Phalaris*, tyrant of Agrigentum during the mid-sixth century B.C., employed the most excruciating tortures in
punishing his subjects. *Dionysius I*, the absolute ruler of Syracuse from 406 to

deceive himself with Caesar's reputation, by finding him so exceedingly eminent in history. Those who cried him up, were either corrupted by his fortune, or terrified by his power; for whilst his empire continued, it was never permitted to any man to say any thing against him. Doubtless if writers had had their liberty, they could have said as much of him as of Catiline:[8] And Caesar is much the worst of the two, by how much it is worse to perpetrate a wicked thing, than to design it. And this may be judged by what is said of Brutus his adversary; for, not daring to speak in plain terms of Caesar, by reason of his power, they, by a kind of reverse, magnified his enemy.[9]

He afterwards gives a summary of the doleful waste and crying miseries brought upon Rome and upon mankind by the imperial wolves his successors; and adds, that, by such a recapitulation, "it will appear what mighty obligations Rome and Italy, and the whole world, had to Caesar."

I shall say no more of these papers either in general or particular. I leave the several arguments maintained in them to justify themselves, and cannot help thinking that they are supported by the united force of experience, reason, and nature, it is the interest of mankind that they assert; and it is the interest of mankind that they should be true. The opinion of the world concerning them may be known from hence; that they have had more friends and readers at home and abroad than any paper that ever

---

368 B.C., was so odious to his subjects and so detested that he could not trust even his wife or children. *Nabis*, who held the Lacedaemonian throne until he was murdered in 192 B.C., was reputed to have surpassed the others in cruelty and oppression.

8. Lucius Sergius *Catilina* (c. 108–62 B.C.), having been refused the consulship, vowed to destroy Rome. In a conspiracy said to have included some of the most prominent Romans of the period, Catiline sought to plunder the Roman treasury, set the city to the torch, and murder all those who had earlier offended him. The conspiracy was uncovered by Cicero who, as consul, successfully prosecuted several of Catiline's associates in Dec. 63 B.C. Catiline managed to escape to Gaul, where he was eventually killed while at the head of an army he had assembled there.

9. Machiavelli's *Discourses on the First Ten Books of Titus Livy*, I.10.4. Machiavelli's remark concerning Rome's obligation to Caesar appears at I.10.8.

appeared in it; nor does it lessen their praise, that they have also had more enemies.

Who were the authors of these letters, is now, I believe, pretty well known. It is with the utmost sorrow I say, that one of them is lately dead, and his death is a loss to mankind. To me it is by far the greatest and most shocking that I ever knew; as he was the best friend that I ever had; I may say the first friend. I found great credit and advantage in his friendship, and shall value myself upon it as long as I live. From the moment he knew me, 'till the moment he died, every part of his behaviour to me was a proof of his affection for me. From a perfect stranger to him, and without any other recommendation than a casual coffee-house acquaintance, and his own good opinion, he took me into his favour and care, and into as high a degree of intimacy as ever was shewn by one man to another. This was the more remarkable, and did me the greater honour, for that he was naturally as shy in making friendships, as he was eminently constant to those which he had already made. His shyness this way was founded upon wise and virtuous considerations. He knew that in a number of friendships, some would prove superficial, some deceitful, some would be neglected; and he never professed a friendship without a sincere intention to be a friend; which he was satisfied a private man could not be to many at once, in cases of exigency and trial. Besides, he had found much baseness from false friends, who, for his best offices, made him vile returns. He considered mutual friends as under mutual obligations, and he would contract no obligation which he was not in earnest to discharge.

This was agreeable to the great sincerity of his soul, which would suffer him to mislead no man into hopes and expectations without grounds. He would let no body depend upon him in vain. The contrary conduct he thought had great cruelty in it, as it was founding confidence upon deceit, and abusing the good faith of those who trusted in us: Hence hypocrisy on one side, as soon as it was discovered, begot hatred on the other, and false friendship ended in sincere enmity: A violence was done to a tender point of morality, and the reputation of him who did it lost and exposed amongst those who thought that he had the most.

He was indeed so tender and exact in his dealings with all sorts of men, that he used to lay his meaning and purposes minutely before them, and scorned to gain any advantage from their mistaking his intentions. He told them what he would and would not do on his part, and what he expected on theirs, with the utmost accuracy and openness. They at least knew the worst; and the only latitude which he reserved to himself was, to be better than his word; but he would let no man hope for what he did not mean. He thought that he never could be too plain with those whom he had to do with; and as men are apt to construe things most in their own favour, he used to foresee and obviate those their partial constructions, and to fix every thing upon full and express terms. He abhorred the misleading of men by artful and equivocal words; and because people are ready to put meanings upon a man's countenance and demeanor, his sincerity extended even to his carriage and manner; and though he was very civil to every body, he ordered it so, that the forms of his civility appeared to mean no more than forms, and could not be mistaken for marks of affection, where he had none: And it is very true, that a man's behaviour may, without one word said, make professions and promises, and he may play the knave by a kind look.

He used to say, and from knowing him long and intimately I could believe him when he said, that he never broke a promise nor an appointment in his life, in any instance where it was practicable to keep them. If he were to make a visit at an hour, or to meet a friend at an hour, he was always there before the hour. He observed the same severe punctuality in every other engagement of his, and had a very ill opinion of such as did not make every promise of every kind a matter of morality and honour. He considered a man's behaviour in smaller matters, as a specimen of what he would do in matters that were greater; and that a principle of faithfulness, or the want of it, would shew itself in little as well as in considerable things; that he who would try your patience in the business of an appointment, would fail you in a business of property; that one who promised at random, and misled you without an intention to mislead you, was a trifling man, and wanted honesty, though he had no treachery, as he who did it with design was a knave; that from what cause soever they deceived you, the deceit was the same, and both were equally to be distrusted; that punctuality or remissness, sincerity or perfidiousness, runs, generally, through the whole of a man's life and actions, and you need only observe his behaviour in one or two, to know his behaviour in all; and a negligent man when he is neglected, has no reason to complain, no more than a false man when he is hated. In many instances, negligence has all the effects of falsehood, and is as far from virtue, though not so near vice.

As Mr. Trenchard was wary and reserved in the choice of his friends, so no small faults, no sudden prejudices nor gusts of humour or passion, could shake their interest in him, or induce him to part with them; nor could any calumnies, however artful, nor the most malicious tales and infusions, however speciously dressed up, lessen his regard for them. In those cases, as in all others, he would see with his own eyes, and have full proof, before he believed or condemned. He knew how easily prejudices and stories are taken up; he knew how apt malice and emulation are to creep into the heart of man, and to canker it; how quickly reports are framed, how suddenly improved; how easily an additional word or circumstance can transform good into evil, and evil into good; and how common it is to add words and circumstances, as well as to create facts. He was aware that too many men are governed by ill nature; that the best are liable to prepossessions and misinformation; and that if we listen to every spiteful tale and insinuation that men are prone to utter concerning one another, no two men in the world could be two days' friends. He therefore always judged for himself, unbiassed by passion or any man's authority; and when he did change, it was demonstration that changed him. He carried his tenderness even to his lowest servants; nor could his steward, who had served him many years, and given him long proof of great integrity and good understanding, ever determine him to turn away a servant, 'till he had satisfied himself that he ought to be turned away. He was not assured but his steward might be prejudiced, notwithstanding his probity: And the steward has told me, that he never went with any complaint to his master, how necessary soever for him to hear, but he went with some uneasiness and diffidence.

No man ever made greater allowances for human infirmities, and for the errors and follies of men. This was a character which he did not bear; but it is religiously true. He knew what feeble materials human nature was made of; perhaps no man that ever was born knew it better. Mankind lay as it were dissected before him, and he saw all their advantages and deformities, all their weaknesses, passions, defects, and excesses, with prodigious clearness, and could describe them with prodigious force. Man in society, man out of society, was perfectly known and familiar to his great and lively understanding, and stood naked to his eye, divested of all the advantages, supplements, and disguises of art. His reasonings upon this subject, as upon all others, were admirable, beautiful, and full of life.

As to his indulgence to human infirmities, he knew that without it every man would be an unsociable creature to another, since every man living has infirmities; that we must take men as they are, or not at all; that it is but mutual equity to allow others what we want and expect to ourselves; that as good and ill qualities are often blended together, so they often arise out of one another: Thus men of great wit and spirit are often men of strong passion and vehemence; and the first makes amends for the last: Thus great humourists are generally very honest men; and weak men have sometimes great good nature. Upon this foundation no man lived more easy and debonair with his acquaintance, or bore their failings better. Good nature and sincerity was all that he expected of them. But in the number of natural infirmities, he never reckoned falsehood and knavery, to which he gave no quarter. Human weaknesses were invincible; but no man was born a knave: He chooses his own character, and no sincere man can love him.

In his transactions with men, he had a surprising talent at bringing them over to his opinion. His first care was that it was sure, and well-grounded, and important; and then he was a prevailing advocate: He entered into it with all his might; and his might was irresistible. He saw it in its whole extent, with all the reasons and all the difficulties, and could throw both into a thou-

sand surprising lights; and nothing could escape him. This a
friend of his used to call bringing heaven and earth into his argument. He had indeed a vast variety of images, a deluge of language, mighty persuasion in his looks, and great natural authority.
You saw that he was in earnest; you saw his excellent judgment,
and you saw his upright soul.

He had the same facility in exposing and taking to pieces
plausible and deceitful reasonings. This he did with vast quickness
and brevity, and with happy turns of ridicule. Many a grave argument, delivered very plausibly and at large, in good and well-
sounding language, he has quite defeated with a sensible jest of
three words, or a pleasant story not much longer. He had a
promptness at repartee, which few men ever equalled, and none
ever excelled. He saw, with great suddenness, the strength and
weakness of things, their justness or ridicule, and had equal excellence in shewing either.

The quickness of his spirit made him sometimes say things
which were ill taken, and for which, upon recollection, he himself
was always sorry. But in the midst of his greatest heat I never
heard him utter a word that was shocking or dangerous: So great
was his judgment, and the guard which he kept over himself and
over the natural impetuosity of his temper. He was naturally a
warm man; but his wisdom and observation gave him great wari-
ness and circumspection in great affairs; and never was man more
for moderate and calm counsels, or more an enemy to rash ones.
He had so little of revenge in his temper, that his personal resentment never carried him to hurt any man, or to wish him hurt,
unless from other causes he deserved it.

He had an immense fund of natural eloquence, a graceful
and persuasive manner, a world of action, and a style strong, clear,
figurative, and full of fire. He attended to sense much more than to
the expression; and yet his expression was noble. Coming late into
the House of Commons, and being but one session there,[10] he could
not exert his great talent that way with freedom; but the few
speeches which he made were full of excellent strong sense; and he

10. Trenchard's tenure in the Commons was brief. He was elected to Parliament in 1722 and died in mid-Dec. 1723.

was always heard with much attention and respect. Whether he would have ever come to have spoke there with perfect ease and boldness, time, from which he is now taken away, could only shew. It is certain, in that short space he acquired very high esteem with all sorts of men, and removed many prejudices conceived against him, before he shewed himself in publick. He had been thought a morose and impracticable man, an imputation which nothing but ill-will, or ignorance of his true character, could lay upon him. He was one of the gayest, pleasantest men that ever lived; an enchanting companion, and full of mirth and raillery; familiar and communicative to the last degree; easy, kind-hearted, and utterly free from all grimace and stateliness. He was accessible to all men. No man came more frankly into conviction; no man was more candid in owning his mistakes; no man more ready to do kind and obliging offices. He had not one ambitious thought, nor a crooked one, nor an envious one. He had but one view; to be in the right, and to do good; and he would have heartily joined with any man, or any party of men, to have attained it. If he erred, he erred innocently; for he sincerely walked according to the best light that he had. Is this the character, this the behaviour, of a morose, of an impracticable man? Yet this was the character of Mr. Trenchard, as many great and worthy men, who once believed the contrary, lived to see.

He was cordially in the interest of mankind, and of this nation, and of this government; and never found fault with publick measures, but when he really thought that they were against the publick. According to the views which he had of things, he judged excellently; and often traced attempts and events to their first true sources, however disguised or denied, by the mere force of his own strong understanding. He had an amazing sagacity and compass of thinking; and it was scarce possible to impose appearances upon him for principles: And they who having the same good affections with him, yet sometimes differed in opinion from him, did it often from the difference of their understandings. They saw not so far into the causes and consequences of things: Few men upon earth did; very few. His active and inquisitive mind, full of velocity and penetration, had not the same limits with those of other men: It was all lightning, and dissipated in an instant the doubts and darkness which bewildered the heads of others. In a moment he unravelled the obscurest questions; in a moment he saw the tendency of things. I could give many undeniable instances, where every jot of the events which he foretold came to pass, and in the manner that he foretold. Without doubt, he was sometimes mistaken; but his mistakes did him no discredit; they arose from no defect in his judgment, and from no sourness of mind.

As he wanted nothing but to see the publick prosper, he emulated no man's greatness; but rejoiced in the publick welfare, whatever hands conducted it. No man ever dreaded publick evils more, or took them more to heart: At one time they had almost broke it. The national confusions, distresses, and despair, which we laboured under a few years ago[11] gave him much anxiety and sorrow, which preyed upon him, and endangered his life so much, that had he staid in town a few days longer, it was more than probable he would never have gone out of it alive. He even dreaded a revolution; and the more, because he saw some easy and secure, who ought to have dreaded it most. This was no riddle to him then, and he fancied that he had lived to see the riddle explained to others.

The personal resentment which he bore to a great man now dead, for personal injuries, had no share in the opposition which he gave to his administration, how natural soever it was to believe that it had. He only considered the publick in that opposition; which he would have gladly dropped, and changed opposition into assistance, without any advantage or regard to himself, if he could have been satisfied that that great man loved his country as well as he loved power.[12] Nor did he ever quarrel with any great man about small considerations. On the contrary, he made great allowances for their errors, for the care of their fortunes and families, and even for their ambition, provided their ambition was honestly directed, and the publick was not degraded or neglected, to satiate their domestick

11. The South Sea Bubble, which burst in 1720.

12. The reference is to Charles Spencer, third Earl of Sunderland (1674–1722), who acted as one of the chief ministers to King George I from 1716 until his death six years later.

pride. He did not vainly expect from men that perfection and heroism which, he knew, were not to be found in men; and he cared not how much good ministers did to themselves, if by it they hurt not their country. He had two things much at heart; the keeping England out of foreign broils, and paying off the publick debts. He thought that the one depended upon the other, and that the fate and being of the nation depended upon the last; and I believe that few men who think at all, think him mistaken. For a good while before he died he was easier, as to those matters, than I had ever known him. He was pleased with the calm that we were in, and entertained favourable hopes and opinions. Nor is it any discredit to the present administration,[13] that Mr. Trenchard was more partial to it than I ever knew him to any other. In this he sincerely followed his judgment; for it is most certain than he had not one view to himself; nor could any human consideration have withdrawn him from the publick interest. It was hard to mislead him; impossible to corrupt him.

No man was ever more remote from all thoughts of publick employments: He was even determined against them; yet he would never absolutely declare that he would at no time engage in them, because it was barely possible that he might. So nice and severe was his veracity! He had infinite talents for business; a head wonderfully turned for schemes, trains of reasoning, and variety of affairs; extreme promptness, indefatigable industry, a strong memory, mighty dispatch, and great adroitness in applying to the passions of men. This last talent was not generally known to be his: He was thought a positive, uncomplying man; and in matters of right and wrong he was so. But it is as true, that he knew perfectly how mankind were to be dealt with; that he could manage their tempers with great art, and bear with all their humours and weaknesses with great patience. He could reason or rally, be grave or pleasant, with equal success; and make himself extremely agreeable to all sorts of people, without the least departure from his native candour and integrity. As he chiefly loved privacy and a domestick life, he seldom threw himself in the way of popularity; but where-ever he sought it, he

13. That of Sir Robert Walpole, which lasted from 1721 to 1742.

had it. One proof of this may be learned from the great town*
where he was chosen into Parliament; no man was ever more
beloved and admired by any place. He found them full of prejudices
against him, and left them full of affection for him. Very different
kinds of men, widely different in principle, agreed in loving him
equally; and adore his memory, now he is gone. The few sour men
who opposed him there, owed him better things, and themselves no
credit by their opposition.

In conversation he was frank, cheerful and familiar, without
reserve; and entertaining beyond belief. His head was so clear,
ready, and so full of knowledge, that I have often heard him make
as strong, fine, and useful discourses at his table, as ever he wrote in
his closet; though I think he is in the highest class of writers that
have appeared in the world. He had such surprizing images, such a
happy way of conceiving things, and of putting words together, as
few men upon earth ever had. He talked without the pedantry of a
man who loves to hear himself talk, or is fond of applause. He was
always excellent company; but the time of the day when he shined
most, was for three hours or more after dinner: Towards the evening he was generally subject to indigestions. The time which he
chose to think in, was the morning.

He was acceptable company to women. He treated them
with great niceness and respect; he abounded in their own chit-chat,
and said a world of pleasant things. He was a tender and obliging
husband; and indeed had uncommon cause to be so, as he well
knew, and has shewn by his will: But he had worthy and generous
notions of the kind regard which men owe to women in general,
especially to their wives; who, when they are bad, may often thank
their husbands. This was a theme that he often enlarged upon with
great wisdom. He was very partial to the fair sex, and had a great
deal of gallantry in his temper.

He was a friendly neighbour: he studied to live well with
every body about him; and took a sensible pleasure in doing good
offices. He was an enemy to litigiousness and strife; and, I think, he
told me, that he never had a law-suit in his life. He was a kind and

* Taunton in Somersetshire.

generous landlord; he never hurried nor distressed any of his tenants for rent, and made them frequent, and unasked, abatements. There were yearly instances of this. He was exact in performing all his covenants with them, and never forgot any promise that he had made them. Nor did he ever deny any tenant any reasonable favour: But he knew his estate well; they could not easily deceive him: And none but such as did so, or attempted it, were known to complain.

To his servants he was a just and merciful master. Under him they had good usage and plenty; and the worst that they had to apprehend in his service, was now and then a passionate expression. He loved to see cheerful faces about him. He was particularly tender of them in their sickness, and often paid large bills for their cure. For this his compassion and bounty he had almost always ill returns. They thought that every kindness done them, was done for their own sake; that they were of such importance to him, that he could not live without them; and that therefore they were entitled to more wages. He used to observe, that this ingratitude was inseparable from inferior servants, and that they always founded some fresh claim upon every kindness which he did them. From hence he was wont to make many fine observations upon human nature, and particularly upon the nature of the common herd of mankind.

Mr. Trenchard had a liberal education, and was bred to the law; in which, as I have heard some of his contemporaries say, he had made amazing progress. But politicks and the Irish Trust,* in which he made a great figure, though very young, took him from the Bar; whither he never had any inclination to return. By the death of an uncle, and his marriage, he was fallen into an easy fortune, with the prospect of a much greater.

He was very knowing, but not learned; that is, he had not read many books. Few books pleased him: Where the matter was not strong, and fine, and laid close together, it could not engage his attention: He out-ran his author, and had much more himself to say upon the subject. He said, that most books were but title pages, and in the first leaf you saw all; that of many books which were valued,

* He was one of the commissioners of the forfeited estates in Ireland in the reign of King William.

half might be thrown away without losing any thing. He knew well the general history and state of the world, and its geography every where. For a gentleman, he was a good mathematician; he had clear and extensive ideas of the astronomical system, of the power of matter and motion, and of the causes and production of things. He understood perfectly the interest of England in all its branches, and the interest and pretensions of the several great powers in Europe, with the state and general balance of trade every where. Upon these subjects, and upon all others that are of use to mankind, he could discourse with marvellous force and pertinency. Perhaps no man living had thought so much and so variously. He had a busy and a just head, and was master of any subject in an instant. He chiefly studied matters that were of importance to the world; but loved poetry, and things of amusement, when the thoughts were just and witty: And no body enjoyed pleasantries more. He had formerly read the classicks, and always retained many of their beautiful passages, particularly from Horace and Lucretius, and from some of the speeches in Lucan.[14] He admired the fire and freedom of the last; as he did Lucretius for the loftiness of his conceptions: And Horace he had almost all by heart. He had the works of Cicero and Tacitus in high esteem: He was not a little pleased when I set about translating the latter. He thought no author so fit to be read by a free people, like this; as none paints with such wisdom and force the shocking deformities of that sort of consuming government, which has rendered almost the whole earth so thin and wretched.

He had a great contempt for logick, and the learning of the Schools;[15] and used to repeat with much mirth an observation of Dr. Smith, late Bishop of Down,[16] his tutor. The doctor used to say, that "Mr. Trenchard's talent of reasoning was owing to his having been so good a logician"; a character for which he was eminent at the

---

14. Quintus *Horatius* Flaccus (65–8 B.C.), the celebrated Augustan poet; Titus *Lucretius* Carus (94–55 B.C.), the great Roman poet, philosopher, and author of *De rerum natura*; Marcus Annaeus *Lucanus* (A.D. 39–65), author of the *Pharsalia*, a verse account of the civil war between Caesar and Pompey. Lucanus was compelled to commit suicide under orders from Nero.

15. That is, for Scholastic philosophy.

16. Edward Smyth (1665–1720), a fellow of the Royal Society, vice chancellor of Dublin University, was consecrated Bishop of Down and Connor in 1699.

university. The truth was, that his reasoning head made him excel in the subtleties of logick. Reason is a faculty not to be learned, no more than wit and penetration. Having as great natural parts as perhaps any man was ever born with, he wanted none of the shew and assistance of art; and many men, who carry about them mighty magazines of learning and quotation, would have made a poor figure in conversation with Mr. Trenchard. He highly valued learned men, when they had good sense, and made good use of their learning: But mere authorities, and terms, and the lumber of words, were sport to him; and he often made good sport of those who excelled in them. He had endless resources in his own strong and ready understanding, and used to strip such men of their armour of names and distinctions with wonderful liveliness and pleasantry. Having lost all the tackle of their art, they had no aids from nature. False learning, false gravity, and false argument, never encountered a more successful foe. Extraordinary learning and extraordinary wit seldom meet in one man: The velocity of their genius renders men of great wit incapable of that laborious patience necessary to make a man very learned. Cicero and Monsieur Bayle, had both, and so had our Milton and George Buchanan.[17] I could name others; but all that I could mention are only exceptions from a general rule. As to Mr. Trenchard, the character of Aper, the Roman orator,[18] suits him so much, that it seems made for him.

> *Aprum ingenio potius & vi naturae quam institutione & literis famam eloquentiae consecutum—communi eruditione imbutus, contemnebat potius literas quam nesciebat: Ingenium ejus nullis alienarum artium inniti videretur.*[19]

DIALOG. DE ORATORIBUS.

17. Pierre Bayle (1647–1706), French philosopher and man of letters whose reputation rests primarily on his *Historical and Critical Dictionary*, a work of immense erudition. George Buchanan (1506–1582), Scottish humanist and, arguably, Scotland's finest scholar.

18. Marcus *Aper* of Gaul (d. A.D. 85), whose rhetorical methods and defense of court oratory were closely studied by Roman rhetoricians.

19. "Aper obtained his reputation for eloquence more from talent and the force of his nature than from education and literature—instructed in general knowledge, he condemned literature rather than was ignorant of it: his talent appeared to rest on no outside training." Tacitus, *Dialogus de Oratoribus*, 2.1–2.

He was not fond of writing; his fault lay far on the other side. He only did it when he thought it necessary. Even in the course of the following letters, he was sometimes several months together without writing one; though, upon the whole, he wrote as many, within about thirty, as I did. He wrote many such as I could not write, and I many such as he would not. But in this edition, to satisfy the curiosity of the publick, I have marked his and my own with the initial letters of our different names at the end of each paper. To him it was owing, to his conversation and strong way of thinking, and to the protection and instruction which he gave me, that I was capable of writing so many. He was the best tutor that I ever had, and to him I owed more than to the whole world besides. I will add, with the same truth, that, but for me, he never would have engaged in any weekly performance whatsoever. From any third hand there was no assistance whatever. I wanted none while I had him, and he sought none while he had me.

His notions of God were noble and refined; and if he was obnoxious to bigots, it was for thinking more honourably of the deity, and for exposing their stupid, sour, and narrow imaginations about him. There was more instruction in three *extempore* sentences of his upon this subject, than in threescore of their studied sermons. He taught you to love God; they only to dread him. He thought the gospel one continued lesson of mercy and peace; they make it a lasting warrant for contention, severity, and rage. He believed that those men, who found pomp and domination in the self-denying example and precepts of Jesus Christ, were either madmen, or worse — not in earnest; that such as were enemies to liberty of conscience, were enemies to human society, which is a frail thing kept together by mutual necessities and mutual indulgences; and that, in order to reduce the world to one opinion, the whole world must be reduced to one man, and all the rest destroyed.

He saw, with just indignation, the mad, chimerical, selfish, and barbarous tenets maintained by many of the clergy, with the mischievous effects and tendency of these tenets: He saw, as every man that has eyes may, that for every advantage which they have in the world, they are beholden to men and societies; and he thought it downright fraud and impudence, to claim as a gift from God, what all mankind knew was the manifest bounty of men, and the policy of states, or extorted from them; that ecclesiastical jurisdiction and revenues could have no other possible original; that it was a contradiction to all truth, to Christianity, and to all civil government, to allow them any other; that the certain effect of detaching the priesthood from the authority of the civil magistrate, was to enslave the civil magistrate, and all men, to the priesthood; and these claims of the clergy to divine right and independency, raised a combustion, a civil schism in the state (the only schism dangerous to society) made the laity the property or the enemies of the clergy, and taught the clergy avowed ingratitude for every bounty, indulgence, privilege, and advantage, which the laity, or any layman, could bestow upon them; since having all from God, they could consider laymen only as intruders, when laymen meddled with celestial rents, and pretended to give them what God had given them. I am apt to think that from this root of spiritual pride proceeds the too common ingratitude of clergymen to their patrons for very good livings. They think it usurpation in laymen to have church benefices in their gift. Hence their known abhorrence of impropriations;[20] and we all know what they mean, when they find so much precipitancy and so many errors in the Reformation. It was a terrible blow to church dominion, and gave the laity some of their own lands again.

Some will say, that these are only a number of hot-headed men amongst the clergy; and I say, that I mean no other: I only wish that the cool heads may be the majority. That there are many such, I know and congratulate; and I honour with all my heart the many bishops and doctors, who are satisfied with the condition of the clergy, and are friends to conscience and civil liberty; for both which some of them have contended with immortal success.

But whatever offence the high claimers of spiritual dominion gave Mr. Trenchard, he was sincerely for preserving the Established Church, and would have heartily opposed any attempt to alter it. He was against all levelling in church and state, and fearful of trying experiments upon the constitution. He thought that it was already upon a very good balance; and no man was more falsely

20. Impropriations: ecclesiastical property that has been appropriated into the hands of lay persons. The Reformation that Gordon mentions refers exclusively to the Reformation in England.

accused of an intention to pull it down. The establishment was his standard; and he was only for pulling down those who would soar above it, and trample upon it. If he offended churchmen, while he defended the legal church, the blame was not his. He knew of no authority that they had, but what the laws gave them; nor can they shew any other. The sanctions of a thousand synods, the names and volumes of ten thousand fathers, weigh not one grain in this argument. They are no more rules to us, than the oracles of Delphos, no more than a college of augurs. Acts of Parliament alone constitute and limit our church government, and create our clergy; and upon this article Mr. Trenchard only asserted what they themselves had sworn. Personally he used them with great civility where-ever he met them; and he was for depriving them of no part of their dignities and reversions. As to their speculative opinions, when he meddled with them, he thought that he might take the same liberty to differ with them, which they took to differ with one another. For this many of them have treated his name very barbarously, to their own discredit. Laymen can sometimes fight, and be friends again. The officers and soldiers of two opposite camps, if they meet out of the way of battle, can be well-bred and humane to each other, and well-pleased together, though they are to destroy one another next day. But, I know not how it happens, clerical heat does not easily cool; it rarely knows moderation or any bounds, but pursues men to their death; and even after death it pursues them, when they are no longer subject to the laws or cognizance of men. It was not more good policy than it was justice in these angry men, to charge Mr. Trenchard with want of religion; as it is owning that a man may be a most virtuous man, and an excellent member of society, without it. But, as nothing is so irreligious as the want of charity; so nothing is more indiscreet.

As passionate as he was for liberty, he was not for a Commonwealth in England. He neither believed it possible, nor wished for it. He thought that we were better as we were, than any practicable change could make us; and seemed to apprehend, that a neighbouring republick[21] was not far from some violent shock. I

21. The Dutch Republic. During the seventeenth century, the Dutch provinces had been able to secure their independence from Spain and joined together in a loose confederation under the stadtholdership of the house of Orange.

wish that he may have been mistaken; but the grounds of his opinion were too plausible.

I have before owned that he was passionate; but he shewed it only in instances where it was not worth while to watch and restrain his temper. In things of moment, or when he had a mind not to be provoked, no man was more sedate and calm. I have often seen him laugh a peevish man out of his peevishness, and without being angry, make others very angry. If he had a mind to dive into any man's designs, in which he was very successful, or meant to gain any end upon him, it was impossible to ruffle him. He was only hasty, when he was inadvertent. There was a rapidity and emotion in his way of talking, which sometimes made him thought warm when he was not. *Etsi vehemens, nondum iratus*; as I think Tully says of himself upon the like occasion.[22] He was likewise apt to give quick answers to impertinent questions, and to mortify men who he thought talked knavishly. Hence chiefly he was called a hot man. Little things sometimes provoked him, but great provocations set him a thinking; and he was capable of bearing great losses, opposition, and disappointments, with signal temper and firmness. He was very merry with those who wrote scurrilously against him, and laughed heartily at what they thought he resented most. Not many days before he died, he diverted himself with a very abuseful book written by a clergyman, and pointed personally at him; by a clergyman highly obliged to his family, and always treated with great friendship by himself.

He had a noble fortune, of which he took such care as a wise man should. He understood husbandry and improvements excellently, and every place where he came was the better for him. But though he was careful to preserve his estate, he was no ways anxious to increase it. He kept a genteel and a plentiful table, and was pleased to see it well filled: He had a great number of servants, and daily employed several tradesmen and many labourers. So that of his whole yearly income he saved little at the year's end, not above two or three hundred pounds. This will appear strange to most people, who generally believed that he saved great sums: But

22. "Although vehement, I was not yet angry." Despite Gordon's attribution, the phrase does not appear in Cicero's writings.

I know what I say, and it is plain from the personal estate which he has left.

As to his family, which I mention last, because it is the last thing upon which a wise man will value himself; it is one of the ancientest in England, and well allied: His ancestors came over with William the Norman; and there has been a good estate in the name ever since. He left no child, and his three sisters are his heirs. I know but one family now remaining of the name, Mr. George Trenchard's, of Dorsetshire, a member of the House of Commons;[23] and I believe the estate in both families is worth near ten thousand pounds a year.

He died of an ulcer in the kidneys, after an illness of five weeks and some days; and he died like a wise man, with great resignation and calmness of spirit, quite free from all false fears or panick terrors, and without one struggle or convulsion. The day before his death he talked to me much and often of an affair which regarded myself; and which, were I to mention it, would shew the great concern and tenderness that he had for me. He died in the fifty-fifth year of his age.[24] I saw him expire, and these hands helped to close his eyes; the saddest office that ever they performed.

In his person he was a strong, well-set man, but of a sickly constitution, and scarce ever in perfect health. He thought too much, and with too much solicitude: This without doubt impaired, and at last wore out, the springs of life: The vigour and activity of his head caused him many bodily disorders, whatever he did, he did intensely; and no man was ever more turned for the *hoc agere*.[25] What Livy says of Cato the Elder, suits Mr. Trenchard extremely; *Versatile ingenium sic pariter ad omnia fuit, ut natum ad id unum diceres, quodcunque ageret.*[26] He had a manly face, and a fair sanguine complexion; regular features, a look of great good sense, and a lively

23. MP for Poole, 1713–41 and 1747–54, George Trenchard was the first son of Sir John Trenchard, MP, Secretary of State to William III.

24. This is apparently an inadvertence. Trenchard in fact died at the age of sixty-one.

25. Essentially, "the matters at hand."

26. "His versatile genius was equally capable of all things, so that, whatever he did, you would say that he was born to do that one thing alone." Livy, 39.40.5.

black eye, so full of fire, that several people have told me that they could not bear to look him in the face. I have heard the same observation made of his father, who, by all accounts, was a gentleman of much wit and spirit.

To conclude: He had extraordinary abilities, extraordinary virtues, and little failings, and these arising from good qualities: He was passionate from the quickness of his parts; and his resentments arose from things which his heart abhorred. I will end his character as Livy does that of Cicero. The words are extremely pertinent:

> *Vir magnus, acer, memorabilis fuit, & in cujus laudes exsequendas, Cicerone laudatore opus fuerit.*[27]
>
> FRAGM. LIVII.

Thus much, I hope, I may be permitted to have said of this great and upright man, and my excellent friend, before the following work; and much more I could have said. His character was as little known, as his name was much. Many sorts of men and causes combined to misrepresent him. Some were provoked by his honest freedom; others emulated his reputation; some traduced him through prejudice, some through folly. But no good man that knew him thoroughly could be his enemy; and what enemies he had, malice, misinformation, or his own virtue, made.

The world has few such men as Mr. Trenchard; and few men in it will be missed so much. His parts, his spirit, and his probity, will be remembered, and perhaps wanted, when the prejudices raised against him will be dead and forgotten with the passions that raised them.

---

27. "He was a great, vigorous, and memorable man, and praising him was a work worthy of a Cicero." Livy, fragment of book 120, quoted by the Elder Seneca in *Suasoriae*, 7.17 (7).

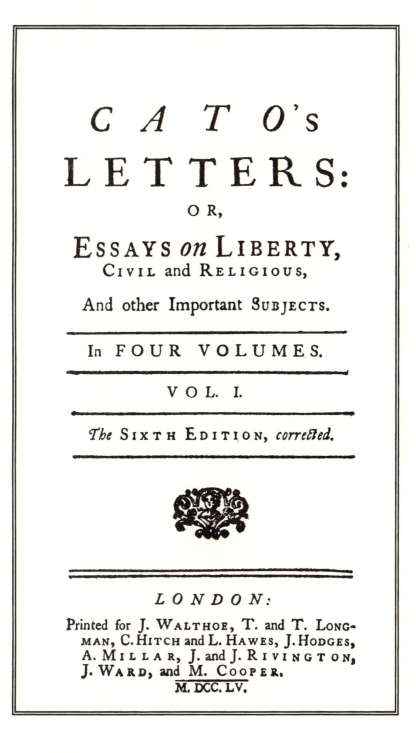

C A T O's
L E T T E R S:

O R,

ESSAYS *on* LIBERTY,
CIVIL and RELIGIOUS,

And other Important Subjects.

In FOUR VOLUMES.

VOL. I.

The SIXTH EDITION, *corrected.*

L O N D O N:

Printed for J. WALTHOE, T. and T. LONG-
MAN, C. HITCH and L. HAWES, J. HODGES,
A. MILLAR, J. and J. RIVINGTON,
J. WARD, and M. COOPER.
M. DCC. LV.

Reasons to prove that we are in no Danger of losing Gibraltar.[1]

SIR,

As I have heard, with concern, the report of our being in danger of losing Gibraltar,[2] lately revived; so I had no small pleasure to see, in the generality of the people, a just sense of the great importance of that place to the trade and security of England.

All men, in truth, shew their opinion of it, by the fears which they express about it; and if we set aside (as unworthy of mention) a few prostitute hirelings, who go about coffee-houses to drop, as far as they dare, stupid and villainous reasons for giving it up: I say, excepting such a contemptible few, I defy those, who for vile ends, or to make good vile bargains, would gladly have it surrendered, to pick out of all the people of England, one honest, rational, and disinterested man, to concur with them in it.

Thank God, in spite of the folly of parties, and the arts of betrayers, we see in all men a steady, warm and unanimous spirit

1. Readers should consult the Note on the Dates of *Cato's Letters*.

2. Gibraltar was captured by a combined British and Dutch fleet in the midsummer of 1704, during the War of the Spanish Succession. Over the next two decades, there were repeated attempts to negotiate a restitution of Gibraltar to the Spanish in return for concessions elsewhere.

for the preservation of Gibraltar; and I hope to see shortly the time, when we shall, with the same frankness and unity, exercise our reason and our eyesight in other matters, in which we are at present misled, either by infatuation, or false interest.

There are two things which surprize me in the many apprehensions which we have had about Gibraltar. The first is, the great diffidence manifested by such fears: Men must be far gone in distrust, before they could come to suspect, that their superiors could ever grow so much as indifferent about a place of such consequence to their country; and to suppose them capable of giving it up, is to suppose them capable of giving up Portsmouth, nay, England itself. Such suppositions must therefore be unjust, and the height of ignorance or spleen. Can it be imagined, that men of honour would forfeit their reputation, patriots sacrifice a bulwark of their country, or wise men venture their heads, by such a traitorous, shameful and dangerous step?

But, say some, perhaps it will be suffered to be taken by surprize; and then all the blame will only rest upon some obscure officer, who may easily be given up or kept out of the way, while those who contrived the roguery, and felt the reward of it, will be as loud in their resentments, as others who love their country well enough to grieve for its disgrace or its losses.

I know, indeed, that all this has been said more than once, and some plausible circumstances urged, to shew that it was not absolutely groundless. But, alas, what a poor plot would here be! A farce of treachery and nonsense, visible to the weakest of mankind, and only fit to raise hatred and contempt towards the wretched framers of it. This would be to deal with us as with a nation of idiots, blind and insensible, who can neither see day-light, nor feel injuries, nor return insolent usage. No, no, we are not as yet to be hood-winked by such thin schemes: We can ask, if need were, a few plain questions, which would easily puzzle such feeble politicians; but at present we have no occasion.

All this, however, shews how much we are apt to suspect foul play in this, and many other cases of the like nature; nor shall I now maliciously enquire, to what prevailing cause such distrust is to be ascribed.

Another thing, at which I am apt to wonder, is, that, considering how much our credit is concern'd to clear ourselves from the charge of any base purpose, of being willing that Gibraltar should be given away, we have not yet done it, at least in any publick and satisfactory manner: The mistaken people will say, and have said, that our silence is a confession of our guilt; and that if their censures and suppositions had not been just, it was in our power publickly to have confuted and removed them; neither of which we have done, but suffered them to remain under painful fears, and ourselves under the suspicion of neither regarding their interest, nor their ease, nor our own credit.

Why did you not, say they, tell all the world how much you were wronged, and belied, in a declaration, said to be the Regent's of France, which expressly asserted, that a bargain was made to give away Gibraltar?[3] Why did you not demonstrate, that you were at least as willing to preserve your own towns, as to conquer countries for other people, who are remarkable for doing you as little service as they possibly can? Why did you suffer it to be suggested, with the least colour of probability, that you would rather throw away what was your own, than not procure for foreign allies, at your expence, what was none of theirs? Why do we fight, why conquer, if we must thus condescend to implore the vanquished, graciously to grant peace to us the conquerors, for which we will humbly pay them with part of our dominions? And how came foreign states, most of them slaves, to be more in your favour, than Old England, which is a nursery of freemen?

All these are malicious questions, though I hope groundless; but as they are proposed by many thousands of his Majesty's liege subjects, in a modest and serious way, methinks it would be a seasonable piece of discretion and good policy, to prove them groundless.

For God's sake, let us answer, if we can answer; and if our innocence can be shewn, as no doubt it can, let it be shewn. It will

3. The reference is to one of the conditions under which France, then governed by the Regent, Louis, Duc d'Orléans, allied itself with England in early 1718. The declaration by which France became a signatory of the Quadruple Alliance authorized the Regent to offer Gibraltar to Spain in return for Spain's compliance with the Alliance's provisions.

not even be enough, that Gibraltar is never given up, but we ought to purge ourselves from the imputation of ever having entertained so criminal an intention. If we can do this, it will recover us some part of the credit and confidence which we have lost by not doing of it. I therefore hope, and humbly propose, that we may soon see some able and sagacious pen, instead of making panegyricks upon us, make apologies for us.

In the mean time, permit me to give here three unanswerable reasons why Gibraltar cannot either be given up, or taken:

First, because Secretary Grimaldo[4] says it.[*]

Secondly, it would make South-Sea stock fall: And,

Thirdly, and lastly, we have wise and honest governors.

G   *I am, &c.*

NO. 2. SATURDAY, NOVEMBER 12, 1720.

The fatal Effects of the South-Sea Scheme, and the Necessity of punishing the Directors.

SIR,

The terrible circumstances of our French neighbours, under the plague in some places,[1] expecting it in others, and dreading it in all, is a loud warning to us, to take all expedients and possible precautions against such a formidable calamity.

We have already had, and still have, a contagion of another sort,[2] more universal, and less merciful, than that at Marseilles: The latter has destroy'd, we are told, about sixty thousand lives; ours has done worse, it has render'd a much greater number of lives miserable, who want but the sickness to finish their calam-

4. José, Marqués de Grimaldo, was Spanish Secretary of War and of Finance during the War of the Spanish Succession. In Nov. 1714, he was appointed Foreign Secretary.

* This letter was written in October 1720.

---

1. In 1720, Marseilles experienced an outbreak of bubonic plague.

2. Gordon is referring to the South Sea crisis.

ity; either by rendering it complete, or by putting an end to them and that together.

Indeed, had the alternative been offered us half a year ago, I think it would have been a symptom of wisdom in us to have chosen rather to fall by the hand of God, than by the execrable arts of stock-jobbers: That we are fallen, is a sorrowful truth, not only visible in every face which you meet, but in the destruction of our trade, the glory and riches of our nation, and the livelihood of the poor.

But complaining does not mend the matter; yet what sensible heart can avoid complaining, when he hears his country, a whole country, a potent nation, a nation happy in its climate, in its prince, and in its laws, groaning under mighty evils brought upon it by mean and contemptible hands, and apprehending evils still more mighty? This gives bitterness to a humane spirit, though it suffer not otherwise than by sympathy. Is there no way left of doing ourselves justice, and has the death of our prosperity extinguished all sense of our injuries?

'Tis true, it is both prudent and religious in private persons, to stifle the notions of revenge, and calmly to expect reparation from God and the law: But jealousy and revenge, in a whole people, when they are abused, are laudable and politick virtues; without which they will never thrive, never be esteemed. How far they are to carry their resentments, I do not pronounce: The measures of it must be determined by circumstances; but still keen resentment ought to be shewn, and some punishment, or punishments, inflicted. When the dignity or interest of a nation is at stake, mercy may be cruelty.

To this spirit of jealousy and revenge, was formerly the Roman commonwealth beholden for the long preservation of its liberty; the Venetian commonwealth owes its preservation to the same spirit;[3] and liberty will never subsist long where this spirit is not: For if any crimes against the publick may be committed with impunity, men will be tempted to commit the greatest of all; I mean, that of making themselves masters of the state; and where

3. Both the Roman and Venetian commonwealths were unusually long-lived. The Roman Republic is customarily regarded as having lasted for about five hundred years, while the Republic of Venice, following a history of close to a thousand years, finally fell in 1797.

liberty ends in servitude, it is owing to this neglect. Caesar thought that he might do what he had seen Marius and Sulla[4] do before him, and so enslaved his country: Whereas, had they been hanged, he would, perhaps, never have attempted it.

I bring these examples to prove, that nations should be quick in their resentments, and severe in their judgments. As never nation was more abused than ours has been of late by the dirty race of money-changers; so never nation could with a better grace, with more justice, or greater security, take its full vengeance, than ours can, upon its detested foes. Sometimes the greatness and popularity of the offenders make strict justice unadvisable, because unsafe; but here it is not so, you may, at present, load every gallows in England with directors and stock-jobbers, without the assistance of a sheriff's guard, or so much as a sigh from an old woman, though accustom'd perhaps to shed tears at the untimely demise of a common felon or murderer. A thousand stock-jobbers, well trussed up, besides the diverting sight, would be a cheap sacrifice to the Manes[5] of trade; it would be one certain expedient to soften the rage of the people; and to convince them that the future direction of their wealth and estates shall be put into the hands of those, who will as effectually study to promote the general benefit and publick good, as others have, lately, most infamously sacrificed both to their own private advantage. Something is certainly due to both the former. The resurrection of honesty and industry can never be hoped for, while this sort of vermin is suffered to crawl about, tainting our air, and putting every thing out of course; subsisting by lies, and practising vile tricks, low in their nature, and mischievous in their consequences.

That a multitude of families are ruined, and suddenly sunk from plentiful circumstances to abject poverty, is affecting and lamentable; though perhaps all owing to their own rash confi-

4. Gaius *Marius* (155–86 B.C.), a self-made man and military commander who became one of the most powerful—and cruelest—tyrants during the period of decline of the Roman Republic. Lucius Cornelius *Sulla* (138–78 B.C.), general and twice consul. During the civil disturbances that shook Italy between 88 and 82 B.C., he succeeded in defeating his opponents and in having himself appointed dictator, at which time he exacted a particularly bloody revenge against his enemies.

5. Manes: the shades or spirits.

dence in the management of known knaves: That innocent children, born, as they imagin'd, to fair fortunes, and brought up accordingly, must now want bread, or beg it, is a catastrophe that must pierce every tender heart, and produce pity and tears: But to see one's country labouring under all the sad symptoms of distress, without the violence of war, without the diabolical refinements of able politicians; but purely from the dull cunning of inferior rogues, void of bravery, void of abilities; wretches that would run away in the field, and be despised in assemblies; this is what should turn pity into rage, and grief into vengeance.

For a nation to suffer itself to be ill used, is of dangerous example; whether those that use it ill be its neighbours or its natives. Patience, in this case, invites fresh injuries; and that people, who would not bear many unjust burdens, must not bear one.

A country, as I said above, ought to do itself justice with speed, as well as with vigour: Delay has often rendered a cure impossible in the body politick, as well as in human bodies: By delays, the edge of resentment goes off, and the offender has leisure to fortify himself by new rogueries.

I would therefore have my countrymen take advantage of the humour that they are in, and make a virtue of their present anger. Let them rouse the bold spirit of a free nation; and shew by all lawful and loyal means, that they who always scorned to be the property of tyrants, will not be the prey of stock-jobbers.

G *I am, &c.*

NO. 3. SATURDAY, NOVEMBER 19, 1720.

The pestilent Conduct of the South-Sea Directors, with the reasonable Prospect of publick Justice.

SIR,

A man robbed in his house, or on the highway, receives from the law all possible satisfaction: He has the restitution of his goods again, where it can be made; he has the life of the offender, if he can be apprehended; and there is a plentiful reward given for every such apprehension. By this salutary method, vengeance is at once taken for the crime committed, and a terrible example made of its author, to prevent its repetition.

The law is the great rule in every country, at least in every free country, by which private property is ascertained, and the publick good, which is the great end of all laws, is secured; and the religious observance of this rule, is what alone makes the difference between good laws, and none. The terror and sanctity of the laws are shewn by the execution of them; and to a contempt of the laws, or to a direct dispensing with them, have been owing most of the shocks and revolutions, that we have, for many ages, sustained in England.

Some laws are, indeed, unwarily made, being procured by passion, craft, or surprize; but such are generally either suffered to wax obsolete, or are repealed, as we have seen in many instances, and may yet see in more.

But I speak here of those laws which have a direct and known tendency to secure to us what we have, and to preserve us what we are: A free people are kept so, by no other means than an equal distribution of property; every man, who has a share of property, having a proportionable share of power; and the first seeds of anarchy (which, for the most part, ends in tyranny) are produced from hence, that some are ungovernably rich, and many more are miserably poor; that is, some are masters of all means of oppression, and others want all the means of self-defence.

What progress we have lately made in England, towards such a blessed state of confusion and misery, by the credulity of the people, throwing their all upon the mercy of base-spirited, hardhearted villains, mischievously trusted with a power to undo them, is too manifest from the woeful condition that we are in. The ruin is general, and every man has the miserable consolation to see his neighbour undone: For as to that class of ravens, whose wealth has cost the nation its all, as they are manifest enemies to God and man, no man can call them his neighbours: They are rogues of prey, they are stock-jobbers, they are a conspiracy of stock-jobbers! A name which carries along with it such a detestable and deadly image, that it exceeds all human invention to aggravate it; nor can nature, with all her variety and stores, furnish out any thing to illustrate its deformities; nay, it gains visible advantage by the worst comparisons that you can make: Your terror lessens, when you liken them to crocodiles and cannibals, who feed, for hunger, on human bodies.

These monsters, therefore, stand single in the creation: They are stock-jobbers; they have served a whole people as Satan served Job; and so far the Devil is injured, by any analogy that you can make between him and them.

Well; but monsters as they are, what would you do with them? The answer is short and at hand, hang them; for, whatever they deserve, I would have no new tortures invented, nor any new death devised. In this, I think, I shew moderation; let them only be hanged, but hanged speedily. As to their wealth, as it is the manifest plunder of the people, let it be restored to the people, and let the publick be their heirs; the only method by which the publick is ever like to get millions by them, or indeed any thing.

But, say some, when did you ever see rogues covered with wealth, brought to the axe or the gallows? I own that the example is rare, more is the shame of this nation, which has had such rich temptations, and such frequent opportunities; we have had publick guilt in abundance, God knows, often protected by party, and often by money. Faction on one side, and riches on the other, have, as it were, made a lane for the great criminals to escape. But all these escapes, which are, indeed, our reproach, cannot give any ground to fear a present one.

This nation has formerly been bought and sold; but arts were used to blind the people's eyes, the effects of the treachery were not immediately felt; and we know that the resentment of the vulgar never follows from their understanding, or their reflection, but from their feeling: A pick-pocket may tickle a plain fellow's ear, till he has got his purse; but if he feel it going, he will knock the thief down.

We have felt our pockets picked, and we know who have done it: vengeance abides them.

I am told, that some of them have the face to pretend, that they ought not to be put to death; but we hope that the legislature will effectually convince them, that this their partiality to themselves is groundless: All their hopes of safety must consist in their money; and without question, they will try to make the wages of their villainy protect their villainy. But I cannot see how any sums can save them; for as they have robbed and cheated all men, except their accomplices, so all men are concerned to see justice done to themselves; and if the ordinary channels of justice could be stopped by bags of money, or by partnership in original guilt, the enraged, the abused people, might be prompted by their uppermost passion, and having their resentment heightened by disappointment, might, it is to be feared, have recourse to extraordinary ways; ways that are often successful, tho' never justifiable.

Here are no parties in this case to disguise truth, and obstruct justice; the calamity is general, so is the resentment: All are sufferers, all will be prosecutors. The cry for justice is loud and united; if it be baulked, I can prophesy no good from so cruel an omission.

If this mighty, this destructive guilt, were to find impunity, nothing remains, but that every villain of a daring and avaricious spirit may grow a great rogue, in order to be a great man. When a people can no longer expect redress of publick and heavy evils, nor satisfaction for publick and bitter injuries, hideous is the prospect which they have before them. If they will tamely suffer a fall from plenty to beggary, they may soon expect another, and a worse, from that to slavery: But I hope better things of England.

I have before my eyes a wise and beneficent prince, a generous and publick-spirited Parliament, an able and disinterested ministry; all contending with each other for the wealth, the glory, the liberty of their country: And I have before my eyes a brave and honest people, lovers of trade and industry, free of their money, and well-deserving of the legislature, passionate for liberty, and haters of chains; but deluded, drained of their money, and abused beyond patience, beyond expression, by mean sharpers, that swagger in the plunder of their country.

Where therefore there is so much capacity, and there are so many good dispositions to help us on one side; such loud and melancholy calls, for that help on another side; such open, such execrable, such publick crimes, from a third quarter; we may hope every thing from the speedy meeting of the King and Parliament.[1] They are our protectors, and we trust that they do not bear the sword in vain.

I doubt not but many schemes will be laid before them, some of them designed for a source of new rogueries, and to prevent enquiries into the old ones. It shall be the business therefore of this paper, to watch and examine such schemes; and to condemn them, or recommend them, just as they deserve.

I have, you see, taken the guilt of our traitors for granted, as I think all men do: But because they shall have all fair play, I undertake hereafter, if it be found necessary, to prove it by an induction of particulars.

G   *I am, &c.*

NO. 4. SATURDAY, NOVEMBER 26, 1720.

Against false Methods of restoring Publick Credit.

SIR,

All men are now taught, by miserable experience, that the project of the South-Sea, through the hard-hearted knavery of some, who have been in the direction of it, and through the folly or rather distraction of the people, has not answered the good and wise ends designed by the Parliament; but instead of that, has ruined thousands of innocent and well-meaning people, to glut harpies and publick robbers with millions: Unhappy fate of poor England, worthy of a better! For this, trade has been neglected: For this, industry discouraged: For this, credit undone; and all, that stock-jobbers might make fortunes, and small sharpers grow mighty men.

Every one, therefore, seems to agree, that something is necessary to be done, in a legal way, to restore, once more, our publick credit. But it is hoped, we are far from consenting, that any

1. Parliament reconvened on Dec. 8, 1720 (O.S.), in order to deal with the financial crisis caused by the bursting of the South Sea Bubble.

thing ought to be done to repair the losses, occasioned by folly and covetousness, out of the estates of those, who always foresaw, who always opposed this mighty mischief; much less at the further expence of the honour and trade of the nation.

To set this matter in a due light, it is necessary to enquire what is meant by the publick credit of the nation.

First, credit may be said to run high, when the commodities of a nation find a ready vent, and are sold at a good price; and when dealers may be safely trusted with them, upon reasonable assurance of being paid.

Secondly, when lands and houses find ready purchasers; and when money is to be borrowed at low interest, in order to carry on trade and manufacture, at such rates, as may enable us to undersell our neighbours.

Thirdly, when people think it safe and advantageous to venture large stocks in trade and dealing, and do not lock up their money in chests, or hide it under-ground. And,

Fourthly, when notes, mortgages, and publick and private security will pass for money, or easily procure money, by selling for as much silver or gold as they are security for; which can never happen, but upon a presumption that the same money may be had for them again.

In all these cases, 'tis abundantly the interest of a nation, to promote credit and mutual confidence; and the only possible way effectually to do this, is to maintain publick honour and honesty; to provide ready remedies for private injustice and oppression; to protect the innocent and helpless from being destroyed by fraud and rapine.

But national credit can never be supported by lending money without security, or drawing in other people to do so; by raising stocks and commodities by artifice and fraud, to unnatural and imaginary values; and consequently, delivering up helpless women and orphans, with the ignorant and unwary, but industrious subject, to be devoured by pick-pockets and stock-jobbers; a sort of vermin that are bred and nourished in the corruption of the state.

This is a method, which, instead of preserving publick credit, destroys all property; turns the stock and wealth of a nation out of its proper channels; and, instead of nourishing the body-politick, produces only ulcers, eruptions, and often epidemical plague-sores: It starves the poor, destroys manufactures, ruins our navigation, and raises insurrections, &c.

The first loss is always the least; one half of the nation is ruined already; I hope we may learn wit from our misfortunes, and save the other half: In order to this, we may expect, that no new projects will be countenanced or received, which have any tendency to prejudice trade, or which cause monopolies, or set up exclusive companies; and that no privileges or advantages be granted, for which ready money might be got.

Some people have the assurance to publish it, for example, that a certain set of stock-jobbers, whose faith and modesty are now well known and felt, expect, among other gifts from the publick, that the island of St. Christophers[1] should be given them, as a further expedient to get more wealth to themselves, and leave the nation none. Now, St. Christophers is worth three hundred thousand pounds sterling, and will yield so much: So that to present them with this island, would be just making them a present of three hundred thousand pounds; a sum almost sufficient to make the fortune of an under–South-Sea clerk; but such a sum as this poor nation cannot at present spare.

I hope, therefore, that it will no longer be impudently alledged, that by parting with such gifts, we lose nothing; since that alone is worth nothing, for which nothing can be got. But the case is otherwise here; and from the nature of our publick gaming, and the spirit of the worthy sharpers who direct it, I dare pronounce before-hand, that every scheme which they themselves propose, to make their bubble and their roguery thrive again, will

1. The island of St. Kitts, in the Leeward Islands of the British West Indies. Originally divided between the British and the French, the island was entirely ceded to the British crown in 1713. The government at one point considered granting concessions on the island to the South Sea Company as a way of alleviating the financial crisis of 1721.

still be built upon the farther expence, upon the farther loss and misery of these unhappy nations.

If our money be gone, thank God, our eyes are left: Sharpened by experience and adversities we can see through disguises, and will be no more amused with moon-shine.

The nation and Parliament have been abused, and they will undoubtedly be revenged; they will not be put off with dark juggling, with knavish projects, to stifle resentments, and divert due vengeance: There is no attending to any new schemes, till the publick robbers are punished, with whom there can never be any accommodation.

To begin then, in the first place, with the criminals, will shew that we are in earnest champions for honesty, for trade, for the nation, all oppressed by money-leaches. All other remedies will be mountebank remedies: It would be madness to concert new schemes, liable to new abuses, without first doing justice to the abusers of the old; impunity for past crimes is a warrant to commit more, especially when they are gainful.

Such mighty mischiefs as these men have done, will be but meanly atoned for by such infamous lives, unless their estates be also confiscated; and even these, great as they are, will repair but part of our misfortunes. But what we can have of them, let us have; their necks and their money.

To begin with any other project, they will take for a confession, that there is a design to save them; and to what that must be owing, we all know: What farther evils it may produce, may even surpass our fears, though already terribly great; but a method of justice presently entered upon, and impartially carried through, will give us patience under our burdens, banish all our fears, give credit to the publick proceedings, and restore hope to the almost despairing people.

G   *I am, &c.*

NO. 5. SATURDAY, DECEMBER 3, 1720.

꙰ *A further Call for Vengeance upon the South-Sea Plunderers; with a Caution against false Patriots.*

SIR,

This great nation, undone by despicable stock-jobbers and their abettors, has hitherto quietly groaned under the merciless hands of its pillagers, and lived for some months upon the pure hopes of redress. We looked towards the Parliament: His Majesty and his ministry being absent, and busied with the affairs of this kingdom abroad,[1] in the glorious aims of settling the peace of Europe, in strengthening the Protestant interest.

The first part of our hopes is now almost accomplished, the Parliament are just upon meeting; and never, sure, did ever session open with greater expectation, or with more to do: Every thing is turned topsy-turvy; and the nation, thrown into convulsions, is waiting for the healing hand of its representatives.

Many expedients will, no doubt, be offered without doors; calculated, in appearance, to improve the stock, but, in reality, designed to save the directors. This is to begin at the wrong end. To pretend to form schemes for the increasing of credit, before the destroyers, the cannibals of credit, are honestly and openly hung up to its manes, is, in some sort, to confess, that we had our instructions and politicks from the criminals themselves, and our best and only reasons out of their purses.

Or if we be not thus wicked, we should, at best, be miserably weak to fall into such a preposterous method; and whether great and general calamities have their root in roguery or folly, is all one to a nation.

In spite of all the remedies that can be applied, multitudes will still remain undone beyond all remedy: Nay, for aught I can see, there is no practical remedy at all for what is past; so effectual

1. In fact, the King had already returned from Hanover by the time this letter was published. Accompanied by Lord Stanhope, his Foreign Secretary, and several other ministers, he had disembarked at Margate on Nov. 10, 1720 (O.S.).

has been the roguery on one side, so rivetted is the ruin on the other.

All, therefore, that seems to me to be left, even to the united wisdom of Great Britain, is the cure of prevention, to stop the progress of the contagion, to take care that those who have already suffered, shall suffer no more, nor make new sufferers: It is certain, that all men have suffered in one sense or other, the criminals excepted. It is hoped that the miserable people will now be honoured with their good company; and that the box on the ear, which wantonly began from them, will in good earnest be returned to them, and end with them. It is some consolation to the inhabitants of a village, who have been bit all round by a mad dog, to see the instrument of the poison, and the author of their pain and danger, honestly hung up, or knocked on the head.

The prevailing woe which has long raged, and still sits hard and heavy upon us, has certainly some authors; the directors are generally taken to be these authors; and if they be duly and publickly punished, they will continue to be taken for the only authors. But if there be nothing done to them, or nothing effectually done, we shall naturally look farther, and make bold to know, that though they have been rogues, yet that others had been greater than they; that others have directed the directors, and were partners in the spoil.

But if they stand single, and are found the only and original plunderers of their country, they will infallibly be given up to publick and crying vengeance; not only by the rules of guilt, but of good policy. A more popular thing cannot be done, nor indeed so popular a thing. The blessings of the people, and the universal affections of Great Britain, will be some of the rewards attending upon those who will be the generous authors of publick justice upon the detestable authors of publick and intense misery.

I will never suppose that any men, or even one man in any publick station, did by any means join with stock-jobbers to undo their country; much less enabled stock-jobbers, to undo their country, and supported them while they were about it. It would be melancholy and terrible, indeed, to imagine that any publick men, at least, any man concerned in the finances, or set over any part of the publick money, by which publick credit is circulated and sustained, should, in defiance of his publick trust, put himself at the head of a conspiracy of stock-jobbers, who were, with merciless and unclean hands, rifling the publick itself, engrossing all its wealth, and destroying at once all publick and private faith.

Such unprecedented treachery, such over-grown guilt, can never be supposed. Our corruptions cannot be yet become so bold and bare-faced, nor we so tame. The thing therefore being so very monstrous, must be impossible, whatsoever suggestions there may be to the contrary; which, were they true, could not fail of calling down double and conspicuous punishment upon such a Verres.[2]

As to those who lately encouraged the scheme, out of an honest purpose to relieve the publick, and pay off its debts, they ought, and no doubt will be the first and the most active to revenge the publick upon those, who, instead of relieving it, have brought the publick into such doleful and dying distress.

By this, they will farther evince the honesty of that purpose, merit still more to conduct our affairs; and their services will undoubtedly be remembered by the honest freeholders of England, at a proper season, to their advantage: Our eyes are upon them, our confidence is in them, and we wish them good success in this great trial of integrity and publick spirit.

I foresee that there will be many loud in their call for publick justice, and yet be the first to prevent it. Their avarice will arm their tongues with zeal, and a proper present disarm it of its eloquence. However, the outside of publick spirit will still be kept on; they will be sure to cry out to the last for punishment, for severe punishment; but they will be as sure to find fault with every expedient proposed for inflicting it. I could name some worthy patriots, of many words, and great weight, who will act this farce rarely. It will not be the first time. What is human life, but a masquerade: And what is civil society, but a mock-alliance between hypocrisy and credulity?

2. Gaius *Verres* (*c.* 120–43 B.C.), Roman magistrate, notorious for his mismanagement of Sicily and for the corruption of his administration.

Magna & misera civitas, eodem anno tantas injurias tantumque; pudorem passa, inter Vineos, Fabios, Icelos, Asiaticos, varia & pudenda sorte agebat; donec successere Mutianus, & Marcellus, & magis alii homines quam alii mores.[3]

These are the words of a great ancient, signal for his wisdom and strong observations. Had he lived now, and written in English, he would have written thus:

Oh London! Oh England! Oh my country! How great! And yet how miserable! What reproach, what calamities, what ruin, hast thou sustained? Sustained in the space of one short year; and less than a year! Sustained from the dregs of human kind! From fellows, vile in their original; and as to their spirit, slaves! What opprobrious delusions, what deadly revolutions, hast thou suffered to be brought upon thee, by the ignoble names and servile hands of B____t, L___b___t, H___h,[4] and the like scum of the vulgar! And after all this, art thou not weary, O my country! of thy own shame? Not yet satiated with devastation and havock? And wilt thou yet again try the old knavery, managed by new knaves?

G   *I am, &c.*

---

3. "Great and unhappy city, suffering in this year such great injury and shame, harried among the Vinii, Fabii, Iceli, and Asiaticii by fickle and ignoble fate; until Mutianus and Marcellus, different men rather than different characters, succeeded." The quotation, slightly modified, appears in Tacitus, *Historiae*, 2.95.

4. John Blunt, John Lambert, and Richard Houlditch, all directors of the South Sea Company.

NO. 6. SATURDAY, DECEMBER 10, 1720.

How easily the People are bubbled by Deceivers. Further Caution against deceitful Remedies for the publick Sufferings from the wicked Execution of the South-Sea Scheme.

SIR,

No experience or sufferings can cure the world of its credulity. It has been a bubble from the beginning; nor is it a bit wiser for this discovery, but still runs into old snares, if they have but new names, often whether they have or no.

Self-love beguiles men into false hopes, and they will venture to incur a hundred probable evils, to catch one possible good; nay, they run frequently into distracting pains and expences, to gain advantages which are purely imaginary, and utterly impossible.

Were the passions properly balanced, men would act rationally; but by suffering one passion to get the better of all the rest, they act madly or ridiculously.

Our prevailing passions in England, of late, have been hope, avarice, and ambition; which have had such a headlong force upon the people, that they are become wretched and poor, by a ravenous appetite to grow great and rich. Our fear and caution were postponed; and by a sanguine struggle for what we had not, we lost what we had. Could such courage be inspired by stock-jobbing? A cowardly science of mean tricks and lies!

Every adventurer in this mighty lottery foresaw that many must be losers, and that what was got by one must be lost by another; but every man hoped that fate would be kinder to him in particular, than to a thousand others; and so this mad hope became general, as are the calamities which it has produced.

This shews the little power that reason and truth have over the passions of men, when they run high. In the late revolution in the Alley,[1] figures and demonstration would have told them, and the directors could have told them, that it was phrenzy; that they were pursuing gilded clouds, the composition of vapour and a little sunshine; both fleeting apparitions! Common sense could have told them, that credit is the most uncertain and most fluctuating thing in the world, especially when it is applied to stock-jobbing; that it had long before been exalted higher than it could well stand, even before it was come to twenty above par;[2] and therefore always tottered, and was always tumbling down at every little accident and rumour. A story of a Spanish frigate, or of a few thieves in the dark dens in the Highlands, or the sickness of a foreign prince, or the saying of a broker in a coffee-house; all, or any of these contemptible causes were able to reduce that same credit into a very slender figure, and sometimes within her old bounds: But particularly, they might have seen, that it was now mounted to such an outrageous height, as all the silver and gold in Europe could not support; and therefore, when people came in any considerable number to sell (and to sell was the whole end of their buying), it would have a dreadful fall, even to the crushing of the nation. This has since dolefully happened: Our hopes, which were our ruin, are gone; and now we behold nothing but the face of the mourner.

But in spite of this mischief, produced by credulity, by manifest and ill-grounded credulity, it is much to be feared that some little art and big promises would make us repeat it, and grow mad again. This seems evident, not only from the folly and feebleness of human nature, ever the prey of craft, and ever caught with shadows; but from our endless gaping after new projects, and our eagerness to run into them. We have been bruised in a mortar, but we are not wiser; while one ruin is yet upon us, we are panting after another, perhaps worked up by the same hands, or by other hands with the same views.

1. Exchange Alley, between Lombard Street and Cornhill in the City of London, an area in which stock promoters did most of their trading.
2. That is, that South Sea stock was overpriced even before it had reached £120 per share.

O the weakness and folly of man! It is like a whirlpool, which destroys and drowns not by halves, but when a part is drawn in, the whole follows.

> Surely the pleasure is as great,
> Of being cheated, as to cheat![3]

Else men would not be such dupes, as every where they are. Whoever would catch mankind, has nothing to do, but to throw out a bait to their passions, and infallibly they are his property. This secret is well known to corrupt courts, who flatter or frighten their obeying believing vassals into all the excesses of misery and obeisance. By this, standing armies have been maintained; by this, wild wars have been waged; by this, an idle, expensive, absurd, and cruel popish hierarchy has been supported.

Once more, O wretched man! Thou willing instrument of thy own bondage and delusion; even mountebanks know this secret of cajoling thee, and picking thy pocket; nay, worse than mountebanks, stock-jobbers know it.

When a people are undone, it is some consolation to reflect, that they had no hand in their own ruin, or did all that they could to prevent it, by the best counsels that they could take, or by the bravest defence that they could make. But alas, poor England! thou hast not that consolation: Thou hast not fallen by able traitors; thou art not the victim of deep design, or artful treason; nor art thou the price of victory in the field; neither art thou out-witted by the subtile dealers in mystery and distinction, nor in this instance deceived by their false alarms.

No, we have no such palliating reflection to reconcile us to our misery, or to abate its pangs: To our deathless shame, we are the conquest, the purchase of stock-jobbers. The British lions crouch to a nest of owls! Can we survive the remembrance without revenge?

But all this is complaining, will some say; and we want remedies, rather than complaints: To bewail our calamities, is indeed natural; but to extricate ourselves out of them, is necessary.

3. The lines appear in Samuel Butler's poem *Hudibras*, part II (1664), canto 3, 1.1.

Here are two hundred millions of imaginary property lost, and at least twenty millions of real property plundered from the honest and industrious, and given to sharpers and pick-pockets: Shall these rooks[4] be suffered to enjoy it? And shall the bubbles be redressed out of other men's estates, no ways chargeable with the mischief? Or must we prostitute the publick honour of the nation to draw in other people (no way concerned) to take the bold bargains of rash men and dupes off their hands? But if none of these methods be taken, our cullies[5] must sit down with their loss, or the traitors be forced to disgorge.

If we make new schemes, or diversify the old, till doom's-day, there will be no paying twenty millions without twenty millions, or without what is equivalent to twenty millions; which will be the same thing to the nation as the parting with twenty millions.

The payment therefore will either be a real payment or a sham payment; and in this case, if *caveat emptor* (let the buyer look to it) be a good general rule in the business of bargains and sale, it will be a good rule here too.

If we have any state chemists,[6] who have art enough to make millions evaporate into smoke; yet I must beg leave to doubt their skill at consolidating smoke into gold.

I hope that I shall not be understood, by what I have said, to oppose an attempt to redeem us out of our present wretched condition. On the contrary, I shall be the first to vote that man a statue of gold, who can strike out an honest and skilful expedient for our recovery, which I own is far past my own skill: I am no candidate for the golden statue.

By all this, I would only caution my countrymen not to be caught again; let them beware of new snares. As to the losers, they have not a great deal to expect; and I can say no more to them here, than that in the countries where the plague rages, the preservation of the whole is the principal care; the infected are, for the most part, left to take care of themselves; and I

4. Rooks: swindlers.
5. Cullies: dupes.
6. State chemists: alchemists.

never heard it suggested, that nine millions of people ought to be exposed to the mortal contagion of that distemper, to preserve a few individuals.

G   *I am, &c.*

NO. 7. SATURDAY, DECEMBER 17, 1720.

Further Cautions about new Schemes for publick Redress.

SIR,

Beware *of the step*, will be allowed by all men, who have any skill in human affairs, to be a commendable caution in all proceedings of moment. In how many instances do we see, that things which begin plausibly, end tragically? People have been often enslaved by princes created by themselves for their protection, often butchered by armies raised by themselves for their defence. The late French King,[1] whenever he was going to shed the blood of his people in any wanton war, though undertaken to gratify his lust of power, or to exalt his own house, never failed to let them know, in an edict made on purpose, that it was all for their good and prosperity; that is, they were to suffer slaughter abroad, oppression and famine at home, purely for their own advantage and felicity.

General propositions are, for the most part, dangerous, and intended to support consequences, which, at first view, they do not seem to mean and imply. They are, therefore, generally plausible in appearance, to catch consent; from which consent, when it is once got, advantages are taken, which were not foreseen; and fresh articles are added, which were not known to have been designed.

In the late long war with France,[2] what was more desirable, what more plausible, than peace? A blessing so universally under-

1. Louis XIV, who was succeeded in 1715 by his great-grandson, Louis XV.
2. The War of the Spanish Succession. England, as a member of the Grand Alliance, declared war on France in May 1702. The two countries remained at war until the Treaty of Utrecht (April 1713).

stood to be one, that the lowest vulgar wanted no words nor persuasions to know its excellency! And when we were insulted with this question, What, will you not treat? To have said, No, would have been an answer so invidious, that scarce any man durst make it; yet all wise men then knew, that to consent to a treaty at that time with France, considering the persons and their interests who were to manage it, was to consent to a conspiracy against England in particular, and to plot against all Europe in general: We were stunned with the word peace; nor could we stand it, though we knew it was hatching treason. In short, to treat, as soft a phrase as it was, signified neither more nor less, than to give to old Lewis[3] his wicked will of all Europe, and to the Tories their Pretender.[4]

Take another instance. In the present Spanish war,[5] which, we are assured, wants nothing but a form to conclude it, we cannot forget the loud attestations that were every where given us, that to declare war was sufficient alone to end the war, and to frighten the Spaniards into a peace: And who, among us, would not willingly be at the expence of a piece of paper, and of the herald's lungs, to scare a turbulent and enterprizing court, as was that of Philip, into moderation and quietness? But the obstinacy of Spain, the length of that war, our great charge in men and money to support it, and the condition of our fleet, worn in the service of our allies, or eaten by worms in the Mediterranean, are all sufficient lessons to us, how little we ought to have trusted to such assurances, or to the word of those that gave them.

Take a third instance. Upon the establishing of the present East-India Company,[6] it was reasonably urged, that such a com-

3. Louis XIV.

4. James Edward ("James III"), the Old Pretender, the son of James II and the Stuart claimant to the British throne.

5. In August 1718, England joined with France, Holland, and Austria in a war against Spain, which was viewed as attempting to overturn the terms imposed on it at the close of the War of the Spanish Succession. Spanish hostilities with England were finally ended in Feb. 1720, when Philip V acceded to the Quadruple Alliance.

6. The reference is to the United East India Company, chartered by the government in 1709 in return for a loan of £1,200,000. The Company was created as a joint operation of the original East India Company, chartered in 1600, and the New East India Company, established as a rival to the old company in 1698. The United East India Company effectively monopolized trade with the East Indies.

pany would be no other than a confederacy of cunning fellows, against fair and general trading, by monopolizing to a few the sole traffick and riches of a great continent. To which it was answered, that there was no such design; but that every man who would subscribe his name in their books, and comply with some easy conditions, would be frankly admitted to share in their trade. But this was all hypocrisy or lying; for no sooner had the projectors by such petty pretences to publick honesty, got the better of opposition, and cooked up their project, but it was found that their trade was impracticable to all but themselves: Every trader was obliged to come into the joint-stock; and all attempts since, for the publick good, have proved ineffectual against so formidable a society.

We have a fourth instance from the first institution of the South-Sea. It was at first pretended, that every proprietor was to have six per cent for his money, without trouble or deductions; and need not engage in the trade, unless he chose it. This drew in a great multitude to vouch for the scheme, and encourage it; but in passing the bill, it was found that the crafty managers had lopt off one per cent to be applied, as they pretended, to carry on the trade of the company, and all were obliged to join in the chimerical Asiento;[7] by which they have since pillaged the proprietors of a million and a half. *See the vast advantage of losing by trade!* A secret well known to the directors!

The fifth instance may be taken from the same South-Sea. What a rare sugar-plumb to the nation was a scheme so finely calculated to pay off the nation's debts! What a tempting bait was here! Even those who saw whither it mischievously tended, and perceived the deceitful hook under it, could not stand the scorn and rebukes of the many, who swallowed it without seeing it. What fatal devastation and poverty it has since produced, by the unparalleled treachery of the directors, and some that are worse than they, the miserable people feel much more sensibly than I can express, pierced as they are with the keen arrows of merciless villainy, and unrelenting distress. We have undone ourselves to pay our debts, and our debts are not paid. What shall I say? We had

7. The *Asiento* was the financially worthless contract to act as exclusive supplier of slaves to Spanish America. By the settlement of Utrecht in 1713, this concession was granted to the British sovereign, who in turn subcontracted it to the South Sea Company for a period of thirty years.

once bread, money, and publick faith: But now! What remains to us? I cannot answer. Our grief, our folly, our losses, our dishonour, our cruel usage, are too big for words.

I have said so much, to prove how wary we ought to be in going into new schemes. We ought at least to know the whole of them, before we consent to a part. It will also behoove us to have an eye to the quarter from whence they come; whether they be directors, or their masters, and confederates; or men of fair and upright characters, whose souls are honest, and their hands clean. As to those who are known to have promoted the mighty cheat, and the ruin of their country; their infamy is so glaring, that, since they will not have modesty and remorse enough to hold their tongues, and to forbear meddling with the concerns of a people beggared by them, we ought to mind no more what they say, than the judge did the house-breaker, who, upon his trial, told his lordship, that he would swear the peace against him, for putting him in fear of his life.

The same may be said of those that are fallen in with the guilty, and unexpectedly speak the same note. We guess at their motives. The powerful getters would save themselves, by letting others get as much; and perhaps are glad to divide their gains, to escape punishment.

If any man would be the unsuspected and fair author of a new project, he can recommend it and himself no better, than by shewing it to be honestly consistent with the punishment of our million knaves, the blood-suckers of England. A new scheme, and an inquisition into the management of the old one, may both successfully go on at the same time; and they who say that they cannot, do but own that they are afraid they should. Are they conscious to themselves, that the directors may hope to escape part of their punishment, by fathering upon others a great share of their guilt, or rather the power of being guilty?

What mean some men by saying, we ought to extinguish the fire, before we inquire into the incendiaries? Are they some of these? Or did they furnish out brands to the rest? Or would they give them time to run away? The truth is, the house is already burned down, many are burned to death, all are miserably scorched: The flame has in a manner wasted itself; but those that talk thus, seem eager to revive it, by new devices to stir the embers. All that we can now do, is to build the house again, if we can; and hang those that fired it, which we are sure we ought. Besides, we have long known who did it; they have been taken in the fact at noon-day, and every day. This thing was not done in a corner, nor at once, nor by one; the villainy was deliberate, gradual, and open.

These gentlemen do however confess, that the house has been set on fire; which confession they would doubtless be glad to avoid, if they could: But the misery is sorely felt, and all Europe are witnesses of it. Can they therefore, after an acknowledgment that the nation has been burned, have the face to be contriving ways to delay the punishment of the burners? Has self-love no share in this? And by the delay of the punishment of others, do they not as good as avow, that they tremble for themselves? For my part, I can see no difference in this case, between delaying it, and frustrating it.

The expedients for retrieving us, if we can be retrieved, are certainly compatible with expedients for revenging us; and the latter will facilitate the former. It will give life to the poor bankrupt heart-broken people, if they see that their destroyers meet due vengeance, and that they are like to be no more the prey of daring parricides.

G   *I am, &c.*

NO. 8. SATURDAY, DECEMBER 24, 1720.

The Arts of able guilty Ministers to save themselves. The wise and popular Conduct of Queen Elizabeth towards publick Harpies; with the Application.

SIR,

There is not in politicks a more established rule, than, *That when a corrupt and wicked ministry intend to pillage a nation, they make use of vile and contemptible instruments, to gather in their plunder, and allow the miscreants part of it; and when the cry for justice becomes strong and universal, they always hang up their faithful rogues.* By this means they stop the people's mouths, and yet keep the money.

But they act by no rule of good policy, but are, in truth, chargeable with folly, or rather with phrenzy, who dream that they can prevent this cry, by the means that first raised it, and by means that will ever produce it. As well might they attempt to prevent the spreading of a deluge, by damming it up; which would prove the direct method to make a whole country its conquest; for it will then know no bounds, but bear down men, beasts, and cities before it; whereas its force and mischief are easily prevented, if proper channels be opened for it, and its torrent be skilfully directed.

The simple multitude, when most provoked, are easily appeased, if they have but fuel for their rage: They will scarce feel their miseries, if they do but fancy that justice is done upon the authors of their miseries. And whatever they suffer; the hanging of a few sorry knaves, who are but the working-tools of a few greater, will hush all the tumult of their spirits, and reconcile them to patience and wretchedness.

The expedient, therefore, to please them, is constantly practised by all wise traitors, by all able oppressors. But when, through the ignorance of their pillagers, the course of justice is entirely stopped; when the abused and enraged people can have no remedy, either real or imaginary, nor one victim to their fury, they will naturally and necessarily look higher; and then who can foresee where their vengeance will end?

If a pirate, who robs upon the sea, be hanged for his robbery, every body is satisfied with the death of the offender: But if the action be avowed, and he produce a commission, the state that gave it becomes answerable.

All these secrets in government were excellently understood by Queen Elizabeth's ministry. Out of her history I have therefore copied the following passage, and the following speech.

> The Queen, upon her return from a progress, held a Parliament at Westminster; wherein, among other things, several good laws were made for the relief of the poor, and of maimed and disabled soldiers and seamen; against fraudulent guardians and trustees; the cheats and impositions of

clothiers; and the robberies and outrages committed upon
the borders of the kingdom towards Scotland. But whereas
great complaints were made in the lower house, relating to
the engrossing practice:[1]

(for it seems there were some, who, under the colour of publick
good, but, in reality, to the great damage of the kingdom, had got
the Queen's letters patents, for the sole privilege and liberty of
vending some particular sorts of wares):

> The Queen therefore, to forestall them, published a proc-
> lamation, declaring those grants to be null and void; and
> also left them to be tried at common law. A method which
> was so acceptable to the lower house, that eighty of that
> body were appointed to wait upon her Majesty with their
> humble thanks, which the Speaker was to present in the
> name of them all. She received them very graciously, and
> gave her answer in the following speech:

> Gentlemen,

> I owe you my best thanks and acknowledgments for your
> respect towards me; not only for your good inclination, but
> those clear and publick expressions thereof, which have
> discovered themselves in retrieving me from a mistake,
> into which I have been betrayed; not so much by the faults
> of my will, as the error of my judgment. This had unavoid-
> ably drawn a blemish upon me, (who account the safety of
> my people my chief happiness) had you not made me
> acquainted with the practice of these lewd harpies and
> horse-leeches. I would sooner lose my heart or hand, than
> ever consent to allow such privilege to engrossers, as may
> turn to the detriment of my people. I am not so blinded
> with the lustre of a crown, as to let the scale of justice be
> weighed down by that of an arbitrary power. The gay title
> of a prince may deceive such as know nothing of the secret
> of governing; as a gilded pill may impose upon the patient:
> But I am not one of those unwary princes; for I am very
> sensible, that I ought to govern for the publick good, and

1. Engrossing consisted of securing or attempting to secure a monopoly of a
commodity in order to resell at a higher price and was punishable at both common law and by statute.

not to regard my own particular; and that I stand accountable to another, a greater tribunal. I account myself very
happy, that, by God's assistance, I have enjoyed so prosperous a government in all respects, and that he has blessed
me with such subjects, for whom I could be contented to
lay down my crown and life. I must entreat you, that let
others be guilty of what faults or misdemeanors soever,
they may not, through any misrepresentation, be laid at my
door. I hope the evidence of a good conscience will, in all
respects, bear me out. You cannot be ignorant, that the servants of princes have, too often, an eye to their own advantage; that their faults are often concealed from their
notice; and that they cannot, if they would, inspect all
things, when the weight and business of a whole kingdom
lies on their shoulders.[2]

Here is a speech, worthy of the occasion, worthy of a wise
prince, worthy of a free people; a speech that has truth, and sense,
and spirit in it. We may be sure from the frankness and vigour of
it, that the ministers who advised it were no sharers in the guilt and
oppression of which it complains: If they had, they would have
chosen words more faint and equivocal; they would have shuffled
in their assertions; they would have talked more cowardly; they
would have kept off from particulars: They could not have hid
their guilt and fears. But here their boldness is the effect of their
innocence, and prompted by it.

Her Majesty frankly owns, that she was drawn into an
error; but that it was only an error of her judgment, she makes
manifest by her alacrity and forwardness to punish those harpies
and horse-leeches, who, in her name, had abused the publick: She
owns it just, that those engrossers should suffer: She owns that the
art and end of reigning, is to advance the publick good; and when
that good is not attained, she consigns to punishment those rooks
and traitors, through whose fault it is not attained. She owns that
she has been abused by her servants; who, under her authority,

2. William Camden's *The History of the Most Renowned and Victorious Princess
Elizabeth, Late Queen of England* (London: Printed for Benjamin Fisher, 1630).
The passage, which concerns the restraints placed on royal monopolies in
1601, appears in book IV, pp. 199–200.

and in the name of the law, had sought their own vile advantages; and she removes from herself all guilt, by giving up the guilty.

Happy Queen! happy in her own qualifications; happy in those of her counsellors: But wise and good as she was, she could not have talked thus, if her ministry had been weak or wicked: Had this been her misfortune, in spite of her sincerity, wisdom and resolution, her speech would have been false, faint, and silly. But her counsellors were able and faithful, and made England prosper; and if we except some rebellions, and some persecutions, both the doings of hot-headed bigots, her people saw nothing during her whole reign but felicity and sunshine.

This has entailed blessings upon her memory, and praise upon that of her counsellors: And, indeed, the happiness or misery of a people will always be the certain measure of the glory or infamy of their rulers, whenever such happiness or misery is evidently deducible from their management.

The above passage out of Queen Elizabeth's history, I thought not impertinent to our present times: Her people had suffered from harpies and horse-leeches: This shews, that the corruption had not reached the court; the hands of her ministers were clean, else her speech would have taken another turn.

Has England suffered less, in this our day, from harpies and horse-leeches? Surely no: All our losses, pillages, and oppressions, since the Conquest, do not balance the present great calamity: From a profusion of all things, we are reduced to a want of every thing: Heaven avert the pestilence and the famine! I am afraid that the latter begins to be sorely felt by many thousands of our poor, and even the rich complain that they can hardly find money to buy bread.

And shall not our harpies be given up? Shall not their blood and money make an undone nation some small amends for their heavy depredations and matchless villainy? Certainly they must: From a ministry as able, and as innocent, as that of Queen Elizabeth, we may expect the behaviour and publick spirit of Queen Elizabeth's ministry: Having no part in the guilt of harpies, they cannot dread the vengeance due to harpies: They have not raised out of their country's calamities, fortunes great as those calamities; they have no discoveries to dread; they have no guilt to hide; they have not conspired with harpies.

G   *I am, &c.*

NO. 9. SATURDAY, DECEMBER 31, 1720.

❦ *Against the projected Union of the Three Great Companies;[1] and against remitting to the South-Sea Company any Part of their Debt to the Publick.*

SIR,

The most successful deluders and oppressors of mankind have always acted in masquerade; and when the blackest villainies are meant, the most opposite spirit is pretended. Vice acts with security, and often with reputation, under the vail of virtue.

Hence atheists have set up for the greatest piety; and, to cover their own real want of it, have cruelly burned those who really had it. The most merciless tyrants have, in the midst of oppression, set up for the patrons of liberty; and, while their hands were deep in blood, impudently adopted the title of clemency; and publick liberty has almost always been given up by those, who passed for the patrons of publick liberty.

The cheating religious orders of the Church of Rome gain the greatest wealth, by a profession of the strictest poverty. The popish inquisitors, while they deliver over to the flames a poor wretch, already half dead with fears, famine, and torture, beseech and adjure the civil magistrate, who must see it done, by the love of God, and the bowels of Jesus Christ, not to hurt his life or limb. And our inquisitors at home began their Occasional Bill[2] with a

1. The Bank of England, the East India Company, and the South Sea Company.
2. The Occasional Conformity Act, which passed Parliament in 1711, was designed to prevent nonconformists who technically satisfied the Test Act—by having received communion in an Anglican Church but who regularly attended a nonconformist "chapel"—from occupying civil or military office. The act was repealed in 1718.

declaration for liberty of conscience; though the purpose of them, and their bill, was to destroy all liberty of conscience.

Companies and joint-stocks are always established for the encouragement and benefit of trade; though they always happen to mar and cramp trade. The Peerage Bill[3] was to be granted as a favour to the Commons of England, by cutting off the Commons of England from all right to peerage. And some people, to save charges to England, are for giving up Gibraltar, which is of such advantage to England; being the security of all our trade. Sweden was once to be destroyed, to preserve the balance of power in the north; and now Sweden must be defended, for the very same reason.[4]

When certain chiefs were at mortal odds, one side opposing (at all adventures) whatever the other projected, it was thought convenient to both sides to come to terms; for one party wanted to fill their coffers, and the other to save their bacon.[5] However, the good of the publick was their sole aim: They, good men! sought no personal advantages, though they have since got considerable ones: But we must believe their sayings, notwithstanding their doings.

Stock-jobbing too must be declared against, whilst the greatest stock-jobbing is promoting. Last year a South-Sea project was to be established to pay off the national debts; and now a project is said to be in embryo, to remit the greatest part of the debt due to the nation by the South-Sea: And if so, the whole nation is to suffer this general loss, out of mere pity to a small part of the nation. Twelve months ago forty millions was not too much to be

3. Introduced into Parliament in 1719 by the Sunderland-Stanhope administration, the bill was designed to prevent any addition to the number of peers, thus creating a permanent majority for their ministry in the House of Lords. The bill was decisively defeated in the Commons.

4. In 1717, Britain came close to war with Sweden over Charles XII's intrigues with members of the Jacobite court and over Swedish privateering on British ships engaged in trading with Russian-occupied Swedish ports. By 1719, however, George I's fears of Russia's growing ambitions in Germany led to a shift in British policy toward Sweden.

5. The reference is to the struggle for power, which lasted from 1717 until the bursting of the South Sea Bubble, between the supporters of the Whig administration of Lord Stanhope and the Earl of Sunderland and those Whigs, led by Robert Walpole and his brother-in-law, Charles, Viscount Townsend, who joined the Tories in opposition.

trusted with one company, high in credit, and its reputation hoisted up by publick authority; but now, when they are bankrupt and undone, and when their directors and undertakers are universally hated and detested, it is to be feared, it seems, that they will become too formidable, if all the stock subscribed into them be continued with them.

There is, therefore, I am told, a project on foot, in Exchange Alley, to deliver up the nation to three companies; and to let them divide us, their cully, among them. In order to prevail upon these three great societies to accept us as a present, to be used as they think fit, I humbly presume that we must behave ourselves as follows: We can do no less than sacrifice the poor half-starved manufacturers to one of them, and oblige ourselves to lay no restraint upon India callicoes, &c. We must also confirm the clause which makes that society perpetual. New trades, more monopolies, and fresh privileges, must be given to another great and virtuous company, which had made so good use of the old: And the Bank of England, which long preserved its integrity, must be brought into the conspiracy; and without doubt something more must be given them, perhaps the increase of their term.[6]

Now, if this mighty project, this noble design, can be accomplished; I suppose that every one will see, or be prevailed upon to see, the absolute necessity why all past errors, and former management, should be forgot; because publick credit, which depends upon temper and moderation, must not be interrupted by ill-timed enquiries, nor disturbed by publick vengeance. How finely we are to be disposed of; and how safe it is to provoke us!

The projectors of such a publick good must deserve well from their country; and I will give city security, that they shall be no losers by it. Where is the wonder, or ill policy of the plunderers and dishonourers of the nation, if the betrayers of their trust should keep a little ill-begotten wealth, to preserve the publick peace? Without doubt, they will give large shares of their prey to those who have power to let them keep the rest; and will readily help their projec-

6. An extension of the guaranteed period of government patronage through long-term borrowing by the Exchequer.

tors and coadjutors with their honest skill and endeavours, to form new projects, to get as much as they have done.

There lives in a certain kingdom, a certain gentleman, of no mean importance there at present, who was agent to one who had the custodium of a forfeited estate there, worth twelve thousand pounds a year; and when he gave in his account to his successor, brought the estate some hundreds of pounds in debt to himself.[7] The other resented this with some menacing expressions, but could get no other answer from him, but that he would abide by his account: "However," says he, "if you will be discreet, I will help you to the man that helped me to this account."

But what now, if, after all, there should be a little job in a corner; and if any gentleman, of remarkable merit, should have amends made for his services, sufferings, and losses of late years? Why, there is nothing uncommon in it; for, *who will serve the Lord for nought?* This certainly can be no reason for rejecting a project, which will restore publick credit, fill the Alley again, raise South-Sea stock to three or four hundred, and help the present proprietors to new bubbles; without doing any other mischief, than that of ruining a few thousand families more, and of not paying off the nation's debts.[8]

These, I confess, are potent reasons; and will, without doubt, have their due weight with all persons interested. But, for myself, who am so unfortunate as often to differ from my betters, I

7. This is likely a personal reminiscence. In 1699 Trenchard was chosen by the House of Commons as one of seven commissioners responsible for taking an account of the forfeited estates in Ireland.

8. Trenchard is here writing ironically of a proposal put forward by Walpole in late 1720 to provide relief for South Sea stockholders. Walpole's Ingraftment Scheme called for the cancellation of £18,000,000 of South Sea capital. This was to be accomplished by exchanging that amount of South Sea stock (supplemented by the South Sea Company's payment to each of the other firms of £1,500,000) for £9,000,000 of Bank of England stock and a like amount of stock in the East India Company. The exchange would thus be effected in a ratio of 1.2 shares at par and cash of South Sea stock for one share at par of Bank or East India stock. The effect of this ingraftment of a significant proportion of the South Sea Company's swollen capital, reducing it from approximately £38,000,000 to about £20,000,000, would, it was hoped, increase the selling price of South Sea stock to around £400. In early 1721 Parliament enacted a statute that would have permitted the three Companies to put Walpole's proposal into effect, but the scheme was never acted upon.

can find nothing in this proposal, which has any tendency to help the present company, or to raise credit, in any respect, or to retrieve us from our great and national calamities; but, on the contrary, to plunge the publick inevitably into irretrievable ruin, by making it impossible, by any medium in nature but that of a sponge, to discharge our national burdens: It will, besides, deprive us of our only colourable pretence, which could justify or excuse the late dreadful scheme; and which, I believe, I may safely say, was the only pretence ever offered to excuse it. I think that it will be listing the three great companies, with all the moneyed interest in England, against England; and will, at last, reduce, and even force, all parties not to oppose what I dread to name, and tremble to think of.

The project abovementioned is calculated, we are told, for the advantage of South-Sea, and for the improvement of their stock; and, in order to this, a great part of that stock is to be given away to the Bank of England, and to the East-India Company; without any apparent consideration to themselves, or any other use to the publick, than the uniting the three great companies in one interest; and consequently, the forming such a potent conspiracy against the whole kingdom, as nothing but a total confusion of all things can dissolve. O Companies, Companies! ye bane of honesty, and ruin of trade; the market of jobbers, the harvest of managers, and the tools of knaves, and of traitors!

It is proposed, that the South-Sea is to give the Bank an hundred and twenty pounds for every hundred pounds of stock in the Bank; which stock is said to be but barely worth ninety pounds; even though we should suppose that they had never divided any of their principal: Which, whether they have done it or not, no body but themselves can know: But at this rate, however, they must divide, whenever they are paid off by the government.

But we are told, that they are to be let also into the profits of banking; from which profits, 'tis said, that they are enabled to divide three per cent upon the old capital, besides the five per cent paid them by the government: But, even upon this foot, the greater their capital is, the less they will be able to divide: And consequently, when nine millions are added to their old capital, they will not be able to divide much above one per cent[9] which is not the interest of the money paid in difference between ninety, which is the real value, and an hundred and twenty, which is the nominal value.

Besides, there is no probability that the Bank can continue to make, for the future, the same gain of banking, as heretofore. The trafficking in publick tallies, from whence that gain chiefly arose, will be at an end, unless there be new funds given, and new debts contracted.

The contract proposed by these people, to be made with the other company, is still worse; for, there they are to give a hundred and twenty pounds for a hundred-pound nominal stock, which is suspected to be worth very little;[10] some men being of the opinion, that the greatest part of the ten per cent divided for some years past, has been pocketed out of other people's money, borrowed by the company upon their bonds: And yet for this choice bargain, they are to give six hundred thousand pounds at present, and subject nine hundred thousand pounds more to be disposed of according to the pleasure, skill, and honesty of the present directors. A pretty sum, and doubtless set apart to answer and accomplish some lovely job, which will appear in proper time, and by which the projectors of the scheme, I dare say, will be no losers!

'Tis said too, that the trade of this company may be enlarged; I suppose they mean, by bringing in more India manufactures, to the ruin of our own.

9. Walpole's proposal provided that the Exchequer pay a five-percent annuity on that portion of Bank stock swapped for South Sea stock. In addition, the capital of the Bank of England in 1720 was approximately £5,500,000, on which it had been paying an annual dividend of £165,000, or three percent. What Trenchard appears to be arguing here is that, even should the capital of the South Sea Company be reduced to £20,000,000, a return of eight percent on that portion of stock surrendered by South Sea stockholders for Bank stock would still generate less than one percent on the stockholders' total investment.

10. The stock of the East India Company underwent a sharp fall (although not as precipitous as that of the South Sea Company) between July and Dec. 1720. Its opening price on July 1 was £450 while it closed on Dec. 15 at £155. It continued, however, to pay an annual dividend of ten percent on the par value of its shares.

Now all this we are given to understand is for the sole benefit of the South-Sea; and if they have not sense to conceive it aright, a worse thing may befall them: We all know, what directors and their old patrons carry halters about their necks, though they have millions in their pockets; and who would not give away a little of other people's money, to save a great deal of their own, with their lives into the bargain? A special set of traitors, to negotiate for the very being of a kingdom!

But I must tell all these forgers of schemes, and inventors of grievances, that the nation, exhausted by past projects, cannot bear new ones, nor furnish out more millions to glut more harpies. The want of bread, long felt by the poor, begins now to be felt by the rich. The purses therefore of the new conspirators must be filled out of the extortions and depredations of the old, or remain empty: They may rack their invention, sift every topick of knavery, and toss and change their projects as much and as long as they please; but we know that nothing but plain honesty can ever save us; and to those who would practise honesty, plain speech is best. Let us honestly hang up those who have deceived and undone us, and let us beware of new deceivers and new destroyers: Let us, with a severity equal to our distress, examine what the directors and their masters have embezzled, and lost to their country, by their merciless villainy, and consuming avarice; and let us have the only satisfaction that they can make us, their lives, and their estates: Let, afterwards, a fair valuation be made of their present capital, and let all the world know it; that the purchaser may buy solid substance, and not a fleeting shadow. This is the honest way to restore credit again; this will prevent the roguish part of stock-jobbing; and this will throw the remaining money into trade once more.

But what, may some say, if we should give away from the South-Sea Company some millions to make new friends, and to save our old friends, so long as we can make that company amends out of the publick, for such a loss? A thing easily done! It is only giving them back again the seven millions already due by them to the publick;[11] or at least the greatest part of those seven millions,

11. The debt due the government by the South Sea Company was somewhat over £7,000,000, under the terms of its agreement of Apr. 1720 by which the company assumed £31,000,000 of government liabilities.

as the same stand secured upon forty millions; and if we do this, behold the advantage that will accrue from it! We will then be under no necessity of hanging our countrymen, or calling up any to disgorge their honest gains: Besides, it is to be hoped that this proposal will be backed with such powerful motives, as to meet with little opposition.

This calls to my mind a comparison, which I have been for some time very apt to make, between the French projectors[12] and those of another country which I know.[13] The first plunder for the publick; the other plunder the publick: The one robs part of the people for the whole people; the other robs the whole people for a small part of the people.

This comparison may be the subject of another letter to you, if you think fit to print this.

T   *I am, &c.*

NO. 10. TUESDAY, JANUARY 3, 1720.

*The Iniquity of late and new Projects about
the South-Sea considered. How fatally they affect
the Publick.*

SIR,

When we compare one nation with another, and balance the power of both, we are not to consider alone the number of people, or the wealth diffused amongst the people; though number and wealth are undoubtedly the first elements of power in a commonwealth; no more than we are to consider the mere extent of territory, or the mere fertility of soil: But we are chiefly to consider, how much of that wealth can be brought together, how it may be most frugally managed, and how most skilfully applied to the publick emolument and defence.

If, in taxing labour and manufactures, we exceed a certain proportion, we discourage industry, and destroy that labour and

12. That is, to John Law and the Mississippi Company.
13. Great Britain.

those manufactures. The like may be said of trade and navigation; they will bear but limited burdens: And we find by experience, that when higher duties are laid, the product is not increased; but the trade is lost, or the goods are run.

Nor can more be extorted from the gentleman and freeholder, than he can spare from the support of his family, in a way suitable to his former condition.

When impositions exceed these bounds, the history of all ages will convince us, that their produce is only bitterness, murmurings, universal discontents; and their end, generally, rebellion, and an overthrow of the then present establishment, or of public liberty.

If therefore one state, for example, possessed of five times as much true, but scattered, wealth, as another state, cannot for all that, from a defect in its constitution, collect so much from the people as the poorer state can; or, if when collected, does yet trust the same to the disposal of blood-suckers and traitors, who intercept the national wealth, and divert it to private purses; or if it be appropriated, before it be raised, to the payment of former debts; or if it be embezzled in pensions and salaries to mercenary men, for traitorous ends; then is such a state really weaker than the other poorer state, and less capable of defending itself against the other, so much its inferior in outward shew and intrinsick power.

This was the state of Spain for near two hundred years; Spain, the mistress of so many nations, and of a new world, richer in silver and gold than the old; Spain, that from terrifying all Christendom with chains, and from threatening all Europe with universal slavery, reduced itself, by mortgaging its publick revenues, to such a despicable condition, that we have seen, in our days, that once formidable kingdom contended for by two small armies of foreigners, within its own bowels:[1] In which contest the natives themselves were little more than spectators; as is very justly observed by the author of a pamphlet printed last year, and written with a spirit which I pretend not to imitate. Had that pamphlet

1. The reference is to military operations in Spain during the War of the Spanish Succession, when British, Portuguese, Dutch, Austrian, and German troops fought Spanish and French forces between 1704 and 1710.

been generally read, and well weighed, it would have prevented most of the mischiefs which we now lamentably labour under. It is entitled, *Considerations upon the State of the Publick Debts in general, and of the Civil List in particular.*[2] I would recommend it to the reading of every one, who is not ashamed of being an honest man.

It is certain, that all the powerful nations of Europe, who were parties in the two last bloody and expensive wars,[3] were reduced, by mortgaging their publick revenues, to the same low and abject condition; and nothing saved any one of them from all the rest, but that all the rest were in the same state of impotence and distress. They were all miserably weak. That people, therefore, who can soonest discharge their publick burdens, will give laws to the rest; and either reduce them to subjection and vassalage, or to a necessity of seizing their mortgaged funds.

There are in the world but two ways of clearing a nation of its publick engagements: The one is, by paying them off; the other is, not to pay them at all. When the one cannot be practised, a small skill in politicks will tell us, that the other must.

It is a jest for any man to flatter himself, that any state will not save the whole people, by the ruin of a part of the people, when the ruin of a part is absolutely necessary to the preservation of the whole. This consideration should, methinks, be worth the attention of the gentlemen inhabitants of the Alley. In truth, nothing would exercise their thoughts more, were it not that every one hopes to save one, by cheating another into a hard and knavish bargain. Will men never have done hoping? They forget how they were caught last year in the South-Sea, with all their hopes and their wisdom about them.

It is, doubtless, the last misfortune to a nation, to be beholden to a sponge for the payment of its debts; such a necessity must be a heavy necessity, attended with many sorrowful circum-

2. This pamphlet of thirty-nine pages was in fact written by John Trenchard and published anonymously. Its correct title is *Some Considerations upon the State of our Publick Debts in general, and of the Civil List in Particular* (London: Printed by J. Roberts, 1720).

3. The War of the Spanish Succession (1701–1715) and its sequel, the War of the Quadruple Alliance (1718–1720), both of which involved the major countries of western Europe, among them England, France, Spain, Austria, Prussia, Holland, Savoy, and Portugal.

stances, and much sore distress. Nothing but the certain fear of foreign force, or domestick tyranny, can justify it. But even a great calamity is eligible, in comparison of a greater. Every person, therefore, who is a creditor to his country, and has demands upon the publick, is nearly concerned to prevent such great and personal, and indeed general misery; which cannot be at all prevented, but by putting the national debts into a method of being honourably discharged. This is the concern of every honest man; this ought to be the care of every worthy citizen; this will be the task of every guiltless great man.

All innocent men, throughout the world, find a private blessing in the general felicity of the publick; and none but mock-patriots, who foolishly or deliberately can lead kingdoms into ruin; desperate hard-hearted parricides, who can wantonly suck out the vitals of their country, whose fortunes are often the plunder of the publick, whose creatures are conspirators, hired against the publick; I say, none but such traitors can find private joy in publick confusion, or their own security in the slavery of their country. Those, it is true, who earn vengeance by committing mighty crimes, would, doubtless, go on to resemble themselves, and to avoid it, if they could, by committing crimes still more mighty. If any amongst us should be capable of practising such great wickedness to get enormous wealth, such persons, if not prevented, might still practise greater to keep it. A fox pursued by the full cry of the hounds, will run into the dog-kennel for shelter; as at the battle of La Hogue, the French fleet fled through the race of Alderney, and ventured rocks and shelves, to escape from the conquering enemy.[4]

It is a folly, and indeed an infatuation, in any persons interested in the publick funds, to form any schemes, or to fall into any schemes for increasing those funds, or for continuing in them, any longer than is absolutely necessary to pay them their debts: When our neighbouring nations have cleared theirs, we too must clear ours, or we are undone. 'Tis said, indeed, that a revolution in

4. In May 1692, English and Dutch naval forces defeated the French fleet at Cap la Hogue, off the Normandy coast. With this victory, mastery of the seas during the War of the League of Augsburg passed from the French to the English. The Race of Alderney lies between Cap la Hogue and the Channel Islands.

government would certainly and effectually do it, and do it at once; and this I take to be the true reason why so many unthinking men appear to wish it; though I hope it is in vain. God avert so dreadful a catastrophe!

Spain has already discharged itself of its publick burdens, by a general sweep:[5] And behold the effect of this! It again shews its head in the world; again it carries its armies into new countries. Holland lies still, free from new broils, and fresh expence: It politically pleads poverty: It takes all ways in its power to recover its losses; and questionless laughs in its sleeve to see another nation grow more mad, and more in debt every year; to see it every year mortgaging new revenues, and every year engaging in wild wars, to support the interests of a state of no concernment to it.

But the most terrible instance of all, is that of France: That government, though to the ruin of great multitudes of other people, has almost, if not quite, got rid of its incumbrances and engagements. The whole wealth of that great kingdom is now got into the hands of the publick. From which formidable situation of theirs, is there not room to fear, that as soon as the present confusion is a little abated,[6] they will renew their designs for empire, and throw Europe into arms again? This is an alarming reflection! And what do the gentlemen of the Alley expect from us, under such an ill-boding circumstance? Trade is already burdened as much as it can bear, and perhaps more than it ought to bear: There is scarce a commodity that can be taxed, but is already taxed. We are marked, we are mortgaged from head to foot. They do not surely expect that the Parliament will give ten shillings in the pound upon land, or that it could be raised if they did.

5. Following the succession of the Bourbons to the Spanish throne in 1700, the Spanish government instituted a series of extraordinary exactions to raise revenues, including the sequestration of the property of dissidents and the suspension of payments on state annuities. Although revenues were substantially increased as a consequence of these measures, Spain's expenditures at the time were so great and its debt so huge that it can hardly be said it was able to "discharge itself of its public burdens."

6. Trenchard and Gordon are here referring to the financial chaos following the bursting of the Mississippi Bubble in the fall of 1720. With the eager support of the French regent, John Law had sought to consolidate the whole of the French national debt by encouraging government creditors to exchange their notes for shares in his Company.

What therefore are we to do in such a calamitous case? Are we to save ourselves at the expence of the gentlemen of the Alley? Or are we to perish together with them? The choice is easy. Can they be so weak, as to form a pretended necessity, to bring their country into such unhappy circumstances; and yet not fear that wise and honester men may take advantage of a real necessity, to get out of such unhappy circumstances?

There is but one thing to be done, to save themselves and their country together; and that is, to put the debts into a method of being certainly and speedily paid off. The present establishment may be saved, though they are undone: But if, through folly or knavery, the establishment sink, they must sink with it. I hope therefore, that they will not be decoyed into any traitorous designs of desperate men: Men, whose characters are but faintly expressed by that of parricides; men, who, had they studied the art of making us miserable, could not have been more accomplished in their trade, nor boast of compleater success. Where is our trade, by which we so long flourished? It is lost. Where is our publick faith, once our own boast, and the envy of foreign nations? It is fled; and one man has no longer any faith in another. Where is our money? Where are our current millions? The people have none. The most part find it hard to buy bread; and many find it impossible. Every man whom you meet complains that he is undone. All our coin is engrossed, pocketed by vile jobbers, their prompters and confederates; publick robbers, who, to keep what they have got, and to escape deserved punishment (if such punishment can possibly be found), would deliver up the wealth and power of England into the griping and polluted hands of a new conspiracy of stock-jobbers, worse than the last, by being more numerous and potent. With these they would combine for common defence, and for publick destruction; with these, contrive new ways to enlarge our miseries, shorten our enjoyments still more, and grind us still smaller; with these, they would form into such a confederacy against their common country, and against common honesty, as would mock even the endeavours of a legislature to dissolve it. Good God! what implacable men! thus mercilessly bent to ruin the very ruins of their country!

What Briton, blessed with any sense of virtue, or with common sense; what Englishman, animated with a publick spirit, or with any spirit, but must burn with rage and shame, to behold the nobles and gentry of a great kingdom; men of magnanimity; men of breeding; men of understanding, and of letters; to see such men bowing down, like Joseph's sheaves, before the face of a dirty *stock-jobber*, and receiving laws from men bred behind counters, and the decision of their fortunes from hands still dirty with sweeping shops!

Surely we shall never suffer this to be our case, and therefore shall never see it. It is ridiculous to think that a nation, free as we are, and bold by being so, will ever submit to such indignities: It is therefore easy to foresee, if once we foolishly take the first step, what will necessarily be the next. One oppression cannot be supported but by another, and a greater; and force and violence alone can do what reason cannot and will not do. These hardships will produce new wants, and new necessities for money; which money, if such men can have their will, will only be to be had from these companies, and from them only upon hard conditions, and in exchange for new privileges, still tending to the detriment of general trade, and ending in the total ruin of the nation.

The nation will be provoked in proportion as it is distressed; ill usage will be returned with rage: And then, I doubt not, when these projectors have rendered the people distracted, they will tell us, that it will not be safe to venture them with another election. They will do every thing in their power to make the kingdom disaffected; and then urge that disaffection as a good reason not to trust them.

This conduct will produce necessarily more and higher discontents; discontents will make armies necessary; armies will inflame those discontents still more vehemently. I dare think no further. But sure there is no one who loves King George, and his government, but will endeavour to prevent these dismal mischiefs, before it be too late.

No man living laments the calamities brought upon his country, more than I do those brought upon mine: Yet I freely own, that I think the paying off the nation's debts, and restoring, by that means, the kingdom to its power, its grandeur, and its security again, was an end worth all the evils which we have yet suffered; an end which ought, if possible, to have been purchased with greater than we have yet suffered, if it could not otherwise have been purchased. I think that it ought to have been done, though attended with many ill circumstances; and might have been done, even upon those hard terms, with justice to private men, and honour to the nation. We are not a people without it; nor is it worth while to dispute about the best cabin in a ship that is sinking.

This prospect gave me some pleasure, and some relief to my thoughts, made anxious by the melancholy and importunate clamours of thousands and ten thousands of my distressed country-men: But when I was told that a project was formed by men of fig-ure, power, and fortune, to give back all, and the only advantage which we were to reap, or could reap, from so many miseries, and which could alone palliate or excuse such a wild and desperate attempt; though this was the only excuse which was ever offered, or can yet be suggested by the wisest men in behalf of it; I confess that I was seized with horror and confusion from such news, and could see nothing before my eyes but total desolation and final ruin.

To tell us, that this is to be done out of tenderness to the miserable, is adding contempt to the injury: It is insulting our understandings, and playing with the publick misfortunes; it is first to make us beggars, then to treat us like idiots. With as much modesty did a grand monarch, who was known to make himself sport, for about half a century, with the lives of men,[7] pretend to ground his desire of peace upon a conscientious inclination to pre-vent the effusion of Christian blood.

Those who have true compassion, virtue, and tenderness, will shew it upon the properest objects; they will prefer the security and welfare of many millions to the security and welfare of some thousands, though they should be many thousands; especially if the latter prove to have been covetous and unthinking men, caught in the snare which they spread for others: For by these wild bargains no man is undone, but he who intended the favour of being undone to somebody else. These gentlemen, pretending to so much tenderness and compassion, will not at least sacrifice those

7. Louis XIV, during whose reign of seventy-two years (1643–1715) France was almost continually at war.

who always foresaw the mischief, and always opposed it, to the relief of such who contributed to it; who made corrupt applications for an early admittance into the advantage of the secret; who swallowed plumbs in their imaginations, and ridiculed as fools or beggars all that kept at a wise and honest distance.

Pity and compassion are charming and engaging sounds, when rightly applied; but pity and compassion do not consist in protecting criminals from justice, and in suffering the devourers of a nation to go off with the plunder of a nation; nor in oppressing the people over again, to make the loser amends: Neither do they consist in giving away the publick treasure of nations to private men, for no reason, or for very bad reasons; nor in engaging a kingdom in wild and romantick expences, to serve wild and romantick purposes; neither do they consist in sacrificing the trade and manufacture of a whole people, and in consequence the bread of a whole people, to the destructive interests of societies of stock-jobbers, combined with publick plunderers for mutual defence.

Our wise and disinterested legislature mean other things; they have told us, that they will not relieve one part of the distressed and deluded bubbles, to the detriment of others, who have as much pretence to relief as themselves; and it is impossible to imagine that they will give up the unoffending and almost despairing people (whose interests they are chosen to assert) to repair the losses of unwary men, and to put thirty millions in the pockets of twenty stock-jobbers.

Can it be supposed, that the Parliament will refuse to make void hasty and private bargains, founded in corruption and fraud, and made without any one honest consideration? And shall this refusal be made for the publick good? And yet shall that very Parliament be thought capable of making void a publick bargain, made for the publick good, with the greatest deliberation, and upon the weightiest motives in the world? Which bargain was indeed the chief, if not the only cause, that drew upon us our present great calamities.

But we are told by the projectors, that the company is not able to pay the publick the sum stipulated; and the King must lose his right, where his right is not to be had. This is impudently as well as stupidly said; for the security is already in the hands of the publick: The nation owes the company near forty millions, and nothing is necessary but to stop the payment of seven.[8]

But it is farther urged by the projectors, that the company will be undone, if so much be stopped from them; and I aver, that the nation is undone, if it be not stopped.

Here a very pleasant observation offers itself: For this very same project, which would mercifully remit to the South-Sea Company the seven millions due by them to the publick,[9] is intended to raise a hundred pounds of their capital stock to three or four hundred pounds in value, I will suppose only to three hundred; and even then their present capital being about twenty-six millions, the whole will be worth about eighty millions;[10] and surely, if the publick give them such an immense advantage, they may well afford to pay the small sum of seven millions due to the publick out of it. Our own laws, and the laws of every country in the world, give precedence to the prerogative, in the business of debtor and creditor; and always secure the debts due to the publick, whatever becomes of those due to private men. Surely we shall not reject the wisdom of nations, and invert the maxims of government, that while we confirm the bargains of particular men, we destroy those made for the benefit of all the men in the kingdom.

But there is yet something more absurd in this project: For the bargain was made with the old company, who were to give three millions and a half, certain, to the publick; and about three millions more, if they could purchase in the annuitants:[11] Which

8. By the time the bubble burst in late 1720, the South Sea Company had converted approximately £40,000,000 of government debt and in turn owed the government somewhat over £7,000,000 in premiums.

9. A provision of Walpole's Ingraftment Scheme called for the remission of all South Sea debts owed the government.

10. In fact, under Walpole's proposal, the Company's capital would be reduced to about £20,000,000. If its shares were selling for £300, or three times their par value, the total value of stock in the Company would be approximately £60,000,000.

11. The agreement of Apr. 7, 1720 (O.S.) (6 Geo. I, c. 4), by which the South Sea Company assumed approximately £31,000,000 of the national debt, called for the company to pay the government an assured amount of slightly over £4,100,000, in addition to an indefinite amount to be determined by the num-

sum they could have afforded to the publick, if they could but have raised their stock thirty per cent upon the whole stock so united: But we have, in fact, seen its imaginary value increased, at one time, more than two hundred millions; which has enabled those in the secret to carry off more than twenty, if not thirty millions.

Valuing the stock, at present, at two hundred, which is less than the stock sells for, the old capital alone is advanced near twelve millions above its first value, and consequently is able to pay seven, without the assistance of the new subscribers: And, if the projectors of the scheme advance the stock to three or four hundred, as they pretend that they will; then the first contractors, and those who stand in their places, will double or treble their capital; though they alone were to pay the publick the poor consideration which has enabled them to do so.

Hard fate of poor England, to be thus the last regarded, even in schemes and deliberations which purely regard England! Private men, who have been bubbled, are to be pitied, but must private men, who have contributed to the publick ruin, and their own, be regarded preferably to the publick? And must publick compassion be shewn to private dupes, rather than to the publick itself?

Poor England! What a name art thou become! A name of infatuation and misery! How art thou fallen! how plundered! And those that have done it, would, to keep their spoil, agree to assist others to squeeze out thy last dregs, and to suck out thy remaining blood. How passive do they think thee! How tame would they make thee! An easy prey for devourers; who, while they hold thee fast, and gripe thee hard with iron claws, aggravate thy misery, by mocking it, and insolently talk of compassion.

What keener indignities can they do us, than thus to jest with us, while we are gasping, while we are expiring, in the midst of the pangs and convulsions into which they have wantonly and wickedly thrown us!

Odd is that compassion which arises from guilt and avarice; and with how much modesty would they christen, with the

ber of government annuities exchanged for South Sea stock. This provision of the agreement could have cost the Company an additional £3,400,000.

deluding title of pity, that conduct, which would prove in effect to be only impunity to the murderers of our prosperity, and the manglers of their country! Thus would they insult our understanding, and deal with us as if we had none.

How long shall we suffer under this pungent usage? this painful disgrace to our sense and our spirit? Patience under indignities, invites fresh indignities. We see our parricides do, as it were, take pains to invent new miseries for us. A hard task! considering those that they have already accomplished. Nay, they act as if they despaired of making us desperate.

They may be mistaken. And indeed, in the whole string of their politicks, I could never discover any one symptom of their skill in human nature, except that which they learned from brokers and pedlars in stocks.

In truth, matters are come to that pass, that an endeavour to make them worse, may probably make them better: *Res nolunt male administrari.*[12] All men suffer; all men are alarmed: Resentment rages high, and gathers thick from all quarters; and though it may seem big with some terrible event, yet it may be prevented by anticipation.

Our eyes are upon the Parliament, and so are the eyes of Europe. We have begun to conceive hope from the bold and upright spirit which appears in our representatives to right us and to revenge us. They have, indeed, a great and unprecedented opportunity given them, of securing to themselves, in the hearts of all Englishmen, a monument of grateful praise and publick spirit, and of perpetuating that praise in the memory of every Briton, till time shall be no more.

T and G.   *I am, &c.*

12. "Matters refuse to be administered badly."

NO. 11. SATURDAY, JANUARY 7, 1720.

꿩 *The Justice and Necessity of punishing great
Crimes, though committed against no subsisting Law
of the State.*

SIR,

S alus populi suprema lex esto: That *the benefit and safety of the people
constitutes the supreme law,* is an universal and everlasting
maxim in government; It can never be altered by municipal statutes: No customs can change, no positive institutions can abrogate,
no time can efface, this primary law of nature and nations. The
sole end of men's entering into political societies, was mutual protection and defence; and whatever power does not contribute to
those purposes, is not government, but usurpation.

Every man in the state of nature had a right to repel injuries, and to revenge them; that is, he had a right to punish the
authors of those injuries, and to prevent their being again committed; and this he might do, without declaring before-hand what
injuries he would punish. Seeing therefore that this right was
inherent in every private man, it is absurd to suppose that national
legislatures, to whom every man's private power is committed,
have not the same right, and ought not to exercise it upon proper
occasions.

Crimes being the objects of laws, there were crimes before
there were laws to punish them; and yet from the beginning they
deserved to be punished by the person affected by them, or by the
society, and a number of men united with him for common security, though without the sentence of a common judge (called by us
the magistrate) formally appointed to condemn offenders.

Laws, for the most part, do not make crimes, but suit and
adapt punishments to such actions as all mankind knew to be
crimes before. And though national governments should never
enact any positive laws, never annex particular penalties to known
offences; yet they would have a right, and it would be their duty to
punish those offences according to their best discretion; much

more so, if the crimes committed are so great, that no human wisdom could foresee that any man could be wicked and desperate enough to commit them.

Lawyers distinguish betwixt *malum prohibitum* and *malum in se*; that is, between crimes that are so in their own nature, and crimes that owe their pravity to a disobedience to positive laws. Of the former sort are all those actions, by which one man hurts another in his reputation, his person, or his fortune; and those actions are still more heinous, if they injure, or are intended to injure, the whole society.

The latter sort consists of such crimes as result from what legislatures enact for the particular benefit of private societies; as laws concerning the regularity of trade, the manner of choosing magistrates, local orders; and from such positive institutions, as receive their force alone from the powers that enact them. Now those crimes were not so before they were declared so; and consequently, no man before was under any obligation to avoid them.

It would be very severe and unjust to punish any man for an undesigned transgression of the latter sort; that is, for such action as he thought that he might lawfully and honestly do, and which he had never notice given him not to do. But to infer from thence, that a villain may despise all the laws of God and nature, ruin thousands of his fellow-subjects, and overturn nations with impunity, because such villainy was too monstrous for human foresight and prevention, is something so absurd, that I am ashamed to confute it.

This is nothing less than asserting, that a nation has not a power within itself to save itself: That the whole ought not to preserve the whole: That particular men have the liberty to subvert the government which protects them, and yet continue to be protected by that government which they would destroy: That they may overturn all law, and yet escape by not being within the express words of any particular law.

There are crimes so monstrous and shocking, that wise states would not suffer them to stand in their statute books; because they would not put such an indignity upon human nature, as to suppose it capable of committing them. They would not mention what they imagined would never be practised. The old Romans, therefore, had no law against parricide; yet there was no want of punishment for parricides from the want of law: Those black and enormous criminals were sewed up in a sack, and thrown into the Tiber.

In Holland, there was no law against men's breaking fraudulently;[1] yet the first man who was known to do so, was immediately executed, and his estate divided among his creditors.

In England, 'tis said, there was no law, till lately, against the burning of ships;[2] yet, if any man had burned the Royal Navy of England, lying at anchor, ought not his crime, which it seems was not felony, to have been declared high-treason?

Many nations have had particular officers appointed on purpose to punish uncommon crimes, which were not within the reach of ordinary justice. The Romans had a dictator; a great and extraordinary magistrate, vested with an extraordinary power, as he was created on extraordinary exigencies; and his commission was limited only by the publick good, and consisted in a very short direction, *Nequid detrimenti respublica capiat*;[3] in English, *To save the state*.

This powerful officer was once created on purpose to put to death Spurius Maelius, for giving *gratis* to the people a large quantity of corn, in a time of famine. This liberality of his was construed by the senate, an ambitious bribe to catch the hearts of the multitude, in order to seize their liberties. *Spurius Maelius— praedives, rem utilem pessimo exemplo, pejore consilio est aggressus.*[4] He undertook a publick and plausible thing, but of ill example, and

1. Breaking fraudulently: to fraudulently declare oneself bankrupt.

2. The reference is to a statute enacted in 1717 (4 Geo. I, c. 12) making it a crime punishable by death for any owner or member of the crew to burn or otherwise destroy a ship to the detriment of the ship's insurers.

3. "That the republic come to no harm," the formula used in the final decrees of the Roman Senate when the customary constitutional protections were about to be waived.

4. "Spurius Maelius, very rich, undertook to do a useful thing in the worst possible manner and with bad intentions." Livy, 4.13.1. Spurius *Maelius* (d. 439 B.C.), a Roman plebeian, is reputed to have distributed corn at his own expense, thus relieving a severe food shortage. He was accused of courting popularity with a view to making himself king and was thrown down from the Tarpeian rock.

with a worse design. *Largitiones frumenti facere instituit.*[5] His avowed pretence was to relieve the poor; *Plebemque hoc munere delinitam, quacunque incederet conspectus alatusque supra modum hominis privati, secum trahere.*[6] He cajoled the people, intending to enslave them; and growing too powerful for a subject, became terrible to the common liberty, which is supported by equality: *Ipse, ut est humanus animus insatiabilis eo quod fortuna spondet, ad altiora & non concessa tendere:*[7] The mind of man is restless, and cannot stand still, nor set bounds to its pursuits. It is not to be expected that one of our million men (and they say that we have several) will sit down and be content with his millions, though he were allowed to keep them (which God forbid!). He will be making new pushes for new acquisitions, having such ample means in his hands. Spurius Maelius would at first have been content with the consulate, or chief magistracy in ordinary; but because he found that even that could not be got without force, he thought that the same force would as well carry him higher, and make him king. *Et quoniam consulatus quoque eripiendus invitis patribus esset, de regno agitare.*[8] The traitor had been suffered to carry a great point; he had abused the publick, and deceived the people. The Senate, therefore, took him to task: and there being no law subsisting, by which he could be put to death— *Consules legibus constricti, nequaquam tantum virium in magistratu ad eam rem pro atrocitate vindicandum quantum animi haberent;*[9] they therefore created a dictator, an officer with power, for a time, to suspend laws, and make laws. The occasion was great—*Opus esse non forti solum viro, sed etiam libero, exsoluto que legum vinculis.*[10]

5. "He undertook to make free distributions of grain." Livy, 4.13.3.

6. "And the plebeians, captivated by this gift, followed him wherever he walked, conspicuous and important beyond the manner of a private citizen." Livy, 4.13.3.

7. "He himself, so insatiable is the human spirit for that which Fortune holds out to him, reached for higher, prohibited things." Livy, 4.13.4.

8. "And since the consulship would have to be seized from the unwilling nobles, he deliberated on how he might become king." Livy, 4.13.4.

9. "The consuls, limited by the laws, had nowhere near as much power in their office in this affair as they had the desire to punish him for his crime." Livy, 4.13.11.

10. "There was need not only of a strong man, but also of one who was free and unbound by the constraints of the law." Livy, 4.13.11.

L. Quincius Cincinnatus[11] was the man; a true and brave old republican, who worthily and boldly did his work, and by the hands of his master of the horse slew the mighty traitor, impudently imploring the publick faith, to which he was a sworn enemy; and complaining of the power of oppression, when the shameless villain had been only seeking a power to oppress. *Fidem plebis Romanae implorare; & opprimi se consensu patrum dicere.*[12] He knew that his villainies were out of the reach of the law, and he did not dream of an extraordinary method of punishing them by the Roman parliament. But he was deceived; and the dictator tells the people, that being a sort of an outlaw, he was not to be proceeded with as with a citizen of Rome: *Nec cum eo tanquam cum cive agendum fuisse.*[13] An unusual death was due to his monstrous wickedness: *Non pro scelere id magis quam pro monstro habendum.*[14] Nor was his blood alone, says the wise dictator, sufficient to expiate his guilt, unless we also pull down his house, where such crying crimes were first conceived; and confiscate to the publick use his estate and his treasures, the price and means of the publick ruin. And his estate was accordingly given to the publick—*Nec satis esse sanguine ejus expiatum, nisi tecta parietesque, inter quae tantum amentiae conceptum esset, dissiparentur; bonaque contacta pretiis regni mercandi publicarentur; jubere itaque questores, vendere ea bona & in publicum redigere:*[15] The treasury had them for the use of the publick.

11. Lucius Quinctius *Cincinnatus* (b. *c.* 519 B.C.), Roman general celebrated for his civic virtue. He was reputed to have twice been chosen dictator to lead Rome's armies against its enemies and to have, in both instances, laid down his office after a series of successes in the field, despite the rewards offered him by a grateful Senate.

12. "He called upon the protection of the Roman plebeians; and he said that he was oppressed by a conspiracy of the patricians." Livy, 4.14.4.

13. "It would not have been proper to deal with him [Maelius] as with a citizen." Livy, 4.15.3.

14. "This ought to be taken as a thing no less monstrous than criminal." Livy, 4.15.7.

15. "For his blood was not sufficient expiation unless the roofs and walls within which such great madness had been conceived also were destroyed and his possessions, tainted as the offering price for a kingdom, were confiscated. He therefore ordered the quaestors to sell the property and place the proceeds in the public treasury." Livy, 4.15.7–8.

Thus did the great, the wise, and the free Romans punish this extraordinary knave, by a power that was not ordinary. They likewise exerted it upon other occasions; nor were they the only people that did so.

The Athenians, grown jealous by having lost their liberties, by the usurpation of a private, but too powerful citizen,[16] durst never trust this great power to any single magistrate, or even to a council. They would not, however, part with it, but reserved it to the whole body of the people, agreeably to the nature of a popular government. In this jealous state, it was a crime to be popular, much more to affect popularity: They would not allow a man to have it in his power to enslave his country. And, indeed, it is wisdom in a state, and a sign that they judge well, to suppose, that all men who can enslave them, will enslave them. Generosity, self-denial, and private and personal virtues, are in politicks but mere names, or rather cant-words, that go for nothing with wise men, though they may cheat the vulgar. The Athenians knew this; and therefore appointed a method of punishing great men, though they could prove no other crime against them but that of being great men. This punishment was called the *ostracism,* or the sentence of a majority in a ballot by oyster-shells; by which a suspected citizen was adjudged to banishment for ten years. They would not trust to the virtue and moderation of any private subject, capable, by being great, to be mischievous; but would rather hurt a private subject, than endanger the publick liberty. Worthy men are thought to have suffered unjustly by this ostracism; and it may be true, for aught that I know; but still it secured the publick, and long secured it. Weak and babbling men, who penetrate no deeper than words, may blame this politick severity in the commonwealth of Athens; but it is justified, in that it was politick.

16. The reference is to *Pisistratus* (605–527 B.C.), Athenian statesman who was successful in making himself tyrant of Athens in 560 B.C. Upon his death in 527 B.C. his sons succeeded to the tyranny until they were expelled in 510 B.C. It was to rid Athens of the Pisistratid faction without perpetual recourse to armed resistance that the institution of ostracism was introduced in the constitutional reforms of 508 B.C.

In Venice, a wise, ancient, and honourable republick, there is a Council of Ten,[17] which exercises this extraordinary power: Every arbitrary prince in the world exercises it; and every free state in the world has an undoubted right to exercise it, though they have never delegated their power to particular magistrates to exercise it for them.

In England, indeed, we have not delegated this power at all, because we very well know who must have had it, and what use would be made of it. The legislature, therefore, has reserved this power to itself, and has an undoubted right to exercise it; and has often done so upon extraordinary occasions. It ought indeed to be exercised but upon extraordinary occasions. Jove's thunderbolts were only launched against such as provoked the thunderbolts of Jove.

I shall, in my next letter to you, apply these general maxims of government to our own particular constitution, and to the present occasion, which calls aloud for Jove's help and thunder.

G   *I am, &c.*

NO. 12. SATURDAY, JANUARY 14, 1720.

Of Treason: All Treasons not to be found in Statutes. The Right of the Legislature to declare Treasons.

SIR,

Treason, properly so called, in Latin, *Crimen laesae majestatis,*[1] is in all countries the same: It is an endeavour to subvert, or to do some notable mischief to the publick; of which every man is a part, and with which he has joined himself for mutual defence, under what form soever the administration is exercised. I own,

---

17. Established as a permanent committee of public safety in 1335, the Council of Ten was originally created to hunt down the remnant of the patrician conspiracy which sought to overthrow the Venetian commercial oligarchy.

---

1. "The crime of *lèse-majesté.*"

that lesser crimes are sometimes called by the same name, and subjected to the same punishment.

An attempt to destroy the chief magistrate of a commonwealth, or the general of an army in the field, or the governor of a town during a siege, are certainly treasons every where; because in such attempts, when they succeed, are often involved the ruin of states. They also are doubtless guilty of high treason, who, being entrusted with the wealth, security, and happiness of kingdoms, do yet knowingly pervert that trust, to the undoing of that people whom they are obliged, by undeserved rewards, as well as by all the ties of religion, justice, honour, and gratitude, to defend and protect.

'Tis the same, if any number of men, though in a lesser trust, or in no trust at all, should deliberately and knowingly destroy thousands of their fellow-subjects, and overturn the trade and publick credit of the nation, to enrich themselves and their accomplices.

These, and crimes of the like nature, are treasons from the nature of things themselves, antecedent to all laws that call them so; and will be treasons, though laws gained by subordination should call them otherwise: And every state has a right to treat those who commit them, as traitors and parricides. In truth, there are as many of these kinds of treasons, as there are different methods of conspiring against kingdoms; and the criminals, though ever so great, deserve death and confiscation; that is, they ought to be destroyed by the people whom they would destroy.

The great principle of self-preservation, which is the first and fundamental law of nature, calls for this procedure; the security of commonwealths depends upon it; the very being of government makes it necessary; and whatever is necessary to the publick safety, is just.

The fate of millions, and the being of states, must not stand and fall by the distinctions of monks, coined in colleges, or by the chicane of petty-foggers; who would bring every thing within the narrow verge of their own knowledge, under their own jurisdiction and cognizance; and would determine all things by the rules of inferior judicatures, the gibberish of private practisers,[2] and the sayings of old women, or of those who are like old women; whose brains are addled by being long jumbled and always turned round within the scanty circle of private courts, not daring to venture at a bold and free thought out of them, however self-evident; like some carriers' horses, that are used to a track, and know not how to travel in an open road.

But questions of this kind belong *ad aliud examen*,[3] and ought to be brought before an higher tribunal: The legislature are the only proper and safe judges: What is done against all, should be judged by all. Nor are their resolutions to be confined by any other rule than *Quid est utile, quid honestum*,[4] general justice, and the general good. Religion, virtue, common sense, and the publick peace and felicity, are the only counsel to be admitted either for the publick or the prisoners.

The conspirators against mankind ought to know, that no subterfuges, or tergiversations; no knavish subtilties, or pedantic quirks of lawyers; no evasions, skulkings behind known statutes; no combinations, or pretended commissions, shall be able to screen or protect them from publick justice. They ought to know, that there is a power in being that can follow them through all the dark labyrinths and doubling meanders; a power that can crush them to pieces, though they change into all the shapes of Proteus,[5] to avoid the fury of Hercules: a power, confined by no limitation, but that of publick justice and the publick good; a power, that does not follow precedents, but makes them; a power, which has this for its principle, that extraordinary crimes ought not to be tried by ordinary rules, and that unprecedented villanies ought to have unprecedented punishments.

But though in all governments, this great power must exist somewhere, yet it can rarely be delegated with prudence to inferior magistrates; who, out of ambition, revenge, or faction, or for

2. Practisers: physicians.

3. "To another consideration."

4. "What is useful and what [is] honorable." The phrase echoes Cicero, *De officiis*, 3.36.

5. Proteus, having received the gift of prophecy, eluded his questioners by assuming a variety of shapes (a tiger, a flame, a whirlwind, etc.).

bribes and preferments, or out of fear and flattery, or in concert with the ill measures or selfish intrigues of statesmen, may pervert so dangerous a trust to the destruction of those whom it was intended to preserve.

This particularly has been the case of England: We know by what means judges were often made, and from what conduct they expected farther preferment, and from whom they looked for protection: For this reason they were, and ought to be, confined in their jurisdiction relating to treason, and the manner of trying it.

Undoubtedly every intention manifested by act to destroy the constitution and government, was treason by the common law of England. But why do I say of England, since it is, and ever was, treason in every country throughout the world? This treason equally extends to those, who would subvert either house of Parliament, or the rights and privileges of the people, as to those who attempt to destroy the person of the King, or dethrone him. And indeed, what can be more absurd, than to suppose it to be the highest crime to attempt to destroy one man, for no other reason but that he is King; and yet not to suppose it the highest crime to destroy that people for whose benefit alone he was made King, and for whose sake indeed there ever was such a thing in the world?

But though this proposition was self-evident, and must ever be assented to as soon as mentioned, yet, by the flattery of priests and servile lawyers, the *salus populi,* or security of the state, soon came to signify only the unbounded power and sovereignty of the prince; and it became treason to hinder one, constituted, and grandly maintained out of the people's labour and wealth, for the publick safety, from destroying the publick safety. Our ancestors found, by lamentable experience, that unworthy men, preferred by corrupt ministers for unworthy ends, made treasons free only of the court; that the least attempt to oppose unlimited and unlawful authority, was often called treason; and that the highest treasons of all, which were those against the commonwealth, might be committed with impunity, applause, and rewards.

It was therefore high time to apply an adequate remedy to an enormous mischief, which struck at the whole state, and at the fortunes and lives of every subject in England. The statute therefore of the 25th of Edward III was enacted, which enumerates the several species or kinds of treasons, which shall continue to be esteemed treasons, and be adjudged so by the King's justices; and are chiefly those which relate to the King's person, his family, and dignity:[6] These the Parliament thought they might safely trust to the examination of the King's judges, under such limitations and regulations as the act presents.

But it is plain, from the same act, that they did not intend to confine all treasons to those recited there, because it is declared in the following words, *viz.*

> If any other case supposed treason, not before specified, shall happen before any justices, they shall stay judgment, till the cause be shewed before the Parliament, whether it ought to be judged treason or not.[7]

So that here is a plain declaration of the legislature (if any man can possibly think such a declaration wanting) that other crimes were treason, and ought to be punished as treason (though not by the King's judges), besides those recited in the act; which were, as has been said, designed only to extend to treasons which were committed against our Lord the King, and his Royal Majesty, as the act expressly says. And 'tis evident, from the whole tenor of it, that it was intended purely to restrain the unlimited and exorbitant jurisdiction assumed by the King's courts, in declaring treasons, and sacrificing by that means, whom they pleased to unlawful power.

But as to the highest and most heinous treasons of all, such as were treasons against the legislature, and against the whole body of the people, for whose safety alone there were any treasons against the King at all, seeing that their safety was, in a great measure, included in his; the Parliament reserved the judgment of every such treason to themselves: They did not alter what was treason, but the judges of it. They knew that treasons against the con-

6. By the Treason Act of 1351, the crime of treason, which was only loosely specified in common law, was given precise definition. According to the statute, the crime consisted, in the main, of aiding the enemies of or levying war against the king within his realm.

7. 25 Edward III. st. 5, c. 2.

stitution could seldom be committed but by ministers and favourites of princes, protected by power, and sheltered by authority; and that therefore it would be absurd to trust the punishment of such potent knaves, and criminal favourites, to judges made by themselves; judges, who would neither have inclination, figure, or character, to reach crimes countenanced, and perhaps authorized, by a Richard II or Edward II.[8]

Such crimes, therefore, were the proper objects of the awful power of a legislature; who will always be supported by the people whom they represent, when they exert themselves for the interest of that people. A power, so supported, can make the loftiest traitor quake. It can fetch corrupt ministers out of their dark recesses, and make their heads a victim to publick vengeance. Every wise and good king will lend a willing ear to their dutiful remonstrances; he will hearken to the importunate cries of his people, and readily deliver up the authors of their misery.

One great part of their care, therefore, has ever been, to call those to an account, who have abused the favour of their royal master, and endeavoured to make him little and contemptible to his people; weakening, by such means, his authority, and hazarding his person. This the people, whom they represented, thought they had a right to expect and demand from them; and this justice they have often done to their King and country.

An excellent *Discourse concerning Treasons and Bills of Attainder*[9] was published soon after his Majesty's accession to the throne, and shewed unanswerably, that our Parliaments, in almost every reign since the Conquest, claimed and exercised this right, upon extraordinary occasions; and none ever, till lately, opposed it, but the criminals who were to suffer by it, and their party: Some gentlemen now living can give the best account, why that book, and the cries of every honest man, had not their desired effect. I hope that no man will be deluded again by any practising the same arts, and for the same reasons too.

8. Richard II, who reigned between 1377 and 1399, and Edward II, from 1307 to 1327, both attempted to impose absolutist regimes and were met by strong baronial opposition. Both were compelled to abdicate.
9. A pamphlet by Richard West (d. 1726), published anonymously in 1716.

The length of this letter will not allow me to draw from all these reasonings upon treason such applications as I promised in my last, and intended in this. I shall therefore defer these applications to another, and perhaps more proper, occasion.[10] In the mean while, I observe with pleasure the noble spirit shewn by our legislature, to punish, with an exemplary severity, the murderers of our credit, and the publick enemies of our liberty and prosperity. This revives every drooping heart, and kindles joy in every face, in spite of all our miseries. And this brings terror, trembling, and paleness upon the guilty; to see death and destruction pursuing them close, and besetting them hard on every side. They are in the circumstances and the agonies of the guilty Cain, who justly feared that every man whom he met would kill him, though there was no law then in being against murder.

T   *I am, &c.*

NO. 13. SATURDAY, JANUARY 21, 1720.

The Arts of misleading the People by Sounds.

SIR,

In surveying the state of the world, one is often at a great loss, whether to ascribe the political misery of mankind to their own folly and credulity, or to the knavery and impudence of their pretended managers. Both these causes, in all appearance, concur to produce the same evil; and if there were no bubbles, there would be no sharpers.

There must certainly be a vast fund of stupidity in human nature, else men would not be caught as they are, a thousand times over, by the same snare; and while they yet remember their past misfortunes, go on to court and encourage the causes to which they were owing, and which will again produce them.

I will own, however, that government makes more fools, and more wise men, than nature makes; and the difference

10. See Letter No. 17 (Feb. 18, 1720).

between nation and nation, in point of virtue, sagacity, and arms, arises not from the different genius of the people; which, making very small allowances for the difference of climate, would be the same under the same regulations; but from the different genius of their political constitutions: The one, perhaps, making common sense dangerous, and enquiries criminal; cowing the spirits of men, and rebuking the sallies of virtue; while the other, at the same time, encourages the improvement of the understanding, rewards the discovery of truth, and cultivates, as a virtue, the love of liberty and of one's country.

Yet even in countries where the highest liberty is allowed, and the greatest light shines, you generally find certain men, and bodies of men, set apart to mislead the multitude; who are ever abused with words, ever fond of the worst of things recommended by good names, and ever abhor the best things, and the most virtuous actions, disfigured by ill names. One of the great arts, therefore, of cheating men, is, to study the application and misapplication of sounds—a few loud words rule the majority, I had almost said, the whole world.

Thus we have heard from our fathers, and seen in our own days, that contemptible insects, born in poverty, educated by charity, and often from cleaning their masters' shoes, preferred unexpectedly and undeservedly to offices and preferments in the Church, have had the front to call themselves the Church itself, and every one its enemy, who despised their meanness, exposed their reverend knavery, and laughed at their grimace.

And thus we have been told of the times, and some men now living remember to have seen them, when unworthy men, who, by faction and treachery, by mean compliances with power, or by insolently daring of authority, having raised themselves to wealth and honours, and to the power of betraying some considerable trust, have had the provoking sauciness to call themselves the government, and their own rogueries his then Majesty's measures; and the next thing was, to pronounce all those enemies to his then Majesty, who would endeavour to rescue their abused King and sinking country out of their devouring and polluted claws.

In King Charles I's time, the great Earl of Strafford and little Archbishop Laud[1] told the nation, that his Majesty's measures were, governing without Parliaments, a power without reserve in the state, a flaming popish hierarchy in the Church, absolute and abject submission in the people, and a barbarian army of Irish papists to support and insure all these worthy measures. But the untimely death of one of these offenders, and the imprisonment of the other, broke all those fine measures.

In the reign of Charles II Pensionary Parliaments,[2] a general depravation of manners, guards increased into armies, and popish religion and a popish successor, popish leagues and Protestant wars, were called by wicked men his Majesty's measures; and all honest men and good subjects were called his Majesty's enemies: And, when that prince saw that these measures of his ministry created endless jealousies to his people, and endless uneasiness to himself, and when he resolved to take other measures of his own, it is thought that they put a short end to all his measures.

When King James came to the crown,[3] though, setting bigotry apart, he had some royal virtues, being a prince of industry and good oeconomy; yet he suffered himself to be governed by a set of sycophants, many of them as foolish as they were mischievous. The establishment of bare-faced Romish popery in the Church, and a lawless tyranny in the prince, became then his Majesty's measures; the ministers, who advised and promoted them, called themselves the government; and whoever opposed his reason, his honesty, and his publick spirit, against those traitors to the publick, was charged with flying in the face of the government, and opposing his Majesty's measures. In what these measures ended, is well known: They

1. Thomas Wentworth, first Earl of Strafford (1593–1641), Lord Lieutenant of Ireland, and William Laud (1573–1645), Bishop of London and later Archbishop of Canterbury, were both trusted counselors to Charles I. They were impeached by a hostile Parliament and sent to the Tower in 1640; Strafford was attainted and executed several months later, while Laud suffered a similar fate in 1645.

2. That is, those Parliaments infamous for the acceptance of bribes by their members. The Cavalier Parliament (so-called because of its royalist majority), which sat from 1661 to 1679, was also known as the Pensionary Parliament.

3. James II, who became King upon the death of his brother Charles II in 1685.

cost his Majesty his kingdoms, and made him an honourable beggar in France all his life for his daily bread.

King William, when he came to the crown,[4] brought with him the hearts, and hands, and the good wishes of every honest man in England; and was supported by these men through a tedious and expensive war,[5] unknown to our ancestors; which, when he had finished, and the exhausted people expected some relaxations from their sufferings, they were given to know by some court parasites that his Majesty's measures was a standing army in time of peace, under the inspection of Parliaments. This unexpected spirit in the court gave such jealousy to those who were best affected to his Majesty's person and government, that with grief I call to mind the difficulties and anxieties which that great prince felt ever afterwards to the end of his reign.

As to Queen Anne, I shall say no more, than that it is shrewdly suspected, that what her Majesty's ministry had the insolence to call her Majesty's measures,[6] broke her Majesty's heart.

Let mankind therefore learn experience from so many misfortunes, and bear no longer to hear the worst things called by the best names; nor suffer hereafter the brightest and most conspicuous virtues of the wisest and most beneficent princes, to be sullied by actions which they do not countenance, nor even know of. Let them not permit the vices of the worst of servants to be laid at the door of the best of masters.

We, in this land, are very sure that we are blessed with the best King in the world, who desires of his people nothing but their

4. William of Orange, son-in-law of James II, who was proclaimed co-sovereign with his wife Mary in Feb. 1689.

5. The reference is to the war between France under Louis XIV on the one hand and the members of the Grand Alliance (the Empire, Sweden, Spain, Bavaria, Saxony, Savoy, England, and Holland) on the other, which lasted from 1689 until the signing of the Treaty of Ryswick in 1697. The guiding force of the Alliance was William of Orange.

6. Among the measures to which Trenchard is referring are the Occasional Conformity Act, the Landed Property Qualification Act (by which the landed gentry attempted to exclude merchants and industrialists from Parliament), the incorporation of the South Sea Company, and the Schism Act (by which all schoolmasters were required to obtain an episcopal license, thus effectively closing all dissenting academies), all undertaken while the Tories controlled Parliament from late 1710 until the accession of George I in 1714.

own greatness and felicity: A prince, ready to prevent their wishes, and to give them more than their duty ought to suffer them to ask. Let us shew our duty to this our great and benevolent sovereign; let us endeavour to alleviate his cares, and ease him of all ungrateful burdens; let us take upon ourselves the heavy labour of cleansing the Augean stables, and of cutting off all the Hydra's heads at once.

The law tells us, that the King can do no wrong: And, I thank God, we have a King that would not, if he could. But the greatest servants to princes may do wrong, and often have done it; and the representatives of the people have an undoubted right to call them to an account for it.

In truth, every private subject has a right to watch the steps of those who would betray their country; nor is he to take their word about the motives of their designs, but to judge of their designs by the event.

This is the principle of a *Whig*, this the doctrine of liberty; and 'tis as much knavery to deny this doctrine, as it is folly to ridicule it. Some will tell us, that this is setting up the mob for statesmen, and for the censurers of states. The word *mob* does not at all move me, on this occasion, nor weaken the grounds which I go upon. It is certain, that the whole people, who are the publick, are the best judges, whether things go ill or well with the publick. It is true, that they cannot all of them see distant dangers, nor watch the motions, and guess the designs, of neighbouring states: But every cobbler can judge, as well as a statesman, whether he can fit peaceably in his stall; whether he is paid for his work; whether the market, where he buys his victuals, be well provided; and whether a dragoon, or a parish-officer, comes to him for his taxes, if he pay any.

Every man too, even the meanest, can see, in a publick and sudden transition from plenty to poverty, from happiness to distress, whether the calamity comes from war, and famine, and the hand of God; or from oppression, and mismanagement, and the villainies of men. In short, the people often judge better than their superiors, and have not so many biases to judge wrong; and politicians often rail at the people, chiefly because they have given the people occasion to rail: Those ministers who cannot make the people their friends, it is to be shrewdly suspected, do not deserve their friendship; it is certain, that much honesty, and small management, rarely miss to gain it. As temporal felicity is the whole end of government; so people will always be pleased or provoked, as that increases or abates. This rule will always hold. You may judge of their affection, or disaffection, by the burdens which they bear, and the advantages which they enjoy. Here then is a sure standard for the government to judge of the people, and for the people to judge of the government.

Blessed be God, and thanks to our sovereign, who has given us a ministry that makes all these cautions unnecessary; who will baffle all calumny, and remove all suspicion of guilt from themselves (if any such suspicion can be), by being foremost to pursue the guilty; and will, doubtless, take double vengeance upon any in publick authority (if any such can be found), who shall appear to have contributed to our publick misfortunes; and, in fine, will promote and encourage a rigorous and strict enquiry, wherever any suspicion is given that enquiry ought to be made.

Such conduct will disperse our fears, restore our credit, give bread to our poor, make trade and manufacture flourish again; and, in some measure, compensate for all our past evils, by giving us a lasting prospect of our future plenty, peace, and felicity.

T   *I am, &c.*

NO. 14. SATURDAY, JANUARY 28, 1720.

The unhappy State of despotick Princes, compared with the happy Lot of such as rule by settled Laws. How the latter, by abusing their Trust, may forfeit their Crown.

SIR,

The best, the wisest, and the most courageous of despotick princes, have frequently lamented the unhappy condition into which their greatness betrayed them. Being often born in purple, and educated in pride and luxury, they seldom can have any feeling of the calamities which the rest of the world suffer. They are, besides, surrounded, for the most part, by the falsest, the most ambitious, and the basest of all men; with such men's eyes they must therefore see, with such men's ears they must likewise hear.

I cannot, in truth, see how, in the nature of things, it can be otherwise: For the mean fawning, the servile flatteries, the deceitful correspondences, the base ingratitude to old benefactors, and the slavish compliances with new friends, and all the other arts and treacheries, which are necessary to be put in practice, in order to rise in such courts, or indeed to become heads of parties even in free governments, make it almost impossible for a truly great or virtuous man to attain to those stations.

A good man will choose to live in an innocent obscurity, and enjoy the internal satisfaction resulting from a just sense of his own merit, and virtue, rather than aim at greatness, by a long series of unworthy arts, and ignoble actions; whilst the ambitious, the cruel, the rapacious, the false, the proud, the treacherous part of mankind, will be ever thrusting themselves forward, and endeavouring to sparkle in courts, as well as in the eyes of the unthinking crowd; and, to make themselves necessary, will be continually either flattering or distressing princes.

Nor can it be expected that men, who have been raised to power by such execrable means, should ever use it to the benefit of mankind, or to any good end. They will always proceed in the same steps where they began; and use, for the support of their greatness, the same vile measures by which they acquired their greatness, till they have at length sacrificed all things in heaven and earth to their ambition.

There is a fine passage, to this purpose, in the short history of the Emperor Aurelian by Vopiscus:

> *Et quaeritur quidem quae res malos principes faciat: Jam primum, licentia, deinde rerum copia, amici improbi, satellites detestandi, eunuchi avarissimi, aulici vel stulti et detestabiles, & (quod negari non potest) rerum publicarum ignorantia. Sed ego a patre meo audivi, Dioclesianum principem, jam privatum, dixisse, nihil esse difficilius quambene imperare. Collegunt se quatuor vel quinque,*

atque unum consilium ad decipiendum principem capiunt: Dicunt quod probandum sit. Imperator, qui domi clausus est, vera non novit. Cogitur hoc tantum scire quod illi loquuntur: Facit judices quos fieri non oportet; amovet a republica quos debebat obtinere. Quid multa? Ut Dioclesianus ipse dicebat, bonus, cautus, optimus venditur imperator.[1] Histor. August. Scriptor. Tom. II. p. 531, 532.

"My friends," (says the great Emperor Dioclesian, to those who advised him to resume the empire)

> you little know how difficult an undertaking it is to per-
> form the duty of a Roman emperor, and to reign well. The
> few who have access to him, will cabal and conspire
> together, and unite in their counsels to deceive and betray
> him. They will study how to flatter him, and never tell him
> what it is their duty to tell him, and what is his interest to
> know; but only what they think will best please him. They
> will shut him up, and, as it were, imprison him in his pal-
> ace; and no one shall be admitted to his ear, but by their
> leave, and in their presence. So that he shall never know
> the condition of his affairs, or be informed of the cries of
> his people, or, indeed, of any thing but what they think fit
> to tell him: By their means he shall prefer undeserving
> men to the best posts of the empire, and disgrace the most
> worthy of his subjects, and the most devoted to his interest.
> But why should I labour this point any more, when even
> the good, the most discerning, when the best and ablest
> emperors are bought and sold?

1. Flavius Vopiscus, "Divus Aurelianus," *Scriptores Historiae Augustae*, 43.1–4. The Latin more properly translates as: "Indeed, it is asked what makes emper-ors evil; first of all, lack of restraint, and then abundance of wealth, wicked friends, loathsome attendants, avaricious eunuchs, foolish and detestable courtiers, and (it cannot be denied) ignorance of public affairs. But I have heard from my father that the emperor Diocletian, while still a private citizen, had said that nothing was more difficult than to rule well. Four or five men come together and adopt one plan aimed at misleading the emperor. They tell him what he must approve. The emperor, who is shut up in his palace, is igno-rant of the truth but knows only what they tell him. He creates judges who ought never to be appointed. He removes from public office those who ought to be retained. Why say more? As Diocletian himself said, the favors of even a good, careful, and virtuous emperor may be sold."

But Dioclesian was an arbitrary prince, whose will was a law to his subjects. But it is far otherwise in limited monarchies, where the prince governs his people by fixed rules and known statutes; and where his faithful States have a right to represent freely, though humbly, their grievances to him, and by his authority to call to account, and punish, such betrayers as are before described.

Happy therefore is that prince, happy in the love of his subjects, happy in the just applause and dutiful acknowledgment of millions of his fellow-creatures, who derive their felicity from him! Thrice happy is that people, where the constitution is so poised and tempered, and the administration so disposed and divided into proper channels, that the passions and infirmities of the prince cannot enter into the measures of his government; where he has in his power all the means of doing good, and none of doing ill; where all beneficent and gracious actions are owned to flow from his clemency and goodness, and where inferior machines are answerable for all such conduct as may prejudice the publick.

Such a government does, in some sense, resemble that of heaven itself, where the sovereign disposer of all things can neither will nor do any thing but what is just and good: He is restrained, by the excellency of his own nature, from being the author of evil; and will call to a severe account all those, who would impute their own unrighteousness to his orders or influence.

Such is the monarchy of England, where the sovereign performs every act of his regal office by his authority, without the fatigue and anxiety of executing the troublesome parts of it in his person. The laws are chosen and recommended to him by his Parliament; and afterwards executed by his judges, and other ministers of justice: His great seal is kept by his chancellor: His naval power is under the direction of his high admiral: And all acts of state and discretion are presumed to be done by the advice of his council. All which officers are answerable for their misbehaviour, and for all actions done within their several provinces, which they have advised or could have prevented by giving their advice, or by making timely and humble remonstrances; which they are obliged to shew that they have done.

His leagues,[2] his commands, and even his authentick speeches, are records. His high office consists in approving laws chosen by common consent; in executing those laws, and in being the publick guardian of the publick safety: And all private orders, which are inconsistent with these great duties, are not the orders of the crown; nor are the actions done in pursuance of them, the actions of the King, but the actions of those that do them. He can do no wrong himself, nor give authority to any one else to do wrong. Every act of his must be lawful, because all unlawful acts are not his. He can give no commands, as a man, which shall interfere with those which he gives as a King. His private will cannot control his publick will. He commands, as a King, his chancellor, and judges, to act according to his known laws; and no private orders to do otherwise can be valid.

The nation has ever acted upon these maxims, and preserved such a dutiful respect to the royal Majesty, as never to suffer any guilt to be laid to him; but has always heaped double vengeance upon such miscreants as would insinuate, that their crimes were approved or countenanced by their royal master.

Here is all the precaution which can be taken by human wisdom to make a happy prince and a happy people. The prince is restrained in nothing, but from doing mischief to his subjects, and consequently to himself; their true interest being ever the same: And the people can never have any motive to refuse just allegiance to their prince, whilst the ligaments of the constitution are preserved entire; that is, whilst parliaments are suffered to meet, and the courts of justice remain open, and such force is not used against them as dissolves all relation. All the subjects of such a prince highly honour, and almost worship, him. He has a vast revenue to support the splendor and magnificence of his court at home, and his royal dignity abroad: He has the power of disposing of all offices: All honours flow from him: His person is sacred, and not answerable for any events: He cannot be accountable for any wrong, which he is incapable of doing; and those who do it, shall be punished by his authority, even though it be supposed possible

2. That is, his alliances.

that they could, by false misrepresentations, deceive him far enough to approve it.

The examples of Richard II who, as our histories tell us, was deposed by the States of his kingdom,[3] and of the late King James, are no instances to disprove the truth of this assertion: For neither of them was deposed by his people before he first deposed himself. No champions for tyranny, or dogmatizers for unlimited dominion, have yet asserted, that a prince may not resign his crown by the consent of his people, when he declines to hold it any longer upon the conditions on which he first accepted it.

Suppose a prince, in any limited monarchy, should make a publick declaration to the States of his kingdom, that, Whereas the crown descended to him by the laws of that country, and that all the power which he was possessed of was conferred upon him by those laws; That he well knew that the preservation of those laws, which he had sworn to observe, and the general good of his people, were the sole considerations of his enjoying that high dignity; and yet, notwithstanding, he refused to hold it any longer, upon the terms upon which he had first accepted it, and sworn to observe; but that he now renounced that title, and would govern them hereafter by his sole will and pleasure: I say, if any should do this, the advocates for lawless power would do well to tell us, whether such a prince did not make as effectual a renunciation and resignation of his government, as if he disabled himself, and resigned it for his ease, or from the satiety of power. And if they allow that he may do all this by words spoken to express his intentions, I should be glad to know, from these men of distinctions, why he may not do it by a series of actions, which will more effectually discover and declare his inward intentions, and may therefore be more depended on than any words can possibly be?

I call upon the two famous universities of this land for an answer: And, till I have a full one, shall continue to believe, that what was done, in regard to the abdication of the late King

3. In fact, Richard was not deposed by the States (i.e., the Estates, or Parliament) but by a conspiracy headed by Henry of Bolingbroke, who was then recognized as King by Parliament in 1399.

James, was just and necessary to be done upon the fundamental principles of government; and, that all his successors since have been rightful and lawful Kings and Queens of this realm; and I particularly glory to say, that no prince has ever better deserved that high title, than our present great and glorious sovereign, King George.

T   *I am, &c.*

NO. 15. SATURDAY, FEBRUARY 4, 1720.

Of Freedom of Speech: That the same is inseparable from publick Liberty.

SIR,

Without freedom of thought, there can be no such thing as wisdom; and no such thing as publick liberty, without freedom of speech: Which is the right of every man, as far as by it he does not hurt and control the right of another; and this is the only check which it ought to suffer, the only bounds which it ought to know.

This sacred privilege is so essential to free government, that the security of property; and the freedom of speech, always go together; and in those wretched countries where a man cannot call his tongue his own, he can scarce call any thing else his own. Whoever would overthrow the liberty of the nation, must begin by subduing the freedom of speech; a thing terrible to publick traitors.

This secret was so well known to the court of King Charles I that his wicked ministry procured a proclamation to forbid the people to talk of Parliaments, which those traitors had laid aside.[1] To assert the undoubted right of the subject, and defend his Majesty's legal prerogative, was called disaffection, and punished as sedition. Nay, people were forbid to talk of religion in their families: For the priests had combined with the ministers to

1. The reference is to the proclamation issued on Mar. 27, 1629, for the purpose of suppressing false rumors touching parliaments.

cook up tyranny, and suppress truth and the law. While the late King James, when Duke of York, went avowedly to mass; men were fined, imprisoned, and undone, for saying that he was a papist: And, that King Charles II might live more securely a papist, there was an act of Parliament made, declaring it treason to say that he was one.[2]

That men ought to speak well of their governors, is true, while their governors deserve to be well spoken of; but to do publick mischief, without hearing of it, is only the prerogative and felicity of tyranny: A free people will be shewing that they are so, by their freedom of speech.

The administration of government is nothing else, but the attendance of the trustees of the people upon the interest and affairs of the people. And as it is the part and business of the people, for whose sake alone all publick matters are, or ought to be, transacted, to see whether they be well or ill transacted; so it is the interest, and ought to be the ambition, of all honest magistrates, to have their deeds openly examined, and publickly scanned: Only the wicked governors of men dread what is said of them; *Audivit Tiberius probra queis lacerabitur, atque perculsus est.*[3] The publick censure was true, else he had not felt it bitter.

Freedom of speech is ever the symptom, as well as the effect, of good government. In old Rome, all was left to the judgment and pleasure of the people; who examined the publick proceedings with such discretion, and censured those who administered them with such equity and mildness, that in the space of three hundred years, not five publick ministers suffered unjustly. Indeed, whenever the commons proceeded to violence, the great ones had been the aggressors.

Guilt only dreads liberty of speech, which drags it out of its lurking holes, and exposes its deformity and horror to day-light. Horatius, Valerius, Cincinnatus, and other virtuous and undesigning magistrates of the Roman commonwealth, had nothing to fear

2. 13 Car. II, st. 1, c. 1 (1661).

3. The correct reading is: . . . *audivit Tiberius probra, quis per occultum lacerabatur, adeoque perculsus est* . . . ("Tiberius heard reproaches that wounded him deeply, and he was disquieted.") Tacitus, *Annales*, 4.42.

from liberty of speech.[4] Their virtuous administration, the more it was examined, the more it brightened and gained by enquiry. When Valerius, in particular, was accused, upon some slight grounds, of affecting the diadem; he, who was the first minister of Rome, did not accuse the people for examining his conduct, but approved his innocence in a speech to them; he gave such satisfaction to them, and gained such popularity to himself, that they gave him a new name; *inde cognomen factum Publicolae est;*[5] to denote that he was their favourite and their friend. *Latae deinde leges. Ante omnes de provocatione, adversus magistratus ad populum,*[6] Livii lib. ii. cap. 8.

But things afterwards took another turn: Rome, with the loss of its liberty, lost also its freedom of speech; then men's words began to be feared and watched; then first began the poisonous race of informers, banished indeed under the righteous administration of Titus, Nerva, Trajan, Aurelius,[7] &c. but encouraged and enriched under the vile ministry of Sejanus, Tigellinus, Pallas, and Cleander:[8] *Querilibet, quod in secreta nostra non inquirant principes, nisi quos odimus,* says Pliny to Trajan.[9]

4. Publius *Valerius* Publicola (d. 503 B.C.), shared the consulship with Lucius Iunius Brutus in the first year of the Roman Republic (509 B.C.). When it was feared that he might seek the crown, he responded by introducing a law by which any man who sought to make himself king could be slain by any Roman with impunity. The *Horatius* to whom Gordon is referring is probably the moderate patrician consul Marcus Horatius Barbatus, who, together with his co-consul, was responsible for passage of a series of laws in 449 B.C. weakening patrician authority and increasing the political power of the plebeians.

5. "Then he was named Publicola." Livy, 2.8.2. Publicola carries the meaning of one who lives among the people.

6. "Then laws were proposed, the first of them a law concerning appeal against the magistrates to the people." Livy, 2.8.1–2.

7. *Titus*, emperor from A.D. 79–81; *Nerva*, A.D. 96–98; *Trajan*, A.D. 98–117; and Marcus *Aurelius*, A.D. 161–180. The four are generally regarded as particularly capable rulers who presided over a prosperous and tranquil empire.

8. Lucius Aelius *Sejanus* (d. A.D. 31), minister to the emperor Tiberius, whose treachery and ambition resulted in his imprisonment and death. Gaius Ofonius *Tigellinus* (d. A.D. 68), advisor to the emperor Nero who was noted for his intrigues and perfidy; he was eventually ordered to commit suicide. *Pallas* (d. A.D. 61), financial secretary to the emperor Claudius, who is reputed to have intrigued in his murder with Nero, his successor, and who, in turn, was put to death by Nero. *Cleander* (d. A.D. 190), a favorite of the emperor Commodus who perverted the administration of justice for his private ends; he was ordered executed.

9. "We may well complain that only those leaders who inquire into our secrets are those we hate." Pliny the Younger, *Panegyricus*, 68.6. Gaius *Plinius* Caecilius Secundus, or Pliny the Younger (A.D. 62–113), was the nephew and

The best princes have ever encouraged and promoted freedom of speech; they knew that upright measures would defend themselves, and that all upright men would defend them. Tacitus, speaking of the reigns of some of the princes above-mention'd, says with ecstasy, *Rara temporum felicitate, ubi sentire quae velis, & quae sentias dicere liceat:*[10] A blessed time, when you might think what you would, and speak what you thought!

The same was the opinion and practice of the wise and virtuous Timoleon,[11] the deliverer of the great city of Syracuse from slavery. He being accused by Demoenetus, a popular orator, in a full assembly of the people, of several misdemeanors committed by him while he was general, gave no other answer, than that he was highly obliged to the gods for granting him a request that he had often made to them; namely, that he might live to see the Syracusians enjoy that liberty of speech which they now seemed to be masters of.[12]

And that great commander, M. Marcellus,[13] who won more battles than any Roman captain of his age, being accused by the Syracusians, while he was now a fourth time consul, of having done them indignities and hostile wrongs, contrary to the League,[14] rose from his seat in the Senate, as soon as the charge against him was opened, and passing (as a private man) into the place where the accused were wont to make their defence, gave free liberty to the Syracusians to impeach him: Which, when they had done, he and they went out of the court together to attend the issue of the cause: Nor did he express the least ill-will or resentment towards these his accusers; but being acquitted, received

---

adopted son of Pliny the Elder. Of his numerous learned writings, only a panegyric on the emperor Trajan and ten books of letters survive.

10. "The rare good fortune of an age where one is allowed to feel what one wishes and to say what one feels." Tacitus, *Historiae*, 1.1. Tacitus is here referring to the reigns of Nerva and Trajan.

11. A Corinthian by birth, *Timoleon* (c. 411–334 B.C.) liberated Greek Sicily from Carthaginian forces in 341 B.C.

12. The account here offered is paraphrased from Plutarch, *Timoleon*, 37.1–3. Plutarch gives the name of his accuser as Demaenetus.

13. Marcus Claudius *Marcellus* (c. 268–208 B.C.), celebrated Roman general who fought in the second Punic War and who conquered the city of Syracuse.

14. That is, contrary to Syracuse's treaty with Rome. The events are related in Plutarch, *Marcellus*, 23.

their city into his protection. Had he been guilty, he would neither have shewn such temper nor courage.

I doubt not but old Spencer and his son,[15] who were the chief ministers and betrayers of Edward II would have been very glad to have stopped the mouths of all honest men in England. They dreaded to be called traitors, because they were traitors. And I dare say, Queen Elizabeth's Walsingham,[16] who deserved no reproaches, feared none. Misrepresentation of publick measures is easily overthrown, by representing publick measures truly: When they are honest, they ought to be publickly known, that they may be publickly commended; but if they be knavish or pernicious, they ought to be publickly exposed, in order to be publickly detested.

To assert, that King James was a papist and a tyrant, was only so far hurtful to him, as it was true of him; and if the Earl of Strafford had not deserved to be impeached, he need not have feared a bill of attainder. If our directors and their confederates be not such knaves as the world thinks them, let them prove to all the world, that the world thinks wrong, and that they are guilty of none of those villainies which all the world lays to their charge. Others too, who would be thought to have no part of their guilt, must, before they are thought innocent, shew that they did all that was in their power to prevent that guilt, and to check their proceedings.

Freedom of speech is the great bulwark of liberty; they prosper and die together: And it is the terror of traitors and oppressors, and a barrier against them. It produces excellent writers, and encourages men of fine genius. Tacitus tells us, that the Roman commonwealth bred great and numerous authors, who writ with equal boldness and eloquence: But when it was enslaved, those great wits were no more. *Postquam bellatum apud Actium; atque*

15. Hugh le Despenser and his son, the younger Hugh. Both father and son became the principal advisors to Edward II. Under pressure from the English barons, Edward consented to their banishment in 1321 but they again established themselves at court and were eventually hanged by the barons a few months before Edward was compelled to abdicate in 1327.

16. Sir Francis Walsingham (1532–1590) was Secretary of State and chief minister to Elizabeth during the last eighteen years of his life.

omnem potestatem ad unum conferri pacis interfuit, magna illa ingenia cessere.[17] Tyranny had usurped the place of equality, which is the soul of liberty, and destroyed publick courage. The minds of men, terrified by unjust power, degenerated into all the vileness and methods of servitude: Abject sycophancy and blind submission grew the only means of preferment, and indeed of safety; men durst not open their mouths, but to flatter.

Pliny the Younger observes, that this dread of tyranny had such effect, that the Senate, the great Roman Senate, became at last stupid and dumb: *Mutam ac sedentariam assentiendi necessitatem.*[18] Hence, says he, our spirit and genius are stupified, broken, and sunk for ever. And in one of his epistles, speaking of the works of his uncle, he makes an apology for eight of them, as not written with the same vigour which was to be found in the rest; for that these eight were written in the reign of Nero, when the spirit of writing was cramped by fear; *Dubii sermonis octo scripset sub Nerone— cum omne studiorum genus paulo liberius & erectius periculosum servitus fecisset.*[19]

All ministers, therefore, who were oppressors, or intended to be oppressors, have been loud in their complaints against freedom of speech, and the licence of the press; and always restrained, or endeavoured to restrain, both. In consequence of this, they have brow-beaten writers, punished them violently, and against law, and burnt their works. By all which they shewed how much truth alarmed them, and how much they were at enmity with truth.

There is a famous instance of this in Tacitus: He tells us, that Cremutius Cordus,[20] having in his *Annals* praised Brutus and

17. "After the battle of Actium, when the interests of peace required that all power should be conferred on one man, great geniuses ceased work." Tacitus, *Historiae*, 1.1. The reference is to the decline of objective historical writing.

18. "Unspoken and fixed necessity to assent." Pliny the Younger, *Panegyricus*, 76.3.

19. A contraction of Pliny the Younger, *Epistulae*, 3.5. Gordon's Latin reads: "Under Nero he wrote eight books concerning linguistic problems—when tyranny made all free and elevated study dangerous."

20. Aulus *Cremutius* Cordus: Roman historian of the Augustan Age and the author of a history of the civil wars and reign of Augustus. He was brought to trial in A.D. 25 for having eulogized Brutus.

Cassius,[21] gave offence to Sejanus, first minister, and to some inferior sycophants in the court of Tiberius; who, conscious of their own characters, took the praise bestowed on every worthy Roman, to be so many reproaches pointed at themselves: They therefore complained of the book to the Senate; which, being now only the machine of tyranny, condemned it to be burnt. But this did not prevent its spreading. *Libros cremandos censuere patres; sed manserunt occultati & editi:*[22] Being censured, it was the more sought after. "From hence," says Tacitus, "we may wonder at the stupidity of those statesmen, who hope to extinguish, by the terror of their power, the memory of their actions; for quite otherwise, the punishment of good writers gains credit to their writings:" *Nam contra, punitis ingeniis, gliscit auctoritas.*[23] Nor did ever any government, who practised impolitick severity, get any thing by it, but infamy to themselves, and renown to those who suffered under it. This also is an observation of Tacitus: *Neque aliud [externi] reges, [aut] qui ea[dem] saevitiae usi sunt, nisi dedecus sibi, atque gloriam illis peperere.*[24]

Freedom of speech, therefore, being of such infinite importance to the preservation of liberty, every one who loves liberty ought to encourage freedom of speech. Hence it is that I, living in a country of liberty, and under the best prince upon earth, shall take this very favourable opportunity of serving mankind, by warning them of the hideous mischiefs that they will suffer, if ever corrupt and wicked men shall hereafter get possession of any state, and the power of betraying their master: And, in order to do this, I will shew them by what steps they will probably proceed to accomplish their traitorous ends. This may be the subject of my next.

21. Gaius *Cassius* Longinus (d. 42 B.C.), the tyrannicide, who committed suicide after being defeated by the armies of Antony and Octavian at Philippi.

22. "The Senate ordered the books burned, but some, having been hidden, remained and were afterward published." Tacitus, *Annales*, 4.35.

23. "On the contrary, the authority of genius, once punished, grows." Tacitus, *Annales*, 4.35.

24. "Nor have foreign kings and those who imitated their cruelty achieved anything except shame for themselves and glory for their victims." Tacitus, *Annales*, 4.35.

Valerius Maximus[25] tells us, that Lentulus Marcellinus,[26] the Roman consul, having complained, in a popular assembly, of the overgrown power of Pompey; the whole people answered him with a shout of approbation: Upon which the consul told them, "Shout on, gentlemen, shout on, and use those bold signs of liberty while you may; for I do not know how long they will be allowed you."

God be thanked, we Englishmen have neither lost our liberties, nor are in danger of losing them. Let us always cherish this matchless blessing, almost peculiar to ourselves; that our posterity may, many ages hence, ascribe their freedom to our zeal. The defence of liberty is a noble, a heavenly office; which can only be performed where liberty is: For, as the same Valerius Maximus observes, *Quid ergo libertas sine Catone? non magis quam Cato sine libertate.*[27]

G   *I am, &c.*

NO. 16. SATURDAY, FEBRUARY 11, 1720.

The Leaders of Parties, their usual Views. Advice to all Parties to be no longer misled.

SIR,

The wise Sancho Pancha desired that his subjects, in the promised island, might be all blacks, because he would sell them. And this seems to be the first modest, and, as I think, the only reasonable desire of the leaders of all parties; for no man will be at the expence and fatigue of body and conscience, which is

25. Roman historian during the reign of Tiberius, *Valerius* Maximus authored a collection of celebrated sayings and accounts of heroic actions. The work was designed as a manual of moral postulates.

26. Gnaeus Cornelius *Lentulus Marcellinus* served as consul in 56 B.C. He reproached Pompey and Crassus for their renewed alliance with Caesar and urged a vigorous resistance to the ambitions of the triumvirate.

27. "What liberty without Cato? No more than Cato without liberty." The quotation appears in Valerius Maximus, 4.2.4.

necessary to lead a faction, only to be disturbed and annoyed by them.

A very great authority* has told us, that " 'Tis worth no man's time to serve a party, unless he can now and then get good jobs by it." This, I can safely say, has been the constant principle and practice of every leading patriot, ever since I have been capable of observing publick transactions; the *primum mobile,* the *alpha* and *omega* of all their actions: They all professed to have in view only the publick good; yet every one shewed he only meant his own; and all the while the great as well as little mob, the *procerum turba mobilium,*[1] contended as fiercely for their leaders, as if their happiness or misery depended upon the face, the clothes, or title of the persons who robbed and betrayed them. Thus the highwayman said to the traveller, "Pray, Sir, leave your watch and money in my hands; or else, by G — , you will be robbed."

Pound a fool in a mortar, and he comes out never the wiser; no experience will make the bulk of mankind so, or put them upon their guard; they will be caught over and over again by the same baits and stale stratagems: No sooner is a party betrayed by one head, but they rail at him, and set up another; and when this has served them in the same manner, they choose a third; and put full confidence in every one of them successively, though they all make the same use of their credulity; that is, put a price upon their calves' heads, and sell them; which, however, they have the less reason to complain of, because they would have all done the same.

I assure you, Sir, that I have not the least hopes in this letter to make men honester, but I would gladly teach them a little more wit; that is, I would advise any one who is contented to be sold, that he receive the money himself, and take good care of one, whatever becomes of his neighbours; as some discreet persons have lately done. Whatever bargains are struck up amongst the betrayers of their country, we must find the money, and pay both

---

* This was said to have been spoken by a certain Lord Chancellor in former times. [It has been suggested that the person to whom Trenchard is here referring is William Cowper, first Earl Cowper, who twice acted as Lord Chancellor (1707–1710; 1714–1718).]

1. "A mob of fickle nobles." The phrase is probably a play on Horace, *Odes,* 1.1.7, who writes of *mobilium turba Quiritium* ("a mob of fickle Roman citizens").

sides. How wise and advantageous would it then be for us, not to interest ourselves in the agreements or squabbles of ambitious men, who are building their fortunes upon our ruin? Once upon a time, a French ambassador desired an audience of the Grand Vizier, and in pompous French fustian[2] notified to him, that his master had won a great victory over the Germans; to which that wise minister answered laconically, "What is it to me, if the whole herd of unbelievers, like dogs, mutually worry one another, so that my master's head be safe?"

This letter of advice is not intended for those who share already in the publick spoils, or who, like jackals, hunt down the lion's prey, that they may have the picking of the bones, when their masters are glutted. But I would persuade the poor, the injured, the distressed people, to be no longer the dupes and property of hypocrites and traitors. But very few can share in the wages of iniquity, and all the rest must suffer; the people's interest is the publick interest; it signifies the same thing: Whatever these betrayers of their country get, the people must lose; and, what is worse, must lose a great deal more than the others can get; for such conspiracies and extortions cannot be successfully carried on, without destroying or injuring trade, perverting justice, corrupting the guardians of the publick liberty, and the almost total dissolution of the principles of government.

Few can receive the advantages arising from publick misfortunes; and therefore methinks few should desire them. Indeed, I can easily see how men of desperate circumstances, or men guilty of desperate crimes, can find their account in a general confusion of all things. I can see how those priests, who aim at tyranny, can find their interest in the loss of publick liberty, in the restraint of the press, and in introducing a religion which destroys Christianity:[3] There are reasons too at hand, why ambitious men should, *per fas & nefas*,[4] grasp at the possession of immense wealth, high honours, and exorbitant power: But that the gentry, the body of the people in a free nation, should become tools and instruments of knaves and

2. Fustian: bombast.
3. That is, Roman Catholicism.
4. "By fair means or foul."

pick-pockets; should list themselves in their quarrels, and fight their
battles; and this too, often at the expence, and by the violation of
good neighbourhood, near relation, private friendship: That men
of great estates and quality, for small and trifling considerations,
and sometimes none at all, should promote wild, villainous projects,
to the ruin of themselves and country, by making precarious their
own titles to their lives, estates, and liberties, is something so stupendous, that it must be thought impossible, if daily experience did not
convince us that it is more than possible.

I have often seen honest Tories foolishly defending knavish Tories; and untainted Whigs protecting corrupt Whigs, even in
instances where they acted against the principles of all Whigs; and
by that means depreciated Whiggism itself, and gave the stupid
herd occasion to believe that they had no principles at all, but were
only a factious combination for preferment and power.

It is high time, at last, for the bubbles of all parties, for
Whigs and Tories, for High Church and Low Church, to come to
an *éclaircissement*,[5] and no longer suffer themselves to be bought
and sold by their drivers: Let them cease to be calves and sheep,
and they will not be used like calves and sheep. If they can be persuaded now and then to confer notes, they will find, that for the
most part the differences between them are not material; that they
take only different measures to attain the same ends; that they
have but one common interest, which is the interest of their country; and that is, to be freed from oppression, and to punish their
oppressors: Whose practice, on the contrary, will always be to form
parties, and blow up factions to mutual animosities, that they may
find protection in those animosities.

Let us not therefore, for the time to come, suffer ourselves
to be engaged in empty and pernicious contentions; which can
only tend to make us the property and harvest of pickpockets: Let
us learn to value an honest man of another party, more than a
knave of our own: Let the only contention be, who shall be most
ready to spew out their own rogues; and I will be answerable that
all other differences will soon be at an end. Indeed, there had been

5. Eclaircissement: enlightenment.

no such thing as party now in England, if we had not been betrayed by those whom we trusted.

Through the villainy and knavish designs of leaders, this nation has lost several glorious opportunities of rescuing the constitution, and settling it upon a firm and solid basis: Let us not therefore, by the like practices, lose the present favourable offer: Let us make earnings of our misfortunes, and accept our calamities as an opportunity thrown into our laps by indulgent providence, to save ourselves; and not again foolishly and ungratefully reject and spurn at the intimations and invitations of heaven, to preserve our prince and country.

Machiavel tells us, that no government can long subsist, but by recurring often to its first principles; but this can never be done while men live at ease and in luxury; for then they cannot be persuaded to see distant dangers, of which they feel no part. The conjunctures proper for such reformations, are when men are awakened by misfortunes, and frighted with the approach and near view of present evils; then they will wish for remedies, and their minds are prepared to receive them, to hear reasons, and to fall into measures proposed by wise men for their security.[6]

The great authority just quoted informs us what measures and expedients are necessary to save a state under such exigencies: He tells us, that as a tyranny cannot be established but by destroying Brutus; so a free government is not to be preserved but by destroying Brutus's sons.[7] Let us therefore put on a resolution equal to the mighty occasion: Let us exert a spirit worthy of Britons, worthy of freemen who deserve liberty. Let us take advantage of the opportunity, while men's resentments boil high, whilst lesser animosities seem to be laid aside, and most men are sick of

6. This is a recurring theme throughout Machiavelli's *Discourses*, but see especially III.1.

7. Lucius Iunius *Brutus* is credited with founding the Roman Republic in 509 B.C. Despite the oath taken by all Romans that they would never again submit to royal authority, his sons were found guilty of conspiring with the Tuscan ambassador to restore the Tarquins to the throne. They were tried and condemned before their father, who personally presided at their execution. Trenchard is here quoting Machiavelli, *Discourses*, III.3.1.

party and party-leaders; and let us, by all proper methods, exemplarily punish the parricides, and avowed enemies of all mankind.

Let neither private acquaintance, personal alliance, or party combination, stand between us and our duty to our country: Let all those who have a common interest in the publick safety, join in common measures to defend the publick safety: Let us pursue to disgrace, destruction, and even death, those who have brought this ruin upon us, let them be ever so great, or ever so many: Let us stamp and deep engrave, in characters legible to all Europe at present, and to all posterity hereafter, what vengeance is due to crimes, which have no less objects in view than the ruin of nations, and the destruction of millions: They have made many bold, desperate, and wicked attempts to destroy us; let us strike one honest and bold stroke to destroy them.

Though the designs of the conspirators should be laid as deep as the center, though they should raise hell itself in their quarrel, and should fetch legions of votaries from thence to avow their proceedings; yet let us not leave the pursuit, till we have their skins and estates: We know, by past experience, that there are those amongst us, who will be glad to quit the chase, when our villains, like beavers, drop what they are usually hunted for; but the nation is now too much provoked, and too much injured, to suffer themselves to be again so betrayed.

We have heaven to direct us, a glorious King to lead us, and a wise and faithful Parliament to assist and protect us: Whilst we have such a King, and such a Parliament, every worthy Briton cries out aloud,

> *Manus haec inimica tyrannis*
> *Ense petit placidam, sub libertate quietem.*[8]

T   *I am, &c.*

8. Literally, "This hand, hostile to tyrants, seeks with the sword peace under liberty," the motto of the great Whig revolutionary theorist Algernon Sidney (1622–1683). David Jacobson, among others, has noted that these lines were paraphrased by John Quincy Adams as "This hand to tyrants ever sworn the foe, / For freedom only deals the deadly blow, / That sheathes in calm repose the vengeful blade, / For gentle peace in freedom's hallowed shade." See *The English Libertarian Heritage: From the Writings of John Trenchard and Thomas Gordon in "The Independent Whig" and "Cato's Letters,"* David L. Jacobson, ed. (San Francisco: Fox & Wilkes, 1994): 50–51 n.

NO. 17. SATURDAY, FEBRUARY 18, 1720.

What Measures are actually taken by wicked and desperate Ministers to ruin and enslave their Country.

SIR,

As under the best princes, and the best servants to princes alone, it is safe to speak what is true of the worst; so, according to my former promise to the publick, I shall take the advantage of our excellent King's most gentle government, and the virtuous administration of an uncorrupt ministry, to warn mankind against the mischiefs which may hereafter be dreaded from corrupt ones. It is too true, that every country in the world has sometimes groaned under that heavy misfortune, and our own as much as any; though I cannot allow it to be true, what Monsieur de Witt[1] has long since observed, that the English court has always been the most thievish court in Europe.

Few men have been desperate enough to attack openly, and barefaced, the liberties of a free people. Such avowed conspirators can rarely succeed: The attempt would destroy itself. Even when the enterprize is begun and visible, the end must be hid, or denied. It is the business and policy of traitors, so to disguise their treason with plausible names, and so to recommend it with popular and bewitching colours, that they themselves shall be adored, while their work is detested, and yet carried on by those that detest it.

Thus one nation has been surrendered to another under the fair name of mutual alliance: The fortresses of a nation have been given up, or attempted to be given up, under the frugal notion of saving charges to a nation; and commonwealths have been trepanned[2] into slavery, by troops raised or increased to defend them from slavery.

1. Jan de Witt (1625–1672), who, in 1653, was made grand pensionary of Holland and from that position exercised control over both foreign and domestic policy. He was murdered by a mob in 1672.
2. Trepanned: ensnared.

It may therefore be of service to the world, to shew what measures have been taken by corrupt ministers, in some of our neighbouring countries, to ruin and enslave the people over whom they presided; to shew by what steps and gradations of mischief nations have been undone, and consequently what methods may be hereafter taken to undo others: And this subject I rather choose, because my countrymen may be the more sensible of, and know how to value the inestimable blessing of living under the best prince, and the best established government in the universe, where we have none of these things to fear.

Such traitors will probably endeavour first to get their prince into their possession, and, like Sejanus, shut him up in a little island,[3] or perhaps make him a prisoner in his court; whilst, with full range, they devour his dominions, and plunder his subjects. When he is thus secluded from the access of his friends, and the knowledge of his affairs, he must be content with such misrepresentations as they shall find expedient to give him. False cases will be stated, to justify wicked counsel; wicked counsel will be given, to procure unjust orders. He will be made to mistake his foes for his friends, his friends for his foes; and to believe that his affairs are in the highest prosperity, when they are in the greatest distress; and that publick matters go on in the greatest harmony, when they are in the utmost confusion.

They will be ever contriving and forming wicked and dangerous projects, to make the people poor, and themselves rich; well knowing that dominion follows property; that where there are wealth and power, there will be always crowds of servile dependents; and that, on the contrary, poverty dejects the mind, fashions it to slavery, and renders it unequal to any generous undertaking, and incapable of opposing any bold usurpation. They will squander away the publick money in wanton presents to minions, and their creatures of pleasure or of burden, or in pensions to mercenary and worthless men and women, for vile ends and traitorous purposes.

3. In A.D. 27 the emperor Tiberius, at the urging of his chief advisor Sejanus, retired to the island of Capreae (Capri), thus permitting Sejanus to intrigue freely.

They will engage their country in ridiculous, expensive, fantastical wars, to keep the minds of men in continual hurry and agitation, and under constant fears and alarms; and, by such means, deprive them both of leisure and inclination to look into publick miscarriages. Men, on the contrary, will, instead of such inspection, be disposed to fall into all measures offered, seemingly, for their defence, and will agree to every wild demand made by those who are betraying them.

When they have served their ends by such wars, or have other motives to make peace, they will have no view to the publick interest; but will often, to procure such peace, deliver up the strong-holds of their country, or its colonies for trade, to open enemies, suspected friends, or dangerous neighbours, that they may not be interrupted in their domestick designs.

They will create parties in the commonwealth, or keep them up where they already are; and, by playing them by turns upon each other, will rule both. By making the Guelfs afraid of the Ghibelines, and these afraid of the Guelfs,[4] they will make themselves the mediums and balance between the two factions; and both factions, in their turns, the props of their authority, and the instruments of their designs.

They will not suffer any men, who have once tasted of authority, though personally their enemies, and whose posts they enjoy, to be called to an account for past crimes, though ever so enormous. They will make no such precedents for their own punishment; nor censure treason, which they intend to commit. On the contrary, they will form new conspiracies, and invent new fences for their own impunity and protection; and endeavour to engage such numbers in their guilt, as to set themselves above all fear of punishment.

They will prefer worthless and wicked men, and not suffer a man of knowledge or honesty to come near them, or enjoy a post under them. They will disgrace men of virtue, and ridicule virtue itself, and laugh at publick spirit. They will put men into employ-

4. The Guelf and Ghibelline parties constituted the two opposing factions vying for political control in northern and central Italy between the thirteenth and fifteenth centuries. The terms as here employed by Trenchard denote political factionalism.

ments, without any regard to the qualifications for those employments, or indeed to any qualifications at all, but as they contribute
to their designs, and shew a stupid alacrity to do what they are bid.
They must be either fools or beggars; either void of capacity to
discover their intrigues, or of credit and inclination to disappoint
them.

They will promote luxury, idleness, and expence, and a
general depravation of manners, by their own example, as well as
by connivance and publick encouragement. This will not only
divert men's thoughts from examining their behaviour and politicks, but likewise let them loose from all the restraints of private
and publick virtue. From immorality and excesses they will fall into
necessity; and from thence into a servile dependence upon power.

In order to this, they will bring into fashion gaming,
drunkenness, gluttony, and profuse and costly dress. They will
debauch their country with foreign vices, and foreign instruments
of vicious pleasures; and will contrive and encourage publick
revels, nightly disguises, and debauched mummeries.

They will, by all practicable means of oppression, provoke
the people to disaffection; and then make that disaffection an
argument for new oppression, for not trusting them any further,
and for keeping up troops; and, in fine, for depriving them of liberties and privileges, to which they are entitled by their birth, and
the laws of their country.

If such measures should ever be taken in any free country,
where the people choose deputies to represent them, then they will
endeavour to bribe the electors in the choice of their representatives, and so to get a council of their own creatures; and where
they cannot succeed with the electors, they will endeavour to corrupt the deputies after they are chosen, with the money given for
the publick defence; and to draw into the perpetration of their
crimes those very men, from whom the betrayed people expect the
redress of their grievances, and the punishment of those crimes.
And when they have thus made the representatives of the people
afraid of the people, and the people afraid of their representatives;
then they will endeavour to persuade those deputies to seize the

government to themselves, and not to trust their principals any longer with the power of resenting their treachery and ill-usage, and of sending honester and wiser men in their room.

But if the constitution should be so stubbornly framed, that it will still preserve itself and the people's liberties, in spite of all villainous contrivances to destroy both; then must the constitution itself be attacked and broken, because it will not bend. There must be an endeavour, under some pretence of publick good, to alter a balance of the government, and to get it into the sole power of their creatures, and of such who will have constantly an interest distinct from that of the body of the people.

But if all these schemes for the ruin of the publick, and their own impunity, should fail them; and the worthy patriots of a free country should prove obstinate in defence of their country, and resolve to call its betrayers to a strict account; there is then but one thing left for such traitors to do; namely, to veer about, and, by joining with the enemy of their prince and country, complete their treason.

I have somewhere read of a favourite and first minister to a neighbouring prince, long since dead, who played his part so well, that, though he had, by his evil counsels, raised a rebellion, and a contest for the crown; yet he preserved himself a resource, whoever got the better: If his old master succeeded, then this Achitophel,[5] by the help of a baffled rebellion, ever favourable to princes, had the glory of fixing his master in absolute power: But, as his brave rival got the day, Achitophel had the merit of betraying his old master to plead; and was accordingly taken into favour.[6]

5. Ahithophel is described as David's chief counselor (2 Samuel 15:12), possessed of great skill but morally corrupt. He advised Absalom in his rebellion against David and, when it became clear that it would fail, hanged himself.

6. It is probable that Trenchard is referring to Thomas Osborne, first Earl of Danby, Lord Treasurer from 1673 to 1679 and a loyal minister to Charles II. Danby had disbelieved allegations, made in 1678 by Titus Oates, that Jesuits were plotting to murder the King and establish Roman Catholicism in England. Oates's testimony, although fabricated, was accepted as genuine by most Whigs, and one of the charges leveled against Danby by Parliament was that he had traitorously concealed the plot.

Happy therefore, thrice happy, are we, who can be unconcerned spectators of the miseries which the greatest part of Europe
is reduced to suffer, having lost their liberties by the intrigues and
wickedness of those whom they trusted; whilst we continue in full
enjoyment of ours, and can be in no danger of losing them, while
we have so excellent a King, assisted and obeyed by so wise a
Parliament.

T   *I am, &c.*

NO. 18. SATURDAY, FEBRUARY 25, 1720.

*The terrible Tendency of publick Corruption to ruin
a State, exemplified in that of Rome, and applied to
our own.*

SIR,

Venalis civitas mox peritura si emptorum invenias![1] "Mercenary
city, ripe for destruction, and just ready to deliver up thy-
self, and all thy liberties, to the first bidder, who is able to buy
thee!" said the great King Jugurtha, when he was leaving Rome.[2]
Rome the nurse of heroes, the mistress of nations, the glory of
empires, and the source, the standard, and pattern of virtue and
knowledge, and, indeed, of every thing which ever was praiseworthy and valuable amongst men, was soon after fallen, fallen ten
thousand thousand fathoms deep in the abyss of corruption and
impiety: No more of that publick spirit appeared, that rendered it
amiable, as well as terrible, to the world: It had conquered by its
virtue more than its arms: It had commanded a willing subjection
from the numerous nations, who readily acknowledged its superior
genius and natural right to empire, and afterwards their own condition to be graced by the dignity of such a mistress.

1. The original reads: *Urbem venalem et mature perituram, si emptorem invenerit.*
("A city for sale, condemned to destruction if it finds a buyer.") Sallust, *Bellum
Iugurthinum*, 35.10.
2. *Jugurtha* was King of Numidia from 111 to 106 B.C.; he carried on a series
of wars with Rome and was eventually defeated and imprisoned.

"But" (says the Abbot Vertot)

about this time another nation seemed to appear upon the stage: A general corruption soon spread itself through all degrees of the state: Justice was publickly sold in the tribunals: The voices of the people went to the highest bidder; and the consuls, having obtained that great post by intrigues, or by bribery, never now made war but to enrich themselves with the spoils of nations, and often to plunder those very provinces, which their duty bound them to protect and defend. The provinces were obliged to supply these prodigious expences: The generals possessed themselves of the revenues of the commonwealth; and the state was weakened in proportion as its members became powerful. It was sufficient colour for rifling the people, and laying new imposts, if they did but give those exactions a new name.

There arose on a sudden, and as it were by enchantment, magnificent palaces, whose walls, roofs, and ceilings were all gilded: It was not enough that their beds and tables were all of silver; that rich metal must also be carved and adorned with *basso relievo's*, performed by the most excellent artists. All the money of the state was in the hands of the great men, the publicans, and certain freedmen richer than their masters.

He says,

It would make a volume to represent the magnificence of their buildings, the richness of their habits, the jewels they wore, the prodigious number of slaves, freed-men, and clients, by which they were constantly attended, and especially the expence and profusion of their tables: They were not contented, if, in the midst of winter, the Falernian wine that was presented them was not strewed with roses; and cooled in vessels of gold in summer: Their side-boards groaned under the weight and load of plate, both silver and gold: They valued the feast only by the costliness of the dishes that were served up; pheasants must be fetched for them through all the dangers of the sea; and, to complete their corruption, after the conquest of Asia, they began to introduce women-singers and dancers into their entertainments.

"What defenders of liberty," says he,

> are here? What an omen of approaching slavery? None could be greater, than to see valour less regarded in a state than luxury? to see the poor officer languishing in the obscure honours of a legion, whilst the grandees concealed their cowardice, and dazzled the eyes of the publick, by the magnificence of their equipage, and the profusion of their expence.[3]

But what did all this profusion and magnificence produce? Pleasure succeeded in the room of temperance, idleness took place of the love of business, and private regards extinguished that love of liberty, that zeal and warmth, which their ancestors had shewn for the interest of the publick; luxury and pride became fashionable; all ranks and orders of men tried to outvie one another in expense and pomp; and when, by so doing, they had spent their private patrimonies, they endeavoured to make reprisals upon the publick; and, having before sold every thing else, at last sold their country.

The publick treasure was squandered away, and divided amongst private men; and new demands made, and new taxes and burdens laid upon the people, to continue and support this extravagance. Such conduct in the great ones occasioned murmurings, universal discontent, and at last civil wars. The people threw themselves under different heads or leaders of parties, who all aspired to make themselves masters of the commonwealth, and of the publick liberty; and, during the struggle, Rome and all Italy was but one slaughter-house. Thousands, hundreds of thousands, fell sacrifices to the ambition of a few: Rivers of blood ran in the publick streets, and proscriptions and massacres were esteemed sport and pastime; till at length two thirds of the people were destroyed, and the rest

---

3. René Aubert, Abbé de Vertot (1655–1735), *The History of the Revolutions that Happened in the Government of the Roman Republic* (2 vols.; London: Printed for W. Taylor, J. Pemberton, and E. Symon, 1720). The quotation appears in the introductory discourse, "The Foundation of the Roman Commonwealth and the Chief Causes of Its Decay."

made slaves to the most wicked and contemptible wretches of mankind.

Thus ended the greatest, the noblest state that ever adorned the worldly theatre, that ever the sun saw: It fell a victim to ambition and faction, to base and unworthy men, to parricides and traitors; and every other nation must run the same fortune, expect the same fatal catastrophe, who suffer themselves to be debauched with the same vices, and are actuated by the same principles and passions.

I wish I could say, that the Abbot Vertot's description of the Roman state, in its last declension, suited no other state in our own time. I hope that we ourselves have none of these corruptions and abuses to complain of: I am sure, if we have, that it is high time to reform them, and to prevent the dismal evils which they threaten. It is wild to think that there is any other way to prevent the consequence, without preventing the corruption, and the causes which produce it: Mankind will be always the same, will always act within one circle; and when we know what they did a thousand years ago in any circumstance, we shall know what they will do a thousand years hence in the same. This is what is called experience, the surest mistress and lesson of wisdom.

Let us therefore grow wise by the misfortunes of others: Let us make use of the Roman language, as a vehicle of good sense, and useful instruction; and not use it like pedants, priests, and pedagogues. Let their virtues and their vices, and the punishment of them too, be an example to us; and so prevent our miseries from being an example to other nations: Let us avoid the rocks upon which they have suffered shipwreck, and set up buoys and sea-marks to warn and guide posterity. In fine, let us examine and look narrowly into every part of our constitution, and see if any corruptions or abuses have crept or galloped into it. Let us search our wounds to the core, without which it is beyond the power of surgery to apply suitable remedies.

Our present misfortunes will rouse up our spirits, and, as it were, awaken us out of a deep lethargy. It is true, indeed, that they came upon us like a storm of thunder and lightning in a clear sky, and when the heavens seemed more serene; but the combustible matter was prepared before: Steams and exhalations had been long gathering from bogs and jakes; and though they some time seemed dispersed and far removed by the heat of a warm sun, yet the firmament was all the while impregnating with fire and brimstone; and now, on a sudden, the clouds thicken, and look black and big on every side, and threaten us with a hurricane.

Let us therefore act the part of skilful pilots, and call all hands to labour at the oars and at the ropes: Let us begin with throwing all our luggage and useless trumpery over-board; then let us lower or take down all superfluous sails, to prevent the boat from being overset; and when we have done all in our power to save the ship, let us implore the assistance of heaven; and I doubt not but we shall out-ride the storm.

Quid times? Caesarem vehis.[4] We have King George on board, and at the helm; the favourite of heaven, and the darling of all good men; who not only gives us full leave, but encourages and assists us, to save ourselves: He will not, like some weak princes amongst his predecessors, screen guilty great men, suffer the faults of others to be laid at his door, nor permit his authority to be prostituted to patronize criminals; nor interpose and stand between his people's just resentment and the punishment of worthless favourites, of which sort of cattle he has none; so that it is our own fault if we are not happy, great, and free.

Indeed, we owe that justice and duty to our great benefactor, as not only fairly and impartially to represent to him our circumstances, and how we came into them; but to do all in our power to put our constitution on such a bottom, if any thing be wanting to it, that he may have the honour and pleasure of reigning over a free and happy people. This will be to make our gift complete, in presenting him with a crown, not beset with any difficulties; a glorious crown, and not to mock him with one of thorns.

I shall soon, in some other letter, offer my thoughts from what sources these mischiefs have flowed upon us, and what methods I conceive are essentially necessary to retrieve them.[5]

T   *I am, &c.*

4. "What do you fear? You carry Caesar." A Greek version of the line appears in Plutarch, *Caesar,* 38.5.

5. See Letter No. 20 (Mar. 11, 1720).

NO. 19. SATURDAY, MARCH 4, 1720.

The Force of popular Affection and Antipathy to particular Men. How powerfully it operates, and how far to be regarded.

SIR,

Opinion and reputation have often the greatest share in governing the affairs of the world. Misled by the great bias of superstition, every where found in human nature, or by ignorance and prejudices, proceeding as often from education itself, as from the want of it, we often take the appearance of things for things themselves, mistake our own imaginations for realities, our delusions for certainties and truth. A very small part of mankind is exempted from the delusive influence of omens, presages, and prognosticks.

These and the like superstitions enter into every scene of private and publick life: Gamesters throw away the cards and dice which they had lost by, and call for others, without any other preference than that they are not the same: Gardeners pretend to plant trees in a fortunate season: Many people will not marry, or do any business, but on certain days accounted prosperous: Even generals have had their fortunate and unfortunate times and seasons; and have often declined coming to battle, when the advantage was apparently on their side, merely because the day, or time of the day, was ill-boding.

Now, though all the whimsies of this kind have no foundation, but in opinion; yet they often produce as certain and regular events, as if the causes were adequate in their own nature to the events. The opinion of a physician or a medicine,[1] does often effect the cure of a patient, by giving his mind such ease and acquiescence as can alone produce health. The opinion of a general, or of a cause, makes an army fight with double vigour; and a confidence in the wisdom and integrity of governors, makes a nation exert its utmost efforts for its own security; whereas by a distrust of its rulers, it often sinks into an universal indifference and despon-

1. Medicine: medical practitioner.

dency. The change alone of a general, or of a minister, has often changed the fortune and disposition of a people, even where there has been no superior endowments in the successor; for if they can be made to believe, that their misfortunes are owing to the ill conduct or ill genius of those who command them, the removal of the supposed cause of their misfortunes will inspire them with new courage and resolution; which are almost always rewarded with success and victory.

From hence the most famous legislators, princes and generals have endeavoured to instill into their followers an opinion of their being more than human, as being descended from, or related to, some god; or have asserted a familiar communion with the gods, a right to explain their wills, and to execute their commands. By these means they obtained an unlimited confidence in their abilities, a cheerful submission to their authority, an assurance of success under their conduct.

Where personal virtues and qualifications, by which the above pretensions are supported, are wanting, as in the successive eastern monarchies; other arts are used to gain admiration, to draw reverence to the persons of their princes, and blind obedience to their power. Those stately tyrants are, for the most part, shut up in their palaces, where every thing is august about them: They seldom shew themselves abroad to their people; and when they do, it is in the most awful and astonishing manner, attended by numerous guards, richly habited, and armed; whilst their own persons are covered with gold and pearl, and glittering with diamonds; and perhaps the horses and elephants they ride on are all in a blaze of gold and precious stones.

The demure faces and deep silence of their ministers and attendants, contribute to spread the general awe; which is still heightened by the solemn clangor of trumpets, and other warlike sounds. All this prepares the gaping and enchanted multitude to swallow, with equal credulity and wonder, the plausible stories artfully given out amongst them, of the sublime and celestial qualities of their emperors, insomuch that even their very images are worshipped.

Indeed, in countries where liberty is established, and people think for themselves, all the above arts and pretences would be ridiculous, and such farce and grimace would be laughed at. The people have sense enough to know, that all this profusion and wealth are their own spoils; that they must labour and want, that others may be idle and abound; and they will see that their poverty is increased, and their miseries aggravated and mocked, by the pomp and luxury of their masters.

Amongst such people virtuous and just actions, or the appearance of virtuous and just actions, are the only ways of gaining esteem, reverence, and submission. They must see, or fancy they see, that the views and measures of their governors tend honestly and only to the publick welfare and prosperity, and they must find their own account in their obedience. A prince who deals thus with his people, can rarely be in danger from disaffected subjects, or powerful neighbours; his faithful people will be his constant guard; and, finding their own security in his government, will be always ready at his call to take effectual vengeance upon those who shall attempt to oppose or undermine his just authority.

However, the wisest and most free people are not without their superstitions and their foibles; and prudent governors will take advantage of them, and endeavour to apply them to the publick benefit. The Romans themselves had their *dies fastos & nefastos*,[2] their fortunate and unfortunate generals; and sometimes empty names have been esteemed endowments and merit. Another Scipio was appointed by the Romans to demolish Carthage, which was first subdued by the great Scipio;[3] and the Athenians called for another Phormio for their war at Lepanto.[4]

Generals and ministers have been oftentimes disgraced, even by wise nations, for making unfortunate expeditions, or for unfortunate conduct in directing the publick affairs, when there was

2. "Days lucky and unlucky."

3. The "great Scipio" is Publius Cornelius *Scipio* Africanus Major, who decisively defeated the Carthaginian armies at the battle of Zama in 202 B.C. In 146 B.C. the Carthaginian army was again annihilated and the city captured by another Scipio, Publius Cornelius *Scipio* Aemilianus (d. 128 B.C.), adopted grandson of Scipio Africanus.

4. *Phormion* (d. 428 B.C.), Athenian admiral and the greatest seaman Greece produced during the Peloponnesian War, twice defeated superior naval forces in the Gulf of Corinth at Naupactus (Lepanto), the site of the great naval victory by Christian forces over the Turkish fleet in 1571.

no deceit or want of virtue, in those generals and ministers; for if a nation or an army take an universal, though an unreasonable disgust at one or a few men, it is ridiculous to bring his or their interest in balance with the satisfaction and affections of millions, or much less than millions. Prudent princes therefore have been always extremely cautious how they employed men in any considerable station, who were either odious or contemptible, even though it happened that they were innocently and unfortunately so.

Indeed this can seldom happen; for a virtuous and modest man will never thrust himself into the service of his prince, nor continue longer in it than he is acceptable to the people: He will know that he can do no real good to a country, which will receive no good at his hands; that the publick jealousy will misrepresent his whole conduct, render his best designs abortive, his best actions useless; that he will be a clog and a dead weight upon the affairs of his prince; and that the general distaste taken at him, will, by degrees, make his prince the object of general distaste.

But when ministers have deservedly incurred the general hatred; when they have been known to have employed their whole power and interest in opposition to the publick interest; when, being trusted with a nation's affairs, they have desperately projected, and obstinately pursued, schemes big with publick ruin; when they have weakened the authority of their prince to strengthen their own, and endangered his safety for the security of their own heads, and the protection of their crimes; when they have thriven by the publick ruin; and, being the known authors of universal calamities, have become the proper objects of such universal detestation, as not to have one real friend in their country, or one sincere advocate even amongst the many that they have bribed to be so: If, after all this, they will go on to brave a nation which they have before ruined, confidently continue at the head of affairs, and obstinately persist to overturn their king and country; this, I say, is aggravating their crimes, by an insolence which no publick resentment can equal.

This was the case of England under the influence of Gaveston and the two Spencers;[5] and this was the case of the

5. Piers Gaveston was a favorite of Edward II and became the focus of baronial hostility to the policies of the King, whom Gaveston dominated. He

Netherlands under the administration of the Duke of Alva;[6] which ministers severally ruined their masters and their country. Nations under such woeful conduct, and unlucky constellations, are often driven into revolts, or lose all courage to defend themselves, either against the attacks from their native traitors, or foreign invaders.

This is famously verified in the story of the Decemviri, a college of magistrates created by the Romans for one year, to compile and establish a body of laws. This term was thought long enough, and undoubtedly was so; but these designing men, under the plausible colour of adding two more tables to the ten already finished and published got their sitting prolonged for another year: Nor at the expiring of that, though the two tables were added, did they dissolve themselves; but, in defiance of the people who chose them, and now every where murmured against them, as well as suffered by them, continued their authority.[7]

The city of Rome saw itself under a new government; *Deploratur in perpetuum libertas, nec vindex quisquam extitit, aut futurus videtur:*[8] The constitution was gone; and though all men complained, yet none offered to help. Whilst the Romans were thus desponding at home, they were despised abroad: The neighbouring nations were provoked, that dominion should still subsist in a city, where liberty subsisted no longer. The Roman territories therefore were invaded by the Sabines and Aequians. This terrified the faction; but I do not find that it troubled the people, who neither feared nor hated foreign invaders half so much as their own domestick traitors. The desperate parricides determined rather to sacrifice their country, than lose their places; so to war they went, but with miserable success. They managed the war no

---

was captured and slain by the barons in 1312. "The two Spencers" are Hugh le Despenser and his son, who shaped Edward's policy between 1322 and 1326.

6. Fernando Alvarez de Toledo, Duke of Alva (1508–1583), governor of the Spanish Netherlands from 1567 until 1573. His administration was a particularly cruel one, typified by his zeal in setting up a tribunal, known as the Court of Blood, to try heretics and malcontents.

7. The events here recounted appear in Livy, 3.33–63.

8. "Liberty was regarded as lost forever and no one arose as its protector or seemed about to do so." Livy, 3.38.2.

better than they did the state; and had no more credit in the camp than in the city: The soldiers would not fight under the detested leaders, but ran away before the enemy, and suffered a shameful rout.

Nor did this loss and disgrace, at once unusual and terrible to Rome, at all move the traitors to resign: They went on misgoverning and debauching, till, the measures of their wickedness being full, they were driven out of their posts by the vigour of the state, and the assistance of the people. The two chief traitors were cast into prison, the rest into banishment.

This soon happily changed the state of affairs, and the spirit of the people; who, having got at length an honest administration, and governors whom they loved and trusted, quickly beat the enemy out of the territories of Rome, that very enemy, who in other circumstances had beaten them.

G   *I am, &c.*

NO. 20. SATURDAY, MARCH 11, 1720.

Of publick Justice, how necessary to the Security and Well-being of a State, and how destructive the Neglect of it to the British Nation. Signal Instances of it.

Sir,

*P*arcere subjectis, & debellare superbos;[1] to pay well, and hang well, to protect the innocent, and punish the oppressors, are the hinges and ligaments of government, the chief ends why men enter into societies. To attain these ends, they have been content to part with their natural rights, a great share of their substance and industry: To quit their equality, and submit themselves to those who had before no right to command them: For this millions live willingly in an innocent and safe obscurity, to make a few great

1. "To spare the meek and to vanquish the proud." The quotation appears in Virgil, *Aeneid*, 6.851–53.

men, and enable them, at their expence, to shine in pomp and magnificence.

But all this pageantry is not designed for those who wear it. They carry about them the dignity of the commonwealth: The honours which they receive are honours paid to the publick, and they themselves are only the pillars and images upon which national trophies are hung; for when they are divested of these insignia, no more respect and homage is due to them, than what results from their own virtue and merit. Yet such is the depravity of human nature, that few can distinguish their own persons from the ensigns and ornaments which they wear, or their duty from their dignity: There seems to be a judgment upon all men in certain stations, that they can never think of the time when they have been, or may again be, out of them.

A good magistrate is the brightest character upon earth, as being most conducive to the benefit of mankind; and a bad one is a greater monster than ever hell engendered: He is an enemy and traitor to his own species. Where there is the greatest trust, the betraying it is the greatest treason. The fasces,[2] the judge, and the executioner, do not make the crime, but punish it; and the crime is never the less, though it escape the vengeance due to it. Alexander, who robbed kingdoms and states, was a greater felon than the pirate whom he put to death, though no one was strong enough to inflict the same punishment upon him. It is no more just to rob with regiments or squadrons, than by single men or single ships; for unless we are determined by the justice of the action, there can be no criterion, boundary, or fixed mark, to know where the thief ends, and the hero begins.

> Must little villains then submit to fate,
> That great ones may enjoy the world in state?

Shall a poor pick-pocket be hanged for filching away a little loose money; and wholesale thieves, who rob nations of all that they have, be esteemed and honoured? Shall a roguery be sanctified by the greatness of it; and impunity be purchased, by deserving the

2. Fasces: the bundle of rods with a projecting axe blade borne before Roman magistrates, which served as the symbol of political authority.

highest punishment? This is inverting the nature of things, confounding virtue and vice, and turning the world topsy-turvy.

Men who are advanced to great stations, and are highly honoured and rewarded at the publick cost, ought to look upon themselves as creatures of the publick, as machines erected and set up for publick emolument and safety. They ought to reflect, that thousands, ten thousands of their countrymen, have equal, or perhaps greater, qualifications than themselves; and that blind fortune alone has given them their present distinction: That the estate of the freeholder, the hazard of the merchant, and the sweat of the labourer, all contribute to their greatness; and when once they can see themselves in this mirror, they will think nothing can be too grateful, nothing too great or too hazardous to be done for such benefactors.

They will consider, that no uncommon application, or distinguishing abilities, will justify this superiority; that many of their fellow-subjects, possessing equal merit, take much more pains for much less considerations; nay, that the business of their own employment is mostly executed by inferior officers, for small rewards; and, consequently, that their great appointments are given to secure their fidelity, and put them far above and out of the reach of bribery and corruption: They ought not to have a thought which is mean or little: Their minds are not to be in the dirt, whilst their heads are in the clouds: They ought to infuse and inspire virtue, resolution, and publick spirit, into the inactive mass, and be illustrious examples of every great and noble quality.

But if they can sink so low beneath themselves; if they can so far descend from the dignity of their characters; if they can choose so to grovel upon the earth, when they may ascend to the heavens; and be so poor and abject, as to combine and confederate with pick-pockets and common rogues; betray their most solemn trusts, and employ all their power and credit to destroy that people, whom they have every motive which heaven and earth can suggest to protect and defend: Then, I say, such wretches ought to be the scorn and detestation of every honest man; and new kinds of vengeance, new tortures, and new engines of misery ought to be invented to make their punishments as much exceed common punishments, as their crimes exceed those of the worst sort of common malefactors, and as their rewards surpass those of the best and worthiest citizens in other stages of life and circumstances of fortune.

There is no analogy between the crimes of private men and those of publick magistrates: The first terminate in the death or sufferings of single persons; the others ruin millions, subvert the policy and oeconomy of nations, and create general want, and its consequences, discontents, insurrections, and civil wars, at home; and often make them a prey to watchful enemies abroad. But amongst the crimes which regard a state, *peculatus*,[3] or robbing the publick, is the greatest; because upon the careful and frugal administration of the public treasure the very being of the commonwealth depends. It is what my Lord Coke[4] calls it, *tutela pacis, & firmamentum belli*;[5] and the embezzling of it is death by the civil law, and ought to be so by all laws. It is the worst sort of treason, as it draws all other sorts of treason after it: It disconcerts all the measures of government, and lays the ground-work of seditions, rebellions, and all kinds of publick miseries.

But these, as well as all other crimes which affect the publick, receive their aggravation from the greatness of the persons who commit them; not only as their rewards are larger, and their temptations less, but as their example recommends, and, as it were, authorizes and gives a licence to wickedness. No one dares to punish another for an offence which he knows, and the other knows, that he every day commits himself. One great man, who gets an hundred thousand pounds by cheating the publick, must wink and connive at ten others who shall wrong it of ten thousand pounds each; and they at ten times as many more, who shall defraud it of one thousand; and so on in lesser progression, till the

3. That is, peculation, or embezzlement from the public purse. Embezzlement in the sense of an offense against a private person was virtually unknown to English criminal law until the end of the eighteenth century.

4. Sir Edward Coke, Lord Coke (1552–1634), Chief Justice of the Court of Common Pleas, 1606 to 1613, and of King's Bench, 1613 to 1616, and one of the leading members of the constitutional party in Parliament upon his election to the Commons in 1620.

5. "Guardian of peace and support for war."

greatest part of the publick revenue is swallowed and devoured by great and little plunderers.

It is therefore of the utmost importance to the security and happiness of any state, to punish, in the most exemplary manner, all those who are entrusted by it, and betray that trust: It becomes the wisdom of a nation, to give ten thousand pounds to purchase a head, which cheats it of six-pence. Valerius Maximus calls severity the sure preserver and avenger of liberty: It is as necessary for the preventing of tyranny, as for the support of it.[6] After the death of the sons of Brutus, executed by the command of their own father, and in his presence, we hear no more of any conspirators in Rome to restore the Tarquins; and had Marius, Caesar, and other corrupters of the people, met with the same punishment, that glorious commonwealth might have subsisted to this day. Lenity to great crimes is an invitation to greater; whereas despair of pardon, for the most part, makes pardon useless. If no mercy were shewn to the enemies of the state, no state would be overturned; and if small or no punishment be inflicted upon them, no state can be safe.

Happy, happy had it been for this unhappy people, if these important and essential maxims of government had been duly regarded by our legislators at the Revolution (and I wish too, that the sincere and hearty endeavours of our present legislators to punish the betrayers of the late unfortunate Queen[7] had met the desired success): For I doubt that all our misfortunes have flowed from these sources, and are owing to these disappointments.

All Europe saw, and all good men in it lamented to see, a mighty nation brought to the brink of destruction by weak and contemptible instruments; its laws superseded, its courts of justice corrupted, its legislature laid aside, its liberties subverted, its religion overturned, and a new one almost introduced, and a violent and despotick government assumed, which was supported by legions

6. The quotation appears in Valerius Maximus, 6.3.11–13.

7. The reference is to the chief Tory ministers to Queen Anne during the last years of her reign, particularly Robert Harley, Earl of Oxford (1661–1724), and his close associate, Henry St. John, Viscount Bolingbroke (1678–1751). Both had extended vague promises to the Pretender of a Jacobite restoration upon the death of the Queen, which would have required that the Act of Settlement be overturned.

and an armed force: They saw this brave people rise under the oppression, and, like Antaeus,[8] gather strength by their late fall: They called for the assistance of the next heir to the crown, to avenge himself and them; and when they had, by his assistance, removed the usurpation, they rewarded him with the immediate possession of the crown. But when they had all the desired success, and subdued all that they had fought with; they soon found, that, by the treachery and corruption of their leaders, they had lost all that they had fought for.

Instead of compleating their deliverance, and punishing the authors of their calamities, and sacrificing them to the Manes of their once lost liberties; upon the most diligent search, there was not a guilty person to be found; not one who had contributed to their misfortunes. Three kingdoms had been undone by mal-administration, and no body had a hand in it. This tergiversation gave fresh heart and courage to the despairing faction: Some imputed it to weakness and fear; others to a consciousness of guilt for what we had done; and all cried out aloud, that if there were no criminals, there could be no crimes; whilst all honest men stood amazed and covered with shame and confusion at these proceedings.

All the while our new betrayers rioted in their sun-shine, laughed at the unseasonable simplicity and folly of a few Whimsicals,[9] who did not know what a revolution was good for: They would not make a rod for themselves:[10] On the contrary, numberless were their projects and stratagems to amass riches, and increase their power. They encouraged and protected a general prodigality and corruption, and so brought the kingdom into the greatest necessities; then took advantage of those necessities: They got publick money into their hands, and then lent that money to the publick again for great premiums, and at great interest, and afterwards squandered it away to make room for new projects: They made bar-

8. A giant, Antaeus was almost impossible to defeat in combat since he received renewed strength each time he touched the ground. Hercules destroyed him by lifting him above his head and squeezing him to death.

9. A faction of the Tory majority during the administration of the Earl of Oxford, the Whimsicals were unalterably committed to the Protestant Succession.

10. That is, they were not about to punish themselves.

gains for themselves, by borrowing in one capacity what they lent in another; and, by a use of their prior intelligence, and knowledge of their own intentions, they wholly governed the national credit, and raised and depressed it at their pleasure, and as they saw their advantage; by which means they beggared the people, and mortgaged all the lands and the stock of the kingdom, though not (like the righteous Joseph)[11] to their master, but to themselves.

Thus the Revolution and the principles of liberty ran backwards again. The banished Tarquin[12] conceived new hopes, and made new attempts for a restoration: All who had shared in the benefits of the former wicked administration; all those who had ever been avowed enemies to an equal government, and impartial liberty; all the grim inquisitors, who had assumed an uncontrollable sovereignty over the free and ungovernable mind, men who have ever pretended a divine right to roguery, united in his interest: With these joined the riotous, the debauched, the necessitous, the poor deluded bigots, as well as all such who had not received rewards equal to their fancied merit, and would not bear to see others revel in advantages, which their own ambition and covetousness had before swallowed for themselves.

This formidable party combined against the new established government, made earnings of the miscarriages and corruptions of those miscreants, who, by their vile and mercenary conduct, betrayed the best prince and best cause in the world, and several times had almost overturned the new restored liberty; but that the gratitude and personal love of the people to that great prince, and the fresh and lively remembrance of the evils which they have suffered, or had been like to have suffered, from the abdicated family, still preserved him upon the throne, in spite of all attempts to the contrary. However, proper advantages were not taken, neither in this nor the following reign, from the many defeats of this restless faction, to settle the Revolution upon such a basis, as not to be shaken but together with the foundations of the earth. There was

11. In response to Pharaoh's dream, Joseph conceived a policy whereby one-fifth of the produce of Egypt was stored during seven years of abundance as provision against the seven lean years to follow (Gen. 41:1–37).

12. The "banished Tarquin" to whom Trenchard is referring is James Stuart, the Old Pretender.

always a lion in the way; the figure or the number of the conspirators, or the difficulty of discovery, or their interest, alliance, or confederacy with men in power, were the reasons whispered; but the
true one was concealed, namely, that one guilty person durst not
heartily prosecute another: The criminals had stories to tell, secrets
not to be divulged; for an innocent and virtuous man alone dares
undertake to bring a great villain to deserved punishment: None
but a Brutus could have destroyed Brutus's sons.

Nothing was ever done to rectify or regulate the education
of youth, the source of all our other evils; but schools of literature
were suffered to continue under the direction of the enemies to all
sound literature and publick virtue: Liberty, being deserted by her
old friends, fell of course into the hands of her enemies; and so
liberty was turned upon liberty: By these means the discontents
were fomented, the evils still increased, and the conspirators still
went on. They had now got new tools to work with, just forged,
and sent glowing hot from the universities: A new generation
arose and appeared upon the publick stage, who had never seen or
felt the misfortunes which their fathers groaned under, nor
believed more of them than what they had learned from their
tutors: So that all things seemed prepared for a new revolution;
when we were surprized by a voice from heaven, which promised
us another deliverance.

We have at last, by the bounteous gift of indulgent providence, a most excellent King, and a wise and uncorrupt Parliament; and yet—but what shall I say, or what shall be left unsaid? I
will go on. We have a prince, I say, who is possessed of every virtue
which can grace and adorn a crown; a Parliament too, than whom
England has never chosen one better disposed to do all those
things which every honest man in it wished, and called for; and
yet—by the iniquity of the times, or the iniquities of particular
men, we are still to expect our deliverance; though I hope that we
shall not expect it long.

Publick corruptions and abuses have grown upon us: Fees
in most, if not in all, offices, are immensely increased: Places and
employments, which ought not to be sold at all, are sold for treble
values: The necessities of the publick have made greater imposi-

tions unavoidable, and yet the publick has run very much in debt; and as those debts have been increasing, and the people growing poor, salaries have been augmented, and pensions multiplied; I mean in the last reign, for I hope that there have been no such doings in this.

Our common rogues now scorn little pilferings, and in the dark; 'tis all publick robbery, and at noon-day; nor is it, as formerly, for small sums, but for the ransom of kings, and the pay of armies: Figures of hundreds and thousands have lost their use in arithmetick: Plumbs* alone are thought worth gathering; and they no longer signify hundreds of thousands, but millions: One great man, who is said in a former reign to have plundered a million and a half, has made his successors think as much to be their due too:[13] Possession of great sums is thought to give a title to those sums; and the wealth of nations is measured out and divided amongst private men, not (as by the West-India pirates) with shovels, but by waggons.

The dregs of the people, and the scum of the Alley, can buy Italian and German sovereigns out of their territories; and their levees have been lately crowded with swarms of dependent princes, like Roman consuls, and Eastern monarchs; and I am told, that some of them have been seen ascending to, and descending from, their chariots, while they leaned upon the necks of prostrate grandees. Oh liberty! stop thy flight. Oh virtue! be something more than a name and empty sound: Return, oh return! inspire and assist our illustrious legislators in the great work which they have so generously undertaken! Assist, assist, if it be but to save those who have always devoutly worshipped thee, and have paid constant incense at they altars.

But what shall be done! Where is the remedy for all these evils? We hope for it, we expect it, we see it; and we call for it, from

* A cant word, known to mean a hundred thousand pounds.

13. It is likely that the reference is to Sir James Craggs, MP for Grampound from 1702 to 1713, who was appointed joint Postmaster-General in 1715. Craggs was able to take advantage of the positions he held to become enormously wealthy. In addition, both he and his son, James Craggs the younger, were active speculators in South Sea stock. By the time of his death in 1721, he had amassed a fortune of more than £1,500,000.

the healing hands of our most gracious King, and his dutiful Parliament. There is a crisis in the health of governments, as well as of private persons. When distempers are at the worst, they must mend, or the patient die: And when the case is desperate, bold and resolute methods must be taken, or he will be suffered to die, for fear of his dying. What then is the remedy? We must begin with letting out some of our adulterate and corrupt blood, one drop of which is enough to contaminate the ocean: We must first take full vengeance of all those whom we can discover to be guilty, and use them as citizens do shoplifters; that is, make those who are caught pay for all that is stolen. Let us not, oh let us not suffer the sins of all Israel to be at this time of day laid upon the head of the scape-goat!

When we have taken this first and necessary step, to prevent an apoplexy or malignant eruptions, let us prescribe strong emeticks, proper sudorificks,[14] and effectual purgatives, to bring up or throw off the noxious juices and morbifick[15] matter that oppresses us, and so wholly to eradicate the causes of our distemper. But, above all, let us avoid the beginning with lenitives[16] and palliating medicines, which will only cover and foment our evils, make them break out more violently, at last perhaps turn into dangerous swellings and epidemical plague sores; and by such means spread a general infection: Let us not suffer any of our great or little rogues to escape publick vengeance.

When we have, by these vigorous methods, removed the peccant humors which are the springs and sources of our distemper, let us use proper applications, gentle remedies, and wholesome diet, to correct and rectify the mass of remaining blood, to invigorate and renew our constitution, restore it to its first principles, and make it sound and active again: Let us see where it abounds, and where it wants; whether the sanguine, the phlegmatick, or the bilious predominates, and reduce them all to a proper balance: Let us look back and examine strictly, by what neglect, by what steps and gradations of intemperance or folly, we are

14. Sudorifics: substances that induce sweat.
15. Morbific: disease-causing.
16. Lenitives: analgesics.

brought into the present condition, and resolve to avoid them for the future.

Let us try no more projects, no more knavish experiments; let us have no more quacking, no more to do with empiricks.[17] Let us act openly and above-board for the publick interest, and not hang out false colours, to catch unwary preys. Let us plainly tell at first what we mean, and all that we mean: If it be honest and advantageous, every good man will defend it, and assist in it; if otherwise, it ought not to be defended at all.

This is the way, and the only way, to preserve and continue the inestimable blessing of our present establishment: Let the people see the benefit of the change, and there is no fear that they will be against their own interest; but state-quacks may harangue and swear till they are black in the face, before they will persuade any one to believe that he is in perfect health, who feels himself sick at heart. Men in such circumstances are always restless, always tumbling about from side to side, changing every posture for present ease; and so often bring death upon themselves, by trying preposterous remedies to avoid it.

T   *I am, &c.*

NO. 21. SATURDAY, MARCH 18, 1720.

A Letter from John Ketch, Esq.[1] *asserting his Right to the Necks of the over-grown Brokers.*

SIR,

In a general call for justice from an injured nation, I beg leave to put in my voice, being myself an eminent sufferer in the ill fate of my country, which no otherwise gains than as I do, by the

17. Emperics: quack practitioners.

1. The hangman responsible for putting to death more than two hundred rebels who were implicated in Monmouth's Rebellion in 1685. His name came to be applied to all public executioners.

exaltation of rogues. Our interests, in this respect, are the same. And as it would be very hard that the blood-suckers of the people should not make the people some amends, by restoring the blood that they have sucked; so it would be as hard that I, who am the finisher of justice, should not have justice done me.

From my best observation upon publick affairs, last summer, I promised myself that I should certainly have full hands this last winter; I therefore applied myself with singular diligence to gain the utmost perfection and skill in the calling wherein God and the law hath placed me: For, I did not think it at all laudable, or agreeable to a good conscience, to accept a post, without proper talents and experience to execute the same, however customary and common such a practice might be: And therefore, without presuming to follow the illustrious example of my betters, in this matter, I thought it became me to become my post. In truth, Sir, if this maxim had prevailed, where it should have prevailed; and if my brethren in place had as well understood, and as honestly executed, their several truths, as I do mine, we should have had a very different face of things, nor would I have had occasion for journeymen.

Thus, Sir, I was firmly and honestly resolved, that the execution of justice should not stick with me, where-ever else it stuck. Moreover, at a time when every thing, but honesty, bore a double price, I bought up a great quantity of silken halters, for the sole use and benefit of any of our topping pick-pockets, who should be found to have noble or genteel blood about them,[2] N. B. This compliment was not intended for the directors,[3] who must expect to wear the same valedictory cravat which is worn by small felons, who come under my hands every Sessions:[4] But I have set apart a good round quantity of these delicate silken turnovers for the benefit and decoration of divers worthy gentlemen, whom I have marked out for my customers in the _____ ; whom it would not be

2. Peers were traditionally extended the courtesy of being hanged with a silken rope.
3. That is, the directors of the South Sea Company.
4. That is, at every sitting of the Court of Quarter Sessions.

good breeding in me, as yet, to name; but I hope they will prove rare chaps.

I did likewise bespeak, at least, a dozen curious axes, spick and span new, with rare steel edges; the fittest that could be made, for dividing nobly betwixt the head and the shoulders of any dignified and illustrious customer of mine, who has, either by birth or by place, a right to die at the east end of the town.[5]

Now, Sir, it unluckily happens, that I cannot pay for any of the implements of national justice, and of my trade, till I have used them: And my creditors, though they own me to be an honest man, yet, wanting faith in all publick officers, begin to fear that I shall never pay for them at all. It is, in truth, a sensible discouragement to them and me, that I have so little to do this winter, when there appear'd so much to be done in my way. Sure never poor deserving hangman had such a shameful vacation!

As having a post, I have consequently the honour of being a true member of the Church of England, as by law established; and therefore under these disappointments I comfort myself with some patience, and more beer. I have, besides that, this further consolation, that if our canary birds find wings to escape me, neither the blame nor the shame shall lie at my door.

You see, Sir, I have merit; and yet you see I labour under discouragements enough to scare any successor of mine from accepting this neglected and pennyless post, till he has a sufficient sum of money in hand paid, and a good pension for life, as is usual upon less occasions, together with ample provision for his children after him.

But, in spite of all these discouragements, I am determined to live in hopes of some topping customers before the Sessions is ended: The publick and I must certainly get at last: God knows we have been eminent sufferers; we have been defrauded on every side.

Being bred a butcher, I can comfort my said customers with an assurance, that I have a delicate and ready hand at cutting

5. That is, to be executed at Tower Hill, the traditional site of executions of the nobility, rather than at Tyburn, where the lowborn were hanged.

and tying; so let them take heart, the pain is nothing, and will be soon over; I am only sorry 'tis so long a coming: No man can be pleased with being defrauded of his just dues.

I have one consolation, Sir, which never leaves me; namely, that though my post has not been so profitable a one as for some time past it should have been, yet it has been a safe one. I doubt not but many of my brethren in place would be glad if they could say as much. I am moreover of opinion, that my post has, for a year past, been one of the most honest and creditable posts in England; nor would I change circumstances or character with some that hold their heads very high, and may hold them higher still before I have done with them. I am sure it cannot be denied, that the hangman of London has for the above space of time been a reputable officer, in comparison. The truth is, that they have got more money than I, but I have more reputation than they; and I hope soon to go snacks[6] with some of them in their money.

I know that knaves of state require a great deal of form and ceremony before they are committed to my care; so that I am not much surprized, that I have not yet laid my hands upon certain exalted criminals. I hope, however, that, when they come, a good number will come at once. But there is a parcel of notorious and sorry sinners, called *brokers*: Fellows of so little consequence, that few of them have reputation enough to stand candidates for my place, were the same vacant (which God forbid!), and yet rogues so swollen with guilt, that poor Derwentwater and Kenmure[7] (my two last customers) were babes and petty larceners to them. Now these are the hang-rogues with whom I would be keeping my hand in use.

Sir, I have been with counsel about them, and my lawyer stands amazed that I have not had them already: "But," says he, "Mr. Ketch, I foresaw that the brokers were only the pimps of great rogues, who were themselves the pimps of greater: So that

6. To go snacks: to have a share in the proceeds.

7. James Radcliffe, third Earl of Derwentwater (1689–1716), and William Gordon, sixth Viscount Kenmure (d. 1716). Both joined in the Stuart rising of 1715 and were taken prisoner at Preston. They were beheaded on Tower Hill in late Feb. 1716.

were these vermin to go up to Tyburn,[8] they would draw many more after them, who would likewise draw others. So, depend upon it, the lion, if it can, will save the jackal. And hence it proceeds, Mr. Ketch, that though it be hard, yet it is not strange, that those rogues, whom all men wish in your hands, are not yet there."

He then told me how the brokers have violated that act of Parliament, which allows them but two shillings and sixpence for transacting a hundred pounds stock, by taking, or rather exacting twenty shillings, and sometimes five pounds.[9] I hope, when I come to strip them, or to commute for stripping them, that I shall be allowed to mete out to them the same measure.

He told me likewise, that during the reign of roguery, they sold for no body but the directors, and their betters; whereas they were obliged in duty to have sold for all men alike, who employed them. Their office is an office of trust, as well as that of the directors. They act, or ought to act, under the restrictions of an act of Parliament,[10] under the sacred obligation of an oath, and under the ties and penalties of a bond; by all which they are obliged to discharge their duty impartially betwixt man and man, and for one man as soon as another. Now it is well known, that they broke their trust to the publick; that they ceased to be common and indifferent officers in the Alley; and yet retaining the name and pretence of their office (by which they also retained the power of deceiving), they became only spies and liars for the directors and their manag-

8. That is, were to ascend Tyburn Hill, which, until 1783, was the main site of public executions in London.

9. Gordon appears to be referring to an act passed in 1697 (8 & 9 Wm III, c. 20) which limited brokerage fees to one-half percent of the value of the transacted stock. This would limit the fee on a stock valued at £100 to ten shillings, not two shillings, sixpence. In any case, the act was superseded by legislation passed in 1708.

10. In fact, the only restriction under which brokers then operated was an act passed in 1708 (6 Anne, c. 68), that empowered the mayor and aldermen of the City of London to license brokers who practiced within the City. Among other limitations, the act forbade brokers to conduct business in Exchange Alley or to deal in securities on their own account. The statute appears to have been seldom enforced and was regarded as an empty gesture. In Dec. 1720, as a consequence of the South Sea Bubble, the Commons again considered legislation regulating brokers and passed a bill to this effect, but it failed in the Lords.

ers, and sellers for them only. They were therefore criminals of the first class, and principal agents in the publick mischief; for, had they not acted thus for one side alone, the directors could not have sold out much at high prices, nor would others have bought in at those prices: So that they are to be considered not only as the instruments of greater traitors, though in that character they are liable to be hanged; but as wilful and deliberate confederates with those traitors; and, consequently, merit every punishment which those higher traitors merit.

My counsel said too, that there were some crimes of so high and malignant a nature, that, in the perpetration of them, all accessories were considered as principals; that those who held a man till he was murdered, were murderers; that those who voluntarily held a candle to others, who robbed a house, were themselves robbers; and that in committing of treason, all are traitors who have had a hand in that treason.

He said, that the brokers were free agents, independent of all companies, and no more attached, in point of duty, to the South-Sea, than to any other; that being *sui juris*[11] (as he called it) they could not excuse their wicked dealings by the pretended commands and authority of any superiors, as some of the South-Sea officers might plead, for that the directors were not their superiors; that their rogueries therefore were voluntary and deliberate rogueries; and that having wilfully sinned with the directors, they ought in justice to suffer with the directors, and hang with them.

He told me, that having share of the gain of villainy with the directors, they ought to have their share of the halter too. They transacted great sums for themselves; though the law, which established them, enacts, that they shall neither buy nor sell for themselves; which is highly reasonable; for how can any man transact honestly for another, whilst he is selling to him his own stock?

He said, that they deceived every man into his own ruin; and ruined the nation, to enrich the directors and themselves: They sold their own stock, and that of the directors, under false and fictitious names, contrary to the obligation of their bond to the

11. "[To be] independent."

City, which obliges them to declare the name of the seller to the buyer, as well as the name of the buyer to the seller; for they knew that no man would have been willing to buy, had he known that the brokers and directors were in haste to sell. Thus they used false dice, and blinded men's eyes, to pick their pockets. "And surely, Mr. Ketch," says the counsellor, "if he who picks a man's pocket is to be hanged, the rogues that pick the pockets of the whole country, ought to be hanged, drawn, and quartered."

But what was most remarkable of all in what the counsellor told me, and what indeed gives me most heart, is, that unless the brokers are hanged, it will be scarce possible that any body else should be hanged. If this be true, their doom is certain, and I shall be able to support my squireship before Easter: For, surely, we shall never save mighty knaves, for the sake of saving little ones; and if so be it is determin'd to gratify the nation with a competent store of hanging and beheading, certainly we must do every thing necessary thereunto.

"Now," says my counsel, "if the brokers do not discover the secrets which they best know, but which they will never discover, if they can save their necks and purses without doing it; then, I doubt me, justice will be impotent for want of evidence. But if they find that they can save nothing by their silence, they will tell all to save something. They are hardened rogues; and, by false oaths, and under-hand dealing, will screen all that are as bad as themselves; but gripe them well, and ten to one but you squeeze the truth out of them."

"For all which reasons, Mr. Ketch," continued he, "I hope soon to give you joy of the brokers, as well as of better customers." And so he dismissed me, without taking a fee; for he told me, that he considered me as an eminent sufferer, by having as yet got nothing, where he wished that I had, before this time, got a great deal.

This, Sir, is the substance of what passed between us; for which I am so much obliged to him, that if ever he falls in my way, I'll use him with the like generosity; and I will owe you, Mr. Journalist, the same favour, if you will be so kind to publish this.

If you knew me, Sir, you would own that I have valuable talents, and am worth your acquaintance. I am particularly possessed of a praiseworthy industry, and an ardent desire of business. In truth, I care not to be idle; and yet it cruelly happens, that I have but one busy day in six weeks, and even then I could do twice as much. Besides, having a tender heart, it really affects me with pity, to be obliged to strangle so many innocents every Sessions; poor harmless offenders, that only commit murders, and break open houses, and rob men of guineas and half crowns; while wholesale plunderers, and mighty rogues of prey, the avowed enemies and hangmen of honesty, trade and truth, the known promoters of villainy, and the merciless authors of misery, want, and general ruin, go on to ride in coaches and six, and to defy a people whom they have made poor and desperate; potent parricides, who have plundered more from this kingdom in six months than all the private thieves and highwaymen ever did, or could do, since the creation.

Sir, I repeat it, that the hanging of such poor felons only, as things now stand, is, comparatively, shedding innocent blood: And so, for the ease of my mind, I beg that I may have those sent me, whom I may truss up with a safe conscience. My teeth particularly water, and my bowels yearn, at the name of the brokers; for God's sake, let me have the brokers.

Upon the whole, Sir, I have reason to hope, from the present spirit raised in the nation (and, they say, it is in a great measure owing to you, that there is such a spirit raised), I say, I hope soon to have the fingering of the throats of these traitors, who have fingered all the money in the nation. Their own guilt, and the incessant cry of the people, will weigh them down, in spite of all arts and screens.

N. B. I have a nice hand at touching a neck of quality; and when any customers come, I shall be ready to give you joy of it, as well as to receive the like from you. Who am,

G

Sir,

your loving friend,

JOHN KETCH

NO. 22. SATURDAY, MARCH 25, 1721.

ֆ   *The Judgment of the People generally sound, where
not misled. With the Importance and Probability of
bringing over Mr. Knight.*[1]

SIR,

From the present spirit of this nation, it is still further evident
to me, what I have always thought, that the people would
constantly be in the interests of truth and liberty, were it not for
external delusion and external force. Take away terror, and men
never would have been slaves: Take away imposture, and men will
never be dupes nor bigots. The people, when they are in the
wrong, are generally in the wrong through mistake; and when they
come to know it, are apt frankly to correct their own faults. Of
which candour in them Machiavel has given several instances, and
many more might be given.

But it is not so with great men, and the leaders of parties;
who are, for the most part, in the wrong through ambition, and
continue in the wrong through malice. Their intention is wicked,
and their end criminal; and they commonly aggravate great crimes
by greater. As great dunces as the governors of mankind often are
(and God knows that they are often great enough), they are never
traitors out of mere stupidity.

Machiavel says, That no wise man needs decline the judgment of the people in the distribution of offices and honours, and
such particular affairs (in which I suppose he includes punishment) for in these things they are almost infallible.[2]

I could give many instances where the people of England
have judged and do judge right; as they generally would, were

1. Robert Knight (1675–1744), cashier of the South Sea Company and, as
such, privy to the various schemes undertaken to inflate the price of the Company's stock. In Jan. 1721, Knight absconded to avoid investigation by Parliament but in the following month was arrested and imprisoned in the Brabant
(the area that now comprises the southern Netherlands and northern
Belgium). Later that year Knight managed to flee to France. He was eventually pardoned and he returned to England in 1742.
2. This observation appears in the *Discourses*, I.47.6.

they not misled. They are, particularly, unanimous in their opinion, that we ought by no means to part with Gibraltar; and this their opinion is grounded upon the same reasons that sway the wisest men in this matter.

They likewise know, that an English war with Muscovy would be downright madness;[3] for that, whatever advantage the same might be to other countries, it would grievously hurt the trade and navy of England, without hurting the Czar.

They know too, that a squabble between Spain and the Emperor about Italy,[4] could not much affect England; and that therefore, were we to go to war with either, upon that account, as things now stand, it could not be for the sake of England.

They know, that our men of war might be always as honestly employed in defending our trade, by which our country subsists, from the depredations of pirates, as in conquering kingdoms for those to whom the nation is nothing obliged, or in defending provinces with which the nation has nothing to do, and from which it reaps no advantage.

They know, that it is of great concernment to any people, that the heir apparent to their crown be bred amongst them;[5] not only that he may be reconciled, by habit, to their customs and laws, and grow in love with their liberties; but that, at his accession to the throne, he may not be engrossed and beset by foreigners, who

3. At one point in 1720 it appeared that England might intervene in the Northern War on the side of Sweden and Prussia and against Russia. Indeed, in late 1719 a joint Swedish-English fleet converged on the Tsar's Baltic fleet with the intention of annihilating it, but the Russian ships retired and an engagement was averted. King George's northern policy appears to be one of the few instances where England's interests were subordinated to Hanoverian concerns.

4. In 1718 the British once again joined with the Austrian Hapsburgs, in the person of the Emperor Charles VI, to force Spain to abide by the terms of the treaties that ended the War of the Spanish Succession. The War of the Quadruple Alliance was brought to a close in 1720 with the surrender by Philip V of Sardinia and Sicily and the abandonment of his Italian claims. However, the Empire's vacillation in supporting the succession of Don Carlos, Philip's son, to the duchies of Parma, Piacenza, and Tuscany, which Austria had agreed to in 1720, remained a source of friction between the two nations.

5. The reference is to Frederick Louis, the King's eldest grandson, who was born in 1707. His father, the Prince of Wales, was thirty-one years old at George I's accession to the English throne and was both ignorant of, and uncomfortable with, English politics and customs.

will be always in the interest of another country; and, consequently, will be attempting to mislead him into measures mischievous to his kingdom, and advantageous to themselves, or their own nation.

The people know, that those are the best ministers, who do the most good to their country, or rather the least mischief: They can feel misery and happiness, as well as those that govern them; and will always, in spite of all arts, love those that do them a sensible good, and abhor, as they ought, those that load them with evils. Hence proceeds the popularity, and the great unenvied characters, of our present governors; who, besides the memorable and prosperous projects which they have brought to maturity, for the good of Great Britain and Ireland, would likewise have obliged us with another present,* but very few years since, which would have completed all the rest, if we had had the courtesy to have accepted it.

It is certain, that the people, when left to themselves, do generally, if not always, judge well; we have just now a glaring instance of it in the loud and unanimous call of all men, that Mr. Knight may be brought over; I say, the call of all men, except the directors and their accomplices, nay, the people judge well, as to the cause of his going away; they more than guess for whose sake, and by whose persuasion, he went; and they are of opinion, that, were he here, the trials of guilt in the House of Commons would be much shorter, and the Tower of London still more nobly inhabited. I am indeed surprized that he is not already in London, considering of what consequence it is to have him here, both to publick and to private men.

Whether the directors and their masters shall be punished or no, is to me one and the same question, as to ask, whether you will preserve your constitution or no; or, whether you will have any constitution at all? It is a contention of honesty and innocence with villainy and falsehood; it is a dispute whether or no you shall be a people; it is a struggle, and, if it be baulked, will, in all probability, be the last struggle for old English liberty. All this is well understood by the people of England.

* The Peerage Bill.

Now, though the inferior knaves are in a fair way of being hanged, yet our top-traitors, having transacted all their villainies in the South-Sea with Mr. Knight alone, or with Mr. Knight chiefly, will think themselves always safe, so long as they can keep him abroad; and while he continues abroad, the nation's vengeance can never be half complete.[6]

As to my own particular, I am so sanguine in this affair, that the very reasons commonly given why he will not be brought over, are to me very good reasons why he will be brought over: I cannot but wonder to hear any doubts about it. I am sure, that those who suggest such doubts, must suggest with the same breath very terrible crimes against some very considerable men.

The business of bringing over Mr. Knight is become the business of the ministry, and incumbent on them only. It is become their duty to their master King George, as they would preserve entirely to him the affections of a willing and contented people, by shewing them, that in consideration of their mighty wrongs (which the said ministry did all in their power to prevent) they shall have all fair play for justice and restitution. And it is in this respect too become the duty of the ministry to the people, whose humours it is their business to watch, whose interest it is their business to study, as much as the interest of the King himself; and it must be owned, to the praise of the present set, that they have constantly consulted and pursued the one as much as the other, with equal skill and honesty; and so far King and people are equally obliged to them.

As to the personal interests of the ministers themselves, I say nothing, the same being supposed always firmly linked with the other two; as doubtless it is at present. Let me only add here, that the bringing over Mr. Knight is a duty which they owe to themselves, their own characters being intimately concerned in it; otherwise. . . .

People indeed begin to say, that the suppressing of evidence ought to be taken for evidence, as in the case of Mr.

6. It was assumed, with justification, that Knight possessed a detailed knowledge of the illicit transfers of stock to certain members of Parliament and to friends of the royal family.

Aislabie,[7] who burned the book which contained the evidence.[8] There is a noble person too,[9] said to be mentioned in the report of the Committee,[10] not to his advantage; but, I thank God, now fully vindicated by patriots as incorrupt as himself, upon the fullest proof of his innocence; and if his acquittal did not meet the universal concurrence of all present, it could be owing only to Mr. Knight's not being at hand to speak what he knew: Had he made his appearance, there had never been a division upon the question, but all would have been then as unanimous in their sentiments about that great man's integrity and clean hands, as all the rest of the kingdom at present are. However, reputation is so nice a thing, that it cannot be made too clear; and therefore we are sure of the hearty assistance of this illustrious patriot to bring over Mr. Knight, if possible, to make his vindication yet more complete.

It is also the interest of another great person,[11] equal to the first in power and innocence, and who, without doubt, has taken common measures with him for the publick good, and will equally share in the grateful applause of good men, and the reproach of bad; for no degrees of virtue will put any one beyond the reach of

7. John Aislabie (1670–1742), MP for Ripon, appointed Chancellor of the Exchequer in 1718 by the Sunderland-Stanhope ministry. A venal man of limited intelligence and enormous ambition, Aislabie had made exorbitant profits through bribes from the South Sea Company and by trading in its stock. In early 1721, he was forced to resign the chancellorship and in March he was expelled from the Commons and sent to the Tower.

8. The reference is to the "green book," a ledger in which Knight, as cashier, entered the recipients and amounts of Company bribes, tendered in the form of South Sea stock of a par value totaling almost £600,000.

9. Most likely the third Earl of Sunderland, one of England's most powerful politicians until the bursting of the South Sea Bubble. It was only through Walpole's efforts that Sunderland was acquitted of wrongdoing by the Commons in Mar. 1721, and then only by a close vote. He resigned his offices in the following month and died the next year, a broken man.

10. In Jan. 1721, the Commons elected a Secret Committee of Inquiry to investigate the South Sea scheme. The Committee's interim report, detailing the bribery that marked the Company's relations with the Court and Parliament, was submitted to the House at the end of February.

11. Robert Walpole (1676–1745), who, with the death or disgrace of England's leading political figures in 1721, assumed responsibility for the nation's government after the South Sea crisis. Despite political differences, Walpole defended both Charles Stanhope, Secretary of the Treasury, and the Earl of Sunderland in the Commons, both of whom were acquitted despite strong public suspicions of their guilt.

envy and calumny, and therefore we cannot be sure that his strenuous and barefaced protection of innocent and oppressed virtue will not be misinterpreted by popular clamour, which often misapplies established and well-known truths; as, that no one who has not part of the gain, will adopt part of the infamy; that it is the property of innocence to abhor guilt in others, as well as not to practise the same itself, and to punish as well as to hate it; that no man who is not a thief, will be an advocate for a thief; that rogues are best protected by their fellows; and that the strongest motive which any man can have for saving another from the gallows, is the fear of the same punishment for the same crimes: And though these, and a thousand other such unwarrantable imputations, ought not, and have not made the least impression upon one conscious of his own virtue; yet it is every man's duty, as well as interest, to remove the most distant causes of suspicion from himself, when he can do it consistent with his publick duty; and therefore we are equally sure of this great man's endeavours too for bringing over Mr. Knight.

Even some of our legislators themselves have not been free from calumny, who are all concerned to have their characters vindicated; and therefore we may be sure will, in the highest manner, resent any prevarication, or trifling chicane, if such a procedure could be possibly supposed in an affair of this nice importance to all England, as well as to many of themselves.

Nay, the whole Parliament of England, who have generously undertaken the scrutiny of the late black knaveries, and the punishment of the knaves, are nearly concerned to see Mr. Knight brought over. They find, in their enquiries, his testimony often referred to, and that the evidence is not complete without him. They know already a good deal of what he could say; and I doubt not but he could say more than they know. They have once addressed his Majesty already, about bringing him over;[12] and I suppose will again, if he do not come speedily. The business of the

12. In Jan. 1721, when the news that Knight had fled England first reached Westminster, the Commons appealed to the King to close all British ports to prevent others implicated in the swindle from escaping and to offer a reward for Knight's capture.

whole nation does, as it were, stand still for it; seeing it is become the business and expectation of the whole nation.

As to remoras[13] from abroad, I cannot see room for any. Quite otherwise; I always thought it very fortunate for England, that Mr. Knight fell into the Emperor's hands;[14] a prince, for whom we have done such mighty, such heroick favours; for whom we consumed our fleet in the Mediterranean, for whom we guarantee'd Italy, for whom we preserved and conquered kingdoms; a prince, in fine, for whose service we have wasted years, fleets, and treasures: And can it be alledged or supposed, with the appearance of common sense, that this great prince, the strict friend, old confederate, and fast ally of England; a prince, who has been, as it were, the ward of England, and brought up in its arms; supported by its interest and counsels, protected and aggrandized by its fleets and armies,[15] will, against all the principles of good policy, against all the ties of gratitude and honour, fly in the face of his friends and benefactors, by refusing to deliver up to this nation and this King, a little criminal, small in his character, but great in his crimes and of the utmost consequence to England in the pursuit of this great enquiry, which merits the consideration; and commands the attention of every Englishman.

We could draw up a long, a very long list of good deeds done, and expensive favours shewn, to the Emperor; without being afraid of being put out of countenance by any German catalogue of returns made us from Vienna. Perhaps there may have been some courtesies procured from thence by England; but we would ask, whether they were intended or procured for England? It seems to me, that this is the first time of asking for ourselves: And shall we, this first time, be denied? Will such an humble mite be refused for millions frankly bestowed, and bestowed beyond all conjecture and expectation? It cannot be; nor, if it could, ought it

13. Remoras: impediments.
14. As a consequence of British efforts, Knight was arrested while on his way from Brussels to Liége in the Brabant, an area that formed part of the Austrian Netherlands, the domain of the Hapsburg Emperor, Charles VI.
15. Trenchard and Gordon are referring to the Quadruple Alliance (1718–1720) by which England and Austria were allied.

to be borne. We know how to shew, that we have sense as well as power, and resentment as well as liberality.

The Emperor therefore cannot be suspected in this matter; I dare say that he will comply with our demands, as soon as they are made, whatever they be. He will not put such contempt upon us, who have purchased more respect at his hands. Besides, it is confidently asserted, that Mr. Knight longs to be at home; which I am apt to believe: He knows, that the kind counsel given him, to go away, was not given him for his own sake; and has reason to fear, that those who sent him away, will keep him away. There is laudanum in Flanders, as well as in England;[16] and that or a poignard may thwart his best inclinations to return. If that should happen, we are at liberty to think the worst; and, I doubt, we cannot think too bad. Unhappy man! he was not a knave for himself alone; and I am apt to believe, were he here, that he would honestly betray those men to the publick, for whom he wickedly betrayed the publick.

Thus then, in all likelihood, neither the Emperor nor Mr. Knight are to be blamed, if Mr. Knight does not return. But, whether he be willing or no, the Emperor has no right, no pretence to keep him. Who will then be to blame, if the universal cry of justice, and of the nation, should not have its effect? The question is easy, were the answer prudent to give. In truth, there needs no answer; all mankind will know how to solve this difficulty.

An honourable messenger has been gone near six weeks, and yet the Commons have occasion to address his Majesty to know what answer he has sent. Wonderful, in a case that is of so much importance, and which requires so much expedition, and so little ceremony! I have sometimes thought a courier must needs have been dispatched to England about it long since, but that he was way-laid, and murdered by our conspirators and their agents upon the road. This may seem a strange fancy; but,

16. Sir James Craggs, one of the government's staunchest supporters of the South Sea scheme, was due to be tried by the Commons on Mar. 29, 1721, but died—apparently from an overdose of laudanum—the evening before.

without being very aged, I have lived long enough to think nothing strange. I have not been once amazed these six months.

In the mean time, the business of the Committee, which is the business of Great Britain, is like to stand still. Those gentlemen have done their duty; and if their evidence be not complete (which however they deny), the fault is not chargeable on them, but they are answerable who keep them from better. This is a reproach not like to be wiped off, but by bringing over Mr. Knight; and then, perhaps, they that deserve it may dread a far worse thing. Here is the riddle, and the solution of the riddle. There are those amongst us, who, clothed as they are with infamy, and cursed and detested by their fellow-creatures universally, do yet dread a greater evil. So precious and prevailing is the love of life! Continue me mine, sweet heaven, upon better terms, or not at all!

I shall conclude, by repeating an observation which I have already made in this letter; namely, that the suppressing the best evidence, contains in it the strongest evidence; and those men will stand condemned, who, in trials of innocence and guilt, stop the mouths of their judges, and deprive the accusers of their witnesses.

T *and* G   *I am,* &c.

NO. 23. SATURDAY, APRIL 1, 1721.

 A memorable Letter from Brutus to Cicero, with an explanatory Introduction.

SIR,

I am going to present you, and the town by your means, with the most valuable performance of all antiquity: It is not likely that it ever had, or ever will have, its fellow. The author of it was, perhaps, the most amiable character, the most accomplished man, that ever the world saw.

Excellent Brutus! of all human race
The best!

COWLEY[1]

He was the author of that glorious letter, which I now send you in English. It was written by the greatest man upon the noblest subject; Brutus upon liberty. It was sent to Cicero, and the occasion this, as I find it very well explained by Monsieur Soreau, and prefixed to his French translation of Brutus's letters.[2]

Octavius Caesar, afterwards called Augustus, having defeated Mark Anthony before Modena,[3] and by that means raised the siege of that place, began now to conceive higher designs than he had yet shewn: He had hitherto declared for the commonwealth, and seemed to act for it; the Senate having trusted him with an army, by the persuasion and interest of Cicero. But after this victory over Anthony, he began to set up for himself, and to meditate the revenge of his uncle, and father by adoption, Julius Caesar; and, finally, to pave himself a way for absolute monarchy. He knew well, that Brutus and Cassius would never, while they lived, suffer him to possess what they would not suffer the first Caesar to enjoy; and therefore, to succeed his uncle, he must destroy them.

But Cicero, who equally loved and admired Brutus, and pretended to great power over the mind of the young Caesar,[4] undertook to write to him in favour of the patrons of liberty, who slew his uncle, to seek their pardon; especially a pardon for Brutus, that he might return to Rome, and be there in safety. This letter of Cicero's contained in it also thanks to Octavius for his services to the Republick, and was entirely unknown to Brutus; but being informed of it by Atticus,[5] he took extreme offence at this step of Cicero's, which seemed to him a confession of sovereignty

1. The quotation is from the Pindaric ode "Brutus" (lines 1–2) by the poet Abraham Cowley (1618–1667).

2. Antoine Soreau, *Lettres de Brutus et de Cicéron* (Paris: Louis Billaine, 1663).

3. The modern name for Mutina, the site of Mark Antony's defeat in 43 B.C.

4. That, is, Octavian.

5. Titus *Pomponius* (109–32 B.C.), surnamed Atticus because of his liberality and generosity toward Athens and his mastery of the Greek language and literature. He was an intimate of all the illustrious men of his day.

in Octavius, by not only owning him master of the lives of the Romans in general, but of his too, who was the deliverer of the Romans, and scorned to owe life to Octavius.

Brutus had another spirit, and other views: He remembered the bold and free words of the great Cato, his uncle, to those of his friends who offered to procure for him the mercy of Caesar, by throwing themselves, on his behalf, at Caesar's feet. "No," says Cato, "I scorn to be beholden to tyranny. I am as free as Caesar; and shall I owe my life to him, who has no right even to my submission."[6]

Brutus found reason to resent, that Cicero should, without his knowledge, thus treat him as a criminal, and Caesar as a sovereign, by begging of Caesar mercy for Brutus. That resentment gave occasion to this letter; in which he treats Octavius as a raw lad, and Cicero as a weak and fearful man. The reasoning through the whole shews Brutus to have been animated by a most sublime and glorious spirit of virtue and liberty; and is so stupendously strong, that his eloquence must have been great as his soul; and yet that great soul was not so dear to him as his liberty.

G   *I am, &c.*

BRUTUS TO CICERO

"I have seen, by the favour of Atticus, that part which concerns me in your letter to Octavius. The affection which you there express for my person, and the pains which you take for my safety, are great; but they give me no new joy: Your kind offices are become as habitual for me to receive, as for you to bestow; and, by your daily discourse and actions on my behalf, I have daily instances of your generous regard for myself and my reputation.

"However, all this hinders not but that the above-mentioned article of your letter to Octavius pierced me with as sensible a grief as my soul is capable of feeling. In thanking him for his services to the Republick, you have chosen a style which shews such lowness and submission, as do but too clearly declare, that you have still a master; and that the old tyranny, which we thought

6. A free translation from Plutarch, *Cato Minor*, 66.2.

destroyed, is revived in a new tyrant. What shall I say to you upon this sad head? I am covered with confusion for your shameful condition, but you have brought it upon yourself; and I cannot help shewing you to yourself in this wretched circumstance.

"You have petition'd Octavius to have mercy upon me, and to save my life. In this you intend my good, but sought my misery, and a lot worse than death, by saving me from it; since there is no kind of death but is more eligible to me than a life so saved. Be so good to recollect a little the terms of your letter! and having weighed them as you ought, can you deny that they are conceived in the low style of an humble petition from a slave to his haughty lord, from a subject to a king? You tell Octavius, that you have a request to make him, and hope that he will please to grant it; namely, to save those citizens who are esteemed by men of condition, and beloved by the people of Rome. This is your honourable request; but what if he should not grant it, but refuse to save us? Can we be saved by no other expedient? Certainly, destruction itself is preferable to life by his favour!

"I am not, however, so desponding, as to imagine that heaven is so offended with the Roman people, or so bent upon their ruin, that you should thus choose, in your prayers, to apply rather to Octavius, than to the immortal gods, for the preservation, I do not say of the deliverers of the whole earth, but even for the preservation of the meanest Roman citizen. This is a high tone to talk in, but I have pleasure in it: It becomes me to shew, that I scorn to pray to those whom I scorn to fear.

"Has then Octavius power to save us, or destroy us? And while you thus own him to be a tyrant, can you yet own yourself his friend? And while you are mine, can you desire to see me in Rome, and at the mercy of an usurper? And yet, that this would be my case you avow, by imploring from a giddy boy, my permission to return. You have been rendering him a world of thanks, and making him many compliments; pray, how come they to be due to him, if he yet want to be petitioned for our lives, and if our liberty depend upon his sufferance? Are we bound to think it a condescension in Octavius, that he chooses that these our petitions should rather be made to him than to Anthony? And are not such low supplications the proper addresses to a tyrant? And yet shall we, who boldly destroyed one, be ever brought basely to supplicate another? And can we, who are the deliverers of the commonwealth, descend to ask what no man ought to have it in his power to give?

"Consider the mournful effects of that dread and despondency of yours in our publick struggles; in which, however, you have too many to keep you in countenance. The commonwealth has been lost, because it was given for lost. Hence Caesar was first inspired with the lust of dominion; hence Mark Anthony, not terrified by the doom of the tyrant, pants and hurries on to succeed him in his tyranny; and hence this Octavius, this green usurper, is started into such a pitch of power, that the chiefs of the commonwealth, and the saviours of their country, must depend for their breath upon his pleasure. Yes, we must owe our lives to the mercy of a minor, softened by the prayers of aged Senators!

"Alas, we are no longer Romans! If we were, the virtuous spirit of liberty would have been an easy over-match for the traitorous attempts of the worst of all men grasping after tyranny; nor would even Mark Anthony, the rash and enterprizing Mark Anthony, have been so fond of Caesar's power, as frightened by Caesar's fate.

"Remember the important character which you sustain, the great post which you have filled: You are a senator of Rome, you have been consul of Rome; you have defeated conspiracies, you have destroyed conspirators. Is not Rome still as dear to you as she was? Or, is your courage and vigilance less? And is not the occasion greater? Or, could you suppress great traitors, and yet tolerate greater? Recollect what you ought to do, by what you have done. Whence proceeded your enmity to Anthony? Was it not, that he had an enmity to liberty, had seized violently on the publick, assumed the disposal of life and death into his own hands, and set up for the sole sovereign of all men? Were not these the reasons of your enmity, and of your advice, to combat violence by violence; to kill him, rather than submit to him? All this was well. But why must resistance be dropped, when there is a fresh call for resistance? Has your courage failed you? Or, was it not permitted to Anthony to enslave us, but another may? As if the nature of servitude were changed, by changing names and persons. No, we do not dispute about the qualifications of a master; we will have no master.

"It is certain, that we might, under Anthony, have had large shares with him in the administration of despotick power; we might have divided its dignities, shone in its trappings. He would have received us graciously, and met us half way. He knew that either our concurrence or acquiescence would have confirmed him monarch of Rome; and at what price would he not have purchased either? But all his arts, all his temptations, all his offers, were rejected; liberty was our purpose, virtue our rule: our views were honest and universal; our country, and the cause of mankind.

"With Octavius himself there is still a way open for an accommodation, if we choose it. As eager as the name of Caesar has made that raw stickler for empire to destroy those who destroyed Caesar; yet, doubtless, he would give us good articles, to gain our consent to that power to which he aspires, and to which, I fear, he will arrive: Alas! what is there to hinder him? While we only attend to the love of life, and the impulses of ambition; while we can purchase posts and dignities with the price of liberty, and think danger more dreadful than slavery, what remains to save us?

"What was the end of our killing the tyrant, but to be free from tyranny? A ridiculous motive, and an empty exploit, if our slavery survive him! Oh, who is it that makes liberty his care? Liberty, which ought to be the care of all men, as 'tis the benefit and blessing of all! For myself, rather than give it up, I will stand single in its defence. I cannot lose, but with my life, my resolution to maintain in freedom my country, which I have set free: I have destroyed a veteran tyrant; and shall I suffer, in a raw youth, his heir, a power to control the senate, supersede the laws, and put chains on Rome? A power, which no personal favours, nor even the ties of blood, could ever sanctify to me; a power, which I could not bear in Caesar; nor, if my father had usurped it, could I have borne in him.

"Your petition to Octavius is a confession, that we cannot enjoy the liberty of Rome without his leave; and can you dream that other citizens are free, where we could not live free? Besides, having made your request, how is it to be fulfilled? You beg him to give us our lives; and what if he do? Are we therefore safe, because we live? Is there any safety without liberty? or rather, can we poorly live, having lost it, and with it our honour and glory? Is there any security in living at Rome, when Rome is no longer free? That city, great as it is, having no security of her own, can give me none. No, I will owe mine to my resolution and my sword; I cannot enjoy life at the mercy of another. Caesar's death alone ascertained my liberty to me, which before was precarious: I smote him, to be safe. This is a Roman spirit; and whithersoever I carry it, every place will be Rome to me; who am Roman enough to prefer every evil to chains and infamy, which to a Roman are the highest of all evils. I thought that we had been released from these mighty evils, by the death of him who brought them upon us; but it seems that we are not; else why a servile petition to a youth, big with the name and the ambition of Caesar, for mercy to those patriots, who generously revenged their country upon that tyrant, and cleared the world of his tyranny? It was not thus in the commonwealths of Greece, where the children of tyrants suffered, equally with their fathers, the punishment of tyranny.

"Can I then have any appetite to see Rome? Or, can Rome be said to be Rome? We have slain our tyrant, we have restored her ancient liberty: But they are favours thrown away; she is made free in spite of herself; and though she has seen a great and terrible tyrant bereft of his grandeur and his life, by a few of her citizens; yet, basely desponding of her own strength, she impotently dreads the name of a dead tyrant, revived in the person of a stripling.

"No more of your petitions to your young Caesar on my behalf; nor, if you are wise, on your own. You have not many years to live; do not be shewing that you over-rate the short remains of an honourable life, by making preposterous and dishonourable court to a boy. Take care that by this conduct you do not eclipse the lustre of all your glorious actions against Mark Anthony: Do not turn your glory into reproach, by giving the malicious a handle to say, that self-love was the sole motive of your bitterness to him; and that, had you not dreaded him, you would not have opposed him: And yet will they not say this, if they see, that, having declared war against Anthony, you notwithstanding leave life and liberty at the mercy of Octavius, and tolerate in him all the power which the other claimed? They will say that you are not against having a master, only you would not have Anthony for a master.

"I well approve your praises given to Octavius for his behaviour thus far; it is indeed praiseworthy; provided his only intention has been to pull down the tyranny of Anthony, without establishing a tyranny of his own. But if you are of opinion, that Octavius is in such a situation of power, that it is necessary to approach him with humble supplications to save our lives, and that it is convenient he should be trusted with this power; I can only say, that you lift the reward of his merits far above his merits: I thought that all his services were services done to the Republick; but you have conferred upon him that absolute and imperial power which he pretended to recover to the Republick.

"If, in your judgment, Octavius has earned such laurels and recompences for making war against Anthony's tyranny, which was only the effects and remains of Caesar's tyranny; to what distinctions, to what rewards, would you intitle those who exterminated, with Caesar, the tyranny of Caesar, for which they felt the blessings and bounty of the Roman people! Has this never entered into your thoughts? Behold here how effectually the terror of evils to come extinguishes in the minds of men all impressions of benefits received? Caesar is dead, and will never return to shackle or frighten the city of Rome; so he is no more thought of, nor are they who delivered that city from him. But Anthony is still alive, and still in arms, and still terrifies; and so Octavius is adored, who beat Anthony. Hence it is that Octavius is become of such potent consequence, that from his mouth the Roman people must expect our doom, the doom of their deliverers! And hence it is too, that we (those deliverers) are of such humble consequence, that he must be supplicated to give us our lives!

"I, as I said, have a soul, and I have a sword; and am an enemy to such abject supplications; so great an enemy, that I detest those that use them, and am an avowed foe to him that expects them. I shall at least be far away from the odious company of slaves; and where-ever I find liberty, there I will find Rome.

And for you that stay behind, who, not satiated with many years, and many honours, can behold liberty extinct, and virtue, with us, in exile, and yet are not sick of a wretched and precarious life; I heartily pity you. For myself, whose soul has never ebbed from its constant principles, I shall ever be happy in the consciousness of my virtue; owing nothing to my country, towards which I have faithfully discharged my duty, I shall possess my mind in peace; and find the reward of well-doing in the satisfaction of having done it. What greater pleasure does the world afford, than to despise the slippery uncertainties of life, and to value that only which is only valuable, private virtue, and publick liberty; that liberty, which is the blessing, and ought to be the birthright, of all mankind?

"But still, I will never sink with those who are already falling; I will never yield with those who have a mind to submit: I am resolved to be always firm and independent: I will try all expedients, I will exert my utmost prowess, to banish servitude, and set my country entirely free. If fortune favour me as she ought, the blessing and joy will be every man's; but if she fail me, and my best endeavours be thrown away, yet still I will rejoice single; and so far be too hard for fortune. What, in short, can my life be better laid out in, than in continual schemes, and repeated efforts, for the common liberty of my country?

"As to your part in this crisis, my dear Cicero, it is my strongest advice and request to you, not to desert yourself: Do not distrust your ability, and your ability will not disappoint you; believe you can remedy our heavy evils, and you will remedy them. Our miseries want no encrease: Prevent, therefore, by your vigilance, any new accession. Formerly, in quality of consul, you defeated, with great boldness, and warmth for liberty, a formidable conspiracy against Rome, and saved the commonwealth; and what you did then against Catiline, you do still against Anthony. These actions of yours have raised your reputation high, and spread it far; but it will be all tarnished or lost, if you do not continue to shew an equal firmness upon as great an occasion; let this render all the parts of your life equal, and secure immortality to that glory of yours, which ought to be immortal.

"From those, who, like you, have performed great actions, as great or greater are expected: By shewing that they can serve the publick, they make themselves its debtors; and it is apt to exact strict payment, and to use them severely if they do not pay: But from those who have performed no such actions, we expect none. This is the difference betwixt the lot of unknown talents, and of those which have been tried; and the condition of the latter is no doubt the harder. Hence it is, that though, in making head against Anthony, you have merited and received great and just praises, yet you have gained no new admiration: By so doing, you only continued, like a worthy consular, the known character of a great and able consul. But if now at last you begin to truckle to one as bad as him; if you abate ever so little in that vigour of mind, and that steady courage, by which you expelled him from the senate, and drove him out of Rome; you will never reap another harvest of glory, whatever you may deserve; and even your past laurels will wither, and your past renown be forgot.

"There is nothing great or noble in events, which are the fruit of passion or chance: true fame results only from the steady perseverance of reason in the paths and pursuits of virtue. The care, therefore, of the commonwealth, and the defence of her liberties, belong to you above all men, because you have done more than all men for liberty and the commonwealth: Your great abilities, your known zeal, your famous actions, with the united call and expectation of all men, are your motives in this great affair; would you have greater?

"You are not, therefore, to supplicate Octavius for our safety; do a braver thing, owe it to your own magnanimity. Rouse the Roman genius within you; and consider that this great and free city, which you more than once saved, will always be great and free, provided her people do not want worthy chiefs to resist usurpation, and exterminate traitors."[7]

---

7. The letter is an extremely loose rendering of Cicero, *Epistulae ad Brutum*, 25. Some indication of Gordon's casual style in translating can be had by comparing Brutus's letter as here offered with a more rigorous translation of the same passage.

NO. 24. SATURDAY, APRIL 8, 1721.

𝕬 *Of the natural Honesty of the People, and their reasonable Demands. How important it is to every Government to consult their Affections and Interest.*

SIR,

I have observed, in a former letter, that the people, when they
are not misled or corrupted, generally make a sound judgment
of things.[1] They have natural qualifications equal to those of their
superiors; and there is oftener found a great genius carrying a
pitch-fork, than carrying a white staff. The poor cook preferred by
the Grand Seignior[2] to be his first vizier, in order to cure the publick disorder and confusion occasioned by the ignorance, corruption, and neglect of the former ministry, made good effectually his
own promise, and did credit to his master's choice: He remedied
the publick disorders, and proved, says Sir Paul Ricaut, an able and
excellent minister of state.[3]

Besides, there are not such mighty talents requisite for
government, as some, who pretend to them without possessing
them, would make us believe: Honest affections, and common
qualifications, are sufficient; and the administration has been
always best executed, and the publick liberty best preserved, near
the origin and rise of states, when plain honesty and common
sense alone governed the publick affairs, and the morals of men
were not corrupted with riches and luxury, nor their understandings perverted by subtleties and distinctions. Great abilities have,
for the most part, if not always, been employed to mislead the honest, but unwary, multitude, and to draw them out of the open and
plain paths of publick virtue and public good.

The people have no bias to be knaves; the security of their
persons and property is their highest aim. No ambition prompts

1. See Letter No. 19 (Mar. 4, 1720).
2. The Ottoman Sultan.
3. Sir Paul Rycaut, *The Present State of the Ottoman Empire* (London: J. Starkey
and H. Brome, 1668). The report appears in bk. I, chap. 11 (pp. 48–49).

them; they cannot come to be great lords, and to possess great titles, and therefore desire none. No aspiring or unsociable passions incite them; they have no rivals for place, no competitor to pull down; they have no darling child, pimp, or relation, to raise: they have no occasion for dissimulation or intrigue; they can serve no end by faction; they have no interest, but the general interest.

The same can rarely be said of great men, who, to gratify private passion, often bring down publick ruin; who, to fill their private purses with many thousands, frequently load the people with many millions; who oppress for a mistress, and, to save a favourite, destroy a nation; who too often make the publick sink and give way to their private fortune; and, for a private pleasure, create a general calamity. Besides, being educated in debauchery, and pampered in riot and luxury, they have no sense of the misfortunes of other men, nor tenderness for those who suffer them: They have no notion of miseries which they do not feel. There is a nation in Europe,[4] which, within the space of an hundred years last past, has been blessed with patriots, who, void of every talent and inclination to do good, and even stinted in their ability for roguery, were forced to be beholden, for most of the mischief which they did, to the superior arts and abilities of humble rogues and brokers.

The first principles of power are in the people; and all the projects of men in power ought to refer to the people, to aim solely at their good, and end in it: And whoever will pretend to govern them without regarding them, will soon repent it. Such feats of errantry may do perhaps in Asia: but in countries where the people are free, it is madness to hope to rule them against their wills. They will know, that government is appointed for their sakes, and will be saucy enough to expect some regard and some good from their own delegates. Those nations who are governed in spite of themselves, and in a manner that bids defiance to their opinions, their interests, and their understandings, are either slaves, or will soon cease to be subjects.

Dominion that is not maintained by the sword, must be maintained by consent; and in this latter case, what security can

4. France.

any man at the head of affairs expect, but from pursuing the people's welfare, and seeking their good-will? The government of one for the sake of one, is tyranny; and so is the government of a few for the sake of themselves: But government executed for the good of all, and with the consent of all, is liberty; and the word *government* is profaned, and its meaning abused, when it signifies any thing else.

In free countries the people know all this. They have their five senses in as great perfection, as have those who would treat them as if they had none. They are not wont to hate their governors, till their governors deserve to be hated; and when this happens to be the case, not absolute power itself, nor the affections of a prince invested with it, can protect or employ ministers detested by the people. Even the Grand Seignior, with all his boundless authority, is frequently forced to give up his first minister (who is sometimes his son-in-law, or brother-in-law) a sacrifice to appease the people's rage.

The people, rightly managed, are the best friends to princes; and, when injured and oppressed, the most formidable enemies. Princes, who have trusted to their armies or their nobility, have been often deceived and ruined; but princes, who have trusted wholly to the people, have seldom been deceived or deserted: The reason is, that in all governments, which are not violent and military, the people have more power than either the grandees or the soldiery; and their friendship is more sincere, as having nothing to desire but freedom from oppression. And whilst a prince is thus beloved by his people, it will rarely happen that any can be so rash and precipitate as to conspire against him; and such conspiracies have never the intended success: but, as Machiavel well observes, When the people are dissatisfied, and have taken a prejudice against their governors, there is no thing nor person that they ought not to fear.[5]

It is therefore of vast importance to preserve the affections of the people even in those governments where they have no share in the administration. The wise states of Holland are so apprized of the truth of this maxim, that they have preserved themselves

5. The sentiments appear in *The Prince*, chap. 19.

and their state by religiously observing it. Their government consists of many little aristocracies, where the magistrates choose each other, and the people have nothing to do; but in spirit and effect it is a democracy, and the dispositions and inclinations of the people have above all things the greatest weight in their counsels. The jealousy of the people makes a vigilant magistracy, who are honest out of fear of provoking them, and, by never doing it, are in great safety.

But, thanks be to heaven and our worthy ancestors, our liberties are better secured. We have a constitution, in which the people have a large share: They are one part of the legislature, and have the sole power of giving money; which includes in it every thing that they can ask for the publick good; and the representatives, being neither awed nor bribed, will always act for their country's interest; their own being so interwoven with the people's happiness, that they must stand and fall together.

But what if our delegates should not be suffered to meet; or, when met, should be so awed by force (as formerly in Denmark[6]) or so corrupted by places and pensions (as in the reign of Charles II) as to be ready to give up publick liberty, and betray the interest of their principals to secure their own? This we may be sure can never happen under his Majesty's most just and gentle reign: However, it has happened formerly; and what has been, may be again in future reigns.

What, in such a case, is to be done? What remedies have our laws provided against so fatal a mischief? Must the people patiently crouch under the heaviest of all evils? Or has our constitution pointed out the means of redress? It would be absurd to suppose that it has not; and, in effect, the people have a legal remedy at hand: It is their undoubted right, and acknowledged to be so in the Bill of Rights passed in the reign of King Charles I and

6. At the close of Denmark's war with Sweden in 1660 and while the *Rigsdag* was in session, a monarchical *coup d'état* effectively established the Danish monarch as a hereditary, absolute prince. The event was regarded as an object lesson to British Whigs, who feared its repetition in England. It is dealt with in Robert Molesworth's *An Account of Denmark* (London: 1694), a work Trenchard and Gordon knew well.

since, by the Act of Settlement of the crown at the Revolution;[7] humbly to represent their publick grievances, and to petition for redress to those whose duty it is to right them, or to see them righted: And it is certain, that in all countries, the people's misfortunes are greater or less, in proportion as this right is encouraged or checked.

It is indeed the best and only just way that they can take to breathe their grievances; and whenever this way has been taken, especially when it has been universally taken, our kings have always accepted so powerful an application. Our parliaments too, who are the keepers and barriers of our liberty, have shewn themselves ready and willing to receive the modest complaints and representations of their principals, and to apply quick remedies to the grievances contained in them. It has, indeed, been always thought highly imprudent, not to say dangerous, to resist the general groans and entreaties of the people, uttered in this manner.

This has been a method, which has always had great weight with good men, and has been always a great terror to bad. It has therefore always been encouraged or discouraged, according to the innocence or guilt or men in power. A prince, who minds the welfare and desires the affections of his subjects, cannot wish for a better expedient to know how his servants are approved, and how his government is liked, than by this way of countenancing his people in laying their hearts, their wishes, and their requests before him; and ministers never can be averse to such representations of the complaints of the people, unless they have given the people occasion to complain.

Titus and Trajan, conscious of their own virtuous administration, and worthy purposes, courted addresses and informations of this kind, from their subjects: They wisely knew, that if the Roman people had free leave to speak, they would not take

---

7. The Bill of Rights to which Gordon is referring is the Petition of Right, passed by Parliament and assented to by the crown in 1628. The Act of Settlement refers to that act containing the Declaration of Rights that accompanied Parliament's offer of the crown jointly to William and Mary in 1689. The Declaration asserted the "true, ancient, and indubitable rights" of Englishmen, including the right to petition the sovereign.

leave to act; and that, whilst they could have redress, they would not seek revenge.

None but desperate parricides will make the people desperate.

G   *I am, &c.*

NO. 25. SATURDAY, APRIL 15, 1721.

🦋 *Considerations on the destructive Spirit of arbitrary Power. With the Blessings of Liberty, and our own Constitution.*

SIR,

The good of the governed being the sole end of government, they must be the greatest and best governors, who make their people great and happy; and they the worst, who make their people little, wicked, and miserable. Power in a free state, is a trust committed by all to one or a few, to watch for the security, and pursue the interest, of all: And, when that security is not sought, nor that interest obtained, we know what opinion the people will have of their governors.

It is the hard fate of the world, that there should be any difference in the views and interests of the governors and governed; and yet it is so in most countries. Men who have a trust frankly bestowed upon them by the people, too frequently betray that trust, become conspirators against their benefactors, and turn the sword upon those who gave it; insomuch that in the greatest part of the earth, people are happy if they can defend themselves against their defenders.

Let us look round this great world, and behold what an immense majority of the whole race of men crouch under the yoke of a few tyrants, naturally as low as the meanest of themselves, and, by being tyrants, worse than the worst; who, as Mr. Sidney observes, use their subjects like asses and mastiff dogs, to work and to fight, to be oppressed and killed for them.[1] Even the good qualities and courage of such subjects are their misfortune, by strengthening the wicked hands of their brutal masters, and strengthening their own chains. Tyrants consider their people as their cattle, and use them worse, as they fear them more. Thus the most of mankind are become the wretched slaves of those, who are or should be their own creatures; they maintain their haughty masters like gods, and their haughty masters often use them like dogs: A fine specimen of gratitude and duty!

Yet this cruel spirit in tyrants is not always owing naturally to the men, since they are naturally like other men; but it is owing to the nature of the dominion which they exercise. Good laws make a good prince, if he has a good understanding; but the best men grow mischievous when they are set above laws. Claudius was a very harmless man, while he was a private man; but when he came to be a tyrant, he proved a bloody one, almost as bloody as his nephew and predecessor Caligula; who had also been a very good subject, but when he came to be the Roman emperor, grew the professed executioner of mankind.[2]

There is something so wanton and monstrous in lawless power, that there scarce ever was a human spirit that could bear it; and the mind of man, which is weak and limited, ought never to be trusted with a power that is boundless. The state of tyranny is a state of war; and where it prevails, instead of an intercourse of confidence and affection, as between a lawful prince and his subjects, nothing is to be seen but jealousy, mistrust, fear, and hatred: An

1. The citation is a paraphrase from Algernon Sidney, *Discourses Concerning Government* (London, 1698). At one point Sidney writes: "They [tyrants] consider nations, as grasiers do their herd and flocks, according to the profit that can be made of them: and if this be so, a people has no more security under a prince, than a herd or flock under their master.... They only look upon us ... as beasts, ... [and] do us any good ... only that we may be useful to them, as oxen are put into plentiful pastures that they may be strong for labour, or fit for slaughter" (chap. 2, sect. 27; p. 213 of the third edition of 1751 [London: Printed for A. Millar]).

2. *Claudius* was Roman emperor from A.D. 41 until his murder in A.D. 54. His reputation as a bloodthirsty tyrant is, in fact, undeserved. *Caligula*, on the other hand, who ranks as one of the most tyrannical of emperors, was reputed to have amused himself by putting innocent people to death. He was murdered after a reign of only four years.

arbitrary prince and his slaves often destroy one another, to be safe: They are continually plotting against his life; he is continually shedding their blood, and plundering them of their property.

Cuncta ferit, dum cuncta timet.[3]

I think it was Justinian, the Emperor, who said, "Though we are above the law, yet we live according to the law."[4] But, by his Majesty's favour, there was more turn than truth in the saying; for princes that think themselves above law, act almost constantly against all law; of which truth Justinian himself is a known instance. Good princes never think themselves above it.

It is an affecting observation, that the power given for the protection of the world, should, in so many places, be turned to the destruction of it.

> As if the law was in force for their destruction, and not for their preservation; that it should have power to kill, but not to protect, them: A thing no less horrid, than if the sun should burn us without lighting us, or the earth serve only to bury, and not feed and nourish us,

says Mr. Waller[5] in a speech of his in Parliament.

Despotick power has defaced the Creation, and laid the world waste. In the finest countries in Asia, formerly full of people, you are now forced to travel by the compass: There are no roads, houses, nor inhabitants. The sun is left to scorch up the grass and fruits, which it had raised; or the rain to rot them: The gifts of God are left to perish; there being none of his creatures, neither man nor beast, left to use and consume them. The Grand Seignior, who (if we may believe some sanctified mouths, not addicted to lying) is the vicegerent of heaven, frustrates the bounty of heaven; and, being the father of his people, has almost butchered them all.

3. "He strikes all, while he fears all."

4. *Justinian* (A.D. 483–565) is best known for his definitive codification of Roman civil law, the *Corpus Juris Civilis*. His rule respecting the prerogative of princes, *Etsi legibus soluti summus, tamen legibus vivimus*, was often cited by Whig writers.

5. Sir William Waller (*c.* 1597–1668), MP for Andover and one of the military leaders of the parliamentary forces between 1642 and 1644. The original suggestion for the New Model Army appears to have been his.

Those few (comparatively very few) who have yet survived the miserable fate of their brethren, and are reserved for sacrifices to his cruelty, as occasion offers, and his lust prompts him, live the starving and wretched property of ravenous and bloody bashaws; whose duty to their master, as well as their own avarice, obliges them to keep the people, over whom they preside, poor and miserable.

But neither bashaws, nor armies, could keep that people in such abject slavery, if their priests and doctors had not made passive obedience a principle of their religion. The holy name of God is profaned, and his authority belied, to bind down wretchedness upon his creatures, and to secure the tyrant that does it. The most consummate of all wickedness, and the highest of all evils, are sanctified by the teachers of religion, and made by them a part of it. Yes, Turkish slavery is confirmed, and Turkish tyranny defended, by religion!

Sir Paul Ricaut tells us, that the Turks maintain, "That the Grand Seignior can never be deposed, or made accountable for his crimes, whilst he destroys carelessly of his subjects under a hundred a day": 'Tis made martyrdom to die submissively by the hand of the tyrant; and some of his highest slaves have declared that they wanted only that honour to complete their felicity. They hold, that it is their duty to submit, though their tyrant "command a whole army of them to precipitate themselves from a rock, or to build a bridge with piles of their bodies for him to pass a river, or to kill one another to afford him pastime and pleasure."[6]

Merciful God! Is this government! And do such governors govern by authority from thee!

It is scarce credible what Monsieur de L'Estoille[7] tells us: He says he travelled in the Indies for above twenty days together, through lanes of people hanged upon trees, by command of the King; who had ordered above a hundred thousand of them to be thus murdered and gibbeted, only because two or three robberies

6. *The Present State of the Ottoman Empire*, bk. I, chap. 3 (pp. 8–9).
7. Pierre de l'Estoile (1546–1611), who authored a history of the reign of Henry III.

had been committed amongst them.[8] Bayle, *Reponse aux Quest. d'un Provinc.* tom. I. p. 595.

It is one of the great evils of servitude, that let the tyranny be ever so severe, 'tis always flattered; and the more severe 'tis, the more 'tis flattered. The oppressors of mankind are flattered beyond all others; because fear and servitude naturally produce, as well as have recourse to, flattery, as the best means of self-preservation; whereas liberty, having no occasion for it, scorns it. Sir Paul Ricaut ascribes the decay of the Ottoman Empire to the force of flattery, and calls the Turkish court, a prison and banniard[9] of slaves.[10]

Old Muley, the Lord's anointed of Morocco,[11] who it seems is still alive, is thought to have butchered forty thousand of his subjects with his own hands. Such a father is he of his people! And yet his right to shed human blood being a genuine characteristick of the church of Morocco, as by law established, people are greedy to die by his hand; which, they are taught to imagine, dispatches them forthwith to paradise: Insomuch that, though, as I am told, every time he mounts his horse, he slices off the head of the slave that holds his stirrup, to shew that he is as good an executioner as he is a horseman, yet there is a constant contention among his slaves, who shall be the happy martyr on that occasion; so that several of them crowding to his stirrup at once, for the gracious favour, his Majesty has sometimes the honour to cut off two heads, and to make two saints, with one blow.

The exercise of despotick power is the unrelenting war of an armed tyrant upon his unarmed subjects: it is a war of one side, and in it there is neither peace nor truce. Tacitus describes it, *Saeva jussa, continuas accusationes, fallaces amicitias, perniciem innocentium*:[12]

8. The quotation appears in Pierre Bayle's *Réponse aux questions d'un provincial*, chap. 60. It can be found in *Oeuvres diverses de Mr Pierre Bayle* (4 vols.; The Hague: Chez P. Husson, etc., 1727–31): III:622.

9. Banniard: a variant of *bagnio*, a Turkish prison.

10. *The Present State of the Ottoman Empire*, bk. I, chap. 3 (p. 9).

11. Ismail, Sultan of Morocco from 1672 until his death fifty-five years later. He was notorious for his bloodshed and cruelty toward both natives and Europeans.

12. "Savage mandates, constant accusations, perfidious friendships, the destruction of the innocent." Tacitus, *Annales*, 4.33.

"Cruel and bloody orders, continual accusations, faithless friendships, and the destruction of innocents." In another place he says, that

> Italy was one continual shambles, and most of its fair cities were defaced or overthrown; Rome itself was in many places laid in ashes, with the greatest part of its magnificent buildings: virtue was despised, and barefaced debauchery prevailed. The solitary islands were filled with illustrious exiles, and the very rocks were stained with slaughters: but, in the city itself, cruelty raged still more; it was dangerous to be noble, it was a crime to be rich, it was capital to have borne honours, and high treason to have refused them; and for virtue and merit, they brought sure and sudden destruction.[13]

These were some of the ravages of absolute dominion! And as to the common people, the same author says, "They were debauched and dispirited, and given up to idleness and seeing shews." *Plebs sordida circo & theatris sueta.*[14]

> Oh! abject state of such as tamely groan
> Under a blind dependency on one!

This is a sort of government, which is too great and heavy a curse for any one to wish, even upon those who are foolish enough, or wicked enough, to contend for its lawfulness; or, which is the same thing, for submission to it: But surely, if ever any man deserved to feel the merciless gripes[15] of tyranny, it is he who is an advocate for it. Phalaris acted justly, when he hanselled[16] his brazen bull with the wretch who invented it.[17]

13. The quotation, which refers to the period immediately following Nero's death in A.D. 69, is taken from Tacitus, *Historiae*, 1.2.

14. "The lowest classes, addicted to the circus and the theater." Tacitus, *Historiae*, 1.4.

15. Gripes: clutches.

16. Hanselled: inaugurated.

17. *Phalaris*, tyrant of Agrigentum, is reputed to have kept a brazen bull in which his victims were enclosed while a fire was kindled beneath them. Their screams were said to represent the bellowings of the bull. Fittingly, the bull's first victim was its inventor.

As arbitrary power in a single person has made greater havock in human nature, and thinned mankind more, than all the beasts of prey and all the plagues and earthquakes that ever were; let those men consider what they have to answer for, who would countenance such a monstrous evil in the world, or would oppose those that would oppose it. A bear, a lion, or a tiger, may now and then pick up single men in a wood, or a desert; an earthquake sometimes may bury a thousand or two inhabitants in the ruins of a town; and the pestilence may once in many years carry off a much greater number: But a tyrant shall, out of a wanton personal passion, carry fire and sword through a whole continent, and deliver up a hundred thousand of his fellow creatures to the slaughter in one day, without any remorse or further notice, than that they died for his glory. I say nothing of the moral effect of tyranny; though 'tis certain that ignorance, vice, poverty, and vileness, always attend it.

He who compares the world now with what it was formerly, how populous once, how thin now; and considers the cause of this doleful alteration, will find just reason to fear, that spiritual and temporal tyranny, if they go on much longer, will utterly extinguish the human race. Of Turkey I have spoken already: The great continent of America is almost unpeopled, the Spaniards having destroyed, 'tis thought, about forty millions of its natives; and for some kingdoms in Europe, especially towards the north, I do not believe that they have now half the inhabitants that they had so lately as a hundred years ago.

Blessed be God, there are still some free countries in Europe, that abound with people and with plenty, and England is the foremost. This demonstrates the inestimable blessing of liberty. Can we ever over-rate it, or be too jealous of a treasure which includes in it almost all human felicities? Or can we encourage too much those that contend for it, and those that promote it? It is the parent of virtue, pleasure, plenty, and security; and 'tis innocent, as well as lovely. In all contentions between liberty and power, the latter has almost constantly been the aggressor. Liberty, if ever it produce any evils, does also cure them: Its worst effect, licentiousness, never does, and never can, continue long. Anarchy cannot be of much duration: and where 'tis so, it is the child and companion of tyranny; which is not government, but a dissolution of it, as tyrants are the enemies of mankind.

Power is like fire; it warms, scorches, or destroys, according as it is watched, provoked, or increased. It is as dangerous as useful. Its only rule is the good of the people; but because it is apt to break its bounds, in all good governments nothing, or as little as may be, ought to be left to chance, or the humours of men in authority: All should proceed by fixed and stated rules, and upon any emergency, new rules should be made. This is the constitution, and this the happiness of Englishmen; as hath been formerly shewn at large in these letters.

We have a constitution that abhors absolute power; we have a King that does not desire it; and we are a people that will never suffer it: No free people will ever submit to it, unless it steal upon them by treachery, or they be driven into it by violence. But a state can never be too secure against this terrible, this last of all human evils; which may be brought upon them by many causes, even by some that at first sight do not seem to threaten any such thing: And of all those causes, none seems more boding than a general distress, which certainly produces general discontent, the parent of revolutions; and in what such a circumstance of affairs may end, no man can ever foresee: Few are brought about without armies; a remedy almost always worse than the disease. What is got by soldiers, must be maintained by soldiers; and we have, in this paper, already seen the frightful image of a military government;[18] a government, which, at best, is violent and bloody, and eternally inconsistent with law and property.

It is therefore a dreadful wickedness to have any share in giving occasion for those discontents, which are so apt to burst into rage and confusion. A state sometimes recovers out of a convulsion, and gains new vigour by it; but it much oftener expires in it. Heaven preserve me from ever beholding contending armies in England! They are different things from what they once were. Our armies formerly were only a number of the people armed occasionally; and armies of the people are the only armies which are

18. See Letter No. 24 (Apr. 8, 1721).

not formidable to the people. Hence it is, that, in the many revolutions occasioned by the strife between the two royal houses of York and Lancaster, there never was any danger of slavery from an armed force: A single battle decided the contention; and next day these popular soldiers went home, and resumed their ordinary arms, the tools of husbandry. But since that time armies have not been so easily parted with; but after the danger was over for which they were raised, have often been obstinately kept up, and by that means created dangers still as great.

Some quacks in politicks may perhaps venture publick disturbances, out of an opinion that they shall be able to prevent them by art, or suppress them by force. But this shews their capacity, as well as their wickedness: For, not to mention the malignity of their hearts, in risking publick ruin, to gratify a private appetite; how can any event be certainly foreseen, when the measure of the cause cannot be certainly known? They can never ascertain the degree of opposition; they cannot foreknow what circumstances may happen, nor into whose hands things may fall. Cicero did not dream, when he employed Octavius for the commonwealth, that his young champion for liberty would ever be the tyrant of his country. Who could foresee that Cromwell would enslave those whom he was employed to defend? But there is no trusting of liberty in the hands of men, who are obeyed by great armies.

From hence may be seen what a fatal and crying crime it would be, in any free country, to break the confidence between the prince and his people. When loyalty is once turned into indifference, indifference will soon be turned into hatred; hatred will be returned with hatred; resentment may produce tyranny, and rage may produce rebellion. There is no mischief which this mutual mistrust and aversion may not bring forth. They must therefore be the blackest traitors, who are the first authors of so terrible an evil, as are they who would endeavour to protect them.

Henry III of Castile[19] said, that he feared the curse of his people more than he did the arms of his enemies: In which saying

19. Henry III, King of Castile, who reigned from 1390 until his death in 1406 at the age of twenty-seven. He is credited with increasing the power of the central government at the expense of the upper aristocracy.

he shewed as much wisdom as humanity; since, while he was beloved at home, he had nothing to fear from abroad, and the curses of his subjects were the likeliest means to bring upon him the arms of his enemies.

G   *I am, &c.*

NO. 26. SATURDAY, APRIL 22, 1721.

The sad Effects of general Corruption, quoted from Algernon Sidney, Esq.

SIR,

I send you, for the entertainment of your readers this week, two or three passages out of the great Algernon Sidney: An author, who can never be too much valued or read; who does honour to the English nobility, and to the English name; who has written better upon government than any Englishman, and as well as any foreigner; and who was a martyr for that liberty which he has so amiably described, and so nobly defended. He fell a sacrifice to the vile and corrupt court of our pious Charles II.[1] He had asserted the rights of mankind, and shewed the odiousness of tyranny; he had exposed the absurdity and vileness of the sacred and fashionable doctrines of those days, passive obedience, and hereditary right; doctrines, which give the lie to common sense, and which would destroy all common happiness and security amongst men! Doctrines, which were never practised by those that preached them! and doctrines, which are big with nonsense, contradiction, impossibility, misery, wickedness, and desolation! These were his crimes, and these his glory.

The book is every way excellent: He had read and digested all history; and this performance of his takes in the whole business of government: It makes us some amends for the loss of Cicero's

---

1. Sidney's participation in the various schemes to prevent the accession of James II to the throne resulted in his trial on a charge of treason in 1683. He was condemned to death and executed in December of that year.

book *De Republica*.[2] Colonel Sidney had all the clear and comprehensive knowledge, and all the dignity of expression, of that great master of eloquence and politicks; his love of liberty was as warm, his honesty as great, and his courage greater.[3]

G

"Liberty cannot be preserved, if the manners of the people are corrupted; nor absolute monarchy introduced, where they are sincere: Which is sufficient to shew, that those who manage free governments ought always, to the utmost of their power, to oppose corruption, because otherwise both they and their government must inevitably perish; and that, on the other hand, the absolute monarch must endeavour to introduce it, because he cannot subsist without it. 'Tis also so natural for all such monarchs to place men in power who pretend to love their persons, and will depend upon their pleasure, that possibly 'twould be hard to find one in the world who has not made it the rule of his government: And this is not only the way to corruption, but the most dangerous of all. For though a good man may love a good monarch, he will obey him only when he commands that which is just; and no one can engage himself blindly to do whatever he is commanded, without renouncing all virtue and religion; because he knows not whether that which shall be commanded is consistent with each, or directly contrary to the laws of God and man. But if such a monarch be evil, and his actions such as they are too often found to be; whoever bears an affection to him, and seconds his designs, declares himself an enemy to all that is good; and the advancement of such men to power, does not only introduce, foment, and increase corruption, but fortifies it in such a manner, that without an entire renovation of that state, it cannot be removed. Ill men may possibly creep into any government; but when the worst are placed nearest the throne, and raised to honours for being so, they will with that force endeavor to draw all men to a conformity of spirit

2. The *De Republica*, a dialogue of which only part survives, deals with Cicero's views on the best form of government and asserts that all political communities must respect the basic human dignity inherent in all men.

3. The extended quotation that follows is taken from Sidney's *Discourses Concerning Government*, chap. 2, sect. 25 (pp. 201–4 of the 1751 edition).

with themselves, that it can no otherwise be prevented than by destroying them, and the principle in which they live.

"Man naturally follows that which is good, or seems to him to be so. Hence it is, that in well-governed states, where a value is put upon virtue, and no one honoured unless for such qualities as are beneficial to the publick; men are from the tenderest years brought up in a belief, that nothing in this world deserves to be sought after, but such honours as are acquired by virtuous actions: By this means virtue itself becomes popular, as in Sparta, Rome, and other places, where riches (which, with the vanity that follows them, and the honours men give to them, are the root of all evil) were either totally banished, or little regarded. When no other advantage attended the greatest riches, than the opportunity of living more sumptuously or deliciously, men of great spirits slighted them. When Aristippus told Cleanthes, that if he would go to court and flatter the tyrant, he need not seek his supper under a hedge; the philosopher answered, that he who could content himself with such a supper, need not go to court to flatter the tyrant.[4] Epaminondas, Aristides, Phocion, and even the Lacedemonian kings,[5] found no inconvenience in poverty, whilst their virtue was honoured, and the richest princes in the world feared their valour and power. It was not difficult for Curius, Fabricius, Cincinnatus, or Emilius Paulus,[6] to content themselves with the narrowest fortune, when

4. Gordon probably has in mind an incident reported by Diogenes Laertius concerning not Cleanthes, but *Diogenes* (404–323 B.C.), the Cynic philosopher. While washing the dirt from his vegetables, he saw *Aristippus* (c. 435–350 B.C.), the philosopher and companion of Socrates, passing by. Diogenes is reputed to have jeered at Aristippus, "If you had learnt to make do with vegetables as your diet, you would not have to fawn before kings." To which Aristippus is said to have replied: "And if you knew how to associate with men, you would not be washing vegetables." Diogenes Laertius, 2.68.

5. *Epaminondas* (c. 418–362 B.C.), Theban general who defeated the Spartan forces in 371 B.C.; *Aristides* (c. 530–468 B.C.), Athenian military commander active in the Persian wars; *Phocion* (d. 318 B.C.), celebrated Athenian statesman and general; the *Lacedemonian kings*, the kings of Sparta. All these figures were known for their love of honor, their virtue and courage, and their contempt for luxury.

6. Manius *Curius* Dentatus (d. 270 B.C.), Roman general and consul celebrated for his fortitude and frugality. Gaius *Fabricius* Luscinus, Roman statesman and military commander of the third century B.C., regarded as a

it was no obstacle to them in the pursuit of those honours which their virtues deserved. 'Twas in vain to think of bribing a man, who supped upon the coleworts[7] of his own garden. He could not be gained by gold, who did not think it necessary. He that could rise from the plough to the triumphal chariot, and contentedly return thither again, could not be corrupted; and he that left the sense of his poverty to his executors, who found not wherewith to bury him, might leave Macedon and Greece to the pillage of his soldiers, without taking to himself any part of the booty. But when luxury was brought into fashion, and they came to be honoured who lived magnificently, though they had in themselves no qualities to distinguish them from the basest of slaves, the most virtuous men were exposed to scorn if they were poor; and that poverty, which had been the mother and nurse of their virtue, grew insupportable. The poet well understood what effect this change had upon the world, who said,

> *Nullum crimen abest facinusque libidinis, ex quo*
> *Paupertas Romana perit.*[8]

JUVENAL

"When riches grew to be necessary, the desire of them, which is the spring of all mischief, followed. They who could not obtain honours by the noblest actions, were obliged to get wealth, to purchase them from whores or villains, who exposed them to sale: And when they were once entered into this track, they soon learned the vices of those from whom they had received their preferment, and to delight in the ways that had brought to it. When they were come to this, nothing could stop them: all thought and remembrance of good was extinguished. They who had bought the commands of armies or provinces from Icelus or Narcissus,[9]

---

model of incorruptible integrity and simplicity. Lucius *Aemilius Paullus* (*c.* 229–160 B.C.), Roman general and conquerer of Macedonia who, despite the treasure he amassed for Rome, lived a spare and simple life.

7. Coleworts: kale.

8. "No crime or lustful act has been absent since the time when Roman poverty perished." Juvenal, *Saturae*, 6.294–95.

9. *Icelus* Marcianus was Galba's freedman; he is said to have accumulated a fortune in bribes during the months that Galba reigned as emperor. The *Nar-*

sought only to draw money from them, to enable them to purchase higher dignities, or gain a more assured protection from those patrons. This brought the government of the world under a most infamous traffick; and the treasures arising from it were, for the most part, dissipated by worse vices than the rapine, violence, and fraud with which they had been gotten. The authors of those crimes had nothing left but their crimes; and the necessity of committing more, through the indigency into which they were plunged by the extravagance of their expenses. These things are inseparable from the life of a courtier; for as servile natures are guided rather by sense than reason, such as addict themselves to the service of courts, find no other consolation in their misery, than what they receive from sensual pleasures, or such vanities as they put a value upon; and have no other care than to get money for their supply, by begging, stealing, bribing, and other infamous practices. Their offices are more or less esteemed, according to the opportunities they afford for the exercise of these virtues; and no man seeks them for any other end than for gain, nor takes any other way than that which conduces to it. The useful means of attaining them are, by observing the prince's humour, flattering his vices, serving him in his pleasures, fomenting his passions, and by advancing his worst designs, to create an opinion in him that they love his person, and are entirely addicted to his will. When valour, industry, and wisdom advanced men to offices, it was no easy matter for a man to persuade the Senate he had such qualities as were required, if he had them not: But when princes seek only such as love them, and will do what they command, 'tis easy to impose upon them; and because none that are good will obey them when they command that which is not so, they are always encompassed by the worst. Those who follow them only for reward, are most liberal in professing affection to them; and by that means rise to places of authority and power. The fountain being thus corrupted, nothing that is pure can come from it. These mercenary

---

cissus to whom Sidney is referring is the onetime secretary to the emperor Claudius, who regularly sold offices for his own enrichment.

wretches having the management of affairs, justice and honour are set at a price, and the most lucrative traffick in the world is thereby established. Eutropius,[10] when he was a slave, used to pick pockets and locks; but being made a minister, he sold cities, armies, and provinces;* and some have undertaken to give probable reasons to believe, that Pallas, one of Claudius's manumised slaves, by these means, brought together more wealth in six years, than all the Roman dictators and consuls had done, from the expulsion of the kings to their passage into Asia. The rest walked in the same way, and the same arts, and many of them succeeded in the same manner. Their riches consisted not of spoils taken from enemies, but were the base product of their own corruption. They valued nothing but money, and those who could bribe them were sure to be advanced to the highest offices; and, whatever they did, feared no punishment. Like effects will ever proceed from the like causes. When vanity, luxury, and prodigality are in fashion, the desire of riches must necessarily increase in proportion to them: And when the power is in the hands of base mercenary persons, they will always (to use the courtier's phrase) make as much profit of their places as they can. Not only matters of favour, but of justice too, will be exposed to sale; and no way will be open to honours or magistracies, but by paying largely for them. He that gets an office by these means, will not execute it *gratis*: He thinks he may sell what he has bought; and would not have entered by corrupt ways, if he had not intended to deal corruptly: Nay, if a well-meaning man should suffer himself to be so far carried away by the stream of a prevailing custom, as to purchase honours of such villains, he would be obliged to continue in the same course, that he might gain riches to procure the continuance of his benefactor's protection, or to obtain the favour of such as happen to succeed them. And the corruption thus beginning in the head, must necessarily

10. Minister to the emperor Arcadius from A.D. 395 until his overthrow in A.D. 399, *Eutropius* was the first eunuch to hold such high office.

* —*Nunc uberiore rapina*
  Peccat in urbe manus.
             CLAUD.
["Now for richer plunder, the hand offends against the City itself." Claudian, *In Eutropium*, 195–96.]

diffuse itself into the members of the commonwealth: Or, if any one (which is not to be expected) after having been guilty of one villainy, should resolve to commit no more, it could have no other effect, than to bring him to ruin; and he being taken away, all things would return to their former channel."

I am, &c.

NO. 27. SATURDAY, APRIL 29, 1721.

General Corruption, how ominous to the Publick, and how discouraging to every virtuous Man. With its fatal Progress whenever encouraged.

SIR,

Sallust, or whoever else was the author of the two discourses to Caesar about settling the commonwealth, observes to that emperor, that those magistrates judge wildly, who would derive their own security from the corruption of the people; and therefore make them wicked men, to make them good subjects: Whereas, says he, "tis the interest of a virtuous prince to make his people virtuous; for, the debauched, having thrown off all restraint, are of all men the most ungovernable."[1]

Pliny tells Trajan, that all his predecessors, except Nerva and one or two more, studied how to debauch their people, and how to banish all virtue, by introducing all vices; first, because they were delighted to see others like themselves; secondly, because the minds of the Romans being depraved by the taste and vices of slaves, they would bear with greater tameness the imperial yoke of servitude.[2]

Thus did these governors and enemies of Rome destroy virtue, to set up power. Nor was such policy at all new or strange: It was then, and always will be, the direct road to absolute monar-

---

1. The lines are a translation of Sallust, *Epistulae ad Caesarem senem de re publica*, 1.1.
2. Pliny the Younger, *Panegyricus*, 45.1–3.

chy, which is in its nature at everlasting enmity with all goodness and honesty. The Roman virtue and the Roman liberty expired together; tyranny and corruption came upon them almost hand in hand.

This shews the importance of an honest magistracy; nothing certainly is more threatening, or more to be apprehended, than a corrupt one. A knave in power is as much to be dreaded, as a fool with a firebrand in a magazine of powder: You have scarce a bare chance for not being blown up.

From the wicked and worthless men, who engrossed all the places at Rome in the latter days of the commonwealth, and from the monstrous prodigalities, infamous briberies, and endless corruptions, promoted by these men, the sudden thraldom of that glorious city might easily have been foreseen. It was scarce possible to be honest, and preferred. Atticus would never accept of any employment, though he was offered the highest. "This refusal," says Monsieur Bayle,

> was doubtless owing to his virtue: There was no rising to offices then, but by means that were infamous; nor was there any such thing as executing these offices according to the rules of justice and the publick good, without being exposed to the resentment and violence of many and great wicked men. He therefore chose to be rather a virtuous private man, than an exalted and publick rogue.
>
> How charming is this example, but how rare! If all men were like Atticus, there would be no danger of a state of anarchy. But as to that we may be easy; for there will be always more rogues and rooks at hand to be devouring and monopolizing places, by all proper vile means, than there will be places to bestow.

Bayle goes on, and tells us of

> a great traveller, who being rallied upon his rambling humour, answered, that he would cease travelling, as soon as ever he could find a country where power and credit were in the hands of honest men, and preferments went by

merit. Nay then, says one who heard him, you will infallibly die travelling.[3]

Corruption, bribery, and treachery, were such ways to power, as Atticus would not tread. Colonel Sidney says, that

> a noble person in his time, who was a great enemy to bribery, was turned out from a considerable post, as a scandal to the court; for, said the principal minister, "he will make no profit of his place; and by that means cast a scandal upon those that do."[4]

And Alexander ab Alexandro[5] tells a story of a very honest man, well skilled in the languages, who having long struggled with difficulties and poverty, while he trusted in vain to his honesty and learning, bethought himself of a contrary road; and therefore turning pimp and pathick, instantly he prospered, and got great riches, power, and places.

Aude aliquid brevibus gyaris & carcere dignum.[6]

Cicero, who lived to see dismal days of ambition and corruption at Rome, was sensible that he could do little or no good with all his abilities and his honesty. "If I saw," says he in a letter to Lentulus,[7]

> if I saw the commonwealth held and governed by corrupt and desperate men, as has happened in my days and formerly, no motive or consideration should engage me in their interests; neither their bribes could move me, nor

3. The quotations are taken from the English translation of Bayle's *Dictionnaire, An Historical and Critical Dictionary* (4 vols.; London: Printed for C. Harper, etc., 1710), s.v. "Atticus," I:420–21 (note F).

4. *Discourses Concerning Government*, chap. 2, sect. 25 (p. 204 in the 1751 edition).

5. The reference is unclear. Gordon appears to be referring to Alexander, the Greek rhetorician, who flourished in the first half of the second century B.C. He is credited with having written several treatises on rhetoric, of which only a Latin abridgment of one remains.

6. "Dare something worthy of small Gyara and the prison." Juvenal, *Saturae* 1.73. Gyara, an island in the Aegean, was, during the empire, used as a prison for political prisoners.

7. Cornelius *Lentulus* Niger (d. 56 B.C.), a close friend of Cicero who much admired his integrity and his dedication to republican principles.

could dangers, which often sway the boldest men, terrify me; nor could any of their civilities, or any of their obligations, soften me.[8]

Talking, in another place, of the Senate, then awed by power, or governed by avarice, he says, *Aut assentiendum est nulla cum gravitate paucis aut frustra dissentiendum:*[9] That is, you must either basely vote with Crassus and Caesar, and one or two men more in power, or vote against them to no purpose. These great men did not seek power, nor use it, to do good to their country, which is the end of power; but to themselves, which is the abuse of power. Where government is degenerated into jobbing, it quickly runs into tyranny and dissolution: And he who in any country possesses himself of a great post for the sake of gainful jobs, as a certain great person once owned that he did, ought to finish his last job under a gallows.

It is natural and necessary for those that have corrupt ends, to make use of means that are corrupt, and to hate all men that are uncorrupt.

I would lay it down as a rule for all nations to consider and observe, that where bribery is practised, 'tis a thousand to one but mischief is intended; and the more bribery, the more mischief. When therefore the people, or their trustees, are bribed, they would do well to consider, that it is not, it cannot be, for their own sakes. Honest and open designs, which will bear light and examination, are hurt and discredited by base and dark expedients to bring them about: But, if you would persuade a man to be a rogue, it is natural that money should be your first argument; and therefore, whoever offers me a bribe, does tacitly acknowledge that he thinks me a knave.

Tacitus, taking notice of the woeful decline of virtue and liberty, towards the end of the Republick, says, that the greatest villainies were committed with impunity, and ruin was the price of

8. *Epistulae ad familiares*, 1.9.11.
9. "One must either, without dignity, agree with a few or dissent from their opinion in vain." Cicero, *Epistulae ad familiares*, 1.8.3.

honesty: *Deterrima quaeque impune, ac multa honesta exitio fuere.*[10] And indeed, where corruption and publick crimes are not carefully opposed, and severely punished, neither liberty nor security can possibly subsist.

The immense briberies practised by Julius Caesar, were sure and terrible presages of Caesar's tyranny. It is amazing what mighty sums he gave away: Caius Curio alone, one of the tribunes, was bought into his interest, at no smaller a price than half a million of our money.[11] Other magistrates too had their shares; and all were bribed, who would be bribed. We may easily conceive how he came by such sums; he got them as wickedly as he gave them away. Nor can I call him generous in this vast liberality; since he purchased the Roman empire with its own money, and gave away a part to get the whole.

Unjust and unfrugal ways of throwing away money, make wicked and violent means necessary to get money; and rapine naturally follows prodigality. They that waste publick money, seldom stop there, but go a wicked step farther; and having first drained the people, at last oppress them. Publick frauds are therefore very alarming, as they are very big with publick ruin. What shall we say then of other times, when publick schemes have been concerted to confound all property, to put common honesty out of countenance, and banish it from amongst men; and when an appetite for power was only an appetite for mischief? Dreadful sure was the prospect! And yet this was the state of Rome in those days; as will be seen further before this letter is ended.

Nor would it have been any advantage or security to Rome, though Caesar and his party had been less able men than in truth they were: Having debauched the people, he did more by corruption towards enslaving them, than he did by his parts, as great as they were. It is somewhere observed, that to do good requires some parts and pains; but any man may be a rogue. The world, says the proverb, little knows what silly fellows govern it.

10. "Every evil remained unpunished and honesty was often one's ruin." Tacitus, *Annales*, 3.28.

11. Gaius Scribonius *Curio* originally took Pompey's side in the civil war. Bribed by Caesar with an immense sum, he subsequently changed sides and became one of Caesar's most active supporters.

Even the difficulties of doing good proceed from the pravity of some men's nature, ever prone to do evil; and so strong is that pravity, that many men frequently slight great temptations to be honest, and embrace slight temptations to be knaves.

It is an observation, which every body is capable of making, that a good character lost is hardly, if ever, recovered. Now the reason of this is, not so much from the malevolence of the world (often too ready to calumniate) as from the inability of a knave to become honest: He is, as it were, doomed to be one: The bias of his spirit is crooked; and if ever he act honestly, it is for a roguish reason. I have known a man, who, having wilfully lost all credit, rejected as wilfully all opportunities to regain it, even when thrown into his lap. He could not help earning fresh detestation, with great labour; when he might have acquired the highest renown with the greatest ease. From hence may be seen how dangerous it is ever to trust a man who has once been a knave; and hence too may be learned, that from men who have done eminent mischief, whether publick or private, greater still is to be dreaded. Vice is a prolifick thing, and wickedness naturally begets wickedness.

Olearius, giving an account of Muscovy, observes, that

> the Great Duke's court hath this in common with those of other princes, that vice takes place of virtue, and gets nearest the throne. Those who have the honour to be nearest his person, are withal more subtle, more deceitful, and more insolent, than the others that have not. They know very well how to make their advantages of the prince's favour, and look for the greatest respects and humblest submissions imaginable, from those who make their addresses to them; which the others render them, as much to avoid the mischief they might do to them, as for the good they expect from them.[12]

This is the character of a court, where one is not much surprized nor troubled to find out tyranny and corruption in abundance:

12. Adam Olearius, *The Voyages and Travels of the Ambassadors Sent by Frederick, Duke of Holstein, to the Great Duke of Moscovy, and the King of Persia* (2 vols. in 1; London: Printed for Thomas Dring and John Starkey, 1662). The passage here cited appears at the end of bk. III, chap. 14 (p. 119).

But one is at once amazed and affected with the mournful account Sallust gives us of the Romans in his time; the Romans, who had been so virtuous a people, so great and so free!

The Romans, he says, were arrived to that pitch of corruption, that they gloried in extravagancy and rapine, and made sarcasms upon virtue. Modesty and a disinterested mind passed with them only for sloth and cowardice. Those that were in power, neglecting virtue, and conspiring against innocence, preferred only their own creatures. *Innocentes circumveniunt, suos ad honorem tollunt:*[13] Wicked deeds, and an infamous character, were no bars to the possessing of power; and those that acted as if rapine were their employment, and plunder the perquisites of their place, were not thought unfit for fresh preferments: *Non facinus, non probrum, aut flagitium obstat, quo minus magistratus capiant: quod commodum est, trahunt, rapiunt.*[14] At last, their great men had no principle but rapaciousness, and observed no law but their lust. The whole commonwealth was become their prey and their pillage: *Postremo, tanquam urbe capta, libidine ac licentia sua, pro legibus utuntur.*[15]

The same author says, that it would have lessened his concern, had he seen such great wickedness perpetrated by men of great qualities. But his grief had not this mitigation: For, says he, wretched creatures with little souls, whose whole genius lay in their tongue and whose utmost talent and ability was to prate glibly, exercised with insolence that power which they had acquired by chance, or by the sloth of others. *Ac me quidem mediocris dolor angerct, si virtute partam victoriam more suo per servitium exercerent: Sed homines inertissimi quorum omnis vis virtusque in lingua sita est, forte, & alterius socordia, dominationem oblatam insolentes agitant.*[16] And for the

13. "They bilked the innocent and raised themselves to high office." Sallust, *Epistulae ad Caesarem senem de re publica*, 3.3–4.

14. "Neither crime nor shame nor disgrace obstructs them from holding office; they seize and plunder where they choose." Sallust, *Epistulae ad Caesarem senem de re publica*, 3.4.

15. "Finally, as if they had taken the city captive, their whims and desires became the only law they acknowledged." Sallust, *Epistulae ad Caesarem senem de re publica*, 3.4–5.

16. "Indeed, I would feel only moderately troubled if they had shown courage in securing that victory which, according to their practice, had allowed them to subjugate others. But these most cowardly of men, whose only courage and

Roman nobility of that time, he says, that, like stupid statues, their names and titles were their only ornament: *Inertissimi nobiles, in quibus, sicut in statua praeter nomen, nibil est additamenti.*[17] Sallust. ad C. Caesarem, de repub. ordinand.

We see what a market these men made of power, and what a degree of degeneracy they introduced. The end of all was, the utter loss of liberty, and a settled tyranny.

G   *I am, &c.*

NO. 28. SATURDAY, MAY 6, 1721.

A *Defence of Cato against his Defamers.*

TO CATO

SIR,

See what it is to be conspicuous! Your honesty, and the truths which you tell, have drawn upon you much envy, and many lies. You cannot be answered; therefore it is fit to abuse you. Had you kept groveling near the earth, in company with most other weekly writers, you might have lulled the town asleep as they do, with great safety to your person, and without any body's saying an unkind word of you: But you have galloped away so fast and so far before them, that it is no wonder the poor vermin, conscious of their own heaviness and want of speed, crawl after you and curse you. It is natural, human sight is offended with splendor: This is exemplified in a man looking at the sun; he makes all the while a world of wry mouths and distorted faces.

Consider yourself, Sir, as the sun to those authors, who behold you with agonies, while they behold you with admiration.

---

ability is in their tongues, insolently maintain a tyranny that was originally gained by chance and through the weakness of another." Sallust, *Epistulae ad Caesarem senem de re publica*, 3.5–7.

17. "Most slothful nobles, among whom, like a statue, nothing is added but a name." Sallust, *Epistulae ad Caesarem senem de re publica*, 9.4.

Great minds alone are pleased with the excellencies of others, and vulgar souls provoked by them. The mob of writers is like the weaver's mob; all levellers.[1] This appears by their unmannerly and seditious speeches concerning you, their monarch. Strange instance of impudence and ingratitude! They live upon you, and scold at you. Your lot is the same with that of many other eminent authors; you feed vermin before you are dead.

Your slanderers, as they are below even contempt, so are they far below all notice: But it is worth considering who set them at work; from whom they receive the wages of prostitution; and what contradictory things the poor creatures are taught to say. Scarce a paper appeared for a considerable time together in which Cato's letters were not extolled; and those who did it endeavoured, to the best of their skill, to write after him: But finding that his labours made theirs useless, and that the recommending of publick spirit was too mighty a task for humble hirelings, they suddenly, and without ceremony, tack about, and, by calumniating Cato, make themselves liars: Such deference have they for their customers, and for themselves!

It is no wonder, therefore, that the same worthy, but waggish pens, represent him, with the same breath, as an abandoned atheist, and a bigoted Presbyterian; while others as plainly prove him a flaming Jacobite, and an arrant republican; that is, one who is high for monarchy, and one who is against all monarchy. I could shew you these pretty consistencies in one and the same paper.

Cato had described and shewed the horrid effects of publick confusion, and contended for punishing the authors of our own: Hence Cato is represented as an enemy to government and order, and a promoter of confusion.

Cato had bestowed real and unfeigned encomiums upon his Majesty, and done all justice to the abilities and honesty of his ministers: Hence Cato is charged with casting reproaches, and making sarcasms upon his Majesty and his ministry.

1. A pun on the Levellers, a political party active during the Civil War and the Commonwealth. The Levellers embraced strong republican views and sought a lessening of the existing distinctions in social rank.

Cato has writ against Turkish, Asiatick, and all sorts of tyranny: Hence Cato is said to be a great incendiary, and an open enemy to our constitution.

Cato contends, that great traitors ought to be hanged: Hence Cato is traduced, as if he affronted the ministry.

Cato asserts, that the good of mankind is the end of government: Hence Cato is for destroying all government.

Cato lays down certain rules for farther establishing his Majesty's throne, and for ensuring to him for ever the minds of his people: Therefore Cato is a Jacobite.

Cato has shewn at large the blessings of a limited monarchy, especially of our own: Therefore Cato is a republican.

Cato has shewn the dreadfulness of popular insurrections and fury; the misery of civil wars, the uncertainty of their end: Therefore Cato stirs up the people to sedition and rebellion.

Cato laments, that great criminals are seldom brought to the gallows: Hence Cato is represented as one that deserves the gallows.

Cato, talking of Turkey, observes with warmth and concern, that the holy name of God was belied, and religion prostituted, to bind down wretchedness upon his creatures, and to protect the tyrant that does it: therefore Cato scurrilously reviles the Church of England.

Cato has shewn the destructive terms of arbitrary power, and how it had almost dispeopled the earth: In answer to this it is said, that Cato wears a dark wig.[2]

Cato has complained, that this great nation has been abused, cheated, and exhausted; its trade ruined; its credit destroyed; its manufactures discouraged, &c. and affirmed, that vengeance is due to those traitors who have done it; that none but traitors will protect traitors; that publick honesty and publick spirit ought to be encouraged, in opposition to publick corruption, bribery, and rapine;[3] that there is regard to be had to the rights, privi-

2. The metaphor is unclear. Possibly, "Cato advocates a vengeful and oppressive government" (from the dark cap worn by judges when passing sentence of death).

3. The reference is, of course, to the South Sea swindle and to those who benefitted from it.

leges, and tempers of the people: That standing armies are dreadful things; that a military government is violent and bloody: That they are the blackest traitors, who would break the confidence between a prince and his subjects: That great men mind chiefly the getting of plumbs;[4] and that honest measures are the best measures. To all which it is replied, that Cato is a whimsical unreasonable man, who talks and expects strange things; and, in fine, that he dreams odd dreams.

By such powerful arguments is Cato answered; by such pretty arts decried. He is really a great criminal; he asserts the rights and property of the people, and calls for justice upon those who would destroy them. He is surely a Jacobite, who would not let certain elevated sages do what they would, and get what they pleased. I would ask, whether the obliging, protecting, and avenging, the injured people, be likely ways to bring in the Pretender? Yet these are the ways which Cato contends for. Or, whether the deceiving, loading, and squeezing of the harmless people, be natural ways to make and keep them well affected? Yet these are the ways which Cato condemns and exposes.

Being detached from all parties, eminently guiltless of all personal views of his own, and going upon principles certainly true in themselves, certainly beneficent to human society; it is no wonder that he is read and approved by every intelligent man in England, except the guilty, their screens, hirelings, and adherents. What he writes, the people feel to be true: If men can be great knaves, in spite of opposition; how much greater would they be, if there were none? And if justice be opposed, openly, shamelessly, and violently opposed, in spite of her champions and defenders; she must certainly be destroyed, if she had none. It is a dismal reflexion, that justice must sometimes be sought for inch by inch, before it can be obtained, and at last is not half obtained; and that the higher and blacker the villainy is, the greater is the security. I hope that this will never be our case; but I could name many a country whose case it has been.

I am not surprized that certain tall traitors are very angry with Cato. "Good now hold your tongue," said a quack to his com-

4. The getting of plumbs: the acquiring of wealth.

plaining patient, under agonies into which he had been cast by the doctor's infallible specifick: "Good now hold your tongue, and be easy; leave the matter to me, and the matter will go well": That is, lie still and die, and I will warrant[5] you. Great grief and distress will have utterance, in spite of art or terror.

On Ascension Day, when the Doge of Venice weds the sea with a ring, the admiral, who conducts the *bucentauro,* or vessel in which that ceremony is performed, does a bold thing: He pawns his head to the Senate, to ensure them, against the danger and effects of tempests and storms.[6] But the thing would still be bolder, if he had first wilfully raised a storm, or bored a hole in the vessel.

I appeal to the sense of the nation, daily uttered in their addresses to the Parliament for relief and vengeance; whether Cato's sentiments be not the same with theirs; I appeal to the sufferings, the heavy, melancholy sufferings of the people, whether either Cato or they speak thus without grounds.

The grounds are too visible, and their allegations too true. Hence the rage of guilt, which is more galled by truth, than innocence is hurt by lies: And hence I have heard it observed, concerning a set of worthies, that they do not care what falsehoods you publish concerning them, but will never forgive you if you meddle with facts.

For certain gentlemen to find fault with Cato's letters, is to avow their own shame. Why was there occasion given for those letters? Some other questions might be asked too, which would discover fresh blackness in these betrayers, were they not already all over black. Who is it that might have checked, and yet did not check, rampant rogues last summer? And from what motives proceeded such omission? Who is it that openly screens open guilt? Who is it that conceals the evidence of guilt? Who is it that browbeats the pursuers of guilt? Who is it that throws obstacles in the Parliament's way? Who is it that lengthens out the process? Who is

5. Warrant: protect.

6. The *sposalizio del mar,* or "wedding of the sea," was performed every year on Ascension Day up to 1789 and symbolized Venice's maritime supremacy. The "bucentauro" (*bucintoro*) is the state galley of the Venetian doges.

it that strives to defeat the enquiry?[7] Who is it that makes malcontents, and then reproaches them for being so?

In vain they fall upon Cato, with lying reproaches, false pictures, and ugly names: Their conduct betrays them; by making him of every party, they shew him to be of none; as he has shewed himself to be of none. I thought it, however, not amiss, thus, once for all, to make his apology, and to shew what are his crimes, and who his enemies. His great guilt is, that he will not spare guilt; and the great objection to his writings is, that they cannot be answered. Let the reader judge whether I have misrepresented him or his foes, who are no other than the late directors, their friends and confederates.

As to the poor weekly journeymen of the press, whose principle is the ready penny, and who, for a morsel, defile paper, and blot reputations without hurting them, they deserve no resentment. It is their profession to do what they are bid, when they are paid for it. A church is not the less sacred, because curs frequently lift up their leg against it, and affront the wall: It is the nature of dogs. They therefore are and ought to be pitied and overlooked; the business of this letter to you being to expose the false and unjust censures of some, who bear a greater figure than such harmless weekly writers, without possessing more honesty.

The conjectures of these creatures about the person of Cato afford matter of mirth. They will needs know him, right or wrong. Let them guess on; whatever they guess, I will venture to pronounce them liars, though they should guess truly: Since without being able to do any thing more than guess, they yet go on to affirm; which no honest man would do without competent evidence. I am,

G   *Sir*

                               your humble servant,
                               PORTIUS

---

7. That is, the ongoing investigations of the Parliamentary secret committee.

NO. 29. SATURDAY, MAY 13, 1721.

🙚 *Reflections occasioned by an Order of Council for suppressing certain impious Clubs that were never discovered.*

SIR,

I would willingly propagate and preserve the following Order of Council, as a monument of his Majesty's great zeal for virtue and religion. It is published in the *Gazette* of the 29th of April, in the following words:

At the Court of St. James's, the 28th day of April, 1721

Present,
The King's Most Excellent Majesty in Council

His Majesty having received information, which gives great reason to suspect, that there have lately been, and still are, in and about the cities of London and Westminster, certain scandalous clubs or societies of young persons, who meet together, and, in the most impious and blasphemous manner, insult the most sacred principles of our holy religion, affront Almighty God himself, and corrupt the minds and morals of one another; and being resolved to make use of all the authority committed to him by Almighty God, to punish such enormous offenders, and to crush such shocking impieties before they increase and draw down the vengeance of God upon this nation: His Majesty has thought fit to command the Lord Chancellor, and his Lordship is hereby required to call together his Majesty's Justices of the Peace of Middlesex and Westminster, and strictly to enjoin them in the most effectual manner, that they, and every of them, do make the most diligent and careful enquiry and search for the discovery of any thing of this and the like sort, tending in any wise to the corruption of the principles and manners of men; and to lay before his Lordship such discoveries as from time to time may be made, to the end

that all proper methods may be taken for the utter sup-
pression of all such detestable practices. His Lordship is
further directed to urge them to the due execution of their
office, in detecting and prosecuting, with vigour, all profaneness, immorality, and debauchery, as they value the
blessing of Almighty God, as they regard the happiness of
their country, which cannot subsist, if things sacred and
virtuous are trampled upon, and as they tender his Majesty's favour, to which they cannot recommend themselves
more effectually, than by shewing the utmost zeal upon so
important an occasion; to which end his Lordship is to
acquaint them, that as his Majesty for himself has nothing
more at heart than to regard the honour of God, so impiously struck at, and is determined to shew all marks of displeasure and discouragement to any who may lie even
under the suspicion of such practices; so he shall always
account it the greatest and most substantial service they can
do to his Majesty or his government, to exert themselves in
discovering any who are guilty of such impieties, that they
may be openly prosecuted, and punished with the utmost
severity and most publick ignominy which the laws of the
land can inflict.

EDWARD SOUTHWELL[1]

To this it is added, in the same *Gazette,*

That his Majesty has been pleased to give orders to the
principal officers of his household, to make strict and diligent enquiry, whether any of his Majesty's servants are
guilty of the horrid impieties mentioned in the Order of
Council inserted above, and to make a report thereof to his
Majesty.

These societies must certainly be as distracted[2] as they are
impious. I have indeed been in doubt till now, whether there really

1. Edward Southwell (1671–1730), from 1699 Clerk of the Privy Council. In
1708, after the Act of Union, Southwell was made Clerk of the Privy Council
of Great Britain.
2. Distracted: deranged.

were any such; but I am in no doubt about the punishment which they deserve: I think that it ought to be the most severe that is due to such raving wickedness, which is such, as neither youth nor wine can excuse, nor indeed extenuate; and till they are further punished, I think that the darkest holes in Bedlam[3] ought to be their portion. But outrageous and godless as they are, they do not merit more detestation and severity, than do those who inhumanly give out, that gentlemen, who abhor such clubs, are members of them: The authors of so dreadful a calumny are much worse than murderers; because they endeavour to take away from men something much dearer than life: They are therefore in the class with daemons, and earn such mighty vengeance as God only can inflict.

The above Order of Council is very just and religious, and of excellent use and example: So much zeal cannot stop at a club or two of pernicious though private sinners; but doubtless extends to other criminals more publick and considerable, and even more destructive. The greatest part of the wickedness done by those thoughtless young wretches, is done to themselves, and like to remain with them; there being little probability that they will ever make many proselytes to their astonishing frenzies: Whereas the other great criminals, for the sole sake of doing good to themselves, have undone almost every man in England, with England itself into the bargain. They set three nations to sale; and themselves fixing the price, were themselves the buyers: They purchased our happiness, and paid us in want and sorrow. Every good man is proof against the contagion of profaneness; but virtue and goodness stood us in no stead against our money-monsters, who, having robbed all honest men, made a jest of honesty itself. Can there be greater evils under the sun, than rampant plunderers, abandoned corruption, and devouring calamity? Or are there any other evils which these do not produce?

We therefore take it for granted, that

> as his Majesty is determined to shew all marks of displeasure and discouragement to any who may even lie under the suspicion of such destructive practices; so he will always

3. Bedlam, or Bethlehem Hospital, England's first lunatic asylum. It was to become infamous for the ill treatment meted out to its inmates.

account it the most substantial service that we can do to him and his government, to exert ourselves in discovering any who are guilty of such unparalleled frauds, such national wickedness; that they may be openly prosecuted, and punished with the utmost severity, and most publick ignominy, that the legislature can inflict.

And,

as his Majesty has been pleased to give orders to the principal officers of his household, to make strict and diligent enquiry, whether any of his Majesty's servants are guilty of the horrid impieties mentioned in the Order of Council inserted above, and to make report thereof to his Majesty:

So we may assure ourselves, that the same severe enquiry has been already made, whether any of those in trust under his Majesty, or about his person, have stained their hands, dishonoured their master, and provoked Almighty God, by promoting or embarking in any of the horrid and spreading mischiefs practised last year by the late South-Sea directors, and their confederates.

An enquiry into religion, and the private morals of men, is not inconsistent with an enquiry into civil and publick villainies; nor can the former ever prove a bone of contention to divert the latter, whatever the wicked and the guilty may hope, and the honest and distressed may apprehend. Fresh objects of horror and aversion cannot lessen our general detestation for those who ought to be beyond all others detested. While we pursue wolves and tigers, and the mightier beasts of prey, who, if they be not destroyed, will continue to destroy, we are not to be diverted by the scent of a fox or badger, though they may annoy a private neighbourhood, and dispeople hen-roosts.

Our publick virtue is the best and surest proof that we can give of our private piety: Piety and justice are inseparable; and prayers said ten times a day, will not atone for a murder or a robbery committed once a month: Appearances go for nothing, when facts contradict them. The readiest way therefore to shew that our hearts are pure, is to shew that our hands are clean, and that we will punish those that have foul ones.

Here is a test of our virtue and innocence!

Let us hang up publick rogues, as well as punish private blasphemers. The observance of religion, and the neglect of justice, are contradictions. Let any man ask himself, whether a nation is more hurt by a few giddy, unthinking, young wretches, talking madly in their drink; or by open, deliberate, and publick depredations committed by a junto of veteran knaves, who add to the injury, and to their own guilt, by a shew of gravity, and a canting pretence to religion? The late directors all pretended to be good Christians. I would ask one question more; namely, whether it had not been better for England, that the late directors, and their masters, had spent their nights and their days in the Hell Fire Club,[4] than in contriving and executing execrable schemes to ruin England? Pray, which of the two is your greater enemy, he who robs you of all that you have, but neither curses nor swears at you; or he who only curses you or himself, and takes nothing from you?

Where justice is exactly observed, religion will be observed; and to pretend to be very strict about the latter, without minding the former, would be highly absurd and ridiculous. Virtue necessarily produces religion, and is itself religion; and profaneness and irreligion will ever and necessarily follow corruption, the prolifick parent of numberless mischiefs.

Private profaneness is not therefore half so terrible to human society, as publick roguery and publick robbery. The happiness of mankind is surely the cause of God; and whenever I hear of arrets[5] and edicts made by popish and tyrannical foreign princes, in favour of religion; I consider them as so many mockeries of God, whose creatures they, at the same time, grind and destroy. As consistently might they pretend great zeal for observing religiously the sixth command, and yet murder by war and famine ten thousand of their subjects a week.

James Naylor was severely punished for blasphemy;[6] is there any comparison, as to their effects, between the crime of James Naylor, and the crimes of the late directors, their seconds,

4. Hell-Fire Club: a club devoted to dissipation and debauchery.

5. Arrets: decrees.

6. James Nayler (1618–1660), English Puritan who in 1651 became a Quaker and soon developed the view that he was Christ incarnate. In 1655, he rode naked into Bristol attended by seven followers. As a result, he was arrested, tried, and brutally punished for blasphemy.

and abettors? James Naylor (being himself deluded) misled a few ignorant people, whose error was their greatest crime: But our modern impostors, our South-Sea deceivers have actually and wilfully plundered their country of near thirty millions of money, and involved it in universal confusion and want.

It is therefore a sensible pleasure to us, to behold his Majesty and his ministry engaged with so much zeal in vindicating our property, as well as our religion. His Majesty, in particular, has condescended, with unparalleled, I am sure uncommon, goodness, to tell the Lord Mayor and Court of Aldermen, that *he has no share in the late wicked management.* This is a piece of royal grace, with which, I believe, never any subjects were blessed before. From hence we may draw a fresh assurance of his Majesty's alacrity and readiness to punish the execrable authors of that wicked management, who are also the greatest enemies to his crown and dignity.

> His Majesty being resolved to make use of all the authority committed to him by Almighty God, to punish such enormous offenders, and to crush such shocking impieties, before they increase and draw down the vengeance of God upon this nation:

I say, his Majesty being thus zealous for religion and the nation, will never suffer the authors of the greatest evil, the highest villainy ever committed in this nation, to escape unpunished. Has ever a heavier judgment befallen our nation, than the last year's merciless rapine? And can there be greater enemies to God and man, than the authors of it? Monsters who were for plucking up all virtue and all property by the roots. Oh, that their success had not increased their guilt! They acted as if they did not believe that there was a God who judged the world, and as if they defied all human tribunals, as well as the divine. These are the atheists terrible to society; this is the atheism woefully and universally felt. Desolation and misery are the occupation and sport of devils, and they their vicegerents who promote them.

He who talks profanely of things sacred, is a wicked man, and as ill bred as he is wicked: But he who wantonly fills a country, a glorious and happy country, with want, woe, and sorrow; what name, what torture, what death, does he not deserve? He is a destroyer-general: He is a mad dog, with ten thousand mouths, who scatters poison, wounds, and death all around him.

I shall conclude in the strong words of the above Order of Council; namely, that as we value the blessing of Almighty God, as we regard the happiness of our country, which cannot subsist, if things sacred and virtuous (and such are private property, publick faith, and publick justice) are trampled upon; and as we tender his Majesty's favour, to which we cannot recommend ourselves more effectually, than by shewing the utmost zeal upon so important an occasion: I say, as we value all these, let us be warm, bold, and active in the discovery and punishment of such enormous offenders; and to crush such shocking mischiefs, before they increase and draw down the vengeance of God upon this nation.

G   *I am, &c.*

P.S. I, who hate to see the punishment of any sort of great wickedness linger, do here propose an expedient to come at a certainty about the blasphemous clubs:* Let a reward be publickly offered for the discovery of any of their members, to be paid upon their legal conviction; and, in the mean time, let us not cast random reproaches upon particular men; lest, by falling upon the innocent, they return double upon ourselves. It is base and dishonest to feign crimes that are not; and where they really are, it is barbarous and diabolical to father them upon the guiltless: He who charges upon another a crime that deserves the gallows, does, if it prove false, pronounce sentence against himself, and proclaim his own right to Tyburn: As, on the other hand, he who screens from the gallows those that deserve it, adopts their title to the halter, and ought to swing in their room.[7]

Can there be greater justice and impartiality than this? And I assure you, Sir, I heartily wish that they may take place.

* Upon the strictest enquiry, it could not be discovered that any such clubs ever existed, except in common fame [that is, by popular belief] and the above Order of Council.

7. Swing in their room: swing in their place.

NO. 30. SATURDAY, MAY 20, 1721.

An excellent Letter from Brutus to Atticus; with an explanatory Introduction.

SIR,

I send you another excellent letter of the great Brutus. They who say that I forged the last, make me as great a compliment as ever was made to man; since whoever could write that letter, is, without reflecting on my contemporaries, certainly the greatest man of the age.

To the former letter I gave you an historical introduction; I shall give you another to this, and own myself obliged for it to Monsieur Soreau.

Brutus and Cassius, after the death of Caesar, having left Rome, Octavius, Caesar's nephew, arrived there: He was no more than nineteen years old; and the first thing of note that happened to him, was a quarrel with Mark Anthony, who treated him like a child, with contempt, and indeed was grown insupportable to all the world. Cicero and Anthony being then declared enemies, Octavius was persuaded by his friends to throw himself into the arms of Cicero. Hence began their friendship, equally desirable to both: Cicero governed the Senate, and Octavius had the hearts of his uncle's soldiers, with great treasure to gain new friends, and carry on new designs. Mark Anthony was the common enemy of both, and of the Republick, which he as outrageously attacked, as Cicero warmly defended.

This quarrel gave occasion to those orations of Cicero, called philippicks; which are eternal monuments of his love for his country, as well as of the marvelous eloquence of that great man.

Cicero and Octavius succeeded; they got the better of Mark Anthony, and drove him out of Rome. But, by his interest and activity, he soon gathered such a force, as he thought sufficient to make himself master of Rome; which therefore he prepared to attack and possess by downright violence. But Octavius having levied, at his own expence, an army, composed mostly of the veteran troops of Caesar, opposed the march of Anthony, and diverted that dreadful storm from the city. Cicero, who had undertaken the defence of Octavius from his first arrival at Rome, and laboured to fortify his cause by the authority of the Senate, was not wanting to extol this first service of Octavius for the Republick. Hence extraordinary honours were decreed him; that he should be made propraetor,[1] and in that quality commander of the army; that a recompence should be given to his troops; that he should be received into the number of the Senators; that he might, before he came of age, demand all the other greatest dignities of the commonwealth; and even that a statue should be erected to him.

In the mean time Anthony, thus repulsed by Octavius, marched into Cisalpine Gaul, to drive from thence Decimus Brutus, its governor, a kinsman of our Brutus, and one of the tyrannicides.[2] That governor, being unprovided of forces sufficient to fight Anthony, retired into the city of Modena, a Roman colony; and there shutting himself up, expected succour from the Senate. Anthony in the interim laid siege to the place, in hopes that being once master of that city, he would soon be so of Gaul, and afterwards be enabled to return into Italy, with a power sufficient to conquer Rome, where he meant to erect a dominion as absolute as was that of Caesar.

That siege occasioned fresh meetings of the Senate; where, in fine, Mark Anthony was declared an enemy to the commonwealth; and both the consuls, Hirtius and Pansa,[3] were sent with an army to relieve Decimus Brutus: With the consuls, Octavius was likewise sent.

During all these transactions, our Brutus and Cassius having staid some time in Italy, after their leaving Rome, were now retired to their governments, Brutus to Macedonia, and Cassius to Syria; and both were levying men, and forming armies, for the defence of the commonwealth.

1. Propraetor: a high-ranking magistrate delegated the function of administering justice in one of the Roman provinces.

2. Decimus Iunius *Brutus* (d. 43 B.C.), one of Caesar's assassins who, after the battle of Mutina, was put to death on Antony's orders.

3. Aulus *Hirtius* and Gaius Vibius *Pansa* Caetronianus, Roman consuls who were both killed by Mark Antony's armies at Mutina in 43 B.C.

As to Cicero, he was now in the zenith of power, and governed all things at Rome: He particularly presided in the Senate, as the most antient consular, during the absence of the two consuls. In this situation he was wonderfully curious to know what was the opinion of Brutus concerning himself and his administration. It is certain that Brutus had his highest esteem; and he thought that if he could procure the esteem of Brutus, it would be an eminent proof of his own virtue and merit, as well as the most glorious reward of that virtue and merit. Brutus had, in all his letters, been very silent with him upon this head. Cicero therefore makes use of Atticus, their common friend, to sift[4] Brutus, and know his sentiments. As soon, therefore, as it was known at Rome, that the siege of Modena was raised, and Anthony defeated by the two consuls and Octavius, Atticus dispatched the news to Brutus, and in his letter sounded him about his thoughts of Cicero.

The following letter is a frank and open answer to that of Atticus. In it he justly condemns Cicero's over violent hatred to Mark Anthony, which betrayed him into as unreasonable an affection and deference for Octavius, his champion against Anthony. Cicero saw his error at last, but saw it too late; the power and credit to which he had raised Octavius, cost him his life, and Rome her liberty. Cicero, who was the author of all the greatness and authority of Octavius, was by Octavius given up to the rage and sword of Mark Anthony, against whom Octavius had been generously defended and supported by Cicero: And Octavius enslaved the commonwealth with those very arms, which the commonwealth had trusted with him for her protection. So early had the pious Augustus learned the arts and gratitude of an absolute monarch!

G   *I am, &c.*

BRUTUS TO ATTICUS[5]

"You tell me, that Cicero wonders why, in any of my letters, I have never discovered to him my sentiments concerning his

4. Sift: probe.
5. The letter that follows is extracted from Cicero, *Epistulae ad Brutum*, 17.1–6.

management and administration at Rome; I therefore discover those sentiments to you, since you are so earnest to know them.

"I know well the sincerity and great uprightness of Cicero's intentions: His passion for the good of the commonwealth is indeed evident and remarkable. But prudent and wise as he is, he has given proofs of a zeal which is imprudent, and a heart that is vain: I leave it to you to judge, which of these swayed him, when, more forward than well advised, he drew upon himself the hatred of so terrible a foe as Mark Anthony. This he meant for the good of the commonwealth; but it has had a contrary effect, since by it, instead of bridling, as he proposed, the dangerous power of Octavius, he has further animated his ambition, and raised his aims. Besides, such is the fatal complaisance of Cicero for that man, that he cannot help speaking of myself and the patriots of my country, with severe and bitter language; which, however, returns double upon himself: If we have put one man to death, he has put many. We killed Caesar, and he the associates of Catiline. If therefore Casca,[6] who gave Caesar the first blow, be a murderer, as Cicero, to please Octavius, calls him; Cicero himself is one, and must confess himself one, and his great enemy Bestia[7] is justified in calling him so.

"How! because we have not the Ides of March, in which we dispatched Caesar, eternally in our mouths, as Cicero has the Nones of December,[8] in which he suppressed the conspiracy of Catiline, and which he is for ever celebrating upon all occasions; does he take advantage of our modesty and his own vanity, and find from hence more reason to blame a glorious deed done by us for mankind, than Clodius[9] and Bestia had to condemn, as they always did, his own severe conduct when he was consul?

"Cicero every where boasts, that he sustained the war against Anthony; yet no body ever saw Cicero out of a gown, and

6. Publius Servilius *Casca*, tribune in the year Caesar was murdered and one of the tyrannicides.

7. Lucius Calpurnius *Bestia*, one of the Catilinarian conspirators and a bitter opponent of Cicero.

8. Catiline's accomplices were executed by Cicero on Dec. 5, 63 B.C.

9. Publius *Clodius* Pulcher (c. 93–52 B.C.), noted for his ruthless and licentious behavior and for his enmity toward Cicero. He was murdered by Titus Annius Milo, whose defense Cicero agreed to undertake.

words were his weapons. But let it be so, that he has defeated Anthony; where is the victory, if, curing one mischief, it introduce a worse? And what avails it to have extinguished the tyranny of Anthony, if he who has done it erect another in its room more terrible, by being more durable? And yet thus will it be if we suffer it. These are articles in the conduct of Cicero, which shew that it is not the tyrant nor the tyranny that he fears; but it is only Anthony that he fears. If a man will have a tyrant, it is all one to me, whether he be more or less outrageous; it is the thing, it is the having a tyrant, which I dread.

"That Cicero is hastening to set up a tyrant, is plain, from actions as visible as sad. Octavius is all in all; a triumph is decreed him; his troops have largesses given them; he is loaded with flatteries, he is covered with honours. What shame for Cicero, to behold all this, and his own abject posture! His publick behaviour, and the speeches and motions which he makes in the Senate, all centering in his master; are they not a scandal to the great figure of that great consular, and a stain upon the renowned name of Cicero?

"You will read this with pain, as with pain I write it; but it is a task which you have put upon me. Besides, I know your thoughts of our publick affairs, and that desperate and extraordinary as they are, you think that, contrary to all appearance, they may be remedied by means that are ordinary. I do not however blame you, my dear Atticus; comfort yourself with hope; it is agreeable to your age, to the sweetness of your temper, and to your regard for your children: I do not therefore wonder that you are indolent and sanguine; which disposition of yours appears still farther to me, from the account which my friend Flavius[10] gave me of what passed between you and him.

"But to return to Cicero: Pray where is the difference between him and the servile Salvidenus?[11] Could that base retainer to Octavius struggle for the glory of his master with more labour and zeal than does Cicero? You will say, perhaps, that Cicero

10. Gaius *Flavius* (d. 42 B.C.), friend of Brutus who accompanied him to Philippi, where he fell in battle.

11. Quintus *Salvidienus* Rufus, an officer in Octavian's army and one of Octavian's advisors. He later sought to change his allegiance to Antony but was betrayed and forced to commit suicide in 40 B.C.

dreads still the remains of the civil war. This is wild: Can any one dread a beaten enemy, and yet apprehend nothing from the formidable power of one who commands a great army, elevated by victory? nor from the rashness of a young man, who may conquer the commonwealth by the means which enabled him to conquer for it? Does Cicero therefore make this mighty court to Octavius, because, having given him so much, he thinks it dangerous not to give him all! Oh the wretched folly of cowardice! thus to lessen your own security by consulting it; and to increase tyranny because you fear it! Is it not better to have nothing at all to fear, than thus to compound for the degrees of fear?

"The truth is, we too much dread poverty, banishment, and death; and our imagination swells their terrors beyond bounds. There are greater evils than these; and Cicero is mistaken if he thinks that there are not. And yet all goes well with him, if he be but humoured, if his opinion be regarded, if his suits be granted; if he be courted and extolled: He has no quarrel to servitude, provided it be accompanied with honour and lustre; if there can be any such thing as honour and lustre in this lowest, this vilest lot of human nature.

"Octavius may indeed call him Father Cicero, refer every thing to his counsel, sooth him with praises, and shew great gratitude and fondness towards him, while he loses nothing by all this, which is only a fair outside and fine words. Facts speak the plainest truth, and they effectually contradict the above appearances. For, can there be a greater insult upon common-sense, than for Octavius to take for a father that man who is no longer in the number of freemen?

"Whither then tend all these compliances, all this zeal of Cicero for Octavius? Why, only to this; that Octavius may be propitious to Cicero. In this little, worthless, shameful point center all the actions and designs of the great Cicero! Hence it is that I value no longer, in the person of Cicero, those arts and accomplishments with which, doubtless, his soul is vastly replenished. What is he the better, himself, for so many excellent precepts, so many noble discourses, every where found in his works, concerning publick liberty, true and solid glory, the contempt of death, exile, and want?

How much better does Philippus[12] understand all those fine rules laid down by Cicero, than Cicero himself does, who pays more homage to Octavius than Philippus, who is father-in-law to Octavius, pays?

"Let Cicero therefore cease glorying thus vainly in our grief, which also ought to be his: For, to repeat what I have already said, what advantage can we draw from a victory, which only translates the pernicious power of Mark Anthony to a new usurper? And yet, by your letter, I perceive that it is still a doubt whether Mark Anthony be entirely defeated.

"After all, since Cicero can live a dependent and a slave, let him live a dependent and a slave. It ought not to be otherwise, if he can thus shamefully forget his reverend age, the illustrious honours which he has borne, and the memorable parts which he has performed.

"For myself, while I live, I will make war upon tyranny; that is, upon all exorbitant power that lifts men above the laws: Nor can any condition of servitude, however advantageous and alluring, divert me from this great, this worthy purpose: Nor could Anthony shake it, though he really were, what you say he is, a man of worth; a character which contradicts my constant opinion of him. The judgment and spirit of our ancestors are mine; they would not have their father for their tyrant, nor would I.

"All this openness to you is the result of my affection for you; nor could I have said so much, had I not loved you as well as Cicero thinks he is beloved by Octavius. That all these sad truths affect not you so much as they do me, is my concern; especially since to an eminent fondness for all your friends, you have added a particular fondness for Cicero. As to myself, I beg you to believe that my affection for him is still the same, though my esteem of him is greatly abated: Nor can I help it, it being impossible to judge ill or well of men and things, but according as they appear ill or well. . . ."

12. Lucius Marcius *Philippus*, Octavian's stepfather and consul in 56 B.C. He is reported to have supported a compromise between the Senate and Mark Antony.

NO. 31. SATURDAY, MAY 27, 1721.

❧ *Considerations on the Weakness and Inconsistencies of human Nature.*

SIR,

The study of human nature has, ever since I could study any thing, been a principal pleasure and employment of mine; a study as useful, as the discoveries made by it are for the most part melancholy. It cannot but be irksome to a good-natured man, to find that there is nothing so terrible or mischievous, but human nature is capable of it; and yet he who knows little of human nature, will never know much of the affairs of the world, which every where derive their motion and situation from the humours and passions of men.

It shews the violent bent of human nature to evil, that even the Christian religion has not been able to tame the restless appetites of men, always pushing them into enormities and violences, in direct opposition to the spirit and declarations of the gospel, which commands us to *do unto all men what we would have all men do unto us.* The general practice of the world is an open contradiction and contempt of this excellent, this divine rule; which alone, were it observed, would restore honesty and happiness to mankind, who, in their present state of corruption, are for ever dealing treacherously or outrageously with one another, out of an ill-judging fondness for themselves.

Nay, the peaceable, the beneficent, the forgiving Christian religion, is made the cause of perpetual hatred, animosity, quarrels, violence, devastation, and oppression; and the apostles, in spite of all their poverty, disinterestedness, and love of mankind, are made to justify their pretended successors of the Church of Rome, in engrossing to themselves the wealth and power of the earth; and in bringing mankind under a yoke of servitude, more terrible, more expensive, and more severe, than all the arts and delusions of paganism could ever bring them under: Of so much more force with the corrupt world are the destructive villainies and falsifications of men, than the benevolent and heavenly precepts of Jesus Christ.

The truth is, and it is a melancholy truth, that where human laws do not tie men's hands from wickedness, religion too seldom does; and the most certain security which we have against violence, is the security of the laws. Hence it is, that the making of laws supposes all men naturally wicked; and the surest mark of virtue is, the observation of laws that are virtuous: If therefore we would look for virtue in a nation, we must look for it in the nature of government; the name and model of their religion being no certain symptom nor cause of their virtue. The Italians profess the Christian religion, and the Turks are all infidels; are the Italians therefore more virtuous than the Turks? I believe no body will say that they are; at least those of them that live under absolute princes: On the contrary, it is certain, that as the subjects of the Great Turk are not more miserable than those of the Pope, so neither are they more wicked.

Of all the passions which belong to human nature, self-love is the strongest, and the root of all the rest; or, rather, all the different passions are only several names for the several operations of self-love. Self-love, says the Duke of Rochefoucauld, is the love of one's self, and of every thing else for one's own sake: It makes a man the idolater of himself, and the tyrant of others. He observes, that man is a mixture of contrarieties; imperious and supple, sincere and false, fearful and bold, merciful and cruel: He can sacrifice every pleasure to the getting of riches, and all his riches to a pleasure: He is fond of his preservation, and yet sometimes eager after his own destruction: He can flatter those whom he hates, destroy those whom he loves.[1]

This is a picture of mankind; and they who say it is a false one, ought to shew that they deserve a better. I have sometimes thought, that it was scarce possible to assert any thing concerning mankind, be it ever so good, or ever so evil, but it will prove true.

1. François, Duc de la Rochefoucauld (1613–1680), whose *Maximes* first appeared at The Hague in 1664. The edition marked "first" and which contained a number of additional maxims, was, in fact, not published until the following year. The maxim here cited appeared as no. 1 in the 1665 Paris "first" edition.

They are naturally innocent, yet fall naturally into the practice of vice; the greatest instances of virtue and villainy are to be found in one and the same person; and perhaps one and the same motive produces both. The observance or non-observance of a few frivolous customs shall unite them in strict friendship and confederacy, or set them a cutting one another's throats.

They never regard one another as men and rational beings, and upon the foot of their common humanity; but are cemented or divided by the force of words and habits. Considerations that are a disgrace to reason! The not being born in the same climate, or on this side such a river, or such a mountain, or the not wearing the like garments, or uttering the like sounds, or having the same thoughts or taste, are all so many causes of intense hatred, sometimes of mortal war. Whatever men think or do, especially if they have found a good name for it, be it ever so foolish or bad, is wisest and best in their own eyes: But this is not all; we will needs be plaguing our neighbours, if they do not quit upon our authority their own thoughts and practices for ours.

It fills me with concern, when I consider how men use one another; and how wretchedly their passions are employed: They scarce ever have proper objects for their passions; they will hate a man for what he cannot help, and what does them no harm; yet bless and pray for villains, that kill and oppress them. There never was such a dreadful tribunal under the sun as the Inquisition: A tribunal, against which the most innocent is not safe, to which the most virtuous men are most exposed; a tribunal, where all the malice, all the sagacious cruelty, all the bitterness, and all the fury and falsehood of devils are exerted, and all the tortures of hell are imitated and practised; yet this very tribunal is so dear to the people, though it terrifies them, enslaves them, and destroys them, that rather than part with it, they would part with all that is left them. Upon the surrender of Barcelona, in the late war, the inhabitants capitulated, that the Inquisition should not be taken from them:[2] And even here in England, we may remember the time when men

2. This claim has no basis in fact. Barcelona was at this time quite hostile to the Inquisition and efforts had been made, even before the start of the War of the Spanish Succession, to limit its authority.

have been knocked down for saying that they had a right to defend their property by force, when a tyrant attempted to rob them of it against law. To such a pitch of stupidity and distraction are people to be brought by those who belie Almighty God, and falsify his word to satiate worldly pride; and such dupes and furies are men to one another!

Every thing is so perverted and abused, and the best things most, that a very wise man had but too much reason to say, that truth did not so much good in the world, as the appearance and pretence of it did evil.[3] Thus the saving of men's souls is so universally understood to be a great and glorious blessing, that for the sake of it men have suffered, and do suffer, the highest misery and bondage from the impostors who pretend to bestow it, in the dark parts of the world, which are by far the greatest parts of the world. And thus civil government is the defence and security of human society; yet Dr. Prideaux makes it a doubt, whether the benefit which the world receives from government be sufficient to make amends for the calamities which it suffers from the follies, mistakes, and mal-administration of those that manage it.[4] And thus to come home to ourselves, a project to pay off the nation's debts was so tempting; so popular and plausible, that almost every body came into it; and yet—the consequences speak themselves.

The Roman Senate could flatter and adore a Nero and a Caligula; the Roman soldiers could butcher a Piso and a Pertinax:[5] It is hard to say which were the most guilty, the Senate while they worshipped tyranny, or the army while they destroyed virtue. So prone are men to propagate publick destruction for personal advantages and security! I can never think without horror and

3. La Rochefoucauld, *Maximes*, no. 73 in the 1665 edition.

4. Humphrey Prideaux, *The Old and New Testaments Connected in the History of the Jews and Neighbouring Nations, From the Declension of the Kingdoms of Israel and Judah to the Time of Christ* (4 vols.; London: Printed for R. Knaplock, 1725). The quotation appears in part II, bk. VI (IV:630).

5. Gaius Calpurnius *Piso*, head of a celebrated conspiracy against Nero in A.D. 65. He was forced to commit suicide rather than face the fury of his troops when the conspiracy was uncovered. Publius Helvius *Pertinax* (A.D. 126–193), Roman emperor who succeeded Commodus and whose administration is regarded as particularly prudent and mild. His attempts to reform the army led to his assassination in March of A.D. 193.

trembling upon that dismal, that bloody maxim of Philip II of Spain,[6] that he would rather be master of a kingdom ruined, miserable, and quiet; than of a kingdom rich, powerful, and turbulent. In pursuance of this maxim, he made his kingdom a desert, by destroying and expelling the most industrious of its inhabitants, the Moors: But Philip was very devout, and would frequently wash a pilgrim's feet; that is, he was very civil and charitable to an idle religious stroller, and a cruel enemy to the general happiness of mankind.

This puts me in mind of the history of John Basilowitz, Great Duke of Muscovy:[7]

> No history of his time but speaks of the unheard-of cruelties exercised by him on all sorts of persons through his whole reign: They are so horrid, that never any tyrant did the like; and yet Bishop Paulus Jovius gives him the character of a good and devout Christian, though he deserves not to be numbered even amongst men: It is true, he would go often to church, say the service himself, sing, and be present at ecclesiastical ceremonies, and execute the functions of the monks: but he abused both God and man, and had no sentiments of humanity.[8] Ambassadors Travels, p. 73, 74.

What a medley is here of devotion and cruelty in the same men! Nor are these examples singular. Louis XI of France[9] was a false, a wicked, and an oppressive prince, and one of the greatest bigots that ever lived; and some of the greatest saints in the Roman calendar[10] were pernicious villains, and bloody monsters. No sect

6. Philip II (1527–1598), who acceded to the Spanish throne in 1556. His attempts to impose religious conformity throughout his empire, including the Netherlands, contributed greatly to Spain's eventual ruin.

7. Ivan IV Vasilovitch, "the Terrible" (1530–1584), proclaimed Grand Duke of Moscow in 1533 and crowned the first Tsar of Russia in 1547.

8. Olearius's *The Voyages and Travels of the Ambassadors Sent by Frederick, Duke of Holstein, to the Great Duke of Moscovy*. The description of Ivan the Terrible quoted here appears in bk. III, chap. 11 (p. 98).

9. It is generally agreed that the policies of Louis XI (1423–1483) laid the foundations of absolutism in France. He has been described as the perfect model of a tyrant.

10. That is, the calendar of the Roman Catholic Church.

of bigots, when they are uppermost, are willing to tolerate another; and all ground their ungodly severity upon their zeal for religion; though their want of charity is a demonstration that they have no religion. It is certain, that without universal charity and forebearance, a man cannot be a Christian.

It is wonderful and affecting, to behold how the ideas of good and evil are confounded! The Turks place great devotion in releasing captive birds from their cages, in feeding indigent and mangey dogs, and building hospitals for them, and in paying a religious reverence to camels: But at the same time that they thus use birds and beasts like men and Christians, they use men and Christians worse than they do beasts; and with them it is a lighter offence to deny bread to a poor Christian, who is famished in his chains, than to the dogs of the street, which are fit for nothing but to breed infection. They will load a poor Christian with irons, cover him with stripes, and think that they do well and religiously in it; yet make it a matter of conscience not to overload a beast of burden.

In popish countries, in cases where nature is left to itself, as much compassion is shewn for the distressed as in other places: Even thieves, robbers, and murderers, are accompanied to the gallows or the wheel with sighs and tears; especially of the tender sex: But when an unhappy innocent is going to be burned, to be cruelly and slowly burned, for his sincerity and piety in speaking truth, and reading the Bible himself, or teaching it to others; nothing is to be seen but a general joy, nor to be heard but loud cries of approbation and consent; and all piety, all sympathy, is denied in an instance which calls for the highest. Tell a Spanish lady of a popish priest hanged in England for sedition or murder, she instantly falls into tears and agonies: Tell her of a kinsman of hers burned for denying transubstantiation, she gives glory to God, and feels a sensible joy.

And, in Protestant countries, how many men are there, who cheat, starve, and oppress all their life long, to leave an estate at their death to religious uses? As if men were to be rogues for God's sake. I have heard of a man, who having given half of his estate to mend highways, for the good of his country, said, that he would willingly give the other half, that England had never a ship, nor a merchant, nor a dissenter from the Church, belonging to it.

Strange inconsistency! By one act of his, two or three miles of causeway were kept in good repair, which was only a kindness to horses' hoofs; by another act of his, he would have made all England miserable and desolate!

The hardships and distresses of this year shew too manifestly the rogueries and depredations of the last: Villainy was let loose amongst us, and every man endeavoured to entrap and ruin another, to enrich himself. Honesty was brow-beaten and driven into corners; humanity was extinguished; all friendship was abolished; and even the distinction of kindred and ties of blood were discarded: A raging passion for immoderate gain had made men universally and intensely hard-hearted: They were every where devouring one another. And yet the directors and their accomplices, who were the acting instruments of all this outrageous madness and mischief, set up for wonderfully pious persons, while they were defying Almighty God, and plundering men; and they set apart a fund of subscriptions for charitable uses: That is, they mercilessly made a whole people beggars, and charitably supported a few necessitous and worthless favourites. I doubt not, but if the villainy had gone on with success, they would have had their names handed down to posterity with encomiums; as the names of other publick robbers have been! We have historians and odemakers now living, very proper for such a task. It is certain, that most people did, at one time, believe the directors to be great and worthy persons: And an honest country clergyman told me last summer, upon the road, that Sir John[11] was an excellent publick-spirited person, for that he had beautified his chancel.

Upon the whole, we must not judge of one another by our fair pretensions and best actions; since the worst men do some good, and all men make fine professions: But we must judge of men by the whole of their conduct, and the effects of it. Thorough honesty requires great and long proof; since many a man, long thought honest, has at length proved a knave. And it is from judging without proof, or too little, of false proof, that mankind continue unhappy.

G   *I am, &c.*

11. Sir John Aislabie, Chancellor of the Exchequer from 1718 to 1721 and one of those who profited most from South Sea Company bribes.

NO. 32. SATURDAY, JUNE 10, 1721.

༖   *Reflections upon Libelling.*

SIR,

I design in this letter to lay before the town some thoughts upon libelling; a sort of writing that hurts particular persons, without doing good to the publick; and a sort of writing much complained of amongst us at this time, with great ground, but not more than is pretended.

A libel is not the less a libel for being true. This may seem a contradiction; but it is neither one in law,[1] or in common sense: There are some truths not fit to be told; where, for example, the discovery of a small fault may do great mischief; or where the discovery of a great fault can do no good, there ought to be no discovery at all: And to make faults where there are none, is still worse.

But this doctrine only holds true as to private and personal failings; and it is quite otherwise when the crimes of men come to affect the publick. Nothing ought to be so dear to us as our country, and nothing ought to come in competition with its interests. Every crime against the publick is a great crime, though there be some greater than others. Ignorance and folly may be pleaded in alleviation of private offences; but when they come to be publick offences, they lose all benefit of such a plea: We are then no longer to consider only to what causes they are owing, but what evils they may produce; and here we shall readily find, that folly has overturned states, and private ignorance been the parent of publick confusion.

The exposing therefore of publick wickedness, as it is a duty which every man owes to truth and his country, can never be a libel in the nature of things; and they who call it so, make themselves no compliment. He who is affronted at the reading of the ten commandments, would make the decalogue a libel, if he durst; but he tempts us at the same time to form a judgment of his life

1. Gordon is here referring to the criminal law, where the falsity of the libel was not an essential element of the offense. In civil actions for libel, on the other hand, the truth of the statement constituted a sufficient defense.

and morals not at all to his advantage: Whoever calls publick and necessary truths, libels, does but apprize us of his own character, and arm us with caution against his designs. I doubt not but if the late directors had been above the Parliament, as they once thought themselves, they would have called the votes of the House of Commons against them, false and scandalous libels.

Machiavel says, Calumny is pernicious, but accusation beneficial, to a state;[2] and he shews instances where states have suffered or perished for not having, or for neglecting, the power to accuse great men who were criminals, or thought to be so; and hence grew the temptation and custom of slandering and reviling, which was the only remedy that the people had left them: So that the evil of calumny was owing to the want of justice, and the people were more blameless than those whom they reviled; who, having forced them upon a licentiousness of speech, did very unkindly chide and punish them for using it. Slander is certainly a very base and mean thing: But surely it cannot be more pernicious to calumniate even good men, than not to be able to accuse ill ones.

I have long thought, that the world are very much mistaken in their idea and distinction of libels. It has been hitherto generally understood that there were no other libels but those against magistrates, and those against private men: Now, to me there seems to be a third sort of libels, full as destructive as any of the former can possibly be; I mean, libels against the people. It was otherwise at Athens and Rome; where, though particular men, and even great men, were often treated with much freedom and severity, when they deserved it; yet the people, the body of the people, were spoken of with the utmost regard and reverence: "The sacred privileges of the people," "The inviolable majesty of the people," "The awful authority of the people," and "The unappealable judgment of the people," were phrases common in these wise, great, and free cities. Other modes of speech are since grown fashionable, and popular madness is now almost proverbial: But this madness of theirs, whenever it happens, is derived from external causes. Oppression, they say, will make a wise man mad; and delusion has not less force: But where there are neither oppressors

2. *Discourses*, I.8.2.

nor impostors, the judgment of the people in the business of property, the preservation of which is the principal business of government, does rarely err. Perhaps they are destitute of grimace, mystery, refinements, shrugs, dissimulation, and reserve, and the other accomplishments of courtiers: But as these are only masks to conceal the absence of honesty and sense, the people, who possess as they do the substance, have reason to despise such insipid and contemptible shadows.

Machiavel, in the chapter where he proves that a multitude is wiser and more constant than a prince, complains, that the credit which the people should be in declines daily; for, says he, every man has liberty to speak what he pleases against them; but against a prince no man can talk without a thousand apprehensions and dangers.[3] I have indeed often wondered, that the inveighing against the interest of the people, and calling their liberties in question, as has been and is commonly done among us by old knaves and young fools, has never been made an express crime.

I must own, I know not what treason is, if sapping and betraying the liberties of a people be not treason, in the eternal and original nature of things. Let it be remembered for whose sake government is, or could be, appointed; then let it be considered, who are more to be regarded, the governors or the governed. They indeed owe one another mutual duties; but if there be any transgressions committed, the side that is most obliged ought doubtless to bear the most: And yet it is so far otherwise, that almost all over the earth, the people, for one injury that they do their governors, receive ten thousand from them: Nay, in some countries, it is made death and damnation, not to bear all the oppressions and cruelties, which men made wanton by power inflict upon those that gave it them.

The truth is; if the people are suffered to keep their own, it is the most that they desire: But even this is a happiness which in few places falls to their lot; they are frequently robbed by those whom they pay to protect them. I know that it is a general charge against the people, that they are turbulent, restless, fickle, and unruly: Than which there can be nothing more untrue; for they

3. *Discourses*, I.58.10.

are only so where they are made so. As to their being fickle, it is so false, that, on the contrary, they have almost ever a strong bent to received customs, and as strong a partiality to names and families that they have been used to: And as to their being turbulent, it is as false; since there is scarce an example in an hundred years of any people's giving governors any uneasiness, till their governors had made them uneasy: Nay, for the most part, they bear many evils without returning one, and seldom throw off their burdens so long as they can stand under them.

But intending to handle this subject more at large in another letter,[4] I return more directly to the business of libels.

As to libels against government, like all others, they are always base and unlawful, and often mischievous; especially when governments are impudently charged with actions and designs of which they are not guilty. It is certain, that we ought not to enter into the private vices or weaknesses of governors, any further than their private vices enter into their publick administration; and when they do, it will be impossible to stop people's mouths: They will be provoked, and shew that they are so, in spite of art and threats, if they suffer hardships and woe from the private gratifications of their superiors, from whom they have a right to expect ease and happiness; and if they be disappointed, they will be apt to deal very freely with their characters.

In truth, most libels are purely personal; they fly at men rather than things; which proceeding is as injudicious as it is unmanly. It is mean to be quarrelling with faces, names, and private pleasures; things perfectly indifferent to the world, or things out of a man's own power; and 'tis silly, as it shews those whom we attack, that we attack them not for what they do, but for what they are: And this is to provoke them without mending them. All this therefore is libelling; an offence against which the laws of almost every country, and particularly of our own, have furnished a remedy in proportion to the consequence and quality of the person offended. And it is as just that reputation should be defended by law, as that property should.

4. The subject is touched upon again in Letter No. 36 (July 8, 1721).

The praise of well-doing is the highest reward that worthy and disinterested men aim at, and it is villainous and ungrateful to rob them of it; and those that do it, are libellers and slanderers. On the other hand, while censure and infamy attend evil-doers, it will be some restraint, if not upon them, yet upon others, from following their example: But if men be ever suffered to do what they please without hearing of it, or being accountable for it; liberty and law will be lost, though their names may remain. And whether acting wickedly with impunity, or speaking falsely with impunity, be likely to do most hurt to human society and the peace of the world, I leave all the world to judge: common equity says, that they both ought to be punished, though not both alike.

All libels, the higher they aim, the more malignity they acquire; and therefore when they strike at the person of the prince, the measure of their guilt is complete. The office of a prince is to defend his people and their properties; an excellent and a painful office; which, where it is executed with honesty and diligence, deserves the highest applause and reward; and whoever vilifies and traduces him, is an enemy to society and to mankind, and will be punished with the consent of all who love either. And yet it is scarce possible, in a free country, to punish by a general law any libel so much as it deserves; since such a law, consisting of so many branches, and being of such vast latitude, would make all writing whatsoever, how innocent soever, and even all speaking, unsafe. Hence it is, that in Turkey, though printing were permitted, it would be of no use, because no body would dare to make any use of it.

As long as there are such things as printing and writing, there will be libels: It is an evil arising out of a much greater good. And as to those who are for locking up the press, because it produces monsters, they ought to consider that so do the sun and the Nile; and that it is something better for the world to bear some particular inconveniencies arising from general blessings, than to be wholly deprived of fire and water.

Of all sorts of libels, scurrilous ones are certainly the most harmless and contemptible: Even truth suffers by ill-manners; and ill-manners prevent the effect of lies. The letter in the *Saturday's*

Post[5] of the 27th past does, I think, exceed all the scurrilities which I have either heard, or seen, from the press or the pulpit. The author of it must surely be mad: he talks as if distraction were in his head, and a firebrand in his hand; and nothing can be more false, than the insinuations which he makes, and the ugly resemblances which he would draw. The paper is a heap of falsehood and treason, delivered in the style and spirit of billingsgate;[6] and indeed most of the enemies to his Majesty's person, title, and government, have got the faculty of writing and talking, as if they had their education in that quarter.

However, as bad as that letter is (and, I think, there cannot be a worse), occasion will never be taken from scurrilous and traitorous writing, to destroy the end of writing. We know that in all times there have been men lying upon the watch to stifle liberty, under a pretence of suppressing libels; like the late King James, who, having occasion for an army to suppress Monmouth's Rebellion,[7] would needs keep it up afterwards; because, forsooth, other rebellions might happen, for which he was resolved to give cause.

I must own, that I would rather many libels should escape, than the liberty of the press should be infringed; yet no man in England thinks worse of libels than I do; especially of such as bid open defiance to the present Protestant establishment.

Corrupt men, who have given occasion for reproach, by their base and dark practices with the late directors, being afraid of truths that affect them from the press, may be desirous of shutting it up: But honest men, with clear reputations, which they know foul mouths cannot hurt, will always be for preserving it open, as a sure sign of liberty, and a cause of it.

5. *The Weekly Journal, or Saturday's Post*, a Tory organ. Gordon is here writing of seditious libel and the letter to which he refers is that signed "Decius," celebrating the anniversary of the restoration of the Stuarts in 1660. Referring to that day, the author at one point writes that "we saw the restoration of the monarchy in the royal house of Stuart, in the person of a prince endowed with a thousand shining qualities. Then those great names, Ormonde, Clarendon, and Southampton, honest hearts and able heads, presided at the helm of affairs. The college of bishops was filled more worthily than in any age since the apolitical one."

6. Billingsgate: coarse and abusive language.

7. An abortive insurrection against James II in 1685 led by James, Duke of Monmouth, the illegitimate son of Charles II.

The best way to escape the virulence of libels, is not to deserve them; but as innocence itself is not secure against the malignity of evil tongues, it is also necessary to punish them. However, it does not follow that the press is to be sunk, for the errors of the press. No body was ever yet so ridiculous to propose a law for restraining people from travelling upon the highway, because some who used the highway committed robberies.

It is commonly said, that no nation in the world would allow such papers to come abroad as England suffers; which is only saying, that no nation in the world enjoys the *liberty* which England enjoys. In countries where there is no liberty, there can be no ill effects of it. No body is punished at Constantinople for libelling: Nor is there any distinction there between the liberty of the press, and the licentiousness of the press; a distinction ever to be observed by honest men and freemen.

G   *I am, &c*

NO. 33. SATURDAY, JUNE 17, 1721.

Cautions against the natural Encroachments of Power.

SIR,

Considering what sort of a creature man is, it is scarce possible to put him under too many restraints, when he is possessed of great power: He may possibly use it well; but they act most prudently, who, supposing that he would use it ill, inclose him within certain bounds, and make it terrible to him to exceed them.

Men that are above all fear, soon grow above all shame. *Rupto pudore & metu, suo tantum ingenio utebatur,*[1] says Tacitus of Tiberius. Even Nero had lived a great while inoffensively, and reigned virtuously: But finding at last that he might do what he

---

1. A slight variation of Tacitus, *Annales*, 6.51. The original reads: *Postremo in scelera simul ac dedecora prorupit, postquam remoto pudore et metu suo tantum ingenio utebatur.* ("Finally, when all shame and fear had disappeared, he followed his own nature and descended into crime and into dishonor.")

would, he let loose his appetite for blood, and committed such mighty, such monstrous, such unnatural slaughters and outrages, as none but a heart bent on the study of cruelty could have devised. The good counsels of Seneca and Burrhus[2] were, for some time, checks upon his wolfish nature; and doubtless he apprehended, that if he made direct and downright war upon his people, they would use resistance and make reprisals: But discovering, by degrees, that they would bear any thing, and his soldiers would execute every thing, he grew into an open defiance with mankind, and daily and wantonly wallowed in their blood. Having no other rival, he seemed to rival himself, and every day's wickedness was blacker than another.

Yet Nero was not the worst of all men: There have been thousands as bad as he, and only wanted the same opportunity to shew it. And there actually have been many princes in the world who have shed more blood, and done more mischief to mankind, than Nero did. I could instance in a late one, who destroyed more lives than ever Nero destroyed, perhaps an hundred to one.[3] It makes no difference, that Nero committed butcheries out of cruelty, and the other only for his glory: However the world may be deceived by the change of names into an abhorrence of the one, and an admiration of the other; it is all one to a nation, when they are to be slaughtered, whether they be slaughtered by the hangman or by dragoons, in prison or in the field; nor is ambition better than cruelty, when it begets mischief as great.

It is nothing strange, that men, who think themselves unaccountable, should act unaccountably, and that all men would be unaccountable if they could: Even those who have done nothing to displease, do not know but some time or other they may; and no man cares to be at the entire mercy of another. Hence it is, that if every man had his will, all men would exercise dominion, and no

2. Lucius Annaeus *Seneca* (*c.* 3 B.C.–A.D. 65), Stoic philosopher who undertook the education of Nero and acted as his preceptor during his first five years as emperor. His name was mentioned in connection with Piso's conspiracy and Nero ordered him to commit suicide in A.D. 65. Sextus Afranius *Burrus* shared in directing Nero's education. By order of Nero, he was poisoned in A.D. 63.

3. Louis XIV of France.

man would suffer it. It is therefore owing more to the necessities of men, than to their inclinations, that they have put themselves under the restraint of laws, and appointed certain persons, called magistrates, to execute them; otherwise they would never be executed, scarce any man having such a degree of virtue as willingly to execute the laws upon himself; but, on the contrary, most men thinking them a grievance, when they come to meddle with themselves and their property. *Suarum legum auctor & eversor*,[4] was the character of Pompey: He made laws when they suited his occasions, and broke them when they thwarted his will. And it is the character of almost every man possessed of Pompey's power: They intend them for a security to themselves, and for a terror to others. This shews the distrust that men have of men; and this made a great philosopher call the state of nature, a state of war;[5] which definition is true in a restrained sense, since human societies and human laws are the effect of necessity and experience: Whereas were all men left to the boundless liberty which they claim from nature, every man would be interfering and quarrelling with another; every man would be plundering the acquisitions of another; the labour of one man would be the property of another; weakness would be the prey of force; and one man's industry would be the cause of another man's idleness.

Hence grew the necessity of government; which was the mutual contract of a number of men, agreeing upon certain terms of union and society, and putting themselves under penalties, if they violated these terms, which were called laws, and put into the hands of one or more men to execute. And thus men quitted part of their natural liberty to acquire civil security. But frequently the remedy proved worse than the disease; and human society had often no enemies so great as their own magistrates; who, wherever they were trusted with too much power, always abused it, and grew mischievous to those who made them what they were. Rome, while she was free (that is, while she kept her magistrates within

4. "The author and transgressor of his own laws." Tacitus, *Annales*, 3.28.

5. The reference here and in the remainder of this paragraph is, of course, to Thomas Hobbes. The theoretical discussion in the first part of the following paragraph, however, is closer to the position put forward by John Locke than to that of Hobbes.

due bounds) could defend herself against all the world, and conquer it: But being enslaved (that is, her magistrates having broke their bounds) she could not defend herself against her own single tyrants, nor could they defend her against her foreign foes and invaders; for by their madness and cruelties they had destroyed her virtue and spirit, and exhausted her strength. This shews that those magistrates that are at absolute defiance with a nation, either cannot subsist long, or will not suffer the nation to subsist long; and that mighty traitors, rather than fall themselves, will pull down their country.

What a dreadful spirit must that man possess, who can put a private appetite in balance against the universal good of his country, and of mankind! Alexander and Caesar were that sort of men; they would set the world on fire, and spill its blood, rather than not govern it. Caligula knew that he was hated, and deserved to be hated; but it did not mend him. *Oderint dum metuant*,[6] was his by-word: All that the monster aimed at, was to be great and terrible. Most of these tyrants died as became them; and, as they had reigned, by violence: But that did not mend their successors, who generally earned the fate of those that went before them, before they were warm in their place. *Invenit etiam aemulos infelix nequitia: Quid si floreat vigeatque?*[7] "If unfortunate villainy thus finds rivals, what shall we say, when it exalts its head and prospers?"

There is no evil under the sun but what is to be dreaded from men, who may do what they please with impunity: They seldom or never stop at certain degrees of mischief when they have power to go farther; but hurry on from wickedness to wickedness, as far and as fast as human malice can prompt human power. *Ubi semel recto deerratum est, in praeceps pervenitur—a rectis in vitia, a vitiis in prava, a pravis in praecipitia*, says a Roman historian;[8] who in this

6. "Let them hate, so long as they fear," attributed to Caligula by Suetonius (*Caligula*, 30).

7. "Even unfruitful wickedness finds imitators. What if it were to flourish and prosper?" Tacitus, *Historiae*, 4.42.

8. "Whenever one wanders from the right, one quickly descends into danger—from propriety to depravity, from depravity to crime, from crime to the abyss." Gaius Velleius Paterculus, *Res Gestae Divi Augusti*, 2.3.4 and 2.10.1. Velleius *Paterculus* (c. 19 B.C.– c. A.D. 31) was a Roman historian and minor military figure. Fragments alone remain of his sycophantic discussion of Tiberius.

speaks the truth, though in other instances he tells many lies; I mean that base flatterer of power, Velleius Paterculus. So that when we see any great mischief committed with safety, we may justly apprehend mischiefs still greater.

The world is governed by men, and men by their passions; which, being boundless and insatiable, are always terrible when they are not controuled. Who was ever satiated with riches, or surfeited with power, or tired with honours? There is a tradition concerning Alexander, that having penetrated to the Eastern Ocean, and ravaged as much of this world as he knew, he wept that there was never another world for him to conquer. This, whether true or no, shews the spirit of the man, and indeed of human nature, whose appetites are infinite.

People are ruined by their ignorance of human nature; which ignorance leads them to credulity, and too great a confidence in particular men. They fondly imagine that he, who, possessing a great deal by their favour, owes them great gratitude, and all good offices, will therefore return their kindness: But, alas! how often are they mistaken in their favourites and trustees; who, the more they have given them, are often the more incited to take all, and to return destruction for generous usage. The common people generally think that great men have great minds, and scorn base actions; which judgment is so false, that the basest and worst of all actions have been done by great men: Perhaps they have not picked private pockets, but they have done worse; they have often disturbed, deceived, and pillaged the world: And he who is capable of the highest mischief, is capable of the meanest: He who plunders a country of a million of money, would in suitable circumstances steal a silver spoon; and a conqueror, who steals and pillages a kingdom, would, in an humbler fortune, rifle a portmanteau, or rob an orchard.

Political jealousy, therefore, in the people, is a necessary and laudable passion. But in a chief magistrate, a jealousy of his people is not so justifiable, their ambition being only to preserve themselves; whereas it is natural for power to be striving to enlarge itself, and to be encroaching upon those that have none. The most laudable jealousy of a magistrate is to be jealous *for* his people;

which will shew that he loves them, and has used them well: But to be jealous *of* them, would denote that he has evil designs against them, and has used them ill. The people's jealousy tends to preserve liberty; and the prince's to destroy it. Venice is a glorious instance of the former, and so is England; and all nations who have lost their liberty, are melancholy proofs of the latter.

Power is naturally active, vigilant, and distrustful; which qualities in it push it upon all means and expedients to fortify itself, and upon destroying all opposition, and even all seeds of opposition, and make it restless as long as any thing stands in its way. It would do what it pleases, and have no check. Now, because liberty chastises and shortens power, therefore power would extinguish liberty; and consequently liberty has too much cause to be exceeding jealous, and always upon her defence. Power has many advantages over her; it has generally numerous guards, many creatures, and much treasure; besides, it has more craft and experience, less honesty and innocence: And whereas power can, and for the most part does, subsist where liberty is not, liberty cannot subsist without power; so that she has, as it were, the enemy always at her gates.

Some have said, that magistrates being accountable to none but God, ought to know no other restraint. But this reasoning is as frivolous as it is wicked; for no good man cares how many punishments and penalties lie in his way to an offence which he does not intend to commit: A man who does not mean to commit murder, is not sorry that murder is punished with death. And as to wicked men, their being accountable to God, whom they do not fear, is no security to use against their folly and malice; and to say that we ought to have no security against them, is to insult common sense, and give the lie to the first law of nature, that of self-preservation. Human reason says, that there is no obedience, no regard due to those rulers, who govern by no rule but their lust. Such men are no rulers; they are outlaws; who, being at defiance with God and man, are protected by no law of God, or of reason. By what precept, moral or divine, are we forbid to kill a wolf, or burn an infected ship? Is it unlawful to prevent wickedness and misery, and to resist the authors of them? Are crimes sanctified by their greatness? And is he who robs a country, and murders ten thousand, less a criminal, then he who steals single guineas, and takes away single lives? Is there any sin in preventing, and restraining, or resisting the greatest sin that can be committed, that of oppressing and destroying mankind by wholesale? Sure there never were such open, such shameless, such selfish impostors, as the advocates for lawless power! It is a damnable sin to oppress them; yet it is a damnable sin to oppose them when they oppress, or gain by oppression of others! When they are hurt themselves ever so little, or but think themselves hurt, they are the loudest of all men in their complaints, and the most outrageous in their behaviour: But when others are plundered, oppressed, and butchered, complaints are sedition; and to seek redress, is damnation. Is not this to be the authors of all wickedness and falsehood?

To conclude: Power, without control, appertains to God alone; and no man ought to be trusted with what no man is equal to. In truth there are so many passions, and inconsistencies, and so much selfishness, belonging to human nature, that we can scarce be too much upon our guard against each other. The only security which we can have that men will be honest, is to make it their interest to be honest; and the best defence which we can have against their being knaves, is to make it terrible to them to be knaves. As there are many men wicked in some stations, who would be innocent in others; the best way is to make wickedness unsafe in any station.

I am, &c.

P. S. This letter is the sequel of that upon human nature;[9] and both are intended for an introduction to a paper which I intend to write upon the restraints which all wise nations put upon their magistrates.

G

The End of the First Volume.

9. See Letter No. 31 (May 27, 1721).

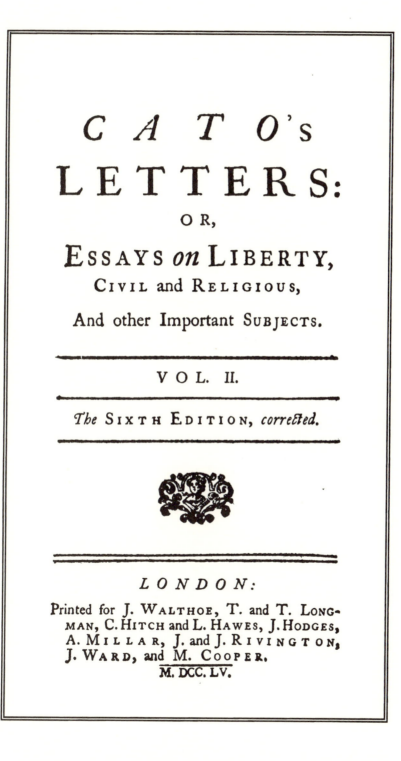

C A T O's
L E T T E R S:
O R,
Essays *on* Liberty,
Civil and Religious,

And other Important Subjects.

V O L. II.

The Sixth Edition, *corrected.*

L O N D O N:
Printed for J. Walthoe, T. and T. Long-
man, C. Hitch and L. Hawes, J. Hodges,
A. Millar, J. and J. Rivington,
J. Ward, and M. Cooper,
M. DCC. LV.

❦ *Of Flattery.*

SIR,

Flattery is a poisonous and pernicious weed, which grows and prevails every where, but most where it does most harm; I mean in courts. If few dare speak the truth to their superiors, how shall he who has no superiors ever come to know the truth? Perhaps there never was an instance in the world, where a prince was told the sincere truth in every thing which concerned him to know, by any servant of his. Truth is of a plain, unalterable nature, and cannot be moulded into fashionable shapes; truth is therefore unfit to be a courtier: But falsehood, being the creature of the imagination, is capable of bearing all modish and pleasing forms; falsehood is therefore an agreeable guest in palaces. To illustrate this, endless examples might be brought; but unfortunate princes are the most pregnant examples. Galba,[1] when he had lost all, and nothing remained to him but his life, which he was also soon to lose, had not one about him to tell him his condition and danger; so cruelly dishonest were his servants! Their flattery prevented the means of his preservation. They therefore were the first murderers of their master.

Nothing more is necessary in order to be flattered, than to be uppermost. Galba was hated for his avarice, and despised for his age and severity; yet, in compliance to an emperor, multitudes

---

1. Servius Sulpicius *Galba* (*c.* 3 B.C.–A.D. 69), Roman military commander who became emperor on the death of Nero in A.D. 68.

of people, and particularly of senators and gentlemen, addressed him to put Otho[2] to death, and to banish all his accomplices: And a rumour being spread, that Otho was slain, the same set of flatterers ran to the palace with noisy congratulations, and deceitfully complained that fate had snatched the usurper from their vengeance.

What marks were here of loyalty to Galba's person, and of zeal and firmness to his interest! yet in so small a space as two hours after, Otho's power having prevailed in Rome, Otho had their hearts and their acclamations in his turn, and Galba's death was demanded of him with the same importunity that the death of Otho had been demanded of Galba, and by the same men.

A melancholy lesson of the vile fraudulency of flatterers, and of the blindness of princes who trust in them! Even Galba, who was thought proof against flatterers (*adversus blandientes incorruptus*[3]) was deceived by them.

The Sieur Amelot de la Houssaye, from whom many of these observations are taken, says truly, that most princes are better armed against fear than against flattery:[4] Terrors animate them, and threats whet their courage; but flattery softens their minds, and corrupts their manners; it makes them negligent and idle, and forget their duty. *Corrupta mens assiduis adulationibus*, says Tacitus of Domitian.[5] Besides, mistaking flattery for complaisance (which is a sign of affection) they think that those who flatter them love them, and from that delusion come to trust and employ their most dangerous enemies. He further says, that Philip II of Spain

---

2. Marcus Salvius *Otho* (A.D. 32–69), dissolute friend of Nero who, upon finding that the emperor Galba would not appoint him his successor, had Galba assassinated and made himself emperor.

3. "Incorruptible against flattery," said by Tacitus of the emperor Galba (*Historiae*, 1.35).

4. Abraham Nicholas Amelot de la Houssaye (1634–1706), whose edition of Balthazar Gracián's *The Art of Prudence: or, Companion for a Man of Sense* (2d ed., corr.; London: Printed for Daniel Brown, etc., 1705) was extremely popular. See maxim 84, where Amelot notes that Pythagoras remarked that those who reprimand us are greater friends than those who flatter us (p. 88).

5. "A man corrupted by unceasing adulation." Tacitus, *Agricola*, 43.4. Titus Flavius *Domitianus*, the younger son of Vespasian and brother of the emperor Titus, was Roman emperor from A.D. 81 to 96. Although the first years of his reign are reputed to have been fairly benign, Domitian's conduct soon degenerated into vice and tyranny.

was wont to interrupt those who went about to flatter him, by saying to them roundly, "Cease trifling, and tell me what it concerns me to know":[6] Words worthy of all princes, who are never entertained by their flatterers but with things useless or pernicious. If princes never heard any thing but what they ought to know, they would never hear flatterers.

Flattery is a false and selfish thing, begot only by fear or favour; and having itself only in view, it observes no rule of equity or merit, but praises and calumniates, just according as men are exalted or depressed. Mezeray[7] tells us, that as long as Henry III of France built magnificent monasteries, and plunged himself into monkish devotions, ill-becoming his dignity, the monks revered him as a saint, and called him one: But no sooner was the religious and seditious League formed against him, but these godly ingrates loaded him with all the reproaches and ill names that they could devise; tyrant, hypocrite, murderer, and abominable, were the titles which they gave him; and at last they butchered him as a heretick:[8] So easily can flatterers make one and the same man a god or devil; and so true is it that flatterers love no man, and only court the fortunes of men. Flattery is venal, and always goes to the best bidder; and it is servile, and always crouches most to those who are uppermost, let them be what they will: *Adulationi foedum crimen servitutis inest.*[9] Most of the evil that princes commit, comes from the lessons and compliance of flatterers; and to such most princes have owed their ruin: Few princes would have done what many of them did, if their false friends had not told them that they

6. The quotation does not appear in Amelot's notes to Gracián's book.

7. François Eudes de Mézeray (1610–1683), author of the *Histoire de France, depuis Faramond jusqu'a maintenant* (3 vols.; Paris: Chez M. Guillemot, 1643–1651). The English translation, by John Bulteel, bears the title *A General Chronological History of France, Beginning before the Reign of King Pharamond and Ending with the Reign of King Henry the Fourth* (London: Printed by T.N. for Thomas Basset, etc., 1683). See pp. 737–796 for his discussion of Henry III.

8. Henry III (1551–1589), the third son of Henry II and Catherine de' Medici to become King of France. The disgust aroused by his compromises with the Huguenots led to the formation of the Holy League, which, in alliance with Philip II of Spain, sought the destruction of the reform party and the elevation of Henry, Duke of Guise, to the French throne. In 1589, partially to retaliate for the murder of the Duke of Guise, Henry was assassinated by Jacques Clément, a Dominican friar.

9. "Adulation is subject to the ignoble charge of servility." Tacitus, *Historiae*, 1.1.

might do what they would: We have had many instances of this at home, and there have been more abroad. It would be a great advantage to princes, if they would remember that there never was a prince in the world but was flattered, and never a prince but was hurt by flattery, and many utterly undone by it. It has made good princes bad, and bad worse: By flattery they have been brought to think themselves more than men, and to act worse than brutes; and, in fine, to live and die as beasts of prey live and die, in blood. Their flatterers having made them worse than men, adored them like gods: But, as Pliny says, *principum exitus docuit ne a diis quidem amari nisi quos homines ament.*[10]

Their business is to tell their great patron what pleases him, though it destroy him; and when they have deprived him of all his friends, his innocence, his felicity, and his possessions, they leave him too; or having ruined his fortune, they take away his life, which is their last and best civility: For flattery ends ever in ingratitude, and often in treason; and for princes to be often distressed by those whom they have obliged most, is nothing new.

Flattery is always great in proportion as its patrons are bad. And therefore Pliny observes, that those emperors who were most hated, were likewise most flattered: For he says, "that dissimulation is more ingenious and artful than sincerity, slavery than liberty, fear than love."[11] Hence flattery is a sign of servitude, and inconsistent with equality, and with liberty, the offspring of equality. It is indeed one of the purposes of flattery to make men worse; it gains by corruption, and lives upon credulity, folly, and vice. It is particularly at perpetual enmity with truth; and flatterers are like liars, not to be believed even when they speak truth. I have somewhere heard flatterers compared to thieves, who break into houses by night; the first thing that they do, is to extinguish the lights: So flatterers, when they have beset a prince, or any other great man, never fail to keep far from him all light and information.

Flattery is cruel, and gives bloody counsels; and flatterers are constant and merciless calumniators: Every word which they do not like, is a libel; every action that displeases them, is treason

10. "The fate of the emperors before you instructs us that no one is loved by the gods whom men do not love." Pliny the Younger, *Panegyricus*, 72.4.

11. Pliny the Younger, *Panegyricus*, 55.2–3.

or sedition: Where there are no faults, they create them. The crimes objected to the honest and excellent Thrasea Petus,[12] were such as these:

> That he had never applauded Nero, nor encouraged others to applaud him; that when the Senate were running into all the extravagancies of flattery, he would not be present, and therefore had not been in it for three years; that he had never sacrificed for Nero's charming voice; that he would never own Madam Poppaea[13] for a goddess, she who had been Nero's mistress, and was then his wife; that he would not vote that a gentleman who had made satirical verses upon Nero should be put to death, though he condemned the man and his libel; but he contended that no law made the offence capital; that they could not, without scandal, and the imputation of cruelty, punish with death, an offence for which the laws had already provided a punishment that was milder.[14]

These were the honourable and virtuous crimes of that great and good man; but they were then high treason, and cost him his life. Memorable are the words of Philip de Comines, speaking of court flatterers:

> If a six-penny tax be to be raised, they cry it ought by all means to be a twelve-penny one. If the prince be offended with any man, they are directly for hanging him. In other instances, they maintain the same character. Above all things, they advise their master to make himself terrible; as they themselves are proud, fierce, and overbearing, in hopes to be dreaded by that means, as if authority and place were their inheritance.[15]

12. Publius Clodius *Thrasea Paetus* (d. A.D. 66), Stoic philosopher celebrated for his independence of mind. He was condemned to death by the Senate by command of the emperor Nero.

13. *Poppaea* Sabina, wife of Otho and mistress, and later wife, of the emperor Nero. She is reputed to have died from a kick that Nero administered to her while she was pregnant with his child.

14. The quotation is a free rendering of Tacitus, *Annales*, 16.21–22.

15. Philippe de Comines, Sieur d'Argenton, author of his *Memoirs* covering the reigns of Louis XI and Charles VIII of France. The quotation appears in bk. V, chap. 19, *The Memoirs of Philip de Comines, Lord of Argenton* (rev. and corr.; London: Printed for John Starkey, 1674): 34.

As all honest truths affect such men, whatever is said against ill men, they construe to be said against them: And even when they are praised, they cry they are abused, and that such praise is rank irony. Now all this is very impolitick: Good men neither fear libels, nor suspect applauses to be ironies. Pliny says justly to Trajan,

> When I speak of your humanity, liberality, frugality, clemency, vigilance, &c. I have no apprehension that your Majesty will think yourself reproached with the contrary vices.[16]

But it was not so in some preceding reigns, when virtue was dangerous, truth capital, and every book that contained either was burnt, and its author put to death: By which violent and unjust proceedings, they hoped to shut up for ever people's mouths, to abolish the liberty of the Senate, and utterly to extinguish the memories of good men. Not satisfied with killing the authors, they exercised their rage upon their works, and appointed a junto called *Triumviri*,[17] to destroy the fruits of the greatest geniuses by fire.

I have scarce ever heard of a more gross or ingenious piece of flattery, than that of Vitellius[18] to Caligula, upon the following occasion: That mad emperor had taken it into his head to be a god, and thought he might debauch some of the she-deities, as well as he had his sisters; he therefore asked Vitellius this question, "Pray, Vitellius," says he, "have you never seen me embrace the Moon?" "O Sir," says the parasite, "that is a mystery which none but a god, such as your Majesty, ought to reveal."[19] Vitellius was one of those, *quibus principum honesta atque inhonesta laudare mos est*;[20] who praise every thing that their prince does, whether good or bad. Flattery therefore is never at the height, till liberty and virtue are utterly

16. Pliny the Younger, *Panegyricus*, 3.4.

17. The term here refers to a governing board consisting of three members.

18. Lucius *Vitellius* (d. A.D. 52), father of the emperor Vitellius. He is reputed to have been the first to worship Caligula as a god.

19. The anecdote appears in Dio Cassius, 59.27.6.

20. "For whom it was the custom to praise the honest and dishonest deeds of the emperor." Tacitus, *Annales*, 2.38.

lost; and with the loss of liberty, shame and honour are lost. Tacitus, who never mentions the woes of his country without seeming to feel them, talking of Sejanus, who having got the whole administration into his hands, was now the chief idol at Rome, makes M. Terentius[21] say with indignation,

> We worshipped his manumised slaves, and prostituted ourselves to his former footmen; and to be acquainted with his porter, was a mighty honour.[22]

As flatterers make tyrants, tyrants make flatterers; neither is it possible that any prince could be a tyrant without them: He must have servile hands to execute his will, servile mouths to approve it. It was with great fear that Nero ordered the murder of his mother, though he had wicked counsellors enough to advise and applaud it; and when he had done it, he was thunder-struck and distracted with apprehensions of the consequences: But finding flattery from all hands, instead of resentment from any, he grew outrageously abandoned, and plunged into all licentiousness and infamy: Had it not been for flatterers, the middle and end of his reign might have been as good as the beginning, than which there was scarce ever a better.

I have said enough to shew the vileness and mischief of flattery; a vice which has finally ruined many nations, and many princes, and one time or other hurt all. Let us be thankful that we are not at the cruel mercy of flatterers, and have a prince who we firmly believe will never be led or perverted by them; we hope that he will never have bad counsel given him, and would reject it, if it were: We know his honest purposes, and great moderation; and confess with gratitude, that during his whole reign no outrages have been committed upon the lives and fortunes of any of his subjects; and that the protection of the law has been as strong and

21. Marcus *Terentius*, an intimate of Sejanus who was implicated in Sejanus's intrigues by the Senate, but was acquitted of the charge.

22. *Annales*, 6.8. The Latin reads *libertis quoque ac ianitoribus eius notescere pro magnifico accipiebatur*. ("It was regarded as nobly done if we grew known to his very freedmen and his janitors.")

extensive, as ever it was, or ought to be. I could say more, but I stop here; for the greatest honour that can be done a prince, is, to suppose him above flattery, and to avoid for his sake the appearance of it, when we speak to him, or of him.

G   *I am, &c.*

NO. 35. SATURDAY, JULY 1, 1721.

Of publick Spirit.

SIR,

The love of one's country, or *publick spirit*, is a phrase in every body's mouth, but it seldom goes deeper; it is talked of without being felt: Some mention it without having any ideas at all of it, but only as a fine thing which every body likes, and a good quality which one would not seem to be without.

Others, when they name it, intend only some poor and selfish gratification of their own: Thus with great men, it is wealth and empire, to do what they list, and to get what they can; which is direct faction, or promoting, under colour of the publick, those views which are inconsistent with it. Thus with the trader and artificer, it is the encouraging only that sort of art or ware in which he himself deals; and this is monopoly and engrossing, ever mischievous to the publick.

In popish countries, it is publick spirit to build and beautify many churches, at the expense of the poor people; who must also maintain, at a further expense, a long band of luxurious ecclesiasticks, to play tricks in them; or, in other words, to keep the heads and pockets of their deluded hearers as empty as they can. It is moreover great publick spirit, to adorn an old skull with pearl and diamonds, and to enrich a venerable rotten tooth with gold and emeralds, of a value sufficient to maintain a city and all its inhabitants, who yet perhaps are starved by doing it. It is likewise very publick-spirited there, for a man to starve his family and his posterity, to endow a monastery, and to feed, or rather gorge, a fraternity of reverend gluttons, professed foes to truth and peace, and to the prosperity of the world; idlers, maintained to gormandize and deceive. This, forsooth, is publick spirit; to rob the country of its hands, to rear up a pernicious and turbulent mob of drones, in principles destructive of liberty, and to bring up enemies to a country at its own charges.[1]

In arbitrary countries, it is publick spirit to be blind slaves to the blind will of the prince, and to slaughter or be slaughtered for him at his pleasure: But in Protestant free countries, publick spirit is another thing; it is to combat force and delusion; it is to reconcile the true interests of the governed and governors; it is to expose impostors, and to resist oppressors; it is to maintain the people in liberty, plenty, ease, and security.

This is publick spirit; which contains in it every laudable passion, and takes in parents, kindred, friends, neighbours, and every thing dear to mankind; it is the highest virtue, and contains in it almost all others; steadfastness to good purposes, fidelity to one's trust, resolution in difficulties, defiance of danger, contempt of death, and impartial benevolence to all mankind. It is a passion to promote universal good, with personal pain, loss, and peril: It is one man's care for many, and the concern of every man for all.

Consider this picture, O ye great patriots and guardians of the earth, and try if you resemble it! Whom have ye exalted for his own merits, whom cast down for the sake of your country? What advantages have you acquired to your nation, with loss to yourselves? And have your people's losses never been your gains?

Out of England these questions cannot well be answered; nor could they in England formerly.

If my character of publick spirit be thought too heroick, at least for the living generation, who are indeed but babes in that virtue; I will readily own, that every man has a right and a call to provide for himself, to attend upon his own affairs, and to study his own happiness. All that I contend for is, that this duty of a man to himself be performed subsequently to the general welfare, and consistently with it. The affairs of all should be minded preferably to the affairs of one, as every man is ready to own when his own particular is embarked with the whole; as indeed every man's will

1. To bring up enemies to a country at its own charges: to raise the enemies of a country at its own expense.

prove to be sooner or later, though for a while some may thrive upon the publick ruins, but their fate seldom fails to meet them at last, them or their posterity.

It is a favourable sign of publick spirit, though not a certain sign, when the interest and reputation of men rise and increase together; and there is policy and wisdom in it. He who acquires money in spite of fame, pays dear for his avarice, while it returns him hatred and curses, as well as gold; and to be rich and detested, is to me no pleasing character. The same holds true in regard to ambition, and every other passion, which breaks its bounds, and makes a captive of its owner. It is scarce possible to be a rogue and be beloved; and when men are arrived to an insensibility of popular censure and opinion concerning their honesty and dishonesty, it is a sign that they are at defiance with the community where they live, and that the rest ought to be upon their guard against them; they do as it were cut themselves off from the society, and teach the people what to call them.

It is true, that great ill men never fail to have great court paid to their fortunes; which court their own self-love always construes to be paid to their persons: But there is a way to undeceive them, and it often happens; let them but sink into meanness, and they will soon find themselves sunk into contempt, which is the end of hatred when the object of hatred diminishes.

There is a sort of men found almost every where, who having got a set of gainful and favourite speculations, are always ready to spread and enforce them, and call their doing so *publick spirit*, though it often turns the world topsy-turvy: Like the mad monk at Heidelberg, who was for knocking every man on the head who did not like Rhenish wine, which it seems was his beloved liquor; perhaps he thought it was as reasonable to make all the world swallow Rhenish, as to make them swallow transubstantiation.

Opinions, bare opinions, signify no more to the world, than do the several tastes of men; and all mankind must be made of one complexion, of one size, and of one age, before they can be all made of the same mind. Those patrons therefore of dry[2]

2. Dry: insipid.

dreams, who do mischief to the world to make it better, are the pests and distressers of mankind, and shut themselves out from all pretence to the love of their country: Strange men! They would force all men into an absolute certainty about absolute uncertainties and contradictions; they would ascertain ambiguities, without removing them; and plague and punish men for having but five senses.

I would assert another proposition, as true as the last, though it may seem stranger; namely, that the taking a thousand or ten thousand pounds a year for the merit of helping to draw a hundred times as much from the people, is not publick spirit, whatever use may call it; and to grasp at all, and put a whole country in two or three pockets, is a sort of publick spirit, which I hope in God never to see, though there have been nations who have sorrowfully felt it.

As liberty can never subsist without equality, nor equality be long preserved without an agrarian law,[3] or something like it; so when men's riches are become immeasurably or surprizingly great, a people, who regard their own security, ought to make a strict enquiry how they come by them, and oblige them to take down their own size, for fear of terrifying the community, or mastering it. In every country, and under every government, particular men may be too rich.

If the Romans had well observed the agrarian law, by which the extent of every citizen's estate was ascertained, some citizens could never have risen so high as they did above others; and consequently, one man would never have been set above the rest, and have established, as Caesar did at last, a tyranny in that great and glorious state. I have always thought, that an enquiry into men's fortunes, especially monstrous fortunes raised out of the publick, like Milton's infernal palace,[4] as it were in an instant, was

3. The agrarian laws (*agrariae leges*) dealt with the distribution of Roman public land and provided for the transfer to the poorer citizens of allotments out of lands owned by the state. The term as here used refers to a law for the more equitable division of landed property.

4. Pandemonium, "city and proud seat of Lucifer" (*Paradise Lost*, X.424–425), which "rises suddenly out of the Deep" (argument to bk. I).

of more importance to a nation, than some other enquiries which I
have heard of.

But, will some say, is it a crime to be rich? Yes, certainly, at
the publick expense, or to the danger of the publick. A man may
be too rich for a subject; even the revenues of kings may be too
large. It is one of the effects of arbitrary power, that the prince has
too much, and the people too little; and such inequality may be the
cause too of arbitrary power. It is as astonishing as it is melancholy,
to travel through a whole country, as one may through many in
Europe, grasping under endless imposts, groaning under
dragoons and poverty, and all to make a wanton and luxurious
court, filled for the most with the worst and vilest of all men. Good
God! What hard-heartedness and barbarity, to starve perhaps half
a province, to make a gay garden! And yet sometimes even this
gross wickedness is called publick spirit, because forsooth a few
workmen and labourers are maintained out of the bread and the
blood of half a million.

In those countries, were the judgment of the people consulted, things would go better: But they are despised, and
esteemed by their governors happy enough, if they do not eat
grass; and having no representatives, or share in the government,
they have no remedy. Such indeed is their misery, that their case
would be greatly mended, if they could change conditions with the
beasts of the field; for then, being destined to be eaten, they would
be better fed: Such a misfortune is it to them that their governors
are not cannibals! Oh happy Britain, mayest thou continue ever so!

For a conclusion: As the preservation of property is the
source of national happiness; whoever violates property, or lessens
or endangers it, common sense says, that he is an enemy to his
country; and publick spirit says, that he should feel its vengeance.
As yet in England, we can speak such bold truths; and we never
dread to see the day, when it will be safer for one man to be a
traitor, than for another man, or for a whole people, to call him so.
Where-ever publick spirit is found dangerous, she will soon be
seen dead.

G   *I am, &c.*

NO. 36. SATURDAY, JULY 8, 1721.

Of Loyalty.

SIR,

Loyalty is a very good word; but, like most others, being wrested first by design, and afterwards by ignorance and custom, from its original and virtuous signification, does now frequently bear a very bad one. In an honest sense, indeed in common sense, it means no more than the squaring our actions by the rules of good laws, and an attachment to a constitution supported by such: And the French word *loyauté*, comes from another French word, which signifies law.

Other meanings have since been fathered upon that word, such as it abhors. To bear stupidly the wild or deliberate ill acts of a tyrant, overturning all law, and to assist him in it, has been impiously called *loyalty*; though it was all the while on the other side: As it is the very office and genius of loyalty to defend law, virtue, and property; and to pull down, as traitors and disloyalists, all who assault them.

Whoever is lawless, is disloyal; and to boast of loyalty to disloyalty, is strange nonsense; a paradox first invented by solemn and pernicious pedants, whose trade it is to pervert the use of words and the meaning of things, to abuse and confound the human understanding, and to mislead the world into misery and darkness.

To obey a prince, who does himself obey the laws, is confessed on all hands to be loyalty: Now, from hence, one would naturally think, that, by every rule of reason, it might be inferred, that to obey one who obeys no law, is a departure from all loyalty, and an outrage committed upon it; and that both he who commands, and he who obeys, are outlaws and disloyalists: And yet these same ungodly pedants shall maintain it to your face, that though loyalty consist in obeying a good prince, it also consists in the very contrary, and in obeying a wicked prince; who, though he be an enemy to God, is the vicegerent of God; and though he commit all wickedness, yet does it by divine right; and though it be a sin to obey him, yet it is a damnable sin to resist him: In short, that all the instruments and partners of his crying crimes are loyalists; and all who defend law, virtue, and mankind, against such monsters, are rebels, and assuredly damned, for preventing or resisting actions which deserve damnation: And thus men become rebels, by acting virtuously against the worst of all rebels, who are restrained by no consideration, human or divine.

Was ever such impudence, impiety, and nonsense, broached amongst pagans? In truth, they never would have been broached amongst Christians, had not sanctity been made a cloak for those who sold godliness for gain, and propagated imposture at the price of all that was virtuous and sacred.

Disloyalty is indeed rarely the crime of subjects and private men; and they who charge it most upon others, are they who practice it most themselves. King Richard II and Edward II were the greatest rebels in England in their own time: The greatest rebel in all Italy, is the Pope. Every lawless prince is a rebel, and the Grand Seignior is the greatest that is or can be in his own dominions. It is true, he is bound by no written law; but in this very thing he is a rebel: No man ought to be exempt from the ties of laws; and the higher any man is, the more ties he ought to be under. All power ought to be balanced with equal restraints, else it will certainly grow mischievous: He who knows no law, but his own lust, seldom observes any other. Besides, there are such things as the external laws of mercy, justice, and truth, legible by every man's natural reason, when it is not blinded by craft; and whoever observes not these, let him be called by what name he will, is a rebel to all the world, and it is loyalty to all the world to pursue him to destruction.

Brutus, who expelled the royal and rebellious race of the Tarquins, was the most loyal man in Rome; and his sons, who would have restored them, were the greatest rebels in Rome: The Roman people therefore acted justly, when they rewarded the father with the chief magistracy; and the father acted justly, when he sacrificed the traitors of his own loins to the liberties and resentments of the Roman people.

Some play with the words *sovereign* and *subject,* and divert themselves with the ridicule of obedience resisting command: But their wit and reasoning are alike wretched, whether they proceed from ignorance or dishonesty, as they often do from both; as if the world were to be guided by sound rather than sense, in things essential to its well-being. The highest and first sovereignty is in the laws, of which the prince has only the sovereign execution: In other words, it is his office and duty to see the laws obeyed; an employment which implies their superiority, and his own subjection.

A learned prince, who knew not much of government, and practised less than he knew,[1] did yet own, that a *King is only the chief servant of the state*. The law ought to be the measure of his power and actions, as much as of any private man's, and more; as his example is of greater influence, and as his opportunities and temptations to break them are greater than any private man's can be: And the only just reason that can be assigned why those crimes which are punished with death in a subject, have been often committed with impunity by a chief magistrate, was, because the station which he was in gave him such strength, and such a party, that to have punished him, the publick quiet must have been risked or shaken: And as to the inferior great traitors, the gain of their crimes and partners of their guilt protected them.

Exalted wickedness is the safest: I could name an English reign, in which, for above twenty years together, there scarce passed a week in which the prince did not venture his crown, and his ministers forfeit their heads.[2] And yet not one of these forfeitures were exacted: So corrupt and wicked was the government, and so tame and acquiescing were the people! Indeed the people in every country deserve the best usage, and in almost all meet with the worst: Their lot is very hard and unequal: They often pay millions, not only in their own wrong, but frequently to strengthen the hands of their oppressors: And this they generally do, without so much as a tumult; yet for one of them to coin a silver sixpence, is death and confiscation.

These things are obvious; yet how little are they considered! It is safer for a great man to rob a country, than for a poor

1. James I.
2. This appears to be a reference to the reign of Charles II.

man to steal a loaf: But the wages of villainy protect villains, and justice is only blind where the object is naked. But these are only complaints, which, we hope, we Britons will never have cause to make.

We have been formerly stunned with the big word *prerogative*, by those who contend for unlimited loyalty: Men, who while they reserve to themselves a right to be the most turbulent of all subjects, would make all others the tamest and the blindest of all slaves.[3] But what prerogative do they mean? I know no prerogative in the crown, which is not at the same time a certain privilege of the people, for their sake granted, and for their sake to be exerted: And where a prerogative is claimed in opposition to the rights and interests of the people, so far a tyranny is claimed; tyranny being nothing else but the government of one man, or of a few men, over many, against their inclination and interest: And where prerogative is exercised more to the hurt than the good of the governed, it is no longer prerogative, but violence and usurpation; and therefore in England several prerogatives have from time to time been taken from the crown, because the crown had abused them.

A certain British king[4] was wont to say, that so long as he could make bishops and judges, he would have what law and gospel he pleased. An impious and arbitrary saying, and a bold one coming from a prince of so mean a spirit, governing a brave and a free people, who were disgraced by his profuse and ridiculous reign, which is one of those that stain our annals. But for all the absurdity of his government, and the smallness of his soul, he found himself able, by the assistance of sycophants, to multiply and entail many evils upon these kingdoms. It is certain, that he and some of his posterity found such complaisant bishops and judges, that the religion and politicks of the court were generally the religion and politicks of Westminster-Hall, and of Henry VII's

3. James I had asserted the doctrine, so much favored by the Tudor monarchs, in his *The Trew Law of Free Monarchies*. The crown's prerogative was held to lie in the fact that the sovereign was duty-bound to govern; this entailed that he possessed all rights necessary to his governing with all required vigor. The Stuart monarchs often invoked the doctrine.

4. James I.

chapel: Absolute power in the crown was pleaded and granted in both those solemn places.

So wicked and merciless a thing is self-interest! Those grave men, who were by profession the guardians of truth and law, gave up both, to keep preferment, or to acquire it. How little are men to be trusted, and how little does religion bind them! They can break the strongest bands, violate the most awful oaths, and commit the most horrid, most extensive treacheries, for the vilest and most uncertain gratifications. I am therefore seldom surprized to hear of the most astonishing things and events, whether they be publick depredations and massacres, or private treacheries and parricides; having my mind constantly filled with examples that answer them, or exceed them, though perhaps they are not exactly of the same nature.

It is certain, that those judges, counsellors, and clergy, who have adjudged a dispensing and lawless power to kings, had, each of them, the guilt of a thousand private murtherers upon their head: They, as it were, signed a dead-warrant for their country; and, as much as in them lay, made themselves the authors of universal barbarity, slavery, infamy, and wretchedness; and of every other evil and wickedness, which is produced by that great source of all evil and wickedness, arbitrary power.

Of this we are sure, that the least publick guilt is greater than the greatest private guilt: Let every man concerned in publick trust, every where, consider this, and examine his own heart: Every step which a publick man takes, every speech which he makes, and every vote which he gives, may affect millions. Whoever acts in a great station against his conscience, might perhaps with more innocence carry a dagger, and like Old Muley stab twenty men a day.

Now were these judges and counsellors above-mentioned, loyalists? Yes, doubtless, if there are such things as loyal traitors. For, even supposing loyalty centered wholly in the person of the prince, than which nothing can be more false; yet even here it loses its name, since it is doing him the highest unkindness, as it separates him from his people, and their hearts from him, and as it tempts him to evil, loads him with infamy and guilt, and lessens his security; in truth, such loyalty is perfidiousness and flattery, and has cost many princes their lives and their kingdoms.

No good prince will pretend that there is any loyalty due to him further than he himself is loyal to the law, and observant of his people, the makers of kings and of laws. If any man, misled by sound and delusion doubt this, let him consider what is the design of magistracy, and what the duty of magistrates; and if he has reason in him, he will find that his duty is only due to those who perform theirs; that protection and allegiance are reciprocal; that every man has a right to defend what no man has a right to take: That the divine right of kings, if they had it, can only warrant them in doing actions that are divine, and cannot protect them in cruelty, depredation, and oppression: That a divine right to act wickedly, is a contradiction and blasphemy, as it is *maledictio supremi numinis*,[5] a reproach upon the Deity, as if he gave any man a commission to be a devil: That a King, in comparison with the universe, is not so much as a mayor of a town, in comparison with a kingdom; and that were Mr. Mayor called King, it would give him no new right; or, if a King were only called Mr. Mayor, it would not lessen nor abrogate his old jurisdiction: That they are both civil officers; and that an offence in the lesser is more pardonable than an offence in the greater: That the doctrines of unbroken hereditary right, and of blind obedience, are the flights and forgeries of flatterers, who belie heaven, and abuse men, to make their own court to power, and that not one of them will stand the trial himself: In fine, the government, honest and legal government, is *imperium legum non hominum*,[6] the authority of law, and not of lust.

These are the principles upon which our government stands, the principles upon which every free government must stand; and that we Britons dare tell such truths, and publish such principles, is a glorious proof of our civil and religious freedom: They are truths which every Briton ought to know, even children and servants: They are eternal truths, that will remain for ever, though in too many countries they are dangerous, or useless, or

5. "Abuse of the Supreme Being."
6. "The rule of law and not of men." The phrase *imperia legum potentiora quam hominum* ("laws superior in authority to men") appears in Livy, 2.1.1–2.

little known: They are truths, to which we are beholden for the present succession, and the present mild administration; and they are the principles of English loyalty, as well as of English liberty.

Before I have done, I would take notice of another mistake very common concerning loyalty: It is indeed a trick, more than a mistake; I mean of those who would assert or rather create a sort of loyalty to ministers, and make every thing which they do not like an offence against their master.

How endless are the arts and instances of deceiving! Yet the stalest artifices are still new. The above is a method which bad ministers have ever taken, but which good ones want not: Innocent ministers will never prostitute the name and authority of the prince, to protect their own faults and mistakes; and every wise and indifferent man will be for preserving him from the imputation of the guilt and folly of his servants, who, whenever they are for thrusting in their master between themselves and the censure or odium of their own actions, do at once acknowledge that their own actions are evil, and that they would barbarously and ungratefully make a screen of their sovereign, and save themselves upon his ruin or disgrace.

What can be more vile, what more disloyal, than this! Yet who were louder in their prate about loyalty, than the worst ministers have ever been; even while they were weakening their master's hands, creating him enemies, and setting him at variance with his people? This is so true, that it has been sometimes impossible to love the prince without abhorring his servants, and to serve them without hurting or abusing him. Yet while they were very loyally undoing him, it was forsooth high disloyalty to resist or expose them. Whoever would recollect instances of this, need not go out of Europe, nor above forty years backwards:[7] And for instances at home, as we can find no present ones, we fear none that are future.

G   *I am, &c.*

---

7. Probably a reference to the Tory ministers to Charles II during the last years of his reign.

NO. 37. SATURDAY, JULY 15, 1721.

ꝗ꙼   *Character of a good and of an evil Magistrate,*
    quoted from Algernon Sidney, Esq.

SIR,

The following are the sentiments of Mr. Sidney:[1] I know it is
objected that he is a republican; and it is dishonestly suggested that I am a republican, because I commend him as an excellent writer, and have taken a passage or two out of him. In answer
to this, I shall only take notice, that the passages which I take from
him are not republican passages, unless virtue and truth be repub-
licans: That Mr. Sidney's book, for the main of it, is eternally true,
and agreeable to our own constitution, which is the best republick
in the world, with a prince at the head of it: That our government
is a thousand degrees nearer a-kin to a commonwealth (any sort of
commonwealth now subsisting, or that ever did subsist in the
world) than it is to absolute monarchy: That for myself, I hope in
God never to see any other form of government in England than
that which is now in England; and that if this be the style and spirit
of a republican, I glory in it, as much as I despise those who take
base methods to decry my writings, which are addressed to the
common sense and experience of mankind. I hope that it is not yet
made heresy in politicks, to assert that two and two make four.

   G

   "The good magistrate seeks the good of the people committed to his care, that he may perform the end of his institution:
and knowing that chiefly to consist in justice and virtue, he
endeavours to plant and propagate them; and by doing this he
procures his own good, as well as that of the publick. He knows
there is no safety where there is no strength, no strength without
union, no union without justice, no justice where faith and truth in
accomplishing publick and private engagements is wanting. This

1. The excerpt is taken from Sidney's *Discourses*, chap. 3, sect. 19 (pp. 342–44)
of the 1751 edition).

he perpetually inculcates; and thinks it a great part of his duty, by precept and example to educate the youth in a love of virtue and truth, that they may be seasoned with them, and filled with an abhorrence of vice and falsehood, before they attain that age which is exposed to the most violent temptations, and in which they may by their crimes bring the greatest mischiefs upon the publick. He would do all this, though it were to his own prejudice. But as good actions always carry a reward with them, these contribute in a high measure to his advantage. By preferring the interest of the people before his own, he gains their affection, and all that is in their power comes with it; while he unites them to one another, he unites all to himself. In leading them to virtue, he increases their strength, and by that means provides for his own safety, glory, and power.

"On the other side, such as seek different ends must take different ways. When a magistrate fancies he is not made for the people, but the people for him; that he does not govern for them, but for himself; that the people live only to increase his glory, or to furnish matter for his pleasure; he does not enquire what he may do for them, but what he may draw from them: By this means he sets up an interest of profit, pleasure, or pomp in himself, repugnant to the good of the publick, for which he is made to be what he is. These contrary ends certainly divide the nation into parties; and while every one endeavours to advance that to which he is addicted, occasions of hatred, for injuries every day done, or thought to be done, and received, must necessarily arise. This creates a most fierce and irreconcilable enmity; because the occasions are frequent, important, and universal, and the causes thought to be most just. The people think it to be the greatest of all crimes to convert that power to their hurt, which was instituted for their good; and that the injustice is aggravated by perjury and ingratitude, which comprehend all manner of ill; and the magistrate gives the name of sedition and rebellion to whatsoever they do for the preservation of themselves and their own rights. When men's spirits are thus prepared, a small matter sets them on fire; but if no accident happens to blow them into a flame, the course of justice is certainly interrupted, the publick affairs are neglected; and when any occasion, whether foreign or domestick, arises, in which the magistrate stands in need of the people's assistance, they whose affections are alienated, not only shew an unwillingness to serve him with their persons and estates, but fear that by delivering him from his distress, they strengthen their enemy, and enable him to oppress them; and he, fancying his will to be unjustly opposed, or his due more unjustly denied, is filled with a dislike of what he sees, and a fear of worse for the future. Whilst he endeavours to ease himself of the one, and to provide against the other, he usually increases the evils of both; and jealousies are on both sides multiplied. Every man knows that the governed are in a great measure under the power of the governor; but as no man, or number of men, is willingly subject to those that seek their ruin, such as fall into so great a misfortune, continue no longer under it than force, fear, or necessity may be able to oblige them. But such a necessity can hardly lie longer upon a great people, than till the evil be fully discovered and comprehended, and their virtue, strength, and power be united to expel it: The ill magistrate looks upon all things that may conduce to that end as so many preparatives to his ruin; and by the help of those who are of his party, will endeavour to prevent that union, and diminish that strength, virtue, power and courage, which he knows to be bent against him. And as truth, faithful dealing, and integrity of manners, are bonds of union, and helps to good, he will always, by tricks, artifices, cavils, and all means possible, endeavour to establish falsehood and dishonesty; whilst other emissaries and instruments of iniquity, by corrupting the youth, and such as can be brought to lewdness and debauchery, bring the people to such a pass, that they may neither care nor dare to vindicate their rights; and that those who would do it may so far suspect each other, as not to confer upon, much less to join in, any action tending to the publick deliverance.

"This distinguishes the good from the bad magistrate; the faithful from the unfaithful; and those that adhere to either, living in the same principle, must walk in the same ways. They who uphold the rightful power of a just magistracy, encourage virtue and justice, and teach men what they ought to do, suffer, or expect

from others; they fix them upon principles of honesty, and generally advance every thing that tends to the increase of the valour,
strength, greatness, and happiness of the nation, creating a good
union among them, and bringing every man to an exact understanding of his own and the publick rights. On the other side he
that would introduce an ill magistrate, make one evil who was
good, or preserve him in the administration of injustice when he is
corrupted, must always open the way for him by vitiating the people, corrupting their manners, destroying the validity of oaths,
teaching such evasions, equivocations, and frauds, as are inconsistent with the thoughts that become men of virtue and courage;
and overthrowing the confidence they ought to have in each other,
make it impossible for them to unite amongst themselves. The like
arts must be used with the magistrate: He cannot be for their
turns, till he is persuaded to believe he has no dependence upon,
and owes no duty to, the people; that he is of himself, and not by
their institution; that no man ought to enquire into, nor be judge
of, his actions; that all obedience is due to him, whether he be good
or bad, wise or foolish, a father or an enemy to his country. This
being calculated for his personal interest, he must pursue the same
designs, or his kingdom is divided within itself, and cannot subsist.
By this means, those who flatter his humour come to be accounted
his friends, and the only men that are thought worthy of great
trusts; while such as are of another mind are exposed to all persecution. These are always such as excel in virtue, wisdom, and
greatness of spirit: They have eyes, and they will always see the
way they go; and leaving fools to be guided by implicit faith, will
distinguish between good and evil, and choose that which is best;
they will judge of men by their actions, and by them discovering
whose servant every man is, know whether he is to be obeyed or
not. Those who are ignorant of all good, careless, or enemies to it,
take a more compendious way: Their slavish, vicious, and base
natures, inclining them to seek only private and present advantage, they easily slide into a blind dependence upon one who has
wealth and power; and desiring only to know his will, care not
what injustice they do, if they may be rewarded. They worship

what they find in the temple, though it be the vilest of idols; and always like that best which is worst, because it agrees with their inclinations and principles. When a party comes to be erected upon such a foundation, debauchery, lewdness, and dishonesty are the true badges of it; such as wear them are cherished; but the principal marks of favour are reserved for them who are the most industrious in mischief, either by seducing the people with the allurements of sensual pleasures, or corrupting their understandings with false and slavish doctrines."

I am, &c.

NO. 38. SATURDAY, JULY 22, 1721.

The Right and Capacity of the People to judge of Government.

SIR,

The world has, from time to time, been led into such a long maze of mistakes, by those who gained by deceiving, that whoever would instruct mankind, must begin with removing their errors; and if they were every where honestly apprized of truth, and restored to their senses, there would not remain one nation of bigots or slaves under the sun: A happiness always to be wished, but never expected!

In most parts of the earth there is neither light nor liberty; and even in the best parts of it they are but little encouraged, and coldly maintained; there being, in all places, many engaged, through interest, in a perpetual conspiracy against them. They are the two greatest civil blessings, inseparable in their interests, and the mutual support of each other; and whoever would destroy one of them, must destroy both. Hence it is, that we every where find tyranny and imposture, ignorance and slavery, joined together; and oppressors and deceivers mutually aiding and paying constant court to each other. Where-ever truth is dangerous, liberty is precarious.

Of all the sciences that I know in the world, that of government concerns us most, and is the easiest to be known, and yet is the least understood. Most of those who manage it would make the lower world believe that there is I know not what difficulty and mystery in it, far above vulgar understandings; which proceeding of theirs is direct craft and imposture: Every ploughman knows a good government from a bad one, from the effects of it: he knows whether the fruits of his labour be his own, and whether he enjoy them in peace and security: And if he do not know the principles of government, it is for want of thinking and enquiry, for they lie open to common sense; but people are generally taught not to think of them at all, or to think wrong of them.

What is government, but a trust committed by all, or the most, to one, or a few, who are to attend upon the affairs of all, that every one may, with the more security, attend upon his own? A great and honourable trust; but too seldom honourably executed; those who possess it having it often more at heart to increase their power, than to make it useful; and to be terrible, rather than beneficent. It is therefore a trust, which ought to be bounded with many and strong restraints, because power renders men wanton, insolent to others, and fond of themselves. Every violation therefore of this trust, where such violation is considerable, ought to meet with proportionable punishment; and the smallest violation of it ought to meet with some, because indulgence to the least faults of magistrates may be cruelty to a whole people.

Honesty, diligence, and plain sense, are the only talents necessary for the executing of this trust; and the public good is its only end: As to refinements and finesses, they are often only the false appearances of wisdom and parts, and oftener tricks to hide guilt and emptiness; and they are generally mean and dishonest: they are the arts of jobbers in politicks, who, playing their own game under the publick cover, subsist upon poor shifts and expedients; starved politicians, who live from hand to mouth, from day to day, and following the little views of ambition, avarice, revenge, and the like personal passions, are ashamed to avow them, yet want souls great enough to forsake them; small wicked statesmen, who make a private market of the publick, and deceive it, in order to sell it.

These are the poor parts which great and good governors scorn to play, and cannot play; their designs, like their stations, being purely publick, are open and undisguised. They do not consider their people as their prey, nor lie in ambush for their subjects; nor dread, and treat and surprize them like enemies, as all ill magistrates do; who are not governors, but jailers and sponges, who chain them and squeeze them, and yet take it very ill if they do but murmur; which is yet much less than a people so abused ought to do. There have been times and countries, when publick ministers and publick enemies have been the same individual men. What a melancholy reflection is this, that the most terrible and mischievous foes to a nation should be its own magistrates! And yet in every enslaved country, which is almost every country, this is their woeful case.

Honesty and plainness go always together, and the makers and multipliers of mysteries, in the political way, are shrewdly to be suspected of dark designs. Cincinnatus was taken from the plough to save and defend the Roman state; an office which he executed honestly and successfully, without the grimace and gains of a statesman. Nor did he afterwards continue obstinately at the head of affairs, to form a party, raise a fortune, and settle himself in power: As he came into it with universal consent, he resigned it with universal applause.

It seems that government was not in those days become a trade, at least a gainful trade. Honest Cincinnatus was but a farmer: And happy had it been for the Romans, if, when they were enslaved, they could have taken the administration out of the hands of the emperors, and their refined politicians, and committed it to such farmers, or any farmers. It is certain, that many of their imperial governors acted more ridiculously than a board of ploughmen would have done, and more barbarously than a club of butchers could have done.

But some have said, It is not the business of private man to meddle with government. A bold, false, and dishonest saying; and whoever says it, either knows not what he says, or cares not, or slavishly speaks the sense of others. It is a cant now almost forgot in England, and which never prevailed but when liberty and the constitution were attacked, and never can prevail but upon the like occasion.

It is a vexation to be obliged to answer nonsense, and confute absurdities: But since it is and has been the great design of this paper[1] to maintain and explain the glorious principles of liberty, and to expose the arts of those who would darken or destroy them; I shall here particularly shew the wickedness and stupidity of the above saying; which is fit to come from no mouth but that of a tyrant or a slave, and can never be heard by any man of an honest and free soul, without horror and indignation: It is, in short, a saying, which ought to render the man who utters it for ever incapable of place or credit in a free country, as it shews the malignity of his heart, and the baseness of his nature, and as it is the pronouncing of a doom upon our constitution. A crime, or rather a complication of crimes, for which a lasting infamy ought to be but part of the punishment.

But to the falsehood of the thing: Publick truths ought never to be kept secrets; and they who do it, are guilty of a solecism, and a contradiction: Every man ought to know what it concerns all to know. Now, nothing upon earth is of a more universal nature than government; and every private man upon earth has a concern in it, because in it is concerned, and nearly and immediately concerned, his virtue, his property, and the security of his person: And where all these are best preserved and advanced, the government is best administered; and where they are not, the government is impotent, wicked, or unfortunate; and where the government is so, the people will be so, there being always and every where a certain sympathy and analogy between the nature of the government and the nature of the people. This holds true in every instance. Public men are the patterns of private; and the virtues and vices of the governors become quickly the virtues and vices of the governed.

Regis ad exemplum totus componitur orbis.[2]

1. That is, the *London Journal.*
2. "The world arranges itself after its ruler's pattern," a somewhat altered transcription of a line from one of the poet Claudian's panegyrics. *Panegyricus de quarto consulatu Honorii Augusti,* lines 299–300.

Nor is it example alone that does it. Ill governments, subsisting by vice and rapine, are jealous of private virtue, and enemies to private property. *Opes pro crimine; & ob virtutes certissimum exitium.*[3] They must be wicked and mischievous to be what they are; nor are they secure while any thing good or valuable is secure. Hence it is, that to drain, worry, and debauch their subjects, are the steady maxims of their politicks, their favourite arts of reigning. In this wretched situation the people, to be safe, must be poor and lewd: There will be but little industry where property is precarious; small honesty where virtue is dangerous.

Profuseness or frugality, and the like virtues or vices, which affect the publick, will be practised in the City, if they be practised in the court; and in the country, if they be in the City. Even Nero (that royal monster in man's shape) was adored by the common herd at Rome, as much as he was flattered by the great; and both the little and the great admired, or pretended to admire, his manners, and many to imitate them. Tacitus tells us, that those sort of people long lamented him, and rejoiced in the choice of a successor that resembled him, even the profligate Otho.[4]

Good government does, on the contrary, produce great virtue, much happiness, and many people. Greece and Italy, while they continued free, were each of them, for the number of inhabitants, like one continued city; for virtue, knowledge, and great men, they were the standards of the world; and that age and country that could come nearest to them, has ever since been reckoned the happiest. Their government, their free government, was the root of all these advantages, and of all this felicity and renown; and in these great and fortunate states the people were the principals in the government; laws were made by their judgment and authority, and by their voice and commands were magistrates created and condemned. The city of Rome could conquer the world; nor could the great Persian monarch, the greatest then upon earth, stand before the face of one Greek city.

3. "Wealth was tantamount to committing a crime and virtue brought certain destruction." Tacitus, *Historiae*, 1.2.
4. *Historiae*, 1.13.

But what are Greece and Italy now? Rome has in it a herd of pampered monks, and a few starving lay inhabitants; the Campania of Rome,[5] the finest spot of earth in Europe, is a desert. And for the modern Greeks, they are a few abject contemptible slaves, kept under ignorance, chains, and vileness, by the Turkish monarch, who keeps a great part of the globe intensely miserable, that he may seem great without being so.

Such is the difference between one government and another, and of such important concernment is the nature and administration of government to a people. And to say that private men have nothing to do with government, is to say that private men have nothing to do with their own happiness and misery.

What is the publick, but the collective body of private men, as every private man is a member of the publick? And as the whole ought to be concerned for the preservation of every private individual, it is the duty of every individual to be concerned for the whole, in which himself is included.

One man, or a few men, have often pretended the publick, and meant themselves, and consulted their own personal interest, in instances essential to its well-being; but the whole people, by consulting their own interest, consult the publick, and act for the publick by acting for themselves: This is particularly the spirit of our constitution, in which the whole nation is represented; and our records afford instances, where the House of Commons have declined entering upon a question of importance, till they had gone into the country, and consulted their principals, the people: So far were they from thinking that private men had no right to meddle with government. In truth, our whole worldly happiness and misery (abating for accidents and diseases) are owing to the order or mismanagement of government; and he who says that private men have no concern with government, does wisely and modestly tell us, that men have no concern in that which concerns them most; it is saying that people ought not to concern themselves whether they be naked or clothed, fed or starved, deceived

5. The coastal plain that lies between the Apennines and the Tyrrhenian Sea. The area was one of the loveliest in the empire.

or instructed, and whether they be protected or destroyed: What nonsense and servitude in a free and wise nation!

For myself, who have thought pretty much of these matters, I am of opinion, that a whole nation are like to be as much attached to themselves, as one man or a few men are like to be, who may by many means be detached from the interest of a nation. It is certain that one man, and several men, may be bribed into an interest opposite to that of the publick; but it is as certain that a whole country can never find an equivalent for itself, and consequently a whole country can never be bribed. It is the eternal interest of every nation, that their government should be good; but they who direct it frequently reason a contrary way and find their own account in plunder and oppression; and while the publick voice is pretended to be declared, by one or a few, for vile and private ends, the publick know nothing of what is done, till they feel the terrible effects of it.

By the Bill of Rights,[6] and the Act of Settlement, at the Revolution; a right is asserted to the people applying to the King and to the Parliament, by petition and address, for a redress of publick grievances and mismanagements, when such there are, of which they are left to judge; and the difference between free and enslaved countries lies principally here, that in the former, their magistrates must consult the voice and interest of the people; but in the latter, the private will, interest, and pleasure of the governors, are the sole end and motives of their administration.

Such is the difference between England and Turkey; which difference they who say that private men have no right to concern themselves with government, would absolutely destroy; they would convert magistrates into bashaws, and introduce popery into politicks. The late Revolution stands upon the very opposite maxim; and that any man dares to contradict it since the Revolution, would be amazing, did we not know that there are, in every country, hirelings who would betray it for a sop.

G   *I am, &c.*

6. A parliamentary enactment (Dec. 1689) of the Declaration of Rights, which repeated the provisions of the declaration and settled the succession to the crown. It formed part of the Revolutionary Settlement.

NO. 39.   SATURDAY,   JULY   29,   1721.

Of the Passions; that they are all alike good or all alike evil, according as they are applied.

SIR,

Nothing is more provoking than to hear men talk magisterially, and with an air of teaching, about things which they do not understand, or which they have an interest to have understood wrong. We have, all of us, heard much of the duty of subduing our appetites, and extinguishing our passions, from men, who by these phrases shewed at once their ignorance of human nature, and yet that they aimed at an absolute dominion over it.

Wrong heads and knavish designs are frequently found together; and creatures that you would not trust with laying out ten shillings for you in an instance where you trust to your own understanding, shall sometimes, by the mere sound of their voice, and an unmeaning distinction, make themselves masters of your mind and your fortune. It is by trusting to these that men come to know so little of themselves, and to be so much the prey of others as ignorant and more dishonest. I know no man so fit as himself to rule himself, in things which purely concern himself. How happy would this plain rule make the world, if they could be brought to observe it, and to remember that brown is as virtuous a colour as black; that the Almighty possesses alike every quarter of the world; and that in his sight fish and flesh in point of merit and innocence are the same! These things are self-evident, and yet the misery of mankind is in a great measure owing to their ignorance of them.

The ancient Stoicks had many admirable and virtuous precepts, but their philosophy was too rigid to be very popular; they taught men an absolute indifference for sensual pain and pleasure; but in this their doctrine was neither useful nor practicable. Men were not to be thus dealt with; they could not cease to be men, nor change nature for philosophy. Besides, these teachers being pagans, and arguing only from the topicks of wisdom strained too high, had no equivalent to offer to their disciples for parting with their appetites and their senses. But when some of their Sophists came into Christianity, and brought along with them the severe notions of their sect, they spread and recommended the same with more success, by tacking to these their opinions the rewards and terrors of the world to come, which had nothing to do with them: However, they said that it had, and quickly found credit enough to make it dangerous to contradict them.

These favourite dreams of theirs, added to some sayings and passages of the gospel, ill understood, were vehemently urged, as if they had been so many certain passports to paradise; and soon turned men's brains, and made them really fond of poverty, hardships, and misery, and even of death itself: Enthusiasm conquered reason, and inflamed nature; and men, to be devout, grew distracted.

This came of stifling the passions, and subduing nature, as the phrase was. But the folly and mischief of this doctrine thus extravagantly pushed, were not greater than its falsehood: For, as there is no such thing as departing from nature, without departing from life, it is certain that they who were remarkable for restraining some of their appetites, were as remarkable for indulging others; so that their boasted mortification was no more than the exchange of one passion for another, and often of a better for a worse. Thus there are many saints in the Romish calendar, who practised a religious abstinence from all sorts of flesh living or dead, and yet made it the duty of their profession, and the business of their lives, to stir up dissension and war amongst men, and to promote slaughter and desolation: They abstained from women, and yet were the authors of infinite rapes and adulteries: Their gentle and sanctified souls would not allow them to kill, much less to eat any part of an animal made to be killed and eaten; but they avowedly and piously preached up human and Christian butcheries, and have smiled over the carcases of a nation massacred at their instigation.

It is the weakness and misfortune of the human race, that a man, by the means of one virtue, or the appearance of it, is often able to do a thousand mischiefs; and it is the quality of human nature, that when any one of its appetites is violently restrained, others break out into proportionable excesses. Thus men grow rash and precipitate, by trampling upon caution and fear; and thus they become cowards, by stifling the love of glory: Whereas, if the appetite for danger were checked by the appetite of self-preservation, and the lazy love of safety by the love of fame, rashness and cowardice would be no more.

It is the highest stupidity to talk of subduing the passions, in the common acceptation of that phrase; and to rail at them in gross,[1] is as foolish. The greatest evils often proceed from the best things abused, or ill applied; and this is particularly true of the passions, which are the constituent parts of a man, and are good or ill as they are managed.

The exercise therefore of reason is nothing else, but the indulging or controlling of the passions, with an impartial hand, and giving them all fair play; it is an equal administration of the appetites, by which they are restrained from outrunning one another: Thus, for example, if men's fears were always as powerful as their hopes, they would rarely run into danger; or, if their hopes balanced their fears, they would never despair.

Every one of the leading passions is as necessary as another; all the difficulty is to keep them well marshalled: They are only terrible by breaking out of their ranks, and when they do, they are all alike terrible, though the world generally thinks otherwise. But it is certain, that those passions to which the kindest ideas are annexed, do as much mischief when they get out of their bounds, as do those to which we annex the harshest ideas; and love and hope, which bear soft and mild names, are in their excesses as active and as formidable passions, as are anger and revenge, the names of which are apt to shock us; and anger and revenge are, in their proper limits, more desirable passions than are love and hope out of their proper limits; that is, they are all equally good, or all equally evil, just as they are let loose or restrained. A man who cuts another's throat out of love to his wife, commits the same wickedness as if he did it out of revenge. Extravagant joy for the Restoration (which was doubtless a great and extraordinary blessing) had well nigh cost England its religion and liberty; and afterwards the

1. To rail at them in gross: to rail at them indiscriminately.

awakening fears of popery saved both. No nation has been more fleshed in blood than the Turks; principally, because the false hopes of Mahomet's lascivious paradise animated them in their butcheries.

The only way therefore of dealing with mankind, is to deal with their passions; and the founders of all states, and of all religions, have ever done so: The first elements, or knowledge of politicks, is the knowledge of the passions; and the art of governing, is chiefly the art of applying to the passions. When the publick passions (by which I mean every man's particular warmth and concern about publick transactions and events) are well regulated and honestly employed, this is called government, or the art of governing; and when they are knavishly raised and ill employed, it is called faction, which is the gratifying of private passion by publick means.

And because passion and opinion are so nearly related, and have such force upon each other, arbitrary courts and crafty churchmen have ever endeavoured to force, or frighten, or deceive the people into an uniformity of thoughts, especially of religious thoughts. A thing tyrannical and impossible! And yet a whole people do often, through ignorance or fear, seem of one mind; and but seem: For, if they come to explain, they would find their ideas differ widely, though their words agree. Whereas in a well-governed free state, diversity of speculations is so far from clogging the publick good, that it evidently promotes the same; all men being equally engaged in the defence of that, by which all men are indifferently protected. So that to attempt to reduce all men to one standard of thinking, is absurd in philosophy, impious in religion, and faction in the state. And though the mortifying of the appetites be a very plausible phrase, and, in a restrained sense, a laudable thing; yet he who recommends it to you does often mean nothing but this, *Make your passions tame, that I may ride them.*

There is scarce any one of the passions but what is truly laudable when it centers in the publick, and makes that its object. Ambition, avarice, revenge, are all so many virtues, when they aim at the general welfare. I know that it is exceeding hard and rare, for any man to separate his passions from his own person and interest; but it is certain that there have been such men. Brutus,

Cato, Regulus, Timoleon, Dion,[2] and Epaminondas, were such, as were many more ancient Greeks and Romans; and, I hope, England has still some such. And though, in pursuing publick views, men regard themselves and their own advantages; yet if they regard the publick more, or their own in subserviency to the publick, they may justly be esteemed virtuous and good.

No man can be too ambitious of the glory and security of his country, nor too angry at its misfortunes and ill usage; nor too revengeful against those that abuse and betray it; nor too avaricious to enrich it, provided that in doing it he violates not the rights of others.

Tacitus giving the character of the emperor Galba, who doubtless was an honest man, and had many virtues, after saying that he coveted no man's money, and was sparing of his own, adds, that he was solicitous to save publick money: *Pecuniae alienae non appetens, suae parcus, publicae avarus*;[3] which publick avarice in him was a publick virtue, and cost him his life; he was not suffered to reign, because would not lavish away the publick money in bribes; *Milites a se eligi, non emi.*[4] So dangerous, and even fatal, was personal virtue in that corrupt state; and so hard and impossible is it, in any state, to stay the progress of corruption! Galba would have reformed the Roman state: But the vices of his predecessors, and long use, made it impracticable; and he lost his life in the attempt. The passions of men were detached from the commonwealth, and placed upon their own personal security or gain; and they had no sense of the publick, and as little knowledge of its affairs: For that great people, and almost the whole world had been long the sole property of a single man, who took counsel only of his lust,

G   *I am, &c.*

2. Marcus Iunius *Brutus* (85–42 B.C.), the tyrannicide; Marcus Porcius *Cato* Uticensis (95–46 B.C.), known as Cato the Younger; Marcus Atilius *Regulus* (d. c. 249 B.C.), Roman commander at the time of the first Punic War, during which he defeated the Carthaginian armies before being taken prisoner in battle; *Dion* (408–353 B.C.), Syracusan commander who was successful in overthrowing the Syracusan tyrant Dionysius in 357 B.C.

3. "He did not covet the property of others; he was frugal with his own, and conscientious with the public's." Tacitus, *Historiae*, 1.49.

4. "He was given to choose, not buy, his soldiers." Tacitus, *Historiae*, 1.5.

NO. 40. SATURDAY, AUGUST 5, 1721.

Considerations on the restless and selfish Spirit of Man.

SIR,

It is melancholy to consider how every thing in the world is abused: The reason is, that men having themselves chiefly in view, consider all things with an eye to themselves only; and thus it is that general blessings cease to be so by being converted into private property, as is always done where it is safe or possible to be done.

Enquiring how it comes to pass that the best things in the world, such as religion, property, and power, are made to do so much hurt; I find it to proceed principally from hence, that men are never satisfied with their present condition, which is never perfectly happy; and perfect happiness being their chief aim, and always out of their reach, they are restlesly grasping at what they never can attain.

So chimerical is the nature of man! his greatest pleasures are always to come, and therefore never come. His content cannot possibly be perfect, because its highest objects are constantly future; and yet it is the more perfect for their being future. Our highest enjoyment is of that which is not: Our pleasure is deceit; and the only real happiness that we have is derived from non-entities. We are never satisfied with being just what we are; and therefore, though you give us all that we desire, or can conceive, yet we shall not have done desiring. The present possessions give but little joy, let them be ever so great; even as great as can be grasped: It is the enjoyment to come that is only or most valued. When we say, that if such a thing happened, we would be easy; we can only mean, or ought only to mean, that we would be more easy than we are: And in that too we are often mistaken; for new acquisitions bring new wants; and imaginary wants are as pungent as real ones. So that there is the same end of wishing as of living, and death only can still the appetites.

Publick blessings would really be so to every man, if every man would be content with his share: But every man would have more; nor would more satisfy him, whatever he may think; but his desires would rise with his possessions or his power, and his last wish would be to have all: Nor would the possession of all quiet the mind of man, which the whole world cannot fill. Indeed, he who has most, wants most; and care, anxious care, as it is the close companion of greatness, so it is furthest from him who has least to care for.

I own, that many have seemed to despise riches and power, and really declined the means of acquiring them: But they deceived themselves, if they thought that this conduct of theirs was owing to a real contempt for the things themselves; when in truth it was only a dislike of the terms upon which they were to be had. Disinterestedness is often created by laziness, pride, or fear; and then it is no virtue. There is not, perhaps, a man living but would be glad of wealth and grandeur, if he could acquire them with speed, and possess them with ease; and almost all men would risk, and do daily risk, ease, reputation, life, and all, to come at them. Do we not see that men venture being beggars to be rich, lose their rest for the sake of quiet, and acquire infamy to earn honour? We live in a hurry, in order to come at the resting-place; and in crowds to purchase solitude. Nor are we the nearer to our end, though the means succeed: Human life is a life of expectation and care; and he who rejects the conditions, must quit it.

Every passion, every view that men have, is selfish in some degree; but when it does good to the publick in its operation and consequence, it may be justly called disinterested in the usual meaning of that word. So that when we call any man disinterested, we should intend no more by it, than that the turn of his mind is towards the publick, and that he has placed his own personal glory and pleasure in serving it. To serve his country is his private pleasure, mankind is his mistress; and he does good to them by gratifying himself.

Disinterestedness, in any other sense than this, there is none. For men to act independently of their passions, is a contradiction! since their passions enter into all that they do, and are the source of it: And the best actions which men perform, often arise from fear, vanity, shame, and the like causes. When the passions of men do good to others, it is called virtue and publick spirit; and when they do hurt to others, it is called selfishness, dishonesty, lust, and other names of infamy. The motive of every man's conduct is fetched from within, and has a good or an ill name according to its effect upon others; and sometimes the great difference between an honest man and a knave, is no other than a piece of humour, or a piece of chance. As the passions of men, which are only the motions raised within us by the motion of things without us, are soothed or animated by external causes, it is hard to determine, whether there be a man in the world who might not be corrupted by some means and applications; the nicety is, to choose those that are proper.

All these discoveries and complaints of the crookedness and corruption of human nature are made with no malignant intention to break the bonds of society; but they are made to shew, that as selfishness is the strongest bias of men, every man ought to be upon his guard against another, that he become not the prey of another. The too great confidence which many men have placed in one, has often ruined millions. How many sorrowful experiences have we, that men will be rogues where they dare; and that the greatest opportunities always make the greatest! Give them what you can, they will still want more than you give; and therefore the highest trusts are the most apt to be broken.

Those who have talked most of the dignity of human nature, seem to have understood it but little. Men are so far from having any views purely publick and disinterested, that government first arose from every man's taking care of himself; and government is never abused and perverted, but from the same cause. Do we not know that one man has slaughtered a million, and overturned nations, for the gaining of one point to himself? and that almost all men would follow evil, if they found their greatest advantage or pleasure in it.

Here therefore lies the source of all the evil which men suffer from men, that every man loves himself better than he loves his whole species, and more or less consults himself in all that he does. He naturally pursues what is pleasant or profitable in his own eyes, though in doing it he entail misery upon multitudes. So that we have no other security against the malice and rapine of each other, but the security of laws or our own force. By laws societies subsist within themselves; and by force they defend themselves against each other. And as in the business of faith and leagues between nation and nation, treaties are made by consent, but kept by fear and power; and observed or violated just as interest, advantage, and opportunities invite, without regard to faith and good conscience, which are only words of good-breeding, with which courts compliment one another and themselves; so between subject and subject, and between magistrates and subjects, concord and security are preserved by the terror of laws, and the ties of mutual interest; and both interest and terror derive their strength from the impulses of self-love.

Thus one man is only safe, while it is the interest of another to let him alone; and men are knaves or honest men, according to the judgment which they make of their own interest and ease, and of the terms upon which they choose to live in the world. Many men are honest, without any virtue, or indeed a thought of honesty; as many others are rogues, without any malice: And both sorts mean only their own personal advantage; but take different roads to arrive at it. This is their great aim; and that constitution which trusts more than it needs to any man, or body of men, has a terrible flaw in it, and is big with the seeds of its own destruction. Hence arose tyrants, and tyranny, and standing armies: Marius, and Caesar, and Oliver Cromwell. How preposterously do men act! By too great confidence in one man, or a few men, they become slaves; and by a general distrust of each other, they continue so!

It may be objected, that since men are such a wretched race, made so by the apostasy of Adam, they are not worth serving; that the most unhappy of them are but what they themselves would make others, and therefore their fate is just upon them.

In answer to this, I readily own what I have been proving, that men are very bad where they dare, and that all men would be tyrants, and do what they please. But still let us preserve justice and equality in the world. Why should he, who is bad himself, oppress others who are no worse than him? Besides, the lot of humanity being an unhappy one, it is an honest ambition, that of endeavouring to mend it, to improve nature by virtue, and to mend mankind by obliging them to observe rules that are good. We do not expect philosophical virtue from them; but only that they follow virtue as their interest, and find it penal and dangerous to depart from it. And this is the only virtue that the world wants, and the only virtue that it can trust to.

G   *I am, &c.*

NO. 41. SATURDAY, AUGUST 19, 1721.

The Emperor Galba's Speech to Piso, with an Introduction.

SIR,

I send you a translation of the speech of the emperor Galba to Piso,[1] when he adopted him his partner and successor in the Empire; a speech full of great sense, great honesty, and noble sentiments. Indeed Galba seems to have come to the government with worthy intentions to mend it. To restore the ancient liberty, was impossible. Things had run long in another channel; people were accustomed to the largesses and false bounty of their princes, to the awful and sounding names of the Caesars, and to the luxury, pomp, and tinsel of a court. The soldiers would have an emperor; nor could the Senate withstand the soldiers: The venerable orders of the commonwealth had been long abolished, her ancient virtues extinct; *Nihil usquam prisci & integri moris;*[2] and the commonwealth itself was forgot: *Quotus quisque reliquus qui rem publicam vidisset!*[3]

1. Lucius Calpurnius *Piso* Licinianus, Roman senator and adopted son of the emperor Galba. He was put to death by order of Galba's successor, Otho, in A.D. 69.
2. "Nothing remained of the old, simple, Roman character." Tacitus, *Annales*, 1.4.
3. "Few indeed were left who had seen the Republic!" Tacitus, *Annales*, 1.3.

says Tacitus, speaking of the end of the reign of Augustus. In short, the emperor was all in all: *Illuc cuncta vergere.*[4] The state was overturned, mangled, and changed: The old laws of equality were utterly lost in the imperial power, and that was supported by the sword. There was no safety but in servitude; *Jussa principis aspectare.*[5] All the other magistrates were but shadows with fine old names.

The chief aim therefore of Galba, since he could not restore, was to reform. A worthy attempt, but he failed in it: So irresistible was the tide of corruption! Two things principally obstructed his design, and shortened his life and reign; the avarice of the soldiery, and the vile conduct of his servants.

As to the soldiers, he had honestly, but unfortunately said, that he *would choose them, but not buy them*; a saying which they never forgave him. Besides, as he practised himself the rigid old Roman discipline, he would oblige his army to practise it; a thing new to them, and intolerable. They had been long used to luxury and sloth, and were grown as fond of the vileness and vices of their princes, as the old republican armies had been of the temperance, modesty, and other virtues of their commanders: They therefore could not bear the severity and frugality of Galba; nor would Galba depart from his temper and his purposes. Money would have made them his friends; but he would part with none. The reflection of the historian upon this conduct of his is fine, but melancholy; *Nocuit antiquus rigor, & nimia severitas, cui jam pares non sumus*:[6] "He was ruined by reviving unseasonably the severe virtue of our ancestors: Alas! we are no longer equal to it." To conclude this head; the soldiers butchered an emperor that would not bribe them.

As to the part of Galba's servants in the tragedy of their master, it was no small one: They made him odious by their own crimes; and in his name committed cruelties and rapine, which blackened his character; and when they had brought him under a

4. "On him all depended." Tacitus, *Annales*, 1.3.
5. "All looked to the orders of the emperor." Tacitus, *Annales*, 1.4.
6. "He was resented for his old-fashioned harshness and excessive severity—qualities to which we are no longer equal." Tacitus, *Historiae*, 1.18.

general dislike, none of his own good qualities could recover him his good name: *Inviso semel principe, seu bene seu male facta premunt.*[7] Their avarice was imputed to him, and called his: *Jam offerebant venalia cuncta praepotentes liberti.*[8] They were resolved to make the most of his short reign; and by doing so made it shorter: *Servorum manus subitis avidae, & tanquam apud senem festinantes.*[9] He paid dear for their wickedness: *Odio flagitiorum oneratum destruebant.*[10] His character, in relation to his friends and servants, was, that he was indulgent to them, if they were good; and blind to their faults, if they were bad. *Ubi in bonos incidisset, sine reprehensione patiens: Si mali forent, usque ad culpam ignarus.*[11]

The rest of his character, taken from Tacitus, from whom I have taken the whole,[12] is, that being seventy years old, he had lived in prosperity during five reigns, more happy in them than in his own: That he was of a family ancient, great, and noble, and master of great wealth: That he had a moderate capacity, and more innocence than abilities: That he neither courted fame, nor despised it: That he coveted no man's money, was sparing of his own, and solicitous to save publick money: That a nobleman of his great birth and quality, having lived so securely in such dangerous times, was a thing so surprizing and rare, that his good fortune passed for wisdom, and his real indolence for real art: That in the vigour of his years he acquired great renown in the German wars: That being proconsul in Africa, he governed that province, and afterwards Spain, with great equity: That he seemed greater than a

7. "Once the emperor was hated, his good and evil deeds were equally unpopular." Tacitus, *Historiae*, 1.7.

8. "Powerful freedmen now offered all for sale." This line is derived from Tacitus, *Historiae*, 1.7.

9. "The hands of slaves, eager for quick gain, hastened in the presence of an old man." Tacitus, *Historiae*, 1.7.

10. "They destroyed him, burdened as he was by hatred for the scoundrels." Tacitus, *Historiae*, 1.6.

11. "With those of his friends who were honest, his patience knew no bounds. And if they happened to be dishonest, he was blind even to a fault." Tacitus, *Historiae*, 1.49.

12. Tacitus discusses Galba's character and the events surrounding his reign in *Historiae*, 1.12–48.

subject, while he was but a subject; and that, in the opinion of all men, he was equal to the empire, if he had never been emperor.

So much for the character of Galba; which I thought necessary to introduce his speech to Piso, who was every way worthy of the adoption and of a better fortune; which, however, was of a-piece: He was long an exile under Nero, who had murdered his brother Crassus; as had Claudius his brother Magnus: He himself was but four days Caesar,[13] and then butchered; as was his eldest brother presently after him. He was of a noble race, both by father and mother, and had an amiable and popular character for the severity of his manners, and his many virtues; and during the few days of his highest power and adversity he behaved himself with great modesty and firmness, and seemed to make good every hope concerning him. But virtue and goodness were then pernicious, and we see what he got by having them. The whole story, and particularly his fate in it, affects me.

I am, &c.

THE SPEECH OF GALBA TO PISO

"Were I, as a private man, to adopt you for my son, by virtue of the law Curiata,[14] in preference of the pontiffs, according to the ordinary usage; glorious even then would be the adoption to us both; as with the blood of the great Pompey and of Marcus Crassus[15] my family would be enriched; and the nobility of your house derive fresh splendor from the signal lustre and renown of the Sulpitian and Lutacian race.[16] I am now a publick person, by the united consent of gods and men called to the empire; and of this same sovereignty, for which our ancestors contended with arms, I, who by war have obtained it, do offer you the possession, while you are neither seeking nor pursuing it: A gift to which I am urged

13. The title granted to Piso by virtue of his having been named the emperor Galba's heir.

14. The reference is to the law governing the adoption of mature persons.

15. Both Gnaeus *Pompeius*, surnamed Magnus (106–48 B.C.), and Marcus Licinius *Crassus* (c. 115–53 B.C.), triumvirs with Caesar, were related, either by blood or marriage, to Licinianus Piso.

16. That is, of two of the great families of Rome.

only by the love of my country and your own excellent qualifications. In this I follow the example of the deified Augustus, who assumed successively, for his partners in power, first his sister's son, Marcellus; next his son-in-law, Agrippa; afterwards his grandsons; lastly, his wife's son Tiberius.[17] But Augustus, who would entail the empire upon his own house, in his own house sought a successor: I choose out of the commonwealth an heir to the commonwealth. Not that I am reduced to this choice by any want of relations to my blood, or of fellow-commanders in war. But neither did I, no more than you, arrive at supreme power by any efforts of ambition; and my thus overlooking your relations, as well as my own, is a proof and monument with what sincerity of intention I prefer you to all men. You have a brother, in nobility your equal, in age your superior; a man worthy of this fortune; did I not in you find one still more worthy. Such is your age, as to be past the giddiness and impetuosity of youth; such has been your course of life, that nothing in your conduct, thus far, is subject to blame. But hitherto you have only had an adverse fortune to contend with. More dangerous and keen are the stimulations of prosperity, to try the temper of the soul, and call forth its weaknesses. For, the strokes of calamity we struggle under and bear: By a flow of felicity we are utterly subdued and corrupted.

"You doubtless will still retain, with your usual firmness, the same honour, faith in friendship, candour and freedom of spirit; endowments which, above all others, adorn the mind of man. But the false complaisance of others will slacken your fortitude. Flattery will force its way to your heart; deceitful soothings, the most pestilent poison to every honest affection, will enchant you; and to his own sordid gain will every particular be wresting your honour and good inclinations. You and I upon this occasion converse together with hearts perfectly open and sincere: Others

17. Marius Claudius *Marcellus* (42–23 B.C.), son of Octavia, the sister of Augustus, and husband of Augustus's daughter Julia; Marcus Vipsanius *Agrippa* (c. 63–12 B.C.), an intimate friend and supporter of Augustus who married first Marcella, Augustus's niece, and then Julia, Augustus's daughter; *Gaius* (20 B.C.–A.D. 4) and *Lucius* (17 B.C.–A.D. 2), the sons of Agrippa and Julia; *Tiberius* Claudius Nero Caesar (42 B.C.–A.D. 37), who became emperor in A.D. 14, was the son of Livia, wife of Augustus, by her former marriage, and adopted son of Augustus.

will choose to make their addresses to our fortune rather than to us. Indeed, to deal faithfully with princes, to reason them into their duty, is a mighty task, and with infinite difficulty performed. But easy is the art of cajoling any prince whatsoever, and in doing it the heart has no share. Could this immense empire subsist, and be swayed without a single ruler, I should glory in resigning, glory in being the first emperor who resigned the power of the Republick into her own hands. But such, long since has been the fatal situation of the state, that all the good which my old age enables me to do to the Roman people, is to leave them a good successor; nor can you, with all your youth, do more for them than afford them in yourself a benevolent prince. Under Tiberius and Caligula and Claudius, we were all of us no more, the Roman world was no more, than as the inheritance of one family. That the empire has in me begun to be elective, is a sign of our ancient liberty revived, and some equivalent for it; the only liberty we are capable of enjoying. Now the Julian and Claudian families[18] being extinct, the best men are likely, in this way of adoption, to become the highest. To be sprung from a sovereign race, is the effect of chance, and further than this requires no deliberation or regard. But in the work of adoption the judgment is exercised, free from bias and restraint; and whenever you want to choose, you are by the general consent directed to the person worthy to be chosen.

"Have always before your eyes the example of Nero, who, secure as he was, and swelling with the pride of his race, a long genealogy of the Caesars his ancestors, was not in reality dethroned by Julius Vindex,[19] the governor of a province unprovided with forces, nor by me, assisted by one legion: No, it was his own brutal tyranny, his own beastly debaucheries, that flung down the tyrant from riding on the necks of mankind. Nor was there till then any instance of an emperor by publick sentence condemned and deposed. We who succeed him by a different title, by war and by publick approbation and choice, shall thence reap publick glory,

18. Ancient patrician houses at Rome. Both Julius Caesar and Augustus were members of the Julian family.

19. Gaius Julius *Vindex*, Governor of Gaul who attempted to liberate the empire from Nero's tyranny (A.D. 68). His armies were finally defeated on the Rhine frontier and Vindex was forced to kill himself.

however the malignity of particulars may pursue us. Nor must you be alarmed, if while the world itself continues in this general uproar, there are two legions which yet remain unreclaimed to obedience. It was my own lot to be called to an unsettled state; and as to my old age, the only objection to my government, it is no longer one, since, when it is known that I have adopted you, I shall seem young in my successor. The loss of Nero will ever be regretted by all the most profligate and bad. To us it belongs, to you and to me, so to govern, that he may not also be regretted by the good.

"To say more in this way of instruction, the present conjuncture suffers not; nor is it necessary; since if I have in you made a worthy choice, I have answered every purpose. One certain rule you have to observe, exceeding wholesome, as well as exceeding short; so to comport yourself towards your subjects, as, were you a subject, you would wish your prince to comport towards you. By this rule you will best distinguish the boundaries of justice and iniquity; best comprehend the art of reigning: for, you must remember that it is not with us as with other nations, such as are barbarous and tyrannized, where a particular lordly house is established, and where all besides are slaves without reserve. But you are about to govern the Romans; a people of too little virtue to support complete liberty, of too much spirit to bear absolute bondage."[20]

G

NO. 42. SATURDAY, AUGUST 26, 1721.

Considerations on the Nature of Laws.

SIR,

The mischiefs that are daily done, and the evils that are daily suffered in the world, are sad proofs, how much human malice exceeds human wisdom. Law only provides against the evils which it knows or foresees; but when laws fail, we must have

20. Galba's speech appears in Tacitus, *Historiae*, 1.15–16.

recourse to reason and nature, which are the only guides in the making of laws. *Stirpem juris a natura repertam,* says Cicero;[1] there never would have been any law against any crime, if crimes might have been safely committed, against which there was no law: For every law supposes some evil, and can only punish or restrain the evils which already exist.

But as positive laws, let them be ever so full and perspicuous, can never entirely prevent the arts of crafty men to evade them, or the power of great ones to violate them; hence new laws are daily making, and new occasions for more are daily arising: So that the utmost that wisdom, virtue, and law can do, is to lessen or qualify, but never totally abolish, vice and enormity. Law is therefore a sign of the corruption of man; and many laws are signs of the corruption of a state.

Positive laws deriving their force from the law of nature, by which we are directed to make occasional rules, which we call laws, according to the exigencies of times, places, and persons, grow obsolete, or cease to be, as soon as they cease to be necessary. And it is as much against the law of nature to execute laws, when the first cause of them ceases, as it is to make laws, for which there is no cause, or a bad cause. This would be to subject reason to force, and to apply a penalty where there is no crime. Law is right reason, commanding things that are good, and forbidding things that are bad; it is a distinction and declaration of things just and unjust, and of the penalties or advantages annexed to them.

The violation therefore of law does not constitute a crime where the law is bad; but the violation of what ought to be law, is a crime even where there is no law. The essence of right and wrong does not depend upon words and clauses inserted in a code or a statute-book, much less upon the conclusions and explications of lawyers; but upon reason and the nature of things, antecedent to all laws. In all countries reason is or ought to be consulted, before laws are enacted; and they are always worse than none, where it is not consulted. Reason is in some degree given to all men; and Cicero says, that whoever has reason, has right reason; that virtue is

1. "The foundation of the law was uncovered from nature itself." Cicero, *De legibus,* 1.6.20.

but perfect reason; and that all nations having reason for their guide, all nations are capable of arriving at virtue.[2]

From this reasoning of his it would follow, that every people are capable of making laws, and good laws; and that laws, where they are bad, are gained by corruption, faction, fear, or surprize; and are rather their misfortune, than the effects of their folly. The acts of Caesar were confirmed by the Senate and the people; but the Senate was awed, and the tribunes and people were bribed: Arms and money procured him a law to declare him lawless. But, as the most pompous power can never unsettle the everlasting land-marks between good and evil, no more than those between pleasure and pain; Caesar remained still a rebel to his country, and his acts remained wicked and tyrannical.

Let this stand for an instance, that laws are not always the measure of right and wrong. And as positive laws often speak when the law of nature is silent, the law of nature sometimes speaks when positive laws say nothing: *Neque opinione, sed natura constitutum esse jus.*[3] That brave Roman, Horatius Cocles, was bound by no written law to defend the wooden bridge over the Tiber, against a whole army of Tuscans;[4] nor was there any law, that I know of, in Rome, against adultery, when the younger Tarquin ravished Lucretia:[5] And yet the virtue of Horatius was justly rewarded, and the vileness of Tarquin justly punished, by the Romans.

It is impossible to devise laws sufficient to regulate and manage every occurrence and circumstance of life, because they are often produced and diversified by causes that do not appear; and in every condition of life men must have, and will have, great allowances made to their own natural liberty and discretion: But

2. Cicero, *De legibus*, 1.6.18–19.

3. "Law is based, not on men's opinions, but on nature." Cicero, *De legibus*, 1.10.28.

4. Publius *Horatius* Cocles is said to have single-handedly defended the Sublician bridge against the whole Etruscan army while the Romans behind him were destroying the bridge.

5. The beauty and nobility of spirit of *Lucretia*, a Roman, is reputed to have so inflamed the passions of *Sextus Tarquinius*, son of the Tarquin king, that when his entreaties proved futile he took her by force. Her suicide, added to the oppressions the Romans endured, was the signal for rebellion, and the Tarquin kings were expelled from Rome.

every man, who consents to the necessary terms of society, will also consent to this proposition, that every man should do all the good, and prevent all the evil, that he can. This is the voice of the law of nature; and all men would be happy by it, if all men would practise it. This law leads us to see, that the establishment of falsehood and tyranny (by which I mean the privilege of one or a few to mislead and oppress all) cannot be justly called law, which is the impartial rule of good and evil, and can never be the sanction of evil alone.

It has been often said, that virtue is its own reward; and it is very true, not only from the pleasure that attends the consciousness of doing well, and the fame that follows it, but in a more extensive sense, from the felicity which would accrue to every man, if all men would pursue virtue: But as this truth may appear too general to allure and engage particular men, who will have always their own single selves most at heart, abstracted from all the rest; therefore in the making of laws, the pleasures and fears of particular men, being the great engines by which they are to be governed, must be consulted: Vice must be rendered detestable and dangerous; virtue amiable and advantageous. Their shame and emulation must be raised; their private profit and glory, peril and infamy, laid before them. This is the meaning of Tully, when he says, *Vitiorum emendatricem legem esse oportet, commendatricemque virtutum.*[6]

Rewards and punishments therefore constitute the whole strength of laws; and the promulgation of laws, without which they are none, is an appeal to the sense and interest of men, which of the two they will choose.

The two great laws of human society, from whence all the rest derive their course and obligation, are those of equity and self-preservation: By the first all men are bound alike not to hurt one another; by the second all men have a right alike to defend themselves: *Nam jure hoc evenit, ut quod quisque ob tutelam corporis sui fecerit, jure fecisse existimetur,*[7] says the civil law; that is, "It is a maxim of the law, that whatever we do in the way and for the ends of self-

6. "Law ought to be a reformer of vice and an incentive to virtue." Cicero, *De legibus,* 1.22.58.
7. "For this comes from the law: that which someone does for the safety of his body, let it be regarded as having been done legally." *Justinian,* 1.1.3, pr. 2.

defence, we lawfully do." All the laws of society are entirely reciprocal, and no man ought to be exempt from their force; and whoever violates this primary law of nature, ought by the law of nature
to be destroyed. He who observes no law, forfeits all title to the
protection of law. It is wickedness not to destroy a destroyer; and
all the ill consequences of self-defence are chargeable upon him
who occasioned them.

Many mischiefs are prevented, by destroying one who
shews a certain disposition to commit many. To allow a licence to
any man to do evil with impunity, is to make vice triumph over
virtue, and innocence the prey of the guilty. If men be obliged to
bear great and publick evils, when they can upon better terms
oppose and remove them; they are obliged, by the same logick, to
bear the total destruction of mankind. If any man may destroy
whom he pleases without resistance, he may extinguish the human
race without resistance. For, if you settle the bounds of resistance,
you allow it; and if you do not fix its bounds, you leave property at
the mercy of rapine, and life in the hands of cruelty.

It is said, that the doctrine of resistance would destroy the
peace of the world: But it may be more truly said, that the contrary
doctrine would destroy the world itself, as it has already some of
the best countries in it. I must indeed own, that if one man may
destroy all, there would be great and lasting peace when nobody
was left to break it.

The law of nature does not only allow us, but oblige us, to
defend ourselves. It is our duty, not only to ourselves, but to the
society; *Vitam tibi ipsi si negas, multis negas,* says Seneca:[8] If we suffer
tamely a lawless attack upon our property and fortunes, we
encourage it, and involve others in our doom. And Cicero says,
"He who does not resist mischief when he may, is guilty of the
same crime, as if he had deserted his parents, his friends, and his
country."[9]

So that the conduct of men, who, when they are ill treated,
use words rather than arms, and practise submission rather than

8. "If one denies life to oneself, one denies it to many." The Younger Seneca,
Phoenissae, 294.
9. Cicero, *De officiis*, 1.7.23.

resistance, is owing to a prudential cause, because there is hazard in quarrels and war, and their cause may be made worse by an endeavour to mend it; and not to any confession of right in those that do them wrong. When men begin to be wicked, we cannot tell where that wickedness will end; we have reason to fear the worst, and provide against it.

Such is the provision made by laws: They are checks upon the unruly and partial appetites of men, and intended for terror and protection. But as there are already laws sufficient every where to preserve peace between private particulars, the great difficulty has hitherto been to find proper checks for those who are to check and administer the laws. To settle therefore a thorough impartiality in the laws, both as to their end and execution, is a task worthy of human wisdom, as it would be the cause and standard of civil felicity. In the theory nothing is more easy than this task: Yet who is able to perform it, if they who can will not?

No man in society ought to have any privilege above the rest, without giving the society some equivalent for such his privilege. Thus legislators, who compile good laws, and good magistrates, who execute them, do, by their honest attendance upon the publick, deserve the privileges and pay which the publick allows them; and place and power are the wages paid by the people to their own deputies and agents. Hence it has been well said, that a chief magistrate is *major singulis, omnibus minor*:[10] "He is above the private members of the community; but the community itself is above him."

Where-ever, therefore, the laws are honestly intended, and equally executed, so as to comprehend in their penalties and operation the great as well and as much as the small, and hold in awe the magistrates as much as the subject, that government is good, that people are happy.

G   *I am, &c.*

---

10. "Above individuals, less than the whole."

NO. 43. SATURDAY, SEPTEMBER 2, 1721.

The natural Passion of Men for Superiority.

SIR,

All men have an ambition to be considerable, and take such ways as their judgments suggest to become so. Hence proceeds the appetite of all men to rise above their fellows, and the constant emulation that always has been, and always will be, in the world, amongst all sorts of men. Nature has made them all equal, and most men seem well content with the lot of parts which nature has given them; but the lot of fortune never thoroughly satisfies those who have the best.

The first spring therefore of inequality is in human nature, and the next in the nature of society. In order that many may live together in perfect equality, it is necessary that some should be above the many, who otherwise will be using frauds and violence to get above one another. Some inequality there must be; the danger is, that it be not too great: Where there is absolute equality, all reverence and awe, two checks indispensible in society, would be lost; and where inequality is too great, all intercourse and communication is lost.

Thus in Turkey, where there are no natural links, nor proper degrees of subordination in the chain of their government, there is a monstrous gap between the subject and the throne. The Grand Seignior preserves no understanding with his people: Nothing is to be seen but the terrors of absolute monarchy, and the abject postures of crouching slaves. Power does not glide there, as it ought every where, down an even and easy channel, with a gentle and regular descent; but pours from a precipice with dreadful din, rapidity, and violence upon the poor and passive valleys below, breaking down all before it, and laying waste where-ever it comes.

All men in the world are fond of making a figure in it. This being the great end of all men, they take different roads to come at it, according to their different capacities, opinions, tempers, and opportunities. No man would choose to have any man his equal, if he could place himself above all men. All would be Pompeys. But though it has fallen to the share but of few men to be above all men; yet as every man may, or thinks he may, excel some men, there is a perpetual spur in every descendant of Adam to be aspiring. Every man has self-love, and self-love is never deserted by hope.

But this spirit in every man of rising above other men, as it constitutes the happiness of private individuals, who take great complacency in their favourable opinion of themselves and their own abilities; so is it the great cause of publick and private evils, wars, frauds, cruelty, and oppression. The ambition of excelling in every station by honest means, is not only lawful, but laudable, and produces great good to society: But as nothing produces good in this world, but what may, and generally does, produce evil; and as fame, riches, and power, may be honestly got, but wickedly used, it ought to be the care of society to provide that such emulation amongst its members be so directed and controlled, as to be always beneficial, but never dangerous. But this is a felicity at which few nations have arrived, and those that had it rarely preserved it long.

It is a nice point of wisdom, perhaps too nice for human judgment, to fix certain and lasting bounds to this spirit of ambition and emulation amongst men. To stop it too soon, frustrates its use; and not to stop it at all, invites its mischief. The Venetians, by discouraging it, have never, or very rarely, felt its advantages; and the Athenians found their ostracism, an expedient invented for this very purpose, ineffectual to prevent their great men, who had done great good to the state, from growing terrible to the state itself: Pericles in particular, by his arts, eloquence, and popularity, made himself master of it, and did almost what he pleased in it all his life; that single man was so potent in that free city, that he broke the power of the Areopagus, the senate of Athens, a court of magistrates that balanced the power of the populace;[1] who, being

1. The Areopagus was at one time the chief administrative council of ancient Athens. In addition, it had the power to appoint to all offices and to punish, both for violations of the law and for immorality. Gordon is wrong in attributing the attacks on the Areopagus primarily to Pericles. Aristotle's *Constitution of Athens* expressly attributes these reforms not to Pericles but to Ephialtes.

set free from that restraint, ran into all manner of licentiousness and corruption.

The people of Athens became the subjects of Pericles: by having done them much good, he found credit enough to destroy their government and their virtue. From the character of a benefactor, he stole into that of a master: so narrow and invisible are the bounds between the benefactor and the betrayer! Valerius Maximus observes very finely, that "the only difference between Pisistratus and Pericles was, that the latter exercised by art the same tyranny that the other had exercised by arms."[2]

Good and evil thus often flowing from the same root, and mischief being frequently introduced by merit, it shews great discernment and virtue in a people, and a happy spirit in their laws, if they can encourage and employ the capacity and genius of their principal men, so as to reap only the good fruits of their services.

This was the practice and good fortune of the old Romans for several ages: Virtue was the only road to glory; it was admired, supported, applauded, and recompensed; but they who had shewn the greatest found no sanctuary from it, when they committed crimes that deserved none. This is particularly verified in the cases of Coriolanus and Manlius Capitolinus.[3] They were both brave men, and had deserved well of their country; were both, in recompence, distinguished with great honours; yet were both afterwards condemned by their country, the one for a conspiracy against it, the other for despising its laws. Their services and crimes were properly separated and rewarded.

Emulation therefore, or the passion of one man to equal or excel another, ought to be encouraged, with these two restrictions: First, that no man, let his merit be what it will, should take his own reward; secondly, that he should have no more than comes to his

2. The quotation appears in Valerius Maximus, 8.9.2.

3. Gnaeus Marcius *Coriolanus*: despite numerous military victories, he was refused the consulship. Banished for opposing the free distribution of corn, Coriolanus retired among his one-time enemy, the Volsci. He then led a Volscian army against Rome but, at the gates of the city, was prevailed upon by his wife and his mother to turn back. Marcus *Manlius* Capitolinus: Roman military commander who held the consulship in 392 B.C. He was held guilty of aspiring to kingly power and was thrown from the Tarpeian rock he had earlier so ably defended.

share. Scipio, afterwards called Africanus, was chosen as the greatest and best man in Rome, to invade the territories of Carthage; and he performed it with great glory to himself, with great emolument to his country. He defeated Hannibal, and conquered Carthage. The like praise is also due to Metellus, Lucullus, to T. Flaminius,[4] Paulus Emilius, and many other Roman commanders, who all conquered for their country, and were rewarded by their country with its laurels and its dignities.

Julius Caesar, being also employed by the commonwealth to conquer for it, succeeded in his commission; but, as a reward, took the commonwealth for his pains: He paid himself with the whole Roman world, for having conquered part of it. Alexander the Great, and most other conquerors, had the same modesty, and the same wages; they took all to themselves.

When men are left to measure their own merit, and the reward due to it, they rarely stint themselves; all that they can get is the least that they expect: And, to descend to lesser instances, the world has always abounded in men, who, though they deserved contempt or a prison, yet could never be satiated with places and power. And all men who have observed the affairs of the world, will remember and acknowledge, that sometimes one man has possessed many posts, to whom the publick suffrage and consent never gave one.

In my reflections upon this subject, I have often amused, and even diverted myself, with an odd imagination; namely, what a wonderful and epidemical cessation of power and place would ensue a sudden and universal removal from thence of every man who deserved neither. I fancied that I saw the whole inhabitants of several countries, towards every quarter of the sky, gaping round them for magistrates, at least for one single magistrate, and finding none; and yet even in this state of anarchy congratulating one another and themselves upon the wonderful amendment of their government. I saw all Asia, the whole ample dominions of the

4. Probably Quintus Caecilius *Metellus* Macedonicus (d. 115 B.C.), Roman general and conqueror of Macedonia; Lucius Licinius *Lucullus* (c. 110–c. 57 B.C.), celebrated as the conqueror of Mithridates the Great, King of Pontus; Titus Quinctius *Flaminius* (230– c. 174 B.C.), who successfully wrested Greece from Macedonia.

Turk, and many potent kingdoms nearer home, all in an absolute state of nature: In the large bosom of the Romish Church, not a priest was to be seen; and in some Protestant countries, the good people were greatly put to it, where to get a man in a proper habit to say publick prayers. Here in England, indeed, I found a different face of things, and more comfort: For, though at present we have no Parliament sitting, and though in other places I saw dismal solitude, and numberless vacancies; yet I perceived many worthy persons in church and state doing their business, and counting their gains, with great attention and alacrity, but greatly distressed how to find new persons for old places.

Imagination apart: I shall conclude in the words of a great English writer. It is true that

> consideration ought to be had of human frailty; and some indulgence may be extended to those who commit errors, after having done important services: But a state cannot subsist, which compensating evil actions with good, gives impunity to dangerous crimes, in remembrance of any services whatever. He that does well, performs his duty, and ought always to do so; justice and prudence concur in this; and it is no less just than profitable, that every action be considered by itself, and such a reward allotted to it as in nature and proportion it best deserves.[5]

G   *I am, &c.*

NO. 44. SATURDAY, SEPTEMBER 9, 1721.

❧   *Men not ruled by Principle, but by Passion.*

SIR,

Mr. Bayle, in the article of Epicurus, says, that "Multitudes of Christians believe well, and live ill: But Epicurus and his followers had, on the contrary, very ill opinions, and yet lived

5. I have been unable to determine the source of this quotation.

well."[1] The truth is, the worst opinions that are can do but little harm, when they are impracticable, or when no advantages are gained by reducing them into practice; and the best can do but little good, when they contradict the darling pleasures and prevailing interests of men.

Dry reasoning has no force: If you would have your doctrine successful, you must prove it gainful. And as in order to lay down good rules for well governing the commonwealth, you must first know the commonwealth; so in order to persuade and govern men, you must know what will please or frighten them. The good that they do to one another, they do not because it is just or commanded; nor do they forbear mutual evil, because it is unjust or forbid: But those things they do out of choice or fear, and both these center in themselves; for choice is pleasure, and fear is the apprehension of pain. So that the best things that men do, as well as the worst, are selfish; and self-love is the parent of moral good and evil.

What Mr. Selden says of humility, may be said of every other virtue. "Humility," says that wise man,

> is a virtue that all preach, none practise, and yet every body is content to hear: The master thinks it good doctrine for his servants, the laity for the clergy, and the clergy for the laity.[2]

Thus we deal with all the virtues; we leave and recommend the practice of them to others, and reserve the advantage and praise of them to ourselves.

All this, and the rest of this letter, is meant to shew that this world is governed by passion, and not by principle; and it ever will be so as long as men are men.

There are rarely any men, never any body of men, but what profess some sort of religion; and every religion professes to promote the peace of mankind, the happiness of human society,

1. The quotation can be found in Bayle, *An Historical and Critical Dictionary*, s.v. "Epicurus," II:1193.

2. John Selden (1584–1654), noted jurist and man of letters. The quotation appears in his *Table Talk: Being the Discourses of John Selden* (3d ed.; London: Printed for Jacob Tonson, 1716), under the heading "Humility" (p. 46).

and the security of the world; and, for proof of this, refers to its principles, doctrines, and decisions. And it is very true, that all parties in religion contend for submission to the state, as long as the state humours them, or submits to them; but their obedience and good humour never hold longer. All their principles ply[3] in the day of trial, and are either thrown away, or distinguished away; which is the same thing, though not so honest. Nature is then the best guide, and passion the most popular preacher.

Men suit their tenets to the circumstances that they are in, or would be in; and when they have gained their point, they forget their tenets. I could give instances of this from all sorts of men, and even from many whose names are great and venerable.

Gregory Nazianzen,[4] that eloquent and eminent Greek Father, being himself orthodox, contended for toleration to the Arians,[5] while the Arians were uppermost, and had the emperor on their side: but as soon as things took a contrary turn, and his own party had the imperial power on their side, he changed his style; and then it was unpardonable boldness and a horrible attempt, for the Arians and Macedonians[6] so much as to meet together to worship God their own way.

St. Austin[7] had the same spirit and inconsistency: He was once in the sentiments of charity and toleration towards hereticks; but his dispute afterwards with the Donatists[8] so inflamed him,

3. Ply: are brought to bear.

4. St. Gregory of Nazianzus (329–389), one of the Fathers of the Eastern Church. A disciple of Origen, he was an eloquent defender of orthodoxy against Arianism.

5. Followers of the Alexandrian theologian Arius (d. 336), who held that the Son of God was himself a created being to whom the Father gave existence. Although defeated by the orthodox party at the Council of Nicea (325), Arianism continued to flourish in the eastern half of the empire until the Council of Constantinople—called by the emperor Theodosius in 381—recognized the Nicene doctrine as the only orthodox one.

6. "The Macedonians" refers to the followers of Macedonius, Bishop of Constantinople and founder of the semi-Arian sect known as the Pneumatomachi, who denied the fully divine nature of the Holy Ghost. The sect was vigorously attacked by St. Gregory of Nazianzus and was anathematized at the Council of Constantinople.

7. St. Augustine of Hippo.

8. A schismatic body of the Church in northern Africa that objected to the consecration of Caecilian as Archbishop of Carthage on the grounds that he

that he changed without any ceremony from white to black, and maintained with violence, that hereticks ought to be compelled, persecuted, and exterminated.

Thus it is that men bear witness against themselves, and practise the evils which they condemn. The Puritans, says Mr. Selden,

> who will allow no free will at all, but God does all; yet will allow the subject his liberty to do, or not to do, notwithstanding the king, who is God upon Earth: The Arminians,[9] who hold that we have free-will, do yet say, when we come to the king, we must be all obedience, and no liberty is to be stood for.[10]

"While Spain was the most renowned power in Europe, the Jesuits," says Mr. Bayle,

> were all Spaniards; as well those born at Paris, or Rome, as those born in old Castile. Ever since the decay of the house of Austria, and the elevation of Lewis le grand, the Jesuits are all French, at Rome, at Vienna, at Madrid, as well as in the College of Clermont.[11] In those days the liberties of the Gallican church appeared to them not well grounded: They never ceased writing for the rights of the Pope against those of our kings. One might fill a library with the defences composed by the Society, and condemned by the

---

had been raised to the see by a *traditor*, that is, a Christian who had surrendered his copy of the scriptures under the compulsion of the Diocletian persecution. The Synod of Arles (314) affirmed the position of Caecilian and held that the validity of sacerdotal acts did not depend upon the personal character of the agent, but its findings apparently had little effect. However, in 411, St. Augustine, a resolute opponent of the sect, arranged a conference on the question at Carthage. The conference found for the orthodox party and a series of brutal penal measures were levied against anyone embracing the heresy.

9. Followers of Jacobus Arminius (1560–1609), Dutch theologian and founder of the anti-Calvinist school in Reform theology. Arminius held that the sovereignty of God is compatible with man's freedom, that man's salvation is dependent on his own acts, and that every believer may, through the mediation of divine grace, be assured of his own salvation.

10. *Table Talk*, s.v. "Free will" (p. 42).

11. In the eighteenth century also known as the College Louis le grand, the foremost Jesuit school in Paris.

parliament and the Sorbon.[12] At present his Majesty has
not trustier pens than theirs in his differences with the
Pope. It is now the turn of the court of Rome to censure
the books of the reverend fathers. It seems the king's prosperity and successes have afforded them new lights.[13]

It is with laymen and civil societies, as with religious: They
have one set of principles when they are in power; another, and a
contrary, when they are out of it. They that command, and they
that obey, have seldom or never the same motives. Men change
with their condition, and opinions change with men. And thus is
verified that maxim of Rochefoucauld's, that the understanding is
the dupe or tool of the heart; that is, our sentiments follow our
passions.[14]

Nor has religion been suffered to mend nature: On the
contrary, being instituted as a restraint, and an antidote against
sin, it has been, and is frequently perverted into a reason for sin-
ning: Yes, to the shame and misfortune of the world, men often
make war upon truth, conscience, and honesty, in behalf of their
religion; and there are others, who, when they have wantonly
wounded virtue, have recourse to religion for a balsam.

All men speak well of religion, either natural or revealed,
and readily practise every thing in religion that is easy, indifferent,
or advantageous to them: But in almost every contention between
religion and the appetites, the victory remains to nature; that is,
men are never dishonest without temptation, and rarely honest
against it.

Thus their principle is interest or pleasure; and when they
say that they act from principle, how can we believe them, unless
we see that they do it against interest? A proof which they rarely
give us! Had the several contracts and treaties between nation and
nation been observed, there would never have been war above

12. The Sorbonne. The pro-Gallican sentiments of its faculty brought it into
frequent conflict with Jesuit theology.
13. *Pensées diverses, écrites à un docteur de Sorbonne a l'occasion de la comète*, in
Oeuvres diverses, III:151.
14. *Maximes*, no. 112 (1665 edition).

once between any; or had every free nation observed its own laws, every free nation would have continued free; or, had private men observed the common laws of equity, and those of mutual compact between each other, every private man would have lived in peace and security. But treaties, compacts, and laws are only so far strong as no body dares break them.

I think it is Juvenal, who somewhere brings in a couple of false witnesses perjuring themselves for hire; one is a religious rogue, and believes in the gods; the other is an infidel, who disbelieves or despises them. But though they disagree in their sentiments, they agree in the thing, with this very small difference; the atheist forswears himself boldly without remorse; the believer forswears himself too, but does it with a small qualm, which is presently over.[15]

> ————Vendet perjuria summa
> Exigua, Cereris tangens aramque pedemque.[16]

Bayle very humourously engages a mandarin of China, of the sect of the Literati, in a dialogue with the Jesuits, and with a Dutch ambassador: The Jesuits tell the mandarin,

> that the Emperor had no subjects in his dominions, whose obedience was so secure to him as that of their converts the Christians; and none whose allegiance was so precarious as that of the Literati, who were atheists.
>
> "Hold," cries the mandarin; "let us not assert too much without proving it: What reason have you to say that the submission of the Christians to the orders of the Emperor is more certain than that of all his other subjects?" "That book inspired by God," answer the Jesuits; "that book, which is the rule of our faith, commands us expressly to submit ourselves to the higher powers: Take the trouble, my lord, to read in it such and such passages: Nothing is more clear, nothing so precisely determined."

15. The reference is to Juvenal, Saturae, 13:86–105.
16. "He will sell his perjuries for a trifle, all the while touching the altar and the foot of Ceres." Juvenal, Saturae, 14.218–19.

"But," says the mandarin turning to the ambassador, "are not you in Europe divided about the meaning of these passages?"

"So divided," replies the Dutchman, "that one room would not contain the volumes written for and against the right of subjects to resist and depose their prince: And both sides take particular care in all their writings to examine accurately every text of scripture, which the reverend fathers refer you to. This discussion of texts has therefore begot two propositions, flatly contradicting each other. One party asserts, that in departing from your obedience, you depart from the Bible: The other says, they resist with the Bible on their side. We have in Christendom many instances of princes attacked by parties of their subjects, bereft of their sovereignty, banished, beheaded, assassinated, and generally for the interest of religion. Nor is there any end of the books published on this occasion; we have every day printed accusations, and every day printed apologies; and both they who accuse and they who defend appeal to God, and refer to his word. As to the Jesuits in particular, it becomes them the least of all men to talk in this manner; no society of men have ever written so much in behalf of popular insurrections; they have openly contended for rebellion, and practised it; they have been the authors of royal assassinations, and have been turned out of states for disturbing them."

"If these things are so," concludes the mandarin, "you gentlemen of the Order of Jesus have no reason to boast in behalf of yourselves and your followers, as if you were better subjects than other men. This your pretended article of faith about the submission of the subject is couched so obscurely in your book of sacred laws, that you will never find it there when you have occasion for a rebellion or a revolution; events which I find are frequent enough in your country."[17]

The same Bayle observes, that the same party of Christians, namely, the French Catholicks, who had maintained, under

17. *Reponse aux questions d'un provincial* (part III, chap. 21), in *Oeuvres diverses*, III:958.

Charles IX[18] and Henry III that it was against all laws, human and divine, for subjects to take arms against their prince, did also maintain, even before the death of Henry III that it was agreeable to laws, human and divine, to take up arms against one's prince. The other party of Christians, namely, the Protestants, were not more consistent. They maintained, during the reigns of Charles IX and Henry III that laws, human and divine, allowed the smaller part of the subjects to arm themselves against the greater part even with the king at their head: But after the death of Henry III when they had got a king of their own religion, they maintained, that both the law of God and the law of man forbid even the greater part of the subjects to arm themselves against the smaller part with the king at their head.[19]

It were needless to give more proofs, and endless to give all that might be given. Almost every thing that men do, is an evidence that their friendship for themselves does effectually extinguish their regard for all the rest of their species; and that they adopt or reject principles, just as these principles promote or contradict their interest and passions.

Nor are religious or moral principles the worse for being thus used; but men shew their own unconquerable malignity and selfishness in using them thus.

Upon the whole, I think it very plain, that if you separate from the principles of men the penalties and advantages which are annexed to them by laws human and divine, or which every man has annexed to them in his own mind, you will hardly leave such a thing as principle in the world; the world is therefore not governed by principle.

G   *I am, &c.*

---

18. Charles IX (1550–1574), Duc d'Orléans, who became King of France on the death of his brother, Francis II. The one outstanding event of his reign was the Massacre of St. Bartholomew.

19. *Reponse aux questions d'un provincial* (part III, chap. 21), in *Oeuvres diverses*, III:958–59.

NO. 45. SATURDAY, SEPTEMBER 16, 1721.

Of the Equality and Inequality of Men.

SIR,

Men are naturally equal, and none ever rose above the rest but by force or consent: No man was ever born above all the rest, nor below them all; and therefore there never was any man in the world so good or so bad, so high or so low, but he had his fellow. Nature is a kind and benevolent parent; she constitutes no particular favourites with endowments and privileges above the rest; but for the most part sends all her offspring into the world furnished with the elements of understanding and strength, to provide for themselves: She gives them heads to consult their own security, and hands to execute their own counsels; and according to the use that they make of their faculties, and of the opportunities that they find, degrees of power and names of distinction grow amongst them, and their natural equality is lost.

Thus nature, who is their parent, deals with men: But fortune, who is their nurse, is not so benevolent and impartial; she acts wantonly and capriciously, often cruelly; and counterplotting justice as well as nature, frequently sets the fool above the wise man, and the best below the worst.

And from hence it is, that the most part of the world, attending much more to the noisy conduct and glaring effects of fortune, than to the quiet and regular proceedings of nature, are misled in their judgment upon this subject: They confound fortune with nature, and too often ascribe to natural merit and excellency the works of contrivance or chance. This however, shews that reason and equity run in our heads, while we endeavour to find a just cause for things that are not just; and this is the source of the reverence which we pay to men whom fortune sometimes lifts on high, though nature had placed them below. The populace rarely see any creature rise, but they find a reason for it in his parts; when probably the true one will be found in his own baseness, or another man's folly.

From the same reasoning may be seen why it is, that, let who will be at the head of a party, he is always extolled by his party as superior to the rest of mankind; and let who will be the first man of his country, he will never fail being complimented by many as the first of his species. But the issue and their own behaviour constantly shew, that the highest are upon a level with the rest, and often with the lowest. Men that are high are almost ever seen in a false light; the most part see them at a great distance, and through a magnifying medium; some are dazzled with their splendor, many are awed by their power. Whatever appears shining or terrible, appears great, and is magnified by the eye and the imagination.

That nature has made men equal, we know and feel; and when people come to think otherwise, there is no excess of folly and superstition which they may not be brought to practise. Thus they have made gods of dead men, and paid divine honours to many while they were yet living: They saw them to be but men, yet they worshipped them as gods. And even they who have not gone quite so far, have yet, by their wild notions of inequality, done as much mischief; they have made men, and often wicked men, to be vice-gods;[1] and then made God's power (falsely so called) as irresistible in the hands of men as in his own, and much more frightful.

It is evident to common sense, that there ought to be no inequality in society, but for the sake of society; but these men have made one man's power and will the cause of all men's misery. They gave him as far as they could the power of God, without obliging him to practise the mercy and goodness of God.

Those that think themselves furthest above the rest, are generally by their education below them all. They are debased by a conceit of their greatness: They trust to their blood; which, speaking naturally, gives them no advantage; and neglect their mind, which alone, by proper improvements, sets one man above another. It is not blood or nature, but art or accident, which makes one man excel others. Aristotle, therefore, must either have been in jest, when he said, that he, who naturally excelled all others, ought to govern all; or said it to flatter his pupil and prince, Alex-

1. Vice-gods: substitute gods.

ander the Great.[2] It is certain, that such a man never yet was found in the world, and never will be found till the end of it. Alexander himself, notwithstanding the greatness of his spirit, and his conquests, had in his own army, and perhaps among the common soldiers, men naturally as great and brave as himself, and many more wise.

Whoever pretends to be naturally superior to other men, claims from nature what she never gave to any man. He sets up for being more than a man; a character with which nature has nothing to do. She has thrown her gifts in common amongst us; and as the highest offices of nature fall to the share of the mean as well as of the great, her vilest offices are performed by the great as well as by the mean: Death and diseases are the portion of kings as well as of clowns; and the corpse of a monarch is no more exempted from stench and putrefaction, than the corpse of a slave.

Mors aequo pulsat pede.[3]

All the arts and endowments of men to acquire pre-eminence and advantages over one another, are so many proofs and confessions that they have not such pre-eminence and advantages from nature; and all their pomp, titles, and wealth, are means and devices to make the world think that they who possess them are superior in merit to those that want them. But it is not much to the glory of the upper part of mankind, that their boasted and superior merit is often the work of heralds, artificers, and money; and that many derive their whole stock of fame from ancestors, who lived an age or many ages ago.

The first founders of great families were not always men of virtue or parts; and where they were so, those that came after them did frequently, and almost generally, by trusting to their blood, disgrace their name. Such is the folly of the world, and the inconvenience of society, to allow men to be great by proxy! An evil that can scarce ever be cured. The race of French kings, called

2. *Politica*, 3.11.15 (1288a).

3. "Death strikes with an impartial foot." Horace, *Odes*, 1.4.13. The original reads: *Pallida Mors aequo pulsat pede pauperum tabernas/regumque turris* ("Pale Death with impartial foot knocks at the poor man's cottage and at princes' palaces.").

by their historians in contempt, *les rois fainéants*[4] and the succession of the Roman Caesars (in both which, for one good prince they had ten that were intolerable, either for folly, or cruelty, and often for both), might be mentioned as known proofs of the above truth; and every reader will find in his own memory many more.

I have been told of a prince, who, while yet under age,[5] being reproved by his governor for doing things ill or indecent, used to answer, *Je suis roy; I am King;* as if his quality had altered the nature of things, and he himself had been better than other men, while he acted worse. But he spoke from that spirit which had been instilled into him from his cradle. *I am King!* What then, Sir? The office of a king is not to do evil, but to prevent it. You have royal blood in your veins: But the blood of your page is, without being royal, as good as yours; or, if you doubt, try the difference in a couple of porringers[6] next time you are ill; and learn from this consideration and experiment, that by nature you are no better than your people, though subject from your fortune to be worse, as many of your ancestors have been.

If my father got an estate and title by law or the sword, I may by virtue of his will or his patent enjoy his acquisition; but if I understand neither law nor the sword, I can derive honour from neither: My honour therefore is, in the reason of things purely nominal; and I am still by nature a plebeian, as all men are.

There is nothing moral in blood, or in title, or in place: Actions only, and the causes that produce them, are moral. He therefore is best that does best. Noble blood prevents neither folly, nor lunacy, nor crimes: but frequently begets or promotes them: And noblemen, who act infamously, derive no honour from virtuous ancestors, whom they dishonour. A man who does base things, is not noble; nor great, if he do little things: A sober villager is a better man than a debauched lord; an honest mechanick than a knavish courtier.

4. Literally, "the idle kings," the term applied to the Merovingian kings, under whom the royal power declined to be replaced by a decentralized feudalism.
5. Louis XIV, who ascended the French throne at the age of five.
6. Porringer: a bowl or cup.

——*Nobilitas sola est atque unica virtus.*

Prima mihi debes animi bona; sanctus haberi
Justitiaeque tenax factis dictisque mereris?[7]

JUV. SAT. 8

We cannot bring more natural advantages into the world than other men do; but we can acquire more virtue in it than we generally acquire. To be great is not in every man's power; but to be good is in the power of all: Thus far every man may be upon a level with another, the lowest with the highest: and men might thus come to be morally as well as naturally equal.

G   *I am, &c.*

NO. 46. SATURDAY, SEPTEMBER 23, 1721.

Of the false Guises which Men put on, and their ill Effect.

SIR,

Men are often capable of doing as much, whether it be good or evil, by the appearance of parts, as by possessing them; and become really considerable by being thought so. Some, by pretending to great interest with the gods, have gained great interest among men; and plagued the earth, to prove themselves favourites of heaven: Others grow great at court, by being thought great in a party; and grow at the same time great in a party, by being thought great at court: Twice liars, they meet with the double wages of lying.

Thus is the world deceived; a thing so easily done, that rarely any man sets about it but he succeeds in it, let his parts be ever so scanty or starved. Murderers have passed for saints, buffoons for wits, and solemn dunces for wise men.

I have been often provoked to see a whole assembly, sometimes neither contemptible for number, nor figure, nor sense, give

7. "Virtue is the one and only nobility.... You owe me above all things the noble qualities of the soul; only by holding fast to justice, by word and deed, do you merit being thought blameless." Juvenal, *Saturae*, 8.20.24–25.

themselves up to the guidance and management of a silly ignorant fellow, important only in grimace and assurance: Nay, parties, potent parties, generally throw themselves into the hands and direction of men, who, though they chop them and sell them, yet want every talent for this sort of negotiation, but what they possess in the credulity of those that trust them. This is the best qualification, and it is sufficient. These are the sidrophils,[1] the cunning men in parties, as ignorant as those in Moorfields;[2] they only know more than those whom they deceive, by pretending to more.

The affectation of wisdom is a prevailing folly in the world; men fall naturally into the practise of it; and it would be pardonable, as it is common, if it went no further than the aiming at a little notice and reverence, which every body may be innocently fond of. But when men seek credit this way, in order to betray, and make use of their grimace as a trap to deceive; when they turn their admirers into followers, and their followers into money; then appearing wisdom becomes real villainy, and these pretenders grow dangerous impostors.

And this is what men frequently get by trusting more to the understanding of others than to their own, though often the better of the two; and therefore we find, in many instances, that fools mislead and govern men of sense. In things where men know nothing, they are apt to think that others know more than they; and so blindly trust to bold pretensions: And here is the great cause and first rise of sharpers and bubbles of all denominations, from demagogues and their followers, down to mountebanks and their mobs.

I think that there is not a more foolish figure in the world than a man affectedly wise: But it is not every body that sees it: and such a one is often the admiration of one sort of people, and the jest of another, at the same time. Where we see much of the outside of wisdom, it is a shrewd sign that there is but little within;

1. The allusion is unclear. Gordon appears to be playing on the word "party," *sidrophils* being a nonce word for lovers of cider; that is, party lovers.
2. Moorfields lies just outside the boundaries of the City of London and is the site of Bethlehem Hospital, Bedlam.

because they who have the least often make the greatest shew: As the greatest hypocrites are the loudest prayers.

The inside of such a man is not worth knowing; and every man must have observed his outside: His words fall from him with an uncommon weight and solemnity; his gait is stately and slow, and his garb has a turn in it of prudence and gravity, of which he that made it is the author, and by that means becomes a considerable instrument and artificer of wisdom.

This will be better illustrated in the character of Lord Plausible,[3] who having long set up for a wise man, and taking eloquence to be the most effectual sign of wisdom, is an orator and a wise man in every circumstance of his life, and to every body; he is eloquent to his footman, to his children, and at his table. Lord Plausible never converses; no, talking carelessly as other people do, would not be wise enough; he therefore does not converse in company, but makes speeches; he meditates speeches in his closet, and pronounces them where he visits. Even while he drinks tea, or plays at cards, his language is lofty and sounding; and in his gait you see the same sublime as in his words. Add to all this, an unrelenting gravity in his looks, only now and then softened by a studied smile. He never laughs without checking his muscles: mirth would be a blot upon wisdom; the good man only creates mirth in others.

Thus he grows important, without suffering in his character for his natural shallowness and acquired folly, unseen by the bulk of his party, who, being for understanding and breeding pretty much in the lower class, think him an oracle, and believe him deep in the counsels and reverence of great men, who use him civilly and laugh at him.

As a man can hardly be severely just and constant to the ways which he approves, without some degree of austereness, or what the world calls so; it is no wonder if this character, always esteemed and often beloved, becomes mimicked by those who have no pretence to it. But I am at a loss whether it be more provoking or merry, to see creatures setting up for a severity of behaviour, without one grain of justice and honour about them; pretending to

3. A somewhat pompous character in William Wycherley's play *The Plain-Dealer* (1674).

wisdom, with great conceit and stupidity; complaisant in every step and degree of corruption, yet preserving a stiffness in their behaviour, as if they were so many rigid Stoicks.

> *Quid? Si vultu torvo & pede nudo*
> *Exiguaeque togae simulet textore Catonem;*
> *Virtutemque repraesentet moresque Catonis.*[4]

There are mimicks of wisdom and virtue in all ages, as well as in that of Horace.

A man may be a lord, or a minister, or a considerable man, without declaring war against gaiety and easiness. But grave fellows, who become grave to gain importance, are by all men of sense disappointed. A wise man may be a merry fellow; and a very silly fellow may be a very grave man. The wisest men of my acquaintance are the merriest men that I know; nor could I ever find what wisdom had to to with an unpleasing and rebuking stateliness, that contradicts it. Mirth, and what these solemn drones call folly, is a piece of wisdom which they want sense to know and practise. Besides, there is a wise way of playing the fool, which wise men know how to practise, without losing their character. But your grave fellows are perhaps afraid of playing the fool, because they would do it too naturally; yet even that would be better than being thus ridiculously wise against nature.

Some men's natural heaviness passes for wisdom, and they are admired for being blockheads. Sometimes forced gravity does the same thing. Nor is it any thing new to place wisdom in grimace; many of the old philosophers did the same, and made their long beards, in particular, an eminent type of it.

> *Jussit sapientem pascere barbam.*[5]

Doubtless, like others who have lived since, they often possessed the sign only. The Schoolmen[6] were reckoned deep and

4. "What? If with fierce look and bare foot, and with the art of a threadbare gown, he were to imitate Cato, would that be sufficient to bring back Cato's virtues and habits?" Horace, *Epistulae*, 1.19.12–14.

5. "He ordered me to grow a wise man's beard." Horace, *Saturae*, 2.3.35.

6. That is, the Scholastic philosophers who dominated western philosophy between the ninth and the sixteenth centuries.

wise men, for talking unintelligibly, and their wisdom was jargon and obscurity.

They that are really wise, need not take much pains to be thought so; and they that do, are not really wise. We cannot live always upon the stretch, either of silence, or of eloquence, or of gaiety: and whoever endeavours it, shews his folly while he seeks renown.

A man of great quality and age, and of great reputation for wisdom, being once surprized by a foreign minister, while he was at play with his little children, was so far from confessing any shame for being thus caught indulging the fancy and fondness of a father, that he told the ambassador, who seemed to have found what he did not expect: "Sir, be in no pain for me; he who is accounted a wise man in the morning, will never be reckoned a fool at night." This is, no doubt, true of a man truly wise . But it is as true, that many men have passed for wise men in the morning, who have been found fools before noon.

Men, affectedly wise, need only be examined to be despised; and we find by experience, that starched gravity creates more jest and laughter amongst men of sense, who are generally frank and pleasant men, than the most remarkable levity and giddiness can do. The reverence therefore paid to such men, if it be real, is constantly the effect of ignorance: We admire them at a distance; but when we see them a little nearer, we begin to admire at our own admiration.

But such examination is never like to be very popular, and consequently such discoveries are not like to be very formidable; the multitude will never make them; there will always be a great deal in resolving to be great and wise, and great success will be ever attending it: *Si populus vult decipi, decipiatur,*[7] is at all times a safe way of reasoning. And hence drones and coxcombs will, by a false show of wisdom, be always bidding fair for the reputation of wisdom, and often for its rewards. This is more easily shewn, than mended.

G   *I am, &c.*

7. "If the people wish to be deceived, let them be deceived." The quotation has been credited to Carlo Cardinal Carafa (1517–1561), legate of Paul IV, in reference to the Parisians.

NO. 47. SATURDAY, OCTOBER 7, 1721.

Of the Frailty and Uncertainty of human Judgment.

SIR,

Human judgment is the best and surest guide that we have to follow, in affairs that are human; and even in spirituals, where the immediate word of God interposes not. But it is so liable to be corrupted and weighed down by the biases that passion, delusion, and interest hang upon it, that we ought never to trust, without caution and examination, either to our own or that of others.

Men are hardly ever brought to think themselves deceived in contending for points of interest or pleasure. But as it is rare that one man's pursuits do not cross and interfere with the pursuits of others, and as every man contends for the reasonableness of his own; though it must be in the nature of things, that they may be both in the wrong, and only one can be in the right: Hence it proceeds that men, who are so naturally alike, become morally so unlike, that sometimes there is more resemblance between a man and a wolf, than between one man and another; and that one and the same man is not one and the same man in two different stations.

The difference therefore between one man's judgment and another's, arises not so much from the natural difference between them; though that too, the structure of their organs being different, may beget different sentiments; as from the difference of their education, their situation and views, and other external causes.

Men, who in private life were just, modest, and good, have been observed, upon their elevation into high places, to have left all their virtuous and beneficent qualities behind them, and to have acted afterwards upon a new spirit, of arrogance, injustice, and oppression. And yet, perhaps, their latter actions had as much the sanction of their own judgment as their first.

England could not boast of a greater patriot than the great Earl of Strafford,[1] while he was yet a private commoner. No man exposed better, or more zealously, the encroachments and oppressions practised by the court upon the kingdom, or contended more loudly for a redress of grievances: But he was no sooner got into the court, but he began openly to counter-act the whole course of his past life: He devised new ways of terror and oppression, heightened all those grievances of which he had complained; and, as the excellent Lord Falkland said of him in the House of Commons, the oppressions which he committed were "so various, so many, and so mighty, as were never committed by any governor in any government since Verres left Sicily."[2] But though the two great parts of his life, were thus prodigiously inconsistent, I do not remember that he ever condemned the worst, though he suffered for it, or recanted the best. It is probable, that his judgment in both cases approved his conduct.

Nor is the judgment of men varied by great and considerable causes only; to the disgrace of our reason we must own, that little ones do it as effectually. A wise man ruffled by an accident, or heated by liquor, shall talk and act like a madman or a fool; as a madman, with a little soothing and management, shall talk like a wise man: And there are instances of very able men, who, having done great service to their prince and country, have undone it all from motives that are shameful to mention. Perhaps they missed a smile from him, when they expected one; or met with a satirical[3] jest, when they expected none: and thus, piqued by a little real mirth or fancied neglect, they have run into all the excesses of dis-

1. The Earl of Strafford, chief advisor to Charles I, was originally a staunch opponent of royal policy. In the Parliament of 1628, he supported the call for resistance to arbitrary taxation and imprisonment and led the move for a bill securing the liberties of Englishmen. It was only in 1629, after having been raised to the peerage and when the breach between King and Parliament appeared to be inevitable, that Strafford joined the King's party.

2. Lucius Cary, second Viscount Falkland (c. 1610–1643), one of the ministers of Charles I during the Civil War. Falkland was universally regarded as a man of principle and of great intellectual integrity, whose support for the King rested solely on his scruples respecting rebellion. He supported Strafford's prosecution and voted for his attainder in 1641. The statement appears in Falkland's speech to the House of Feb. 9, 1640.

3. Satyrical: lascivious.

loyalty and rebellion, and either ruined their country, or themselves and their families in attempting it. Others, misled by a gracious nod, or a squeeze by the hand, or a few fair promises no better than either, have, by running all the contrary lengths of complaisance and subserviency, done as much mischief to their country, without intending it any, and perhaps thinking that they did it none. There are examples of the same men practising both these extremes.

So mechanical a thing is human judgment! So easily is the human machine disconcerted and put out of its tone! And the mind subsisting in it, and acting by it, is calm or ruffled as its vehicle is so. But though the various accidents and disorders happening to the body, are the certain causes of disorders and irregular operations in the mind; yet causes that are internal affect it still more; I mean the stimulations of ambition, revenge, lust, and avarice. These are the great causes of the several irregular and vicious pursuits of men.

Neither is it to be expected, that men disagreeing in interest, will ever agree in judgment. Wrong, with advantages attending it, will be turned into right, falsehood into truth; and, as often as reason is against a man, a man will be against reason: And both truth and right, when they thwart the interests and passions of men, will be used like enemies, and called names.

It is remarkable that men, when they differ in any thing considerable, or which they think considerable, will be apt to differ in almost every thing else. Their differences beget contradiction, contradiction begets heat, heat quickly rises into resentment, rage, and ill-will. Thus they differ in affections, as they differ in judgment; and the contention, which began in pride, ends in anger.

The acquiescing sincerely in the judgment of another, without the concurrence of our own, and without any advantage, real or fancied, moving us to such acquiescence, is a compliment which I do not know that one man ever paid to another: An unanswerable argument, why no man should be provoked at those whom he cannot convince; since they, having reasons, or thinking that they have reasons, on the contrary side, as strong as his, or stronger, have as much cause to be provoked with him for not acquiescing in theirs. Yet there are but few debates of consequence in this world, where the arguments are not seconded by wrath, and often supplied by it.

But this is not the way of dealing with men; nor is there any other way of persuading them into your judgment, but by shewing it their interest. Their minds are so corrupted by their appetites, that, generally speaking, their judgment is nothing but their interest in theory; and their interest is their judgment reduced into practice. This will account for the contradictory parts which men play, and the contrary parties that they occasionally choose. This serves them with reasons for the unreasonable things that they do, turns roguery into honesty, madness into merit.

In truth, whenever men leave their own judgment for the judgment of others, as they sometimes do, they either do it for gain, or glory, or pleasure, or for the avoiding of shame, or some such cause; all which motives are interest, as is every thing else that they do for their own sakes. Thus honesty is often only the fear of infamy, and honour the appetite of applause: Thus men rush into danger and death, to gratify love or anger, or to acquire fame: And thus they are faithful to their word and engagement, to avoid the reproach of treachery.

Men are so apt to link their approbation to their profit and pleasure, that their interest, though ever so vile, absurd, and unjustifiable, becomes really their judgment. I do not think that human art and imagination could have invented tenets more false and abominable, more chimerical or mischievous, than are those of the *infallibility of the Pope,* and the *irresistibleness of tyrants;* that is, that one man, living in the hourly practice of error, or vice, or folly, and often of them all, shall judge for the whole earth, and do what God has not done; that is, fashion the minds of all the human race like his own, and make them his sacrifices, where he cannot make them his slaves: And that another man shall have a divine right to represent God and govern man, by acting against God and destroying man.

These are such monstrous absurdities, such terrible, ridiculous, and inhuman inventions, as could arise from nothing but pride and avarice on one side, and fear and flattery on the other; and could be defended by nothing but the most brutish force, or the most abandoned impudence. Yet we have seen these monstrous absurdities defended, and God Almighty declared their defender; even him, who is the God of mercy and truth, made, blasphemously, the author of cruelty and lies.

In this light do these things appear to one who considers them without embarking in them, and receiving any advantage from them. But those who gain or subsist by them, see them in a different light: I doubt not but their judgment, as they call it, does actually blend with their interest, or for the most part does; and therefore they are really in earnest in maintaining it. Folly, falsehood, and villainy, are no longer called by their own names, nor thought to deserve them, by those that reap advantages from them. Even those, who have practised the greatest of all evils, even that of destroying God's people, have thought that in doing it they did God good service. Our blessed Saviour foretold it; and his words have been fulfilling ever since, and perhaps will be till he return.

Oliver Cromwell fought God in all his oppressions; and though I am sure that he was an usurper, I am not sure that he was a hypocrite, at least all along; though it is most probable that he was one at first. But he had so long personated a saint, that he seems at last to have thought himself one; and when he saw his latter end approaching, he was so far from shewing any compunction for the part which he had acted, that he, on the contrary, boasted that he had been the cause of much good to this nation; and added such ejaculations and prayers, as shewed that he possessed his mind in peace, and was not without confidence in God.

The emperor of Morocco, than whom a more inhuman butcher never lived, makes God the author of all his barbarities; and when he murders a slave (as he does every day some) out of wantonness or wrath, he lifts up his eyes and says, "Tis God that does it": No man talks more of God and religion, and he certainly thinks himself a most religious man.

Let all this serve to shew, how little men's judgment is to be trusted when interest follows it, and is probably both the cause and the effect. Let it abate our confidence in particular men, who may make our trust in them the means of their misleading us: Let us learn to believe no man the more, for that he believes himself; since men are as obstinate in error, especially in gainful error, as they are in truth; and more so, where truth is not gainful: And lastly, let us swallow no man's judgments, without judging of it and him; and yield up our reason to no man's authority, nor our interest to any man's direction, any farther than prudence or necessity obliges us. Let us remember what the world has ever got by implicit faith of any kind whatsoever.

G   *I am, &c.*

NO. 48. SATURDAY, OCTOBER 14, 1721.

 The general unhappy State of the World, from the Baseness and Iniquity of its Governors in most Countries.

SIR,

While I have been reading history, or considering the state of human affairs, how woefully they are neglected, how foolishly managed, or how wickedly disconcerted and confounded, in the most and best countries: When I have remembered how large, every where, is the source of mischief, how easily it is set a running, and how plentifully it flows; how it is daily breaking into new channels, and yet none of the old ones are ever suffered to wax dry: I have been apt to wonder, that the general condition of mankind, though already vastly unhappy, is not still worse.

Pope Aeneas Sylvius must have had such reflections as these, when he said, that this world did, in a great measure, govern itself.[1] He had many examples before his eyes, how easy it was to govern wretchedly, and yet continue to govern. The papacy itself

1. The reference is to Enea Silvio de Piccolomini (1405–1464), who upon being raised to the papal throne took the name Pius II. His *Commentaries*, a history of his life and times, was widely read.

might particularly have furnished him with many examples. It is a fairy dominion, founded upon non-entities, inventions, and abominations; supported by lies and terrors; exercised with cruelty, craft, and rapine; and producing meanness, delusion, and poverty, where-ever it prevails.

What could appear more strange, incredible, and shameful, than to see a mean monk, residing in a corner of the world, and ruling and plundering it all; living in crimes, pride and folly, and controlling Christendom by the sounds of humility, holiness, and infallibility; subsisting upon the spoils and industry of nations, and engaging nations in a blind conspiracy against themselves, for the defence of their oppressor; pronouncing the peace of God to mankind, and animating mankind to continual quarrels and slaughters; declaring himself the vicar of Christ, and making unrelenting war against the followers of Christ; and, finally, the father of Christendom, and the destroyer of Christians.

All this villainy and impudence was obvious to common sense, and felt by long experience. But how little do men see, when they are taught to be afraid of their eye-sight! Even the Reformation, one of the greatest blessings that ever befell Europe, has but partially removed this mighty and enormous usurpation. The root of the evil still remains: and men are not yet weary of fighting about words, subtleties, chimeras, and about the shape of their thoughts and imagination; a thing as much out of their own power, as the shape of their limbs, or the motion of the winds: The issue and design of all which is, that their leaders in strife reap the fruits of it, and gather the spoils, the whole spoils of those battles, in which craft only blows the trumpet, while ignorance wields the sword, and runs all the danger.

If in this, as in other wars, none would fight but those that are paid, or find their account in fighting, the combatants would soon be reduced to a few; and they too would quickly leave a field where there was no booty.

Will the world never learn, that one man's corn grows not the worse, because another man uses different words in his devotion? That pride and anger, wealth and power, are of no religion? And that religion is inseparable from charity and peace?

I am told, that the famous combustion raised some years ago at Hamburgh, by one Krumbultz,[2] a divine, and in which that free city had like to have perished, was occasioned by this momentous question, namely, whether in the Lord's Prayer we should say, *Our Father,* or, *Father, our.* A hopeful point of debate, to be the cause of civil dissension, and a true specimen of the importance and consequences of ecclesiastical disputes, and of the spirit of those that manage them!

It is a shameful satire upon the wickedness of some, and the weakness of others, thus to endanger the peace of society and their own, for the sake of a sound; to be thus eager for trifles; thus to concern heaven and earth in behalf of conceits, which of themselves concern neither: but, as they are generally managed, do both provoke God, and hurt men. But so it will ever be, as long as men, in possession of reverence, find their ends and gratifications in fetching knotty distinctions out of the plain word of God and making them of equal importance with it.

Thus unhappy has the greatest part of the world been, and is, in its ghostly government; two words which are a contradiction to each other; since the mind and understanding, in which alone all religion that is rational doth reside, can never be altered or controlled by any other means than that of counsel, reasoning, and exhortation; which method is utterly inconsistent with force and positive authority, as the same are implied in the idea of government.

Nor can I say, that mankind have been more happy in their civil lot, and in the administration of their temporal affairs; which are almost every where in a wretched situation, and they themselves under the iron hand of the oppressor. The whole terraqueous globe cannot shew five free kingdoms; nor perhaps half so many kings, who make the ease and prosperity of their people their care.

In enslaved countries (that is, in all countries, except our own, and a very few more) the good of the governed is so far from entering into the hearts and counsels of the governors, that it is

2. Christian Krumbholz (1662–1725), pastor of St. Peter's in Hamburg and champion of orthodox Lutheranism. Krumbholz was active in the struggle against the Pietists in that city at the turn of the century.

opposite to the genius of their politicks, either to do them good, or to suffer them to acquire it for themselves. Their happiness and security, which are the very ends of magistracy, would be terrible to their magistrates; who, being the publick enemies of their country, are forced, for their own safety, to leave their people none.

How vile is that government, and those governors, whose only strength lies in whips and chains; a sort of instrument of servitude, which it would much better become the baseness of these men's natures to wear themselves, than to inflict upon others! A prince of slaves is a slave; he is only the biggest and the worst; just as the chief of the banditti is one of them. Such a prince is but a national executioner, and for a scepter he carries a bloody knife.

Such, for the most part, by far the most part, are the governors of the world: They derive their whole greatness, plenty, splendor, and security, from the misery, poverty, peril, and destruction of the governed. Whoever makes just, equal, and impartial laws, does, by doing so, but declare to the people, *Be wicked at your peril:* But he who rules them by terrors and standing armies, does, in effect, tell them in a terrible tone, *Be happy if you dare.*

Who, that has human compassion, can help feeling the sorrows of his wretched race, and behold, unconcerned, the forlorn and abject state of mankind? Monks deceiving, alarming, and sponging them; their governors taxing, mulcting, and squeezing them! Soldiers harrassing, oppressing, and butchering them! And, in short, all the bitter evils and crying miseries in human power to inflict, deliberately and daily inflicted upon them! Nor do things mend; on the contrary, the mischiefs and misfortunes of the world grow hourly greater, and its inhabitants thinner.

All these black considerations would lead a man, who had no other spirit or guide but that of nature, to think that providence, tempted by the sins of men, had long ago renounced them, or signed a decree of vengeance against them, which has ever since been dreadfully executed, and continues to be.

If one was to consider mankind in theory only, his own species would make no small figure in his imagination; he would see them formed by a divine hand, and according to a divine model; possessed of all the advantages of strength and contrivance, guided by reason, made wise by observation, and cautious by their own foresight and the experience of others; directed by laws and human constitutions; rendered discerning by the frequent trials of good and evil, and many of them enlightened by divine revelation: He would see them lords of the creation, arbiters of their own condition and felicity, invested with the use and property of sea and land, and with dominion over every other creature.

Thus mankind appear in speculation, powerful, wise, just, equal, and happy. But viewed in another light, they make another appearance. They use one another worse than they do the beasts of the field; and, by the wretched and monstrous oeconomy and government, almost every where found amongst them, they would seem not to have more understanding, as they have certainly less happiness. The beasts no where appoint or suffer one of their own herd to monopolize the whole soil, to engross every advantage to himself, to deprive them of all, to kill and destroy, to disperse and to starve them at his pleasure. Every one of them equally enjoys the shelter and pasture, the air and the water, which nature makes common to them all.

But men, their masters, cannot boast such security and justice: they generally live at the mere mercy of one, one of themselves, whose views suffer him to have no mercy. He is often a madman, often an idiot, often a destroyer; and the whole art of his government consisting in oppressing and terrifying, no other talent is required but a merciless spirit and brutal force.

Such is an arbitrary prince, and the descendants of Adam know few others. Sometimes a creature is seen to start into imperial power, whom the world never knew before, or knew only for his infamy: Taken out of the stews[3] or out of a dungeon, into a throne; and without knowing how to rule himself, he rules an empire; living a recluse, and seen by nobody, he governs all but the women or parasites, who govern him: Millions of men, and their properties, are at the sole discretion of one who has none; and a creature void of humanity disposes wantonly of a great part of human kind.

3. Stews: brothels.

This is the dismal state of all Asia and of all Africa, except a few free towns. The spirit of their monarchs, which is generally alike, may be seen in a story (among many others) which Knox tells us of the King of Ceylon, who, being in danger of drowning, was saved by the officious affection or ambition of one of his slaves, who leaped into the water, and ventured his own life to preserve his master's. This, one would think, was the greatest and most heroick kindness that one man could do another. But mark how the monarch requites it! why, the first thing he did after he came to himself, was to order the belly of his preserver to be ripped up, for daring to touch the person of his sacred Majesty.[4]

Nature has prepared many advantages and pleasures for the use of mankind, given them taste to enjoy them, and sagacity to improve them: But their governors, almost universally, frustrate the kind purposes of nature, render her beneficence abortive, and mar all human happiness. They have successfully studied the arts of misery, and propagated the practice.

It is a melancholy reflection, that when human affairs are put into a bad way, where they do not speedily recover, they never recover, or rarely ever. One great reason is, that power is always on the worst side, either promoting mischief, or preventing its removal; and the champions of dishonesty and oppression are more artful and better paid than the patrons of justice and innocence.

It has hitherto been the good fortune of England (and I hope always will be) when attempts have been made upon its liberty, to recover it before it was gone, at least before the sense of it was gone. And therefore it still subsists in spite of all the powerful, popular, and sanctified attacks that have been made, and frequently made, upon it. Let us make much of it; while it remains, it will make us amends for all the losses and miscarriages which we have fallen under, or may fall under, and will enable us to get the better of them. It is the root of our felicity, and all our civil advantages grow from it. By it we exceed almost all other nations, many

4. Robert Knox (1640?–1720), *An Historical Relation of the Island* [of] *Ceylon in the East Indies: Together With an Account of the Detaining in Captivity* [of] *the Author . . . and of the Author's Miraculous Escape* (London: Printed by R. Chiswell, 1681), p. 87.

more degrees than some of them exceed us in sun and soil: We are men, and they are slaves. Only government founded upon liberty, is a publick blessing; without liberty, it is a publick curse, and a publick warrant for depredation and slaughter.

Let us therefore remember the mighty difference between ourselves and other nations, and the glorious cause of it, and always dearly cherish it. We are not the prey of monks, or janizaries, or dragoons, nor the blind slaves of unaccountable will and pleasure. Our lives and properties are secured by the best bulwark in the world, that of laws made by ourselves, and executed by our magistrates, who are likewise made by us; and when they are dishonestly executed, or wilfully neglected, our constitution affords a remedy, a tried and a practicable remedy. And as no nation ever lost its liberty but by the force of foreign invaders, or the domestick treachery of its own magistrates; we have the sea and a great navy for our defenders against the former; and exorbitancies of the other are prevented or restrained by an excellent counterpoise, in the frame of our legislature.

That we may be for ever able to boast of all these blessings, these glorious and uncommon blessings, is the cordial wish and passionate prayer of

G   *Yours, &c.*

NO. 49. SATURDAY, OCTOBER 21, 1721.

Of the Power of Prejudice.

SIR,

Men boast of their reason, and might justly, if they used it freely, and applied it properly; but considering that generally in their moral conduct they are guided by such reasons as are a shame and a contradiction to reason, it seems to be thrown away upon them: Indeed so little, or so wrong, is the use which they make of it, that it would be really [better] for their reputation if they had none.

But though the many scarce use it all, and none so much as they ought; yet every man thinks he does, and never wants something which he calls reason, for the justification of his folly or wickedness. Prejudice or passion steps into its room, takes its name; and, under the appearance of reason, does things which reason abhors. And thus reason, as well as religion, is forced to furnish its enemies with arms against itself; and the abuse of it is worse and more dangerous than the absolute want of it; as an idiot is less terrible and less odious than a knave, and as a harmless pagan is a much more amiable character than an outrageous persecuting bigot. So that as no religion at all is better than a mischievous religion; that is to say, any religion that prompts men to hurt one another; so the absence or inactivity of the faculties is better than the quickness of faculties wickedly applied.

Of all the many false lights that mislead men from their reason, prejudice is one of the foremost and most successful; and though no two things upon earth are more opposite in their natures, or more destructive of each other, than reason and prejudice are; yet they are often made to pass for each other: And as some men will give you very good reasons for their being in the wrong themselves, there are those too, who will give you as good, why others should not be in the right; that is, the prejudices of some would be thought wisdom, and the wisdom of others is miscalled prejudice. The worst things that men do, called by a good name, pass for the best; and the best, blackened by an ill name, pass for the worst. Such is the force of prejudice in the world, and so successfully does this foe to reason ape reason!

Prejudice is an obstinate and unreasonable attachment to an opinion, supported only by a wilfulness to maintain it, whether regarding men or things: It links the good with the bad, the bad with the good, and hates or loves by the lump. Thus if a man be called a saint, his worst actions are sainted with him; his very ignorance and cruelty, and even his dirtiness and his dreams, are made sacred and meritorious; as may be seen at large in the Romish legends, where the principal qualification for saintship seems to have consisted in stark raving madness, and in an implacable and bloody fury towards all sense and sobriety. And thus, even with us, if a man passes for a good man, his bad deeds are often thought good ones, by those that think him so, and only because they think him so.

On the other side, if a man be called an atheist, the odium of that name, where it is believed true, is made a blot upon his best actions and greatest virtues, and to defeat them as well as soil them. That there are such men as atheists, can only be imagined by those, who, doubting of a deity themselves, may naturally enough suppose that there are others who quite disbelieve one: For my own particular, I cannot think that there are any such men; but if there were, I cannot think that truth and sobriety in an atheist are worse than in another man. That black is not white, and that two and two make four, is as true out of the mouth of an atheist, as out of the mouth of an apostle: A penny given by an atheist to a beggar, is better alms than a half-penny given by a believer; and the good sense of an atheist is preferable to the mistakes of a good Christian: In short, whatever reputed atheists do well, or speak truly, is more to be imitated and credited, than what the greatest believers do wickedly, or say falsely; and even in the business of bearing testimony, or making a report, in which cases the credit and reputation of the witness gives some weight, or none, to what he says, more regard is to be had to the word of an unbeliever who has no interest on either side, than to the word of a believer who has.

So that as no man is to be believed an atheist, unless he is evidently proved one; which, where he himself denies it, can be done by God only: So neither are the good or bad actions of an atheist worse, with respect to the world at least, for his being one; though the sin of a saint is more sinful than that of a pagan. As it is therefore the blackest and most barbarous villainy to charge any man with atheism, who is no atheist; it is the greatest folly to think that any man's crimes are the less for the name of him that commits them; or that truth is less or more truth, for the ill or good name of him that speaks it.

Prejudice has long taught men, contrary to all reason, to think otherwise; and to consider, not what was done or said, but who were the men that said or did it. A happy expedient, I must own, to acquire dominion, and to exercise it, and to keep, for that end; mankind ignorant and base, as their teachers and governors too generally keep them! And therefore, in most parts of the world, truth is a capital crime; and the Pope and Mahomet, the Alcoran and the mass-book, and the like sounds, with a competent assistance of fire and sword, are sufficient to convince and govern all true Catholicks and Mussulmen.

But we live in a land of liberty; and have, I hope, well-nigh wiped off the scandal of being led or animated by noise or names, as were many of our forefathers; whose reason, being in other men's keeping, was generally turned upon them, and co-operated with other causes towards keeping them in bondage. They were decoyed or frightened into folly and chains; some saw not their condition, others wanted courage or power to mend it. But with liberty light has sprung in, and we have got rid of the terror and delusion occasioned by solemn and ill sounding names; a sort of bugbears that frighten only in the dark: We have learned, that we are as fit to use our own understandings, as they are whose understandings are no better than ours; and that there is no merit in sounds, nor in those actions which a wicked man may practise as well as a good man, without departing from his character.

True learning and prejudices cannot subsist together; and therefore, though in societies of pedants, little else is to be found but prejudices, bitterness, ignorance, and ill-breeding; I am amazed to hear, that in societies of gentlemen, formed for the promoting of knowledge, and liberty of enquiry, a province utterly inconsistent with the narrow spirit of prejudice, there are yet found instances of the greatest. I hope, however, that it is not true, what I am told, that the Royal Society refused admitting Mr. Whiston[1] and another ingenious gentleman as members, because the one was an Arian, and the other a Black. Who would imagine, that natural complexion, or religious opinions, could any way affect the discovery of fossils and cockleshells, or the improvement of mustard and pickles? But I dare say, that this is only a story raised, to

1. William Whiston (1667–1752), mathematician, who also wrote on theological questions. In 1703 Whiston replaced Sir Isaac Newton as Lucasian professor of mathematics at Cambridge, but his outspoken adherence to Arianism led to his expulsion from the university in 1710.

bring that learned body into ridicule and contempt: If it were true, it would justify the jest made upon them by a gentleman, who, being asked by some of them, whether he had a mind to be a member? told them, "No, gentlemen, 'tis impossible; you see I have a mole on my upper lip, and I am subject to talk in my sleep."

It is scarce credible, but that we see it, how violently and shamefully prejudice flies in the face of reason, and often gets the better of it, in instances too where reason seems to be strongest and most obvious. I shall mention a remarkable one.

Alexander and Caesar are never mentioned but with applause, or thought of but as amiable characters, and the true patterns of princes and heroes, though it is certain that there never lived more wicked men; they turned the world upside down, and usurped its power; they paved their way to dominion with dead bodies, and were the oppressors and butchers of [the] human race. Here is fact, plain undeniable fact, against prejudice and opinion.

Oliver Cromwell, on the contrary, is scarce ever mentioned but with detestation, or thought of but as a monster; though it is as certain that he never did the hundredth part of the mischief that was done by either of the other two. He had at least as good a right to Great Britain as they had to the globe, and ruled it with more equity and less blood. He was, doubtless, an usurper, but a little one; and though wicked enough, really an innocent man compared to them. Nor was he at all below them in parts and courage. What therefore is the cause of this mighty and unjust difference, where the lesser wickedness is most magnified, and least excused; and where the blackest criminals and the highest usurpers are admired and extolled?

There is yet one effect of prejudice more impious than all the rest; I mean, the daring presumption of those men who wantonly apply the judgments of God to others, and of calling those things judgments which are not so. Probably nothing ever yet happened to one man, but has happened to another, and a different man: The wicked live in as much prosperity, and die with as few agonies, as do the righteous; who, I think, are allowed to be here below much the more unhappy of the two. Who has told us, what

God can only tell, that misfortunes are judgments, or that death is one? That death which is common to all men? And as to the different and disastrous manners of dying; have not fire and sword, famine and pestilence, poison and torture, wild beasts and accidents, destroyed as many good men as evil men?

How foolish and insolent are we! When we are angry, unreasonably angry with one another, we presumptuously think that God, the good and all-wise God, is so too; by which we profanely suggest, that he is a being as weak, ridiculous, and passionate as ourselves. Whereas that often pleases God, which is hated by man; and that which is really a blessing, is often thought a curse: and therefore some wickedly think the judgment of God due to others for things that entitle them rather to God's favour. So wickedly do men differ in their sentiments and affections!

They who call the misfortunes of others judgments upon them, plainly enough own, though not in words, that they wish for judgments upon others, or are glad when they happen. What can we say of such an anti-Christian spirit as this?

When the heathens were uppermost, they charged the Christians with being the cause of all the evils and misfortunes that befell the Roman empire, such as inundations, plagues, earthquakes, and the like; and one of the fathers writ a book, to prove, that all those things had been from the beginning;[2] and whoever makes the like charge now against any man, or body of men, may be silenced, if he has modesty, sense, or shame, in him, by the same answer.

G   *I am, &c.*

---

2. The reference is to St. Augustine's *De civitate Dei*, which was intended as a response to those who attributed the sack of Rome by the Visigoths in 410 to the fact that the city's gods had been abandoned.

NO. 50. SATURDAY, OCTOBER 28, 1721.

An Idea of the Turkish Government, taken from Sir Paul Ricaut.

SIR,

Sir Paul Ricaut's *State of the Ottoman Empire,* is what I have quoted before in these letters: It is written with fidelity and judgment, and gives us a good idea of that horrible and destroying government; a government fierce and inhuman, founded in blood, supported by barbarity; and a government that has a declared enmity to all that is good and lovely in the eyes of mankind.

I have therefore transcribed the following passage from him,[1] to shew my countrymen the abject, the deplorable condition of that people, and the brutish and destructive genius of their government, and I do it with a benevolent view, to make them more and more in love with their own, and passionate for its preservation.

No man's authority is, or ought to be, of any weight for or against truth, when every man sees it, or may see it: but since weak men, and they that are worse, make a difficulty of crediting the reasonings and relations of any men about any thing, unless they know and approve his opinions in every thing; I think it not amiss to acquaint my readers, that Sir Paul was a sincere monarchy-man, and an unquestionable friend to our civil and religious establishment; but having long seen the dismal terrors and desolations of absolute monarchy, he could not help observing the infinite distance between that and a limited one; as may be seen in the following quotation.

For my own particular, I think it contrary to common sense to concern myself with the character of a writer, in those writings which do not concern his character: And therefore in matters of reason or fact, Cicero is as much regarded by me as Dr.

---

1. The excerpt that follows is taken from Rycaut's *The Present State of the Ottoman Empire,* bk. I, chap. 17 (pp. 75–79).

Tillotson; and I credit Livy as much as I do Dr. Prideaux.[2] For this reason, in reading authors, Christian or heathen, monarchical or republican, I do not consider their system, but their sense; which I shall therefore, as often as I see necessary, give in their own words, where I cannot mend them: And as often as they speak my thoughts as well, or better than I could speak them myself, I shall not scruple being beholden to them.

G   *I am, &c.*

"He that is an eye-witness and strict observer of the various changes and chances in the greatness, honours, and riches of the Turks, hath a lively emblem before him of the unconstancy and mutability of human affairs. Fortune so strangely sports with this people, that a comedy or a tragedy on the stage, with all its scenes, is scarce sooner opened or ended, than the fate of divers great men, who in the day-time being exhaled into high sublimity by the powerful rays of the Sultan's favour, fall or vanish in the night, like a meteor. The reason hereof, if duly considered, may be of great use as things stand here; that is, the power of the Grand Seignior; for in this constitution, the benefit of the emperor is consulted before the welfare of the people.

* * *

"And this course does not only evidence the power of the Grand Seignior; but likewise increases it: For none are advanced in these times to office, but pay the Grand Seignior vast sums of money for it, according to the riches and expectations of profit from the charge. Some pay, as the bashaws of Grand Cairo and Babylon, three or four hundred thousand dollars upon passing the commission; others one, others two hundred thousand; some fifty thousand, as their places are more or less considerable; and the money is most commonly taken up at interest at 40 or 50 per cent

2. John Tillotson (1630–1694), appointed Archbishop of Canterbury in 1691. Tillotson's Whig credentials were impeccable; he was on intimate terms with William and Mary and was regarded with particular enmity by the Jacobites. Humphrey Prideaux (1648–1724), theologian and Orientalist of some note. Prideaux's Whiggish sympathies, as well as his Low Church sentiments, colored his numerous publications.

for the year, and sometimes at double, when they are constrained to become debtors to the covetous eunuchs of the seraglio. So that every one, at his first entrance into office, looks upon himself (as indeed he is) greatly indebted, and obliged, by justice or injustice, right or wrong, speedily to disburden himself of the debts, and improve his own principal in the world; and this design must not be long in performance, lest the hasty edict overtake him before the work is done, and call him to an account for the improvement of his talent.

"Taking then all circumstances together, the covetous disposition of a Turk, the cruelty and narrowness of soul in those men commonly that are born and educated in want; think what oppression, what rapine and violence must be exercised, to satisfy the appetite of these men, who come famished with immense desires and strange considerations to satisfy!

Diu sordidus, repente dives mutationem fortunae male [tegebat], accensis egestate longa cupidinibus immoderatus.[3]

Tacit.

"So that justice in its common course is set to sale; and it is very rare, when any law-suit is in hand, but bargains are made for the sentence; and he hath most right, who hath most money to make him *rectus in curia*,[4] and advance his cause; and it is the common course for both parties at difference, before they appear together in presence of the judge, to apply themselves singly to him, and try whose donative and present hath the most in it of temptation; and it is no wonder if corrupt men exercise this kind of trafficking with justice, for having before bought the office, of consequence they must sell the fruit.

"Add hereunto a strange kind of facility in the Turks, for a trifle or small hire, to give false witness in any case, especially (and that with a word) when the controversy happens between a Chris-

3. "Having long been poor and suddenly becoming rich, he barely concealed his change of fortune; his cupidity having been excited by long poverty, he lacked all restraint." Tacitus, *Historiae*, 1.66.
4. Literally, "upright in the senate-house."

tian and a Turk; and then the pretence is for the Mussulmanleek,[5] as they call it; the cause is religious, and hallows all falseness and forgery in the testimony.

"This consideration and practice made an English ambassador, upon renewing the Capitulations,[6] to insert an article of caution against the testimony of Turks, as never to be admitted or pleaded in any court of Turkish justice, against the English interest.

"In the times of the best emperors, when virtue and deserts were considered, and the empire flourished and increased, men had offices conferred upon them for their merits, and good services were rewarded freely and with bounty, without sums of money and payments. But now it is quite contrary, and all matters run out of course; a manifest token, in my opinion, of the declension and decay of the empire! However, this serves in part the great end of the empire; for bashaws and great men, having a kind of necessity upon them to oppress their subjects, the people thereby lose their courage; and by continual taxes and seizures upon what they gain, poverty subdues their spirits, and makes them more patiently suffer all kind of injustice and violence that can be offered them, without thoughts or motion to rebellion: And so the Lord Verulam says in his *Essays,* that it is impossible for a people overladen with taxes ever to become martial or valiant; for no nation can be the lion's whelp, and the ass between two burdens.[7]

"By this means the Turk preserves so many different sorts of people, as he hath conquered, in due obedience, using no other help than a severe hand, joined to all kind of oppression: But such as are Turks, and bear any name of office or degree in the service of the empire, feel but part of this oppression, and live with all

5. That is, Islam.

6. The reference is to the treaty granting the British extraterritorial jurisdiction within the borders of the Ottoman Empire.

7. Francis Bacon, Baron Verulam and Viscount St. Albans (1561–1626), noted English philosopher and statesman. The sentiment appears in "Of Inlarging the Bounds of Kingdoms and States" (essay No. 32) in *Lord Bacon's Essays, or Counsels Moral and Civil,* trans. from the Latin by William Willymott (2 vols.; London: Printed by H. Parson, etc., 1720), I:194.

freedom, having their spirits raised by a licence they attain to insult over others that dare not resist them.

"But the issue and conclusion of the spoils that these great men make on subjects is very remarkable: For, as if God were pleased to evidence his just punishment more evidently and plainly here than in other sins, scarce any of all these bashaws that have made haste to be rich, have escaped the Grand Seignior's hands; but he either wholly divests them of all, or will share the best part of the prey with them. Amongst whom I have observed none passes so hardly as the bashaws of Grand Cairo, because it is the richest and most powerful of all the governments of this empire; and so, either in his journey home, or after his return, he loses his life by publick command, or at least is rifled of his goods as ill got, which are condemned to the Grand Seignior's treasury: And it is strange yet to see with what heat these men labour to amass riches, which they know by often experiences have proved but collections for their master; and only the odium and curses which the oppressed wretches have vented against their rapine; remain to themselves.

Rebus secundis avidi, adversis autem incauti.[8]

Tacit.

*   *   *

"The Turk understands well how profitable it is for the constitution of this estate, to use evil instruments, who may oppress and poll his people, intending afterwards for himself the whole harvest of their labours; they remaining with their hatred, while the prince, under colour of performing justice, procures both riches and fame together.

"If it be suspected that any great man intends to make combustion or mutiny in his government, or that his wealth or natural abilities render him formidable, without further inquisition or scrutiny, all discontent of the Grand Seignior is dissembled, and perhaps a horse, or sword, or sable vest, is reported to be pre-

8. "No less intractable in success than careless in adversity." Tacitus, *Annales,* 1.68.

sented, and all fair treatment is counterfeited, till the executioner gets the bow-string about his neck, and then they care not how rudely they deal with him: Just like the birds in Plutarch, that beat the cuckoo, for fear that in time he should become a hawk.[9]

"And to make more room for the multitude of officers that crowd for preferments, and to act the cruel edicts of the empire with the least noise; oftentimes when a great personage is removed from his place of trust, and sent with a new commission to the charge, perhaps, of a greater government; and though he depart from the regal seat with all fair demonstrations of favour, yet before he hath advanced three days in his journey, triumphing in the multitude of his servants and his late hopes, the fatal command overtakes him, and, without any accusation or cause, other than the will of the Sultan, he is barbarously put to death, and his body thrown into the dirt of a foreign and unknown country, without solemnity of funeral or monument; and he is no sooner in his grave, than his memory is forgotten.

"Hence are apparent the causes of the decay of arts amongst the Turks; and of the neglect and want of care in manuring and cultivating their lands; why their houses and private buildings are made slight, and not durable for more than ten or twenty years; why you find there no delightful orchards, and pleasant gardens and plantations; and why, in those countries where nature hath contributed so much on her part, there are no additional labours of art to complete all, and turn it into a paradise: For men, knowing no certain heir, nor who shall succeed them in their labours, contrive only for a few years' enjoyment. And moreover, men are afraid of shewing too much ostentation or magnificence in their palaces, or ingenuity in the pleasures of their gardens, lest they should bring on them the same fate that Naboth's vineyard occasioned to its master.[10] And therefore men neglect all applications to the studies of arts and sciences, but only such as are necessary to the mere course of living: For the fear and crime of being

9. Plutarch, *Aratus*, 30. The fable is taken from Aesop.

10. Having refused to sell his vineyard to the king, Naboth was falsely accused of blasphemy by Queen Jezebel and he, together with his family, were stoned to death (1 Kings 21:8–14).

known to be rich, makes them appear outwardly poor; and so become naturally Stoicks and philosophers in all the points of a reserved and cautious life.

"And here I am at a stand, and cannot conclude, without contemplating a while, and pleasing myself with the thoughts of the blessedness, the happiness, the liberty of my own country; where men, under the protection and safe influence of a gracious and the best prince in the world [He might with more propriety have said, *the best constitution in the world*],[11] enjoy and eat of the fruit of their own labour; and purchase to themselves, with security, fields and manors, and dare acknowledge and glory in their wealth and pomp, and yet leave the inheritance to their posterity."

NO. 51. SATURDAY, NOVEMBER 4, 1721.

Popularity no Proof of Merit.

SIR,

Popularity is the fondness and applause of many, following the person of one, who, in their opinion, deserves well of them; and it must doubtless be a sensible pleasure to him who enjoys it, if he enjoy it upon good terms, and from reputable causes: But where it is only to be acquired by deceiving men with words, or intoxicating them with liquors, or purchasing their hearts with bribes, a virtuous man would rather be without it; and therefore virtuous men have been rarely popular, except in the beginning, or near the first rise of states, while they yet preserved their innocence.

Where parties prevail, a principal way to gain popularity is, to act foolishly for one side, and wickedly against the other: And therefore some publick talkers have grown popular, by calling those whom they disliked by bitter and ill-bred names; or by rioting and making a noise for some sounds, which they had taken a liking to; or by insulting and abusing those that affronted them, by being more sober and sensible than themselves: And some, to be

11. The interpolation is Gordon's.

revenged on those that never hurt them, have given themselves up a blind prey to certain leaders, who deluded them, and sold them, and yet earned popular applause of them for so serving them.

So that popularity is often but the price which the people pay to their chiefs, for deceiving and selling them: And this price is so implicitly paid, that the very vices and fooleries of a popular chief become popular too, and were perhaps amongst the first causes that made him so. Some gentlemen of this cast owe their figure to the weakness of their heads, or the strength of their barrels;[1] and grow considerable by their having small parts, or by drinking away those that they have.

These are the instruments that cunning men work with; and therefore sometimes a knave, who is not popular, shall get a weak man, who is so, to do those things with applause, for which he himself would be hated and condemned: And the hand that executes shall be blessed, when the head that contrives would be cursed, for one and the same thing.

This shews that names are principal reasons to determine the multitude to popular love and hatred; and it proceeds not so much from their being untaught as ill taught: When they are instructed not to reason but to rage, not to judge but to mistake, a better discernment and wiser behaviour are not to be hoped from them.

Demetrius, and the other craftsmen, shrine-makers to Diana, at Ephesus, were more popular men than St. Paul, and raised a mob to confute his arguments for Christianity:[2] For it had not yet entered into the heads of the people, that religion and rage were contradictory things, and that antiquity and reverence could not sanctify impiety, falsehood, and folly.

In like manner, Barabbas, a rioter and a murderer, had more votes to save him than our blessed Saviour had;[3] who was thought by that zealous, deluded, and outrageous people, to be the greater criminal of the two, for having told them sober, and saving

1. Their barrels: their bodies.

2. Demetrius is reputed to have accused Paul of violating the sanctity of the goddess Diana by proclaiming Diana's statue a mere idol (Acts 19:24–27). As a consequence, a riot broke out in the city and Paul and his companions came close to losing their lives.

3. The event is related in Acts 15:6–14.

truth, which was new to them, though everlasting in itself; and therefore condemned because it was new.

Now, in neither of these instances were the people, though they acted thus impiously and madly, originally in the fault; but those who taught them; and who, having for religion taught them trifles, folly, and fury, were alarmed by the rational and prevailing doctrines of mercy, wisdom, and truth. They therefore blaspheme against the author of truth, yet charge him with blasphemy. As to the populace, they did as they were taught, and uttered the cry which was put into their mouths.

The people, when they are left to themselves, and their own understandings and observation, will judge of men by their good or bad actions, and are capable of separating vice from virtue, and the just from the unjust: And therefore, when their government is not corrupted, the best and most virtuous men will always be the most popular, and he who does best will be esteemed best: But when strong liquor, or money, or false terrors intervene, and government is turned into faction; the judgment of the people is vitiated, and worse than none. They then prefer the worst men to the best, if they have stronger drink, or more money, or are covered with any other false merit, by those whose word they take, and whose authority they submit to; and the most popular man is he who bribes highest, or imposes upon them best.

That these things are common, and almost universal, is not strange: Generally speaking, where-ever there is power, there will be faction; and where-ever there is money, there will be corruption: So that the heads of faction, and the promoters of corruption, have from their very characters, which ought to render them detestable, the means of popularity.

Who was better beloved at Rome than Spurius Melius, while he was meditating the slavery of the Roman people? Who could ever boast such potent parties, such numerous followers, such high applause and regard, such trophies and statues, as Marius and Sulla, Pompey and Caesar, Augustus and Anthony could boast; while they were overturning the state, oppressing mankind, butchering one half of the world, and putting shackles upon the other? And, in fine, who was ever a greater impostor, and more admired prophet, than Mahomet was? All these men were enemies to liberty, truth, and peace; the plagues and scourges of the earth: But they deceived and destroyed their people with their own consent, and by the highest wickedness gained the highest popularity.

The two Dukes of Guise, Francis and Henry, father and son, were the two most popular men that ever France saw, and grew so by doing it more mischief than ever two men till then had done. They were perpetually, during a course of many years, destroying its peace, violating its laws, usurping its authority, pushing at the crown, raising and carrying on rebellions, committing massacres, and filling it with blood and desolation:[4] They had no one publick end, and did no one publick thing, but what was pernicious to France; yet France adored them.

Whoever is the author of a civil war, is author of all its cruel consequences; plunders, devastations, burnings, rapes, slaughters, oppression and famine. A frightful catalogue of crimes to line at one man's door! yet both these dukes had them all to answer for over and over, yet were vastly beloved. Even when they were dead, they continued the authors of long publick miseries, by leaving their destructive schemes and their party behind them; a fierce, lawless, and powerful party, that maintained the civil war long after them; and having destroyed Henry III was like to prove too hard even for the great Henry IV nor did he overcome it but by infinite courage, industry, and patience, and the renouncing of his religion: Nay, at last, his murder was owing to the spirit of the League,[5] first concerted, and afterwards constantly headed and animated, by these two dukes successively.

Had ever any country two greater foes? yet were ever two men greater darlings of any country? For Henry, Duke of Guise, particularly, he had so much the hearts of the people, that their

4. François de Lorraine, second Duke of Guise, and Henri de Lorraine, the third Duke: Both were in the forefront of the Catholic party during the Wars of Religion in France. They were active in planning and executing the persecution of the Huguenots, including the St. Bartholomew's Day massacre, and in the founding of the Holy League.

5. Henry IV, who, in 1598, issued the Edict of Nantes, by which the Huguenots were granted equal political rights with the Catholics, was assassinated in Paris in 1610 by the fanatic François Ravaillac. It has generally been assumed that Ravaillac had been prompted to this act by certain members of the League, although he repeatedly denied this under torture.

passion for him ran not only to dotage, but idolatry; and they blasphemed God, to do the duke honour: They worshipped his image; they invoked him in their prayers; they touched religiously the hem of his garment, and with the same spirit and design rubbed their beads upon his clothes; nay, following him in multitudes as he passed their streets, saluted him with hosannas to the son of David.

Thus they treated and adored this idol; a lewd man, a publick incendiary and destroyer, but represented to them as their saviour. He had for the ends of ambition put himself at the head of the Catholick cause; the surest warrant in the world for mischief and homage!

Our good fortune, or our better constitution, has hitherto restrained us against our will from running into all these excesses of distraction and folly. But we have had our popular idols too; wretched idols, who could not furnish us from their parts or reputation with one reason for our stupidity in admiring them. Sometimes paltry and turbulent priests, destitute of all virtue and goodbreeding, weak and immoral patricians, or loud and ignorant plebeians, have run away with our reverence, without being able to merit our esteem; without religion they have been popular in the cause of religion, and contended popularly for loyalty by faction and rebellion.

To every reader, instances of this nature will occur within his own memory and observation. To name them with the other great names above-mentioned, would be an honour too mighty for them, who were but small wicked men, though greatly popular.

I have often remembered, with compassion, an unfortunate great man still living, but utterly ruined by his popularity and false friends. His good-nature has been often mentioned, and is grown almost proverbial: Nor do I deny it; though by it he never served himself, his family, or the publick. On the contrary, it has proved his failing and his crime. If one were to enquire for the causes of his popularity in the probity of his life, the piety of his mind, his publick abilities, private oeconomy, or conjugal or domestick virtues, these are topicks upon which his friends do not extol him: And for his loyalty, take loyalty in what sense you will, he will be found to have given preposterous proofs of it, and to have been engaged in all the depths of rebellion and perjury, and is still engaged.[6]

From what has been said, it will not seem strange that some of the most popular men in the world have been the most mischievous in their behaviour and opinions. What fighting and burning has there been for transubstantiation! what declaiming, damning, and rebelling, for passive obedience! what fierce contention, and how many foolish arguments for persecution! All which opinions are a contradiction to religion and scripture, an affront to common-sense, and utterly destructive of all civil and religious liberty, and of all human happiness: Nor would any of them, or any like them, have ever entered into the heart of any man, unless he were first deceived, or found his account in deceiving. But even crimes, contradictions, and folly, will be popular in a state, when they bring gain or selfish gratifications to those who are in possession of a power to render folly, contradiction, and crimes, advantageous to the pernicious pursuits which they are engaged in.

G   *I am, &c.*

NO. 52.   SATURDAY,   NOVEMBER   11,   1721.

Of Divine Judgments; the Wickedness and Absurdity of applying them to Men and Events.

SIR,

I have in a former letter to you,[1] not long since, shewn the rashness of men in applying to one another the judgments of God. I shall in this consider that subject farther, and endeavour to cure that prevailing and uncharitable spirit.

Almost all sorts of men pretend, in some instances, to be in the secrets of the Almighty, and will be finding out the unsearch-

---

6. This apparently is a reference to Robert Harley, Earl of Oxford, a man of great personal character, who was involved in attempts to restore the Stuart Pretender. Harley was one of the founders of the South Sea Company and, in 1711, became its first governor.

---

1. See Letter No. 47 (Oct. 7, 1721).

able purposes of his providence; they will be prying into the hidden things of God, and assigning such ends and motives for his all-wise dispensations, as are only suitable to their own weakness, or prejudices, or malice: They give him the same passions that they themselves possess, and then make him love and hate what and whom they themselves love and hate: They are pleased with flattery and sounds, and provoked by trifles and names; and so they think is he. And as they thus sanctify all their own doings, affections, and fancies, with a fiat and approbation from heaven, and belie and provoke God, to make him their friend; so they take it for granted that he is an enemy to all their enemies; and that therefore every evil, or seeming evil, that befalls their enemies, or those whom they dislike, is a manifest judgment from God, and a justification of whatever they can do against them: So that God is often made the author of every mischief which they themselves commit; but they that feel it, think more rationally that they are animated by a contrary spirit.

God made man after his own likeness, perfect, amiable, merciful, and upright; and men are bold and foolish enough to make God after theirs; and almost every one has his own God, one fashioned according to his own temper, imaginations, and prejudices. In this sense they worship as many false gods, as they have wrong notions of the true one; and so in some sort polytheism does yet remain even in the Christian world. They only agree in calling what they worship by the same name; but they conceive him in such a different manner, they differ so widely about his nature and will, and either give him such contradictory attributes, or so contradict one another in explaining these attributes, that it is plain they do not mean one and the same being. Some make God hate what he certainly loves, others make him love what he certainly hates; and all take it amiss if you think that they own and adore any God but the true God. But let them think what they will, many of them still worship the old gods of the heathens, gods that were delighted with baubles, shew, and grimace, and with cruelty, revenge, and human sacrifices.

From this mistaken and impious spirit it proceeds, that when calamities and disasters befall others, especially those that differ from us, we call them judgments, and say that the hand of God is against them: But when the same evils or worse befall ourselves, the style is changed, and then *whom God loveth he chasteneth;* or if we own them to be judgments, yet still they are judgments upon us for other people's sins.

Thus all the misfortunes that happened to Spain for many hundred years, whether they came from the enemy, or the elements, were divine judgments upon them for suffering the idolatrous Moors to inhabit that good Catholick country;[2] and therefore, like true Catholicks, they brought the greatest judgment of all upon it, by destroying and banishing that numerous and industrious people. Thus the bigotted pagans, when Alarick, king of the Huns, sacked Rome,[3] charged the Christians with being the cause of that and of every other calamity that befell the empire: The Christians despised their gods, and therefore their gods, out of a particular spite to the Christians, afflicted the whole world with miseries; and so plagues, wars, hurricanes, and earthquakes, which were evils that had been in the world from the beginning of it, and will be to the end, were, notwithstanding, all so many judgments, occasioned by the poor Christians! Hence the beginning of penalties, severities, and persecutions against them; and thus the Christians came in time to return the charge upon the heathens, to use the same way of reasoning, and to make the like reprisals, and with as little equity, truth, or clemency: And thus, lastly, all parties in religion have ever dealt with one another.

We are commanded *not to judge, lest we be judged;* and we are told that *vengeance is the Lord's,* and that *judgments are in his hand:* All which are to convince us, that we have no certain or probable rule to apply God's judgments by; and that the surest rule is the rule of charity, *which wisheth all things, hopeth all things.* The good and evil that happen to man in this world, are no sure marks of the approbation and displeasure of Almighty God, who makes his sun to shine and his rain to fall upon the just and the unjust:

2. By 719 the Muslims had conquered all but the extreme northern part of the Iberian peninsula. They were not finally expelled until Granada fell to the armies of Ferdinard and Isabella in 1492.

3. Alaric, who sacked Rome in A.D. 410, was the leader of the Visigoths, and not a Hun.

Good-fortune and calamities are the portion of the good and of the bad; and if there be any inequality, the wicked seem to have the advantage. The world had more people and temporal prosperity in the times of heathenism, than since its abolishment; Mahometanism possesses much more of the globe than Christianity possesses; the papists are more numerous than the Protestants are, and have greater and better countries. The apostles and saints were the poorest men in the world, and debauched men are often uppermost, and thrive best; and as the righteous are at least as subject to distempers and affliction while they live, as the wicked are, so the wicked die with as little pain and as few pangs as the righteous die.

That there is a providence, and a gracious providence presiding over the world, is manifest and undeniable; but how it works, and from what particular motives, in a thousand instances, none but the author of it can tell; though almost all pretend to tell, and are for ever diving into the secret counsels of the most high, with as much temerity as ill success.

To the discredit of this practice, it is observable, that none but the fierce and uncharitable, none but ignorant and narrow-spirited bigots and barbarians come into it or encourage it. Men of charitable and benevolent minds, enlarged by reason and observation, condemn it as irreligious; they know that it is often malicious and dishonest, always ridiculous and dangerous; they know the ways of God to be past finding out; they see human affairs so perplexed and unaccountable; men sometimes rising and sometimes falling, both by virtue and vice; such vicissitudes and revolutions in the fortunes of men and of nations, often without any change in these men and nations from virtue to vice, or from vice to virtue; people growing greater without becoming better, and poorer without growing worse: They behold good and evil so promiscuously dispensed; sometimes thousands of men, women, and children, of different spirits, merit, and morals, suffering equally under the same publick calamity, and deriving equally the like advantages from publick prosperity; they behold the adversity of some to be the visible cause of the prosperity of others, who are no better than them; and the prosperity of some the visible cause of the adversity of others, who are no worse than the former; and one and the same thing producing good and evil to those who alike deserve or do not deserve good and evil: They see so little equity or consistency in the proceedings of men; sometimes good men exalted, without any regard had to their virtue; sometimes wicked men cast down, without any resentment of their crimes; sometimes good men punished for being good, and wicked men raised and rewarded for being wicked; sometimes both good and bad suffering or prospering alike, sometimes good-fortunes following the good, and ill-fortune the bad, often taking a contrary freak. I say, wise and honest men, seeing all these things in this great confusion and uncertainty, find sufficient reason to be afraid of making bold with heaven, and of christening by the name of its judgments any of these events and evils that afflict any part of mankind.

But bigots, and they, who, to serve ill ends, interest heaven in all that they do, deal more freely and profanely with their great maker and judge, whose counsels and judgments being incomprehensible, it is impiety and a contradiction to go about to explain and apply them. The Turks make God the author of every thing that they do, and of every evil that others suffer from them. They measure his will by the event; and, with them, whatever is successful, is lawful and just: The murder of a prince, or his murdering of others, is never sinful if it succeed: God, they say, blesses and approves the event, else he would prevent it. So that, upon this principle, there can be no such thing as wickedness and villainy amongst them; for who knows but it may succeed, and then it is good? or if it does not succeed, who could foresee but it would? This impious tenet of that brutish people arms them with fierceness and outrage against one another, and all the world; it animates them to commit rapine and butcheries, and then sears their consciences, and prevents all remorse. Nay, they glory in executing cruelty, because it is the judgment of God, and they are his agents.

I wish I could keep this dreadful principle out of Christendom; but I am sorry to say, that it is common amongst us. Whoever applies the judgment of God to others, has this Turkish spirit in him: And all men that make such applications, reason so foolishly, so falsely, and often so maliciously in their defence, that every instance which I have ever yet met with in all my reading and observation (except the declared instances in sacred writ) exposes them.

Upon the murder of Henry III of France, by Jacques Clément, a Dominican friar, the deputy of the famous French League,[4] then at Rome, tells the Pope, in an audience given upon that occasion, that the assassin was chosen by God, and divinely inspired to murder his prince, and calls it a glorious exploit: And though that execrable and bloody monk used all the methods of falsehood, lies, and forgeries, to get access to the King, in order to destroy him; yet the deputy solemnly tells his Holiness, that it was notorious that the thing came not from men. The League distressed, resisted, and at last murdered their prince: And all these their own wicked doings were, forsooth, the judgments of God upon him, for suffering heresy in the land.

The Huguenots, on the other hand, made a judgment of that murder too; but a judgment on their side, for his frequent breach of faith and edicts with them, and for his barbarities towards them. They said, it was a remarkable providence of God, that he was assassinated in the same chamber where he had concerted the furious massacre of St. Bartholomew[5]—in the very chamber, nay, on the same day, the same hour, and on the same spot! Here are judgments encountering judgments! let who will reconcile them. I think both sides sufficiently rash and ridiculous in making them, as are all those that do, whatever side they are of.

The conquest of the Greeks by Mahomet II and their slavish subjection to the Turks,[6] is ascribed by the Jesuit Maimbourg to the Schism, which he says they were guilty of in withdrawing their

4. The Holy League, which was unalterably opposed to a Protestant successor to Henry III and whose members were implicated in his murder in 1589.

5. So-called because it began on St. Bartholomew's Day, 1572. It was ordered by King Charles IX under pressure from his mother, Catherine de' Medici. Taking advantage of the presence of large numbers of Huguenots who were in Paris for the marriage of Henry of Navarre to the King's sister, Catherine prevailed upon the King to order the massacre as an act of public safety. The carnage began on the Aug. 24, 1572, and continued in the city for three more weeks. Altogether more than 50,000 people throughout France are estimated to have been slaughtered.

6. By 1456, the Ottoman Turks under the Sultan Mohammed II, the conqueror of Constantinople, had succeeded in gaining control over all of Greece.

obedience from the See of Rome. Here, according to him, was the judgment and the cause of the judgment.[7] Bayle observes upon this occasion, that Rome being taken by Charles V in 1527, was as barbarously pillaged by his troops, as was Constantinople by the Turks, when they took it: And he asks, whether Maimbourg would take it well to be told by the Greeks that that desolation of Rome was a judgment upon her for her pride and ambition, in demanding, imperiously, of the Greek Church an absolute uniformity and obedience to her discipline and dictates? He says, that Maimbourg, since he was dealing in judgments, might as well have given this another turn,[8] with which Chalcondylis would have furnished him.[9] That historian relates, that when Mahomet invaded and subdued Greece, the then inhabitants of Rome, who thought themselves the descendants of the old Romans, who came from Aeneas, who came from Troy,[10] asserted positively, that all the destruction brought upon the Greeks by the barbarians, was but a judgment upon them for all the ravages which their Greek ancestors had committed against the subjects of Priamus, and in the destruction of Troy some thousand years before.[11]

The death of Oliver Cromwell was, it seems, attended or followed by a very high wind; which was nothing strange: But as Oliver had been a usurper, and a great deceiver, and was greatly hated; most of the vulgar, and many that would be thought much wiser took it into their heads, that that same storm was a loud judgment and declaration of the wrath of heaven against him, and that Satan was fetching away his soul in a whirlwind. But his friends

7. Louis Maimbourg (1610–1686), *Histoire du schisme des Grecs*, vol. 4 of *Les Histoires du Sieur Maimbourg* (12 vols.; Paris: Sebastien Mabre-Cramoisy, 1686), bk. VI, *passim*. See also Maimbourg's *l'Histoire de l'heresie des iconoclastes* (vol. 3 of the collected histories).

8. *An Historical and Critical Dictionary*, s.v. "Mahomet II," III:1118 (note O).

9. Laonicus Chalcondyles (*c.* 1430–*c.* 1490), Athenian Byzantine author of a history in ten books covering the period 1298–1463, in which the fall of the Greek Empire and the rise of the Ottoman Turks is described. The work was published in French under the title *L'histoire de la decadance de l'empire grec et establissement de celvy des Turcs* (Paris: Chez Nicolas Chesneau, 1577).

10. Louis Maimbourg, *Histoire du schisme des Grecs*, bk. VI.

11. Aeneas, a Trojan prince, is reputed by Virgil to have voyaged to Italy after the fall of Troy and to have become King of Latium.

turned it quite another way; particularly Mr. Waller, who made all that tumult and bellowing in the elements, to be partly the call of heaven, summoning away so great a man; partly the sighs and sympathy of nature for his last agonies and departure. The copy of verses that Waller made on that occasion is one of the noblest in our language; I shall conclude with a few lines out of it.[12]

> We must resign; Heav'n his great soul does claim,
> In storms as loud as his immortal fame.
> His dying groans, his last breath shakes our isle;
> And trees, uncut, fall for his fun'ral pile.
> New Rome in such a tempest lost her king,
> And, from obeying, fell to worshipping.
> Nature herself took notice of his death,
> And, sighing, swell'd the sea with such a breath,
> That, to remotest shores, her billows roll'd,
> Th' approaching fate of their great ruler told.

G   *I am, &c.*

NO. 53. SATURDAY, NOVEMBER 18, 1721.

*Dr. Prideaux's Reasoning about the Death of Camby-
ses, examined; whether the same was a Judgment for
his killing the Egyptian God Apis.*

SIR,

The talent of writing history is so rare on this side the Alps, and more on this side the Channel, that I think most of our southern neighbours have far exceeded us in it; as much, perhaps, as some of the ancients have exceeded them. By far the most part of our English histories are pitiful performances, unworthy of a free, polite, and learned nation. But though many of our neighbours excel us in the histories of their own countries, we can boast of two universal histories, which do honour to the authors,

12. The verses constitute lines 1–4, 7–8, and 31–34 of Edmund Waller's "Upon the late Storme and of the death of his Highness (the Lord Protector) Ensuing the same," first published in London in 1659.

and their country. The first is Sir Walter Raleigh; one of the worthiest and ablest men that this or any other country ever produced. He had a soul as vast as the work which he undertook, and his work resembles him;[1] for though it has much in it that is foreign to history, it is noble, nervous, and instructive; its spirit, clearness, and style, are admirable; and for narration, penetration, knowledge, sentences, and observation, he has few competitors in antiquity.

The other is the very reverend, learned, and aged Dr. Prideaux, Dean of Norwich; who has given us a body of universal history, written with such capacity, accuracy, industry, and honesty, as make it one of the best books that ever came into the world,[2] and shew him to be one of the greatest men in it. No book was ever more universally read and approved. It is indeed a great publick service done to mankind, and entitles the author to the highest publick gratitude and honour.

But though I never saw any great work to which I found fewer objections; yet, as a memorable proof how inseparably mistakes and prejudices cleave to the mind of man, the great and candid Dr. Prideaux is not without them; I therefore do not upbraid him with them, but rather admire him for having so few. There are however some of his theological observations, which seem to me not only ill-grounded, but to have a tendency to create in his readers wrong notions of the Deity, and to encourage them to mistake the common accidents of life, and the common events of nature, for the judgments of God, and to apply them superstitiously as such.

Of this kind is the observation which he makes upon the death of Cambyses, the Persian emperor, who had slain the Egyptian Apis.[3] For the better understanding of this, we must know,

1. Sir Walter Raleigh's *The History of the World* (London: Walter Byrre, 1614), a work that achieved immense popularity.

2. The reference is to Prideaux's *The Old and New Testaments Connected*. The quotations and paraphrases from Prideaux that appear in this letter are taken from part I, bk. III of this work (I:237–44 and 340–41).

3. *Cambyses*, King of Persia and the son of Cyrus the Great, is said to have been so offended by the superstitions of the Egyptians following his conquest of Egypt in 525 B.C. that he killed their god Apis—whose form was that of a bull—and plundered the Egyptian temples.

that the chief god of the Egyptians was Osiris; him they worshipped in the shape of a bull, and that not only in imagery, but also in reality; for they kept a bull in the temple of Osiris, which they worshipped in his stead. The Doctor adds, that in imitation of this idolatry was it that Aaron made the golden calf in the wilderness, and Jeroboam those in Dan and Bethel, and did set them up there to be worshipped by the children of Israel, as the gods that had brought them out of the land of Egypt.[4]

When this the god and bull of the Egyptians died, they looked out for another, with such proper marks and spots as were certain indications of his divinity; and when they found one, they expressed their joy in great and publick festivity. In such a fit of rejoicing Cambyses found the city of Memphis,[5] when he returned to it from his unprosperous expedition into Aethiopia. The Egyptians had just then found a new god amongst the cattle, and had lodged him at his crib in his temple with great solemnity. Cambyses had a mind to see this deity of theirs: And, says Dr. Prideaux,

> this Apis being brought to him, he fell into a rage, as well he might, at the sight of such a god; and, drawing out his dagger, run it into the thigh of the beast; and then reproaching the priests for their stupidity and wretchedness in worshipping a brute for a God, ordered them to be severely whipped, and all the Egyptians in Memphis to be slain, who should be found any more rejoicing there on this occasion. The Apis being carried back to the temple, languished of his wounds, and died.

As to the death of Cambyses, and the manner of it, take it also in the Doctor's words.

> As he mounted his horse, his sword falling out of the scabbard, gave him a wound in the thigh, of which he died: The Egyptians remarking, that it was in the same part of the body where he had afore wounded the Apis, reckoned

---

4. Jeroboam became king of the northern tribes of Israel, which had broken away from the house of David. To reenforce his subjects' independence of Jerusalem, Jeroboam introduced the practice of calf-worship and erected idols at Dan and Bethel (1 Kings 12:19–30).

5. The capital of the Old Kingdom of ancient Egypt.

it as an especial judgment from heaven upon him for that fact; and perchance they were not much out in it: For it seldom happening in an affront given to any particular mode of worship, how erroneous soever it may be, but that religion in general is wounded thereby; there are many instances in history, wherein God had very signally punished the profanations of religion in the worst of times, and under the worst modes of heathen idolatry.

Without inquiring whether this be any compliment to truth and religion, I freely own, that the distressing or disturbing of any sort of people in any sort of worship, however false and ridiculous, where the same does not violate property or human society, is an invasion of the rights of nature and conscience, and no man can do it with a wise and honest design: And what men do of this kind, out of bitterness of spirit or self-ends, no one will justify. If people will play the fool in their devotion, they only expose themselves, but hurt not others; and whoever does hurt to them, does but warrant them to return it: And hence is the sure beginning of tyranny, and of eternal civil and religious war. Every man reckons every religion false or foolish, which he does not embrace; and his own the best, though it be the worst. And if in this universal obstinacy of every man in every religious opinion which he has imbibed, a dispute by the sword, and arguments of authority and force, were encouraged, or but permitted, confusion and slaughter would be their chief employment. Or if one man's will were to be a law to other men's thoughts, the effects would be every where alike; that is, the stupidity and slavery of Turks would be the portion and character of Englishmen.

But I cannot think that the wounding of a bull, even of a consecrated bull, and the whipping of his priests, were such crimes as, beyond all the other crimes of Cambyses, called for the avenging judgments of God upon him. He had others to answer for of a far more black, malignant, and detestable nature: He put his brother to death for his merit, and for a dream that he had concerning him. He killed, by a kick in the belly, his beloved wife Meroe, who was also his sister, and then with child by him, for lamenting the death of her murdered brother.

He caused several of his principal followers to be buried alive, without any cause deserving of it, and daily sacrificed some or other of them to his wild fury. And when Croesus[6] (formerly King of Lydia, the old and faithful friend and counsellor of his father Cyrus) advised him against those proceedings, and laid before him the ill consequences which they would lead to, he ordered him to be put to death; and when those who received his orders, knowing he would repent of it next day, did therefore defer the execution, he caused them all to be executed for it, though at the same time he expressed great joy that Croesus was alive: And out of a mere humour, only to shew his skill in archery, he shot to death the son of Prexaspes, who was the chief of his favourites.

He caused the magistrates of Memphis to be put to death, for answering truly to a question which he asked them. In his mad march over the Lybian sands, to invade a people that had done him no harm, he destroyed most of his vast army, fifty thousand in one place: The rest were reduced by famine to feed on each other.

Which now is most likely, and most becoming the divine wisdom and goodness, that the great God of heaven and earth should be more offended with this black catalogue of cruelties and crimes, than with a hasty blow given to a brute worshipped as God; which the doctor owns had justly provoked the rage of Cambyses? And is the Almighty more provoked at an affront put upon an idol, and upon the attendants of an idol, which falsely and impudently is made to represent him, than at a terrible and raging tyranny, that spreads blood and desolation over the face of the earth?

Cambyses, upon his invading Egypt, did another thing as bad as the wounding of Apis; I shall relate it in the Doctor's own words:

Finding that the garrison of Pelusium, a strong frontier town, were all Egyptians, in an assault which he made upon the city, he placed a great number of cats, dogs, sheep, and others of those animals which the Egyptians

6. *Croesus*, King of Lydia, lost his empire to Cyrus in 548 B.C. Although sentenced to death, he was reprieved by Cyrus, to whom he became an intimate friend and family advisor.

reckoned sacred, in the front of the army; and therefore the soldiers not daring to throw a dart, or shoot an arrow, that way, for fear of killing some of those animals, Cambyses, made himself master of the place without any opposition. For these being the gods which the Egyptians then adored, it was reckoned the highest impiety to kill any of them; and when they died of themselves, they buried them with great solemnity.

The Doctor makes no reflection upon this; though, upon the same principle, it must have been an affront to religion; and if none of these sacred creatures were killed, it was owing to no tenderness in Cambyses, who exposed them to so much danger. But if true religion be hurt by putting an affront upon a false one, how came it to be a merit in the primitive Christians to pull down the heathen temples, and to destroy the idols of the heathen, as they almost every where did where they had power, often in opposition to power? And upon what foot and motive is it that penalties and incapacities are put upon any sect of religion in any country? And how came the Jews to exercise such fury upon the Gods and worship of the Gentiles, as many of the Jewish leaders, especially the Maccabees,[7] did, often out of their own country, often without provocation?

The primitive Fathers are every where full of sarcasms against the heathenish worship, which they treat constantly with ridicule and reproach, with contempt and bitterness: Did Christianity suffer by this behaviour of theirs; or did not Christianity rather gain advantage and new beauties, by comparing it with the absurdities, the fopperies, nonsense, corruptions, and vanities of the pagans? Truth cannot suffer by exposing falsehoods, which can no more bear the face of truth, than darkness can the face of the sun. No two things are more unlike than true and false religion; and the same treatment can never affect both in any respect, as the same arguments cannot defend truth and error. Indeed, true religion is defended and recommended by the very means

7. Following the outlawing of Jewish religious practices by the Seleucid conqueror of Jerusalem in 168 B.C., the Maccabeus family organized a guerrilla army which successfully retook the city in 164 B.C. The family continued to rule Judea until it fell to the Romans in 63 B.C.

that expose and destroy a false one. I have therefore often wondered at a saying of Mr. Collier's,[8] though not that it was said by him; namely, that the transition is easy from ridiculing a false religion to the ridiculing a true one; or words to that effect. Than which nothing could be more unjustly said: They are as opposite as law and the violation of law; as unlike as justice and oppression, and as different as Christ and Belial. How should the worship of daemons resemble the worship of the true God? And if they cannot be mistaken for each other, how can they be annoyed by the same weapons? The Fathers were so far from such an imagination, that in their railleries and reasonings upon the devout fooleries of the Gentiles, they did not treat them with a bit the more reverence or regard for their being established by a law.

So much may serve to shew, that the true religion can have no sympathy with the false, nor suffer in its sufferings. As to the death of Cambyses, I do not see any sign of a judgment in it, unless every death occasioned by an accident, or an instrument, is a judgment. Indeed every disaster, before it can be called a judgment in this sense of the word, must be proved a miracle; and common effects from visible and common causes, as they are no miracles, so neither can they be called judgments, unless God, the author of judgments, declares them so, as he did not in the case before us. Many a good man has been killed in a more terrible manner, as were all the saints and martyrs.

Now where is the miracle of a sword falling out of the sheath, when a man is mounting his horse? And where was it more likely to fall than on his leg or his thigh? If indeed it had got out of the scabbard of its own accord, and mounted up to his head and cut it off, it might have looked like a judgment; but yet I should have looked out rather for any cause of it, than the killing of a deified bull.

G   *I am, &c.*

8. Jeremy Collier (1650–1726), nonjuring ecclesiastic with strong Jacobite sympathies and the author of *An Ecclesiastical History of Great Britain, Chiefly of England, From the First Planting of Christianity to the End of the Reign of Charles the Second* (2 vols.; Printed for Samuel Keble, 1708), in which the sentiment appears.

NO. 54. SATURDAY, NOVEMBER 25, 1721.

The Reasoning of Dr. Prideaux about the Fate of Brennus the Gaul, and of his Followers, examined; whether the same was a Judgment for an Intention to plunder the Temple of Delphos.

SIR,

I shall bestow this paper in considering what Dr. Prideaux says of Brennus the Gaul,[1] his expedition, death, and crime. This man, at the head of a great number of his countrymen, sent abroad to seek new habitations, passing through Hungary, Illyriam, and Macedonia, plundering, pillaging, and destroying as they went, at last invaded Greece, and

marched on towards Delphos, to plunder the temple in that city of the vast riches which were there laid up. But he there met a wonderful defeat: For on his approaching the place, there happened a terrible storm of thunder, lightning, and hail, which destroyed great numbers of his men; and at the same time there was as terrible an earthquake, which rending the mountains in pieces, threw down whole rocks upon them, which overwhelmed them by hundreds at a time; by which the whole army being much dismayed, they were the following night seized with such a panick fear, that every man supposing him that was next to him to be a Grecian enemy, they fell upon each other; so that before there was day-light enough to make them see the mistake, one half of the army had destroyed the other. By all this the Greeks, who were now come together from all parts to defend their temple, being much animated, fell furiously on them; and although now Acichorus[2] was come up with Brennus, yet both their forces together could not stand the assault; but great numbers of them were slain,

---

1. The *Brennus* to whom Prideaux and Gordon are referring was the leader of a Gallic army that invaded Greece in 279 B.C. He is not to be confused with the more famous Brennus, who is reputed to have captured Rome in 390 B.C.

2. *Acichorius* was one of the generals accompanying Brennus during his expedition into Macedonia and Greece.

and great numbers were wounded; and amongst these last
was Brennus himself, who had received several wounds;
and although none of them were mortal, yet seeing all now
lost, and the whole expedition, which he had been the
author of, thus ended in a dismal ruin, he was so confounded at the miscarriage, that he resolved not to outlive
it: And therefore calling to him as many of the chief leaders as he could get together amidst calamitous hurry, he
advised them to slay all the wounded, and with the remainder make as good a retreat backward as they could; and
then having guzzled down as much wine as he could drink,
he ran himself through and died. The rest being to march
through enemies' countries, they were, as they passed, so
distressed for want of provisions, which they were every
where to fight for, so incommoded at night by lodging
mostly upon the ground in a winter season, and in such a
manner harrassed and fallen upon where-ever they came
by the people of those countries through which they
passed, that what with famine, cold, and sickness, and what
with the sword of their enemies, they were all cut off and
destroyed: So that of the numerous company which did
first set out on this expedition, not so much as one man
escaped the calamitous fate of miserably perishing in it.[3]

This is the story of Brennus, which I have told in the Doctor's own words: Now follows his reflection upon it:

Thus God was pleased in a very extraordinary manner to
execute his vengeance upon those sacrilegious wretches,
for the sake of religion in general, how false and idolatrous
soever that particular religion was, for which that temple at
Delphos was erected. For, to believe a religion true, and
offer sacrilegious violences to the places consecrated to the
devotions of that religion, is absolute impiety, and a sin
against all religion; and there are many instances of very
signal judgments with which God hath punished it even
amongst the worst of heathens and infidels; and much

3. This and the previous quotation are taken from Prideaux's *The Old and New
Testaments Connected*, part II, bk. I (III:35–37).

more may they expect it, who, having the truth of God established among them, shall become guilty hereof.

If this unhappy end of Brennus and his followers was a judgment, as doubtless this reverend and worthy author thinks, I cannot see why an intention to pillage a stupid idol of his useless wealth and devout baubles, given and used for the ends of idolatry and delusion, should be reckoned the cause of it. I would be glad to know how any part of mankind would have suffered in their religion and fortune, though the shrine and temple of Apollo had been stripped of their superstitious and ill-got finery; or how God Almighty came to shew himself thus miraculously the guardian of an idol, set up to rival him, and to deceive the world by uttering oraculous lies; or, how the taking away those riches that were acquired by belying God and deceiving man, and employed for the ornament and support of a blasphemous imposture, could be called sacrilege or robbing of God, who was really robbed by an idol of that only which he can be robbed of, divine worship and homage.

But because people are apt to be misguided and terrified by words, especially by such as are applied to devotion and holy things, I shall here bestow some reflections upon the awful word *sacrilege*, and shew that it is ill understood.

Sacrilege, we are told by some, signifies the robbing or stealing from God any thing which is peculiarly his. Now nothing can be stolen from God, nor can any thing be concealed from him. Every thing being his, it is as much his in the hands of one man as in the hands of another; for, let who will have the use of it, the property cannot be altered: God, who has all things, can never be put out of possession of any thing; and as nothing can be taken from him, so neither can any thing be given to him, because all the world and every thing in it is already his; and it is absurd to imagine that any form of words, or change of place or position, can enlarge or lessen his property in any thing. All that we have, we have from him; and to return him his own gifts back again, which we want, and he does not, is no compliment nor any part of religion or of reason: It is shewing ourselves wiser than him, in setting apart for his use those things which he has graciously created and set apart for ours. Can we feed him? Or can we clothe, adorn, or enrich him? Can we build him a city to dwell in, or furnish him with guards for the security of his person?

Sacrilege therefore is either the robbing of men, or no robbery at all. And this crime is greater or less, according to the measure or mischief done. To rob a poor man of his loaf, is a greater crime, *in foro conscientiae*,[4] than to rob a rich man of an ox: To rob a man of a small part of a thing that is necessary to him, is a greater crime, than the robbing him of a great superfluity; and if I rob a man of a thing that will do him hurt, I hope I do him less an injury, than if I robbed him of a thing which does him good. But if I take a thing which no man has a right to, I myself have a right to it, by possessing it.

To apply all this to the business of sacrilege; if a man take away any of the books, vestments, or utensils, made use of in devotion, he only robs the congregation, who must buy more; and many being more able than one to bear this loss, the offence, as to its effects, is less than if he robbed but one man. But if he take away from a heathen temple, plate, or hidden treasure, laid up there, but not used, he indeed does an action that he has no right to do, but an action that however does good to the world, by turning into use that which was of none, or of bad use.

Dead treasure, first drawn from the people in superstitious offerings, and then laid up in a heathen temple, and kept and used for impious and idolatrous ends, but never to return again into the world, for the necessary purposes of life and commerce, is the plunder of mankind; and the worst of all plunders, because it never circulates; and people are greatly the worse for it, in respect both of soul and body, but never can be the better. It is first taking from them, and afterwards denying them, the great and chief means of life and convenience. He therefore, whoever he be, that takes it from thence, let him take it in what manner he will, does a better and more publick thing than he who keeps it there.

4. "In the court of conscience."

No man can be robbed of a thing in which he has no property. Of this sort was Apollo's wealth; and no body was robbed in taking it away. So that whoever takes away golden images, or other dead wealth, the means and objects of false adoration, is guilty of no other crime, than that of disturbing erroneous consciences: Nor need such consciences be much disturbed, since the crime being committed without their consent, they have no share in it. And therefore if such idolatrous images, and such superstitious, useless, and pernicious riches, be taken away by a lawful authority, or in a lawful war, it is no crime at all. So that in every sense Brennus committed a greater crime in plundering one village, than he could have committed, had he plundered, as he intended, the temple of Delphos.

If Brennus had believed in Apollo, he sinned against his conscience, in designing to rob him. But we do not know that Brennus, or those that followed him, believed thus. I do not remember that Apollo was the god of the Gauls, or that the druids owned him: All nations agreed not in worshipping the same gods, but often disputed about the quality, birth, and precedence of their gods. And if Brennus despised or disregarded Apollo, he committed no sacrilege; at least with respect to himself, it was no sacrilege, but only rapine; but if, believing in him, though an idol, he would have sinned in pillaging him, as doubtless he would, here is an argument, that a good conscience may be an erroneous conscience; and that if no man must act against his own conscience, though it be erroneous, as doubtless he must not, then much less has any other man whatsoever a right to punish or distress him for it. If God approve, who is it that condemns? And none but God knows the heart of another.

If Brennus had worshipped Apollo, he was guilty of idolatry, in the opinion of all Christians: And if he had robbed him, he was guilty of sacrilege in the opinion of most. Now we hear of no judgment falling upon those that worshipped Apollo, and supported that idol with superstitious donations; all which was idolatry. And is idolatry, which God has declared abominable in his eyes, a less sin than robbing an idolatrous temple, which action

God has no where declared a sin? The good kings of the Jews destroyed all idols and idolatrous temples, where-ever they had power; and the wrath of God was kindled against all that did not. If it was therefore a sin against the true God, not to destroy them; how came it to be sin only to rob them?

I think all this is enough to shew, that an intention to plunder Apollo of his idle and unhallowed wealth, was not the probable cause of any judgment upon Brennus and his followers: But if there must be a judgment in the case, there were reasons for it much more powerful, and much more likely to provoke God to send it. He was a wild and barbarous robber, at the head of an army of savages, who cruelly ravaged many nations, made spoil of all men's property, and inhumanly massacred those that defended their own. They were invaders, plunderers, and murderers, who, by numbers, barbarity, rapine, and slaughter, laid waste whole countries, and destroyed, unprovoked, men and property. In this general pillage, they had already passed through and desolated Hungary, Illyrium, Macedonia, and were now got into Greece. Was not here guilt enough to call down a thousand judgments? And after all this bloody and brutish violence done to the world, and to the laws of God and man; can we imagine that these Gauls suffered that terrible doom for barely intending a thing, in which neither God would have been dishonoured, nor man injured? At least in any degree of comparison, with the least of the other great and terrible calamities, which they suffered from these destroying barbarians?

I shall now add something more particularly concerning the wretched end of these Gauls, and enquire how far it can be reckoned a judgment. And here I am of opinion, that either every calamity, publick or private, must be accounted a judgment; which doctrine, I believe, no man holds; or else we must determine, by what means we can know a judgment from a calamity: Nor do I know of any sufficient marks to direct us in this matter, but an immediate miracle, and declaration from Almighty God, that he means it so: And in such a miraculous declaration, the crime must be expressly specified, for which such judgment is inflicted;

because for every crime judgments are not indicted, nor always for the latest crimes; but sometimes overtake the sinner, long after the sin is committed. All this I take to be self-evident. We must remember that men, biassed by passions and prejudices, do often confound good and evil, and mistake the greatest wickedness for the greatest merit, and the highest merit for the highest wickedness: Publick massacres have been applauded, publick incendiaries have been sainted, publick tyrants deified. While on the other side, public virtue has passed for a publick crime, truth for blasphemy, and Christianity has been rewarded with fire and sword. So that men thus blind and perverse do frequently entitle vice to the blessing and favour of God, and virtue and merit to his severest judgments.

Where-ever therefore there is a great complication of crimes, and sometimes of great crimes, how can we distinguish for which of them the judgment is sent, unless he that sends it declare the same? If he send it for more crimes than one, how shall we distinguish where he, who only can, does not? And if the judgment be sent for one sin only, by what certain token can we discover it? If one man hurt or disoblige twenty, in twenty different ways; rob one, steal from another, deceive a third, calumniate a fourth, wound a fifth, bear false witness against a sixth, and so on till he has as many enemies as crimes, and afterwards die by a disaster or the law; every one of the twenty will be apt to call it a judgment, and a particular judgment, for the particular offence done to himself. Now where is the rule, by which certainly to know either that this man's death was a judgment, or to find out the certain crime that brought it upon him? Or is ever such a rule like to be found, as long as all sorts of evils befall all sorts of men?

As to the thunder, lightning, hail, and earthquakes, that destroyed so many of the Gauls, were they not the usual operations and effects of nature? And have they not been from the beginning? Have not whole cities and countries been destroyed by them? And has not their impartial fury been felt by the good and the bad, without distinction? In destroying storms by land and sea, are the wicked only overtaken? And do not the virtuous perish undistinguished with the latter? And are not just men, going upon just expeditions, frequently overwhelmed by them? And do not wicked men, in wicked enterprizes, often escape them? When an impetuous shock of an earthquake overturns a city, or opens a devouring chasm to swallow it up; do the dwellings of the righteous remain unmoved, and their persons unhurt!

Nor is it at all wonderful and uncommon, that this ignorant multitude, dismayed by so many and so alarming misfortunes, thus suddenly checked in their progress, at a great distance from home, beset with enemies in an enemy's country, unskilled in the phaenomena of nature, suffering many calamities, and dreading more, fell into a panick; and, having lost their senses, attacked one another, by a mistake, in the dark. Wicked armies have fallen into the like terror upon the sight of an eclipse: And the same unaccountable fear, but without the same effect, seized the victorious Macedonian army of Alexander the Great, the very night before they fought one of their greatest and most successful battles.[5] And we have still a much later instance at home: At the battle of Naseby,[6] King Charles I who was in it, being pressed by some of his own people that were behind them, bid them keep back; which words being repeated by others to those next them, and by these to others, the word *back* was catched up, and running from man to man through all the ranks, was understood as a sign to fly; and accordingly the royal army fled, and the field was lost. And thus a chance word threw a whole army into a panick. None of the royal party have yet told us, that this was a judgment upon that king and his cause; nor, I dare say, would they have believed the other party, had the other party alledged that it was.

Considering all these calamities and losses suffered by the Gauls, and the consternation which they were in, I suppose there was no great miracle in their being vanquished by the Greeks, who were now come together from all parts, to fall furiously on a defeated enemy. And as small is the wonder of Brennus's killing

5. The reference is to the battle of Arbela in Sept. 331 B.C., on the eve of which a lunar eclipse occurred.

6. A crucial battle in the English Civil War fought near Naseby in June 1645, in which Charles I's army was decisively defeated by the Puritans' newly organized New Model Army.

himself: He was a resolute man, and took this method to cure himself of that grief and disappointment which he could not bear, and to preserve himself from falling alive into the hands of his enemies, to whom he had given a right of using him very ill.

Neither is it any thing surprizing that the rest,

> being to march through enemies' countries, were, as they passed, so distressed for want of provisions, which they were every where to fight for; so incommoded at night by lodging mostly on the ground in a winter season, and in such a manner, harassed and fallen upon where-ever they came by the people of those countries through which they passed, that what with famine, cold, and sickness, and what with the sword of their enemies, they were all cut off and destroyed.[7]

All this misfortune is thus fairly accounted for, and the thing is not uncommon. The whole nation of the Cimbrians[8] were destroyed in much greater numbers, when they left their old habitations in quest of new; though it does not appear that they intended to rob temples. And yet Xerxes[9] destroyed and plunder'd all the idolatrous temples in the East, except that of Diana at Ephesus, without thriving the worse for it.

They were all cut off and destroyed! for which plain, natural, and necessary causes are assigned; and yet it was a judgment! Surely this is strange and unaccountable! Doubtless there were degrees and great differences of guilt and innocence amongst Brennus's followers; and why should they, who were not all equally guilty, all equally suffer? Why should subjects and soldiers be punished for the sins of a prince or a general? Soldiers are often pressed into the service, and rarely or never know the reasons of the commander's orders; and it is mutiny and death to disobey

7. *The Old and New Testaments Connected*, part II, bk. I (III:35–37).

8. A north German tribe who invaded the Roman empire in large numbers and was eventually defeated by Marius in 101 B.C.

9. King of Persia from 486 to 465 B.C., *Xerxes* embarked on an expedition against the Greeks in 480 B.C. in which large parts of the Greek world were eventually laid waste.

him. And princes often run into wild wars, without the consent of their subjects, and against their interest; and yet if their subjects oppose them in it, they are guilty of resistance, which is reckoned rebellion; a very terrible and crying crime, to which the judgment of God has been pronounced due: And yet the judgments of God, which sometimes fall upon princes for an unjust war, fall also upon their subjects, who were utterly guiltless of it, What strange doctrine is this? that every man in a nation shall suffer for the sins of one man, whom they could not restrain; or that any man shall suffer for the crimes of another? And that the best men in an army or a nation shall bear the calamities inflicted upon them for the sins of the worst; as if it were a crime in a good man to live where his lot has cast him, without his own consent, next door to a wicked man, or within ten miles of him?

This paper, which I could make much longer, grows already too long. I shall conclude with observing, that we either apply God's judgments at random, without his authority, always in opposition to his commands, and, for aught we know, as often contrary to his ends and intention; or we do it out of prejudices to men and opinions: And by this we give advantage to infidels and men of no religion, to reproach us with presumption upon our own principles, in meddling with the secret councils of God, in confounding his mercy and justice, in making him act capriciously, and in confounding one religion with another, the good with the bad, as if we thought them all alike. Let us give no more ground for this reproach; and as a specimen of our candour and equitable judgment, let us own, in the instance before us, that the liberty, prosperity, and peace of the world, and, amongst the rest, the liberty of Greece, were things somewhat more sacred and inviolable than Apollo's consecrated baubles.

I am, & c.

P. S. The story about King Charles I relate upon memory, and may mistake in names or circumstances.[10]

G

---

10. Regardless of Gordon's memory or his sources, the story is apocryphal.

NO. 55. SATURDAY, DECEMBER 2, 1721.

The Lawfulness of killing Julius Caesar considered, and defended, against Dr. Prideaux.

SIR,

I shall, in this paper, consider and discuss a great point; namely, whether the killing of Julius Caesar was a virtue, or a crime? And because Dr. Prideaux, who condemns it, does not only speak his own sense, but that of a great party, I shall here transcribe what he says of it.

> He was murdered in the Senate-house, by a conspiracy of Senators. This was a most base and villainous act; and was the more so, in that the prime authors of it, Marcus Brutus, Decimus Brutus, Cassius, and Trebonius,[1] and some others of them, were such as Caesar had in the highest manner obliged; yet it was executed under the notion of an high heroick virtue, in thus freeing their country from one whom they called a tyrant; and there are not wanting such as are ready, even in our days, to applaud the act. But divine justice declared itself otherwise in this matter: For it pursued every one of them that were concerned herein with such a just and remarkable revenge, that they were every man of them cut off in a short time after, in a violent manner, either by their own or other men's hands.[2]

These are the Doctor's words, and this his judgment, which is roundly passed; but how justly, I hope to make appear before I have ended this letter. He has not told us what it was, that, in his opinion, rendered the person of Caesar so very inviolable. That Caesar had for his title, only power and success gained by violence, and all wicked means, is most certain. That the acquiring and exercising of power by force, is tyranny, is as certain; nor did

1. Marcus Iunius *Brutus*: the tyrannicide; Decimus Iunius *Brutus*, (d. 43 B.C.), one of Ceasar's assassins who, after the battle of Mutina, was put to death on Antony's orders; Gaius *Cassius* Longinus (d. 42 B.C.), the tyrannicide; Gaius *Trebonius* (d. 43 B.C.), active in the plot to assassinate Caesar, he detained Antony outside the Senate chamber.

2. *The Old and New Testaments Connected*, part II, bk. VII (IV:700).

ever any reasonable man say, that success was a proof of right. They who make the person of Caesar sacred, declare the person of a tyrant, and an usurper to be sacred; for no man ever lived, to whom those two characters do more notoriously belong. And if all the privileges and impunity belonging to a lawful magistrate, who protects his people, and rules himself and them by law, and their own consent, do also appertain to a lawless intruder, who is stronger than all, by being worse than all; and under the mock name of a publick magistrate, is a publick oppressor, scourge, usurper, executioner, and plunderer; then all these blessed consequences follow: That there is an utter end of all publick and private right and wrong, every magistrate may be a tyrant, every tyrant is a lawful magistrate; it is unlawful to resist the greatest human evil; the necessary means of self-preservation are unlawful; though it be lawful and expedient to destroy little robbers, who have as much right, and more innocence, than great ones, and who are only so for subsistence; yet it is impious and unlawful to oppose great robbers, who, out of lust, avarice, cruelty, or wantonness, take away life and property, and destroy nations at pleasure: That real, great, and general mischief, is defended by giving it a good name, by which he who commits it is protected; violence, fraud, and oppression, may be committed with security, if they be but called magistracy; and the execrable authors of them are not only safe, but sacred, if they be but called magistrates: Though it be unlawful to be a publick destroyer and murderer, yet it is unlawful to destroy him; that is, it is unlawful to prevent or punish that which is most impious and unlawful: And, finally, that any man who can oppress and enslave the world, and destroy nations, with the most and best men in them, may do all this with impunity.

If Julius Caesar was a lawful magistrate, then every man who has force and villainy enough, may make himself a lawful magistrate; and lawful magistrates are, or may be made by force and villainy. But if magistracy is not acquired by overturning with the sword all law and magistracy, then Julius Caesar was no magistrate; and if he was not, how came he by the rights and impunity with which lawful magistrates only are vested?

Against any man using unlawful force, every man has a right to use force. What crime would it have been in any Roman, or body of Romans, even without any commission from Rome, to have slain Alarick, or Attila,[3] or Brennus, when they invaded the Roman territories? And what more right had Caesar than they? In truth, his crime was infinitely greater than theirs, as he added the sins of ingratitude, treachery, and parricide,[4] to that of usurpation. The Goths and Gauls did indeed violate the laws of nations, in molesting and invading a country, that owed them neither subjection nor homage: But Caesar violated the laws of nature, and of his country, by enslaving those whom he was entrusted and bound to defend.

Every body, I believe, will own, that when he first made war upon his country, his country had a right to make war upon him; and to destroy him, who fought to destroy them. How came that right to cease, after he had, by his success in villainy and usurpation, added to his crimes, and made death still more his due? Or, is it lawful to resist and kill a robber before he has taken away your money, but not after he has done it? And does a villain grow sacred and inviolable, by the mere merit of completing his villainy? If Caesar had forfeited his life, as he certainly had by all the laws of Rome; why was it not lawful to take it away by the hands of thirty men, as by the arms of thirty thousand, and in the Senate as well as in the field?

The reason why one private man must not kill another in society, even when he does that which deserves death, is, that in society no man must be his own judge, or take his own revenge; but the more equitable law must give it him, and there are judges established for that purpose. But if the offender set himself above the law and the judges, he leaves a right to the person injured to seek redress his own way, and as he can get it. Whoever puts himself in a state of war against me, gives me a right of war against him; and violence is a proper remedy for violence, when no other is left.

3. King of the Huns from A.D. 434 to 453. He ravaged the Eastern empire and, in 452, invaded Italy and sacked some of its most important cities.
4. Parricide, in that Caesar was guilty of the murder of the Republic.

That right which, in the state of nature, every man had, of repelling and revenging injuries, in such a manner as every man thought best, is transferred to the magistrate, when political societies are formed, and magistracy established; but must return to private men again, when the society is dissolved: Which dissolution may happen either through the natural demise of the persons entrusted with the publick authority, where there is no provision made in the constitution for others to succeed them; or when, by a superior unlawful force, they are restrained from answering the great end of their trust, in protecting the innocent; an end for which alone men part with their natural rights, and become the members and subjects of society.[5]

It is a most wicked and absurd position, to say, that a whole people can ever be in such a situation, as not to have a right to defend and preserve themselves, when there is no other power in being to protect and defend them; and much more, that they must not oppose a tyrant, a traitor, an universal robber, who, by violence, treachery, rapine, infinite murders and devastations, has deprived them of their legal protection.

Now, that all these black characters belonged to Caesar, is indisputable fact; nor was there ever a traitor and a tyrant in the world, if he was not one. He broke, outrageously broke, every tie that can bind a human soul; honour, virtue, religion, law, trust, humanity, and every thing that is sacred and valuable amongst men. He was a subject and servant of the Roman commonwealth, greatly honoured and trusted by it; he was a Senator and high priest; he had been consul; he was general of one of its greatest armies, governor of one of its greatest and best provinces. All this power and credit, all these offices and forces, he turned, ungratefully, barbarously, and traitorously, upon his masters, and made a prey of his country with its own money and arms.

The means by which he did this mighty and consummate evil, were suitable to the end. He stuck at nothing; nor was any pitch of baseness too high or too low for him. He even submitted his person to infamous and unnatural prostitution, for the ends of ambition; and from a boy was in every faction for embroiling and

5. These views were earlier put forward by John Locke in his *Treatise of Civil Government* and were an integral part of the radical Whig canon.

overturning the state; first in the bloody measures of Marius; afterwards in the more terrible conspiracy of Catiline, to murder the consuls and the Senate, to burn Rome, and to enslave the commonwealth: And though he failed in that conspiracy, he went on conspiring; he corrupted the people, and headed parties of desperadoes, to frighten those whom he could not bribe: He oppressed the provinces, and destroyed their inhabitants; he robbed the publick temples; he slaughtered the armies of the republick; he seized the publick treasure; at last, he seized the world, and extinguished its liberty. Hear the dismal dread of the Roman Senate and people, upon that dreadful occasion, as the same is described by Lucan.

> ——*Fuit haec mensura timoris,*
> *Velle putant quodcunque potest——*
> *Omnia Caesar erat; privatae curia vocis*
> *Testis adest. Sedere patres, censere parati,*
> *Si regnum, si templa sibi, jugulumque senatus,*
> *Exiliumque petat.——*[6]

LUCAN. PHARSAL. l. 3. v. 108

Thus fell Rome, the glory and mistress of the earth, and the earth with it, under the yoke of a tyrant, whose parts increased his guilt, and made him the more dreadful. From the numberless mischiefs which he had done to get power, the highest were apprehended from him now he was possessed of it; and it was not doubted, but he would have proceeded to massacre and conflagration, had he been provoked by opposition.

> ————*Namque ignibus atris*
> *Creditur ut captae rapturus moenia Romae.*[7]

LUCAN. UT SUPRA, V. 99

6. "The measure of their fear was this: They thought him able to do whatever he wished. Caesar was all. The Senate met to witness the utterances of a private citizen. The Fathers sat, prepared to comply even were he to demand a kingdom or that a temple be erected to him or if he were to ask for the execution or exile of the Senators themselves." Lucan, *Pharsalia*, 3.100–101, 108–111.

7. "For it was believed that, as if Rome had fallen, he would destroy the walls with dark fires." Lucan, *Pharsalia*, 3.98–100.

And therefore most of the Senators were fled with Pompey, and Rome was left defenceless to the sword of the usurper.

What now had the Romans to do in this calamitous case, under this enormous oppressor; owing them duty and allegiance as one of their own citizens, but, like a barbarous conqueror and an alien, holding them in bonds with his sword at their throats? Law, liberty, and appeals, were no more! A tyrant was their chief magistrate; his will their only law. Because he had murdered one half of the people, had he therefore a right to govern the rest? And because he had robbed them of most of their property, were they obliged to give him the remainder? Does the success of a criminal sanctify his crime, or are crimes sanctified by their greatness? If only an intention to destroy the state, was high treason and death; how did the executing of that execrable intention become lawful government, and acquire a right of allegiance?

I say, what remained now to the Romans to be done for relief? As to legal process against Caesar, there could be none; *omnia Caesar erat!*[8] Nor was there any publick force great enough to oppose him: He had before destroyed or corrupted the armies of the commonwealth. Or, if a new army could have been drawn together, ought an opportunity to have been given him to have destroyed that too? Or, was it lawful to kill him, and twenty or thirty thousand men with him, and perhaps with the like slaughter on the other side, and with the loss of the best and bravest Romans whom his ambition had left unmurdered; and yet was it unlawful to kill him, without all this apparatus, expence, and mischief? Strange! that the killing by surprize a single traitor and parricide, who had forfeited his life by all the laws of God and man, should be esteemed a heinous and crying crime; and yet that the surprizing and cutting to pieces a whole army should be reckoned heroick virtue!

It was a known maxim of liberty amongst the great, the wise, the free ancients, that a tyrant was a beast of prey, which might be killed by the spear as well as by a fair chase, in his court as well as in his camp; that every man had a right to destroy one who would destroy all men; that no law ought to be given him who took

8. "Caesar was all things." Lucan, *Pharsalia*, 3.108.

away all law; and that, like Hercules's monsters, it was glorious to rid the world of him, whenever, and by what means soever, it could be done.

If we read the stories of the most celebrated heroes of antiquity (men of whom the present world is not worthy) and consider the actions that gained them their highest reverence and renown, and recommended their names to posterity with the most advantage; we shall find those in the first rank of glory, who have resisted, destroyed, or expelled tyrants and usurpers, the pests, the burdens, and the butchers of mankind. What can be more meritorious, what more beneficent to the world, than the saving of millions of men at the expense of one grand murderer, one merciless and universal plunderer? And can there be any better or other reason given for the killing of any guilty man, but the preserving of the innocent? Indeed, an action so glorious to those that did it, and so benevolent and advantageous to those for whom it was done, could never have been censured in the world, if there had not lived in all ages abject flatterers, and servile creatures of power, always prepared to sanctify and abet any [of] the most enormous wickedness, if it were gainful: And these are they who have often misled good men in the worst prejudices.

Timoleon, one of the wisest and most virtuous men that ever blessed this earth, spent a long and glorious life in destroying tyrants; he killed, or caused to be killed, his own brother, when he could not persuade him to lay down an usurped power, and no other means were left to save his country.[9] And if this action cost him afterwards much grief and melancholy, it was owing to his own tender heart, and the curses and reproaches of a mother otherwise indulgent. He was even censured for this his sorrow, as if it had got the better of his love to mankind; and when he at last overcame it, he shewed that it was not occasioned for having slain a tyrant, but his brother; for he immortalized the rest of his life in doing nothing else but destroying tyrants, and restoring liberty.

9. Timoleon is reputed to have had so ardent a love of liberty that when his brother Timophanes attempted to make himself tyrant of Corinth, Timoleon murdered him rather than see his native city enslaved.

But if the killing Caesar were so great a crime, how comes Catiline to be still so universally detested, for only intending what Caesar accomplished! It is true, Caesar did not burn Rome; nor did he save it out of any tenderness to it, but saved it for himself: He spared fire, only because the sword was sufficient. I would here ask another question: If Oliver Cromwell had died by any of the numerous conspiracies formed to take away his life; would posterity have condemned the action for this reason alone, that it was done the only way that it could be done?

But there is an instance in the Roman history, that will set this matter yet in a fuller light; it is the story of Spartacus, a Thracian slave and gladiator, who bid fair for being lord of the Roman world.[10] He seems to me to have had personal qualifications and abilities, as great as those of Caesar, without Caesar's birth and education, and without the measure of Caesar's guilt. For I hope all mankind will allow it a less crime in any man to attempt to recover his own liberty, than wantonly and cruelly to destroy the liberty of his country.

It is astonishing to consider, how a poor slave, from the whip and the chain, followed only by about seventy fugitive gladiators, should begin a revolt from the most powerful state that ever the world saw; should gather and form, by his courage and dexterity, a formidable army; should inspire resolution and fidelity into the very dregs of mankind; should qualify his sudden soldiers, composed of thieves and vagabonds, to face and defeat the Roman legions, that were a terror to the world, and had conquered it; should keep together, without pay or authority, a raw and lawless rabble, till he had vanquished two Roman armies, and one of them a Praetorian army:[11] And even when Crixius, his fellow-commander, envying his glory and success, had withdrawn from him, and carried with him a great number of his forces, and was cut to

10. In 73 B.C. *Spartacus* led a revolt at Capua, which numerous fugitives and slaves soon joined. Spartacus was successful in defeating no fewer than seven Roman armies before being caught by an army under Marcus Licinius Crassus and killed in 71 B.C.

11. That is, a permanent corps of elite troops assigned directly to a Roman general as his bodyguard. During the empire, members of the praetorian guard attended the emperor and served directly under his command.

pieces with twenty thousand of his men, by Q. Arrius the praetor,[12] yet he still continued to conquer. He beat that very Arrius that had killed Crixius; he defeated Lentulus the consul; he overcame L. Gellius, another consul;[13] and in all likelihood, had he not been weakened by the above defection of Crixius, he had beat Crassus too, and seen himself lord of Rome.

Now I would ask the advocates of lawless power, the friends to the life and name of Caesar, whether Spartacus, if he had succeeded in his last battle against Crassus, had been lawful and irresistible King of Rome? And whether the Senate and people of Rome, with the greatest part of the known world, would have owed him duty and allegiance? Or, would he not have continued still a thief and a robber? And if he had continued so, then, by all the laws of nature and self-preservation, as well as by the municipal laws of every country in the world, every man was at liberty to seize him how he could, and to kill him if he resisted, or ran away.

Tell me, O ye unlimited slaves, ye beasts of lawless power, ye loyal levellers of right and wrong! how came Caesar by a better title to dominion than Spartacus had, whose sword was as good, though not quite so prosperous and destructive, as Caesar's? Tell me where lay the difference between them, unless in their different success; and that Spartacus was as great a man, but Caesar a greater traitor and tyrant?

Indeed, had Sir Robert Filmer,[14] or any other of the honest and sage discoverers of Adam's right heir, lived in those days (as they have done since, and plainly pointed him out) and complimented Caesar, as doubtless they would, with a lineal and hereditary title from Aeneas, wandering prince of Troy; he might have been called the Lord's Anointed, as well as others, and his assassination been accounted rebellion, and worse than the sin of witch-

12. Quintus *Arrius* was successful in defeating an army of German slaves under Crixius, one of Spartacus's Celt commanders, in 72 B.C.

13. Both Gnaeus Cornelius *Lentulus* Clodianus and Lucius *Gellius* Poplicola served as consuls in 72 B.C. and both suffered disastrous defeats at Spartacus's hands.

14. Sir Robert Filmer (d. 1653) was author of the most influential essay asserting the divine right of kings, *Patriarcha, Or the Natural Power of Kings Asserted*, published in 1680. Filmer argued that royal authority descended directly from the authority accorded Adam by God himself.

craft. But as I do not find that Caesar, though he valued himself upon his descent from the pious Trojan hero, did yet claim any dictatorial right by virtue of his illustrious parentage; I have therefore taken liberty to treat him as a mere traitor, an usurper, and a tyrant.

G   *I am, &c.*

NO. 56. SATURDAY, DECEMBER 9, 1721.

A *Vindication of Brutus, for having killed Caesar.*

SIR,

Having proved in my last, I think unanswerably, that Caesar was rightly killed; I will here enquire, whether Brutus and the other tyrannicides did right in killing him? And methinks, if it has been shewn that he ought to have been slain, as an enemy to every Roman citizen, and virtuous man; every Roman citizen, and every virtuous man, had a right to slay him.

But since there are in our world so many little and cramped spirits, who dare not think out of the vulgar path, though ever so crooked and dark, and perhaps first struck out by ignorance or fraud: Narrow minds, which, locked up in received systems, see all things through false mirrors, and as they are represented by strong prejudices, prevailing customs, and very often by corruption and party-interest: I shall, as I have occasion, endeavour to disperse these thick and deceitful mists from before weak eyes; and shall consider the present question, as well as all others that come before me, as they appear in their own nature, independent on the quirks of pedants, and the narrow jurisdiction of inferior tribunals: I shall bring them before the great tribunal of heaven; and assert the cause of liberty and truth, by arguments deduced from common-sense, and the common good of mankind.

It is generally alledged against Brutus, and some of those who joined with him in this great action, that they were highly obliged by Caesar; which is a strange objection. How were they obliged? He gave Brutus a life, which he could not take from him without murder; and did a mighty generous thing in not murdering Brutus for defending his country, animated by his own virtuous spirit, and the known laws of Rome! This is the obligation of a highwayman, who, taking away your money, which is all he wants, kindly leaves you your life. Are you obliged in honour, conscience, or common-sense, to spare the robber, because he was not a murderer? Or are you obliged not to pursue and take him, and to kill him, if he refuse to submit? In truth, Caesar was one of the greatest robbers and murderers that ever lived: Every man slain in that unjust, bloody, and unnatural war, which he wantonly and maliciously made upon his country, was murdered: And the world was the mighty spoil which he gained by universal murder and rapine. He was, in short, a man so consummately wicked, that the strongest words which you can use, and the bitterest instances which you can bring, to paint out him and his actions, will be but faint, compared to him and his actions.

As to the places and favours conferred upon Brutus, by Caesar; they were not Caesar's but Rome's. He was only *rapti largitor*.[1] Caesar had no right to the publick, nor to dispose of it, or its emoluments. It was all barefaced usurpation. Besides, when favours of this, or any kind, with-hold a man from his duty, they are mischievous baits and corruptions, and ought to bind no man, as they never will a virtuous man: And we see how Brutus, who was the most virtuous man upon earth, understood and disregarded them.

They were only the artful shackles of a tyrant, intended to bind the bold and free mind of Brutus to his interest: But he, who owed no allegiance but to the commonwealth, scorned the deceitful smiles and generosity of its oppressor; who was bribing him to be his slave, with the gifts and offices of his country, to which he himself had no title, but Brutus had every title. This therefore was a piece of impudent civility, which Brutus could not but detest, as it was a shameful and melancholy proof of Caesar's tyranny, and of his own and Rome's vassalage. They were hollow and destructive favours; it was high-treason to be the author of them: And was not

1. "Dispenser of seized property."

death signally due to such high-treason? Brutus therefore made the properest return.

Caesar had usurped the Roman world, and was cantoning[2] it out to his creatures as became a tyrant, and paying his personal creatures with the publick bounty. As the worst tyrants must have some friend; and as the best men do them the most credit, and bring them the most support, if such can be got; Caesar had sense enough to know, that he could never buy Brutus too dear; and so paid him great court. But Brutus saw the tyrant's design, and his own shame; and every civility was a fresh provocation. It was as if a thief breaking into a house to rob a lady of her jewels, spoke thus to her son; "Sir, pray permit me, or assist me, to cut your mother's throat, and seize her treasure, and I will generously reward you with your life, and lend you one or two of her diamonds to sparkle in as long as I think fit."

Could such a villainous civility as this engage the son, especially a virtuous son, to any thing but revenge? And would not the only way that he could take it, be the best way?

Caesar took from Brutus his liberty, and his legal title to his life and his estate, and gave him in lieu of it a precarious one during his own arbitrary will and pleasure: Upon the same terms he gave him some mercenary employments, as hire for that great good man's assistance to support his tyranny. Could the great and free soul of Brutus brook this? Could Brutus be the instrument or confederate of lawless lust? Brutus receive wages for an oppressor! That great, virtuous, and popular Brutus; who, if the commonwealth had subsisted, might, from his reputation, birth, abilities, and his excellent worth, have challenged the most honourable and advantageous offices in it, without owing thanks to Caesar.

So that the injuries done by Caesar to Brutus were great, heinous, and many; and the favours none. All the mercy shewn by Caesar was art and affectation, and pure self-love. He had found in the Roman people so universal a detestation of the bloody measures of Marius, Cinna,[3] and Sulla: He saw the whole empire so

2. Cantoning: dividing.

3. Lucius Cornelius *Cinna* (d. *c.* 84 B.C.) is alleged to have brutalized Rome's population with his cruelties. He was eventually assassinated by one of his officers.

reduced and enervated by repeated proscriptions and massacres, that he thought it his interest to establish his new-erected dominion by different measures; and to reconcile, by a false and hypocrital shew of clemency, the minds of men, yet bleeding with their late and former wounds, to his usurpation. That Caesar, the usurping and destructive Caesar, who had slaughtered millions, and wantonly made havock of the human race, had any other sort of mercy, than the mercy of policy and deceit, will not be pretended by any man, that knows his and the Roman story. Brutus therefore being the most reverenced and popular man in Rome, it became the craft of the tyrant to make Brutus his friend; it was adding a sort of sanctity to a wicked cause: Whereas the death of Brutus by Caesar, would have made Caesar odious and dreadful even amongst his own followers.

But it is said, that Brutus submitted to Caesar, and was bound by his own act. Here the allegation is true, but the consequence false. Did not Brutus submit to Caesar, as innocent men are often forced to submit to the galleys, the wheel, and the gibbet? He submitted, as a man robbed and bound submits to a housebreaker, who, with a pistol at his heart, forces from him a discovery of his treasure, and a promise not to prosecute him. Such engagements are not only void in themselves, but aggravate the injury, and become themselves fresh injuries. By the law of nature and reason, as well as by the positive institutions of every country, all promises, bonds, or oaths, extorted by duress, that is, by unlawful imprisonments or menaces, are not obligatory: It is, on the contrary, a crime to fulfil them! because an acquiescence in the impositions of lawless villains, is abetting lawless villains.

Besides, it was not in the power of Brutus to alter his allegiance, which he had already engaged to the commonwealth, which had done nothing to forfeit the same. For how lawful soever it be for subjects to transfer their obedience to a conqueror, in a foreign war, when the former civil power can no longer protect them; or to a new magistrate made by consent, when the old had forfeited or resigned: It is ridiculous to suppose, that they can transfer it to a domestick traitor and robber, who is under the same ties and allegiance with themselves, and, by all acts of violence, treason, and usurpation, extorts a submission from his oppressed masters and fellow-subjects. At least such allegiance can never be pre-engaged, whilst any means in nature are left to rid the world of such a monster.

It is a poor charge against Brutus, that Caesar intended him for his heir and successor. Brutus scorned to succeed a tyrant: And what more glorious for Brutus, than thus to own that the dangerous and bewitching prospect of the greatest power that ever mortal man possessed, could not shake the firm and virtuous heart of Brutus, nor corrupt his integrity? To own that no personal considerations, even the highest upon earth, could reconcile him to a tyrant; and that he preferred the liberty of the world to the empire of the world!

The above charges therefore against Brutus can hardly come from any but those, who, like the profane and slavish Esau, would sell their birthright for a mess of pottage;[4] would sacrifice their duty to their interest; and, unconcerned what becomes of the rest of mankind, would promote tyranny, if they might but shine in its trappings. But an honest mind, a mind great and virtuous, scorns and hates all ambition, but that of doing good to men, and to all men; it despises momentary riches, and ill-gotten power; it enjoys no vicious and hard-hearted pleasures, arising from the miseries of others: But it wishes and endeavours to procure impartial, diffusive, and universal happiness to the whole earth.

This is the character of a great and good mind; and this was the great and sublime soul of the immortal Brutus.

From this mention of the slippery and dangerous favours of tyrants, I would just observe, as I go along, that, to any man who values virtue or liberty, twenty pounds a year in a free country, is preferable to being first minister to the Great Turk; whose ministers, by their station and allegiance, are obliged to be oppressors, and are often rewarded with the bow-string[5] for their most faithful services to their master, and for services perhaps performed by his command.

4. Esau was the son of Isaac and the elder twin brother of Jacob. His short-sightedness was borne out by the fact that Jacob was able to entice him into exchanging his inheritance for a bowl of gruel (Gen 25:24–30).

5. The term refers to the string used for killing people by strangulation, a common method of execution in the Ottoman Empire.

But to return to Brutus: He had on his side the law of self-preservation, the spirit of the Roman constitution, and of those laws of liberty, which had subsisted near five hundred years, but were now destroyed by the usurper. And during all those long and renowned ages of liberty, the destroying of tyrants was ever accounted glory and heroism. And, as every law of the commonwealth was against Caesar, who was an open enemy to the commonwealth; the commonwealth, and all its laws, were for Brutus, its greatest and best subject. Caesar's laws were none, and worse than none; but the whole life and actions of Brutus were agreeable to the constitution of his country.

Suppose Brutus, having killed Caesar, had succeeded him: He could not have been a greater usurper than Caesar was. And yet would he, in that case, have been less sacred and inviolable than Caesar? I hope the oppressing of mankind is not a less crime than the killing of their oppressor.

Our Brutus could not have greater ties of affection to the tyrant Caesar, who usurped Rome, and destroyed its liberties, than the elder Brutus had to his own sons, whom he put to death, for a plot to restore the tyrant Tarquin, a thousand times more innocent than Caesar: And as to the sudden manner of putting him to death, Mutius Scaevola is immortalized for a bold attempt, to kill by surprize the Tuscan king Porsenna, who was a foreign enemy, making unjust war upon Rome, to restore Tarquin:[6] And the like immortality is bestowed upon Judith, for killing Holofernes deceitfully, when it could be done no other way.[7] Now both these men were publick enemies; but neither of them a publick traitor: Caesar was both; and *dolus an virtus quis in hoste requirat?*[8] Was ever Aratus mentioned with reproach, or does Dr. Prideaux mention him with reproach, for surprizing and expelling Nicocles, tyrant of

6. Gaius Mucius *Scaevola*, reputed to have attempted to kill Porsenna, the King of Etruria. When brought before him, Mucius exhibited his indifference to pain by placing his right hand on an altar of burning coals while calmly informing Porsenna that hundreds of young Romans were dedicated to preserving the Republic or dying in the attempt.

7. The event is recounted in the Book of Judith, one of the apocryphal books of the Old Testament, particularly Judith 13:1–8.

8. "Guile or courage—what difference when dealing with an enemy?" Virgil, *Aeneid*, 2.390.

Sicyon;[9] or has he not gained deathless fame by that worthy action? And how comes the little tyrant Nicocles to be less sacred than the greater tyrant Caesar, who did millions of mischiefs more than Nicocles?

Let us now see what Dr. Prideaux says of Caesar. After having told us, that he was excited by ambition and malice; that he justly had for the reward thereof that destruction by which he fell; the Doctor adds these words:

> He is said to have slain eleven hundred and ninety-two thousand men; which proves him to have been a terrible scourge in the hand of God, for the punishment of the wickedness of that age. And, consequently, he is to be reputed the greatest pest and plague that mankind had therein: But notwithstanding this, his actions have with many acquired great glory to his name: Whereas true glory is due only to those who benefit, not to those who destroy, mankind.[10]

All this is honestly and justly said; but I cannot reconcile it to what he has said before, about the death of that destroyer. Sure, upon his own principles, never was true glory more due to any mortal man, than to Brutus! His life and studies were laid out in doing good to mankind; whereas Caesar was indeed the greatest pest and plague that mankind had. For, besides all the wickedness that he did with his own wicked hands and counsels, he frustrated all the purposes, virtue, and bravery, of the old Romans, in establishing liberty, and in conquering, polishing, and setting free great part of the barbarous world. All the battles that they fought, were fought for him; all the blood that they spilt, was spilt for him. Caesar took all, and overturned all. Besides, all the numberless and heavy mischiefs that the Roman world suffered from succeeding tyrants, were, in a great measure, owing to Caesar, who established a government by tyrants. He was in this sense the author of all the barbarity, rapine, and butcheries, brought upon the empire, by the Goths, Huns, Vandals, and other barbarians, who easily mastered

9. *Aratus* (271–213 B.C.), a Sicyonian statesman who is said to have killed the tyrant Niccoles and thus restored the city to liberty.
10. *The Old and New Testaments Connected*, part II, bk. VII (IV:701).

an empire, weakened, and already almost destroyed, by the folly, madness, cruelty, and prodigality, of the imperial tyrants, his successors.

The Doctor takes notice, that Cassus Parmensis,[11] being the only remaining tyrannicide, was put to death by the command of Augustus. And he observes upon it, that murder seldom escapes the vindictive hand of God, and especially the murder of princes. All this may be true; and yet, what is all this to Julius Caesar? If Caesar was a prince, any robber or murderer that has force and villainy enough, may be a prince; and blood, and wounds, and treason, constitute a prince. Every soldier in Caesar's army had as good a right to the government of Rome, as Caesar had. Was his style like that of a prince, or the father of his country, when he told his soldiers, according to Petronius, and agreeably to what he did afterwards;

> ————*Ite furentes,*
> *Ite mei comites, & causam dicite ferro.*
> *Judice fortuna cadat alea: Sumite bellum;*
> *Inter tot fortes armatus nescio vinci.*[12]

Was not this setting up open violence and the sword for a title? If Rob Roy had conquered Scotland, with his barbarous Highland host; would he have been a prince, Prince of Scotland?[13] Was Cromwell a prince? And would Massianello and Jack Straw, had they succeeded, have been princes?[14]

As to Caesar's parts, they added vastly to his crimes, and were, as he applied them, only a great capacity to do great mischief. *Curse on his virtues, they have undone his country!* Besides, there were doubtless many men in Rome who had equal parts, and infi-

11. Cassius *Parmensis* is listed among those implicated in Caesar's murder.

12. "To arms, comrades, while hot with anger! Let us plead our cause with the sword. Let fate determine our fortune. Choose war! Among so many brave warriors I cannot be conquered." Petronius, *Satyricon*, 122.

13. Rob Roy (1671–1734), Scottish cattle thief and brigand, was able to take advantage of the Jacobite Rebellion in 1715 to expand his area of operations. He was caught and sentenced to transportation in 1727.

14. Tommaso Aniello, known as Masaniello, an Amalfi fisherman, led a tax revolt against the Spanish viceroy at Naples in 1647. Jack Straw was one of the chief lieutenants of Wat Tyler, who led a major peasant revolt in 1381.

nitely more merit. Brutus particularly had. The Devil has much greater abilities than Caesar had, and is also a prince, a very great prince; the executioner of God's vengeance too, the greatest executioner: And yet are we not expressly commanded to resist him? The plague is often the instrument of God's judgment; are we therefore not to resist the plague, by proper diet and antidotes? The bite of an adder may be the judgment of God; is it therefore a sin to tread upon the adder's head, and kill him? Or are antidotes against all other plagues lawful; but none lawful against the worst, the most lasting and destructive of all plagues, the plague of tyranny? Or is an adder less sacred than a tyrant? And why? I hope God made adders as well as Caesar. A storm may be a judgment; must we not therefore discharge a great gun against it, in order to disperse it? Or pray how comes one sort of the instruments of God's judgment to be more sacred than another? I am sure, God detests tyrants; and if they be God's ministers, so are plagues and serpents, and so is Satan himself.

Brutus was one of the properest persons to kill Caesar; as he was of all the men in Rome the most reverenced and popular. His wisdom, and virtue, and publick spirit, were known and adored: The consent of the Senate, and of all good men, was with him; none but the prostitute creatures of power, and those that ambitiously sought it, with their deceived and hireling followers, condemned him; nor durst even they at first. But Brutus, out of his too great goodness and generosity, spared Anthony, who ought to have accompanied Caesar. But while the wild Anthony remained, the root of the evil was not quite plucked up. He began a new war upon his country. The Senate, however, declared for the tyrannicides; declared Mark Anthony a publick enemy for making war upon Decimus Brutus, who was one of them; and sent both the consuls with an army against Anthony, in defence of Brutus: And had it not been for the treacherous and ungrateful young Caesar,[15] the commonwealth would have been, in all likelihood, thoroughly established. But this young traitor, like his uncle

15. That is, Gaius Octavian (Augustus), whom Caesar had adopted and made his principal heir.

Julius,[16] turned the arms of the commonwealth upon the common-wealth, and joined with its enemy Mark Anthony to oppress it.

The terrible proceedings and bloody proscriptions that fol-lowed this agreement are well known. Nor is it at all strange, that not one of the tyrannicides survived the civil war, or died a natural death. They were almost all soldiers and commanders, and were either mostly slain in battle, or by the command of the conquerors: Their enemies got the better, and they had no where to fly to. The world was possessed by the usurpers. If Brutus and Cassius killed themselves, rather than fall into their enemies' hands, and adorn the triumphs of successful traitors; several of the chiefs of the other party did also kill themselves during the war; particularly Dolabella, and many of the principals of his party at Antioch, when Cassius besieged them there.[17] Was this also a judgment?

Brutus and Cassius killed themselves! What then? Was it not done like Romans, like virtuous old Romans, thus to prefer death to slavery? It was a Roman spirit; and those who possessed it, did as much disdain to be tyrants, as to submit to tyranny; a spirit that scorned an ignominious life, held only at the mercy of an usurper, or by flattering his villainy, and abetting his usurpations; and a spirit, which those that want it can never admire. Great souls are not comprehended by small! It is undoubtedly true, that by the precepts of Christianity we are not at liberty to dispose of our own lives; but are to wait for the call of heaven to alleviate or end our calamities: But the Romans had no other laws to act by, but the natural dictates of uncorrupted reason. I call upon the great pretenders to philosophy and refined morals, to assign one fair reason, why a Roman, why Brutus and Cassius, should prefer a miserable life to an honourable death; should bear vassalage, chains, and tortures of body or mind, when all those evils were to be avoided by doing only that, which, by the course of nature, every man must soon do. It is better not to be, than to be unhappy;

16. Octavian's mother was the daughter of Julia, the sister of Julius Caesar. Caesar was therefore his great-uncle.

17. The reference is to Publius Cornelius *Dolabella* (*c.* 80 B.C.–43 B.C.), who, on Caesar's death, associated himself with the assassins but soon switched his allegiances. The Senate declared him an enemy of the republic and, on being captured, Dolabella committed suicide.

and the severest judgment on the wicked is, that they shall live for ever, and can never end their miseries: Much less can it be any service to society, to keep alive by art or force a melancholy, miserable, and useless member, grown perhaps burdensome too by age and infirmities.

In this light we must view the actions of the old Romans, guided only by nature, and unrestrained from suicide by any principles of their religion. We find, on the contrary, in history, many examples of the great and magnanimous heroes of antiquity, choosing voluntary death, often in the midst of health, with the greatest calmness of mind; sometimes from satiety of life and glory, either when they could gain no more, or apprehending that the future caprices of unconstant fortune might sully the past; and oftener still, to avoid submitting to disgrace and servitude.

A voluntary death from such motives as these, was, among the ancients, one of the paths to immortality; and, under certain circumstances, none but mean and abject minds declined it. Roman ladies often chose it. Cleopatra, Queen of Egypt, chose a long premeditated death, rather than be led captive to Rome. And when Perseus sent to P. Aemilius,[18] beseeching him with all earnestness, that so great a prince, late lord of Macedon, and good part of Greece, might not be led, like a slave, in chains at his chariot wheel, to grace his triumph; he received this short answer, that "it was in his own power to prevent it": Thus signifying to him, that he deserved the disgrace, if he would live to bear it.

Even under the dispensations of a new religion, which God Almighty condescended personally to teach mankind; human nature has prevailed so far over revealed truths, that in multitudes of instances a voluntary death is approved, at least not condemned, by almost the greatest part of the world. Men in extreme pain and agonies do often refuse physick,[19] and the means of preserving their lives, days, weeks, and months longer. Men in lingering and desperate distempers go, uncalled, to mount a breach in a siege, or into the midst of the battle, to meet certain death. Great com-

18. The armies of Perseus, King of Macedon, were defeated at Pydna in 168 B.C. by a Roman force under the command of Lucius Aemilius Paullus.
19. Physic: medicine.

manders have done the same, when the day went against them, rather than survive being beaten. Commanders of ships have blown up themselves and their ships, rather than be the prey of the conqueror. Towns besieged, when they could defend themselves no longer, have first burnt their town, then precipitated themselves desperately amongst their enemies, to procure an honourable death and revenge. Even common malefactors often choose to die, rather than discover their accomplices; and always get credit by doing so. And the stories of the Decii, of Celanus, of the great Cato, and even of Otho,[20] and many other of the great examples of antiquity, made immortal by this act of ancient heroism, are still read with admiration.

I shall, for a conclusion of this long paper, give my readers the sentiments of the excellent Mr. Cowley, concerning Brutus and Caesar, in his ode entitled *Brutus*.

> Can we stand by and see
> Our mother robb'd, and bound, and ravish'd be,
>   Yet not to her assistance stir,
> Pleas'd with the strength and beauty of the ravisher?
> Or shall we fear to kill him, if before
>   The cancell'd name of friend he bore?
> Ingrateful Brutus do they call?
> Ingrateful Caesar, who could Rome enthral!
> An act more barbarous and unnatural
> (In th' exact balance of true virtue try'd)
> Than his successor Nero's parricide!
>
>   *   *   *
>
> What mercy could the tyrant's life deserve
> From him who kill'd himself rather than serve?

20. Publius *Decius* Mus, grandfather, father, and son, collectively known as the Decii: All three are reputed, over the course of some sixty years, to have sacrificed themselves in battle by rushing into the thickest part of the enemy, thus animating the soldiers under them and serving as examples of overwhelming devotion to the state. Quintus Rufius *Calenus*, general who served under Caesar and, following Caesar's death, commanded Mark Antony's forces in northern Italy. He died just as he was about to march against Octavian's armies. Marcus Porcius *Cato* Uticensis, Cato the Younger, who fortified himself in the city of Utica against Caesar's armies. Rather than fall alive into Caesar's hands, Cato stabbed himself after reading Plato's treatise on the immortality of the soul. The emperor *Otho* fell upon his sword after his armies had been decisively defeated by those of Vitellius in A.D. 69.

* * *

What joy can human things to us afford,
When we see perish thus by odd events,
By ill men and wretched accidents,
The best cause, and best man that ever drew a sword?
   When we see
The false Octavius and wild Anthony,
  God-like Brutus! conquer thee?[21]

G   *I am, &c.*

NO. 57. SATURDAY, DECEMBER 16, 1721.

Of false Honour, publick and private.

SIR,

I have more than once complained in these letters, that the best things being most abused are capable of doing the greatest harm: Nor is it a new observation, whatever new occasion there may be, at all times, to repeat it. Men have been ever deceived by good names into an approbation of ill things, sanctified by these names. Imposture and delusion have been called religion, and thought so; oppression and rapine have been called government, and esteemed government. Teachers have degenerated into deceivers, submission into slavery, taxation into plundering, protection into destruction, and magistrates into murderers, without changing their names: Power and right have been ever confounded; and success, or the want of success, has turned villainy into virtue, and virtue into villainy.

Hence it is that little crimes and small criminals have been detested and punished, while great malefactors have been generally reverenced and obeyed: and that little rogues have been called thieves, and hanged; and great thieves have been styled conquerors and princes, and sometimes deified. Your Alexanders and

21. The quotation is patched together from sections of several stanzas of Abraham Cowley's ode "Brutus": stanza 3, lines 1–11; stanza 2, lines 3–4; and stanza 5, lines 1–7.

Caesars were only felons above the gallows; and so have been many others of much less figure than they. Great crimes protect themselves, and one another; so that, in effect, crimes are not always punished because they are crimes, but because they are not mighty crimes: Nor, in the inflicting of punishments, has the offence or the offender been considered, but only the figure of the offender; who, if he were poor and necessitous, has been put to death; if great and ambitious, has been protected or preferred. And thus it is, that halters and garters, axes and white staves, palaces and dungeons, have been often miserably confounded and misplaced.

Thus are the boundaries and distinction between good and evil almost lost in the world. To illustrate this in every instance that deserves illustration, would be to write a folio instead of a letter; at present I shall confine myself to the consideration of false honour, which has done much more mischief to mankind than ever real honour did good, as it is more conducing to the little personal gratifications, and the crooked self-ends of particular men.

True honour is an attachment to honest and beneficent principles, and a good reputation; and prompts a man to do good to others, and indeed to all men, at his own cost, pains, or peril. False honour is a pretence to this character, but does things that destroy it: And the abuse of honour is called honour, by those who from that good word borrow credit to act basely, rashly, or foolishly.

A man cannot act honourably in a bad cause. That he thinks it a good cause, is not a good excuse; for folly and mistake is not honour: Nor is it a better excuse, that he is engaged in it, and has pledged his faith to support it, and act for it; for this is to engage his honour against honour, and to list his faith in a war against truth. To say that he is ashamed to desert it, is to say that he is ashamed to do an honest thing; and that he prefers false shame to true honour, which engages the man that possesses it to hate and break all criminal engagements. If a man enter into a party or society, because he thinks it an honest society; is he obliged to continue in it, when he finds it a society of knaves? And does his honour oblige him to be a knave too, or to desert those that are knaves? Or, does a robber, who leaves the gang, violate his honour, which was only an obligation to rob?

A good conscience, an honest heart, and clean hands, are inseparable from true honour; nor does true honour teach any man to act against his judgment. It must be convinced before it acts, and mere authority has no weight with it. In human matters, it does not consider what is commanded, but what ought to be commanded; and before it executes an injunction, enquires whether the same be rational and just. When superior orders are unjust, the honour of obedience is taken away; for honour is not the instrument of evil; it is therefore false and pretended honour, to execute and vindicate a bad action by an unjust command. Indeed, no command of any consequence ought to be obeyed, but what is or ought to be law, and is not forbidden by any law.

But this is only reasoning, which has but little force with men when it combats their interest and worst passions. To them therefore who follow the guides of gain and ambition, what I have here said is not addressed; but to those who, contrary to their interest, follow and approve others whose only principle is interest.

False honour has more power over men than laws have; and those who despise all the ties of laws, and of religion and humanity, are often very exact in observing all the fantastical and wicked rules of false honour. There are no debts so punctually paid as those contracted at play: though there are express laws against play, and against paying of money won at play; nay, 'tis penal to pay such debts. And yet those that are thus exact in paying to their own ruin, and in defiance of law, whatever debts they contract to avowed sharpers, who live by cheating and picking pockets, and are the destruction of families, and a publick nuisance: I say, those men thus exact in unrighteousness and their own wrong, shall run in debt to honest tradesmen, without any purpose of paying them, and, unconcerned, see them broke, imprisoned, and undone, for want of such payment. So lawlessly just are they to rogues that ruin them, and so barbarously unjust to industrious and credulous men, who feed and clothe them!

Is this honour! What dupes are we to words and to our own vice and folly! It is but small comfort to us, that this voluntary

madness prevailed of old amongst our barbarous German ancestors; of whose distracted propensity to gaming Tacitus gives us this
astonishing account:

> *Aleam sobrii inter seria exercent, tanta lucrandi perdendive temer-*
> *itate, ut cum omnia defecerunt, extremo ac novissimo jactu, de*
> *libertate & de corpore contendant. Victus voluntariam servitutem*
> *adit, quamvis junior, quamvis robustior, adligari se ac venire*
> *patitur. Ea est in re prava pervicacia: ipsi fidem vocant.*[1]

Gaming is one of their most serious employments, and
even sober they are gamesters! To this rash vice they are so
violently addicted, that when they have wantonly lost all,
they have not done, but desperately stake their liberty and
their persons upon the last throw. The loser goes calmly
into bondage; and though the younger and the stronger,
suffers himself tamely to be bound and sold by him that
wins. Such is their vicious perseverance in folly! they themselves call it honour.

Our modern gamesters do not indeed go quite this length;
they only sell themselves, with their families and posterity, to beggary: For as to their bodies, no body will stake any thing against
them. But in point of honour, in gaming, we still retain the strict-
ness of these our polite ancestors at play, and generously pay to
the last morsel of bread, and venture famine rather than a dun[2]
from one that has foiled us at the art of picking pockets. As to
other duns, honest and necessitous duns, we matter them not; and
debts of real honour and conscience, do not at all touch our
honour.

Thus is honour set up against virtue and law. Good laws
not executed are worse than none, and only teach men to despise
law: whereas reverence and obedience go together. No law will or

1. "Among their serious activities during their sober hours they play dice, but
with such recklessness whether they win or lose that, when all else has been
lost, they stake themselves and their own liberty on a last and final throw; the
loser faces voluntary slavery. Though he be much younger and much stronger
than his opponent, he permits himself to be bound and sold. Such is their
persistence, which they call their 'good faith,' in this vicious practice." Tacitus,
Germania, 24.2.

2. A dun: a request for payment.

can ever be executed by inferior magistrates, while the breach of it is openly encouraged by the example of superior. Does any man think that the best laws, even inspired laws, against duelling, would have any effect, if there was at the same time a duelling-office kept open at St. James's? The example of those that should execute laws, or see them executed, is stronger than the authority of those that make them. The example of Vespasian[3] did more towards the restraint of luxury, than all the sumptuary laws of Rome could do till his time.

> *Praecipuus adstricti moris auctor Vespasianus fuit. Obsequium inde in principem, & aemulandi amor, validior quam poena ex legibus & metus.*[4]

> Vespasian was himself a special instance and author of temperance and frugality. From hence grew in the people a reverence for the example of the prince, and an emulation to conform their manners to his; a tie much stronger than the dread of laws and all their penalties.

It is moreover become a mighty piece of honour to repair one crime by another, and a worse; and when one has done you an injury, he must, by the rules of honour, fight to defend it. Having affronted or harmed you, contrary to justice and honour, he makes you satisfaction by taking away your life, according to the impulses of true honour; so here is a war of honour against honour and justice and common sense.

Another piece of honour is an adherence to error, after conviction, and not to change a bad religion for a better. To have been born in a certain faith, is just as good sense as to have been born a lawyer or mathematician; and yet that same is often the best and truest reason against change! And therefore we often adhere against all our reason, to what others said or did for us without our consent, and when we had no reason. Because perhaps some peo-

3. Titus Flavius *Vespasianus*, Roman emperor from A.D. 69 until his death from natural causes in A.D. 79.

4. "Vespasian especially kept to a strict regimen, which encouraged a feeling of deference toward the emperor and the desire to follow his example, more powerful motives than all the penalties and terrors of the law." Tacitus, *Annales*, 3.55.

ple promised for us when we were a day old, that we should forty years afterwards, and all our life, count beads, worship unsavoury bones, be governed by deceivers, and believe contradictions; are we therefore obliged to do all this, though we find it to be against all religion? Must we be hypocrites, because our ancestors were fools? Are old falsehoods and fooleries the standard of our honour? Are we never to mend a wretched condition, and never to make use of our conscience? If so, then here is a war of honour against conscience, a war of faith against belief, and a war of religion against persuasion!

Another piece of false honour has sometimes been that of serving a prince at the expence of one's country, though the serving of that country was the only duty and only business of the prince, and of every man in office under him. But this, though a truth as self-evident as any in the Bible, has been so little understood or practised, that the wicked execution of impious engagements made to a tyrant, against those made to society, has been called honour. And it has frequently been the honour of a courtier, to execute all the ill purposes of a court against his country. And here was the war of honour against duty.

The honour of a party is to adhere to one another, right or wrong; and though their chief be a knave and a traitor, their honour is engaged to be honest to him in all his rogueries and treason. And this is a war of honour against honesty.

The honour and *bona fide*[5] of some princes have been of that odd and unprincely contexture, that they were never once restrained by the same, from deceiving, plaguing, invading, robbing, and usurping upon their neighbours, and doing things which would have entitled a plain subject to the gibbet. Their honour seems to have been deeply concerned to have no honour: And though their faith was engaged to protect their subjects; yet their honour, on the other side, was engaged to pillage and enslave them. And here grew the royal war of honour against faith and equity!

How many peaceable nations have been robbed, how many millions of innocents butchered, out of mere honour,

5. "Good faith."

princely honour? This honour is indeed so wild, mischievous, and extravagant, that words, the most warm and significant words, fail in describing it. I shall therefore subjoin a few instances of its spirit, and conclude.

His Grace, Villiers, first Duke of Buckingham, engaged his country in two mad wars at once with the two greatest powers in Europe, because his honour had suffered a rebuff in his attempts to debauch two great foreign ladies.[6] Europe was to be embroiled; lives, treasure, and the safety of kingdoms to be risked and thrown away, to vindicate, forsooth, his Grace's debauched honour.

Cambyses, to revenge an affront put upon his father many years before by an Egyptian king, in the business of sending him a wife, involved the world in a flame of war; and at the expence of perhaps a million of lives, and the destruction of kingdoms, did at last heroically vindicate his father's honour and his own, upon the bones of a dead king, whom he caused to be dug up, and, after many indignities, cast into the fire.[7]

White elephants are rare in nature, and so greatly valued in the Indies, that the King of Pegu[8] hearing that the King of Siam had got two, sent an embassy in form, to desire one of them of his royal brother, at any price: But being refused, he thought his honour concerned to wage war for so great an affront. So he entered Siam with a vast army, and with the loss of five hundred thousand of his own men, and the destruction of as many of the Siamese, he made himself master of the elephant, and retrieved his honour.[9]

6. George Villiers, first Duke of Buckingham (1592–1628), held enormous political power under James I and Charles I. In 1624 England became engaged in a war with Spain, while two years later the country went to war with France over France's treatment of the Huguenots at La Rochelle. While on a mission to Spain, Buckingham is reputed to have attempted the seduction of the wife of the Count of Olivares, chief minister to Philip IV. And, during a diplomatic mission to France in 1625, he is reported to have made amorous advances to the French Queen Mother. It has been suggested that these personal entanglements played a role in shaping British foreign policy.

7. The events are recounted in Prideaux's *The Old and New Testaments Connected*, part I, bk. III (I:237–44).

8. That is, the King of Burma.

9. The reference is to the Siamese-Burmese War of 1563–1569, which ended with the capture of Siam's capital and the establishment of Siam as a Burmese vassal state.

Darius (I think it was Darius the Mede) found his honour concerned to chastise the Scythians for having invaded Asia a hundred and thirty years before; and lost a great army to vindicate his honour, which yet was not vindicated;[10] that is, he missed the white elephant.

In short, honour and victory are generally no more than white elephants; and for white elephants the most destructive wars have been often made. What man free, either by birth or spirit, could, without pity and contempt, behold, as in a late French reign[11] he frequently might behold, a swarm of slavish Frenchmen, in wooden shoes, with hungry bellies, and no clothes, dancing round a maypole, because their *Grand Monarque,* at the expence of a million of their money, and thirty or forty thousand lives, had acquired a white elephant, or, in other words, gained a town or victory?

Instances are endless, or else I could name other people, who have employed themselves several years in catching white elephants by sea and land; but I am in haste to conclude.

G   *I am, &c.*

NO. 58. SATURDAY, DECEMBER 23, 1721.

Letter from a Lady, with an Answer, about Love, Marriage, and Settlements.

TO CATO

S IR,

Though love, abstracted from marriage, is a subject too low for a statesman, a politician, and I might add a philosopher; yet as it relates to that holy state (as our Church is pleased to call it) it is worthy the greatest notice; for though many take upon them

10. Darius I, King of Persia (521–486 B.C.). In 512 B.C. Darius penetrated Europe on a punitive expedition against the Scythians.
11. That is, that of Louis XIV.

to ridicule all lawful and honourable love, and marriage, which crowns and proves it, yet I will venture to affirm, that hardly any person lives a long life without desiring at some part of it to enter into that state: It is like religion, implanted in our natures; and all men have a notion that 'tis the way to happiness, though all do not practise it: The reasons of this want of practise are many; besides the degeneracy of human nature, the imperfections of both sexes make them afraid of so close an affinity; the want of constancy in the male sex, and, above all, the love of money in both, is the greatest scandal and hindrance to this most honourable state in life.

I cannot excuse either sex (though by this time, both from my subject and handling of it, you will guess me to be of the weakest) from this last vice, the love of money; and I might add to it ambition; for it seems to me grown the rule of marriage, there being few alliances contracted of late years, but where this is the chief motive on the man's side, and almost so on the woman's: No wonder the ladies should have catched the vice; for when a woman finds herself slighted for no other want but that of a large fortune, she must needs think it worth purchasing at any rate, and neglect all other merit as useless.

I do not pretend to say that virtue and merit, in our sex, is to be met with in every corner of the streets, as I am too sensible the contrary is; but sure I am it is to be found, and judgment was given to the men in order to distinguish it. But, say your sex, is money then to be despised? Must the contrary be sought? And has a lady less merit for having a large fortune? Not always, but indeed too often; nay, nothing can hinder it but natural good sense and temper, joined to great care taken in the education; without that a superior fortune makes a worse woman, consequently a worse wife.

I was led into this thought, and which occasioned this letter, by a disappointment that a young lady I had a friendship for met with lately, with relation to this subject, which cost her her life.

She was addressed to by a gentleman, whose good sense and agreeableness would, she thought, atone for some natural defects and infirmities, which she had penetration enough to find out in his temper and disposition; among which his love of money was not the least: He was superior to her in fortune; but she was a gentlewoman born, and bred so, and in every respect, but money, his equal: She resolved to suit herself to his humour; and fancied herself cut out to please and make him happy, not out of vanity, but inclination to do so. She had pride, and did not greatly care to be obliged, even by the man whom she loved; but fancied she could save up a fortune to him in a few years, and, with the refusing of presents, and resigning of settlements, atone in great measure for the want of it. He thought it worth while to deceive her for a considerable length of time, for what reason I cannot guess, she being a woman of undoubted character, which he had known for some years before, and all her actions answered: But in short he left her, and that in so abrupt and rude a manner, as made her bear it worse; not shewing the least abatement of his passion the last time he saw her, more than at the first. I wish that he had trusted her with the secret of forsaking her; for I dare say she would have taken it handsomely, and (for his advantage) given him up.

The disappointment met her under an indisposition of body, else I believe she had good sense, reason, and resentment enough, to have got the better of it. But she died, and without reproaching of him, or behaving herself unhandsomely; she said she was inclined to believe that there was a fate in things of that nature, and wished him happier than (she doubted) he deserved.

He is now upon the brink of marriage to a lady, that I dare say he does not like half so well as this lady whom he left for her; but she had more money abundantly, which he does not want; and then, though, as I said before, money is no objection, nor need a woman be sought out that wants it, yet I would not have a man venture to leave a woman for no other reason, lest he (as too probably he may) chance to repent it.

Sir, if you think this subject, or our sex, worthy your notice, we shall be obliged to you; you are an author, I might say it to your face, capable of serving any cause that you undertake; ours is a charitable one: I am out of the question myself, with relation to making my fortune, or it might not have been so proper for me to have started this subject, though obscure; but I have a general love for mankind, and particularly for my own sex; whose cause I commit to you, as into the hands of a most powerful advocate, and (I hope) a willing patron. My sincerity on this subject cannot be doubted, when I most humbly subscribe myself of that sex whose cause I recommend; *viz.*

A Woman

TO THE LADY WHO WROTE THE FOREGOING

MADAM,

Y ou will easily believe me, when I acquaint you, that I am not a little proud of the honour you have done me, in thinking me worthy of the correspondence of a lady, to whom nature has shewn herself so indulgent. She seldom leaves her own work imperfect; and therefore I doubt not but she has been propitious to you more ways than one: And I am persuaded, that if you had been the first object of the inconstant Strephon's adoration,[1] he had never worshipped any false goddess.

I can assure you, madam, you could never have recommended yourself so much to me, or have obliged me more, than in engaging me in this agreeable manner in the cause of helpless innocence, and distressed virtue; and in giving me an opportunity to consider the greater and better half of the world in their nearest and most engaging relation. I am, by profession, a knight-errant: It is my business to right wrongs, and redress injuries; and none more than those done to your tender sex.

It is a subject which employs my softest and most delicate thoughts and inclinations; which I can in nothing gratify so much, as by contributing to the ease and happiness of that sex, to whom we owe most of our own.

> That cordial drop heav'n in our cup has thrown,
> To make the nauseous draught of life go down;

1. Strephon is the fickle shepherd who makes love to Urania in Sir Philip Sidney's *Arcadia* (1580).

And to atone for the thousands, ten thousands of evils, to which human condition is subject.

Hercules himself laid down his club, and took up a distaff: And,

———furious Mars,
The only governor and god of wars,
When tir'd with heat and toil, does oft resort
To taste the pleasures of the Paphian court.

I do not therefore depart from my character, or desert my duty, in considering this subject, and attending upon the concerns of the fair: With their cause the cause of liberty is blended; and scarce any man will be much concerned for publick happiness, unless he enjoys domestick: Publick happiness being nothing else but the magistrate's protecting of private men in their property, and their enjoyments. It is certain, that a man's interest, in point of happiness and pleasures, is in no instance so much concerned as in that of marriage; which being the happiest or unhappiest state in the world, must mostly contribute to his happiness or misery.

The beauty, the vigour, the wit, and consequently the preferment of his posterity, do much depend upon the choice of his wife, and possibly upon his inclinations to her, and hers to him. We are very careful of the breed of our horses, of our cocks, and our dogs, and as remarkably neglectful of the education of our children; and yet we dedicate two thirds of our substance to our posterity: For so much is the difference between the purchase of estates of inheritance, and of estates only for our own lives.

Our wealth does also depend in a great measure upon domestick sympathy and concord; and it is a true proverb, that *A man must ask leave of his wife to be rich*: So great a share of his substance and prosperity must remain in her power, and at her discretion, and under her management, that if he would thrive and be happy himself, he must make her so.

In order to this, he ought to choose one whose temper, good sense, and agreeableness, shall make him find his pleasure in obliging her; and by constancy and endearing actions make her wholly his own, and to do all in her power to oblige him. No man can live in a constant state of hypocrisy in his own family; but if he has distastes, they will certainly break out; or at least be found out by one who is always about him, and whose constant business it is to observe him, and his humours and affections. And therefore it is his best and only way to find out such a one as he need not counterfeit a kindness to.

In all my observation, a good husband rarely misses to make a good wife. The hearts of women are naturally so tender, their passions towards their husbands so strong, their happiness and the respect which they meet with in the world are so much owing to their husbands, that we seldom find a married woman who will not, with a little real, and often with but a seeming kindness, do whatever a prudent husband will desire of her; and often, to oblige him, more than he desires. And what can be more barbarous, than to use one ill who throws herself into his power, and depends upon his protection; who gives up all that she has to his mercy, and receives it afterwards at his pleasure?

It is miserable folly, to put yourself in a circumstance of being uneasy in your own house, which ought to be a retreat from all the ruffles and disappointments that you meet with elsewhere: In consequence of this, you must seek your pleasures abroad at great expence, and the hazard of your health, and to the neglect of your affairs. Your wife too, when she finds herself neglected by one in whom she had fixed her whole happiness, will not bear the place and mansion of her misery, but will fall into a despondency, and an indifference to your interest; and will be apt to look out in her turn for pleasures abroad, when she can have none at home. Women for the most part place their felicity in their husbands, and in their families; and generally pursue those views, till the unkindness, neglect, and folly of their husbands render them impracticable.

Whatever excuse there may be for men overrun with debts, or otherwise very necessitous, to aim only at money in marriage, and thereby to throw themselves into a miserable and nauseous imprisonment for life, to prevent falling into one but little worse; I cannot find one tolerable reason in nature, why any man in easy circumstances, and who does not want the common necessaries of life, should purchase the superfluities at so dear a price.

But it is stupendous that men of figure and fortune, who have in their power the means of enjoying not only the conveniencies, but the luxury and vices of life (if such can be called enjoyments), should yet barter away all their happiness for a little seeming additional wealth, which for the most part produces real poverty.

It is certain, that ten men of birth and estates have been undone by marrying great fortunes, for one who has been enriched by it. Most men pay twenty per cent for such portions, as long as they have any thing to pay.[2] Ten thousand pounds additional fortune, when laid out in land, will not produce three hundred pounds a year clear; which sum will scarce maintain the tea-table, and keep the supernumerary baubles in repair; and it will cost as much more to shew them. Besides, when the usual presents are made, and an expensive marriage is solemnized, gaudy clothes and equipage are bought, and perhaps a London house furnished; a considerable part of this portion will be disbursed, and the forlorn hero of this shewy, noisy farce, will discover, too late, how much more eligible it had been to have married a lady well born, of a discreet, modest, and frugal education, and an agreeable person, with less money, than a haughty dame with all her quality airs about her, or Mr. Thimbleman's daughter, though bedecked with as many trinkets as Tallboy or Jerry Blackacre upon the stage.[3]

But before we can complete this account, we must balance what must be given in lieu of this lady's wealth, besides the entire loss of conjugal and domestick happiness. It is truly said, that *gold may be bought too dear*; and I may safely say, that the dearest purchase now in England, is a wife with a great fortune, not excepting that of South-Sea stock last year.

For every thousand pounds the lady brings, she must have a hundred pounds a year, at least during her own life, and often a rent-charge, which alone is worth the purchase money which she

2. That is, most men are expected to settle approximately twenty percent of the value of the proposed marriage settlement on their wives.

3. Both Master Talboy, Amie's lover in Richard Brome's *A Jovial Crew* (1641), and Jerry Blackacre, the young squire "bred to the law" in William Wycherley's *The Plain-Dealer* (1674), tended toward the foppish. "Thimbleman" is a slang term for a professional cheat; thus, "Mrs. Thimbleman's daughter" appears to be a reference to the occupation of the lady's father.

brings, if she outlives her husband;[4] and then she brings nothing towards the issue, which, modestly speaking, are as much hers as her husband's; and it is certain, that during her living with him, she spends more than the interest of it: For (besides her private expence) the gay furniture, the rich beds, the China ware, the tea-table, the visiting-rooms, rich coaches, &c. must be chiefly placed to her account; and she shares equally in the table expence, and in that of the children and gardens: And yet, over and above all this, a man must settle the remainder of his estate and substance out of his own power, and entail it upon whatever heir chance and his wife bring him; perhaps upon an ungrateful and disobedient one, made so by his independency upon his father; often upon a foolish and unimprovable one; sometimes, perhaps, upon a spurious one.

I do not complain of this usual method of settlement, as thinking it reasonable that any man should give a large sum of money in dowry with his daughter, without taking proper precautions to provide for her and his own posterity: But I censure the present great abuse of giving and demanding such fortunes, which have inverted the very ends of marriage, and made wives independent on their husbands, and sons on their fathers; fortunes, which make men bargain for their wives, as they would for cattle; and, instead of creating conjugal friendship and affection, and all sorts of domestick happiness, have produced nothing but strife, aversion, and contention, where there ought to be perfect sympathy and unanimity; and have brought into the world a race of monkeys and baboons, instead of creatures with human shape and souls.

Why should men of fortune and understanding bring themselves, without any motive from reason or interest, into these unhappy circumstances? Why should any man, without any consideration, at least any valuable consideration, divest himself of the greatest part of the property of his own estate? Why make himself only tenant for life, when he is in possession of an inheritance; and render himself by that means unable to provide against the many emergencies of life? Why subject himself to the insolence of an ungrateful heir, or be forced to leave it to an unworthy one? Why

4. The "rent charge" to which Gordon refers is the right conferred on a widow, created by deed or will, to a stipulated rent on certain property during her lifetime.

be obliged to bear the caprices and dishonour of a wanton and peevish wife, perhaps made so by his neglect, arising from his aversion, the ordinary effect of marriage against inclination? when he might have chosen one every way suited to the same; and, by contenting himself with less fortune, have kept the greatest part of his estate in his own power, and with it the further means of obliging her, and of making her future fortune and expectations to depend upon her own conduct, complaisance, and affectionate behaviour?

T

You have given me, madam, a very pregnant and affecting instance of a gentleman, who, made false by avarice, has lost, and wickedly lost, a virtuous, prudent, and fond wife, while he sought money more than merit; and cruelly broke his faith, and with it a tender heart, for the infamous sake of lucre; which may deservedly prove a canker in his soul and his substance, and bring him a lady with qualities proper to revenge the other's just quarrel and barbarous wrongs. And I, on my part, can give you an instance of a gentleman of great fortune and figure, who, by acting according to the former wiser rules, has made himself happy in an amiable, discreet, and observant lady, and enjoys with her all the blessings of mutual confidence and tender affection. He is complaisant without art, and she without fear. I am,

G

With perfect respect,
Madam,
your most humble
and most obedient servant,
CATO

POSTSCRIPT

I have, in several of my late letters, observed some slips that have escaped from the pen of the great and learned Dr. Prideaux;[5] but as I have done this with no design of blemishing a

5. See Letters 53, 54, and 55 (Nov. 18 and 25, and Dec. 2, 1721).

character which cannot be blemished, I think myself obliged to own once more, his great merit, the service done by him to mankind, the honour to his country, and the pleasure and information which I in particular have received from his worthy labours.

It is possible, that out of detestation to principles which subvert and tear up by the roots all liberty and civil happiness, I may have used some warm expressions against those that maintain them. Such expressions therefore can be applied only to those who have been ever the avowed and active enemies of every thing lovely, valuable, or praiseworthy amongst men. But as to Dr. Prideaux, however he is fallen into prejudice, perhaps early imbibed, and not since examined by him with his usual accuracy; or however he might intend to serve a pious cause with adventitious helps and precarious supports, which it wanted not: Certain it is, from the whole course of his excellent performance, that he had sincerely at heart the interest of true religion and liberty. A spirit of virtue, piety, good sense, and integrity, and an aversion to oppression, cruelty, and tyranny, shine through his whole history, and animate the same; and neither he nor his history can be too much commended.

But the Doctor is an eminent instance, how little any man ought to be guided by the mere authority of another; since one of the greatest and worthiest men living is capable of falling into such obvious errors. From the greatness of his name and credit alone I was led to these animadversions, and with reluctance I made them. Falcons do not prey upon flies. Other writers, whose characters add no weight to their mistakes, are safe from any censure of mine. For this reason I shall not trouble myself with the party-falsehoods, and pious ribaldry, and blunders, of a modern voluminous writer of English history. His contract and dialogue between Oliver Cromwell and the Devil, is a harmless piece of history, and as entertaining as the rest.[6]

T   *I am, &c.*

6. The reference is to Lawrence Echard's *History of England; From the Beginning of the Reign of King Charles the First to the Restoration of King Charles the Second* (London: Printed for Jacob Tonson, 1718). The dialogue between Cromwell and the Devil appears on p. 713.

NO. 59. SATURDAY, DECEMBER 30, 1721.

❧   *Liberty proved to be the unalienable Right of all Mankind.*

SIR,

I intend to entertain my readers with dissertations upon liberty, in some of my succeeding letters;[1] and shall, as a preface to that design, endeavour to prove in this, that liberty is the unalienable right of all mankind.

All governments, under whatsoever form they are administered, ought to be administered for the good of the society; when they are otherwise administered, they cease to be government, and become usurpation. This being the end of all government, even the most despotick have this limitation to their authority: In this respect, the only difference between the most absolute princes and limited magistrates, is, that in free governments there are checks and restraints appointed and expressed in the constitution itself: In despotick governments, the people submit themselves to the prudence and discretion of the prince alone: But there is still this tacit condition annexed to his power, that he must act by the unwritten laws of discretion and prudence, and employ it for the sole interest of the people, who give it to him, or suffer him to enjoy it, which they ever do for their own sakes.

Even in the most free governments, single men are often trusted with discretionary power: But they must answer for that discretion to those that trust them. Generals of armies and admirals of fleets have often unlimited commissions; and yet are they not answerable for the prudent execution of those commissions? The Council of Ten, in Venice, have absolute power over the liberty and life of every man in the state: But if they should make use of that power to slaughter, abolish, or enslave the senate; and, like

---

1. The advantages of liberty serve as the main topic of this and the succeeding nine letters.

the *Decemviri* of Rome,[2] to set up themselves; would it not be lawful for those, who gave them that authority for other ends, to put those ten unlimited traitors to death, any way that they could? The crown of England has been for the most part entrusted with the sole disposal of the money given for the Civil List,[3] often with the application of great sums raised for other publick uses; yet, if the lord-treasurer had applied this money to the dishonour of the King, and ruin of the people (though by the private direction of the crown itself) will any man say that he ought not to have compensated for his crime, by the loss of his head and his estate?

I have said thus much, to shew that no government can be absolute in the sense, or rather nonsense, of our modern dogmatizers, and indeed in the sense too commonly practised. No barbarous conquest; no extorted consent of miserable people, submitting to the chain to escape the sword; no repeated and hereditary acts of cruelty, though called succession, no continuation of violence, though named prescription; can alter, much less abrogate, these fundamental principles of government itself, or make the means of preservation the means of destruction, and render the condition of mankind infinitely more miserable than that of the beasts of the field, by the sole privilege of that reason which distinguishes them from the brute creation.

Force can give no title but to revenge, and to the use of force again; nor could it ever enter into the heart of any man, to give to another power over him, for any other end but to be exercised for his own advantage: And if there are any men mad or foolish enough to pretend to do otherwise, they ought to be treated as idiots or lunaticks; and the reason of their conduct must be derived from their folly and frenzy.

All men are born free; liberty is a gift which they receive from God himself; nor can they alienate the same by consent, though possibly they may forfeit it by crimes. No man has power over his own life, or to dispose of his own religion; and cannot

2. In 451 B.C. the Roman constitution was suspended and ten patricians were granted absolute political power while preparing a code of laws for the city. These magistrates were known as the *decemviri*.

3. The allowance allotted the crown by Parliament to meet the expenses of the royal household. The first Civil List Act was passed in 1697.

consequently transfer the power of either to any body else: Much less can he give away the lives and liberties, religion or acquired property of his posterity, who will be born as free as he himself was born, and can never be bound by his wicked and ridiculous bargain.

The right of the magistrate arises only from the right of private men to defend themselves, to repel injuries, and to punish those who commit them: That right being conveyed by the society to their publick representative, he can execute the same no further than the benefit and security of that society requires he should. When he exceeds his commission, his acts are as extrajudicial as are those of any private officer usurping an unlawful authority, that is, they are void; and every man is answerable for the wrong which he does. A power to do good can never become a warrant for doing evil.

But here arises a grand question, which has perplexed and puzzled the greatest part of mankind: Yet, I think, the answer to it easy and obvious. The question is, who shall be judge whether the magistrate acts justly, and pursues his trust? To this it is justly said, that if those who complain of him are to judge him, then there is a settled authority above the chief magistrate, which authority must be itself the chief magistrate; which is contrary to the supposition; and the same question and difficulty will recur again upon this new magistracy. All this I own to be absurd; and I aver it to be at least as absurd to affirm, that the person accused is to be the decisive judge of his own actions, when it is certain that he will always judge and determine in his own favour; and thus the whole race of mankind will be left helpless under the heaviest injustice, oppression, and misery, that can afflict human nature.

But if neither magistrates, nor they who complain of magistrates, and are aggrieved by them, have a right to determine decisively, the one for the other; and if there be no common established power, to which both are subject; then every man interested in the success of the contest, must act according to the light and dictates of his own conscience, and inform it as well as he can. Where no judge is nor can be appointed, every man must be his own; that is, when there is no stated judge upon earth, we must have recourse to heaven, and obey the will of heaven, by declaring ourselves on that which we think the juster side.

If the Senate and people of Rome had differed irreconcilably, there could have been no common judge in the world between them; and consequently no remedy but the last: For that government consisting in the union of the nobles and the people, when they differed, no man could determine between them; and therefore every man must have been at liberty to provide for his own security, and the general good, in the best manner he was able. In that case the common judge ceasing, every one was his own: The government becoming incapable of acting, suffered a political demise: The constitution was dissolved; and there being no government in being, the people were in the state of nature again.

The same must be true, where two absolute princes, governing a country, come to quarrel, as sometimes two Caesars in partnership did, especially towards the latter end of the Roman empire; or where a sovereign council govern a country, and their votes come equally to be divided. In such a circumstance, every man must take that side which he thinks most for the publick good, or choose any proper measures for his own security: For, if I owe my allegiance to two princes agreeing, or to the majority of a council; when between these princes there is no longer any union, nor in that council any majority, no submission can be due to that which is not; and the laws of nature and self-preservation must take place, where there are no other.

The case is still the same, when there is any dispute about the titles of absolute princes, who govern independently on the states of a country, and call none. Here too every man must judge for himself what party he will take, to which of the titles he will adhere; and the like private judgment must guide him, whenever a question arises whether the said prince be an idiot or a lunatick, and consequently whether he be capable or incapable of government. Where there are no states, there can be no other way of judging; but by the judgment of private men the capacity of the prince must be judged, and his fate determined. Lunacy and idiotism are, I think, allowed by all to be certain disqualifications for government; indeed they are as much so, as if he were deaf, blind, and dumb, or even dead. He who can neither execute an office, nor appoint a deputy, is not fit for one.

Now I would fain know, why private men may not as well use their judgment in an instance that concerns them more; I mean that of a tyrannical government, of which they hourly feel the sad effects, and sorrowful proofs; whereas they have not by far the equal means of coming to a certainty about the natural incapacity of their governor. The persons of great princes are known but to few of their subjects, and their parts to much fewer; and several princes have, by the management of their wives, or ministers, or murderers, reigned a good while after they were dead. In truth, I think it is as much the business and right of the people to judge whether their prince be good or bad, whether a father or an enemy, as to judge whether he be dead or alive; unless it be said (as many such wise things have been said) that they may judge whether he can govern them, but not whether he does; and that it behoves them to put the administration in wiser hands, if he be a harmless fool, but it is impious to do it, if he be only a destructive tyrant; that want of speech is a disqualification, but want of humanity, none.

That subjects were not to judge of their governors, or rather for themselves in the business of government, which of all human things concerns them most, was an absurdity that never entered into the imagination of the wise and honest ancients: Who, following for their guide that everlasting reason, which is the best and only guide in human affairs, carried liberty, and human happiness, the legitimate offspring and work of liberty, to the highest pitch that they were capable of arriving at. But the above absurdity, with many others as monstrous and mischievous, were reserved for the discovery of a few wretched and dreaming Mahometan and Christian monks, who, ignorant of all things, were made, or made themselves, the directors of all things; and bewitching the world with holy lies and unaccountable ravings, dressed up in barbarous words and uncouth phrases, bent all their fairy force against common sense and common liberty and truth, and founded a pernicious, absurd, and visionary empire upon their ruins. Systems without sense, propositions without truth, religion without reason, a rampant church without charity, severity without justice, and government without liberty or mercy, were all the blessed handy-works of these religious mad-men, and godly pedants; who, by pretending to know the other world, cheated and confounded this. Their enmity to common sense, and want of it, were their warrants for governing the sense of all mankind: By lying, they were thought the champions of the truth; and by their fooleries, impie-ties, and cruelty, were esteemed the favourites and confidents of the God of wisdom, mercy, and peace.

These were the men, who, having demolished all sense and human judgment, first made it a principle, that people were not to judge of their governor and government, nor to meddle with it; nor to preserve themselves from publick destroyers, falsely calling them-selves governors: Yet these men, who thus set up for the support and defenders of government, without the common honesty of dis-tinguishing the good from the bad, and protection from murder and depredation, were at the same time themselves the constant and avowed troublers of every government which they could not direct and command; and every government, however excellent, which did not make their reveries its own rules, and themselves alone its peculiar care, has been honoured with their professed hatred; whilst tyrants and publick butchers, who flattered them, have been deified. This was the poor state of Christendom before the Reformation; and I wish I could say, of no parts of it since.

This barbarous anarchy in reasoning and politicks, has made it necessary to prove propositions which the light of nature had demonstrated. And, as the apostles were forced to prove to the misled Gentiles, that they were no gods which were made with hands; I am put to prove, that the people have a right to judge, whether their governors were made for them, or they for their governors? Whether their governors have necessary and natural qualifications? Whether they have any governors or no? And whether, when they have none, every man must not be his own? I therefore return to instances and illustrations from facts which cannot be denied; though propositions as true as facts may, by those especially who are defective in point of modesty or discernment.

In Poland, according to the constitution of that country, it is necessary, we are told, that, in their diets, the consent of every man present must be had to make a resolve effectual:[4] And therefore, to prevent the cutting of people's throats, they have no remedy but to cut the throats of one another; that is, they must pull out their sabres, and force the refractory members (who are always the minority) to submit. And amongst us in England, where a jury cannot agree, there can be no verdict; and so they must fast till they do, or till one of them is dead, and then the jury is dissolved.

This, from the nature of things themselves, must be the constant case in all disputes between dominion and property. Where the interest of the governors and that of the governed clash, there can be no stated judge between them: To appeal to a foreign power, is to give up the sovereignty; for either side to submit, is to give up the question: And therefore, if they themselves do not amicably determine the dispute between themselves, heaven alone must. In such case, recourse must be had to the first principles of government itself; which being a departure from the state of nature, and a union of many families forming themselves into a political machine for mutual protection and defence, it is evident, that this formed relation can continue no longer than the machine subsists and can act; and when it does not, the individuals must return to their former state again. No constitution can provide against what will happen, when that constitution is dissolved. Government is only an appointment of one or more persons, to do certain actions for the good and emolument of the society; and if the persons thus interested will not act at all, or act contrary to their trust, their power must return of course to those who gave it.

Suppose, for example, the Grand Monarch, as he was called, had bought a neighbouring kingdom, and all the lands in it, from the courtiers, and the majority of the people's deputies; and amongst the rest, the church-lands, into the bargain, with the consent of their convocation or synod, or by what other name that assembly was called; would the people and clergy have thought themselves obliged to have made good this bargain, if they could

4. The unanimity rule, known as the *liberum veto*, effectively governed Polish parliamentary practice until the Third Polish Partition in 1795.

have helped it? I dare say that neither would; but, on the contrary, that the people would have had the countenance of these reverend patriots to have told their representatives in round terms, that they were chosen to act for the interest of those that sent them, and not for their own; that their power was given them to protect and defend their country, and not to sell and enslave it.

This supposition, as wild as it seems, yet is not absolutely and universally impossible. King John actually sold the kingdom of England to his Holiness:[5] And there are people in all nations ready to sell their country at home; and such can never have any principles to with-hold them from selling it abroad.

It is foolish to say, that this doctrine can be mischievous to society, at least in any proportion to the wild ruin and fatal calamities which must befall, and do befall the world, where the contrary doctrine is maintained: For, all bodies of men subsisting upon their own substance, or upon the profits of their trade and industry, find their account so much in ease and peace, and have justly such terrible apprehensions of civil disorders, which destroy every thing that they enjoy; that they always bear a thousand injuries before they return one, and stand under the burdens as long as they can bear them; as I have in another letter observed.[6]

What with the force of education, and the reverence which people are taught, and have been always used to pay to princes; what with the perpetual harangues of flatterers, the gaudy pageantry and outside of power, and its gilded ensigns, always glittering in their eyes; what with the execution of the laws in the sole power of the prince; what with all the regular magistrates, pompous guards and standing troops, with the fortified towns, the artillery, and all the magazines of war, at his disposal; besides large revenues, and multitudes of followers and dependants, to support and abet all that he does: Obedience to authority is so well secured, that it is wild to imagine, that any number of men, formidable enough to disturb a settled state, can unite together and hope to

5. As part of the settlement ending his struggle with Pope Innocent III, which had resulted in an interdict being placed on England in 1209, John gave England to the Papacy and received it back as a fief.

6. See, for example, Letter No. 32 (June 10, 1721).

overturn it, till the publick grievances are so enormous, the oppression so great, and the disaffection so universal, that there can be no question remaining, whether their calamities be real or imaginary, and whether the magistrate has protected or endeavoured to destroy his people.

This was the case of Richard II, Edward II, and James II and will ever be the case under the same circumstances. No society of men will groan under oppressions longer than they know how to throw them off; whatever unnatural whimsies and fairy notions idle and sedentary babblers may utter from colleges and cloisters; and teach to others, for vile self-ends, doctrines, which they themselves are famous for not practising.

Upon this principle of people's judging for themselves, and resisting lawless force, stands our late happy Revolution, and with it the just and rightful title of our most excellent sovereign King George, to the scepter of these realms; a scepter which he has, and I doubt not will ever sway, to his own honour, and the honour, protection, and prosperity of us his people.

T   *I am, &c.*

NO. 60. SATURDAY, JANUARY 6, 1721.

All Government proved to be instituted by Men, and only to intend the general Good of Men.

SIR,

There is no government now upon earth, which owes its formation or beginning to the immediate revelation of God, or can derive its existence from such revelation: It is certain, on the contrary, that the rise and institution or variation of government, from time to time, is within the memory of men or of histories; and that every government, which we know at this day in the world, was established by the wisdom and force of mere men, and by the concurrence of means and causes evidently human. Government therefore can have no power, but such as men can give, and such as they actually did give, or permit for their own sakes: Nor can any government be in fact framed but by consent, if not of every subject, yet of as many as can compel the rest; since no man, or council of men, can have personal strength enough to govern multitudes by force, or can claim to themselves and their families any superiority, or natural sovereignty over their fellow-creatures naturally as good as them. Such strength, therefore, where-ever it is, is civil and accumulative strength, derived from the laws and constitutions of the society, of which the governors themselves are but members.

So that to know the jurisdiction of governors, and its limits, we must have recourse to the institution of government, and ascertain those limits by the measure of power, which men in the state of nature have over themselves and one another: And as no man can take from many, who are stronger than him, what they have no mind to give him; and he who has not consent must have force, which is itself the consent of the stronger; so no man can give to another either what is none of his own, or what in its own nature is inseparable from himself; as his religion particularly is.

Every man's religion is his own; nor can the religion of any man, of what nature or figure soever, be the religion of another man, unless he also chooses it; which action utterly excludes all force, power, or government. Religion can never come without conviction, nor can conviction come from civil authority; religion, which is the fear of God, cannot be subject to power, which is the fear of man. It is a relation between God and our own souls only, and consists in a disposition of mind to obey the will of our great Creator, in the manner which we think most acceptable to him. It is independent upon all human directions, and superior to them; and consequently uncontrollable by external force, which cannot reach the free faculties of the mind, or inform the understanding, much less convince it. Religion therefore, which can never be subject to the jurisdiction of another, can never be alienated to another, or put in his power.

Nor has any man in the state of nature power over his own life, or to take away the life of another, unless to defend his own, or what is as much his own, namely, his property. This power therefore, which no man has, no man can transfer to another.

Nor could any man in the state of nature, have a right to violate the property of another; that is, what another had acquired by his art or labour; or to interrupt him in his industry and enjoyments, as long as he himself was not injured by that industry and those enjoyments. No man therefore could transfer to the magistrate that right which he had not himself.

No man in his senses was ever so wild as to give an unlimited power to another to take away his life, or the means of living, according to the caprice, passion, and unreasonable pleasure of that other: But if any man restrained himself from any part of his pleasures, or parted with any portion of his acquisitions, he did it with the honest purpose of enjoying the rest with the greater security, and always in subserviency to his own happiness, which no man will or can willingly and intentionally give away to any other whatsoever.

And if any one, through his own inadvertence, or by the fraud or violence of another, can be drawn into so foolish a contract, he is relievable by the eternal laws of God and reason. No engagement that is wicked and unjust can be executed without injustice and wickedness: This is so true, that I question whether there be a constitution in the world which does not afford, or pretend to afford, a remedy for relieving ignorant, distressed, and unwary men, trepanned into such engagements by artful knaves, or frightened into them by imperious ones. So that here the laws of nature and general reason supersede the municipal and positive laws of nations; and no where oftener than in England. What else was the design, and ought to be the business, of our courts of equity? And I hope whole countries and societies are no more exempted from the privileges and protection of reason and equity, than are private particulars.

Here then is the natural limitation of the magistrate's authority: He ought not to take what no man ought to give; nor exact what no man ought to perform: All he has is given him, and those that gave it must judge of the application. In government there is no such relation as lord and slave, lawless will and blind submission; nor ought to be amongst men: But the only relation is that of father and children, patron and client, protection and allegiance, benefaction and gratitude, mutual affection and mutual assistance.

So that the nature of government does not alter the natural right of men to liberty, which in all political societies is alike their due: But some governments provide better than others for the security and impartial distribution of that right. There has been always such a constant and certain fund of corruption and malignity in human nature, that it has been rare to find that man, whose views and happiness did not center in the gratification of his appetites, and worst appetites, his luxury, his pride, his avarice, and lust of power; and who considered any publick trust reposed in him, with any other view, than as the means to satiate such unruly and dangerous desires! And this has been most eminently true of great men, and those who aspired to dominion. They were first made great for the sake of the publick, and afterwards at its expence. And if they had been content to have been moderate traitors, mankind would have been still moderately happy; but their ambition and treason observing no degrees, there was no degree of vileness and misery which the poor people did not often feel.

The appetites therefore of men, especially of great men, are carefully to be observed and stayed, or else they will never stay themselves. The experience of every age convinces us, that we must not judge of men by what they ought to do, but by what they will do; and all history affords but few instances of men trusted with great power without abusing it, when with security they could. The servants of society, that is to say, its magistrates, did almost universally serve it by seizing it, selling it, or plundering it; especially when they were left by the society unlimited as to their duty and wages. In that case these faithful stewards generally took all; and, being servants, made slaves of their masters.

For these reasons, and convinced by woeful and eternal experience, societies found it necessary to lay restraints upon their magistrates or publick servants, and to put checks upon those who would otherwise put chains upon them; and therefore these societies set themselves to model and form national constitutions with such wisdom and art, that the publick interest should be consulted and carried at the same time, when those entrusted with the administration of it were consulting and pursuing their own.

Hence grew the distinction between arbitrary and free governments: Not that more or less power was vested in the one than in the other; nor that either of them lay under less or more obligations, in justice, to protect their subjects, and study their ease, prosperity, and security, and to watch for the same. But the power and sovereignty of magistrates in free countries was so qualified, and so divided into different channels, and committed to the direction of so many different men, with different interests and views, that the majority of them could seldom or never find their account in betraying their trust in fundamental instances. Their emulation, envy, fear, or interest, always made them spies and checks upon one another. By all which means the people have often come at the heads of those who forfeited their heads, by betraying the people.

In despotick governments things went far otherwise, those governments having been framed otherwise; if the same could be called governments, where the rules of publick power were dictated by private and lawless lust; where folly and madness often swayed the scepter, and blind rage wielded the sword. The whole weath of the state, with its civil or military power, being in the prince, the people could have no remedy but death and patience, while he oppressed them by the lump, and butchered them by thousands: Unless perhaps the ambition or personal resentments of some of the instruments of his tyranny procured a revolt, which rarely mended their condition.

The only secret therefore in forming a free government, is to make the interests of the governors and of the governed the same, as far as human policy can contrive. Liberty cannot be preserved any other way. Men have long found, from the weakness and depravity of themselves and one another, that most men will act for interest against duty, as often as they dare. So that to engage them to their duty, interest must be linked to the observance of it, and danger to the breach of it. Personal advantages and security, must be the rewards of duty and obedience; and disgrace, torture, and death, the punishment of treachery and corruption.

Human wisdom has yet found out but one certain expedient to effect this; and that is, to have the concerns of all directed by all, as far as possibly can be: And where the persons interested are too numerous, or live too distant to meet together on all emergencies, they must moderate necessity by prudence, and act by deputies, whose interest is the same with their own, and whose property is so intermingled with theirs, and so engaged upon the same bottom, that principals and deputies must stand and fall together. When the deputies thus act for their own interest, by acting for the interest of their principals; when they can make no law but what they themselves, and their posterity, must be subject to; when they can give no money, but what they must pay their share of; when they can do no mischief, but what must fall upon their own heads in common with their countrymen; their principals may then expect good laws, little mischief, and much frugality.

Here therefore lies the great point of nicety and care in forming the constitution, that the persons entrusted and representing, shall either never have any interest detached from the persons entrusting and represented, or never the means to pursue it. Now to compass this great point effectually, no other way is left, but one of these two, or rather both; namely, to make the deputies so numerous, that there may be no possibility of corrupting the majority; or, by changing them so often, that there is no sufficient time to corrupt them, and to carry the ends of that corruption. The people may be very sure, that the major part of their deputies being honest, will keep the rest so; and that they will all be honest, when they have no temptations to be knaves.

We have some sketch of this policy in the constitution of our several great companies, where the general court, composed of all its members, constitutes the legislature, and the consent of that court is the sanction of their laws; and where the administration of their affairs is put under the conduct of a certain number chosen by the whole. Here every man concerned saw the necessity of securing part of their property, by putting the persons entrusted under proper regulations; however remiss they may be in taking care of the whole. And if provision had been made, that, as a third part of the directors are to go out every year, so none should stay in above three (as I am told was at first promised), all juggling with courtiers, and raising great estates by confederacy, at the expence of the company, had, in a great measure, been prevented; though there were still wanting other limitations, which might have effectually obviated all those evils.

This was the ancient constitution of England: Our kings had neither revenues large enough, nor offices gainful and numerous enough in their disposal, to corrupt any considerable number of members; nor any force to frighten them. Besides, the same Parliament seldom or never met twice: For, the serving in it being found an office of burden, and not of profit, it was thought reasonable that all men qualified should, in their turns, leave their families and domestick concerns, to serve the publick; and their boroughs bore their charges. The only grievance then was, that they were not called together often enough, to redress the grievances which the people suffered from the court during their intermission: And therefore a law was made in Edward III's time, that Parliaments should be holden once a year.[1]

But this law, like the late Queen's Peace,[2] did not execute itself; and therefore the court seldom convened them, but when they wanted money, or had other purposes of their own to serve; and sometimes raised money without them: Which arbitrary proceeding brought upon the publick numerous mischiefs; and, in the reign of King Charles I, a long and bloody civil war. In that reign an act was passed, that they should meet of themselves, if they were not called according to the direction of that law; which was worthily repealed upon the restoration of King Charles II:[3] And in the same kind fit, a great revenue was given him for life, and continued to his brother. By which means these princes were enabled to keep standing troops, to corrupt Parliaments, or to live without them; and to commit such acts of power as brought about, and indeed forced the people upon the late happy Revolution. Soon

1. The statute was passed in 1362 (4 Edw. III, c. 14) and was similar in nature to one previously enacted in 1330.

2. The Peace of Utrecht, a series of treaties signed in Apr. 1713, which ended the War of the Spanish Succession. The settlements agreed to were overturned when Philip V of Spain, in 1717 and 1718, sent an expeditionary force that seized Sardinia and Sicily.

3. The reference is to the Triennial Act of 1641 (16 Car. I, c. 1). It was repealed in 1664 upon passage of a new act (16 Car. II, c. 1).

after which a new act was passed, that Parliaments should be rechosen once in three years: Which law was also repealed, upon his Majesty's accession to the throne,[4] that the present Parliament might have time to rectify those abuses which we labour under, and to make regulations proper to prevent them all for the future. All which has since been happily effected; and, I bless God, we are told, that the people will have the opportunity to thank them, in another election, for their great services to their country. I shall be always ready, on my part, to do them honour, and pay them my acknowledgments, in the most effectual manner in my power. But more of this in the succeeding papers.

T   *I am, &c.*

NO. 61. SATURDAY, JANUARY 13, 1721.

How free Governments are to be framed so as to last, and how they differ from such as are arbitrary.

SIR,

The most reasonable meaning that can be put upon this apothegm, that *virtue is its own reward,* is, that it seldom meets with any other. God himself, who having made us, best knows our natures, does not trust to the intrinsick excellence and native beauty of holiness alone, to engage us in its interests and pursuits, but recommends it to us by the stronger and more affecting motives of rewards and punishments. No wise man, therefore, will in any instance of moment trust to the mere integrity of another. The experience of all ages may convince us, that men, when they are above fear, grow for the most part above honesty and shame: And this is particularly and certainly true of societies of men, when they are numerous enough to keep one another in countenance; for when the weight of infamy is divided amongst many, no one sinks under his own burden.

---

4. 6, 7 W. & M., c. 2 (1694). In 1716, a new statute was passed (1 Geo. I, st. 2, c. 38), extending the life of Parliament from its previous three to seven years.

Great bodies of men have seldom judged what they ought to do, by any other rule than what they could do. What nation is there that has not oppressed any other, when the same could be done with advantage and security? What party has ever had regard to the principles which they professed, or ever reformed the errors which they condemned? What company, or particular society of merchants or tradesmen, has ever acted for the interest of general trade, though it always filled their mouths in private conversation?

And yet men, thus formed and qualified, are the materials for government. For the sake of men it is instituted, by the prudence of men it must be conducted; and the art of political mechanism[1] is, to erect a firm building with such crazy and corrupt materials. The strongest cables are made out of loose hemp and flax; the world itself may, with the help of proper machines, be moved by the force of a single hair; and so may the government of the world, as well as the world itself. But whatever discourses I shall hereafter make upon this great and useful subject, I shall confine myself in this letter to free monarchical constitutions alone, and to the application of some of the principles laid down in my last.

It is there said, that when the society consists of too many, or when they live too far apart to be able to meet together, to take care of their own affairs, they can not otherwise preserve their liberties, than by choosing deputies to represent them, and to act for them; and that these deputies must be either so numerous, that there can be no means of corrupting the majority; or so often changed, that there shall be no time to do it so as to answer any end by doing it. Without one of these regulations, or both, I lay it down as a certain maxim in politicks, that it is impossible to preserve a free government long.

I think I may with great modesty affirm, that in former reigns the people of England found no sufficient security in the number of their representatives. What with the crowd of offices in the gift of the crown, which were possessed by men of no other merit, nor held by any other tenure, but merely a capacity to get into the House of Commons, and the disservice which they could

1. Mechanism: mechanics.

and would do their country there: What with the promises and
expectations given to others, who by court-influence, and often by
court-money, carried their elections: What by artful caresses, and
the familiar and deceitful addresses of great men to weak men:
What with luxurious dinners, and rivers of Burgundy, Champaign,
and Tokay, thrown down the throats of gluttons; and what with
pensions, and other personal gratifications, bestowed where wind
and smoke would not pass for current coin: What with party
watch-words and imaginary terrors, spread amongst the drunken
'squires, and the deluded and enthusiastick bigots, of dreadful
designs in embryo, to blow up the Church, and the Protestant
interest; and sometimes with the dread of mighty invasions just
ready to break upon us from the man in the moon: I say, by all
these corrupt arts, the representatives of the English people, in
former reigns, have been brought to betray the people, and to join
with their oppressors. So much are men governed by artful applications to their private passions and interest. And it is evident to
me, that if ever we have a weak or an ambitious prince, with a
ministry like him, we must find out some other resources, or acqui-
esce in the loss of our liberties. The course and transiency of
human affairs will not suffer us to live always under the present
righteous administration.

So that I can see no means in human policy to preserve the
publick liberty and a monarchical form of government together,
but by the frequent fresh elections of the people's deputies: This is
what the writers in politicks call rotation of magistracy. Men, when
they first enter into magistracy, have often their former condition
before their eyes: They remember what they themselves suffered,
with their fellow-subjects, from the abuse of power, and how much
they blamed it; and so their first purposes are to be humble, modest, and just; and probably, for some time, they continue so. But
the possession of power soon alters and vitiates their hearts, which
are at the same time sure to be leavened, and puffed up to an
unnatural size, by the deceitful incense of false friends, and by the
prostrate submission of parasites. First, they grow indifferent to all
their good designs, then drop them: Next, they lose their modera-

tion; afterwards, they renounce all measures with their old acquaintance and old principles; and seeing themselves in magnifying glasses, grow, in conceit, a different species from their fellow-subjects; and so by too sudden degrees become insolent, rapacious and tyrannical, ready to catch at all means, often the vilest and most oppressive, to raise their fortunes as high as their imaginary greatness. So that the only way to put them in mind of their former condition, and consequently of the condition of other people, is often to reduce them to it; and to let others of equal capacities share of power in their turn: This also is the only way to qualify men, and make them equally fit for dominion and subjection.

A rotation therefore, in power and magistracy, is essentially necessary to a free government: It is indeed the thing itself; and constitutes, animates, and informs it, as much as the soul constitutes the man. It is a thing sacred and inviolable, where-ever liberty is thought sacred; nor can it ever be committed to the disposal of those who are trusted with the preservation of national constitutions: For though they may have the power to model it for the publick advantage, and for the more effectual security of that right; yet they can have none to give it up, or, which is the same thing, to make it useless.

The constitution of a limited monarchy, is the joint concurrence of the crown and of the nobles (without whom it cannot subsist) and of the body of the people, to make laws for the common benefit of the subject; and where the people, through number or distance, cannot meet, they must send deputies to speak in their names, and to attend upon their interest: These deputies therefore act by, under, and in subserviency to the constitution, and have not a power above it and over it.

In Holland, and some other free countries, the states are often obliged to consult their principals; and, in some instances, our own Parliaments have declined entering upon questions of importance, till they had gone into the country, and known the sentiments of those that sent them; as in all cases they ought to consult their inclinations as well as their interest. Who will say, that the Rump, or fag-end of the Long Parliament of forty-one, had any right to expel such members as they did not like?[2] Or to watch for their absence, that they might seize to themselves, or give up to any body else, the right of those from whose confidence and credulity they derived the authority which they acted by?

With thanks to God, I own, that we have a prince so sensible of this right, and who owes his crown so entirely to the principles laid down, and I think fully proved in these letters; that it is impossible to suspect, either from his inclinations, his interest, or his known justice, that he should ever fall into any measures to destroy that people, who have given him his crown, and supported him in it with so much generosity and expense; or that he should undermine, by that means, the ground upon which he stands. I do therefore the less regard the idle suspicions and calumnies of disaffected men, who would surmise, that a design is yet on foot to continue this Parliament; a reflection the most impudent and invidious that can be thrown upon his Majesty, his ministers, or his two houses; and a reflection that can come from none but professed, or at least from concealed, Jacobites.

It is no less than an insinuation, that our most excellent sovereign King George has a distrust of his faithful subjects; that he will refuse them the means of their own preservation, and the preservation of that constitution which they chose him to preserve; that he will shut his ears against their modest, just, and dutiful complaints; and that he apprehends danger from meeting them in a new and free-chosen Parliament. This is contrary to the tenor of his whole life and actions; who, as he has received three crowns from their gift, so he lies under all the ties of generosity, gratitude, and duty, to cherish and protect them, and to make them always great, free, and happy.

It is a most scandalous calumny upon his faithful servants, to suggest that any of them, conscious of guilt and crimes, feared any thing from the most strict and rigorous inspection into their proceedings. Some of them have already stood the fiery trial, and come off triumphant with general approbation. They have,

2. In Dec. 1648, the Puritan army was ordered to forcibly exclude ninety-six Presbyterian members from the Long Parliament, which had originally convened in Nov., 1640. The remaining sixty members were henceforth known as the Rump Parliament.

besides, the advantage of his Majesty's most gracious pardon, which they did not want, and which was not passed for their sakes. Who therefore can suspect, that patriots so uncorrupt, so prudent, and so popular, will dishonour their master, give up the constitution, ruin their country, and render themselves the objects of universal scorn, detestation, and cursing, by advising the most odious, dangerous, and destructive measures, that ever counsellors gave a prince?

It is a most ungrateful return to our illustrious representatives, to suggest, that men who have left their domestick concerns to serve their country at their own expence, and without any personal advantages, and have bestowed their labours upon the publick for a much longer time than their principals had at first a right to expect from them; and have, during all that time, been rectifying the abuses which have crept into our constitution; and have assisted his Majesty in going through two very useful and necessary wars,[3] and have regulated our finances, and the expence of our guards and garrisons, and corrected many abuses in the fleet and the civil administration; and have taken effectual vengeance of all those who were concerned in promoting, procuring, aiding, or assisting the late dreadful South-Sea project: I say, after so many things done by them for the publick honour and prosperity, it is the basest ingratitude to surmise, that any of them would give up that constitution which they were chosen, and have taken so much pains, to preserve.

I do indeed confess, if any invasion were to be feared from Muscovy, Mecklenburg, Spain, or Civita Vecchia;[4] if new provinces were to be obtained abroad, new armies to be raised, or new fleets to be equipped, upon warlike expeditions; if new provision were wanting for the Civil List, and new taxes to be levied, or new companies to be erected to pay off the publick debts; if the universities were to be farther regulated, or any inspection were necessary into

3. Trenchard is apparently referring to "The Fifteen," the Jacobite Rebellion in Scotland, led by James Edward, the Pretender, which lasted from Sept. 1715 to Feb. 1716, and to the War of the Quadruple Alliance against Spain (1718–1720).

4. Civita Vecchia: a seaport town approximately thirty-five miles from Rome and the chief port of the Papal States.

the increase of fees and exactions of civil officers; if there were the least ground to suspect bribery or corruption in a place where it should not be; or if there were any new project on foot to banish tyrannical and popish principles far out of the land: I say, that in such a scene of affairs, I dare not be altogether so positive in my assertion, that we ought to venture, and at all events to leave to chance, that which we are in possession of already. But as we are at present in the happy state of indolence and security, at peace with all the world and our own consciences; as little more money can be raised from the people, most of it being already in hand, which, according to the rules of good policy, unite dominion and property; as our benefactors too are generous and honourable, our boroughs not insensible or ungrateful, nor the counties themselves inexorable to shining merit; So it is much to be hoped, that another Parliament may be chosen equally deserving, and as zealous for the publick interest; or, at worst, there are honest and tried measures at hand, which will undoubtedly make them so. And I offer this as a conclusive, and I think a most convincing, argument, that the kingdom will be obliged with a new election.

T   *I am, &c.*

NO. 62. SATURDAY, JANUARY 20, 1721.

An Enquiry into the Nature and Extent of Liberty; with its Loveliness and Advantages, and the vile Effects of Slavery.

SIR,

I have shewn, in a late paper, wherein consists the difference between free and arbitrary governments, as to their frame and constitution;[1] and in this and the following, I shall shew their different spirit and effects. But first I shall shew wherein liberty itself consists.

1. See Letter No. 61 (Jan. 13, 1721).

By liberty, I understand the power which every man has over his own actions, and his right to enjoy the fruit of his labour, art, and industry, as far as by it he hurts not the society, or any members of it, by taking from any member, or by hindering him from enjoying what he himself enjoys. The fruits of a man's honest industry are the just rewards of it, ascertained to him by natural and eternal equity, as is his title to use them in the manner which he thinks fit: And thus, with the above limitations, every man is sole lord and arbiter of his own private actions and property. A character of which no man living can divest him but by usurpation, or his own consent.

The entering into political society, is so far from a departure from his natural right, that to preserve it was the sole reason why men did so; and mutual protection and assistance is the only reasonable purpose of all reasonable societies. To make such protection practicable, magistracy was formed, with power to defend the innocent from violence, and to punish those that offered it; nor can there be any other pretence for magistracy in the world. In order to this good end, the magistrate is entrusted with conducting and applying the united force of the community; and with exacting such a share of every man's property, as is necessary to preserve the whole, and to defend every man and his property from foreign and domestick injuries. These are the boundaries of the power of the magistrate, who deserts his function whenever he breaks them. By the laws of society, he is more limited and restrained than any man amongst them; since, while they are absolutely free in all their actions, which purely concern themselves; all his actions, as a publick person, being for the sake of society, must refer to it, and answer the ends of it.

It is a mistaken notion in government, that the interest of the majority is only to be consulted, since in society every man has a right to every man's assistance in the enjoyment and defence of his private property; otherwise the greater number may sell the lesser, and divide their estates amongst themselves; and so, instead of a society, where all peaceable men are protected, become a conspiracy of the many against the minority. With as much equity may one man wantonly dispose of all, and violence may be sanctified by mere power.

And it is as foolish to say, that government is concerned to meddle with the private thoughts and actions of men, while they injure neither the society, nor any of its members. Every man is, in nature and reason, the judge and disposer of his own domestick affairs; and, according to the rules of religion and equity, every man must carry his own conscience. So that neither has the magistrate a right to direct the private behaviour of men; nor has the magistrate, or any body else, any manner of power to model people's speculations, no more than their dreams. Government being intended to protect men from the injuries of one another, and not to direct them in their own affairs, in which no one is interested but themselves; it is plain, that their thoughts and domestick concerns are exempted entirely from its jurisdiction: In truth, men's thoughts are not subject to their own jurisdiction.

Idiots and lunaticks indeed, who cannot take care of themselves, must be taken care of by others: But whilst men have their five senses, I cannot see what the magistrate has to do with actions by which the society cannot be affected; and where he meddles with such, he meddles impertinently or tyrannically. Must the magistrate tie up every man's legs, because some men fall into ditches? Or, must he put out their eyes, because with them they see lying vanities? Or, would it become the wisdom and care of governors to establish a travelling society, to prevent people, by a proper confinement, from throwing themselves into wells, or over precipices; or to endow a fraternity of physicians and surgeons all over the nation, to take care of their subjects' health, without being consulted; and to vomit, bleed, purge, and scarify them at pleasure, whether they would or no, just as these established judges of health should think fit? If this were the case, what a stir and hubbub should we soon see kept about the established potions and lancets? Every man, woman, or child, though ever so healthy, must be a patient, or woe be to them! The best diet and medicines would soon grow pernicious from any other hand; and their pills alone, however ridiculous, insufficient, or distasteful, would be attended with a blessing.

Let people alone, and they will take care of themselves, and do it best; and if they do not, a sufficient punishment will follow their neglect, without the magistrate's interposition and penalties. It is plain, that such busy care and officious intrusion into the personal affairs, or private actions, thoughts, and imaginations of men, has in it more craft than kindness; and is only a device to mislead people, and pick their pockets, under the false pretence of the publick and their private good. To quarrel with any man for his opinions, humours, or the fashion of his clothes, is an offence taken without being given. What is it to a magistrate how I wash my hands, or cut my corns; what fashion or colours I wear, or what notions I entertain, or what gestures I use, or what words I pronounce, when they please me, and do him and my neighbour no hurt? As well may he determine the colour of my hair, and control my shape and features.

True and impartial liberty is therefore the right of every man to pursue the natural, reasonable, and religious dictates of his own mind; to think what he will, and act as he thinks, provided he acts not to the prejudice of another; to spend his own money himself, and lay out the produce of his labour his own way; and to labour for his own pleasure and profit, and not for others who are idle, and would live and riot by pillaging and oppressing him, and those that are like him.

So that civil government is only a partial restraint put by the laws of agreement and society upon natural and absolute liberty, which might otherwise grow licentious: And tyranny is an unlimited restraint put upon natural liberty, by the will of one or a few. Magistracy, amongst a free people, is the exercise of power for the sake of the people; and tyrants abuse the people, for the sake of power. Free government is the protecting the people in their liberties by stated rules: Tyranny is a brutish struggle for unlimited liberty to one or a few, who would rob all others of their liberty, and act by no rule but lawless lust.

So much for an idea of civil liberty. I will now add a word or two, to shew how much it is the delight and passion of mankind; and then shew its advantages.

The love of liberty is an appetite so strongly implanted in the nature of all living creatures, that even the appetite of self-preservation, which is allowed to be the strongest, seems to be contained in it; since by the means of liberty they enjoy the means of preserving themselves, and of satisfying their desires in the manner which they themselves choose and like best. Many animals can never be tamed, but feel the bitterness of restraint in the midst of the kindest usage; and rather than bear it, grieve and starve themselves to death; and some beat out their brains against their prisons.

Where liberty is lost, life grows precarious, always miserable, often intolerable. Liberty is, to live upon one's own terms; slavery is, to live at the mere mercy of another; and a life of slavery is, to those who can bear it, a continual state of uncertainty and wretchedness, often an apprehension of violence, often the lingering dread of a violent death: But by others, when no other remedy is to be had, death is reckoned a good one. And thus, to many men, and to many other creatures, as well as men, the love of liberty is beyond the love of life.

This passion for liberty in men, and their possession of it, is of that efficacy and importance, that it seems the parent of all the virtues: And therefore in free countries there seems to be another species of mankind, than is to be found under tyrants. Small armies of Greeks and Romans despised the greatest hosts of slaves; and a million of slaves have been sometimes beaten and conquered by a few thousand freemen. Insomuch that the difference seemed greater between them than between men and sheep. It was therefore well said by Lucullus, when, being about to engage the great King Tigranes's army, he was told by some of his officers, how prodigious great the same was, consisting of between three and four hundred thousand men: "No matter," said that brave Roman, drawing up his little army of fourteen thousand, but fourteen thousand *Romans*: "No matter; the lion never enquires into the number of the sheep."[2] And these royal troops proved no better; for the Romans had little else to do but to kill and pursue; which yet they could scarce do for laughing; so much more were they diverted than animated by the ridiculous dread and sudden flight of these imperial slaves and royal cowards.

2. The armies of *Tigranes* the Great, King of Armenia, were decisively defeated by a considerably smaller Roman force under Lucius Licinius *Lucullus* in 69 B.C. The events are recounted in Appian, *Roman History*, 12.85.

Men eternally cowed and oppressed by haughty and insolent governors, made base themselves by the baseness of that sort
of government, and become slaves by ruling over slaves, want
spirit and souls to meet in the field freemen, who scorn oppressors,
and are their own governors, or at least measure and direct the
power of their governors.

Education alters nature, and becomes stronger. Slavery,
while it continues, being a perpetual awe upon the spirits,
depresses them, and sinks natural courage; and want and fear, the
concomitants of bondage, always produce despondency and baseness; nor will men in bonds ever fight bravely, but to be free.
Indeed, what else should they fight for; since every victory that
they gain for a tyrant, makes them poorer and fewer; and, increasing his pride, increases his cruelty, with their own misery and
chains?

Those, who, from terror and delusion, the frequent causes
and certain effects of servitude, come to think their governors
greater than men, as they find them worse, will be as apt to think
themselves less: And when the head and the heart are thus both
gone, the hands will signify little. They who are used like beasts,
will be apt to degenerate into beasts. But those, on the contrary,
who, by the freedom of their government and education, are
taught and accustomed to think freely of men and things, find, by
comparing one man with another, that all men are naturally alike;
and that their governors, as they have the same face, constitution,
and shape with themselves, and are subject to the same sickness,
accidents, and death, with the meanest of their people; so they possess the same passions and faculties of the mind which their subjects possess, and not better. They therefore scorn to degrade and
prostrate themselves, to adore those of their own species, however
covered with titles, and disguised by power: They consider them as
their own creatures; and, as far as they surmount themselves, the
work of their own hands, and only the chief servants of the state,
who have no more power to do evil than one of themselves, and
are void of every privilege and superiority, but to serve them and
the state. They know it to be a contradiction in religion and reason,
for any man to have a right to do evil; that not to resist any man's

wickedness, is to encourage it; and that they have the least reason
to bear evil and oppression from their governors, who of all men
are the most obliged to do them good. They therefore detest slavery, and despise or pity slaves; and, adoring liberty alone, as they
who see its beauty and feel its advantages always will, it is no wonder that they are brave for it.

Indeed liberty is the divine source of all human happiness.
To possess, in security, the effects of our industry, is the most powerful and reasonable incitement to be industrious: And to be able
to provide for our children, and to leave them all that we have, is
the best motive to beget them. But where property is precarious,
labour will languish. The privileges of thinking, saying, and doing
what we please, and of growing as rich as we can, without any
other restriction, than that by all this we hurt not the publick, nor
one another, are the glorious privileges of liberty; and its effects, to
live in freedom, plenty, and safety.

These are privileges that increase mankind, and the happiness of mankind. And therefore countries are generally peopled in
proportion as they are free, and are certainly happy in that proportion: And upon the same tract of land that would maintain a
hundred thousand freemen in plenty, five thousand slaves would
starve. In Italy, fertile Italy, men die sometimes of hunger amongst
the sheaves, and in a plentiful harvest; for what they sow and reap
is none of their own; and their cruel and greedy governors, who
live by the labour of their wretched vassals, do not suffer them to
eat the bread of their own earning, nor to sustain their lives with
their own hands.

Liberty naturally draws new people to it, as well as
increases the old stock; and men as naturally run when they dare
from slavery and wretchedness, whithersoever they can help themselves. Hence great cities losing their liberty become deserts, and
little towns by liberty grow great cities; as will be fully proved
before I have gone through this argument. I will not deny, but that
there are some great cities of slaves: But such are only imperial
cities, and the seats of great princes, who draw the wealth of a continent to their capital, the center of their treasure and luxury. Babylon, Antioch, Seleucia, and Alexandria, were great cities peopled

by tyrants; but peopled partly by force, partly by the above reason, and partly by grants and indulgencies. Their power, great and boundless as it was, could not alone people their cities; but they were forced to soften authority by kindness; and having brought the inhabitants together by force, and by driving them captive like cattle, could not keep them together, without bestowing on them many privileges, to encourage the first inhabitants to stay, and to invite more to come.

This was a confession in those tyrants, that their power was mischievous and unjust; since they could not erect one great city, and make it flourish, without renouncing in a great measure their power over it; which, by granting it these privileges, in effect they did. These privileges were fixed laws, by which the trade and industry of the citizens were encouraged, and their lives and properties ascertained and protected, and no longer subjected to the laws of mere will and pleasure: And therefore, while these free cities, enjoying their own liberties and laws, flourished under them, the provinces were miserably harrassed, pillaged, dispeopled, and impoverished, and the inhabitants exhausted, starved, butchered, and carried away captive.

This shews that all civil happiness and prosperity is inseparable from liberty; and that tyranny cannot make men, or societies of men, happy, without departing from its nature, and giving them privileges inconsistent with tyranny. And here is an unanswerable argument, amongst a thousand others, against absolute power in a single man. Nor is there one way in the world to give happiness to communities, but by sheltering them under certain and express laws, irrevocable at any man's pleasure.

There is not, nor can be, any security for a people to trust to the mere will of one, who, while his will is his law, cannot protect them if he would. The number of sycophants and wicked counsellors, that he will always and necessarily have about him, will defeat all his good intentions, by representing things falsely, and persons maliciously; by suggesting danger where it is not, and urging necessity where there is none; by filling their own coffers, under colour of filling his, and by raising money for themselves, pretending the publick exigencies of the state; by sacrificing particular men to their own revenge, under pretence of publick security; and by engaging him and his people in dangerous and destructive wars, for their own profit or fame; by throwing publick affairs into perpetual confusion, to prevent an enquiry into their own behaviour; and by making him jealous of his people, and his people of him, on purpose to manage and mislead both sides.

By all these, and many more wicked arts, they will be constantly leading him into cruel and oppressive measures, destructive to his people, scandalous and dangerous to himself; but entirely agreeable to their own spirit and designs. Thus will they commit all wickedness by their master's authority, against his inclinations, and grow rich by the people's poverty, without his knowledge; and the royal authority will be first a warrant for oppression, afterwards a protection from the punishment due to it. For, in short, the power of princes is often little else but a stalking-horse to the intrigues and ambition of their minister.

But if the disposition of such a prince be evil, what must be the forlorn condition of his people, and what door of hope can remain for common protection! The best princes have often evil counsellors, the bad will have no other: And in such a case, what bounds can be set to their fury, and to the havock they will make? The instruments and advisers of tyranny and depredation always thrive best and are nearest their ends, when depredation and tyranny run highest: When most is plundered from the people, their share is greatest; we may therefore suppose every evil will befall such a people, without supposing extravagantly. No happiness, no security, but certain misery, and a vile and precarious life, are the blessed terms of such a government—a government which necessarily introduces all evils, and from the same necessity neither must nor can redress any.

The nature of his education, bred up as he ever is in perpetual flattery, makes him haughty and ignorant; and the nature of his government, which subsists by brutish severity and oppression, makes him cruel. He is inaccessible, but by his ministers, whose study and interest will be to keep him from knowing or helping the state of his miserable people. Their master's knowledge in his own affairs, would break in upon their scheme and power; they are not likely to lay before him representations of grievances caused by themselves; nor, if they be the effects of his own barbarity and command, will he hear them.

Even where absolute princes are not tyrants, there ministers will be tyrants. But it is indeed impossible for an arbitrary prince to be otherwise, since oppression is absolutely necessary to his being so. Without giving his people liberty, he cannot make them happy; and by giving them liberty, he gives up his own power. So that to be and continue arbitrary, he is doomed to be a tyrant in his own defence. The oppression of the people, corruption, wicked counsellors, and pernicious maxims in the court, and every where baseness, ignorance, and chains, must support tyranny, or it cannot be supported. So that in such governments there are inevitable grievances, without possible redress; misery, without mitigation or remedy; whatever is good for the people, is bad for their governors; and what is good for the governors, is pernicious to the people.

G   *I am, &c.*

NO. 63. SATURDAY, JANUARY 27, 1721.

Civil Liberty produces all Civil Blessings, and how; with the baneful Nature of Tyranny.

SIR,

I go on with my considerations upon liberty, to shew that all civil virtue and happiness, every moral excellency, all politeness, all good arts and sciences, are produced by liberty; and that all wickedness, baseness, and misery, are immediately and necessarily produced by tyranny; which being founded upon the destruction of every thing that is valuable, desirable, and noble, must subsist upon means suitable to its nature, and remain in everlasting enmity to all goodness and every human blessing.

By the establishment of liberty, a due distribution of property and an equal distribution of justice is established and secured. As rapine is the child of oppression, justice is the offspring of liberty, and her handmaid; it is the guardian of innocence, and the terror of vice: And when fame, honour, and advantages, are rewards of virtue, she will be courted for the dower which she brings; otherwise, like beauty without wealth, she may be praised, but more probably will be calumniated, envied, and very often persecuted; while vice, when it is gainful, like rich deformity and prosperous folly, will be admired and pursued. Where virtue is all its own reward, she will be seldom thought any; and few will buy that for a great price, which will sell for none. So that virtue, to be followed, must be endowed, and her credit is best secured by her interest; that is, she must be strengthened and recommended by the publick laws, and embellished by publick encouragements, or else she will be slighted and shunned.

Now the laws which encourage and increase virtue, are the fixed laws of general and impartial liberty; laws, which being the rule of every man's actions, and the measures of every man's power, make honesty and equity their interest. Where liberty is thoroughly established, and its laws equally executed, every man will find his account in doing as he would be done unto, and no man will take from another what he would not part with himself: Honour and advantage will follow the upright, punishment overtake the oppressor. The property of the poor will be as sacred as the privileges of the prince, and the law will be the only bulwark of both. Every man's honest industry and useful talents, while they are employed for the publick, will be employed for himself; and while he serves himself, he will serve the publick: Publick and private interest will secure each other; all will cheerfully give a part to secure the whole, and be brave to defend it.

These certain laws therefore are the only certain beginnings and causes of honesty and virtue amongst men. There may be other motives, I own; but such as only sway particular men, few enough, God knows: And universal experience has shewn us, that they are not generally prevailing, and never to be depended upon. Now these laws are to be produced by liberty alone, and only by such laws can liberty be secured and increased: And to make laws certainly good, they must be made by mutual agreement, and have for their end the general interest.

But tyranny must stand upon force; and the laws of tyranny being only the fickle will and unsteady appetite of one man, which may vary every hour; there can be no settled rule of right or wrong in the variable humours and sudden passions of a tyrant, who, though he may sometimes punish crimes, perhaps more out of rage than justice, will be much more likely to persecute and oppress innocence, and to destroy thousands cruelly, for one that he protects justly. There are instances of princes, who, being out of humour with a favourite, have put to death all that spoke well of him, and afterwards all that did not: Of princes, who put some of their ministers to death, for using one or two of their barbers and buffoons ill; as they did others of their ministers, for using a whole country well: Of princes, who have destroyed, a whole people, for the crimes or virtues of one man; and who, having killed a minion in a passion, have, to revenge themselves upon those who had not provoked them, destroyed in the same unreasonable fury, a hundred of their servants who had no hand in it, as well as all that had; who yet would have been destroyed, had they not done it: Of princes, who have destroyed millions in single mad projects and expeditions: Of princes, who have given up cities and provinces to the revenge or avarice of a vile woman or eunuch, to be plundered, or massacred, or burned, as he or she thought fit to direct: Of princes, who, to gratify the ambition and rapine of a few sorry servants, have lost the hearts of their whole people, and detached themselves from their good subjects, to protect these men in their iniquity, who yet had done them no other service, but that of destroying their reputation, and shaking their throne.

Such are arbitrary princes, whose laws are nothing but sudden fury, or lasting folly and wickedness in uncertain shapes. Hopeful rules these, for the governing of mankind, and making them happy! Rules which are none, since they cannot be depended upon for a moment; and generally change for the worse, if that can be. A subject worth twenty thousand pounds today, may, by a sudden edict issued by the dark counsel of a traitor, be a beggar tomorrow, and lose his life without forfeiting the same. The property of the whole kingdom shall be great, or little, or none, just at the mercy of a secretary's pen, guided by a child, or a dotard, or a foolish woman, or a favourite buffoon, or a gamester, or whoever is uppermost for the day; the next day shall alter entirely the yesterday's scheme, though not for the better; and the same men, in different humours, shall be the authors of both. Thus in arbitrary countries, a law aged two days is an old law; and no law is suffered to be a standing law, but such as are found by long experience to be so very bad, and so thoroughly destructive, that human malice, and all the arts of a tyrant's court, cannot make them worse. A court which never ceaseth to squeeze, kill, and oppress, till it has wound up human misery so high, that it will go no further. This is so much fact, that I appeal to all history and travels, and to those that read them, whether in arbitrary countries, both in Europe and out of it, the people do not grow daily thinner, and their misery greater; and whether countries are not peopled and rich, in proportion to the liberty which they enjoy and allow.

It has been long my opinion, and is more and more so, that in slavish countries the people must either throw off their cruel and destroying government, and set up another in its room, or in some ages the race of mankind there will be extinct. Indeed, if it had not been for free states, that have repaired and prevented in many places the mischiefs done by tyrants, the earth had been long since a desert, as the finest countries in it are at this day by that means. The gardens of the world, the fruitful and lovely countries of the lower Asia, filled formerly by liberty with people, politeness, and plenty, are now gloriously peopled with owls and grasshoppers; and perhaps here and there, at vast distances, with inhabitants not more valuable, and less happy; a few dirty huts of slaves groaning, starving, and perishing, under the fatherly protection of the Sultan, a prince of the most orthodox standard.

The laws therefore of tyrants are not laws, but wild acts of will, counselled by rage or folly, and executed by dragoons. And as these laws are evil, all sorts of evil must concur to support them. While the people have common-sense left, they will easily see whether they are justly governed, and well or ill used; whether they are protected or plundered: They will know that no man ought to be the director of the affairs of all, without their consent; that no consent can give him unlimited power over their bodies and minds; and that the laws of nature can never be entirely abrogated by positive laws; but that, on the contrary, the entering into society, and becoming subject to government, is only the parting with natural liberty, in some instances, to be protected in the enjoyment of it in others.

So that for any man to have arbitrary power, he must have it without consent; or if it be unadvisedly given at first, they who gave it soon repent when they find its effects. In truth, all those princes that have such power, by keeping up great armies in time of peace, effectually confess that they rule without consent, and dread their people, whose worst enemies they undoubtedly are. An arbitrary prince therefore must preserve and execute his power by force and terror; which yet will not do, without calling in the auxiliary aids and strict allies of tyranny, imposture, and constant oppression. Let this people be ever so low and miserable, if they be not also blind, he is not safe. He must have established deceivers to mislead them with lies, to terrify them with the wrath of God, in case they stir hand or foot, or so much as a thought, to mend their doleful condition; as if the good God was the sanctifier of all villainy, the patron of the worst of all villains! He must have a band of standing cut-throats to murder all men who would sacrilegiously defend their own. And both his cut-throats and his deceivers must go shares with him in his tyranny.

Men will naturally see their interests, feel their condition; will quickly find that the sword, the rack, and the sponge,[1] are not government, but the height of cruelty and robbery; and will never submit to them, but by the united powers of violence and delusion: Their bodies must be chained, their minds enchanted and deceived; the sword kept constantly over their heads, and their spirits kept low with poverty, before they can be brought to be used at the wanton and brutish pleasure of the most dignified and lofty oppressor. So that God must be belied, his creatures must be fettered, frightened, deceived, and starved, and mankind made

1. Sponge: parasite.

base and undone, that one of the worst of them may live riotously and safely amongst his whores, butchers, and buffoons.

Men, therefore, must cease to be men, and in stupidity and tameness grow cattle, before they can become quiet subjects to such a government; which is a complication of all the villainies, falsehood, oppression, cruelty, and depredation, upon the face of the earth: Nor can there be a more provoking, impudent, shocking, and blasphemous position, than to assert all this group of horrors, or the author of them, to be of God's appointment.

> If such kings are by God appointed,
> Satan may be the Lord's anointed.[2]

And whoever scatters such doctrine, ought, by all the laws of God, reason, and self-preservation, to be put to death as a general poisoner, and advocate for publick destruction.

All men own, that it is the duty of a prince to protect his people; And some have said, that it is their duty to obey him, when he butchers them. An admirable consequence, and full of sweet consolation! His whole business and office is to defend them, and to do them good; therefore they are bound to let him destroy them. Was ever such impudence in an enlightened country? It is perfectly agreeable to the doctrines and followers of Mahomet: But shall Englishmen, who make their own laws, be told, that they have no right to the common air, to the life and fortune which God has given them, but by the permission of an officer of their own making; who is what he is only for their sakes and security, and has no more right to these blessings, nor to do evil, than one of themselves? And shall we be told this by men, who are eternally the first to violate their own doctrines? Or shall they after this have the front[3] to teach us any doctrine, or to recommend to us any one virtue, when they have thus given up all virtue and truth, and every blessing that life affords? For there is no evil, misery, and

2. The couplet appears to be Gordon's own variation on two lines from the anonymous poem, "The Vicar of Bray":

> Kings are by God appointed,
> And damned are those who dare resist,
> Or touch the Lord's Anointed.

3. Front: impudence.

wickedness, which arbitrary monarchies do not produce, and must produce; nor do they, nor can they, produce any certain, general, or diffusive good.

I have shewn, in my last, that an arbitrary prince cannot protect his people if he would; and I add here, that he dares not. It would disgust the instruments of his power, and the sharers in his oppression, who will consider the property of the people as the perquisites of their office, and claim a privilege of being little tyrants, for making him a great one: So that every kindness to his subjects will be a grievance to his servants; and he must assert and exercise his tyranny to the height for their sakes, or they will do it for him. And the instances are rare, if any, of any absolute monarch's protecting in earnest his people against the depredations of his ministers and soldiers, but it has cost him his life; as may be shewn by many examples in the Roman history: For this the emperor Pertinax was murdered,[4] and so was Galba.

Machiavel has told us, that it is impossible for such a prince to please both the people and his soldiers: The one will not be satisfied without protection, nor the other without rapine:[5] To comply with the people, he must give up his power; to comply with his soldiers, he must give up his people. So that to continue what he is, and to preserve himself from the violence of his followers, he must countenance all their villainies and oppression, and be himself no more than an imperial thief at the head of a band of thieves; for which character he is generally well qualified by the base and cruel maxims of that sort of power, and by the vile education almost always given to such a prince by the worst and most infamous of all men, their supple and lying sycophants.

Even the Christian religion can do but little or no good in lands of tyranny, since miracles have ceased; but is made to do infinite harm, by being corrupted and perverted into a deadly engine in the hands of a tyrant and his impostors, to rivet his subjects' chains, and to confirm them thorough wretches, slaves, and

4. The reference is to Publius Helvius *Pertinax*, Roman emperor, whose zeal for reform and strict discipline led to his assassination. He was killed by his praetorian guard in A.D. 193, after a reign of only 187 days.
5. *The Prince*, chap. 19.

ignorants. I cannot indeed say, that they have the Christian religion at all amongst them, but only use its amiable name to countenance abominable falsehoods, nonsense, and heavy oppression; to defend furious and implacable bigotry, which is the direct characteristick and spirit of Mahometism, and destroys the very genius and first principles of Christianity. All this will be further shewn hereafter. I shall conclude with observing, that arbitrary monarchy is a constant war upon heaven and earth, against the souls as well as bodies and properties of men.

G   *I am, &c.*

NO. 64. SATURDAY, FEBRUARY 3, 1721.

Trade and Naval Power the Offspring of Civil Liberty only, and cannot subsist without it.

SIR,

I have in former letters begun to shew, by an induction of particulars, and shall hereafter more fully shew, that population, riches, true religion, virtue, magnanimity, arts, sciences, and learning, are the necessary effects and productions of liberty;[1] and shall spend this paper in proving, that an extensive trade, navigation, and naval power, entirely flow from the same source: In this case, if natural advantage and encouragements be wanting, art, expence, and violence, are lost and thrown away. Nothing is more certain, than that trade cannot be forced; she is a coy and humorous dame, who must be won by flattery and allurements, and always flies force and power; she is not confined to nations, sects, or climates, but travels and wanders about the earth, till she fixes her residence where she finds the best welcome and kindest reception; her contexture is so nice and delicate, that she cannot breathe in a tyrannical air; will and pleasure are so opposite to her nature, that but touch her with the sword, and she dies: But if you give her gentle and kind entertainment, she is a grateful and beneficent

1. See especially Letters 59 through 63 (Dec. 30, 1721, to Jan. 27, 1721).

mistress; she will turn deserts into fruitful fields, villages into great cities, cottages into palaces, beggars into princes, convert cowards into heroes, blockheads into philosophers; will change the coverings of little worms into the richest brocades, the fleeces of harmless sheep into the pride and ornaments of kings, and by a further metamorphosis will transmute them again into armed hosts and haughty fleets.

Now it is absolutely impossible, from the nature of an arbitrary government, that she should enjoy security and protection, or indeed be free from violence, under it. There is not one man in a thousand that has the endowments and abilities necessary to govern a state, and much fewer yet that have just notions how to make trade and commerce useful and advantageous to it; and, amongst these, it is rare to find one who will forego all personal advantages, and devote himself and his labours wholly to his country's interest: But if such a phoenix should arise in any country, he will find it hard to get access to an arbitrary court, and much harder yet to grapple with and stem the raging corruptions in it, where virtue has nothing to do, and vice rides triumphant; where bribery, servile flattery, blind submission, riotous expence, and very often lust and unnatural prostitutions, are the ladders to greatness; which will certainly be supported by the same methods by which it is obtained.

What has a virtuous man to do, or what can he do, in such company? If he pity the people's calamities, he shall be called seditious; if he recommend any publick good, he shall be called preaching fool; if he should live soberly and virtuously himself, they will think him fit only to be sent to a cloister; if he do not flatter the prince and his superiors, he will be thought to envy their prosperity; if he presume to advise his prince to pursue his true interest, he will be esteemed a formidable enemy to the whole court, who will unite to destroy him: In fine, his virtues will be crimes, reproaches, and of dangerous consequence to those who have none. As jails pick up all the little pilfering rogues of a country, so such courts engross all the great ones; who have no business there but to grow rich, and to riot upon the publick calamities, to use all the means of oppression and rapine, to make hasty fortunes before the bow-string overtakes them, or a sudden favourite supplants them.

Now what encouragement or security can trade and industry receive from such a crew of banditti? No privileges and immunities, or even protection, can be obtained but for money, and are always granted to such who give most; and these again shall be curtailed, altered, abrogated, and cancelled, upon the change of a minister, or of his inclinations, interest, and caprices: Monopolies, exclusive companies, liberties of pre-emption, &c. shall be obtained for bribes or favour, or in trust for great men, or vile and worthless women. Some merchants shall be openly encouraged and protected, and get exemptions from searches and duties, or shall be connived at in escaping them; others shall be burdened, oppressed, manacled, stopped, and delayed, to extort presents, to wreak revenge, or to give preference of markets to favourites. Governors of port-towns, or of colonies, who have purchased their employments at court, shall be indulged and countenanced in making reprisals upon the traders, and to enable them to satisfy the yearly presents due to minions: Admirals and commanders of men of war shall press their sailors, to be paid for not doing it; and military officers and soldiers shall molest and interrupt them in the course of their commerce and honest industry.

Nor shall it be in the power of the most vigilant, active and virtuous prince, to prevent these and a thousand other daily oppressions; he must see with his ministers' eyes, and hear with their ears; nor can there be any access to him but by their means, and by their leave: Constant spies shall watch and observe the first intentions, or least approaches to a complaint; and the person injured shall be threatened, way-laid, imprisoned, perhaps murdered; but if he escape all their treacheries, and can get to the ear of his prince, it is great odds but he will be treated and punished as a calumniator, a false accuser, and a seditious disturber of his Majesty's government: No witness will dare to appear for him, many false ones will be suborned against him; and the whole posse of ministers, officers, favourites, parasites, pathicks,[2] strumpets, buf-

---

2. Pathics: catamites, that is, boys upon whom sodomy is performed.

foons, fiddlers,[3] and pimps, will conspire to ruin him, as a common enemy to their common interests.

But if all these mischiefs could be avoided, the necessities of such a prince, arising from the profusion and vast expence of his court, from his foolish wars, and the depredations, embezzlements, and various thefts of his ministers and servants, will be always calling for new supplies, for new extortions, which must be raised by all the means by which they can be raised: New and sudden impositions shall be put upon trade, new loans be exacted from merchants; commodities of general use shall be bought up by the prince's order, perhaps upon trust, and afterwards retailed again at extravagant advantages: Merchants shall be encouraged to import their goods, upon promises of easy and gentle usage; these goods when imported shall be subjected to exorbitant impositions and customs, perhaps confiscated upon frivolous pretences. But if these, and infinite other oppressions, could be prevented for some time, by the vigilance of a wise prince, or the care of an able minister; yet there can be no probable security, or even hopes of the continuance of honest and prudent measures in such a government: For one wise prince so educated, there will be twenty foolish ones; and for one honest minister, there will be a thousand corrupt ones.

Under such natural disadvantages, perpetual uncertainties, or rather certain oppressions, no men will embark large stocks and extensive talents for business, breed up their children to precarious employments, build forts, or plant colonies, when the breath of a weak prince, or the caprice of a corrupt favourite, shall dash at once all their labours and their hopes; and therefore it is impossible that any trade can subsist long in such a government, but what is necessary to support the luxury and vices of a court; and even such trade is, for the most part, carried on by the stocks,[4] and for the advantage of free countries, and their own petty merchants are only factors to the others. True merchants are citizens of the world, and that is their country where they can live best and most secure; and whatever they can pick up and gather

3. Fiddlers: cheats.
4. That is, the large trading companies whose capital is publicly subscribed.

together in tyrannical governments, they remove to free ones. Tavernier[5] invested all the riches he had amassed by his long ramble over the world, in the barren rocks of Switzerland: And being asked by the last king of France, how it came to pass that he, who had seen the finest countries on the globe, came to lay out his fortune in the worst? He gave his haughty Majesty this short answer, that he was willing to have something which he could call his own.

As I think it is evident, by what I have said before, that trade cannot long subsist, much less flourish, in arbitrary governments; so there is so close and inseparable a connection between that and naval power, that I dare boldly affirm, that the latter can never arrive to any formidable height, and continue long in that situation, under such a state. Where there is an extensive trade; great numbers of able-bodied and courageous sailors, men bred up to fatigues, hardships, and hazards, and consequently soldiers by profession, are kept in constant pay; not only without any charge to the publick, but greatly to its benefit; not only by daily adding to its wealth and power, but by venting and employing abroad, to their country's honour and safety, those turbulent and unruly spirits that would be fuel for factions, and the tools and instruments of ambitious or discontented great men at home. These men are always ready at their country's call, to defend the profession which they live by, and with it the publick happiness: They are, and ever must be, in the publick interest, with which their own is so closely united; for they subsist by exporting the productions of the people's industry, which they constantly increase by so doing: They receive their pay from the merchants, a sort of men always in the interests of liberty, from which alone they can receive protection and encouragement. And as this race of men contribute vastly to the publick security and wealth, so they take nothing from it: They are not quartered up and down their native country, like the bands

5. Jean Baptiste Tavernier, Baron d'Aubonne (1605–1689), who authored an account of his travels: *Les six voyages de Jean Baptiste Tavernier . . . qu'il a fait en Turquie, en Perse et aux Indes* (2 vols.; Paris: Gervaise Clouzier, 1676-1677). The work was quickly translated into English as *The Six Voyages of John Baptista Tavernier . . . through Turkey, into Persia, and the East Indies, finished in the year 1670* (London: Printed for John Starkey and Moses Pitt, 1678), and it achieved considerable popularity.

of despotick princes, to oppress their subjects, interrupt their industry, debauch their wives and daughters, insult their persons, to be examples of lewdness and prodigality, and to be always ready at hand to execute the bloody commands of a tyrant.

No monarch was ever yet powerful enough to keep as many seamen in constant pay at his own expence, as single cities have been able to do without any at all: The pay of a sailor, with his provision, is equal to that of a trooper in arbitrary governments; nor can they learn their trade, by taking the sea-air for a few summer months, and wafting about the coasts of their own country: They gain experience and boldness, by various and difficult voyages, by being constantly inured to hardships and dangers. Nor is it possible for single princes, with all their power and vigilance, to have such regular supplies of naval provisions, as trading countries must have always in store. There must be a regular and constant intercourse with the nations from whom these supplies come; a certain and regular method of paying for them; and constant demands will produce constant supplies. There are always numerous magazines in the hands of private merchants, ready for their own use or sale. There must be great numbers of shipwrights, anchor-smiths, rope and sail-makers, and infinite other artificers, sure always of constant employment; and who, if they are oppressed by one master, may go to another. There must be numbers of ships used for trade, that, upon occasions, may be employed for men of war, for transports, for fireships, and tenders. Now all these things, or scarce any of them, can ever be brought about by arbitrary courts; stores will be embezzled, exhausted, and worn out, before new ones are supplied; payments will not be punctually made; artificers will be discouraged, oppressed, and often left without employ: Every thing will be done at an exorbitant expence, and often not done when it is paid for; and when payments are made, the greatest part shall go in fees, or for bribes, or in secret trusts.

For these reasons, and many others, despotick monarchs, though infinitely powerful at land, yet could never rival Neptune, and extend their empire over the liquid world; for though great and vigorous efforts have been often made by these haughty tyrants of mankind, to subject that element to their ambition and their power, being taught by woeful experience, arising from perpetual losses and disappointments, of what vast importance that dominion was to unlimited and universal sovereignty; yet all their riches, applications, and pride, have never been able, in one instance, to effect it. Sometimes, indeed, trade, like a phantom, has made a faint appearance at an arbitrary court, but disappeared again at the first approach of the morning light: She is the portion of free states, is married to liberty, and ever flies the foul and polluted embraces of a tyrant.

The little state of Athens was always able to humble the pride, and put a check to the growing greatness, of the towering Persian monarchs, by their naval power; and when stripped of all their territories by land, and even their capital city, the seat of their commonwealth, yet had strength enough left to vanquish numerous fleets, which almost covered the sea, and to defeat an expedition carried on by armies that drank up rivers, and exhausted all the stores of the land.[6]

The single city of Venice has proved itself an over-match in naval power to the great Ottoman Empire, though possessed of so many islands, useful ports, environed with so many sea-coasts, and abounding with all sorts of stores necessary to navigation; and in the year fifty-six gave the Turks so signal an overthrow at the Dardanelles, as put that state in such a consternation, that they believed their empire at an end; and it is thought if the Venetians had pursued their victory, they had driven them out of Constantinople, and even out of Europe; for the Grand Seignior himself was preparing to fly into Asia.[7] The little island of Rhodes defended itself for some ages against the whole power of the Sultan, though

6. The reference is to the battle of Salamis in 480 B.C., where the Athenian navy dealt a crushing defeat to the Persian fleet after most of central Attica, including Athens, had fallen before the Persian army.

7. In 1656, during the course of one of the many wars between the two powers over the eastern Mediterranean islands, the Venetian navy decisively defeated the Ottoman fleet in the Dardanelles and briefly threatened Constantinople itself.

encompassed by his dominions; and it was with great difficulty, hazard, and expence, that he at last overcame them,[8] and drove the inhabitants to Malta, where they have ever since braved his pride, and live upon the plunder of his subjects: And notwithstanding all his numerous and expensive efforts to share with the Christians the dominion of the sea; yet there are no other seeds or traces of it left through his great and extensive territories, but what are found in the free piratical states of Algiers, Tunis, and Tripoli.

Neither the Sophi[9] of Persia, the Great Mogul, the many kings who command the banks of the Ganges, nor all the haughty potentates of Asia and Africa, are able to contend at sea with the English or Dutch East-India Companies, or even to defend their subjects against but a few pirates, with all their population, and their mines of gold and diamonds.

Spain in all her pride, with the wealth of both Indies, with dominions so vast and extensive, that the sun rises and sets within them, and a sea-line, which if extended would environ the earth, yet was not able to dispute their title to that element with a few revolted provinces, who grew up through the course of an expensive war to that amazing greatness, that in less than a century they saw themselves, from a few fisher-towns encompassed with bogs and morasses, become a most formidable state, equal to the greatest potentates at sea, and to most at land; to have great kings in a distant world submit to be their vassals; and, in fine, to be protectors of that mighty nation from whom they revolted. Here is a stupendous instance of the effects of liberty, which neighbouring monarchs with twenty times the territory tremble at, and posterity will hardly believe.

France, with all its oeconomy, address, and power, with its utmost and most expensive efforts, and the assistance of neighbouring and even rival kings, has not been able to establish an empire upon that coy element. She saw it, like a mushroom, rise

8. Between 1480 and 1522, the Turks made several attempts against Rhodes, the stronghold of the Knights Hospitalers of St. John. Despite its immensely strong fortifications, the island finally fell to Ottoman forces in 1522.

9. The surname of the ruling dynasty of Persia from 1500 to 1736, hence the title of its emperor.

in a night, and wither again the next day. It is true, that at an immense expence and infinite labour, she got together a formidable fleet, and with it got victories, and took thousands of rival ships; yet every day grew weaker as her enemies grew stronger, and could never recover a single defeat, which in Holland would have been repaired in a few more weeks than the battle was days in fighting:[10] So impossible is it for art to contend with nature, and slavery to dispute the naval prize with liberty.

Sweden and Denmark, though possessed of the naval stores of Europe, nations who subsist by that commerce, and are constantly employed to build ships for their neighbours; yet are not able, with their united force, to equip, man out, and keep upon the sea for any considerable time, a fleet large enough to dispute with an English or Dutch squadron: And I dare venture my reputation and skill in politicks, by boldly asserting, that another vain and unnatural northern apparition[11] will soon vanish and disappear again, like the morning-star at the glimmering of the sun, and every one shall ask, Where is it?

T   *I am, &c.*

NO. 65. SATURDAY, FEBRUARY 10, 1721.

Military Virtue produced and supported by Civil Liberty only.

SIR,

I have shewn in my last, that trade and naval power are produced by liberty only; and shall shew in this, that military vir-

10. During the reign of Louis XIV, France saw the creation of a virtually new navy; while the nation possessed only twenty warships in 1661, by 1677 that number had increased to 270. Far from having quickly withered, the French navy continued as a powerful force. Indeed, during the first half of the eighteenth century, the French navy had clearly surpassed that of the Dutch and, outside of England, was the strongest in Europe.

11. The reference is to Russia, which had risen to the rank of a great power under Peter the Great (d. 1725).

tue can proceed from nothing else, as I have in a good measure shewn already.

In free countries, as people work for themselves, so they fight for themselves: But in arbitrary countries, it is all one to the people, in point of interest, who conquers them; they cannot be worse used; and when a tyrant's army is beaten, his country is conquered: He has no resource; his subjects having neither arms, nor courage, nor reason to fight for him; He has no support but his standing forces; who, for enabling him to oppress, are sharers in his oppression; and fighting for themselves while they fight for him, do sometimes fight well: But his poor people, who are oppressed by him, can have no other concern for his fate, than to wish him the worst.

In attacks upon a free state, every man will fight to defend it, because every man has something to defend in it. He is in love with his condition, his ease, and property, and will venture his life rather than lose them; because with them he loses all the blessings of life. When these blessings are gone, it is madness to think that any man will spill his blood for him who took them away, and is doubtless his enemy, though he may call himself his prince. It is much more natural to wish his destruction, and help to procure it.

For these reasons, small free states have conquered the greatest princes; and the greatest princes have never been able to conquer free states, but either by surprizing them basely, or by corrupting them, or by forces almost infinitely superior, or when they were distracted and weakened by domestick divisions and treachery.

The Greeks thought scarce any number of Persians too great for their own small armies, or any army of their own too small for the greatest number of Persians. Agesilaus[1] invaded the great Persian Empire, the greatest then in the world, at the head of no more than ten thousand foot, and four thousand horse, and carried all before him; he defeated the Asiatick forces with so much ease, that they scarce interrupted his march; he subdued

1. King of Sparta, who successfully engaged the forces of Artaxerxes, King of Persia, in Asia Minor until recalled home to oppose Athenian and Boeotian forces in 394 B.C.

their provinces as fast as he entered them, and took their cities without sitting down before them: And had he not been recalled by his countrymen to defend his own city against a confederacy of other Greek cities, much more terrible foes than the greatest armies of the great king, it is very probable that that brave old Spartan would have soon robbed him of his empire.

And not long before this, when Cyrus made war upon his brother Artaxerxes for the crown,[2] thirteen thousand auxiliary Greeks entertained by him for that end, routed the emperor's army of nine hundred thousand men, and got the victory for Cyrus, had he outlived the battle to enjoy it. And though they had now lost the prince they fought for, and afterwards Clearchus their general,[3] who with other of their officers was treacherously murdered by the Persians when they had brought him to a parley; though they were in great straits, destitute of horses, money, and provisions, far from home, in the heart of an enemy's country, watched, and distressed by a great army of four hundred thousand men, who waited for an occasion to cut them off in their retreat, if they attempted it: yet these excellent soldiers, excellent by being freemen, commanded by the famous Xenophon,[4] made good that retreat of two thousand three hundred miles over the bellies of their enemies, through provinces of Persians, and in spite of a vast host of Persians, who coasted and harassed them all the way.

Alexander of Macedon, with his free Greeks, attacked the Persians, and beat them at all disadvantages in the open fields, when they were five, ten, nay, twenty times his number; and having, passed the Hellespont, with not fifteen thousand pounds in his treasury, and not above thirty-five thousand men in his army, he made himself master of that great and overgrown empire, with as much expedition as he could travel over it; and though he fought three battles for it, he scarce lost in them all one regiment of his men.

2. In 401 B.C., *Cyrus*, the younger son of *Darius II*, collected a sizeable number of mercenaries and moved against his older brother, the King of Persia, intending to take the throne. He came close to victory but lost his life in battle.

3. *Clearchus* (*c.* 450–401 B.C.), the Spartan officer commissioned by Cyrus to recruit and act as commander of his Greek mercenary force.

4. *Xenophon* (*c.* 428–*c.* 354 B.C.), the prominent Athenian historian and military commander who led Cyrus's Greek army out of Asia Minor.

Leonidas, at the head of four thousand Greeks, fought Xerxes at the head of six and twenty hundred thousand Persians, according to Herodotus, in the straits of Thermopylae for two days together, and repulsed them at every assault with vast slaughter; nor did they at last get the better of him, till being led by a treacherous Greek a secret way over the mountains, they fell upon him in the rear, and surrounded him with their numbers; neither did he then desert his post, though all his men retreated, except three hundred Spartans, who resolutely stood by him, and were all slain with him upon the spot, with twenty thousand Persians round them.[5]

The Romans, enjoying the same liberty, and animated by it, vanquished all the enslaved nations of the known world, with the same ease, and upon the same unequal terms. The subduing of free countries cost them long labour and patience, great difficulty, and a world of blood; and they suffered many defeats before they got a decisive victory: The inhabitants being all freemen, were all brave, all soldiers, and were exhausted before their states could be conquered: And the Volscians, Aequians, Tuscans, and Samnites,[6] preserved their liberties, as long as they had men left to defend them. The Samnites particularly declared in their embassy to Hannibal, that having often brought great numbers of men into the field against the Romans, and sometimes defeated the Roman armies, they were at last so wasted, that they could not resist one Roman legion.

But when the Romans came to war against great and arbitrary kings, they had little else to do but to shew their swords; they gained battles almost without fighting, and two or three legions have routed three or four hundred thousand men. One battle generally won a kingdom, and sometimes two or three. Antiochus[7] was so frightened with one skirmish with Acilius at Thermopylae, that he ran away out of Greece, and left all that he possessed there to

5. The events are recounted in Herodotus, 7.204–39.

6. Native Italian tribes with whom Rome was engaged in warfare.

7. *Antiochus III*, the Great (*c.* 242–187 B.C.), Seleucid king of Syria, whose armies were defeated by Roman forces first under the tribune Glabrio *Acilius* at Thermopylae and then by Lucius Cornelius *Scipio* Asiaticus at the battle of Magnesia in Asia Minor.

the Romans; and being beaten afterwards by Scipio, the brother of Africanus, he quitted to them all his kingdoms and territories on this side Mount Taurus. And Paulus Aemilius, by one battle with Perseus, became master of Macedonia. Tigranes, Ptolemy, and Syphax, all monarchs of mighty territories,[8] were still more easily vanquished. So that the great kingdoms of Asia, Aegypt, Numidia, and Macedon, were all of them much more easily overcome, and suffered much fewer defeats, than the Samnites alone, though inhabiting a small barren province.

The only dreadful foes which the Romans ever found, were people as free as themselves; and the most dreadful of all were the Carthaginians. Hannibal alone beat them oftener, and slew more of their men in battle, than all the kings in the world ever did, or could do. But for all the great and repeated defeats which he gave them; though he had destroyed two hundred thousand of their men, and many of their excellent commanders; though, at the same time, their armies were cut off in Spain, and with them the two brave Scipios; and though they had suffered great losses in Sicily, and at sea, yet they never sunk nor wanted soldiers, nor their soldiers courage; and as to great commanders, they had more and better than ever they had before: And having conquered Hannibal, they quickly conquered the world.

This vast virtue of theirs, and this unconquerable spirit, was not owing to climate or complexion, but to liberty alone, and to the equality of their government, in which every Roman had a share: They were nursed up in the principles of liberty; in their infancy they were instructed to love it; experience afterwards confirmed their affections, and shewed them its glorious advantages: Their own happy condition taught them a contempt and indignation for those wretched and barbarous governments, which could neither afford their subjects happiness nor protection: And when they attacked such governments and their wretched people, they found themselves like lions amongst sheep.

8. The references are to *Tigranes*, King of Armenia, whose armies were crushed by a much smaller Roman force in 69 B.C.; *Ptolemy XIII*, brother and husband of Cleopatra, who was decisively defeated by Julius Caesar in 47 B.C.; and *Syphax*, chief of Numidia and ally of Carthage, whose forces were routed by a Roman army in 203 B.C.

It is therefore government alone that makes men cowardly or brave: And Boccalini well ridicules the absurd complaint of the princes of his time, that their subjects wanted that love for their country which was found in free states, when he makes Apollo tell them, that no people were ever in love with rapine, fraud, and oppression; that they must mend their own administration, and their people's condition; and that people will then love their country, when they live happily in it.[9] The old Romans were masters of mankind; but the present race of people in Rome are not a match for one of the Swiss cantons; nor could these cantons ever be conquered, even by the united forces of the house of Austria. Charles Duke of Burgundy was the last that durst invade them; but though he had been long a terror and constant rival to Louis XI of France, a crafty, politick, and powerful monarch, and often too hard for him; he paid dear for his bravery in attacking the Switzers, and lost by doing it three armies, and his own life.[10] They were a free people, and fought in their own quarrel; the greatest incitement upon earth to boldness and magnanimity. The Switzers had a property, though in rocks; and were freemen, though amongst mountains. This gives them the figure which they make in Europe; such a figure, that they are courted by the greatest princes in it, and have supported some of them in their wars, when their own native slaves could not support them.

The Dutch, having revolted from the greatest potentate then in Europe, defended themselves against all his power for near a hundred years, and grew rich all the time, while he grew poor;[11] so poor, that Spain has never yet recovered its losses in that war:

9. Trajano Boccalini, *I Ragguagli di Parnasso: or Advertisements from Parnassus; in two centuries*, Henry, Earl of Monmouth, trans. (London: Printed for Humphrey Moseley, 1656). The interchange appears in advertisement 99 of the first century, pp. 195–96.

10. The Hapsburgs made several attempts to subdue the Swiss cantons between the beginning of the fourteenth and the middle of the fifteenth centuries, but all proved unsuccessful. In 1474, the Swiss went to war with Charles the Bold of Burgundy, and won major victories at Grandson and Morat in 1476 and at Nancy in 1477, where Charles himself fell.

11. The war between the provinces of the Spanish Netherlands and Spain lasted from 1568 until 1648, when Spain finally recognized the independence of the United Provinces. During that period the United Provinces rose to become an important European power.

And though they are in their constitution more formed for trade than war, yet their own bravery in their own defence is astonishing to those that know not what the spirit of liberty can do in any people: Even their women joined to defend their walls; as the women of Sparta once did, and as the women of Barcelona more lately did, though the united force of the two monarchies of France and Spain had at last the honour to take that city, especially when we, who had engaged them in the war, had also given them up.

These same Dutch in that war, when they were closely besieged in one of their towns by the Spanish Army, let in the sea upon their country, trusting rather to the mercy of that element, than to the mercy of an invading tyrant; and the sea saved them.[12] It must be remembered too, that they had the power of the Emperor, as well as that of Spain, to contend with; both these mighty monarchs having joined their counsels and arms to subdue seven little provinces, which yet they never were able to subdue: The city of Ostend alone cost them a three years siege, and an hundred and thirty thousand men; and when they took it, they only took a heap of rubbish, to which it was reduced before it was surrendered.[13]

In free states, every man being a soldier, or quickly made so, they improve in a war, and every campaign fight better and better. Whereas the armies of an absolute prince grow every campaign worse; especially if they be composed of his own subjects, who, being slaves, are with great difficulty and long discipline made soldiers, and scarce ever made good ones; and when his old troops are gone, his new ones signify little. This was eminently shewn in the late war with France, which degenerated in arms every year; while the English and Dutch did as evidently mend. And doubtless, if the French barrier of fortified towns had been

12. In 1573, the city of Leyden, under siege by the Spanish and on the verge of starvation, cut the dikes, thus flooding the Spanish army from their trenches and camps. The city was finally relieved by a Dutch fleet that sailed across the inundated countryside.

13. Spanish forces besieged Ostend for a period of three years and seventy-one days, from 1601 until 1604. The invading Spanish army is calculated to have lost approximately 60,000 men by casualty and disease, not the 130,000 claimed by Gordon.

quite broken through, as it was very near, one battle would have completed the conquest of France, and perhaps it would not have cost a battle.

And if free states support themselves better in a war than an absolute prince, they do likewise much sooner retrieve their losses by it. The Dutch, when they had been beaten twice at sea by Cromwell's admirals and English seamen, with great slaughter and loss of ships, did notwithstanding, in two months time, after the second great defeat, fit out a third fleet of a hundred and forty men of war, under the famous Van Trump:[14] Upon this Lord Clarendon observes, that,

> there cannot be a greater instance of the opulency of that people, than that they should be able, after so many losses, and so late a great defeat, in so short a time, to set out a fleet strong enough to visit those who had so lately overcome them.[15]

This is what no arbitrary prince in Europe, or upon the face of the earth, could have done; nor do I believe, that all the arbitrary monarchs in Europe, Africa, and Asia, with all their united powers together, could do it at this day. The whole strength of the Spanish monarchy could not fit out their famous armada, without the assistance of money from the little free state of Genoa; and that invincible armada, being beaten by the English, and quite destroyed, Spain has never been able, with all her Indies, and her mountains of silver and gold, to make any figure at sea since, nor been able to pay that very money which equipped that its last great fleet.

14. The reference is to the naval battles between England and the Dutch in 1653. At the battles of Beachy Head and of the Gabbard Bank, English fleets scored decisive victories over the Dutch fleet under Maarten van Tromp. On July 31, the fleets again met at the battle of Scheveningen; the Dutch fleet, encountering a much smaller British force, suffered severe losses, including thirty men-of-war and the death of van Tromp himself.

15. Edward, Earl of Clarendon, *The history of the rebellion and civil wars in England begun in the year 1641* (3 vols. in 6; Oxford: Printed at the theater, 1712), bk. XIV, sect. 29 (III.2.488).

The little city of Tyre gave Alexander the Great more resistance, and cost him more labour to take it, than to conquer the great monarchy of Asia;[16] and though, when with infinite labour and courage he had taken it, he burnt it to the ground, slew eight thousand Tyrians in the sackage of their town, crucified two thousand more, and sold all the rest for slaves; yet some of the citizens, with their wives and children, having escaped to Carthage (a colony of their own), and others being conveyed away and saved by their neighbours the Sidonians during the siege, they returned and rebuilt their desolated city; and in so small a time as nineteen years afterwards, endured another siege of fifteen months from Antigonus, the most powerful of all Alexander's successors;[17] nor could he take it at last, but upon honourable terms. What an instance of the blessings and power of liberty and trade!

From the moment that the Romans lost their liberty, their spirit was gone, and their valour scarce ever after appeared. In the beginning of Augustus's reign, the best and bravest of them perished by the sword, either in the civil war, where, Romans fighting against Romans, multitudes were slain, with Brutus and Cassius, the last brave men that ever drew a sword for the commonwealth; or in the bloody proscriptions that followed, in which all the excellent men and assertors of liberty, who escaped the battle, were gleaned up and murdered by soldiers and informers, and, amongst the rest, the divine Cicero. Afterwards, when Augustus had got the world to himself, *jura omnium in se traxit*;[18] flatterers were his only favourites, and none were preferred to magistracy, but the servile creatures of his power; liberty was extinct, and its spirit gone; and though there was a universal peace, yet the power of the empire

16. Tyre, an island less than half a mile from the mainland and the main base of the Persian fleet, was able to withstand a siege of some eight months against Alexander's forces in 332 B.C. before finally capitulating.

17. *Antigonus* (d. 301 B.C.), one of Alexander's generals and an illegitimate son of Philip of Macedon. Following the death of Alexander, he attempted to reunite all portions of the Alexandrian empire under his control.

18. "He had drawn all the laws into himself." This is most probably a paraphrase of Tacitus, *Annales*, 1.2: *Munia senatus, magistratuum, legum in se trahere* ("He drew to himself the functions of the senate, the magistrates, and the laws").

continually decayed. Augustus himself was so sensible of this, that the loss of two or three legions under Varus in Germany,[19] frightened him, and had almost broke his heart; not from any tenderness in it, for he had butchered myriads, and enslaved all; but he knew that now Roman legions were hard to be got, and scarce worth getting. Having destroyed so many brave Romans, and made the rest base by slavery, and by the corruptions which support it, he knew the difficulty of forming a Roman army.

His successors were worse; they went on in a perpetual series of slaughters, dreading and destroying every thing that had the appearance of virtue or goodness; and even so early as Tiberius's reign, that emperor, says Tacitus, knew *magis fama quam vi stare res suas*,[20] that his empire was supported more by the reputation of Roman greatness, than by the real strength of the Romans, who grew every day more and more weak and wretched; and though they had now and then a little sun-shine in the reign of a good emperor, yet the root of the evil remained: They were no longer freemen, and for far the most part, their government was nothing else but a constant state of oppression, and a continual succession of massacres. Tyrants governed them, and soldiers created and governed the tyrants, or butchered them if they would not be butchers.

As to military virtue, it was no more: The Praetorian bands were only a band of hangmen with an emperor at their head; Italy and the provinces were exhausted; the Roman people were nothing but an idle and debauched mob, that cared not who was uppermost, so they had but a little victuals, and saw shews; The provincial armies were foreign hirelings, and there was not a Roman army in the Roman empire. *Inops Italia, plebs urbana imbellis nihil in exercitibus validum praeter externum.*[21] This was said not long after the death of Augustus; nor do I remember an instance of one

19. In A.D. 9, *Arminius*, German general, treacherously attacked three legions of Roman troops under Publius Quinctilius *Varus* and destroyed them.

20. "His fortunes rested more on his prestige than on force." Tacitus, *Annales*, 6.30.

21. "The poverty of Italy, the unwarlike urban population, the feebleness of the armies except for the leavening of foreigners." Tacitus, *Annales*, 3.40.

great Roman captain after Germanicus and Corbulo;[22] the first murdered by Tiberius, his uncle and father by adoption; and the other by Nero, for whom he reconquered and settled the East; and after Vespasian and Titus, every Roman emperor of remarkable bravery was a foreigner, and every victory gained by them, was gained by foreigners; who, being all mercenaries, were perpetually setting up and pulling down their own monarchs. At length, being possessed of the whole power of the empire, they took it to themselves; and thus it ended, and became dismembered by several nations, and into several governments, according to their fortune; and it is remarkable, that though those nations had frequent wars amongst themselves about the countries which they invaded, yet they had nothing to apprehend from the Romans while they were seizing Roman provinces.

Tyrants are so sensible, that when they have lost their army, they have lost all, that amongst their other destructive expedients to preserve themselves, whatever becomes of their people, one of their methods is, to lay whole countries waste, and to keep them waste, to prevent an invader from subsisting; and their best provinces are by this means turned often into wildernesses. For this reason a march to Constantinople is scarce practicable to an enemy from any quarter.

I will conclude with answering an objection: It may be said, that the armies of tyrants often fight bravely, and are brave; and I own it to be true in many instances: But I desire it may be remembered, that in arbitrary countries nothing flourishes except the court and the army. A tyrant must give his spoilers part of the spoil, or else they will fight but faintly for it, or perhaps put him to death if he do not. The most absolute princes must therefore use their soldiers like freemen, as they tender their own power and their lives; and under the greatest tyrants the men of war enjoy great privileges, even greater than in free states. The privileges

22. *Germanicus* Julius Caesar (24 B.C.–A.D. 19), nephew and adopted son of Tiberius, who led the Roman forces in Germany. He is reputed to have been poisoned by Gnaeus Calpurnius Piso, one of Tiberius's favorites, while visiting Antioch. Gnaeus Domitius *Corbulo*, Roman general of some prominence. In A.D. 66 the emperor Nero, jealous of his abilities, invited him to Greece and there ordered him to commit suicide.

and immunities which they enjoy, constitute a sort of liberty, dear to themselves, but terrible always to the subject, and often pernicious to the prince: It being the certain condition of a tyrant, that to be able to oppress his people, or plague his neighbours, he must empower his soldiers to destroy himself.

The chief forces therefore of an arbitrary prince consist of freemen: Such were the Praetorian bands of the Roman emperors, and such are the Turkish janizaries; and both of them, though they maintained the tyranny, have frequently killed the tyrants; and such are the Grand Seignior's zaims, timariots, or horsemen,[23] who have lands given them in the provinces, and are the only nobility and gentry there: And such too were the Mamalukes of Egypt,[24] which country at last they usurped for themselves, having put the king their master to death. I might mention here the Swiss Guards, and gendarmes of a neighbouring prince,[25] which are his janizaries. As to the Turkish janizaries, I own the Sultan may put particular men of them to death, but no sultan dares touch their privileges as a body; and two or three of their greatest emperors were deposed and destroyed by them for attempting it.

Mere slaves can defend no prince, nor enable him even to rule over slaves: So that by giving liberty, or rather licentiousness, to a few, the slavery of all is maintained.

All this does, I think, fully prove, that where there is no liberty, there can be no magnanimity. It is true, enthusiasm has inspired armies, and most remarkably of all the Saracen armies, with amazing resolution and fury; but even that was fierceness for liberty of opinion to themselves, and for subduing all men to it; and besides, this courage of enthusiasm is rarely eminent, except in the first rise of states and empires.

G   *I am, &c.*

23. Zaims and timariots were feudal vassals of the Ottoman sultan and comprised the Ottoman cavalry during battle.

24. Originally slaves and later employed as warriors by the rulers of Egypt, the Mamelukes became sultans of Egypt in 1250 and continued to rule until the Turkish conquest in 1517.

25. The Pope.

NO. 66. SATURDAY, FEBRUARY 17, 1721.

❦   *Arbitrary Government proved incompatible with true Religion, whether Natural or Revealed.*

SIR,

I shall shew, in this paper, that neither the Christian religion, nor natural religion, nor any thing else that ought to be called religion, can subsist under tyrannical governments, now that miracles are ceased. I readily confess, that such governments are fertile in superstition, in wild whimsies, delusive phantoms, and ridiculous dreams; proper to terrify the human soul, degrade its dignity, deface its beauty, and fetter it with slavish and unmanly fears, to render it a proper object of fraud, grimace, and imposition; and to make mankind the ready dupes of gloomy impostors, and the tame slaves of raging tyrants. For, servitude established in the mind, is best established.

But all these bewildered imaginations, these dark and dreadful horrors, which banish reason, and contract and embitter the heart, what have they to do with true religion, unless to destroy it? That religion, which improves and enlarges the faculties of men, exalts their spirits, and makes them brave for God and themselves; that religion, which gives them great and worthy conceptions of the Deity; and that religion which inspires them with generous and beneficent affections to one another, and with universal love and benevolence to the whole creation? No man can love God, if he love not his neighbour; and whoever loves his neighbour, will neither injure, revile, nor oppress him: Nor can we otherwise shew our love to God, than by kind, humane, and affectionate actions to his creatures: "A new commandment," says our blessed Saviour, "I give unto you, that ye love one another."[1]

Almighty God, the great author of our nature, and of all things, who has the heavens for his throne, and the earth for his footstool, is raised far above the reach of our kindness, our malice, or our flattery. He derives infinite happiness from his own infinite

1. John 15:17.

perfections; nor can any frail power or actions of ours lessen or improve it: religion therefore, from which he can reap no advantage, was instituted by him for the sake of men, as the best means and the strongest motive to their own happiness, and mutual happiness; and by it men are taught and animated to be useful, assisting, forgiving, kind and merciful one to another. But to hurt, calumniate, or hate one another, for his sake, and in defence of any religion, is a flat contradiction to *his* religion, and an open defiance of the author of religion: And to quarrel about belief and opinions, which do not immediately and necessarily produce practical virtue and social duties, is equally wicked and absurd. This is to be wicked in behalf of righteousness, and to be cruel out of piety. A religion which begets selfishness and partiality only to a few, and its own followers, and which inspires hatred and outrage towards all the rest of the world, can never be the religion of the merciful and impartial maker and judge of the world. Speculations are only so far a part of religion, as they produce the moral duties of religion, general peace, and unlimited charity, publick spirit, equity, forbearance, and good deeds to all men: And the worship of God is no longer the worship of God, than as it warms our minds with the remembrance of his gracious condescensions, his indulgent care, bounty, and providence, exercised towards us; and as it raises and forms our affections to an imitation of such his divine and unrestrained goodness, and to use one another kindly by his great example, who uses us all so. So that our worthy, tender, and beneficent behaviour to one another, is the best way to acknowledge his to us: It is the most acceptable way that we can worship him, and the way which he will best accept our worship: And whatever devotion has not this effect, or a contrary effect, is the dry or mad freaks of an enthusiast, and ought to be called by another and a properer name.

This is a general idea of true religion; these are the certain and only marks of it: All which, as they are opposite to the essence and spirit of an arbitrary government; so every arbitrary government is an enemy to the spirit of true religion, and defeats its ends. In these governments, in defiance of religion, humanity, and common sense, millions must be miserable to exalt an embellish one or a few, and to make them proud, arrogant, and great: Protection and security are no more; the spirit of the people is sunk, their industry discouraged and lost, or only employed to feed luxury and pride; and multitudes starve, that a few may riot and abound. All love to mankind is extinct, and virtue and publick spirit are dangerous or unknown; while vice, falsehood, and servile syco-phancy, become necessary to maintain precarious safety and an ignominious life: And, in fine, men live upon the spoils of one another, like ravenous fishes and beasts of prey: They become rapacious, brutish, and savage to one another, as their cruel gover-nors are to them all; and, as a further imitation of such masters, their souls are abject, mean, and villainous. To live upon prey, and worry [the] human race, is the genius and support of tyrants, as well as of wolves and tigers; and it is the spirit and practice of men to resemble their governors, and to act like them. Virtue and vice, in courts, run like water in a continual descent, and quickly over-flow the inferior soil.

> *Torva Leaena lupum, &c.* [2]

Now, what can be found here to answer the spirit and precepts of the Christian religion, which is all love, charity, meek-ness, mutual assistance, and mutual indulgence; and must either destroy tyranny, which destroys all these, or be destroyed by it? A religion given by God, to inspire men with every social virtue, and to furnish them with every argument for social happiness, will never find quarter, much less protection, from a government, which sub-sists by an unrelenting war against every virtue, and all human felic-ity. On the contrary, all its divine doctrines shall be perverted, all its divine principles mangled, and both its principles and its precepts corrupted, disguised, and wrested, to be made free of the court: Truth will be made to patronize imposture, and meekness to sup-

2. Virgil, *Eclogue*, 2.63–64. The lines read:

> *Torva laeana lupum sequitur, lupus ipse capellem,*
> *florentem cytisum sequitur lasciva capella,*
> *te Corydon, o Alexi: trahit sua quemque voluptas.*

("The fierce lioness follows the wolf, the wolf himself follows the goat, the lascivious goat the flowering clover, and Corydon follows you, Alexis. Each is drawn by his own desire.")

port tyranny: Obedience to equal laws, and submission to just authority, shall be turned into a servile and crouching subjection to blind rage and inhuman fury; complaisant and respective behaviour into slavish flattery, and supple homage to power; meekness and humility into dejection, poorness of spirit, and bodily prostrations; charity, benevolence, and humanity, into a fiery and outrageous zeal to propagate fashionable and gainful opinions: Christian courage shall be changed into cruelty and brutish violence; impartial justice into savage severity; protection into oppression and plundering; the fear of God into the fear of man; and the worship of the Deity into an idolatrous adoration of a tyrant.

Though God Almighty sent his only son into the world to teach his will to men, and to confirm his mission by wonders and miracles; yet, having once fully manifested himself and his law, he has left it to be propagated and carried on by human means only, according to the holy writings inspired by him; and if the powers of the world will not submit to those directions, and will neither pursue them themselves, nor suffer their subjects to pursue them, nor leave them the means of doing it; then the Christian religion must take the fate of all sublunary[3] things, and be lost from amongst men, unless heaven interpose again miraculously in its favour. Now the experience of all ages will convince us, that all tyrannical princes will be against the religion which is against them; and either abolish it, or, which is much worse, pervert it into a deadly and unnatural engine, to increase and defend that pride and power, which Christianity abhors; and to promote those evils and miseries, which Christianity forbids, and, were it left to itself, would prevent or relieve. A religion modelled by usurped power, to countenance usurpation and oppression, is as opposite to the Christian religion, as tyranny is to liberty, and wickedness to virtue. When religion is taught to speak court-language, and none are suffered to preach it, but such as speak the same dialect; when those who are ministers of the gospel, must be also the ministers of ambition, and either sanctify falsehood and violence, by the word of mercy and truth, or hold their tongues; when preferments and worldly honours are on the side of imposture, and galleys, racks

3. Sublunary: earthly.

and dungeons, are the rewards of conscience and piety; the good and efficacy of Christianity will be as effectually gone, as if it were formally exchanged for Mahometanism; and under those circumstances, if its name be retained, it is only retained to do evil, and might be as innocently banished with the thing.

The Christian religion has as rarely gained by courts, as courts have improved by the Christian religion; and arbitrary courts have seldom meddled with it, but either to persecute it, or debate and corrupt it; nor could the power and fury of tyrants ever hurt or weaken it so much, as their pretended favours and countenance have done: By appearing for it, they turn their power most effectually against it. Their avowed persecution of Christianity, did only destroy Christians; but afterwards, while they set up for protecting none but the true Christians, that is, those that were as bad as themselves, and having no religion of their own, adopted blindly the religion of their prince; and whilst they were for punishing all who were not true Christians, that is, all that were better than themselves, and would take their religion from no man's word, but only from the word of God; they lifted Christians against Christians, and disfigured, and undermined, and banished Christianity itself, by false friendship to its professors: And these professors thus corrupted, joining a holy title to an impious cause, concurred in the conspiracy, and contended fiercely in the name of Christ for secular advantages, which Christ never gave nor took, and for a secular sovereignty, which he rejected, and his gospel forbids. Thus one sort of tyranny was artfully made to support another, and both by a union of interests maintained a war against religion, under colour of defending it, and fought the author of it under his own banner; that is, as Dr. Tillotson finely says, they lied for the truth, and killed for God's sake.[4]

4. Archbishop Tillotson, in comparing the Church of England with the Roman Church, wrote: "Our religion doth not clash and interfere with any of the great moral duties to which all mankind stand obliged by the law and light of nature; as fidelity, mercy and truth. We do not teach men to break faith with hereticks and infidels; nor to destroy and extirpate those who differ from us, with fire and sword." Sermon 9: "Of Constancy in the Profession of the True Religion," *The Works of the Most Reverend Dr. John Tillotson* (2 vols.; London: William Rogers, etc., 1712), I:70.

The many various and contradictory opinions of weak enthusiasts, or of designing men, and all the different and repugnant interpretations of scripture, published and contended for by them, could have done but small prejudice to religion and society, if human authority had not interposed with its penalties and rewards annexed to the believing or not believing fortuitous speculations, useless notions, dry ideas, and the inconsistent reveries of disordered brains; or the selfish inventions of usurping Popes, ambitious synods, and turbulent and aspiring doctors, or the crafty schemes of discontented or oppressive statesmen: For all these have been the important causes, and the wicked fuel, of religious wars and persecutions.

It is so much the general interest of society to perform and to encourage all its members to perform the practical duties of religion, that if a stronger and more prevailing interest were not thrown by power into the contrary scale, there would be no difference amongst men about the nature and extent of their duties to magistrates, to parents, children, and to friends and neighbours: And if these social duties (the only duties which human society, as such, is concerned to promote) were agreed upon and practised, the magistrate would have no more to do with their opinions than with their shape and complexion; nor could he know, if he would, by what method to alter them. No man's belief is in his own power, or can be in the power of another.

The utmost length that the power of the magistrate can in this matter extend, beyond that of exhortation, which is in every man's power, can be only to make hypocrites, slaves, fools, or atheists. When he has forced his subjects to belie their consciences, or to act against them, he has in effect driven them out of all religion, to bring them into his own; and when they thus see and feel the professed defender of religion overturning all its precepts, exhorting by bribes, rebuking by stripes,[5] confiscations and dungeons, and making Christianity the instrument of fury, ambition, rapine, and tyranny; what can they think, but either that he is no Christian, or that Christianity is not true? If they come to suspect it of imposture, they grow infidels; if they grow into a belief that reli-

5. Stripes: whippings.

gion countenances bitterness, outrage, and severities, nay, commands all these, they become bigots; the worst and most mischievous character of the two: For, unbelievers, guided by the rules of prudence or good nature, may be good neighbors and inoffensive men; but bigotry, standing upon the ruins of reason, and being conducted by no light but that of an inflamed imagination, and a sour, bitter, and narrow spirit, there is no violence nor barbarity which it is not capable of wishing or acting.

Happiness is the chief end of man, and the saving of his soul is his chief happiness; so that every man is most concerned for his own soul, and more than any other can be: And if no obstruction be thrown in his way, he will for the most part do all in his power for his own salvation, and will certainly do it best; and when he has done all that he can, he has done all that he ought: people cannot be saved by force; nor can all the powers in the world together make one true Christian, or convince one man. Conviction is the province and effect of reason; when that fails, nothing but the grace of God can supply it: And what has the power and penalties of men to do either with reason or grace; which being both the gifts of God, are not to be conquered by chains, though they may be weakened, and even banished, by worldly allurements blended with Christianity, and by the worldly pride of its professors?

The methods of power are repugnant to the nature of conviction, which must either be promoted by exhortation, kindness, example, and arguments, or can never be promoted at all: Violence does, on the contrary, but provoke men, and confirm them in error; nor will they ever be brought to believe, that those who barbarously rob them of their present happiness, can be charitably concerned for their future.

It is evident in fact, that most of the different religious institutions now subsisting in the world, have been founded upon ambition and pride; and were advanced, propagated, and established, by usurpation, faction, and oppression: They were begun for the most part by enthusiasts, or by designing and unpreferred churchmen; or at least occasioned by the continued usurpations and insults of cruel and oppressive ones, and always in times of faction and general discontent. Turbulent and aspiring men, discarded and discontented courtiers, or ambitious and designing statesmen, have taken advantage from these general disorders, or from the hot and giddy spirits of an enthusiastical or oppressed people, and from thence have formed parties; and setting themselves at the head, formed national establishments, with the concurrence of weak princes, sometimes in opposition to them, by the assistance of factious clergymen and factious assemblies, often by tumults and popular insurrections; and at last, under pretence of saving men's souls, they seized their property. A small acquaintance with ecclesiastical history, and the history of the Turks and Saracens, will shew such causes as these to have given rise to most of the national religious establishments upon earth: Nor can I see how any future one can arise by other means, whilst violence and worldly interest have any thing to do with them.

Such therefore as is the government of a country, such will be made its religion; and no body, I hope, is now to learn what is, and ever will be, the religion of most statesmen; even a religion of power, to do as little good and as much mischief as they please. Nor have churchmen, when they ruled states, had ever any other view; but having double authority, had generally double insolence, and remarkably less mercy and regard to conscience or property, than others who had fewer ties to be merciful and just: And therefore the sorest tyrants have been they, who united in one person the royalty and priesthood. The Pope's yoke is more grievous than that of any Christian prince upon earth; nor is there a trace of property, or felicity, or of the religion of Jesus Christ, found in the dominions of this father of Christendom; all is ignorance, bigotry, idolatry, barbarity, hunger, chains, and every species of misery. The Caliphs of Egypt, who founded the Saracen empire there, and maintained it for a great while, were at once kings and priests; and there never lived more raging bigots, or more furious and oppressive barbarians. The monarchy of Persia, which is also a severe tyranny, has the priesthood annexed to it; and the Sophi is at the same time the Caliph. The Turkish religion is founded on imposture, blended with outrageous and avowed violence; and by their religion, the imperial executioner is, next to their Alcoran, the most sacred thing amongst them: And though he be not himself chief priest, yet he creates and uncreates him at pleasure, and is, without the name of *mufti,* the chief doctor, or rather author of their religion; and we all know what sort of a religion it is.

In fact, as arbitrary princes want a religion suited to the genius of their power, they model their religion so as to serve all the purposes of tyranny; and debase, corrupt, discourage, or persecute all religion which is against tyranny, as all true religion is: For this reason, not one of the great absolute princes in Europe embraced the Reformation, nor would suffer his people to embrace it, but they were all bitter and professed enemies to it: Whereas all the great free states, except Poland, and most of the small free states, became Protestants. Thus the English, Scotch, the Dutch, the Bohemians, and Sweden and Denmark (which were then free kingdoms), the greatest part of Switzerland, with Geneva, and all the Hans-towns,[6] which were not awed by the Emperor, threw off the popish yoke: And not one of the free popish states, out of Italy, could be ever brought to receive the Inquisition; and the state of Venice, the greatest free state there, to shew that they received it against their will, have taken wise care to render it ineffectual: And many of the popish free states would never come into persecution, which they knew would impoverish and dispeople them; and therefore the states of Arragon, Valencia, and Catalonia, opposed, as much as they were able, the expulsion of the Moors, which was a pure act of regal power, to the undoing of Spain; and therefore a destructive and barbarous act of tyranny. As to the Protestant countries, which have since lost their liberties, there is much miserable ignorance, and much bitter and implacable bigotry, but little religion, and no charity, amongst them.

We look upon Montezuma, and other tyrants, who worshipped God with human sacrifice, as so many monsters, and hug ourselves that we have no such sons of Moloch here in Europe; not considering, that every man put to death for his religion, by the Inquisition and elsewhere, is a real human sacrifice, as it is burning and butchering men for God's sake.

6. That is, the towns that earlier comprised the Hanseatic League.

I think no body will deny, but that in King James's time,[7] we owed the preservation of our religion to our liberties, which both our clergy and people almost unanimously concurred to defend, with a resolution and boldness worthy of Britons and freemen. And as the cause and blessings of liberty are still better understood, its spirit and interest daily increase. Most of the bishops, and many of the inferior clergy, are professedly in the principles of civil and religious liberty, notwithstanding the strong and early prejudices of education. And I hope soon to see them all as thorough advocates for publick liberty, as their predecessors were, upon grounds less just, in the times of popery; and then there will be an end of the pernicious and knavish distinction of Whig and Tory; and all the world will unite in paying them that respect which is due to their holy office.

I shall conclude with this short application; that as we love religion, and the author of it, we ought to love and preserve our liberties.

G   *I am, &c.*

NO. 67. SATURDAY, FEBRUARY 24, 1721.

❧ *Arts and Sciences the Effects of Civil Liberty only, and ever destroyed or oppressed by Tyranny.*

SIR,

Having already shewn, that naval trade and power cannot subsist but in free countries alone,[1] I will now shew, that the same is true of domestick arts and sciences; and that both these, and population, which is their constant concomitant, and their chief cause as well as their certain effect, are born of liberty, and nursed, educated, encouraged, and endowed, by liberty alone.

Men will not spontaneously toil and labour but for their own advantage, for their pleasure or their profit, and to obtain

7. That is, the reign of James II, 1685 to 1688.

1. See Letter No. 64 (Feb. 3, 1721).

something which they want or desire, and which, for the most part, is not to be obtained but by force or consent. Force is often dangerous; and when employed to acquire what is not ours, it is always unjust; and therefore men, to procure from others what they had not before, must gain their consent; which is not to be gained, but by getting them in lieu of the thing desired, something which they want and value more than what they part with. This is what we call trade; which is the exchange of one commodity for another, or for that which purchases all commodities, silver and gold.

Men, in their first state, content themselves with the spontaneous productions of nature, the fruits of the field and the liquid stream, and such occasional supplies as they now and then receive from the destruction of other animals. But when those supplies become insufficient to support their numbers, their next resource is to open the bosom of the earth, and, by proper application and culture, to extort her hidden stores: And thus were invented tillage and planting. And an hundred men thus employed can fetch from the bowels of our common mother, food and sustenance enough for ten times their own number; and one tenth part more may possibly be able to supply all the instruments of husbandry, and whatever is barely necessary to support these husbandmen: So that all the rest of the people must rob or starve, unless either the proprietors of the land will give them the produce of their estates for nothing, or they can find something wherewithal to purchase it.

Now in countries where no other arts are in use, but only husbandry and the professions necessary to it, and to support those who are employed about it; all the other inhabitants have no means of purchasing food and raiment, but by selling their persons, and becoming vile slaves and vassals to their princes, lords, or other proprietors of the land; and are obliged, for necessary sustenance, to follow them in their wild wars, and their personal and factious quarrels, and to become the base instruments of their ambition and pride. Great men will rather throw their estates into forests and chases, for the support of wild beasts, and for their own pleasure in hunting them, than into farms, gardens, and fruitful fields, if they can get nothing from the productions of them.

This is the forlorn condition of mankind, in most of the wild empires of the East; this was their condition in all the Gothick governments;[2] and this is the condition of Poland and of the highlands of Scotland; where a few have liberty, and all the rest are slaves. And nothing can free mankind from this abject and forlorn condition, but the invention of arts and sciences; that is, the finding out of more materials and expedients to make life easy and pleasant; and the inducing people to believe, what they will readily believe, that other things are necessary to their happiness, besides those which nature has made necessary. Thus the luxury of the rich becomes the bread of the poor.

As soon as men are freed from the importunities of hunger and cold; the thoughts and desire of conveniency, plenty, ornament, and politeness, do presently succeed: And then follow after, in very quick progression, emulation, ambition, profusion, and the love of power: And all these, under proper regulations, contribute to the happiness, wealth, and security of societies. It is natural to men and societies, to be setting their wits and their hands to work, to find out all means to satisfy their wants and desires, and to enable them to live in credit and comfort, and to make suitable provision that their posterity may live so after them.

Necessity is the mother of invention; and so is the opinion of necessity. Whilst things are in their own nature necessary to us, or, from custom and fancy, made necessary; we will be turning every thought, and trying every method, how to come at them; and where they cannot be got by violence and rapine, recourse will be had to invention and industry. And here is the source of arts and sciences; which alone can support multitudes of people, who will never be wanting to the means which bring them support.

Where-ever there is employment for people, there will be people; and people, in most countries, are forced, for want of other employment, to cut the throats of one another, or of their neighbours; and to ramble after their princes in all their mad conquests, ridiculous contentions, and other mischievous maggots; and all to get, with great labour, hazard, and often with great hunger and slaughter, a poor, precarious, and momentary subsistence.

2. That is, the governments of the medieval period.

And therefore whatever state gives more encouragement to its subjects than the neighbouring states do, and finds them more work, and gives them greater rewards for that work; and by all these laudable ways makes [the] human condition easier than it is elsewhere, and secures life and property better; that state will draw the inhabitants from the neighbouring countries to its own; and when they are there, they will, by being richer and safer, multiply faster. Men will naturally fly from danger to security, from poverty to plenty, and from a life of misery to a life of felicity.

And as there will be always industry where-ever there is protection; so where-ever there is industry and labour, there will be the silver, the gold, the jewels, and power, and the empire. It does not import who they are that have conquered, or inhabit the countries where silver and gold are natives, or who they are that toil for them in the mines; since they will be the possessors of the coin, who can purchase it afterwards with the goods and manufactures which the proprietors of the mine and their people want. One artificer in England, or Holland, can make manufacture enough in a week to buy as much silver and gold at the mine, as a labourer there can dig and prepare in a month, or perhaps two; and all the while that Spain and Portugal lessen their inhabitants, we increase ours: They lose their people by sending them away to dig in the mines; and we, by making the manufactures which they want, and the instruments which they use, multiply ours. By this means every man that they send out of their country is a loss to it, because the reason and produce of their labour goes to enrich rival nations; whereas every man that we send to our plantations, adds to the number of our inhabitants here at home, by maintaining so many of them employed in so many manufactures which they take off there; besides so many artificers in shipping, and all the numerous traders and agents concerned in managing and venting the produce of the plantations, when it is brought hither, and in bringing it hither: So that the English planters in America, besides maintaining themselves and ten times as many Negroes, maintain likewise great numbers of their countrymen in England.

Such are the blessings of liberty, and such is the difference which it makes between country and country! The Spanish nation lost much more by the loss of their liberties, followed with the expulsion of the Moors, than ever they got by the gold and silver mountains of Mexico and Peru, or could get by all the mines of gold, silver, and diamonds upon earth.

Where there is liberty, there are encouragements to labour, because people labour for themselves: and no one can take from them the acquisitions which they make by their labour: There will be the greatest numbers of people, because they find employment and protection; there will be the greatest stocks, because most is to be got, and easiest to be got, and safest when it is got; and those stocks will be always increasing by a new accession of money acquired elsewhere, where there is no security of enjoying it; there people will be able to work cheapest, because less taxes will be put upon their work, and upon the necessaries which must support them whilst they are about it: There people will dare to own their being rich; there will be most people bred up to trade, and trade and traders will be most respected; and there the interest of money will be lower, and the security of possessing it greater, than it ever can be in tyrannical governments, where life and property and all things must depend upon the humour of a prince, the caprice of a minister, or the demand of a harlot. Under those governments few people can have money, and they that have must lock it up, or bury it to keep it; and dare not engage in large designs, when the advantages may be reaped by their rapacious governors, or given up by them in a senseless and wicked treaty: Besides, such governors condemn trade and artificers; and only men of the sword, who have an interest incompatible with trade, are encouraged by them.

For these reasons, trade cannot be carried on so cheap as in free countries; and whoever supplies the commodity cheapest, will command the market. In free countries, men bring out their money for their use, pleasure, and profit, and think of all ways to employ it for their interest and advantage. New projects are every day invented, new trades searched after, new manufactures set up; and when tradesmen have nothing to fear but from those whom they trust, credit will run high, and they will venture in trade for many times as much as they are worth: But in arbitrary countries, men in trade are every moment liable to be undone, without the guilt of sea or wind, without the folly or treachery of their correspondents, or their own want of care or industry: Their wealth shall be their snare; and their abilities, vigilance, and their success, shall either be their undoing, or nothing to their advantage: Nor can they trust any one else, or any one else them, when payment and performance must depend upon the honesty and wisdom of those who often have none.

T

Ignorance of arts and sciences, and of every thing that is good, together with poverty, misery, and desolation, are found for the most part all together, and are all certainly produced by tyranny. In all the great empires of Morocco, Abyssinia, Persia, and India, there is not amongst the natives such a thing as a tolerable architect; nor one good building, unless we except a palace built by a Portuguese for the Abyssinian emperor; and perhaps there may be in all these vast continents a few more good houses built by Europeans. The Aethiopians have scarce such a thing as an artificer among them; their only weavers are the Jews, who are likewise their smiths, whose highest employment in iron is to make heads for their spears; and for artists of their own, their wretched trumpeters and horn-winders seem to be the highest. When the Jesuits built a few churches and chapels in their country, the whole nation were alarmed, taking them for so many castles and fortresses. The rest of their condition is a-piece; they are abjectly miserable, in spite of their soil, which in many places is luxuriant, and yields three crops a year; Of such small effect are the gifts of God to his creatures, when the breath of a tyrant can blast them!

In Persia, the carpenters and joiners have but four tools for all their work, and we may guess what sort of work they make; they have a hatchet, a saw, and a chisel, and one sort of plainer, brought thither not long since by a Frenchman. As to printing, they have none; nor any paper but coarse brown stuff, which cannot be folded without breaking to pieces. In painting, they do not go beyond birds and flowers, and are utterly ignorant of figures and history.

Egypt was once the mother of arts and sciences, and from thence Greece had them: But Egypt losing its liberties, lost with them all politeness, as all nations do; and the pyramids were built by the first Egyptian tyrants, while the knowledge of arts was not yet lost in barbarism, and before the country was dispeopled, else they never had been built. Nor could all the power of the Ottoman Empire build such in the place now, though the Turks were not savages in the sciences, as they are. "Till the time of Ramphsinitus," says Herodotus, "the Egyptians report, that liberty flourished, and the laws were the highest power."[3] Then he tells us, that Cheops,[4] the successor of that king, falling into all debauchery and tyranny, employed a hundred thousand of his people in drawing of stone; Diodorus Siculus says, three hundred and sixty thousand were employed in this inhuman drudgery;[5] and then he began a pyramid. The Egyptians grew afterwards in ignorance, barbarity, and vileness, and almost any body that invaded them, mastered them; and when they were defended, the free Greeks defended them, a band of them being generally entertained for that end by the Egyptian kings. It is true, one or two of the Ptolemies, particularly the first, attempted to revive arts and learning amongst them; but the attempt came to nothing: They were slaves, incapable either of tasting or producing the embellishments and excellencies of liberty, of which they had been long deprived; and therefore the Greek artists, and the Greek professors in Egypt, had the glory of every improvement to themselves, as indeed they were the authors of all. The Romans afterwards left there many monuments of their grandeur and politeness: But when their free government ended, as tyranny succeeded, so did barbarity all over the empire, and no where more than in Egypt, which is at this day the prey of robbing and thieving Arabs, and of oppressive and devouring Turks.

I shall here subjoin a summary account given us by that judicious traveller Monsieur Bernier, concerning the condition of

3. Herodotus, 2.124. "Rampsinitos" is Ramses III.

4. Fourth Dynasty Egyptian ruler who, with his successors, was responsible for building the colossal pyramids at Gizeh.

5. Diodorus Siculus, 1.63.9.

the three great eastern empires, best known to us. It is in his last chapter of *The History of the Great Mogul.*

There is, says he,

almost no person secure from the violence of the governors, timariots, and farmers of the royal rents; nor can the princes, though they were disposed, hinder these violences, nor prevent the tyranny of their servants over their people; which should be the chief employment of a king. This tyranny is often so extensive, that it leaves to the peasant and tradesman neither food nor raiment, but robs them of the common necessaries of life, and they live in misery, and die with hunger: They either beget no children; or, if they do, see them perish in their infancy, for want of food: Sometimes they desert their huts and land, to become lackeys to the soldiers, or fly to neighbouring nations (where their condition is not mended). In short, the land is not tilled but by force, and therefore wretchedly tilled; and great part of it lies waste and is lost: There is no body to clear the ditches and water-courses; no body to build houses, or to repair those that are ruinous. The timariot will not improve the ground for his successor, not knowing how soon he may come; nor will the peasant work for a tyrant, and starve while he does it: And neither timariot nor peasant will labour for bread which others are to eat. So the peasant is left to starve, and the land to become a desert.

Hence it is, that we see those vast states in Asia run and running to wretched ruin: Most of their towns are raised with dirt and earth; and you see nothing but ruinous towns, and deserted villages: And hence it is, that those celebrated regions of Mesopotamia, Anatolia, Palestine, with those admirable plains of Antioch, and so many other countries, anciently so well manured, so fertile, and so full of people, are all at present half deserted, abandoned, and untilled, or become pestilent and uninhabitable bogs. Egypt is in the like condition; and within these fourscore years, above the tenth part of its incomparable soil is lost by poverty, and want of hands to scour the channels of the Nile, and remove the sand which covers their fields.

From the same causes, arts languish and starve in those countries: For with what heart can an artisan labour and study for ignorant beggars, who are not judges of his work, and cannot pay him for it, or for grandees who will not? He is so far from any prospect of reward, that he is not only without all hopes of wealth, office or lands; but, to avoid being thought rich, must live poorly: He must never eat a good meal, never wear a decent coat, never appear to be worth sixpence. Nay, he is happy if he can escape the korrah, a terrible whip exercised by the great lords upon the artists; proper encouragement of ingenuity!

Indeed, the knowledge and beauty of arts had been lost in those countries long since, were it not that the kings and grandees give wages to certain handicraftsmen, who work in their houses, and, to escape the whip, do their best: Besides, the rich merchants, who share their gains with men of power, to be protected by them, give these handicraftsmen a little more pay, and but a little. We must not therefore think, upon seeing rich eastern stuffs here, that the workman there is in any condition or esteem: He works not for himself: Only necessity and the cudgel makes him work; and let him work how he will, he is doomed to live miserably, to clothe himself meanly, to eat poorly.

Traffick also in those countries is faint and decaying: For how many are there that care to take much pains; to make dangerous voyages, and take long journeys; to be constantly running up and down; to write much, to live in perpetual anxiety and care, and to risk all hazards and chances; and all for a precarious gain, which is at the mercy of the next greedy governor?[6]

This whole chapter of Bernier deserves every man's reading: I have only room to add part of another paragraph. talking of the Turkish empire: "We have travelled," says he,

6. The passage appears in François Bernier, *The history of the late revolution of the empire of the great Mogul: together with the most considerable passages, for 5 years following that empire* (2 vols.; London: Printed and sold by Moses Pitt, Simon Miller, and John Starkey, 1671), translated from the original *Histoire de la dernière révolution des états du Grand Mogul*. Gordon is here quoting from the section of the work titled "Letter to the Lord Colbert Concerning Indostan," pp. 69–74.

through almost all the parts of it; we have seen how woefully it is ruined and dispeopled; and how in the capital city the raising of five or six thousand men requires three whole months: And we know what a fall it must have had before now, had it not been for the supplies of Christian slaves and captives brought thither every year from all parts. Without doubt, if the same sort of government continue, that state will destroy itself: It is at this day maintained by its own weakness, and must at last fall by it. The governors are frequently changed, to make room for new oppressors; but neither has any one governor, or one subject in the whole empire, a penny that he can call his own, to maintain the least party; nor, if he had money, are there any men to be had in these wide desolate provinces. A blessed expedient this, to make a state subsist! An expedient, much like that of a brama of Pegu,[7] who, to prevent sedition, commanded that no land should be tilled for some years together; and having thus destroyed half the kingdom with hunger, he turned it into forests: Which method, however, did not answer his end, nor prevent divisions in that state, which was reduced so low, that a handful of Chinese fugitives were like to have taken and mastered the capital city Ava.[8]

Thus far Bernier. Sir Paul Ricaut tells us, that it is a reigning maxim in the Turkish policy, to lay a great part of their empire waste.[9] A maxim, which they need take no pains to practise; since, without destroying deliberately their people and provinces, which yet they do, the dreadful spirit of their government creates desolation fast enough in all conscience.

The whole city of Dhili,[10] the capital of India, is obliged to follow the Great Mogul their emperor, when he takes a journey, their whole dependence being upon the court and the soldiery; for they cannot support themselves: Nor is the country round them,

7. A Burmese brahman, that is, a member of the highest-ranking caste.

8. "Letter to Colbert," in *History of the Great Mogul*, pp. 91–92.

9. *The Present State of the Ottoman Empire*, bk. I, chap. 15 (p. 68).

10. Delhi. The account appears in Bernier's "Second Letter to Monsieur de Merveilles" on his journey to Kachemire (Kashmir), in his *History of the Great Mogul*.

which is either waste, or its inhabitants starving, able to support them. So that the citizens of this mighty metropolis, are only the wretched sutlers[11] to a camp: They are forced to leave their houses empty, and stroll after their monarch, whenever he is graciously disposed to take a jaunt; and are absent sometimes from home a year and a half together.

The Jesuit Nicholas Pimenta, who was in Pegu about an hundred and twenty years ago, gives this account of it: "The last king," says he,

> was a mighty king, and could bring into the field a million and sixty thousand men, taking one out of ten: But his son had, by his wars, his oppressions, his murders, and other cruelties, made such quick dispatch of his subjects, that all that were left did not exceed seven thousand, including men, women, and children. What an affecting influence is here of the pestilential nature of tyranny![12]

It is not unlikely that some of these fatal wars were made by this inhuman prince, for white elephants; and that he either made or provoked invasions upon that score, as I have instanced in another paper:[13] And here I shall add something to make this conjecture still more probable. Mr. Ralph Fitch, a merchant of London, was at Pegu thirteen or fourteen years before Pimenta, in the reign of the above potent king; and he says,

> Such is the esteem that this king has for an elephant of this colour, that amongst his other titles, he is called King of the White Elephants; a title, which to him seems as lofty as any of the rest. And that no other prince round about him may wear his glorious title, therefore none of them must keep a white elephant, though nature gave it them; but

11. Sutlers: provisioners attached to a military post.

12. Nicholas Pimenta, "Indian Observations . . . written from divers Indian Regions; principally relating the Countries and accidents of the Coast of Coromandel, and of Pegu." Pimenta's essay appears in Samuel Purchas, ed., *Hakluytus Posthumus, or, Purchas his Pilgrimes: Contayning a History of the World in Sea Voyages and Lande Travells by Englishmen and others* (5 vols.; London: Printed for William Stansby for Henrie Fetherstone, 1625). The quotation can be found in vol. II, x.1746.

13. See Letter No. 57 (Dec. 16, 1721).

must send it to him, or an army shall fetch it; for rather
than not have it, he will make war for it.[14]

He says, that the houses of these creatures are splendidly
gilt, and so are the silver vessels out of which they are fed. When
they go to the river to be washed, which they do every day, six or
seven men bear up a canopy of cloth of gold or silk over them; and
as many more march with drums and musical instruments before
them; and when they come out of the water, their feet are washed
in great silver basins by persons of quality, whose office it is thus to
serve them.[15] Bernier says, the Great Mogul allows fixed pensions
(sometimes very large ones) to every elephant, with proper attendance; nay, two men are employed in the sultry months, to stand,
one on each side, to fan them.[16]

I only mention this, to shew how much more care these
tyrants take of their beasts, than of their people. And it is too true
of all arbitrary princes; their stable of horses is dearer to them than
their subjects, and live infinitely better.

This is almost universally true where-ever there are such.
Nay, they value their dogs more than they do the lives of men.
When the Grand Seignior goes a hunting, a great number of peasants must enclose the ground for several leagues round, and keep
in the game; this they must often do for many days together, sometimes in ice and snow, with hungry bellies. By which means their
work is neglected, their grounds are destroyed, and they themselves are many times killed in the sport, or starved in attending it;
and it often happens, that forty or fifty of his own followers perish
in a day. Sultan Mahomet's grand falconer had once the honesty
and boldness to represent to his master all this destruction and carnage which attended his endless passion for hunting; but all the
answer which he received from this father of the faithful, was, "By

14. Ralph Fitch, "The Voyage of Master Ralph Fitch, Merchant of London to
Ormus, and so to Goa in the East India," in Samuel Purchas, ed., *Purchas his
Pilgrimes*, II.x.1738.

15. Ralph Fitch, in Purchas, ed., *Purchas his Pilgrimes*, II.x.1738.

16. At no point does Bernier make this precise claim. But see his discussion of
elephants in his "Letter to Monsieur de la Mothe le Vayer" containing a
description of Delhi and Agra, in his *History of the Great Mogul*.

all means take care of the dogs, let them have clothing and other accommodations."

This paper upon arts and population grows too long: I shall therefore reserve to another what I have to say further upon this subject.

G   *I am, &c.*

Property and Commerce secure in a free Government only; with the consuming Miseries under simple Monarchies.

SIR,

I here send you what I have to say further upon arts, industry and population. To live securely, happily, and independently, is the end and effect of liberty; and it is the ambition of all men to live agreeably to their own humours and discretion. Nor did ever any man that could live satisfactorily without a master, desire to live under one; and real or fancied necessity alone makes men the servants, followers, and creatures of one another. And therefore all men are animated by the passion of acquiring and defending property, because property is the best support of that independency, so passionately desired by all men. Even men the most dependent have it constantly in their heads and their wishes, to become independent one time or other; and the property which they are acquiring, or mean to acquire by that dependency, is intended to bring them out of it, and to procure them an agreeable independency. And as happiness is the effect of independency, and independency the effect of property; so certain property is the effect of liberty alone, and can only be secured by the laws of liberty; laws which are made by consent, and cannot be repealed without it.

All these blessings, therefore, are only the gifts and consequences of liberty, and only to be found in free countries, where power is fixed on one side, and property secured on the other; where the one cannot break bounds without check, penalties or forfeiture, nor the other suffer diminution without redress; where the people have no masters but the laws, and such as the laws appoint; where both laws and magistracy are formed by the people or their deputies; and no demands are made upon them, but what are made by the law, and they know to a penny what to pay before it is asked; where they that exact from them more than the law allows, are punishable by the law; and where the legislators are equally bound by their own acts, equally involved in the consequences.

There can be no good, where there are none of the causes of good; and consequently all the advantages of liberty must be lost with liberty, and all the evils of tyranny must accompany tyranny. I have in my last taken a view of the eastern monarchies, with regard to the miserable decay of their people and arts; I shall in this confine myself, for instances, to Europe, and begin with Muscovy, by far the greatest empire for territory in Christendom: And because the best short account that I have seen of that government, is given by Giles Fletcher, who was there in the latter end of Queen Elizabeth's time, I shall here recite part of that account.[1]

Talking of the many wicked and barbarous arts used by the late czars of Russia, to drain and oppress their people, he says;

"They would suffer their people to give freely to the monasteries (as many do, especially in their last wills), and this they do, because they may have the money of the realm more ready at hand, when they list to take it, which is many times done; the friars parting freely with some, rather than lose all.

"John Basilowitz pretended to resign the crown to the Prince of Cazan,[2] and to retire for the rest of his life to a monastery: He then caused this new king to call in all the ecclesiastical charters, and to cancel them. Then pretending to dislike this fact,

1. The excerpt is taken from Giles Fletcher, *Of the Russe Commonwealth or, Maner of Gouernement by the Russe Emperour* ... (London: Printed by T.D. for Thomas Charde, 1591): 43–47.
2. The Prince of Kazan.

and the misrule of the new king, he resumed the sceptre, possessed as he was of all the church lands; of which he kept what he would, and gave new charters for the rest. By this he wrung from the ecclesiasticks a vast sum; and yet hoped to abate the ill opinion of his government, by shewing a worse.

"When they want to levy a new tax, they make a shew of want, as was done by Duke Theodore; who, though left very rich by his father, yet sold most of his plate, and coined the rest, that he might seem in necessity: Whereupon presently came out a new tax upon his people.

"They would sometimes send their messengers into the provinces to forestall and engross the commodities of the country, taking them at small prices, what they themselves listed, and selling them again at excessive prices to their own merchants, or to strangers. If they refuse to buy them, then they force them into it: The like they do, when any commodity thus engrossed, foreign or native, such as cloth of gold, broad cloth, and the like, happens to decay, by lying upon hand; it is forced upon the merchants at the emperor's price, whether they will or no.

"Besides the engrossing of foreign commodities, and forcing them upon the merchants, they make a monopoly for a season of all such commodities as are paid the prince for rent or custom; and this they do to enhance the price of them: Thus they monopolize furs, corn, wood, &c. during all which time none must sell of the same commodity, till the emperor's be all sold.

"The above-mentioned John Basilowitz sent into Permia[3] (a country of the poor Samoides) for certain loads of cedar, though he well knew that none grew there; and the inhabitants returned answer, that they could find none. Whereupon he taxed the country in twelve thousand rubles. Again, he sent to the city of Moscow to provide for him a measure full of fleas, for a medicine. They answered, that the thing was impossible; and if they could get them, yet they could not measure them, because of their leaping out. Upon which he set a mulct upon them of seven thousand rubles.

3. Permia lies just to the west of the Ural Mountains in central Russia.

"To these may be added, their seizures and confiscations upon such as are under displeasure, and the connivance at the oppression and extortions of the governors of the provinces, till their time be expired; and then turning all their wicked plunder into the emperor's treasury, but never a penny back again to the right owner, how great or evident soever the injury be.

"As to the people, they are of no rank or account, and esteemed no better than villains; and so they subscribe themselves in all their writings to any of the nobility, as they of the nobility do to the emperor: And indeed, no bond slaves are kept more in awe and subjection, than the common people are, by the nobility, officers, and soldiers; so that when a poor *mousick*[4] (one of the commonalty) meets any of them upon the highway, he must turn himself about, as not daring to look them in the face, and fall down with his head to the very ground.

"And as to the lands and goods of these miserable people, they are so exposed to the rapine of the nobility and soldiers, besides the taxes, customs, and seizures, and other publick exactions laid upon them by the emperor, that they are utterly discouraged from following their trades and professions; because the more they have, the more danger they are in, not only of their goods, but even of their lives: And if they happen to have any thing, they convey it into monasteries, or hide it in woods or under ground, as men do when they are in fear of a foreign invasion. So that many villages and towns are entirely without inhabitants; and in the way towards Moscow, betwixt Volaghda and Yareslave,[5] for about an hundred English miles, there are least fifty villages, some half a mile long, some a whole mile long, that stand wholly desolate, without a single inhabitant. The like desolation is seen in all other places of the realm, as I have been told by those that travelled the country.

"In every great town the emperor hath a drinking-house, which he rents out: Here the labouring man and artificer many times spends all from his wife and children. Some drink away all that they wear about them, to their very shirts, and so walk naked;

4. Muzhik: a Russian peasant.
5. Between Vologhda and Yaroslavl.

and all for the honour of the emperor. Nay, while they are thus drinking themselves naked, and starving their families, no body must call them away, upon any account, because he would hinder the emperor's revenue.

"The capital punishments upon the people are very cruel; but if theft or murder be committed upon them by one of the nobility, he is seldom punished, or so much as called to account for it, because the people are the slaves of the nobility: Or if these crimes are committed by a gentleman soldier, perhaps he may be imprisoned at the emperor's pleasure, or perhaps fined—and that is all."

I make this quotation chiefly upon memory, having only taken down some hints when I read it; but I can assert it to be a just one, and almost wholly in the Doctor's words.

I know much has been said of the improvements made by the present Czar,[6] and of his many projects in favour of arts and trade: And it is very true, that he is a prince of a very active and inquisitive genius. But though he has made himself a more power-ful prince than any of his predecessors were, I do not find that the numbers of his people are increased, or their general wretched condition much mended. He has a vast army constantly on foot; he keeps vast numbers of his poor subjects constantly employed in making havens and canals; great taxes are raised, great and daily waste is made of his people, who are likewise miserably oppressed by his boyars,[7] to whom he still leaves the raising of money, and the direction of trade: So that the general oppression remains; trade is deadened and distressed; the people burdened beyond measure; sudden and arbitrary duties are laid upon commodities imported; the old way of monopolies is continued; the state of the exchange, and the allay[8] and uncertain value of the current coin, are as bad as they can be; arts and ingenuity are really discour-aged, and those who have skill in any art must conceal it, to avoid

6. Peter I, the Great.
7. Boyars were members of the Russian aristocracy ranking immediately below the ruling princes.
8. Allay: admixture of metals.

working for nothing; there are grievances without number, and like to be, for he who complains is certainly undone, and petitions are answered with stripes, sometimes with death itself. In short, the condition of the Russian people is much upon the same foot as it was in Dr. Fletcher's time; and whoever doubts it, may find full conviction from Captain Perry's state of Russia, under the present Czar.[9]

In Poland, nothing can be more miserable than the condition of the peasants, who are subject to the mere mercy of the great lords, as to life and death and property; and must labour five days in a week, nay sometimes six, for these lords; and if they cannot subsist themselves and their families upon one day's labour in seven, they must famish. The state of the other northern kingdoms is, with respect to the people, as wretched as any yet named: They have many soldiers, endless taxes, dreadful poverty, few people, and gaudy courts. It is indeed said of some arbitrary princes in some parts of Europe, that they are merciful to their subjects, and do not use them barbarously; that is, they do not deliberately butcher them, but only take all that they have, and leave them to starve peaceably upon the rest: All the riches of the country are to be seen at court, and the people are wretchedly poor. *Cantabit vacuus*.[10] A countryman once complained to General Kirk,[11] that his soldiers had plundered him of all that he had in the world: "Thou art a happy man," says the General, "for then they will plunder thee no more."

The woeful decay of people and plenty in many states in Italy is so astonishing, that were it not obvious to every eye that sees it, and so well attested to those who have not seen it, by those who have, it would seem beyond all belief.

"When I came into the Pope's territories at Pont Centino," says Dr. Burnet,

9. John Perry, *The State of Russia Under the Present Czar* (London: Printed for Benjamin Tooke, 1716).

10. "Empty-handed, he will sing." Juvenal, *Saturae*, 10.22.

11. Percy Kirke (1646?–1691), military commander active in crushing the rebellion of the Duke of Monmouth in 1685, reputed to have engaged in the worst atrocities in dealing with those who had rebel sympathies.

there was a rich bottom all uncultivated, and not so much as stocked with cattle: But as I passed from Montifiascone to Viterbo, this appeared yet more amazing; for a vast champaign country lay almost quite deserted. And that wide town, which is of so great compass, hath few inhabitants, and those looked poor and miserable. When I was within a day's journey of Rome, I fancied the neighbourhood of so great a city must mend the matter; but I was much disappointed: For a soil that was so rich, and lay so sweetly, that it far exceeded any thing I ever saw out of Italy, had neither inhabitants in it, nor cattle upon it, to the tenth part of what it could bear. The surprize this gave me increased upon me, as I went out of Rome on its other side, chiefly all the way to Naples, and on the way to Civita Vecchia; for that vast and rich champaign country, which runs all along to Terracina, which from Civita Vecchia is a hundred miles long, and is in many places twelve or twenty miles broad, is abandoned to such a degree, that as far as one's eye can carry one, there is often not so much as a house to be seen. The severity of the government hath driven away the inhabitants; and their being driven away hath reduced it to such a pass, that it is hardly possible to people it.

He adds, that in Rome itself,

it is not possible for the people to live and pay taxes; which has driven, as it is believed, almost a fourth part of the people out of Rome during this pontificate.[12]

He tells us elsewhere, that the Pope buys in all the corn of St. Peter's patrimony.

He buys it at five crowns their measure, and even that is slowly and ill paid. So that there was eight hundred thousand crowns owing upon that score when I was at Rome. In selling this out, the measure is lessened a fifth part, and the

12. Gilbert Burnet, *Some Letters Containing an Account of What Seemed Most Remarkable in Travelling Through Switzerland, Italy, and Some Parts of Germany, &c. in the Year 1685 and 1686. Written by G. Burnet, D.D. to the Honorable R[obert] B[oyle]* (London: Printed and are to be sold by J. Robinson, 1689). The quotation appears in Letter IV (pp. 186–87).

price of the whole is doubled; so that what was bought at five crowns, is sold out at twelve; and if the bankers, who are obliged to take a determined quantity of corn from the chamber, cannot retail out all that is imposed upon them, but are forced to return some part of it back, the chamber discounts to them only the first price of five crowns.[13]

It is observed by another noble author of our country, that Mario Chigi, brother to Pope Alexander the Seventh, by one sordid cheat upon the sale of corn, is said within eight years to have destroyed above the third part of the people in the ecclesiastical state;[14] and that that country, which was the strength of the Romans in the Carthaginian wars, suffered more by the covetousness and fraud of that villain, than by all the defeats received from Hannibal.

The country of Ferrara was formerly very populous, and the lands being fertile, were well cultivated; but since the Pope has got possession of it, it is almost depopulated; the lands are nigh desolate; and, for want of people, it is like the rest of the ecclesiastical state, unhealthy to live in. His Holiness has reduced the inhabitants from above an hundred thousand, to about twelve thousand. In the city itself, grass grows in the streets, and most of the houses are empty.

The Great Duke's dominions[15] lie much in the same dismal solitude. When Sienna and Pisa were free states, they swarmed with people, and were rich in trade and territory: Sienna alone was computed to have had above half a million of subjects; but in a matter of an hundred and fourscore years, during which time it has been in the possession of his Highness of Tuscany, they are

13. A somewhat garbled transcription from Burnet's "Remarks Upon the Temporal Government of the Pope," in the supplement to his *Travels* (pp. 326–27 of the 1689 edition).

14. Gordon's memory is possibly faulty. Bishop Burnet, in the supplement to his *Travels*, observed: "It was Donna Olympia [Maidalchini, sister-in-law to Pope Innocent X] that, during the pontificate of Innocent X, began to put taxes and imposts upon corn and made such laws which have ruined the most part of the great nobility and gentry that live under the ecclesiastical government, who had their revenues consisting in corn." "Remarks Upon the Temporal Government of the Pope" (p. 326).

15. The territories belonging to the dukes of Tuscany, the Medicis, until the extinction of the line in 1737.

sunk below twenty thousand, and these miserably poor. The same is the abject condition of Pisa, Pistoja, Arezzo, Cortona, and many other great towns. Florence, his capital particularly, which, in the days of liberty, could, by the ringing of a bell, bring together, of its own citizens and the inhabitants of the valley Arno, a hundred and thirty-five thousand well armed men in a few hours' time, is now so poor and low, that it could not bring together three tolerable regiments in thirteen months.

The city of Pisa alone was reckoned, when it was free, to have had a hundred and fifty thousand inhabitants, all happy in liberty and commerce; and now they are about ten thousand, without liberty, and commerce, and bread. Formerly an hundred of its citizens could fit out an hundred galleys, and maintain them during a war, at their own charge; and now the whole city could not furnish out nor maintain one. Their stately palaces are desolate, like their territory; or let out for stables, or any other sorry use, at three or four pounds a year rent. Their streets are covered with grass; their territory, by being waste, is grown unwholesome; and their few remains of people are starving. And that great state, which the Great Duke could not master without the armies of Spain, are not now able to contend with his infamous crew of tax-gatherers. The people are famished slaves, their houses are ruins, their trade is gone, their land unmanured, and yet their taxes are not lessened; and if there be any plenty amongst them, 'tis only plenty of beggars.

The same is the condition of the Milanese, and other countries under the same sort of government; the people starve in the best soils: Whereas in Switzerland, and in the territories of Genoa, Lucca, and the Grisons, they are numerous, and live happily in the worst. "The people in France" (says the author of the supplement to Dr. Burnet's travels),

> especially the peasants, are very poor, and most of them reduced to great want and misery; and yet France is an extraordinary good country. The people of Switzerland (which is a country of mountains) cannot be said to be very rich, but there are very few, even of the peasants, that are miserably poor. The most part of them have enough to live

on. Every where in France, even in the best cities, there are swarms of beggars; and yet scarce any to be seen throughout all Switzerland. The houses of the country people in France are extremely mean; and in them no other furniture is to be found, but poor nasty beds, straw chairs, with plates and dishes of wood and earth. In Switzerland, the peasants have their houses furnished with good featherbeds, good chairs, and other convenient household-stuffs; their windows are all of glass, always kept mended and whole; and their linen, both for bedding and their tables, is very neat and white.[16]

This was written above thirty years ago, when France was in a much better condition than it has been since. The glory of their late Grand Monarch cost them much misery, and many myriads of people. And yet even thirty years ago their miseries were great and affecting! "As I came from Paris to Lyons" (says Dr. Burnet),

I was amazed to see so much misery as appeared not only in villages, but even in big towns; where all the marks of an extreme poverty shewed themselves, both in the buildings, the clothes, and almost in the looks of the inhabitants. And a general dispeopling in all the towns, was a very visible effect of the hardships under which they lay.[17]

What blessed circumstances that great kingdom is in now, Mr. Law, who is amongst us,[18] can best tell; though we all pretty well know. It is really a science, and no easy one, to know the names, numbers, and quality of their taxes; which are so many, so various, and so heavy, that one of their own writers calls them, inventions proper to impoverish the people, and to enrich the dictionaries. Bulion, treasurer to Louis XIII,[19] told his master, that his

16. "Remarks Upon Switzerland" (p. 316). The supplement, added to the main body of Burnet's letters with the third edition of 1687, although unattributed, was almost certainly written by Burnet himself.

17. *Burnet's Travels*, Letter I (p. 2).

18. John Law, the person most responsible for the Mississippi Bubble, returned to England in Oct. 1721.

19. Claude Bullion, one of Richelieu's subordinates, entrusted with the kingdom's finances.

subjects were too happy, they were not yet reduced to eat grass. And the cruel spirit and politicks of that minister were afterwards so well improved, that I am apt to think their present felicity is no part of their misfortunes.

Such instances shew what hopeful methods such governors take to increase people, trade, and riches.

As to the politer arts, I own several of them have flourished under some of the Popes themselves, and some other arbitrary princes; such as painting, architecture, sculpture, and musick. But these arts, and the improvements of them, were so far from owing any thing to that sort of government, that by liberty alone, and the privileges given to the professors of them, they came to excel in them; nor would they ever have excelled upon the common foot and condition of their other subjects: So that to make them excellent, they made them free. And thus even tyrants, the enemies of liberty, were, for their furniture, luxury, pomp, pleasure, and entertainment, forced to be beholden to liberty; and for those particular purposes, they gave it to particular men. But for the rest of their subjects, they were left by them in the condition of brutes, both in point of livelihood and knowledge; For it is liberty more than shape, that makes the difference; since reason without liberty proves little better, and sometimes worse, than none. Servitude mars all genius; nor is either a pen or a pencil of any use in a hand that is manacled.

G   *I am, &c.*

The End of the Second Volume.